ACCLAIM FOR TODD WILBUR'S
TOP SECRET RECIPES SERIES

"There's something almost magically compelling about the idea of making such foods at home."
—*Boston Herald*

"The mission: Decode the secret recipes for America's favorite junk foods. Equipment: Standard kitchen appliances. Goal: Leak the results to a ravenous public."
—*USA Today*

"This is the cookbook to satisfy all your cravings."
—Juli Huss, author of *The Faux Gourmet*

TODD WILBUR is the bestselling author of *Top Secret Recipes*, *More Top Secret Recipes*, and *Top Secret Restaurant Recipes* (all available from Plume). When not taste-testing recipes on himself, his friends, or TV talk-show hosts, Todd lives in Las Vegas, Nevada.

Visit the Top Secret Recipes website at:
www.topsecretrecipes.com

ALSO BY TODD WILBUR

Top Secret Recipes
More Top Secret Recipes
Top Secret Restaurant Recipes
Top Secret Recipes Lite!
Low-Fat Top Secret Recipes
Top Secret Recipes: Sodas, Smoothies, Spirits, & Shakes

More Kitchen Clones of America's Favorite Brand-Name Foods

Todd Wilbur

With Illustrations by the Author

A PLUME BOOK

This book was not prepared, approved, licensed or endorsed by any of the owners of the trademarks or brand names referred to in the book. Terms mentioned that are known or believed to be trademarks or service marks have been indicated as such. See section on "Trademarks."

PLUME
Published by the Penguin Group
Penguin Putnam Inc., 375 Hudson Street, New York, New York 10014, U.S.A.
Penguin Books Ltd, 80 Strand, London WC2R 0RL, England
Penguin Books Australia Ltd, 250 Camberwell Road, Camberwell, Victoria 3124, Australia
Penguin Books Canada Ltd, 10 Alcorn Avenue, Toronto, Ontario, Canada M4V 3B2
Penguin Books (N.Z.) Ltd, 182–190 Wairau Road, Auckland 10, New Zealand

Penguin Books Ltd, Registered Offices: Harmondsworth, Middlesex, England

First published by Plume, a member of Penguin Putnam Inc.

First Printing, November 2002
10 9 8 7 6 5 4 3 2 1

This is an omnibus edition encompassing *Top Secret Recipes Lite!: Learn the Secrets of Creating Lower-Fat Versions of Your Favorite Foods*, *Low-Fat Top Secret Recipes: Creating Kitchen Clones of America's Favorite Brand-Name Foods*, and *Top Secret Recipes: Sodas, Smoothies, Spirits, & Shakes*.

Copyright © Todd Wilbur, 1998, 2000, 2002
All rights reserved

 REGISTERED TRADEMARK—MARCA REGISTRADA

LIBRARY OF CONGRESS CATALOGING-IN-PUBLICATION DATA
Wilbur, Todd.
Top secret recipes treasury : more kitchen clones of America's favorite brand-name foods ; with illustrations by the author / Todd Wilbur.
p. cm.
Includes bibliographical references and index.
ISBN 0-452-28407-4 (trade paper)
1. Cookery, American.   2. Brand name products—United States.   I. Title.

TX715 .W65865 2002
641.5973—dc21   2002031195

Printed in the United States of America
Set in Gill Sans Light

Without limiting the rights under copyright reserved above, no part of this publication may be reproduced, stored in or introduced into a retrieval system, or transmitted, in any form, or by any means (electronic, mechanical, photocopying, recording, or otherwise), without the prior written permission of both the copyright owner and the above publisher of this book.

BOOKS ARE AVAILABLE AT QUANTITY DISCOUNTS WHEN USED TO PROMOTE PRODUCTS OR SERVICES. FOR INFORMATION PLEASE WRITE TO PREMIUM MARKETING DIVISION, PENGUIN PUTNAM INC., 375 HUDSON STREET, NEW YORK, NEW YORK 10014.

TOP SECRET RECIPES
TREASURY II

CONTENTS

PART 1: TOP SECRET RECIPES LITE!

Introduction   3

TOP SECRET RECIPES LITE! CLONES

APPLEBEE'S® LOW-FAT BLACKENED CHICKEN SALAD   19
APPLEBEE'S® LOW-FAT VEGGIE QUESADILLA   22
ARBY'S® LIGHT MENU ROAST CHICKEN DELUXE   25
ARBY'S® LIGHT MENU ROAST TURKEY DELUXE   28
CHILI'S® GUILTLESS GRILL® GUILTLESS CHICKEN SALAD   30
CHILI'S® GUILTLESS GRILL® GUILTLESS CHICKEN SANDWICH   33
CHILI'S® GUILTLESS GRILL® GUILTLESS PASTA PRIMAVERA   36
EINSTEIN BROS.® BAGELS: 39
   PLAIN   41
   CINNAMON SUGAR   42
   JALAPEÑO   43
   CHOPPED GARLIC   44
   CHOPPED ONION   45
   EVERYTHING   45
ENTENMANN'S LIGHT® FAT-FREE CHEESE-FILLED CRUMB
   COFFEE CAKE   47
ENTENMANN'S LIGHT® FAT-FREE GOLDEN LOAF   51
ENTENMANN'S LIGHT® FAT-FREE OATMEAL RAISIN COOKIES   54
EL POLLO LOCO® SALSA   57
GARDENBURGER® ORIGINAL VEGGIE PATTY   58

HOSTESS LIGHTS® LOW-FAT CUPCAKES   62
HOSTESS LIGHTS® LOW-FAT TWINKIES®   66
KELLOGG'S® LOW-FAT FROSTED BROWN SUGAR CINNAMON
    POP-TARTS®   70
KRAFT FREE® CATALINA DRESSING   74
KRAFT FREE® CLASSIC CAESAR DRESSING   76
KRAFT FREE® THOUSAND ISLAND DRESSING   78
KRAFT® LIGHT DELUXE MACARONI & CHEESE DINNER   80
NABISCO® REDUCED-FAT CHEESE NIPS®   83
NABISCO® SNACKWELL'S® CHOCOLATE CHIP COOKIES   86
NABISCO® SNACKWELL'S® FUDGE BROWNIE BARS   89
NABISCO® SNACKWELL'S® GOLDEN SNACK BARS   92
RED LOBSTER® LEMON-PEPPER GRILLED MAHI-MAHI   95
RED LOBSTER® NANTUCKET BAKED COD   97
SWISS MISS® FAT-FREE CHOCOLATE FUDGE PUDDING   99
SWISS MISS® FAT-FREE TAPIOCA PUDDING   101
T.G.I. FRIDAY'S® FAT-FREE CHEESECAKE   103
T.G.I. FRIDAY'S® JACK DANIEL'S® GRILL SALMON   106
WEIGHT WATCHERS® SMART ONES® CHOCOLATE ÉCLAIR   109

TOP SECRET RECIPES LITE! CONVERSIONS

REDUCED-FAT APPLEBEE'S® BAJA POTATO BOATS   115
FAT-FREE BOSTON MARKET® BUTTERNUT SQUASH   118
FAT-FREE BOSTON MARKET® CINNAMON APPLES   120
REDUCED-FAT BOSTON MARKET® CREAMED SPINACH   123
REDUCED-FAT BURGER KING® BK BROILER®   125
REDUCED-FAT BURGER KING® BIG KING®   128
REDUCED-FAT BURGER KING® WHOPPER®   131
REDUCED-FAT CHI-CHI'S® MEXICAN "FRIED" ICE CREAM   134
REDUCED-FAT CHI-CHI'S® SWEET CORN CAKE   137
REDUCED-FAT CINNABON® CINNAMON ROLLS   139
LOW-FAT DENNY'S® MOONS OVER MY HAMMY®   143
REDUCED-FAT DENNY'S® THE SUPER BIRD®   146

LOW-FAT DOLLY MADISON® BUTTERCRUMB CINNAMON   149
REDUCED-FAT DOLLY MADISON® CARROT CAKE   152
FAT-FREE EINSTEIN BROS.® CREAM CHEESE SHMEAR®:   155
    ROASTED GARLIC   155
    STRAWBERRY   156
    JALAPEÑO SALSA   157
    MAPLE WALNUT RAISIN   157
REDUCED-FAT EL POLLO LOCO® FLAME-BROILED CHICKEN   159
FAT-FREE EL POLLO LOCO® PINTO BEANS   161
FAT-FREE EL POLLO LOCO® SPANISH RICE   162
LOW-FAT EL POLLO LOCO® BURRITOS: 163
    B.R.C.®   163
    CLASSIC CHICKEN   164
    SPICY HOT CHICKEN   164
    LOCO GRANDE®   165
REDUCED-FAT HOOTERS® BUFFALO CHICKEN WINGS   166
LOW-FAT HOOTERS® BUFFALO SHRIMP   169
FAT-FREE KELLOGG'S® RICE KRISPIES TREATS®   172
LOW-FAT KFC® BUTTERMILK BISCUITS   175
FAT-FREE KFC® COLE SLAW   178
LOW-FAT KFC® MASHED POTATOES & GRAVY   180
REDUCED-FAT KFC® TENDER ROAST CHICKEN®   182
REDUCED-FAT MCDONALD'S® BIG MAC®   185
LOW-FAT MCDONALD'S® BREAKFAST BURRITO   189
REDUCED-FAT OLIVE GARDEN® CHICKEN CAESAR SANDWICH   192
FAT-FREE OLIVE GARDEN® ITALIAN SALAD DRESSING   195
REDUCED-FAT OLIVE GARDEN® PASTA E FAGIOLI   197
LOW-FAT OLIVE GARDEN® TIRAMISU   199
REDUCED-FAT OTIS SPUNKMEYER® APPLE CINNAMON MUFFINS   203
REDUCED-FAT OTIS SPUNKMEYER® BANANA NUT MUFFINS   206
LOW-FAT RED LOBSTER® CHEDDAR BAY BISCUITS®   209
FAT-FREE RED LOBSTER® TARTAR SAUCE   212
REDUCED-FAT SHONEY'S® HOT FUDGE CAKE   213

Reduced-Fat Shoney's® Country Fried Steak   217
Low-Fat Taco Bell® Beef Soft Taco   219
Reduced-Fat Taco Bell® Grilled Chicken Burrito   222
Reduced-Fat Taco Bell® Mexican Pizza   225
Reduced-Fat Wendy's® Single with Cheese   228
Low-Fat Wendy's® Frosty®   231
Reduced-Fat White Castle® Cheeseburgers   232

PART II: LOW-FAT TOP SECRET RECIPES

Guest Introduction: A Word From Fat Gram Freddy   237

LOW-FAT TOP SECRET RECIPES CLONES

Applebee's® Low-Fat Asian Chicken Salad   247
Applebee's® Low-Fat & Fabulous™ Brownie Sundae   249
California Pizza Kitchen® Tuscan Hummus   252
California Pizza Kitchen® Dakota Smashed Pea & Barley Soup   254
California Pizza Kitchen® Grilled Eggplant Cheeseless Pizza   256
California Pizza Kitchen® Vegetarian Pizza   260
Chevys™ Fresh Salsa   264
Entenmann's Light® Low-Fat Cinnamon Raisin Sweet Rolls   266
Entenmann's Light® Low-Fat Gourmet Cinnamon Rolls   269
Gardenburger® Classic Greek Veggie Patty   272
Gardenburger® Fire-Roasted Vegetable Veggie Patty   276
Gardenburger® Savory Mushroom Veggie Patty   280
Girl Scout Cookies® Reduced-Fat Lemon Pastry Cremes   284
Healthy Choice® Traditional Pasta Sauce   287
Healthy Choice® Chunky Tomato, Mushroom & Garlic Pasta Sauce   288
Keebler® Reduced-Fat Pecan Sandies®   290

Koo Koo Roo® Original Skinless Flame-Broiled
   Chicken™   292
Koo Koo Roo® Santa Fe Pasta   295
Little Debbie® Oatmeal Lights®   298
Nabisco® Honey Maid® Grahams: 301
   Honey   301
   Cinnamon   302
   Chocolate   304
Nabisco® Old Fashion Ginger Snaps   307
Nabisco® Reduced-Fat Oreo® Cookies   310
Nabisco® SnackWell's® Apple Raisin Snack Bars   314
Nabisco® SnackWell's® Banana Snack Bars   317
Planters® Fat-Free Fiddle Faddle®   320
Rainforest Cafe® Reggae Beat Seasoning®   323
Rainforest Cafe® The Plant Sandwich   325
Rainforest Cafe® Rumble in the Jungle Turkey Pita®   328
Seven Seas® Free Red Wine Vinegar Fat-Free
   Dressing   331
Seven Seas® Free Viva Italian Fat-Free Dressing   333
Tootsie Roll® Midgees   335

LOW-FAT TOP SECRET RECIPES **CONVERSIONS**

Reduced-Fat Applebee's® Tequila Lime Chicken   341
Reduced-Fat Bennigan's® Buffalo Chicken Sandwich   344
Low-Fat California Pizza Kitchen® Sedona White Corn
   Tortilla Soup   347
Reduced-Fat Carl's Jr.® Ranch Crispy Chicken
   Sandwich   349
Reduced-Fat Carl's Jr.® Charbroiled Chicken Club
   Sandwich™   353
Reduced-Fat Carl's Jr.® Charbroiled Santa Fe Chicken
   Sandwich™   356

Reduced-Fat Carl's Jr.® Bacon Swiss Crispy Chicken Sandwich™ 359

Fat-Free Chevys® Garlic Mashed Potatoes 363

Reduced-Fat Chevys® Texas BBQ Wrap 365

Reduced-Fat Chevys® Mesquite-Grilled BBQ Chicken Quesadilla 369

Reduced-Fat Chili's® Boneless Buffalo Wings 373

Reduced-Fat Chili's® Fajita Salad 376

Reduced-Fat Chili's® Margarita Grilled Tuna 379

Reduced-Fat Chili's® Southwestern Eggrolls 384

Reduced-Fat KFC® Macaroni & Cheese 388

Fat-Free KFC® Potato Salad 391

Reduced-Fat McDonald's® Arch Deluxe® 394

Low-Fat McDonald's® Egg McMuffin® 398

Reduced-Fat Olive Garden® Chicken Parmigiana Sandwich 401

Reduced-Fat Olive Garden® Fettucine Alfredo 404

Reduced-Fat Olive Garden® Zuppa Toscana 406

Reduced-Fat Otis Spunkmeyer® Chocolate Chip Muffins 408

Reduced-Fat Otis Spunkmeyer® Wild Blueberry Muffins 411

Reduced-Fat Outback Steakhouse® Walkabout Soup® 414

Low-Fat Outback Steakhouse® Caesar Salad Dressing 416

Reduced-Fat Outback Steakhouse® Alice Springs Chicken® 418

Reduced-Fat Panda Express® Orange-Flavored Chicken 422

Reduced-Fat Rainforest Cafe® Tropical Chicken Quartet® 425

Low-Fat Screaming Yellow Zonkers® 429

Reduced-Fat Sonic Drive-In® No. 1 Burger 432

Reduced-Fat Sonic Drive-In® Hickory Burger 435

Reduced-Fat Sonic Drive-In® Jalapeño Burger   438
Reduced-Fat Taco Bell® Beef Burrito Supreme®   441
Low-Fat Taco Bell® Chicken Soft Taco   444
Reduced-Fat T.G.I. Friday's® BBQ Chicken Wings   447
Reduced-Fat T.G.I. Friday's® Dijon Chicken Pasta   450
Reduced-Fat T.G.I. Friday's® Potato Skins   453
Reduced-Fat Wendy's® Chicken Caesar Fresh Stuffed Pita®   456
Low-Fat Wendy's® Classic Greek Fresh Stuffed Pita®   459
Reduced-Fat Wendy's® Junior Bacon Cheeseburger   462
Reduced-Fat Wendy's® Spicy Chicken Fillet Sandwich   465

PART III: TOP SECRET RECIPES: SODAS, SMOOTHIES, SPIRITS, & SHAKES

Introduction   471

SODAS

A&W® Cream Soda   480
A&W® Root Beer   481
Coca-Cola®   483
Orange Slice®   487
7UP®   488
Sonic Drive-In® Cherry Limeade   490
Sonic Drive-In® Strawberry Limeade   491
Sonic Drive-In® Ocean Water®   492
Squirt®   493
T.G.I. Friday's® November Sea Breeze Fling®   494
T.G.I. Friday's® Strawberry Surprise Fling®   495

SMOOTHIES

Applebee's® Bananaberry Freeze   500

Baskin-Robbins® Peach Smoothie   502
Baskin-Robbins® Strawberry Smoothie   503
Baskin-Robbins® Strawberry Banana Smoothie   504
Baskin-Robbins® Wild Berry Banana Smoothie   505
Jamba Juice® Banana Berry   506
Jamba Juice® Citrus Squeeze   507
Jamba Juice® Cranberry Craze   509
Jamba Juice® Orange-A-Peel   510
Jamba Juice® Peach Pleasure   511
Jamba Juice® Strawberries Wild   512
Orange Julius®:   513
   Pineapple Julius®   514
   Strawberry Julius®   514
Red Robin® Chillin' Mango Smoothie   515
Red Robin® Groovy Smoothie   516
Starbucks® Tazoberry® Tea: 517
   Tazoberry® & Cream   518
T.G.I. Friday's® Tropical Oasis smoothie   519

SHAKES

Arby's® Jamocha Shake   525
Baskin-Robbins® B.R. Blast®:   526
   Cappuccino   526
   Mocha   527
Cinnabon® Icescape®:   528
   Strawberry   528
   Orange   529
   Mochalatta®   529
Cinnabon® Mochalatta Chill®   530
Dairy Queen® Blizzard®:   531
   Baby Ruth®   532
   Banana Pudding   532
   Banana Split   534

BERRY BANANA 534
CHOCOLATE CHIP 535
CHOCOLATE CHIP COOKIE DOUGH 535
HAWAIIAN 536
WHOPP'N'WILD 536
YUKON CRUNCHER 537
JACK IN THE BOX® OREO® COOKIE SHAKE 538
MCDONALD'S® MCFLURRY®: 539
    BUTTERFINGER® 539
    M&M'S® 540
    OREO® COOKIE 540
    REESE'S® 540
MCDONALD'S® SHAKES: 542
    CHOCOLATE 542
    STRAWBERRY 542
    VANILLA 542
MCDONALD'S® SHAMROCK SHAKE® 544
SONIC DRIVE-IN® CREAM PIE SHAKES: 545
    BANANA 545
    CHOCOLATE 546
    COCONUT 546
    STRAWBERRY 547
STARBUCKS® FROZEN FRAPPUCCINO: 548
    COFFEE 548
    CARAMEL 550
    MOCHA 550
WENDY'S® FROSTY 551

OTHER SIPS

ARIZONA® GREEN TEA WITH GINSENG AND HONEY 555
ARIZONA® ICED TEA WITH GINSENG 556
CINNABON® STRAWBERRY LEMONADE 557
GENERAL FOODS INTERNATIONAL COFFEES®: 558

Café Vienna   558
French Vanilla Café   559
Hazelnut Belgian Café   559
Suisse Mocha   560
Viennese Chocolate Café   560
Hawaiian Punch® Fruit Juicy Red   561
Hot Dog on a Stick® Muscle Beach Lemonade®   562
Minute Maid® All Natural Lemonade   564
Nestea® Natural Lemon Flavored Iced Tea   565
Red Robin® Freckled Lemonade   566
Red Robin® Strawberry Ecstacy   567
7-Eleven® Cherry Slurpee®   568
Snapple® Iced Tea: 570
   Cranberry   570
   Diet Lemon   570
   Lemon   571
   Orange   571
   Peach   571
   Raspberry   571
   Strawberry   571
Sunny Delight®   573
Yoo-hoo® Chocolate Drink   575
Yoo-hoo® Mix-Ups®:   576
   Chocolate-Banana   576
   Chocolate-Mint   576
   Chocolate-Strawberry   577

SPIRITS
SCHNAPPS & LIQUEURS

Bailey's® Original Irish Cream   583
DeKuyper® Thrilla Vanilla® French Vanilla Liqueur   584
DiSaronno® Amaretto   585
Grand Marnier® Liqueur   586

Hiram Walker® Anisette Liqueur 587
Hiram Walker® Crème de Banana Liqueur 588
Hiram Walker® Crème de Cacao Liqueur 589
Hiram Walker® Crème de Menthe Liqueur 590
Hiram Walker® Crème de Strawberry Liqueur 591
Hiram Walker® Razz Attack® Raspberry Schnapps 592
Hiram Walker® Root Beer Schnapps 593
Kahlúa® Coffee Liqueur 594
Marie Brizard® Watermelon Liqueur 595
Midori® Melon Liqueur 596

SPIRITS
COCKTAILS

Applebee's® Bananaberry Split 602
Applebee's® Blue Skies 603
Applebee's® Perfect Margarita 604
Applebee's® Summer Squeeze 605
Bahama Breeze® Bahama Mama 606
Bahama Breeze® Caribbean Magic 607
Bahama Breeze® Malimbo Breeze 608
Bahama Breeze® Verry Berry Good 609
Bennigan's® Emerald Isle Iced Tea 610
Bennigan's® Irish Coffee 611
Bennigan's® O'Malley's Orange Cooler 613
Bennigan's® Raspberry Road Iced Tea 614
The Cheesecake Factory® Caribbean Cooler 615
The Cheesecake Factory® Key Lime Martini 616
The Cheesecake Factory® J.W. Pink Lemonade 617
The Cheesecake Factory® Twilight Zone 618
The Cheesecake Factory® Tropical Martini 619
Chevys® 100% Blue Agave Margarita 620
Chevys® House Rocks Margarita 621
Chevys® Lava Lamp Margarita 622

Chevys® The Sunburn Margarita   623
Chevys® Ultimate Orange Margarita   624
Chevys® Watermelon Fresh Fruit Margarita®
   (on the rocks)   625
Chili's® Calypso Cooler   626
Chili's® Chambord 1800 Margarita   628
Chili's® Jamaican Paradise   629
Chili's® Mandrin Blush   630
Chili's® Margarita Presidente   631
Chili's® Tropical Sunburn   632
Chili's® Twisted Lemonade   633
Claim Jumper® Absolutely Electric Lemonade   634
Claim Jumper® Bermuda Sunset   635
Claim Jumper® Hawaiian Punch   636
Claim Jumper® Mai Tai   637
Claim Jumper® Otter Pop   638
Claim Jumper® Root Beer Float   639
Claim Jumper® Shark on the Beach   640
Claim Jumper® Tropical Storm   641
Hard Rock Cafe® The Hard Rock Hurricane   642
Hard Rock Cafe® Lynchburg Lo-Rider   643
Hard Rock Cafe® Shooters: 644
   Lemon Drop   644
   Purple Hooter   646
House of Blues® Eve's Revenge Martini   647
House of Blues® HOB Blue Martini   648
House of Blues® HOB Cruiser   649
House of Blues® Mo' Betta Blues   650
Joe's Crab Shack® Joe Makin' Me Java   651
Joe's Crab Shack® Joe's Ya Ya   652
Joe's Crab Shack® Red Snapper   653
Joe's Crab Shack® Secret Passion Punch   654
Joe's Crab Shack® Shark Tooth   655

Joe's Crab Shack® Swamp Moss   656
Olive Garden® Chocolate Almond Amoré   657
Olive Garden® Italian Margarita   658
Olive Garden® Strawberry Siciliano   659
Olive Garden® Venetian Sunset   660
Outback Steakhouse® Coral Reef 'Rita   661
Outback Steakhouse® Don't Koala Me,
   I'll Koala You Cooler   662
Outback Steakhouse® Great Barrier Punch   663
Outback Steakhouse® Melbourne Cooler   664
Outback Steakhouse® Wallaby Darned   665
P.F. Chang's® Buddha's Dream   667
P.F. Chang's® Heat Wave   668
P.F. Chang's® Nutty Uncle Chang's Favorite   669
P.F. Chang's® The Poolside   670
Planet Hollywood® The Comet   671
Planet Hollywood® Cool Running   672
Planet Hollywood® Meet Jack Black   673
Planet Hollywood® Shooters: 674
   Blue Hawaii   674
   Bubble Gum   674
   Grape Crush   674
   Peanut Butter & Jelly   675
Planet Hollywood® Sweet Death Becomes Her   676
Planet Hollywood® Terminator   677
Red Lobster® Bahama Mama   678
Red Lobster® Butter-tini Funtini   679
Red Lobster® The Hawaiian Funtini   680
Red Lobster® Red Passion Colada   681
Red Robin® Absolut Lemonade   682
Red Robin® Jamaican Shake   683
Red Robin® Sand in Your Shorts   684
Red Robin® T.N.T.   686

T.G.I. Friday's® Banana Split blender blaster   687
T.G.I. Friday's® Electric Lemonade   688
T.G.I. Friday's® Hawaiian Volcano   689
T.G.I. Friday's® June Bug   690
T.G.I. Friday's® Lights of Havana   691
T.G.I. Friday's® Strawberry Shortcake blender blaster   692
Z'Tejas® Z' Big Stick Margarita   693
Z'Tejas® Famous Chambord Raspberry Margarita   695

SPIRITS
MIXERS

Beau Rivage® Bloody Mary Mix   699
Mara® Simple Syrup   700
Mr & Mrs T® Bloody Mary Mix   701
Mr & Mrs T® Sweet & Sour Mix   702
Restaurant-Style Mai Tai Mix   703
Restaurant-Style Pina Colada Mix   704
Restaurant-Style Sweet & Sour Mix   705

Bibliography   707

Trademarks   709

Index   713

TOP SECRET RECIPES
LITE!

INTRODUCTION

Before I begin, let me assure you that my love for the gooey, greasy, cheesy, sugary, sloppy, slippery, creamy, saucy, and chocolaty famous American convenience foods cloned in previous *Top Secret Recipes* books has not diminished in the least. I'm still in ecstasy when sinking my teeth into a hot double-stacked burger slathered in secret sauce, or when chomping down hard into a chocolate bar loaded with caramel, nougat, and a fistful of nuts.

I don't care who you are, or how healthy you claim to eat, or how much you boast you never divert your car in a rush through a fast-food drive-thru joint for a quickie. It's a sure bet that you have at least one favorite, sinfully delicious food that you often crave, that's high in fat and calories. I'm talking about the kind of food that gives you an ecstatic rush as you eat it, and practically gets you high from the oral gratification. I'm talking about the type of grub that washes over your tastebuds in that all-too-short belly-stuffing journey, making you close your eyes for just a moment while you chew to let out a little "mmmm." It's the euphoric palatal experience that ends much too soon. And it's the experience that's quickly followed by the post-nosh guilt, as you realize the pants are a bit more snug today, and will be a lot more snug tomorrow.

Sure, I still enjoy eating America's favorite brand-name foods, and I still dig cloning them at home, just as much as ever. But I also realize that no matter how good the stuff tastes, these higher-fat foods can't be on the menu every day if I want to maintain a 6-foot-tall, 180-pound frame. Sure, if I gave in to my cravings, I'd be eating huge portions of Olive Garden Tiramisu, Taco Bell Mexican Pizza, KFC Cole Slaw, and Big Mac after Big Mac (I'll have fries with that, please). And I could eat Hooters Buffalo Wings every day of the year and not get sick of them ... until around Thanksgiving. Okay, make that Christmas.

But I don't pig out wildly on these foods because I know that, while these products are delicious and popular, some of them contain significant amounts of fat. And we've all been informed by the scads of nutritionists and dieticians on anti-fat crusades that if we want to stay fit, we're going to have to turn away from the greasy goodies and start looking in the direction of "low-fat alternatives." I've heard it, you've heard it; and as much as I don't want to hear it anymore, I know I will, and so will you. And the real bummer is, it's all true.

This news was even more of a bummer in the early days of the move away from foods higher in fat. Back then, smart, tasty alternatives were hard to come by. Food manufacturers were coming out with products that tasted only slightly better than potting soil. Maybe that's why when we hear the words "low-fat" or "fat-free" today, while we know it's the right thing to choose, a part of us is thinking "yech!"

But the good news is that in the last several years, fat-reduced foods have been much improved. There are many more better-tasting staple products such as mayonnaise, cheese, sour cream, and butter-flavored additives available than ever before. With these products and the skillful use of thickeners, starches, and fruit purees, it's now easier to enjoy foods that taste as though they're pumped with fat, when the nutrition facts say otherwise. The tricks we're learning to remove the fat from our meals and snacks, both in the food production plants and in the home kitchens, are quickly turning the "yechs" into "yums."

As I was creating the previous *Top Secret Recipes* books, I began to devise simple ways to use lower-fat ingredients and special cooking techniques that would eliminate much of the fat, yet retain the flavor of the original product. This was a casual exercise, for my own meals, and I was at first only moderately effective. But as I explored and experimented further over the years, and started to use the many new fat-free ingredients that were becoming available, I found that it was possible to eliminate at least 50 percent of the fat in most cloned convenience foods, with minimal effort and standard ingredients. The big surprise was that in many cases I could get the fat down much lower than that—as low as 15 to 20 percent of the original product.

Isn't it amazing that only twenty-five years ago we could eat the same higher-fat foods available today without feeling that we had done something horribly wrong. Today we still have the same classic burgers, famous fried food, top-selling candy bars, snack cakes, and cookies that have been around for years; and these items are as popular as ever. But in this last decade of the millennium we are continuously force-fed information about what is good and bad for our bodies. How often have you heard that we should eat no more than 2200 calories a day and that we should limit our fat intake to around 60 grams? Sure we hear it, and we know it. But that information doesn't keep us from loving our favorite junk foods. It just makes us feel much worse when we cave in.

Food manufacturers are aware of our dilemma, and they realize that creating products that address our nutritional concerns *and* that satisfy our strongest, most insatiable cravings, is a quick trip down mega-profits street. Millions and millions of dollars have been spent on reduced-fat product development, and for conversion of previously higher-fat products to trendy lower-fat versions. Just look for the green packages. Not only can these healthier alternatives be found in growing numbers in supermarket aisles, but also fast-food outlets and restaurant chains have been making lower-fat choices available. It's the latest food craze, and the cost to the consumer is usually high. Ironically, many times the lower-fat or light versions of a product are more expensive or smaller in size (or both) than the higher-fat counterpart.

And as these food companies with their "healthy alternatives" are wrestling for shelf space and customers, scores of cookbook authors have jumped into the fray. Low-fat cookbooks have been some of the most popular books sold in recent years, with some scoring high on bestseller lists. Many of these books have some great ideas and delicious recipes (and some definitely don't), but not one gives us recipes for the type of food for which we really want homemade reduced-fat versions. I'm talking about the kind of food that sales figures show is the most popular food—convenience food, fast food, and junk food. America's favorite foods.

If you are discouraged to find that supermarkets are filled with record numbers of overly expensive and not-so-fresh low-fat products; or if you have wished for reduced-fat versions of your favorite brand-name foods; or if you have yearned for a low-fat cookbook that actually provides recipes to make dishes at home that taste good rather than tasting low-fat, then I'm hoping to make your day.

This book will show you how to make low-fat and fat-free food at home that will taste just like these reduced-fat products you find in restaurants and supermarkets, at a fraction of the cost. At the same time, this book will show you how to cook reduced-fat food at home that tastes as good as the popular brands that're usually higher in fat.

TWO, TWO, TWO BOOKS IN ONE

What you have here is like two books in one. The first section is a collection of recipes that taste like existing low-fat and fat-free products. These are famous products such as Nabisco Snack-Well's Cookies, Weight Watchers Éclairs, Hostess Lights Twinkies, Kellogg's Low-Fat Pop-Tarts, and Gardenburger Veggie Patties. These products are created by the manufacturers as lower-fat versions of their existing higher-fat products, or as an entirely new line of products created solely for the fat-conscious eaters. Some of these products, such as Einstein Bros. Bagels, are just naturally low in fat, without much attention drawn to that fact.

When creating these clone recipes for the products in the first half of the book, I've made every attempt to keep fat gram numbers the same as the real item. This was not always easy. In fact, it was rarely easy, and next to the boxes, cans, and bottles of ingredients on the kitchen counter could always be found a well-stained calculator, ready to spew running fat totals.

With the recipes in the first half of the book, you can now

recreate your favorite low-fat and fat-free foods with everyday ingredients. This gives you the opportunity to enjoy a product that may not be available where you live, and, in most cases, you will find that creating the product at home from scratch saves a significant amount of money, versus buying the real thing. Plus fresh food is always better than the packaged stuff, which may contain preservatives.

The second section is the fat-reduction extravaganza. This part of the book is filled with recipes to clone items that don't exist as lower-fat or fat-free food. I call these recipes "TSR Lite Conversions," and it is here where you will find recipes to recreate America's favorite brand-name foods, but with significantly reduced numbers in the fat column. Every recipe reduces the fat grams by at least 50 percent when compared to the original product—and in many cases, by significantly more than that.

The recipes in this section make it possible for you to get lower-fat versions of products that would otherwise be impossible to enjoy. With these recipes you can now have a cinnamon roll that tastes like Cinnabon Cinnamon Rolls with only 4 grams of fat, while the actual product contains 24 grams of fat. You can savor the flavor of Boston Market's Creamed Spinach for just one-fourth the fat grams (6g fat) of the original (24g fat). You can eat two clone hamburgers (13g fat each) with the same taste of a Big Mac, but still not consume as much fat as just one of the real burgers (31g fat).

Here are some other examples of the incredible fat savings when compared to the original:

	Original	*TSR Conversion*
Burger King BK Broiler	29 grams	6 grams
Chi-Chi's "Fried" Ice Cream	34 grams (est.)	7 grams
Hooters Buffalo Wings	30 grams (est.)	10 grams
KFC Buttermilk Biscuits	10 grams	2.5 grams
McDonald's Breakfast Burrito	19 grams	2.5 grams
Olive Garden Tiramisu	38 grams (est.)	2.9 grams
Otis Spunkmeyer Banana Nut Muffins	12 grams	5 grams

	Original	*TSR Conversion*
Red Lobster Cheddar Biscuits	7 grams	3 grams
Shoney's Country Fried Steak	37 grams	10 grams
Taco Bell Mexican Pizza	36 grams	10 grams
Wendy's Frosty	11 grams	2 grams

There are even several TSR conversions that cut out all the fat. With these recipes you can now enjoy fat-free versions of Olive Garden's Italian Salad Dressing, Boston Market Butternut Squash, and Red Lobster Tartar Sauce. And even though KFC's famous cole slaw contains more than 10 grams of fat per serving, you now have a TSR conversion to recreate a fat-free clone—and it's made with only five ingredients!

THE TOP SECRET TRICKS

As I created the recipes in previous *Top Secret Recipes* books, I gave priority to one very important guideline: All ingredients for the recipes must be available in the local supermarket. This is often difficult, as manufacturers love to pack their ingredients list with additives, flavorings, stabilizers, and preservatives with long names that consumers like you and me will never be able to track down at the neighborhood Safeway. We must then find substitutes for the commercial components, while dismissing preservatives entirely, since our homemade versions won't be sitting on the shelves for weeks at a time. I would hope.

Adhering to this rule presented a bigger challenge than ever when creating these reduced-fat recipes. That's because in the low-fat and fat-free food manufacturing world, companies use obscure gums and thickeners and modified starches to replace the missing fat in their products. These additional ingredients are necessary to give a product the textural qualities of fat. Although carrageenan, xanthan gum, cellulose gel, and carob bean gum are missing from supermarket aisles, we do have access to many products that can stand in nicely. The trick is in determining the best ingredient for each situation. Lots of time is logged over a stovetop and mixing bowl figuring out if a recipe works better with pectin or gelatin or cornstarch or arrowroot, or other available thickeners and additives that may help to give the finished product a pleasant texture.

A baked product may be best with some fruit puree mixed in. Raisin or prune or banana purees lend a nice flavor to cakes and brownies and cookies, and they help a snack retain moisture and give it a pleasant, chewy consistency. Unsweetened applesauce can make magic happen. And sweetened condensed skim milk works great with its sweet fat-free gooeyness.

In creamy sauces and dressings, we might use fat-free versions of sour cream, mayonnaise, strained nonfat yogurt, cream cheese, or evaporated milk. For creamy desserts, fat-free puddings and Dream Whip come in very handy.

Also included in our arsenal will be products to replace the butter in many of the recipes. Fleischmann's Fat Free Buttery Spread, I Can't Believe It's Not Butter Spray, and Butter Buds Sprinkles are excellent weapons in the TSR fight against fat.

I've even made a special effort to find substitutes for soy lecithin and whey, common in baked goods, but only available in health food stores. Even though some low-fat cookbooks include these items in their recipes, I felt that they were not common enough to include. You will also find that I leave in some optional suggestions for ingredients, such as cake decorating items like clear vanilla, brown paste food coloring, and meringue powder, but that these are not necessary to complete the recipe. They are only suggested to make a better clone. There is, however, one case where bulgur wheat is essential. That's in the *Top Secret Recipes* version of the Gardenburger Original Veggie Patty. You just can't create that one without bulgur wheat, which you can sometimes find in supermarkets (it's becoming increasingly more popular), but in many cities may require a trip to the health food store.

Prepare to have several of these ingredients on hand as you go forth into the world of lower-fat kitchen cloning.

While these ingredients help greatly in our fight against fat, there are a great many tricks that involve the cooking process itself. In some recipes, for example, we'll leave the skin on chicken pieces while they bake to lock in the juiciness, then we'll strip it off during the final cooking stages. And we'll recreate fried products such as Shoney's Country Fried Steak and Hooters Buffalo Chicken Wings by breading the meat and spraying it with a light coating of vegetable oil cooking spray before baking the portions in a very hot oven.

By using this book, you'll surely learn to use some ingredients and cooking techniques that will help you reduce the fat from many of your own favorite recipes. And food companies will surely continue to develop additional ingredients in the future that will further add to your personal reduced-fat cooking bag of tricks.

A TRIBUTE TO OUR GOOD FRIEND, MR. FAT

Most of us remember a time when we ate only for taste, with little regard for ingredients and cooking methods. Only a dozen or so years ago much of our food was fried in animal tallow. Butter, heavy cream, and oil were added to foods indiscriminately, in large amounts. Eggs were eaten every morning, and red meat every night. Then a little ice cream would be thrown in for dessert.

After all, this is America, a supreme technologically advanced superpower, land of the free, home of the brave, and the world's fattest nation. It's the country where the average citizen eats 130 pounds of fat per year, or the equivalent of a stick of butter every day. This is the country where, according to Joseph Piscatella in *Choices for a Healthy Heart*, "the typical adult American male weighs 20 to 30 pounds too much, and the typical female is overweight by 15 to 30 pounds."

Even though there are entire areas of the globe where coronary heart disease is not known, obesity is the American way. But it's a recent problem that goes back not as far as you might think. Prior to World War II, Americans were primarily blue-collar laborers, working hard in factories, burning off massive amounts of calories, and staying lean. Like professional athletes, these workers could eat large amounts of food and, as fuel, it would burn off with the daily activity.

But after the war, automation eased the workloads. The country began a shift to a more white-collar society working to process the increasing amounts of information. Modern-day conveniences were being developed to make life easier. Automobile sales were skyrocketing and television became America's favorite leisure-time activity.

These developments were the beginning of our nation's new sedentary lifestyle. The fat and calories that were once burned off were just sitting there as folks leisurely rested in a car every day while driving to work and then, at the office, sat for many hours behind a desk. Back home, after sitting again for dinner, more sitting was still to come in front of the tube until bedtime. Sitting upon sitting upon sitting, without adjustments to the heavy diets, led to the inevitable consequences: millions of cases of obesity, high cholesterol, and coronary heart disease. This was not a good thing.

To make matters worse, after the war many soldiers returning from overseas wanted the luxury of gourmet meals smothered in thick creamy sauces, butter and cheese, and entrées of red meat. These thick greasy ingredients became known as luxury items and were much sought after at the time, especially for those who had been denied them for so long. It would eventually become clear that our diets would have to change.

Millions of heart attacks later, in the 1980s, the tide was turning as growing numbers of Americans began to heed the advice of the dieticians who had been emphasizing the need to cut down on the fat choking off our precious arteries. They told us that while our bodies do need some fat to function, too much of the stuff leads to high cholesterol and coronary heart disease. They told us that the body is limited in the amount of proteins and carbohydrates it stores, but there is no limit to the amount of fat it can accumulate.

It was in the late eighties that the increasing interest to reduce the fat in our foods began to show up in numerous products on grocery store shelves. But, it wasn't until the 1990s that the trend really took off.

The three words "Reduced in Fat" became the most appealing descriptor for products in supermarkets. Slapping the words "low-fat" or "fat-free" on the products, and using green on the packaging to indicate reduced fat, maintained brand loyalty and kept the customers in a manufacturer's corner. Those who held out converting their brands in the earliest part of the decade would eventually give in to create low-fat clones of their existing products as well. The low-fat rush was on.

Consumers demanded low-fat alternatives like never before. Just look at the trend: In 1994, there were 70 percent more reduced-fat products than in the year before. In 1995, that number went up again, to 1,914 new products. In 1996, it was up again, to 2,076. And today this number continues to climb.

At this rate, we'll exit this last decade of the millennium with green as the most commonly used color on product packaging in supermarket aisles. And that trend will continue to grow as scientists perfect magical new fat replacers that will allow us to eat formerly higher-fat foods without digesting a single gram—the fat will just pass right through. Newfangled substitutes, like Olestra and Salatrim, are now being marketed in snack food production by companies such as Nabisco, Frito-Lay, and Hershey. And you can expect to hear much more about these and other fat replacers in the near future; and about new developments on the horizon, such as a way to coat french fries with pectin to keep the oil from soaking in.

Yes, the low-fat revolution is on. And, with so many products to choose from, consumers are finding they can now limit the amount of fat in their diet and satisfy their cravings. The best of both worlds.

I'VE GOT YOUR LABEL RIGHT HERE

In 1990, when the Food and Drug Administration passed laws that standardized labeling of nutrition information on all products, confusion over what our food was offering us in regard to fat and calories came to an end. Or did it?

Prior to 1990, nutrition labeling was required only of products that had added nutrients or when nutrition claims appeared on the label. Cereals fortified with "8 essential vitamins and minerals" were to list those extra nutrients and include the percentage of daily recommended allowance satisfied by a single serving.

Today, in addition to Daily Value percentages, the labels are printed in large, easy-to-read type, with the heading "Nutrition Facts." Manufacturers are required to list calories, fat, saturated fat, cholesterol, fibers, sodium, and several other important nutritional contents on a per serving measurement.

Serving sizes must closely reflect the amount people eat (although that's certainly open for debate), and similar products must measure the same amount for nutritional analysis. For example, each brand of cookies measures approximately 1 ounce for analysis, for salad dressing it's 2 tablespoons, and for ice cream it's ½ cup.

One of the most misunderstood and confusing labeling practices concerns the fat claims now splashed across the front of product packages to encourage sales. There is much confusion about the combinations of two words, of which one is always "fat." "Reduced-Fat," "Low-Fat," "Fat-Free": Each of these terms means something different. Then, when we throw "Light," "Lean," and "Extra Lean" into the mix, it can all become a bit confusing.

Allow me to shed some light:

Reduced-Fat: This means that the product has at least 25 percent less fat per serving than the original food. Reduced-Fat Nabisco Cheese Nips have 3.5 grams of fat per serving, whereas the original full-fat Cheese Nips contain 6 grams of fat per serving.

Low-Fat: The product must contain 3 grams of fat or less per serving. The Reduced-Fat Cheese Nips mentioned above don't quite qualify as low-fat—they're ½ gram too heavy. However, Nabisco Reduced Fat 'Nilla Wafers (2 grams of fat per serving) qualify for the "low-fat" label. Nevertheless, Nabisco chose to go with "Reduced Fat." (Probably to stay consistent with its other products.)

Fat-Free: While you may assume that a product must contain no fat at all to qualify for this label, that is not entirely true. Adding up all of the fat grams contained within one package of a "fat-free" product might indeed reveal dozens of grams of fat. To qualify as "fat-free" a product is required to contain less than ½ a gram of fat *per serving*. An entire jar of fat-free mayonnaise may contain a total of 30 grams of fat, but since it holds 64 servings, with each serving under ½ gram of fat, the mayo is still considered "fat-free."

Light: This one means two things, and can be misleading.

Either the food must have one-third fewer calories or half the fat of the referenced food, or it means that a low-fat or low-calorie food has a sodium content that is reduced by half of the referenced food. Read the label carefully to determine exactly what "light" is referring to.

"Lite!" as it is used in the title of this book, refers to the low-fat claims of the original products cloned in the first section. For the second section, it refers to the amount by which the recipes have been reduced in fat—at least 50 percent.

Low-Calorie: The product has no more than 40 calories per serving.

Calorie-Free: The product has less than 5 calories per serving.

Lean: Found on meat packaging, this means that the product has less than 10 grams of total fat per serving.

Extra Lean: Also found on meat packaging, this means that the product has less than 5 grams of total fat per serving.

David Lean: Directed the movie *Lawrence of Arabia*. Rarely used.

All of the rules that apply to the labels on the food you find in your supermarket are used in the same manner within this book. If the recipe says "*Top Secret Recipes* Low-Fat version of Taco Bell Beef Soft Taco" you can expect a serving of the finished product to have 3 grams of fat or less.

SPECIAL AUTHOR'S NOTE

The nutritional facts (fat and calories) included with each of the clone recipes were compiled with the help of manufacturers' labels, and fat gram and calorie content reference material. Care was taken to make very accurate calculations, but these numbers can vary slightly from brand to brand for certain ingredients. In these cases I used the numbers from the most popular brands available.

Most of the fat and calorie information for the manufacturers' original products comes from that company's printed nutritional information materials produced by corporate offices. Any nutrition information that was not available was calculated based on full-fat versions of the low-fat clone recipe. When these are estimated figures, I have indicated so.

As with my other books, none of these recipes has been created with the cooperation of the manufacturers. No manufacturers have endorsed this work, but I thank each and every one of them for creating the great food that has become so popular as to warrant its inclusion here.

Please know that I did not swipe, heist, or bribe, or otherwise obtain any formulas through coercion or illegal means. However I do admit to occasionally kidnapping samples of the restaurant food in doggie bags (after paying for them, of course), and transporting it to my hardly secret laboratory for further examination and experimentation.

While the product dissections may have appeared cruel, I assure you that no foodstuffs were harmed in the creation of this book.

SO LET'S GET COOKING!

Now, if you're ready to munch out on some fat-saving clones, get out some ingredients and measuring spoons, and tie on that apron. Or, better yet, start being really, really nice to the person you intend to persuade to do all of the cooking for you.

Whoever decides to give these recipes a try will find the recipes easy to follow, even for the novice chef. So dive right in, and get ready to enjoy lower-fat clones that are so good you don't even miss the fat.

If you'd like some more kitchen clone recipes, be sure to check out the other *Top Secret Recipes* books, also from Plume.

You may also want to surf on over to the official Web site, *Top Secret Recipes on the Web,* for dozens more recipes you won't find anywhere else, and new weekly content:

http://www.topsecretrecipes.com

Until next time, happy cloning!

—Todd Wilbur

TOP SECRET RECIPES
LITE!
CLONES

APPLEBEE'S LOW-FAT BLACKENED CHICKEN SALAD

TOP SECRET RECIPES VERSION OF

The big secret to keeping a tasty salad low in fat is to develop a dressing that's low in fat, or even better, fat-free. This recipe clones one of Applebee's most popular low-fat dishes from its "Low-Fat and Fabulous" selections. It's one dish that customers have raved about, because it's so delicious it just doesn't seem possible it could contain only 7 grams of fat. The burst of flavor from the marinated and blackened chicken helps to hide the lack of fat. And the dressing, which is made so incredibly light by using a fat-free mayonnaise base, is indescribably delicious.

DRESSING
¼ cup fat-free mayonnaise
¼ cup Grey Poupon Dijon
   mustard
1 tablespoon prepared mustard
¼ cup honey
1 tablespoon white vinegar
⅛ teaspoon paprika

CHICKEN MARINADE
1 cup water
3 tablespoons lime juice
2 tablespoons soy sauce
½ tablespoon Worcestershire
   sauce

2 chicken breast fillets

CAJUN SPICE BLEND

½ tablespoon salt
1 teaspoon sugar
1 teaspoon paprika
1 teaspoon onion powder

1 teaspoon black pepper
½ teaspoon garlic powder
½ teaspoon cayenne pepper
½ teaspoon white pepper

½ tablespoon butter

SALAD

8 cups chopped iceberg lettuce
½ cup shredded red cabbage
½ cup shredded carrot
½ cup shredded fat-free mozzarella cheese

½ cup shredded fat-free cheddar cheese
1 hard-boiled egg white, diced
1 large tomato, diced

1. Make the dressing by first combining the mayonnaise with the mustards in a small bowl. Whisk thoroughly until the ingredients are well combined. Mix in the honey, then the vinegar and paprika. Store the dressing in a covered container in the refrigerator until the salads are ready.
2. Combine the water, lime juice, soy sauce, and Worcestershire in a medium bowl, and stir. Add the chicken fillets to the marinade, cover the bowl, and keep it in the refrigerator for several hours. Marinate the chicken overnight, if you've got the time.
3. When the chicken is well marinated, preheat a frying pan or skillet (an iron skillet, if you've got it) over medium/high heat. Also, preheat your barbecue grill to medium/high heat.
4. Combine the spices for the Cajun spice blend in a small bowl. Sprinkle a teaspoon of the spice blend over one side of each chicken fillet. Cover the entire top surface of the chicken with an even coating of the spice blend.
5. Melt the butter in the hot pan, then sauté the chicken fillets for 2 to 3 minutes on the side with the spices. While the first side cooks, sprinkle another teaspoon of spice over the top of each chicken breast, coating that side as you did the other. Flip the chicken over, and sauté for another 2 to 3 minutes. The surface

of the chicken should end up with a charred-looking black coating.
6. Finish the chicken off on your barbecue grill. Grill each breast on both sides for 2 to 3 minutes, or until done.
7. While the chicken is cooking, prepare the salads by splitting the lettuce into two large bowls. Toss in the red cabbage and carrots. Mix the cheeses together, then top the salad with the cheese blend and hard-boiled egg white. Sprinkle half of the diced tomato over each salad.
8. Slice the chicken breasts crosswise to ½-inch-thick pieces. Spread the chicken over the top of the salads and serve immediately with dressing on the side.

- SERVES 2 AS AN ENTRÉE.

Nutrition Facts
SERVING SIZE—1 SALAD   FAT (PER SERVING)—7G
TOTAL SERVINGS—2   CALORIES (PER SERVING)—420

• • • •

APPLEBEE'S LOW-FAT VEGGIE QUESADILLA

The menu description's got the scoop: "Fresh mushrooms, red pepper, onion, broccoli, & carrots smothered in nonfat shredded Cheddar/Mozzarella blend & sandwiched between two wheat tortillas. Served with fat-free sour cream & shredded lettuce. Less than 10 grams of fat."

The TSR version of this tasty favorite appetizer comes in with a fat gram count that's even slightly lower than that, at only 6 grams. The fat-free cheese is where you're spared the major fat gram dosage. And the fat-free sour cream on the side, which nicely completes this guilt-free veggie-filled finger food, certainly helps to keep the waistline in check.

½ tablespoon canola oil
½ cup sliced mushrooms
⅓ cup shredded carrot
⅓ cup chopped broccoli
2 tablespoons diced onion
1 tablespoon diced red bell pepper
1 teaspoon soy sauce
dash cayenne pepper

dash black pepper
dash salt
2 10-inch whole wheat flour tortillas
¼ cup shredded fat-free cheddar cheese
¼ cup shredded fat-free mozzarella cheese
nonstick cooking spray

ON THE SIDE
fat-free sour cream
Pace picante salsa

shredded lettuce

1. In a frying pan that has a bigger diameter than the tortillas, sauté the vegetables in the oil over medium/high heat for 5 to 7 minutes. Season with soy sauce, peppers, and salt.
2. Pour the vegetables into a bowl, and place the frying pan back on the heat, but reduce the heat to medium/low.
3. Place one of the tortillas in the pan, and sprinkle half of the cheeses on the tortilla. Spread the vegetables over the cheese, then sprinkle the rest of the cheeses over the vegetables. Put the second tortilla on top, and cook for 1 to 2 minutes, or until heated through and the cheese is melted. Flip the quesadilla over and cook for 1 to 2 more minutes.
4. Slide the quesadilla onto a cutting board and slice it like a pizza into 6 equal pieces. Serve hot with fat-free sour cream, salsa, and shredded lettuce on the side.

- SERVES 2 AS AN APPETIZER.

Nutrition Facts

SERVING SIZE—½ QUESADILLA   FAT (PER SERVING)—6G
TOTAL SERVINGS—2   CALORIES (PER SERVING)—274

• • • •

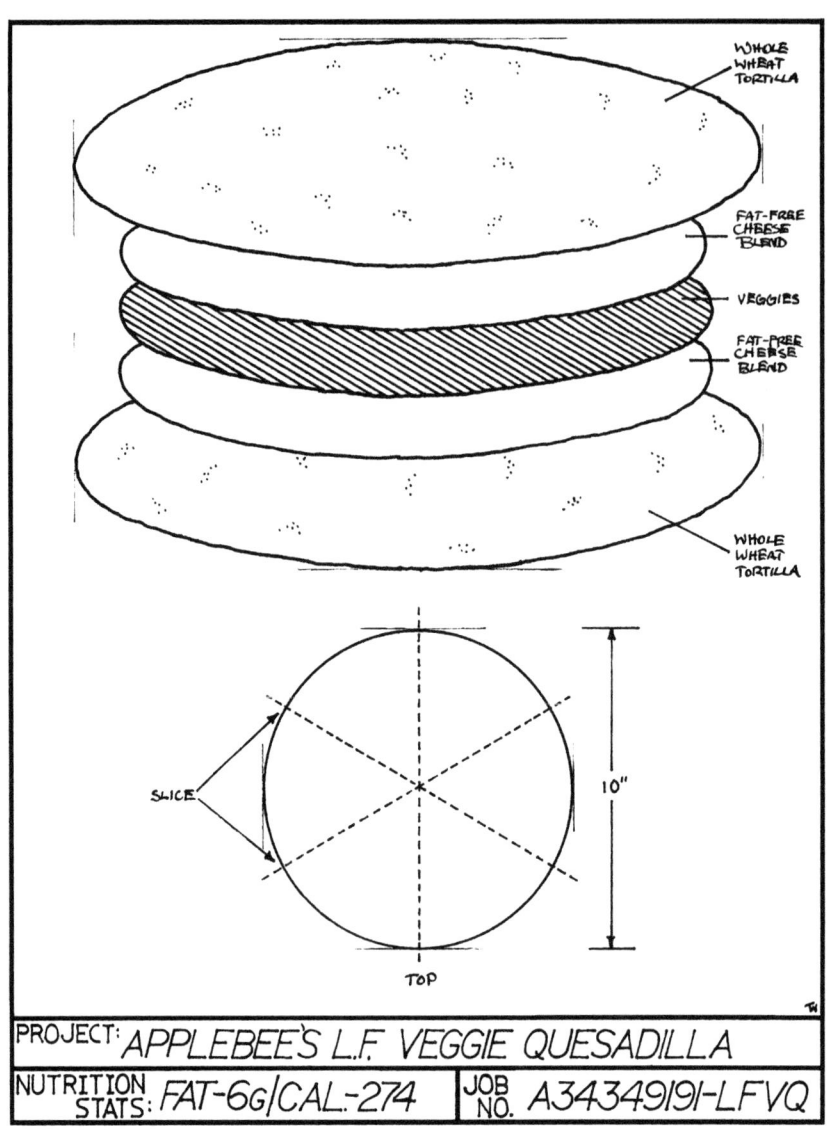

ARBY'S LIGHT MENU ROAST CHICKEN DELUXE

TOP SECRET RECIPES VERSION OF

Here's an awesome kitchen clone for a selection off of Arby's 3-item "Light Menu." As other fast food chains were zigging by creating giant gooey burgers with fat grams in the 40-plus range, this 3,100-outlet roast beef sandwich chain opted to zag, offering a selection of scrumptious sandwiches with only 6 to 10 grams of fat each.

The secret to recreating the special Arby's taste in the Roast Chicken Deluxe is in the marinade. Let your chicken soak in it for several hours, or even overnight, if you've got the patience. It also helps if you have a meat slicer to get that paper-thin, deli-style cut to the chicken. If you don't have a slicer, just do what I do. It's called the "poor man's meat slicer"—a very sharp knife and a steady hand.

CHICKEN MARINADE
2 tablespoons water
1 tablespoon vegetable oil
2 teaspoons ketchup
½ teaspoon sugar
½ teaspoon salt

¼ teaspoon paprika
⅛ teaspoon onion powder
⅛ teaspoon coarse black pepper
⅛ teaspoon savory
dash garlic powder

2 chicken breast fillets
butter-flavored spray or spread
4 whole wheat hamburger buns

2 tablespoons light mayonnaise
1 medium tomato, sliced
1 cup shredded lettuce

1. First make the marinade for the chicken breasts. In a small bowl, combine all of the ingredients for the marinade and stir well. Add the chicken breasts to the bowl and cover. Marinate the chicken for several hours. Overnight is even better.
2. When you are ready to make the sandwiches, preheat the oven to 400 degrees. Prepare to roast the chicken breasts by removing them from the marinade and placing them in a foil-lined baking pan. Bake for 20 to 25 minutes or until the chicken is fully cooked. When the chicken is cool enough to handle, slice each breast very thinly with a sharp knife. If you have a meat slicer, that works even better.
3. Preheat a frying pan or griddle to medium heat. Apply butter-flavored spread or spray to the faces of the top and bottom wheat buns. Grill the bun faces lightly on the hot cooking surface until light brown.
4. Build each sandwich by first placing one-quarter of the sliced chicken on the bottom bun.
5. Spread mayonnaise on the face of the top bun.
6. Invert the top bun. On the bun, stack a tomato slice or two, then ¼ cup of lettuce on top of that.
7. Slap the top portion of the sandwich onto the bottom and serve while the chicken is still warm. Repeat the process to make the remaining sandwiches.

- MAKES 4 SANDWICHES.

Nutrition Facts

SERVING SIZE—1 SANDWICH   FAT (PER SERVING)—6.5G
TOTAL SERVINGS—4   CALORIES (PER SERVING)—201

• • • •

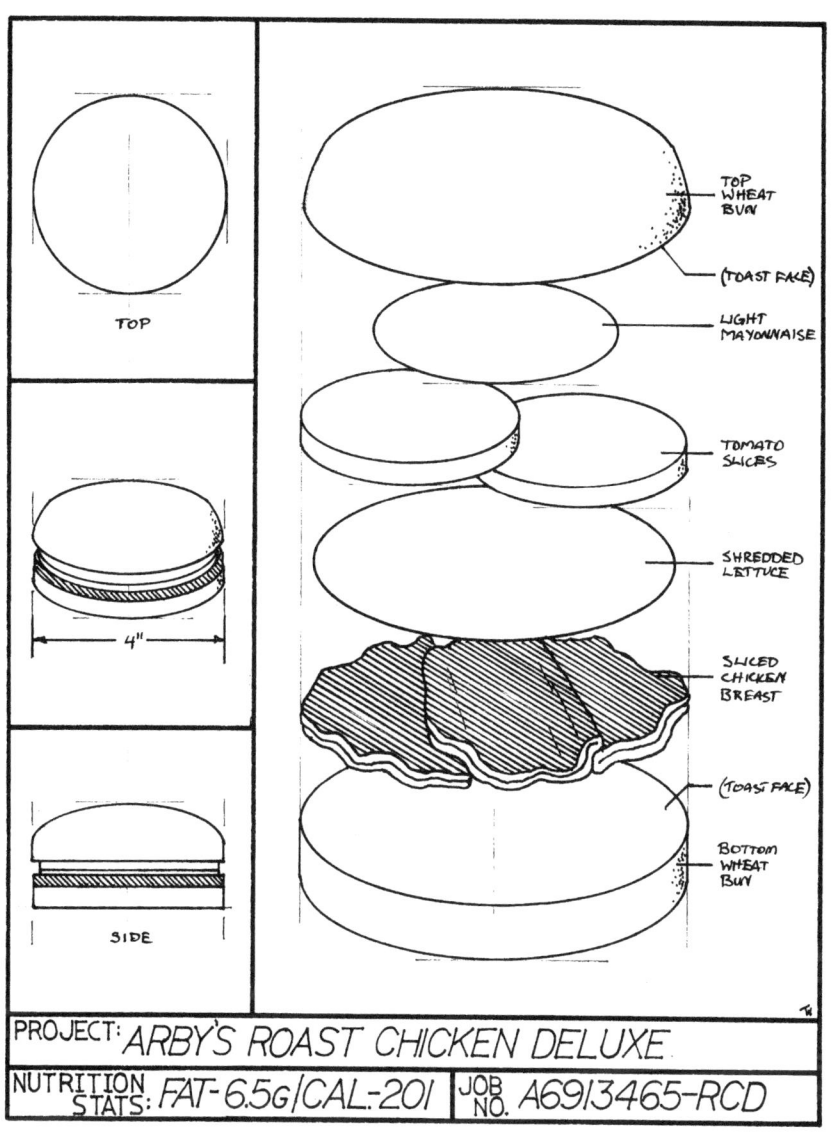

ARBY'S LIGHT MENU ROAST TURKEY DELUXE

It was in 1991 that Arby's saw a market for a selection of sandwiches that weighed in with very little fat. The chain was able to create three sandwiches that had 10 grams of fat or less, with whole wheat hamburger buns, light mayonnaise, lettuce, and tomato. Of the three selections, it is the Roast Turkey Deluxe that has the least fat, with only 6 grams per sandwich.

Now you can make a clone of that light creation, with deli-sliced roast turkey breast that you can pick up at any deli counter at your local supermarket. You can also find the turkey in pre-packaged portions near the luncheon meats.

butter-flavored spray or spread
1 whole wheat hamburger bun
2 ounces deli-sliced roast turkey breast
salt
½ tablespoon light mayonnaise
1 to 2 tomato slices
¼ cup shredded lettuce

1. Preheat a frying pan or griddle to medium heat. Apply butter-flavored spread or spray to the faces of the top and bottom wheat buns. Grill the faces of the buns lightly on the hot pan.
2. Build the sandwich by first placing the sliced turkey on the bottom bun. Salt the turkey.
3. Spread the mayonnaise on the face of the top bun.
4. Invert the top bun. On the bun, stack the tomatoes, then the lettuce on top of that.
5. Turn the top of the sandwich over onto the bottom and serve.

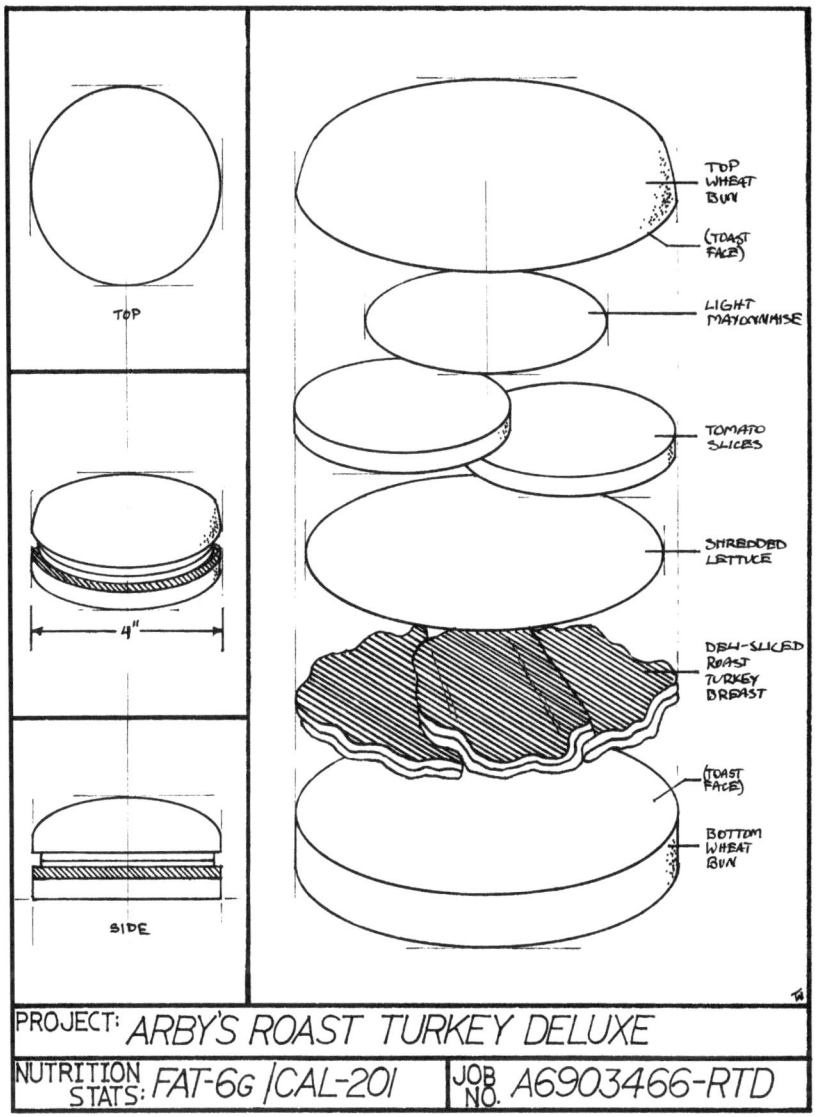

- MAKES 1 SANDWICH.

Nutrition Facts
 SERVING SIZE—1 SANDWICH   FAT (PER SERVING)—6G
 TOTAL SERVINGS—1   CALORIES (PER SERVING)—201

• • • •

CHILI'S GUILTLESS GRILL GUILTLESS CHICKEN SALAD

TOP SECRET RECIPES VERSION OF

This salad was one of the first six selections offered when Chili's Guiltless Grill premiered on the chain's menu in 1993. You'll love the Southwestern flavors in this delicious and healthy salad clone. The marinated grilled chicken has a sweet, smoky taste, and the pico de gallo lends a nice zing to the dish. Top it all off with irresistible Southwest dressing and you'll have a meal-size salad that comes in at only 5 grams of fat.

Fat-free sour cream and low-fat milk help to keep the slightly spicy dressing remarkably low in fat grams. It's a dressing that's so tasty you'll want to use it for other low-fat salad creations.

CHICKEN MARINADE

1 cup water
¼ cup pineapple juice
1 tablespoon soy sauce
½ teaspoon salt
¼ teaspoon liquid smoke
¼ teaspoon onion powder
dash garlic powder

2 chicken breast fillets

LOW-FAT SOUTHWEST DRESSING

¼ cup low-fat milk
1 tablespoon vinegar
2 tablespoons minced tomato
1 tablespoon minced white onion
2 teaspoons minced canned ortega chili
1 teaspoon sugar
¼ teaspoon salt
⅛ teaspoon chili powder
⅛ teaspoon cumin
dash thyme
dash oregano
½ cup fat-free sour cream

PICO DE GALLO
1 large tomato
¼ cup diced Spanish onion
1 teaspoon chopped fresh jalapeño pepper, seeded
1 teaspoon finely minced fresh cilantro
pinch of salt

4 cups chopped iceberg lettuce
4 cups chopped green leaf lettuce
1 cup shredded red cabbage
¼ cup shredded carrot
2 cups alfalfa sprouts
⅔ cup canned dark red kidney beans
2 green onions, diced (green part only)

1. Make the chicken marinade by combining the ingredients in a medium bowl. Add the chicken fillets and marinate for at least 24 hours.
2. Prepare the dressing by combining all ingredients, except the sour cream, in a blender. Blend on low speed for about 15 seconds or until the onion is pulverized.
3. Pour the mixture into a medium bowl and add the sour cream. Whisk until smooth. Cover and chill.
4. Prepare the pico de gallo by combining all of the ingredients in a small bowl. Cover and chill.
5. When you are ready to build the salads, cook the chicken fillets on a preheated barbecue or indoor grill set to high for 4 to 7 minutes per side, or until done.
6. To build the salad, first toss the lettuces, cabbage, and shredded carrot together. Divide this lettuce mixture and arrange it on two plates.
7. Divide the sprouts and sprinkle them over the lettuce around the edge of each plate.
8. Divide the kidney beans and sprinkle them over the lettuce on each plate.
9. Divide the pico de gallo and sprinkle it over the top of the salads.
10. Divide the green onion and sprinkle it over the top of each salad.
11. Slice the chicken fillets into bite-size pieces and arrange

over the top of each salad. Serve with the low-fat dressing on the side.

- MAKES 2 LARGE ENTRÉE SALADS.

Nutrition Facts
SERVING SIZE—1 SALAD   FAT (PER SERVING)—5G
TOTAL SERVINGS—2   CALORIES (PER SERVING)—558

• • • •

CHILI'S GUILTLESS GRILL GUILTLESS CHICKEN SANDWICH

Here's another item that has been on Chili's Guiltless Grill menu from the start. It's a chicken sandwich that gets its sweet smoky flavor from the marinated chicken that is grilled over an open flame. The chicken is stacked on whole wheat buns with lettuce and tomato; and a tasty, yet simple-to-make honey mustard sauce is drizzled over the top. If your chicken fillets are too plump, just give 'em a few whacks with a tenderizing mallet and rejoice in the extra calories you work off.

MARINADE
1 cup water
1/4 cup pineapple juice
1 tablespoon soy sauce
1/2 teaspoon salt
1/4 teaspoon liquid smoke
1/4 teaspoon onion powder
dash garlic powder

4 chicken breast fillets

FAT-FREE HONEY MUSTARD DRESSING
2 tablespoons Grey Poupon Dijon mustard
2 tablespoons honey
1 tablespoon fat-free mayonnaise
1 teaspoon vinegar

4 whole wheat hamburger buns
1 cup shredded lettuce
4 large tomato slices

1. Prepare the chicken marinade by combining the marinade ingredients in a medium bowl. Add the chicken fillets, cover, and refrigerate for several hours. Overnight is even better.
2. When the chicken has marinated, cook the fillets on a preheated barbecue or indoor grill set to a high temperature for 4 to 7 minutes per side or until done.
3. While the chicken is grilling, make the fat-free dressing by mixing together the dressing ingredients in a small bowl.
4. Build each sandwich by first stacking one-quarter of the lettuce on the bottom hamburger bun.
5. Stack the tomato slice on the lettuce.
6. Stack the chicken fillet on the tomato.
7. Cover each sandwich with the top bun and serve with the fat-free honey mustard dressing on the side.

- SERVES 4.

Nutrition Facts

SERVING SIZE—1 SANDWICH   FAT (PER SERVING)—8G
TOTAL SERVINGS—4   CALORIES (PER SERVING)—378

• • • •

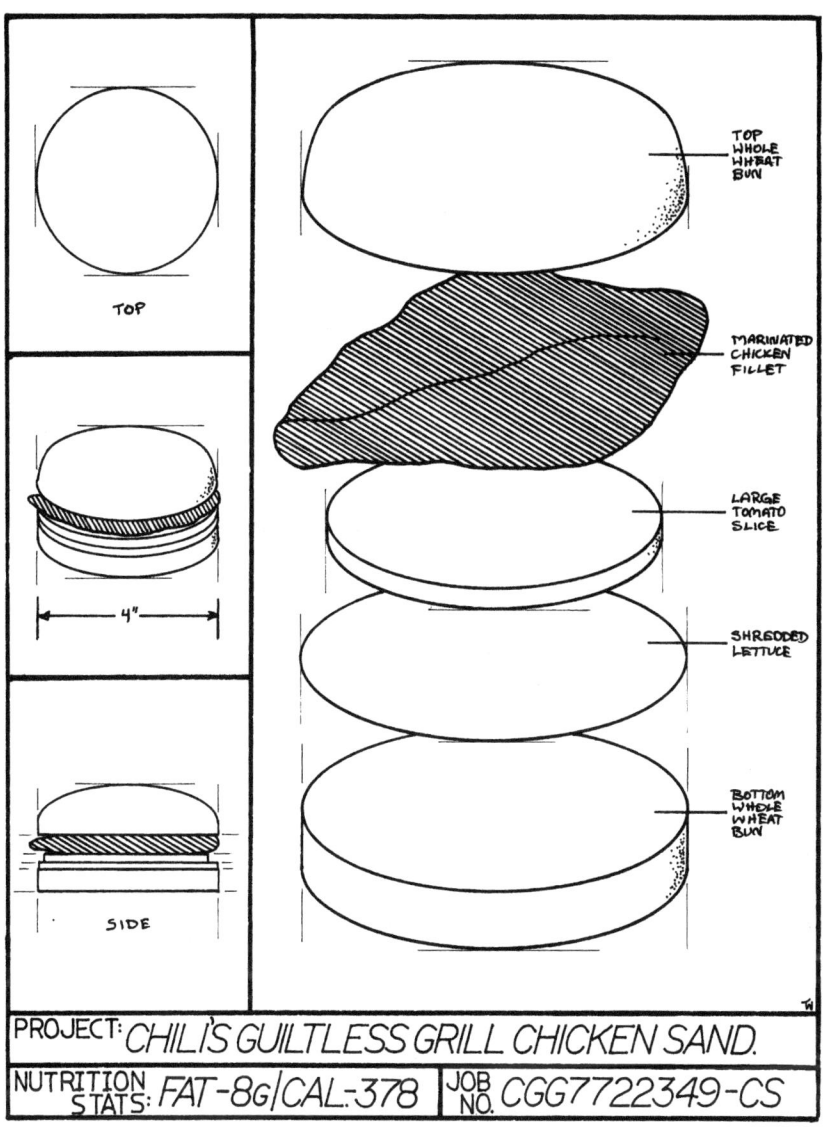

CHILI'S GUILTLESS GRILL GUILTLESS PASTA PRIMAVERA

TOP SECRET RECIPES VERSION OF

According to one Chili's spokesperson, "The Guiltless Grill selections are extremely popular. Guiltless Grill was a smash from the start." And to ensure that customers keep coming back to these lighter selections on the menu, Chili's often rotates items and introduces new ones. The Guiltless Pasta Primavera is one of the new kids on the block among the Guiltless Grill selections. This clone recipe of the recent favorite dish makes two huge dinner-size portions, just like the restaurant serves. The recipe should even be enough for three, perhaps four—if there's a big dessert coming.

CHICKEN MARINADE
1 cup water
¼ cup pineapple juice
1 tablespoon soy sauce
½ teaspoon salt
¼ teaspoon liquid smoke
¼ teaspoon onion powder
dash garlic powder

2 chicken breast fillets

SAUCE
2 15-ounce cans tomato sauce
1½ cups water
½ cup diced onion
2 cloves garlic, minced
1 tomato, diced
1 tablespoon dried parsley
1 tablespoon brown sugar
2 teaspoons lemon juice
2 teaspoons red wine vinegar
1 teaspoon dried basil
1 teaspoon dried oregano
½ teaspoon salt
¼ teaspoon pepper

1 1-pound package penne pasta	¼ red bell pepper, seeded and sliced
4 quarts water	
1 summer squash, sliced	¼ green bell pepper, seeded and sliced
1 zucchini, sliced	
1 slice red onion, halved and separated	salt
	pepper

1. Prepare the chicken marinade by combining the marinade ingredients in a medium bowl. Add the chicken breast fillets to the marinade, cover, and refrigerate for 24 hours. If you're in a hurry, you can get by with a minimum of four hours' marinating time, although the flavors will not be as intense.
2. When the chicken is marinated, prepare the sauce by combining all of the ingredients in a large saucepan over high heat. Bring the sauce to a boil, then reduce the heat to low and simmer for 1 to 1½ hours or until the diced tomato is soft, the onions are translucent, and the sauce thickens.
3. About 20 minutes before the sauce is done, prepare the penne pasta by bringing 4 quarts of water to a boil. Dump the penne into the water, stir, and cook for 11 to 15 minutes or until it is *al dente*, or tender but not soft. Drain.
4. As the pasta cooks, grill the chicken fillets on a preheated barbecue or indoor grill set to a high temperature for 4 to 7 minutes per side or until done.
5. As the pasta and chicken cook, steam the vegetables in a steam basket over boiling water or in a steamer, for 8 to 10 minutes or until tender. Salt and pepper the vegetables to taste.
6. Build the dish by arranging half of the pasta on a plate. Distribute half of the vegetables over the pasta and spoon the marinara sauce over the top. Slice a chicken fillet into bite-size pieces and arrange over the top of the pasta. Repeat for the second serving.

- MAKES 2 LARGE DINNER-SIZE PORTIONS.

Nutrition Facts

Serving size—
 1 dinner-size portion
Total servings—2

Fat (per serving)—15g
Calories (per serving)—1200

• • • •

TOP SECRET RECIPES VERSION OF

EINSTEIN BROS. BAGELS

According to legend, in 1683 a Jewish baker shaped dough into the form of a riding stirrup to honor King John Sobieski of Poland, a skilled horseman who had saved the Austrian people from Turkish invaders. Three hundred years later, this Boulder, Colorado, chain is the biggest seller of what has become America's favorite low-fat munchies. Since the first Einstein Bros. Bagel store opened in 1995, the chain has quickly expanded into 38 states. Today there are around 450 Einstein Bros. Bagel stores serving 16 varieties of the chewy bread snack. The company also owns Noah's bagels, giving them another 140 stores. Each company has its own style of bagel, but both brands often win awards in local bagel contests. The company strives to open a new Einstein Bros. or Noah's somewhere in the country each business day.

Here are clones for six of the chain's most popular bagels. You'll notice that the special ingredient that sets these bagels apart from others is molasses. It's an ingredient that adds a unique sweetness and slightly dark color to these tasty, soft bagels. Check out pages 155 to 158 for fat-free flavored cream cheese recipes.

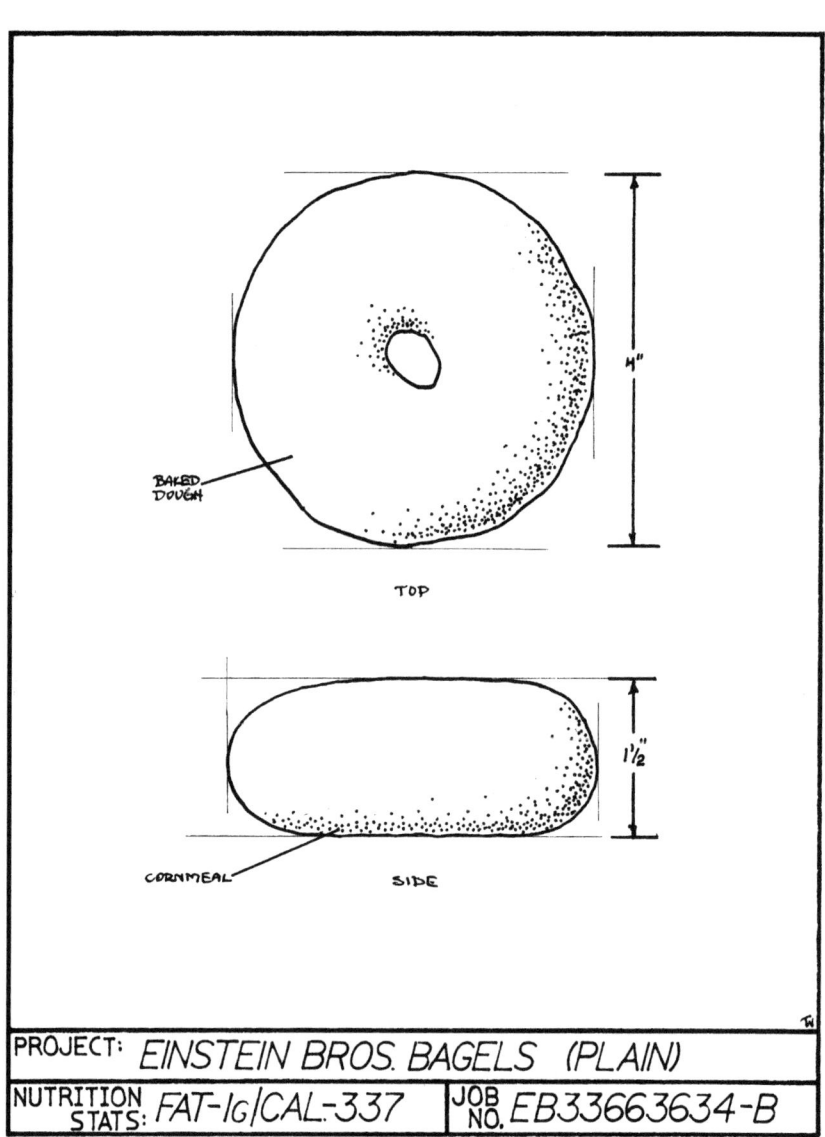

PLAIN

1 cup very warm water
(110 to 115 degrees,
not steaming)
½ tablespoon yeast
1 tablespoon plus 1 teaspoon
light corn syrup
1 tablespoon plus 1 teaspoon
molasses
½ teaspoon vegetable oil
1 teaspoon salt
2 cups bread flour (plus about
⅔ cup to incorporate while
kneading)
1½ tablespoons sugar
(for water bath)
cornmeal (for dusting)

1. Combine the warm water and yeast in a medium bowl and stir until the yeast is dissolved. Be sure the water is not too hot, or it may kill the yeast.
2. Add the corn syrup, molasses, and oil to the bowl and stir thoroughly. Add the salt.
3. Pour the 2 cups of bread flour into the bowl and incorporate it with the other ingredients.
4. Sprinkle a little of the reserved flour over the dough in the bowl and turn it out onto a surface that has been dusted with more of the reserved flour. Knead the dough, while working in the remaining reserve flour (depending on your climate you may not have to use all of the reserve flour, but you will surely use most of it). The dough should become very smooth and elastic, dry to the touch, and not tacky. You will have to knead for 6 or 7 minutes to get the right consistency.
5. Put the dough back into the bowl or another container, cover, and let it rise in a warm place for 30 to 40 minutes. The dough should double in size.
6. Punch down the dough and cut it into 4 even portions. Working with one portion of the dough at a time, form the dough into a ball. Turn the edge of the dough inward with your fingers while punching a hole in the center with your thumbs. Work the dough in a circle while stretching it out and enlarging the center hole, so that it looks like a doughnut. The hole should be between 1 to 1½ inches in diameter. Place the 4 portions of shaped dough onto a greased board or baking sheet, cover (a clean towel works well), and allow

the dough to rise for 20 to 30 minutes. The dough should nearly double in size.
7. Preheat the oven to 400 degrees.
8. Fill a medium saucepan ⅔ full of water and bring it to a boil. Add 1½ tablespoons of sugar to the water.
9. Working with one bagel at a time, first enlarge the hole if it has closed up to less than ¾ of an inch. Be careful not to overwork the dough at this point or it won't have the proper consistency. Drop the bagel into the water, cover the saucepan, and boil for 20 seconds. Flip the bagel over, and boil for another 20 seconds. Immediately take the bagel out of the water with a slotted spoon, let the water drip off for about 10 seconds, then place the bagel onto a baking sheet that has been dusted with cornmeal. Repeat for the remaining bagels. Be sure the bagels do not touch each other.
10. Bake the bagels for 26 to 30 minutes, or until they are light brown.

- MAKES 4 BAGELS.

Nutrition Facts

SERVING SIZE—1 BAGEL FAT (PER SERVING)—1 G
TOTAL SERVINGS—4 CALORIES (PER SERVING)—337

CINNAMON SUGAR

1 cup very warm water
 (110 to 115 degrees,
 not steaming)
½ tablespoon yeast
1 tablespoon plus 1 teaspoon
 light corn syrup
1 tablespoon plus 1 teaspoon
 molasses
½ teaspoon vegetable oil

1 teaspoon salt
2 cups bread flour (plus about
 ⅔ cup to incorporate while
 kneading)
1½ tablespoons sugar
 (for water bath)
2 tablespoons superfine sugar
1½ teaspoons cinnamon
nonstick spray

1. Follow steps 1 to 8 for the plain bagels.
2. Combine superfine sugar and cinnamon in a small bowl (or use a premixed cinnamon/sugar, such as the one made by Schilling). If you have an empty shaker bottle—an empty spice bottle works well—you can put the cinnamon and sugar in it and use it to sprinkle an even coating on the bagel when the time comes.
3. Working with one bagel at a time, first enlarge the hole if it has closed up to less than ¾ of an inch. Be careful not to overwork the dough at this point or it won't have the proper consistency. Drop the bagel into the water, cover the saucepan, and boil for 20 seconds. Flip the bagel over, and boil for another 20 seconds. Immediately take the bagel out of the water with a slotted spoon, let the water drip off for about 10 seconds, sprinkle a light coating of the cinnamon/sugar over the entire surface of the bagel, then place the bagel onto a lightly greased baking sheet. Repeat for the remaining bagels. Be sure the bagels do not touch each other.
4. Bake the bagels for 26 to 30 minutes, or until they are light brown.

- MAKES 4 BAGELS.

Nutrition Facts

SERVING SIZE—1 BAGEL   FAT (PER SERVING)—1 G
TOTAL SERVINGS—4   CALORIES (PER SERVING)—360

JALAPEÑO

⅓ cup canned jalapeño slices (nacho slices)
⅛ teaspoon red pepper flakes
1 cup very warm water (110 to 115 degrees, not steaming)
½ tablespoon yeast
1 tablespoon plus 1 teaspoon light corn syrup
1 tablespoon plus 1 teaspoon molasses
½ teaspoon vegetable oil
1 teaspoon salt
2 cups bread flour (plus about ⅔ cup to incorporate while kneading)
1 ½ tablespoons sugar (for water bath)
cornmeal (for dusting)

1. Finely mince the jalapeño slices, then combine with the red pepper flakes in a small bowl and set aside.
2. Follow all of the steps for the plain bagels, adding the jalapeño mixture to the dough in step 2.
3. Rise and bake using the same steps as for the plain bagels.

- MAKES 4 BAGELS.

Nutrition Facts
SERVING SIZE—1 BAGEL
TOTAL SERVINGS—4
FAT (PER SERVING)—1G
CALORIES (PER SERVING)—340

CHOPPED GARLIC

1 cup very warm water
   (110 to 115 degrees,
   not steaming)
½ tablespoon yeast
1 tablespoon plus 1 teaspoon
   light corn syrup
1 tablespoon plus 1 teaspoon
   molasses
2 teaspoons vegetable oil

1 teaspoon salt
2 cups bread flour (plus about
   ⅔ cup to incorporate while
   kneading)
1½ tablespoons sugar
   (for water bath)
cornmeal (for dusting)
1 tablespoon dry minced garlic
1 teaspoon sesame seeds

1. Follow the same steps as for the plain bagels through step 9. After the bagels have been arranged on the cornmeal-dusted baking sheet, and while they are still moist, sprinkle a scant teaspoon of dry minced garlic over the top of each one. Sprinkle about ¼ teaspoon of sesame seeds over the top of each bagel as well.
2. Bake the bagels for 26 to 30 minutes, or until they are light brown.

- MAKES 4 BAGELS.

Nutrition Facts
SERVING SIZE—1 BAGEL
TOTAL SERVINGS—4
FAT (PER SERVING)—3G
CALORIES (PER SERVING)—366

CHOPPED ONION

1 cup very warm water (110 to 115 degrees, not steaming)
½ tablespoon yeast
1 tablespoon plus 1 teaspoon light corn syrup
1 tablespoon plus 1 teaspoon molasses
½ teaspoon vegetable oil
1 teaspoon salt
1 teaspoon poppy seeds
2 cups bread flour (plus about ⅔ cup to incorporate while kneading)
1½ tablespoons sugar (for water bath)
cornmeal (for dusting)
1 tablespoon dry minced onion

1. Follow the directions for the plain bagels through step 9, but add the poppy seeds to the mixture in step 2.
2. After the bagels have been arranged on the cornmeal-dusted baking sheet, and while they are still moist, sprinkle a scant teaspoon of dry minced onion over the top of each one.
3. Bake the bagels for 26 to 30 minutes, or until they are light brown.

- MAKES 4 BAGELS.

Nutrition Facts
SERVING SIZE—1 BAGEL
TOTAL SERVINGS—4
FAT (PER SERVING)—1 G
CALORIES (PER SERVING)—340

EVERYTHING

1 cup very warm water (110 to 115 degrees, not steaming)
½ tablespoon yeast
1 tablespoon plus 1 teaspoon light corn syrup
1 tablespoon plus 1 teaspoon molasses
1 teaspoon vegetable oil
1 teaspoon salt
2 cups bread flour (plus about ⅔ cup to incorporate while kneading)
1½ tablespoons sugar (for water bath)
cornmeal (for dusting)
1 tablespoon dry minced onion
1 tablespoon dry minced garlic
½ teaspoon poppy seeds
½ teaspoon caraway seeds
½ teaspoon sesame seeds
½ teaspoon kosher salt

1. Follow the directions for the plain bagels through step 9.
2. After the bagels have been arranged on the cornmeal-dusted baking sheet, and while they are still moist, sprinkle a scant teaspoon each of dry minced onion and dry minced garlic over the top of each bagel. Combine the poppy seeds, caraway seeds, sesame seeds, and kosher salt in a small bowl. Sprinkle ¼ of the mixture over the top of each bagel.
3. Bake the bagels for 26 to 30 minutes, or until they are golden brown.

- MAKES 4 BAGELS.

Nutrition Facts

SERVING SIZE—1 BAGEL FAT (PER SERVING)—2G
TOTAL SERVINGS—4 CALORIES (PER SERVING)—356

• • • •

TOP SECRET RECIPES VERSION OF

ENTENMANN'S LIGHT FAT-FREE CHEESE-FILLED CRUMB COFFEE CAKE

Take a close look at the Entenmann's logo sometime. You'll see a drawing of the same type of horse-drawn delivery wagon that William Entenmann drove back in 1898 in Brooklyn, New York, when he started his home-delivery baking service. The successful family business was passed on through the generations with little change in philosophy or goals. Then in 1951, the family realized the best way to reach the growing numbers of customers was by selling the products in New York-area supermarkets. The delivery business went retail, but the company was still a local New York-area business.

All that changed in 1982, when General Foods purchased the company. Not only did distribution go national, but at the same time food scientists at General Foods were working hard to develop the first line of fresh-baked fat-free cakes and pastries. When those products hit store shelves in 1989, the fat-shunning fad was in its infancy, and Entenmann's was able to grab a big chunk of the market.

Now you can sink your teeth into a big chunk of this homemade version of the popular cheese-filled crumb cake. This clone recipe of the popular treat makes two cakes the same size as the original, by dividing a standard 9 x 13-inch pan in half with a large piece of aluminum foil.

CAKE
½ cup Duncan Hines yellow cake mix
2½ cups cake flour (unsifted)
3 tablespoons Butter Buds Sprinkles
1 package rapid-rise yeast (2¼ teaspoons)
¾ teaspoon baking soda
½ teaspoon salt
1¼ cups fat-free milk
¾ teaspoon vanilla
1 tablespoon white vinegar

FILLING
2 8-ounce packages fat-free cream cheese
⅓ cup powdered sugar
1 tablespoon cornstarch
1 teaspoon Butter Buds Sprinkles
½ teaspoon white vinegar
½ teaspoon vanilla
¼ teaspoon salt

TOPPING
1 tablespoon yellow cake mix
¼ cup plus 1 tablespoon sugar
¼ cup all-purpose flour
2 teaspoons Butter Buds Sprinkles
½ teaspoon baking powder
dash salt
2 to 3 tablespoons fat-free ricotta cheese

GLAZE
1 cup powdered sugar
½ teaspoon vanilla (clear is best)
1 tablespoon plus 1 teaspoon fat-free milk
¼ teaspoon Butter Buds Sprinkles
pinch of salt

1. Preheat the oven to 350 degrees.
2. To make the cake, in a large bowl, combine the cake mix, cake flour, Butter Buds, yeast, baking soda, and salt.
3. In a separate, smaller bowl, combine the milk, vanilla, and vinegar, then microwave on high heat for 1½ to 2 minutes until very warm. Add the wet ingredients to the dry and beat until the mixture is well combined. Cover the bowl and set it in a warm place to rise for 10 minutes.
4. While the cake batter rises, make a custom cake pan using a 16- to 18-inch piece of foil and a 9 x 13-inch baking pan. Fold the foil in half lengthwise, then bend it up again about 1 inch to

the left and right of the middle fold. Place this foil down into the pan. This will make a liner for the baking pan with a foil divider down the middle. Spray the foil with nonstick cooking spray.
5. Pour 1 cup of the batter into each side of the pan. Bake for 5 minutes, then remove it from the oven and cool for 15 minutes.
6. As the cake cools, prepare the filling by first warming the cream cheese in the microwave on 50 percent power for 3 minutes. Add the remaining filling ingredients and beat with an electric mixer until smooth.
7. Prepare the crumb topping by combining all of the topping ingredients, except the cheese, in a small bowl. Cut the fat-free ricotta into the mixture with a knife or pastry blender until it makes crumbs about one-half to one-quarter the size of a pea.
8. Divide the cheese filling and spread half onto the top of each cake. Cover the filling with the remaining batter. Sprinkle the crumb topping over the top of the batter. Bake for 25 to 30 minutes, or until the cake begins to brown. Remove the pan from the oven and allow the cake to cool completely.
9. Make the glaze by combining the glaze ingredients in a small bowl. When the cake is cool, drizzle the glaze over the top. Store uncovered for the first day.

- MAKES 2 CRUMB CAKES.

TIDBITS

It is important to eat these cakes shortly after adding the glaze. Once the cakes are stored in a sealed container, moisture will begin to liquefy the glaze. If you plan to keep the cakes longer than a day or two, hold off on frosting the cakes until just before you eat them.

Nutrition Facts
SERVING SIZE—2.6-OUNCE SLICE   FAT (PER SERVING)—0G
TOTAL SERVINGS—18   CALORIES (PER SERVING)—140

• • • •

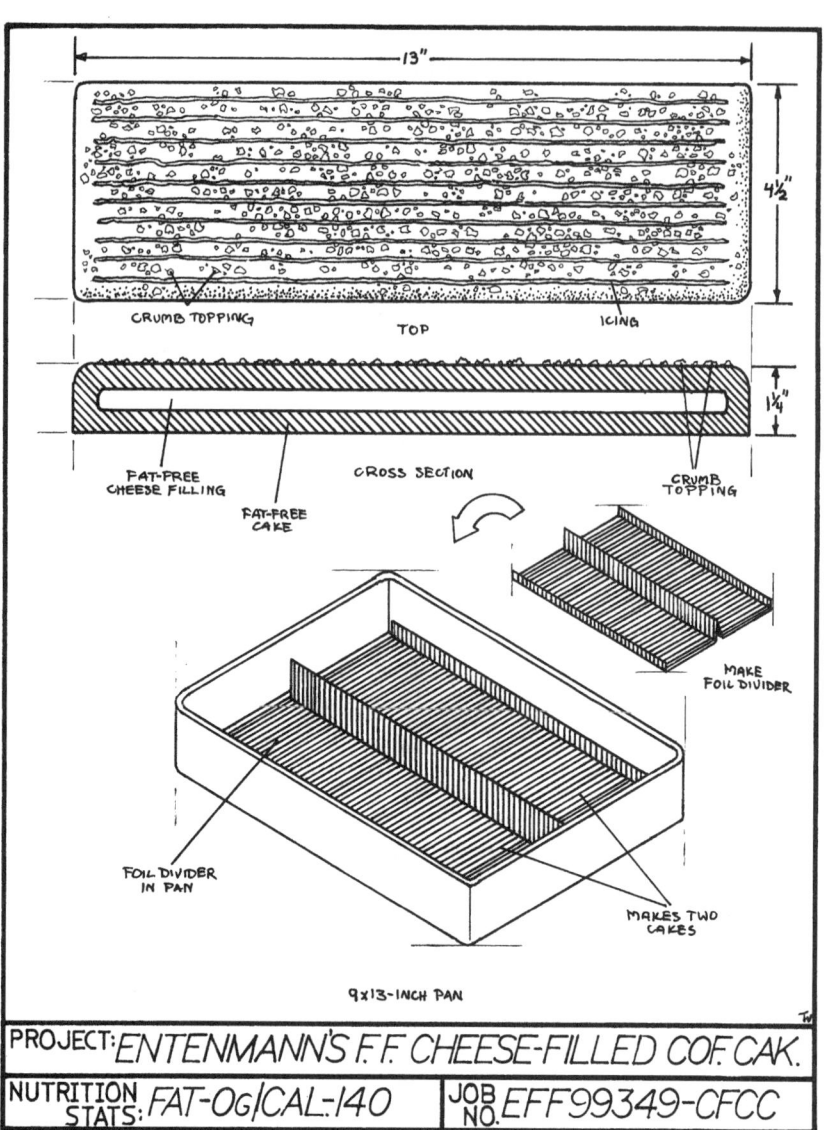

ENTENMANN'S LIGHT FAT-FREE GOLDEN LOAF

TOP SECRET RECIPES VERSION OF

How would you like this job? Three times a day, each day, the chief bakers at Entenmann's gather in "scoring sessions," wherein they taste and rate products that come off the factory line. If a product doesn't earn at least an 8 out of 10 rating, it never makes it onto a delivery truck.

In the last ten years, Entenmann's has become known as a company that makes delicious baked fat-free products that do not taste fat-free. Today the company boasts around 50 products that carry the low-fat and fat-free labels. One of those products is a delicious pound cake, called Golden Loaf, cloned with this recipe. It makes an excellent dessert or snack when sliced and served with strawberries and low-fat whipped topping, or beneath a big scoop of light ice cream. I've also included this recipe to use with one of my favorites: the reduced-fat tiramisu found on page 199.

However you decide to serve this versatile dessert, you will amaze your guests when you tell 'em it's fat-free fare. And, yes, I realize that the reduced-fat yellow cake mix contains fat, but we have stretched out the product with cake flour so that each slice of these cakes (the recipe makes two) contains less than ½ gram. Check it out.

1 18.25-ounce package reduced-fat yellow cake mix (Betty Crocker Sweet Rewards)
¾ cup cake flour (unsifted)
1 teaspoon vanilla
2 tablespoons Butter Buds Sprinkles
½ cup sugar
1 cup egg substitute
1⅔ cups water

1. Preheat the oven to 325 degrees.
2. Mix together all the ingredients in a large bowl with an electric mixer on medium speed.
3. Spray two 9 x 5-inch loaf pans with nonstick spray. Pour half of the batter into each pan and bake for 25 minutes. Using a knife, slice down the middle of each cake (about ½-inch into the cake). This will give the cakes the same look on top as the original. Bake for an additional 20 to 25 minutes, or until the cakes are golden brown on top. Cut each cake into 13 slices.

- MAKES 2 POUND CAKES, 13 SLICES EACH.

Nutrition Facts

SERVING SIZE—1.7-OUNCE SLICE FAT (PER SERVING)—0G
TOTAL SERVINGS—26 CALORIES (PER SERVING)—106

• • • •

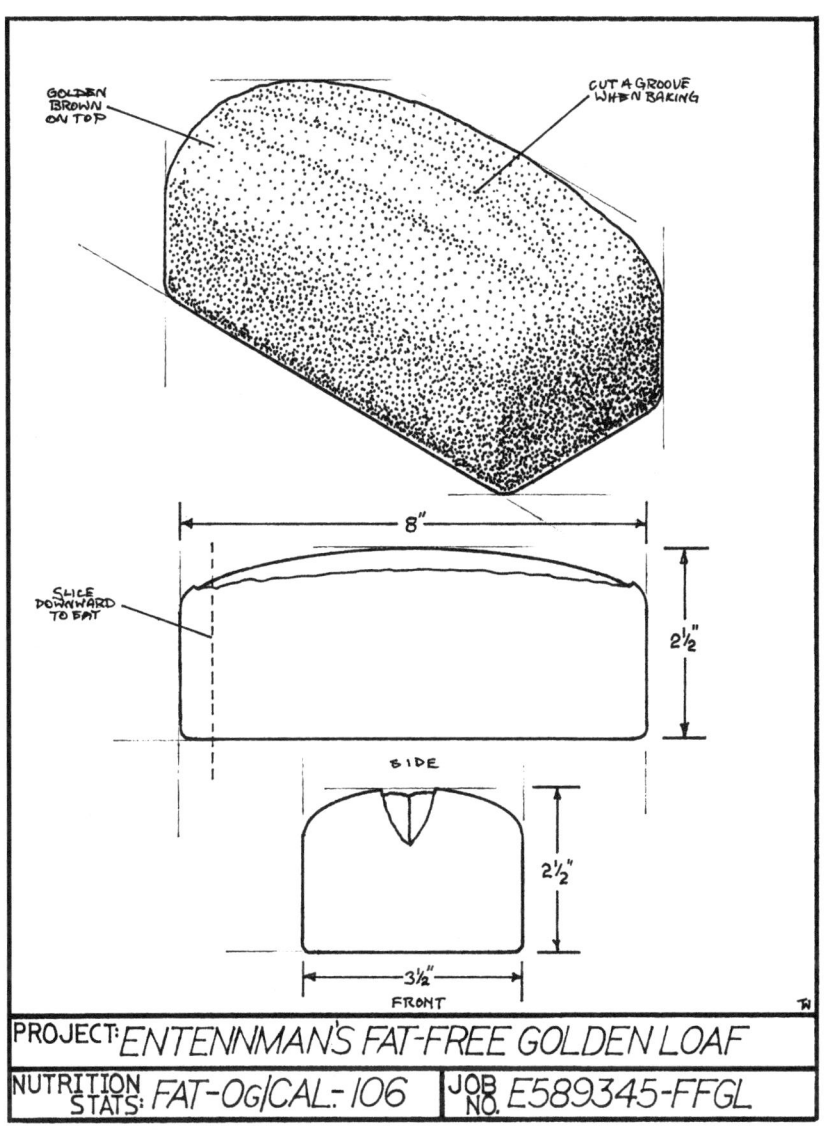

ENTENMANN'S LIGHT FAT-FREE OATMEAL RAISIN COOKIES

TOP SECRET RECIPES VERSION OF

These chewy little fat-free cookies have become quite popular in recent years. And they're pretty tasty considering there's a big goose egg in the fat column. A typical oatmeal cookie would have somewhere in the neighborhood of 3 grams of fat ... each. Since we're removing all the fat, we'll have to resort to some of our *Top Secret* tricks to keep these clones nice and chewy like the original.

The sweetened condensed milk, molasses, and raisin puree will certainly help by not only giving the cookies a delicious flavor, but will also create the perfect chewy texture. Sweetened condensed milk can be found in a fat-free variety that is made with skim milk, and raisin puree is easy to make in a blender. Plus, that raisin flavor is just what we want for this recipe.

2 egg whites
½ cup sugar
3 tablespoons sweetened condensed skim milk
1 teaspoon vanilla extract
2 tablespoons molasses
2 tablespoons raisin puree (see tidbit)
½ cup quick-cooking oats

¾ cup unbleached flour
¾ cup whole wheat flour
¼ cup dry nonfat milk
½ teaspoon salt
½ teaspoon baking powder
½ teaspoon baking soda
¼ teaspoon cinnamon
½ cup dark raisins

1. Preheat the oven to 325°.
2. Whip the egg whites with an electric mixer until they form soft peaks. Add the sugar, a little bit at a time, while beating.
3. Add the condensed milk, vanilla, molasses, and raisin puree and beat until well combined.
4. Use a blender or food processor to grind the oats into coarse flour. Pulse the machine a few times to pulverize the oats, but don't grind too long. You still want to see some of the oats in the cookie.
5. Combine the ground oatmeal with the remaining ingredients, except for the raisins, in another bowl and mix by hand.
6. Pour the dry mixture into the wet. Mix by hand until well combined.
7. Add the raisins to the cookie dough, and mix once again by hand.
8. Drop the dough by the tablespoonful onto a greased cookie sheet. Form the cookies into circles, and press down on them to flatten a bit.
9. Bake the cookies for 10 to 15 minutes or until they begin to turn slightly brown around the edges.

- MAKES 2 DOZEN COOKIES.

TIDBIT

Make raisin puree by combining ¼ cup raisins with ½ cup water in a blender. Blend on high speed until smooth.

Nutrition Facts
SERVING SIZE—2 COOKIES   FAT (PER SERVING)—0G
TOTAL SERVINGS—12   CALORIES (PER SERVING)—120

• • • •

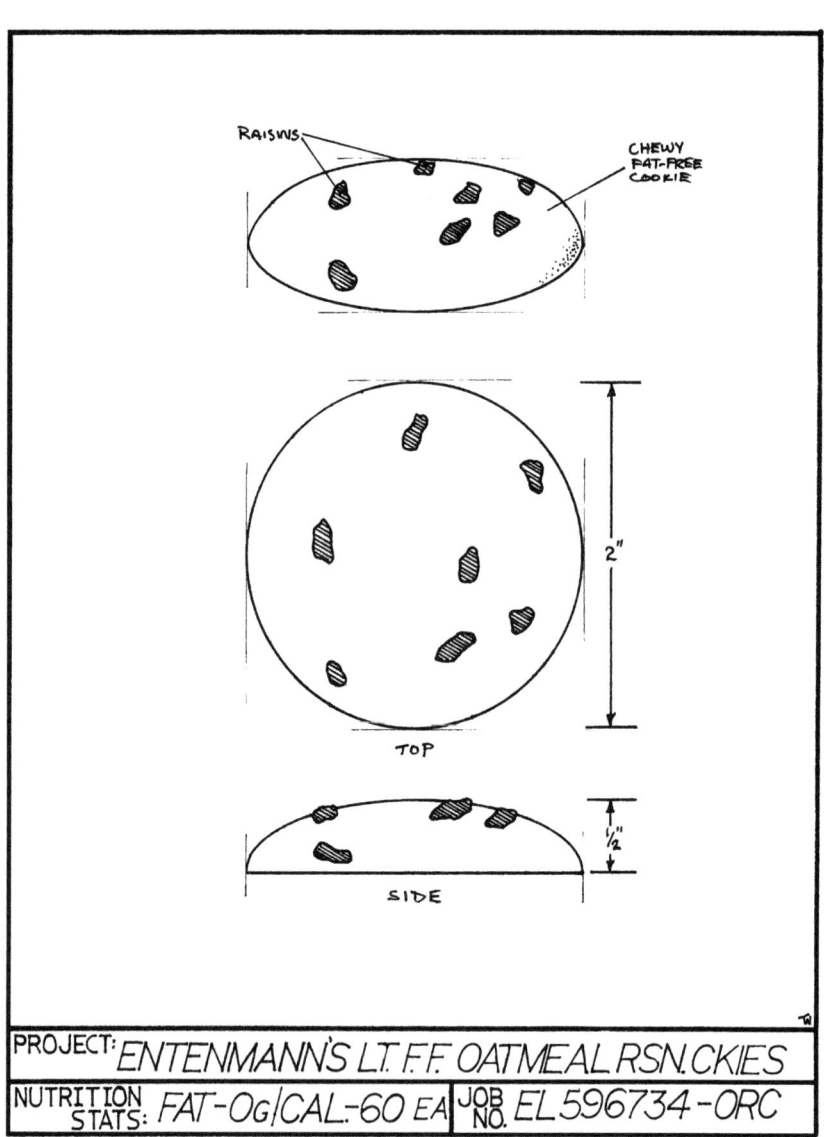

EL POLLO LOCO SALSA

Along with your order from this 250-unit Western U.S. chain, comes a delicious, yet simple to clone, fat-free salsa. If you don't have a food processor, never fear. You can also make the salsa by hand, with a large, sharp knife and some steady-handed, energetic, calorie-burning mincing action. Keep your head down, legs slightly spread, and watch the fingers. You don't want the salsa too red.

2 medium tomatoes, quartered
½ fresh jalapeño pepper, stem and seeds removed
2 leaves fresh cilantro
¼ teaspoon salt

Combine all the ingredients in a food processor. Pulse 3 to 5 times on low speed until the vegetables are well chopped. Be careful that you don't overchop and puree the ingredients. Pour everything, including the liquid, into a medium bowl. Cover and chill for several hours.

- MAKES 1 CUP.

Nutrition Facts
SERVING SIZE—1 OUNCE
TOTAL SERVINGS—8
FAT (PER SERVING)—0G
CALORIES (PER SERVING)—6

• • • •

TOP SECRET RECIPES VERSION OF

GARDENBURGER ORIGINAL VEGGIE PATTY

In the early eighties, at his Gardenhouse restaurant, Chef Paul Wenner created a unique meatless patty to replace hamburgers. The patty, which contained mushrooms, brown rice, onions, oats, and low-fat cheeses, was dubbed the Gardenburger and quickly became a hit. Soon, Wenner closed his restaurant and began to concentrate on marketing his meatless, low-fat creation to a hungry, health-conscious America. Today Gardenburger patties can be found in more than 35,000 food service outlets around the world, and more than 20,000 stores.

Now you can make a surprisingly accurate clone of the real thing with the same type of ingredients Wenner uses. Most of the ingredients can be found at your local supermarket, although you may have to go to a health food store for the bulgur wheat. And if you jog over there, you can burn off what little calories you gain from this amazing kitchen clone.

2 tablespoons bulgur wheat
1 pound mushrooms, quartered (4 cups steamed)
1 cup diced onion (½ cup steamed)
½ cup rolled oats
⅔ cup cooked brown rice
½ cup shredded low-fat mozzarella cheese
2 tablespoons shredded low-fat cheddar cheese
2 tablespoons low-fat cottage cheese
½ teaspoon salt
½ teaspoon garlic powder
dash pepper
2 tablespoons cornstarch
olive oil cooking spray

1. Add ¼ cup boiling water to the bulgur wheat in a small bowl and let it sit for about 60 minutes. The wheat will swell to about double in size.
2. Steam the quartered mushrooms for 10 minutes or until tender, then remove them from your steamer, and replace with the onion. Steam the diced onion for 10 minutes or until the pieces are translucent. Keep these two ingredients separate, and set aside.
3. Add ½ cup of water to the oats and let them soak for about 10 minutes, until soft.
4. Drain any excess water from the bulgur wheat and oats, then combine the grains with the steamed mushrooms, rice, cheeses, and spices in a food processor and pulse 4 or 5 times until ingredients are chopped fine, but not pureed. You want a coarse texture with some identifiable chunks of grain, mushroom, and cheese.
5. Pour the mixture into a bowl with the steamed onion and cornstarch, and mix well.
6. Preheat the oven to 300 degrees and set a large skillet over medium/low heat.
7. Spray the skillet with a light coating of olive oil cooking spray. Measure ½ cup at a time of the patty mixture into the pan and shape with a spoon into a 3¾-inch patty that is approximately ½-inch thick. Cook the patties in batches for 2 to 4 minutes per side, or until light brown on the surface.
8. When all of the patties have been cooked in the skillet, arrange them on a lightly sprayed baking sheet and bake for 20 to 25 minutes in the oven. Be sure to turn them over halfway through the cooking time. You can serve the patties immediately, or freeze them, like the original, when they have cooled.
9. If you freeze the patties, you can reheat them several ways. Simply spray a light coating of olive oil cooking spray on each side and heat each patty in a pan over medium heat for 3 to 4 minutes per side until it is hot in the center. You can also use a grill to prepare the patties. Just be sure to spray each frozen patty with the oil, and be sure the flames are low. Cook for 3 to 4 minutes per side. Those are the best cooking methods;

however, you can also prepare a frozen patty by microwaving it for 30 to 35 seconds, then turning the patty over and zapping it for another 30 to 35 seconds. Finally, you can heat a frozen patty in the microwave for 30 to 35 seconds, then place the partially defrosted patty in a toaster or toaster oven and cook it on medium heat until it's hot in the center.

- MAKES 6 VEGGIE PATTIES.

TIDBITS

If your food processor is too small to hold all of the ingredients, simply divide the ingredients and process one half at a time, or cut the recipe in half. Bulgur wheat can be found in most health food stores, and even some supermarkets carry it.

Nutrition Facts

SERVING SIZE—1 PATTY
TOTAL SERVINGS—6
FAT (PER SERVING)—3G
CALORIES (PER SERVING)—135

• • • •

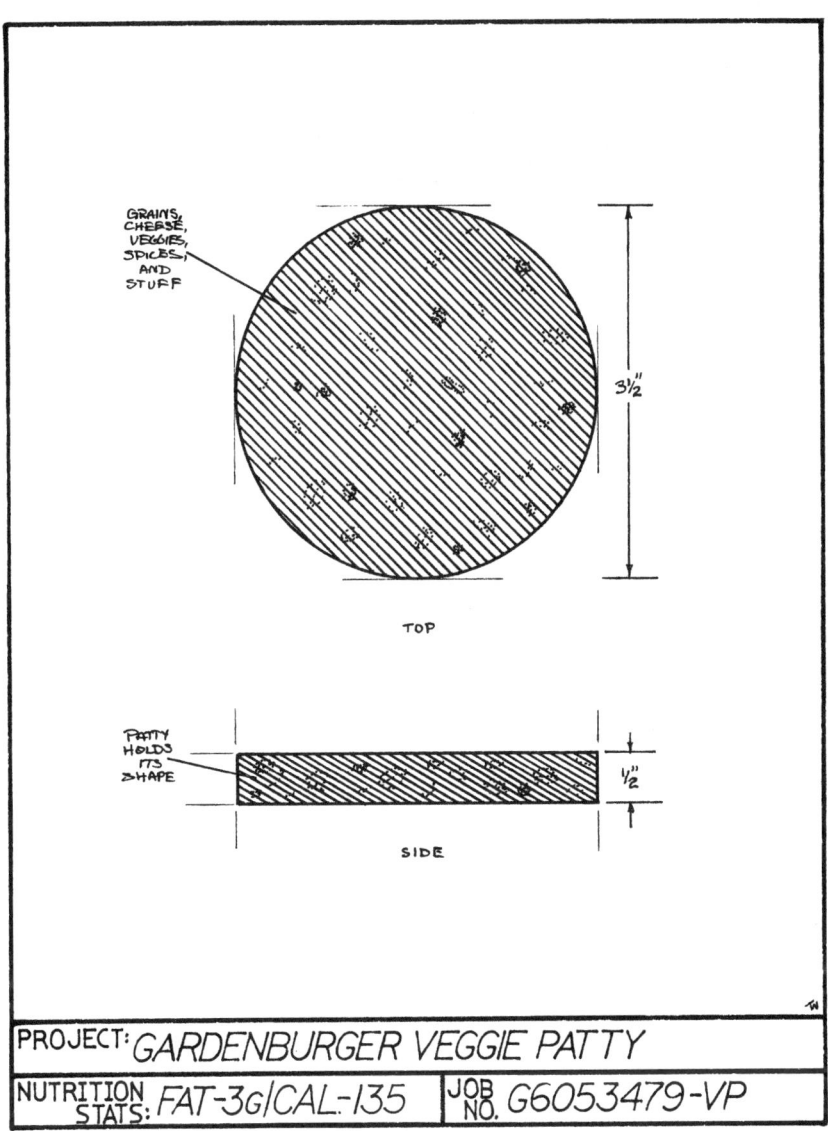

HOSTESS LIGHTS LOW-FAT CUPCAKES

The Twinkie company, otherwise known as Hostess, was one of the first to introduce reduced-fat baked goods to the masses. In 1990 the company took its most popular products and created lower-fat versions under the "Hostess Lights" label. Among the company's well-known low-fat offerings is this popular cupcake, with its trademark seven loops of white icing on the top of frosted, crème-filled cake. Here's a way you can recreate these popular cupcakes at home, with applesauce in the cake to help replace the fat, and filling made with marshmallow crème.

CAKE
1 cup sugar
1/3 cup unsweetened applesauce
1/4 cup egg substitute
1 teaspoon vanilla
1 1/4 cups cake flour (unsifted)
1/2 cup cocoa
1 teaspoon baking soda
1/2 teaspoon salt
1/2 cup buttermilk
1/2 cup whole milk

FILLING
1 7-ounce jar marshmallow crème
1/3 cup shortening
2 tablespoons powdered sugar
1/4 teaspoon salt
1 teaspoon water
1/4 teaspoon vanilla

CHOCOLATE FROSTING

1 cup sugar
⅓ cup cocoa powder
¼ teaspoon salt (rounded)
⅓ cup very hot water
1 teaspoon vanilla
1 teaspoon dark brown food paste coloring (optional)
1¼ to 1½ cups powdered sugar, sifted

WHITE FROSTING

⅓ cup powdered sugar, sifted
1 teaspoon fat-free milk
1 teaspoon meringue powder (optional)

1. Preheat the oven to 350 degrees.
2. To make the cake, beat together the sugar, applesauce, egg substitute, and vanilla in a large bowl for one minute.
3. In a separate medium bowl combine the cake flour, cocoa, baking soda, and salt and use a wire whisk to break up any lumps of cocoa.
4. Add the dry ingredients to the previous wet ingredients and mix together. Add the buttermilk and whole milk, then beat the mixture until smooth.
5. Spoon the batter into a 12-cup muffin tin, sprayed lightly with nonstick spray. Bake for 20 to 24 minutes or until a toothpick inserted into the center of the cake comes out clean. Turn the cupcakes out onto a cooling rack.
6. As the cupcakes cool, prepare the filling by combining ¼ teaspoon salt with 1 teaspoon water in a small bowl or cup. Microwave for 10 to 20 seconds on high, then stir until the salt is dissolved.
7. Beat the marshmallow crème with the shortening in a medium bowl with an electric mixer until smooth and fluffy. Add the powdered sugar, salt, water, and vanilla and beat well.
8. When the cakes have cooled, use a toothpick to poke a hole in the top of each cupcake. Swirl the toothpick around inside the cake to make room for the filling. Fill each cupcake with about 2 teaspoons of the filling.
9. For the chocolate frosting, measure 1 cup of sugar and ⅓ cup of cocoa powder into a deep 1½- to 2-quart Pyrex bowl.

Add a rounded ¼ teaspoon of salt and mix the ingredients together.
10. Add the ⅓ cup of very hot water and the vanilla to the mixture and stir until all ingredients are well combined.
11. Loosely cover the bowl with plastic wrap and microwave at 50 percent power for 2 minutes. Stir carefully to continue dissolving the sugar crystals. Then replace the plastic wrap tightly over the bowl. Microwave on high in 30-second increments (to avoid boiling over) for 2 minutes. The mixture should begin to bubble, but watch it carefully so that it doesn't boil over. Remove the mixture from the microwave, poke holes in the plastic wrap so that steam will escape, and let the mixture stand for 15 minutes.
12. Carefully uncover the bowl (the contents will be very hot). Add 1 teaspoon dark brown food paste coloring to the hot syrup (this is an optional step that creates dark frosting like the original).
13. Stir in the sifted powdered sugar, ½ cup at a time. Mix thoroughly after each addition. You may need to add a few drops of water to the frosting to make it easier to spread. Spread about 2 teaspoons of frosting on each cupcake. You may want to moisten your knife to help the frosting spread on smoothly.
14. Make the white frosting for the design on the top of the cupcakes by mixing ⅓ cup sifted powdered sugar with 1 teaspoon nonfat milk. Add 1 teaspoon of meringue powder to the mixture, if you like, to make the frosting more opaque, like the original. Use a pastry bag with a #3 tip and make small loops down the middle of the top of each frosted cupcake.

- MAKES 12 CUPCAKES.

TIDBITS

You can create small pastry bags for the filling and the white frosting decoration by cutting the corner off of small plastic storage bags. First add the filling or frosting to the bag, then just clip the tip of a corner with scissors. Also, the cupcakes are best if eaten within a couple days of filling.

Nutrition Facts

SERVING SIZE— 1 CUPCAKE FAT (PER SERVING)—1.5G
TOTAL SERVINGS—12 CALORIES (PER SERVING)—220

• • • •

Technical drawing of cupcake:

TOP view: White frosting, Chocolate frosting, Seven glorious loops; 2½"

SIDE (cross section): Chocolate frosting, Filling, Chocolate cake; 2½" wide top, 1¾" wide bottom, 1¼" tall

PROJECT: HOSTESS LIGHTS LOW-FAT CUPCAKE
NUTRITION STATS: FAT-1.5G/CAL-220
JOB NO. HL4634962-LFC

TOP SECRET RECIPES VERSION OF

HOSTESS LIGHTS LOW-FAT TWINKIES

Howdy Doody peddled them on his 1950s TV show. Archie Bunker got one in his lunchbox every day. Even President Jimmy Carter was a fan, supposedly ordering a Twinkie vending machine installed in the White House. Yes, Twinkies are an American favorite. And if the oblong little snack cake isn't being eaten, it's being talked about; usually by talk show hosts joking about the snack food's supposedly long shelf life.

The crème-filled cakes we know today are not exactly the same as the early Twinkies. When the snack cake was first conceived by Hostess plant manager James Dewar in 1930, it was as a way to use the cake pans for the strawberry "Little Short Cake Fingers," which sat idle for all but the six-week strawberry season. The filling in those original cakes was flavored with bananas, and they were called "Twinkle Fingers." But when bananas got scarce during World War II the filling was changed to the vanilla flavor we know today, and the name was shortened to "Twinkies."

The latest reformulation of the Twinkie came in 1990, when a low-fat version was first introduced. Now Twinkie lovers could have their cakes and eat 'em too, with only half the fat of the original.

You should know that these clones are twice the size of the Hostess version, with the fat and calories double as well. By weight, however, this clone's nutrition stats are right on track with the original.

CAKE

1 cup egg substitute
1 egg white
1 ⅔ cups sugar
½ teaspoon vanilla
⅛ teaspoon lemon extract

2 cups unsifted cake flour
1 tablespoon baking powder
½ teaspoon salt
½ cup fat-free milk
1 ½ teaspoons vegetable oil

12 12 x 12-inch pieces of aluminum foil

nonstick cooking spray

FILLING

¼ teaspoon salt
2 teaspoons water
1 7-ounce jar marshmallow crème

⅓ cup shortening
2 tablespoons powdered sugar
¼ teaspoon vanilla

1. Preheat the oven to 325 degrees.
2. In a large glass or metal bowl (copper is best—don't use plastic), beat together the egg substitute egg white until thick and lemon-colored. Add sugar, vanilla, and lemon extract and beat until smooth.
3. In another bowl, mix together the flour, baking powder, and salt.
4. Fold the dry mixture into the wet. Don't overmix.
5. In a small microwave-safe bowl, combine the fat-free milk with the oil. Heat this mixture in the microwave on high for 1 ½ minutes, or until it is very hot, but not boiling.
6. Fold the hot milk mixture into the batter. Do not beat and don't overmix.
7. Prepare the cake molds by folding each square of foil in half and then in half again, so that each piece is a 6-inch square. Wrap each of these foil pieces around a spice bottle. Fold the ends and leave the side open, so that when the foil is removed it makes a small pan (see diagram on page 67). Spray the inside of each mold with nonstick cooking spray. Then, arrange the molds in one or two baking dishes so that they can't tip over when baking.
8. Fill each mold about halfway with batter. Bake the cakes for

25 to 30 minutes or until the tops of the cakes turn light brown. Remove the cakes from the oven, and when they have cooled enough to touch, peel the foil off of each one and place them flat side (the top when baking) down onto wax paper or a cooling rack.

9. As the cakes cool, prepare the filling by combining ¼ teaspoon salt with 1 teaspoon water in a small microwave-safe bowl or cup. Microwave for 10 to 20 seconds on high, then stir until the salt is dissolved.
10. Beat the marshmallow crème with the shortening in a medium bowl with an electric mixer until smooth and fluffy. Add the powdered sugar, salt, water, and vanilla and beat well.
11. When the cakes have cooled, use a toothpick to poke three holes along the flat side of the cake (the top when baking). Swirl the toothpick around inside the cake to make room for the filling.
12. Squirt crème filling into each of the three holes in each of the cakes. Be careful not to overfill the cakes or you will have a sticky explosion that must be eaten immediately.

- MAKES 12 SNACK CAKES.

TIDBITS

If you want the cake to be yellow, like the original, you will have to be selective when choosing egg substitute. Scramblers brand egg substitute seems to make the cake the deepest yellow. Or, if you don't use Scramblers, you can add a couple drops of yellow food coloring. These snack cakes are best if eaten within a couple days of filling.

Nutrition Facts
SERVING SIZE—1 SNACK CAKE   FAT (PER SERVING)—3G
TOTAL SERVINGS—12   CALORIES (PER SERVING)—280

• • • •

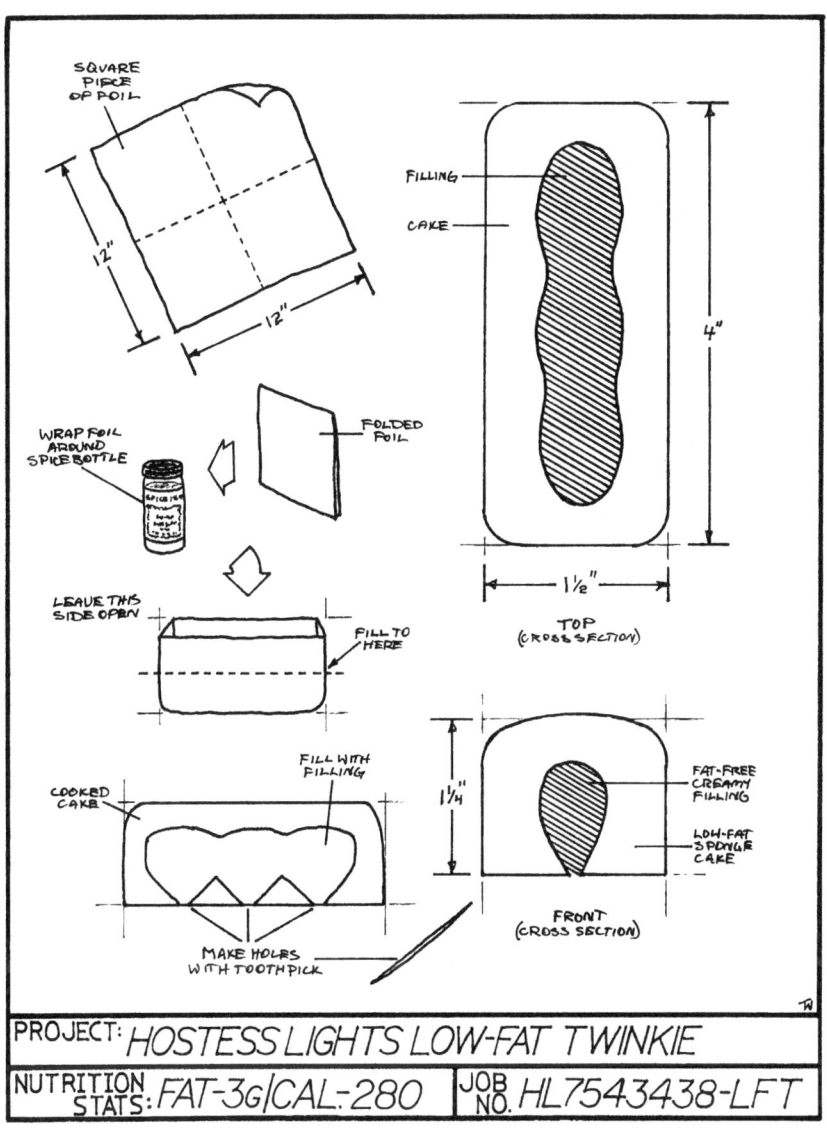

KELLOGG'S LOW-FAT FROSTED BROWN SUGAR CINNAMON POP-TARTS

TOP SECRET RECIPES VERSION OF

Not even Tony the Tiger is a match for the world's most beloved toaster pastries. While Kellogg's Frosted Flakes is the best-selling cereal in the U.S., Pop-Tarts are an even bigger seller for the food manufacturer, with $330 million in sales in 1996. The two-to-a-pack rectangular snacks were born in 1964, when Kellogg's followed a competitor's idea for breakfast pastries that could be heated through in an ordinary toaster. With the company's experience in cereals and grains it was able to create pastries in a variety of flavors. Pop-Tarts have always dominated the toaster pastry market, but in the first half of the 1990s Nabisco was coming on strong with its own toaster pastries called Toastettes. Toastettes became so appealing to consumers because the package held eight pastries, while Pop-Tarts still had six to a box. In June of 1996, Kellogg's added two more Pop-Tarts to each box without changing the price, and Toastettes sales quickly dropped by 45 percent.

Another move against competitor Nabisco came that same year when Kellogg's introduced its new line of low-fat Pop-Tarts. Nabisco had earlier introduced low-fat toaster pastries in its SnackWell's line, but the Kellogg's low-fat version of its popular product once again dominated.

This recipe makes eight clones, or a box's worth of the toaster pastries. Be sure to roll the dough very flat when preparing the pastries, and toast them on the very lowest setting of your toaster. Watch the pastries closely and pop 'em up if the frosting begins to turn brown.

DOUGH

2 tablespoons shortening
1/3 cup powdered sugar
3 tablespoons low fat
   (1 percent fat) buttermilk
1 tablespoon light corn syrup
1/2 teaspoon baking soda

rounded 1/4 teaspoon salt
scant 1/8 teaspoon baking powder
1 2/3 cups all-purpose flour
   (plus about 1/4 cup
   reserved for rolling dough)
3 tablespoons water

FILLING

3 tablespoons dark brown sugar
3 tablespoons sugar
3 tablespoons all-purpose flour

dash cinnamon
dash salt

1 egg white, beaten

FROSTING

1 tablespoon dark brown sugar
4 teaspoons fat-free milk
1 1/4 cups powdered sugar

dash salt
dash cinnamon

1. In a large bowl combine the shortening, powdered sugar, buttermilk, corn syrup, baking soda, salt, and baking powder using an electric mixer.
2. Add the flour and mix by hand to incorporate.
3. Mix in the water by hand, then use your hands to form the dough into a ball. Cover and set aside.
4. To make the filling, combine the ingredients in a small bowl and whisk together. Set aside.
5. To build the pastries, divide the dough in half, then roll one half out onto a floured surface, using additional flour on the rolling pin to prevent the dough from sticking. Roll the dough to no more than 1/16-inch thick. Use a knife or pizza wheel to cut the dough into four 3 x 8-inch rectangles.
6. Brush the beaten egg white over the entire surface of one half of each rectangle. Sprinkle a rounded 1/2 tablespoon of the filling over the surface of the brushed half of the pastry, being sure to leave a margin of about 1/4-inch from the edge

of the dough all of the way around. Fold the other side of the dough over onto the filling. Press down on the edge of the dough all of the way around with the tines of a fork to seal it. Use the fork to poke several holes in the top of the pastry. Fill the remaining three dough rectangles, and then repeat the process with the remaining half portion of dough.
7. Arrange the pastries on a lightly greased cookie sheet and bake in a preheated 350-degree oven 8 to 10 minutes. The pastries should be only very light brown, not dark brown (the pastries will be reheated and browned in a toaster before eating, like the real thing). Remove the pastries from the oven and cool completely.
8. Make the frosting by combining the brown sugar and milk in a small bowl. Microwave on half power for 10 to 20 seconds and stir until the sugar is dissolved. Add the remaining ingredients and stir well until smooth.
9. Spread a thin layer of the frosting over the top of each pastry and allow it to dry. Now leave the pastries out so that they dry completely. Overnight is best.
10. To reheat the pastries, toast them in a toaster oven or toaster on the lightest setting only. Watch carefully so that the pastries do not burn.

- SERVES 8.

Nutrition Facts

SERVING SIZE—1 PASTRY FAT (PER SERVING)—3G
TOTAL SERVINGS—8 CALORIES (PER SERVING)—219

• • • •

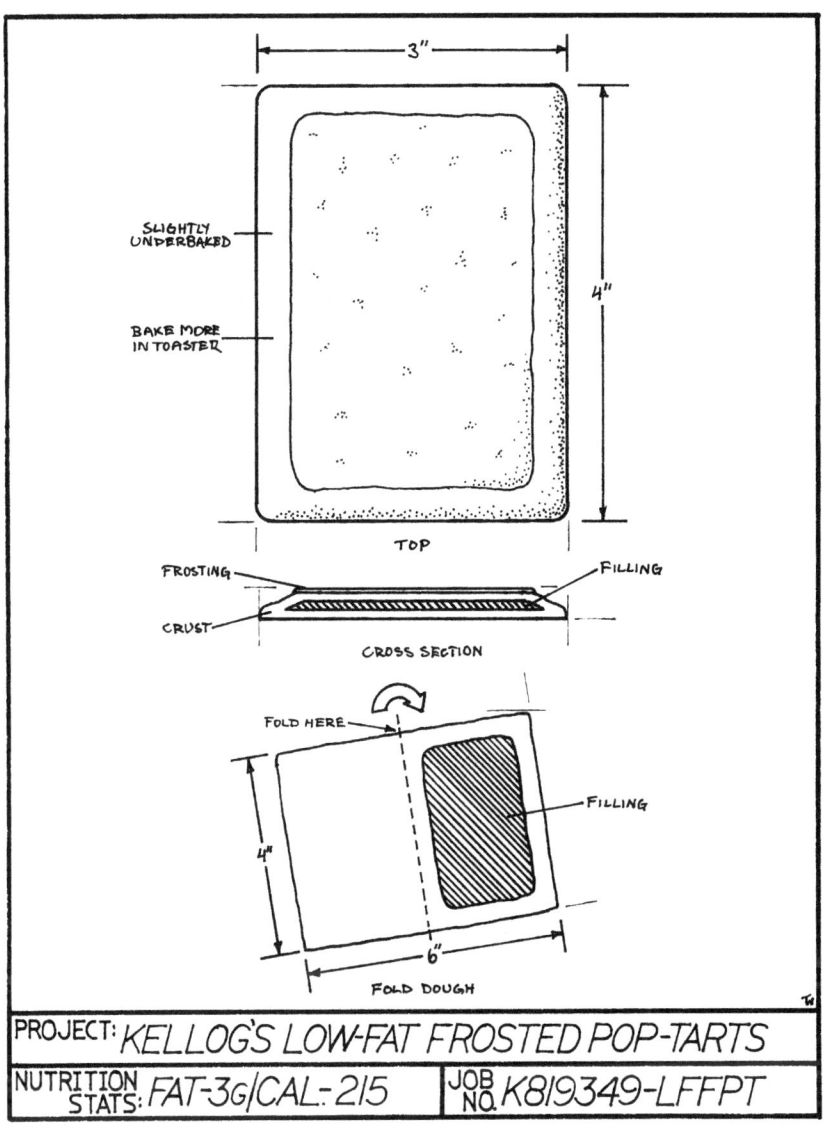

KRAFT FREE CATALINA DRESSING

In 1958, Kraft became one of the first companies to introduce low-calorie salad dressings, with dietetic versions of Italian, French, Bleu Cheese, and Thousand Island dressings. Then, in 1990, Kraft scored another series of hits with its line of fat-free dressings. Today, fat-free and low-fat dressings are just about as popular and diverse as the full-fat varieties.

Here's a TSR clone recipe to create a fat-free dressing like the popular Catalina variety from the innovative food conglomerate. Where the fat should be, cornstarch and gelatin help thicken the dressing and give it a pleasing texture that will ensure you don't even miss those big-time fat grams of the traditional stuff.

1 cup water
⅓ cup sugar
⅓ cup white vinegar
3 tablespoons tomato paste
1 teaspoon cornstarch
½ teaspoon Knox unflavored gelatin
¾ teaspoon salt
dash garlic powder

1. Combine all the ingredients in a saucepan and stir to dissolve the gelatin and cornstarch.
2. Set the pan over medium heat until the mixture begins to boil. Boil for 1 minute, stirring often, then remove the pan from the heat, cover it, and let it cool.
3. Pour the dressing into a covered container and refrigerate it for several hours or overnight until chilled.

- MAKES 1 CUP.

Nutrition Facts
SERVING SIZE—2 TABLESPOONS FAT (PER SERVING)—0G
TOTAL SERVINGS—8 CALORIES (PER SERVING)—40

• • • •

KRAFT FREE CLASSIC CAESAR DRESSING

Thanks to fat-free mayonnaise and low-fat buttermilk, we can make a homegrown version of this popular fat-free Kraft creation. You might at first say, "Wait a minute ... how can this be fat-free when there's buttermilk and two kinds of grated cheese in there?" Yes, indeed, those products do contain fat. But, as long as a serving of the finished product contains less than ½ gram of fat—as it does here—it's considered fat-free. Be sure to give yourself plenty of time to allow this dressing to chill in the refrigerator for several hours before serving.

1 tablespoon sugar
½ teaspoon salt
2 tablespoons hot water
½ cup fat-free mayonnaise
2 tablespoons low-fat buttermilk (1 percent fat)
4 teaspoons white vinegar
2 teaspoons grated Romano cheese
2 teaspoons grated Parmesan cheese
dash coarse ground black pepper
dash dried oregano
dash garlic powder

1. Dissolve the sugar and salt in a small bowl with the hot water. Set aside.
2. Combine the remaining ingredients in a medium bowl and stir well.
3. Add the water/sugar/salt mixture to the other ingredients and stir once more to combine. Place the dressing in a covered container in the refrigerator and chill for several hours.

- MAKES A LITTLE OVER ¾ CUP.

TIDBITS

If the dressing seems too thick, just add some more water, a tablespoon at a time, until it has the desired consistency.

Nutrition Facts
    SERVING SIZE—2 TABLESPOONS   FAT (PER SERVING)—0G
    TOTAL SERVINGS—7   CALORIES (PER SERVING)—35

• • • •

KRAFT FREE THOUSAND ISLAND DRESSING

TOP SECRET RECIPES VERSION OF

Once upon a time we drenched our salads with generous portions of popular dressings such as this one and considered it a healthy pre-entrée course. Just two tablespoons of the full-fat version of Thousand Island dressing packs about 10 grams of fat, and we normally use about ¼ cup on a salad. That's 20 grams of fat in our bellies, before the main course has even started. Yikes! But, today we know better. So, never fear, a *Top Secret Recipe* is here. And you won't get even one gram of fat from a serving of this TSR formula that clones the most popular fat-free Thousand Island dressing on the supermarket shelves.

1 tablespoon sugar
⅛ teaspoon salt
2 tablespoons hot water
½ cup fat-free mayonnaise
2 tablespoons ketchup
1 tablespoon white vinegar
2 teaspoons sweet pickle relish
1 teaspoon finely minced white onion
dash black pepper

1. Dissolve the sugar and salt in the hot water in a small bowl.
2. Combine the remaining ingredients with the water mixture. Stir well.
3. Place the dressing in a covered container and refrigerate it for several hours so that the flavors blend.

- MAKES ABOUT 1 CUP.

TIDBITS

If the dressing seems too thick, just add some more water, a tablespoon at a time, until it has the desired consistency.

Nutrition Facts

Serving size—2 tablespoons Fat (per serving)—0g
Total servings—6 Calories (per serving)—40

• • •

TOP SECRET RECIPES VERSION OF

KRAFT LIGHT DELUXE MACARONI & CHEESE DINNER

The difference between the "deluxe" version of Kraft's Macaroni & Cheese Dinner and the original is the cheese. The deluxe dinner has an envelope of cheese sauce, while the original dinner, introduced to the nation back in 1937, comes with powdered cheese. The original Kraft Macaroni & Cheese Dinner is the most popular packaged dinner product around, and one of the top six best-selling of all dry goods sold in the supermarket—probably because it only takes about 7 minutes to prepare, and a box costs just 70 cents. And who doesn't like macaroni and cheese? But it's the deluxe version—the more expensive version—with its pouch of gooey, yellow cheese sauce, which Kraft reformulated as a reduced-fat product in 1997. The new version boasts 50 percent less fat and 10 percent fewer calories than the deluxe original, and tastes just as good. So here's a simple clone that requires you to get your hands on Cheez Whiz Light, reduced-fat cheddar cheese, and elbow macaroni. Then you're on your way to an amazing clone of what cartoon Texan Hank Hill from the TV show *King of the Hill* refers to as "veggies."

8 cups water
1¾ cups uncooked elbow macaroni
⅓ cup reduced-fat
   (2 percent milk) shredded
   cheddar cheese

½ cup Cheez Whiz Light
1 tablespoon whole milk
½ teaspoon salt

1. Bring 8 cups (2 quarts) of water to a boil over high heat in a large saucepan. Add the elbow macaroni to the water and cook for 10 to 12 minutes or until tender, stirring occasionally.
2. As the macaroni boils, prepare the sauce by combining the cheddar cheese, Cheez Whiz, and milk in a small saucepan over medium/low heat. Stir the cheese mixture often as it heats, so that it does not burn. Add the salt. When all of the cheddar cheese has melted and the sauce is smooth, cover the pan and set it aside until the macaroni has cooked.
3. When the macaroni is ready, drain the water off, but do not rinse the macaroni.
4. Using the same pan you prepared the macaroni in, combine the macaroni with the cheese sauce and mix well.

- SERVES 4.

TIDBITS

If you would like your macaroni and cheese to have a color that is similar to the happy, fluorescent orange tint of the original, you can add a little paprika—about ⅛ teaspoon—to the cheese sauce just before you remove it from the heat.

Nutrition Facts

SERVING SIZE—1 CUP
TOTAL SERVINGS—4
FAT (PER SERVING)—5G
CALORIES (PER SERVING)—290

• • • •

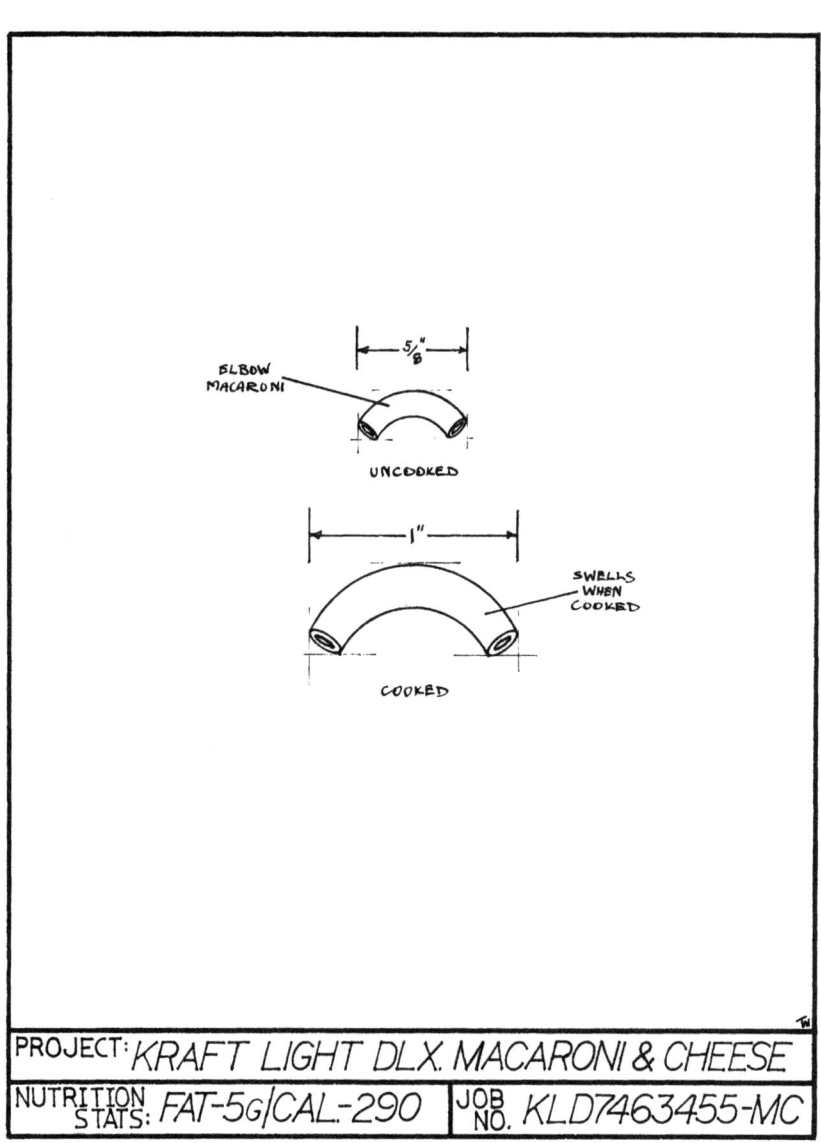

TOP SECRET RECIPES VERSION OF NABISCO REDUCED-FAT CHEESE NIPS

In the last several years, since 1992, Nabisco has taken great effort to produce reduced-fat versions of all the popular products created by the food giant. This product loyalty–retaining move is just good business. According to one Nabisco spokesperson, "We want to bring back the people who have enjoyed our products, but went away for health and diet reasons." Indeed, that's exactly what we see happening, as customers are now grabbing for all those boxes with the green on them. The box for these cheesy crackers is indeed splashed with green and has big letters at the top that say: "Reduced Fat: 40% less fat than original Cheese Nips."

The secret ingredient for this clone of the popular little square crackers is the fat-free cheese sprinkles by Molly McButter. One 2-ounce shaker of the stuff will do it, and you won't use it all. Just keep in mind that cheese powder is pretty salty, so you may want to go very easy on salting the tops of the crackers.

1 cup sifted all-purpose flour (plus about ½ cup for kneading and rolling)
1 teaspoon baking soda
¼ teaspoon baking powder

nonstick cooking spray

½ cup Molly McButter fat-free cheese sprinkles.
2½ tablespoons shortening
⅓ cup plus 1 tablespoon low-fat buttermilk (1 percent fat)

½ teaspoon salt (optional for tops)

1. Sift together 1 cup of flour, the baking soda, baking powder, and cheese sprinkles in a large bowl.
2. Cut in the shortening with a fork and knife with a crosswise motion until the dough is broken down into rice-size pieces. The mixture will still be very dry.
3. Stir in the buttermilk with a fork until the dough becomes very moist and sticky.
4. Sprinkle a couple tablespoons of the reserved flour over the dough and work it in until the dough can be handled without sticking, then turn it out onto a floured board, being sure to reserve ¼ cup of flour for later. Knead the dough well for 60 to 90 seconds, and be sure the flour is incorporated. Wrap the dough in plastic wrap and chill for at least one hour.
5. Preheat the oven to 325 degrees. Spray a light coating of cooking spray on a baking sheet.
6. Remove the dough from the refrigerator and use the remaining reserved flour to dust a rolling surface. Roll about one-third of the dough to about 1/16-inch thick. Trim the edges square (a pizza slicer works great for this), then transfer the dough to the baking sheet. Use the rolling pin to transfer the dough. Simply pick up one end of the dough onto the rolling pin, and roll the dough around it. Reverse the process onto the baking sheet to transfer the dough.
7. Use a pizza slicer to cut across and down the dough, creating 1-inch square pieces. Use the blunt end of a skewer or a cut toothpick to poke a hole in the center of each piece.
8. Sprinkle a very light coating of salt over the top of the crackers (this is optional—the crackers will already be quite salty) and bake for 8 to 10 minutes. Mix the crackers around like Scrabble tiles (so those on the edge don't burn) and bake for another 3 to 5 minutes, or until some are just barely turning a light brown. Repeat the rolling and baking process with the remaining dough.

- MAKES APPROXIMATELY 300 CRACKERS.

Nutrition Facts

SERVING SIZE—31 CRACKERS FAT (PER SERVING)—3.5G
TOTAL SERVINGS—ABOUT 10 CALORIES (PER SERVING)—105

• • • •

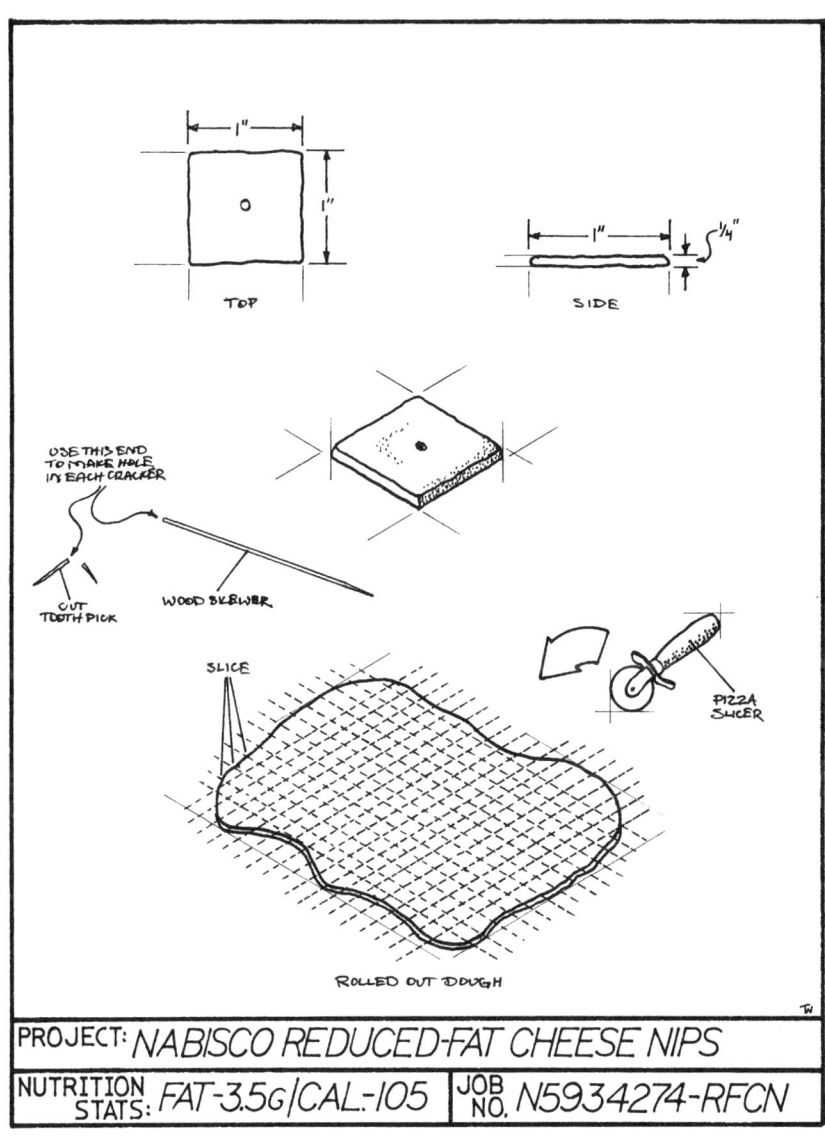

TOP SECRET RECIPES VERSION OF

NABISCO SNACKWELL'S CHOCOLATE CHIP COOKIES

Nabisco debuted its first six SnackWell's line of products in 1992 to rave reviews and more than impressive sales. The company was having a very hard time keeping up with the extraordinary demand, and customers would find empty shelves in the supermarkets where SnackWell's cookies were once stacked. That supply problem would eventually be addressed in a series of humorous commercials, featuring the shelf-stocking "Cookie Man" who was attacked by ravenous women in search of the fast-selling products. The ads' announcer told everyone not to worry, that the products would soon be on the way to the stores.

Today, supply has caught up with demand, and the stores seem to be able to keep plenty of the products in stock, including the bite-size chocolate chip cookies, which can be cloned with this recipe. The cookies are easily made so small by rolling the dough into long, plastic-wrapped logs, which you then chill, slice, and bake.

1 egg white
¼ cup sugar
1 tablespoon brown sugar
1 tablespoon corn syrup
1 tablespoon shortening
1½ tablespoons egg substitute

¾ cup all-purpose flour
¼ teaspoon plus a pinch of salt
¾ teaspoon baking soda
½ teaspoon baking powder
½ cup mini chocolate chips

1. Preheat the oven to 325 degrees.
2. Beat the egg white until thick.

3. Add the granulated sugar to the egg white and continue beating until the mixture forms soft peaks.
4. While beating, add the brown sugar, corn syrup, shortening, and egg substitute.
5. In a separate bowl, combine the flour, salt, baking soda, and baking powder.
6. Combine the dry mixture with the wet and mix well. Add the chocolate chips and incorporate them into the dough.
7. Divide the dough in half, then roll each portion into a long, thin log about the same diameter as a nickel and wrap each in plastic wrap. Put the dough into the refrigerator and chill it for a couple hours (you may also use the freezer for roughly half the time if you're in a hurry).
8. When the dough has thoroughly chilled, remove each log of dough from the plastic wrap and cut into ¼-inch-thick slices. Place slices on a cookie sheet coated lightly with nonstick spray about ½-inch apart, and bake for 10 to 12 minutes or until the cookies turn light brown.

- MAKES 12 DOZEN BITE-SIZE COOKIES.

Nutrition Facts

SERVING SIZE—13 COOKIES   FAT (PER SERVING)—3.3G
TOTAL SERVINGS—11   CALORIES (PER SERVING)—105

• • • •

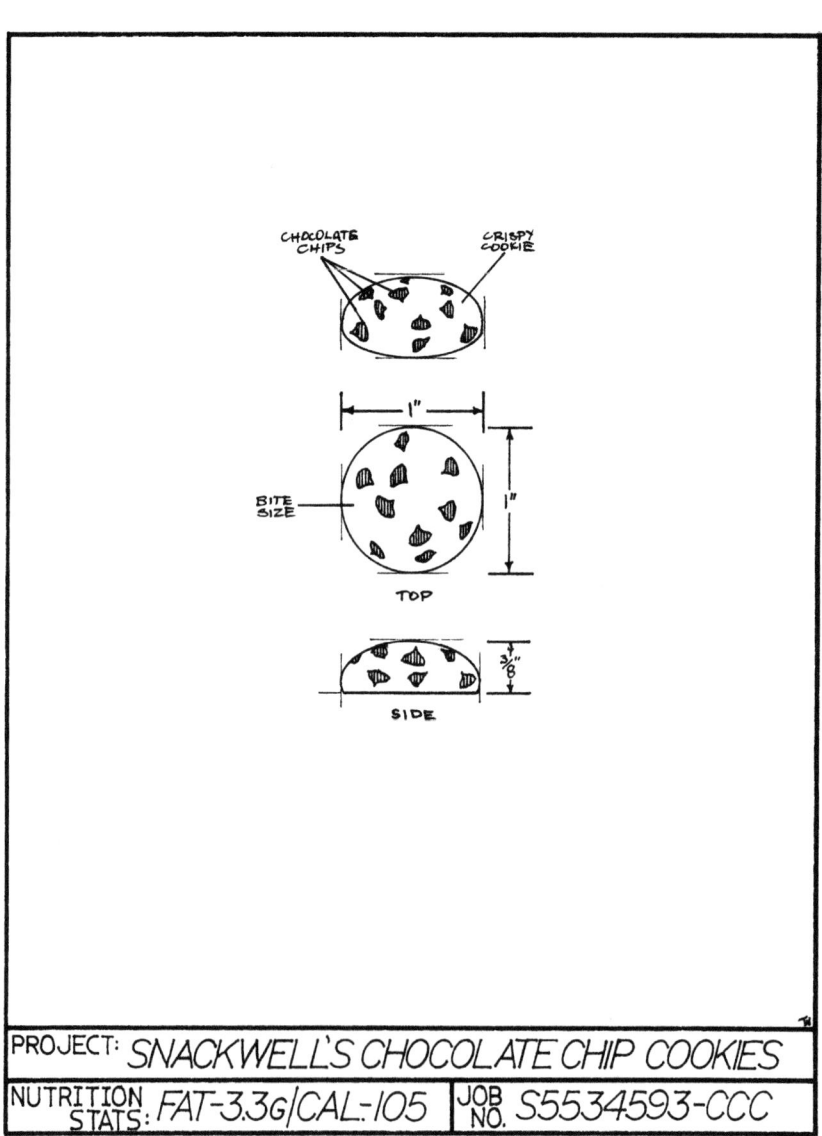

NABISCO SNACKWELL'S FUDGE BROWNIE BARS

TOP SECRET RECIPES VERSION OF

One of the favorite SnackWell's creations are the very low-fat snack bars that now come in several varieties, including apple raisin, banana, golden cake, and this one, which tastes like a brownie. But, while a single brownie might contain around 6 to 10 grams of fat, this snack bar weighs in with just a fraction of that—at only 2 grams of fat per serving.

The secret to keeping the fat to a minimum in this recipe is the use of egg whites, corn syrup, and chocolate syrup. These fat-free ingredients help to replace much of the fat that would be found in a traditional recipe, while keeping the finished product moist and chewy, and filled with flavor.

2 egg whites
1 cup plus 5 tablespoons sugar
2 tablespoons corn syrup
2 tablespoons shortening
1/2 cup Hershey's chocolate syrup
1/2 cup fudge topping
1/4 cup warm water

1 teaspoon vanilla
1 1/2 cups all-purpose flour
1/4 cup cocoa
3/4 teaspoon salt
1/4 teaspoon baking soda
nonstick cooking spray

1. Preheat the oven to 350 degrees.
2. In a large bowl, whip the egg whites with an electric mixer until they become thick. Do not use a plastic bowl for this.
3. Add 1 cup of sugar to the egg whites and continue to beat until the mixture forms soft peaks.
4. To the egg white and sugar mixture, add the corn syrup, shortening, chocolate syrup, fudge, water, and vanilla.

5. In a separate bowl, combine the flour, cocoa, salt, and baking soda.
6. While beating the wet mixture, slowly add the dry mixture.
7. Lightly grease a 9 x 13-inch pan with a light coating of nonstick cooking spray. Be sure to coat the sides as well as the bottom of the pan. Dump about 3 tablespoons of the remaining sugar into the pan, then tilt and shake the pan so that a light layer of sugar coats the entire bottom of the pan and about halfway up the sides. Pour out the excess sugar.
8. Pour the batter into the pan, spreading it evenly around the inside. Sprinkle a light coating of sugar—about two tablespoons—over the entire top surface of the batter. Gently shake the pan from side to side to evenly distribute the sugar over the batter. Bake for 25 to 28 minutes or until the cake begins to pull away from the sides of the pan.
9. Remove the cake from the oven and turn it out onto a cooling rack. When the cake has cooled, place it onto a sheet of wax paper on a cutting board and slice across the cake 6 times, creating 7 even sections. Next cut the cake lengthwise twice, into thirds, creating a total of 21 snack bars. When the bars have completely cooled, store them in a resealable plastic bag or an airtight container.

- MAKES 21 SNACK BARS.

Nutrition Facts

SERVING SIZE—1 BAR	TOTAL FAT (PER SERVING)—2G
SERVINGS—21	CALORIES (PER SERVING)—144

• • • •

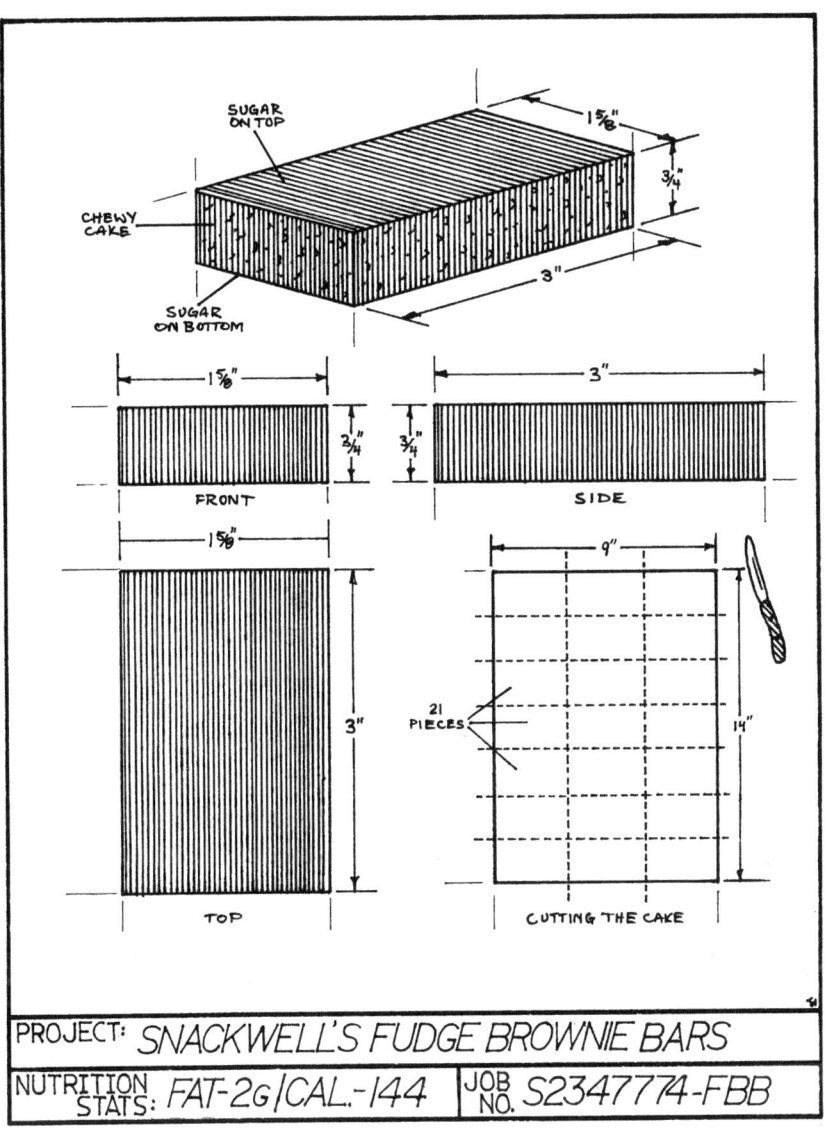

NABISCO SNACKWELL'S GOLDEN SNACK BARS

Bite into one of these chewy cake bars and you won't believe that it's so low in fat. That's because we replace a lot of the fat you would find in most cakes with sweetened condensed milk, and some egg substitute. That gives us room to throw some shortening in there and still keep the fat count at less than 2 grams per serving, just like the real thing. Also, take note of the technique used to give the snack bars that sugar-crystal coating on the top and bottom of the bars, just as you will find on the original SnackWell's creation.

2 egg whites
1 cup plus 5 tablespoons sugar
2 tablespoons corn syrup
3 tablespoons shortening
¼ cup sweetened condensed skim milk
¼ cup egg substitute

3 tablespoons low-fat (2 percent) milk
1 ½ teaspoons vanilla
¼ teaspoon lemon extract
1 ½ cups all-purpose flour
1 teaspoon salt
¼ teaspoon baking soda
nonstick cooking spray

1. Preheat the oven to 350 degrees.
2. In a large bowl, whip the egg whites with an electric mixer until they become thick. Do not use a plastic bowl for this.
3. Add 1 cup of sugar to the egg whites and continue to beat until the mixture forms soft peaks.
4. Add the corn syrup, shortening, condensed milk, egg substitute, low-fat milk, vanilla, and lemon extract to the mixture while beating.

5. In a separate bowl, combine the flour, salt, and baking soda.
6. While beating the wet mixture, slowly add the dry ingredients.
7. Lightly grease a 9 x 13-inch pan with a light coating of nonstick cooking spray. Be sure to coat the sides as well as the bottom of the pan. Dump about 3 tablespoons of sugar into the pan, then tilt and shake the pan so that a light layer of sugar coats the entire bottom of the pan and about halfway up the sides. Pour out the excess sugar.
8. Pour the batter into the pan, spreading it evenly around the inside. Sprinkle a light coating of sugar—about two tablespoons—over the entire top surface of the batter. Gently shake the pan from side to side to evenly distribute the sugar over the batter. Bake for 25 to 28 minutes or until the cake begins to pull away from the sides of the pan.
9. Remove the cake from the oven and turn it out onto a cooling rack. When the cake has cooled, place it onto a sheet of wax paper on a cutting board and slice across the cake 6 times, creating 7 even slices. Next cut the cake lengthwise twice, into thirds, creating a total of 21 snack bars. When the bars have completely cooled, store them in a resealable plastic bag or an airtight container.

- MAKES 21 SNACK BARS.

Nutrition Facts

SERVING SIZE—1 BAR	TOTAL FAT (PER SERVING)—1.8G
SERVINGS—21	CALORIES (PER SERVING)—113

• • • •

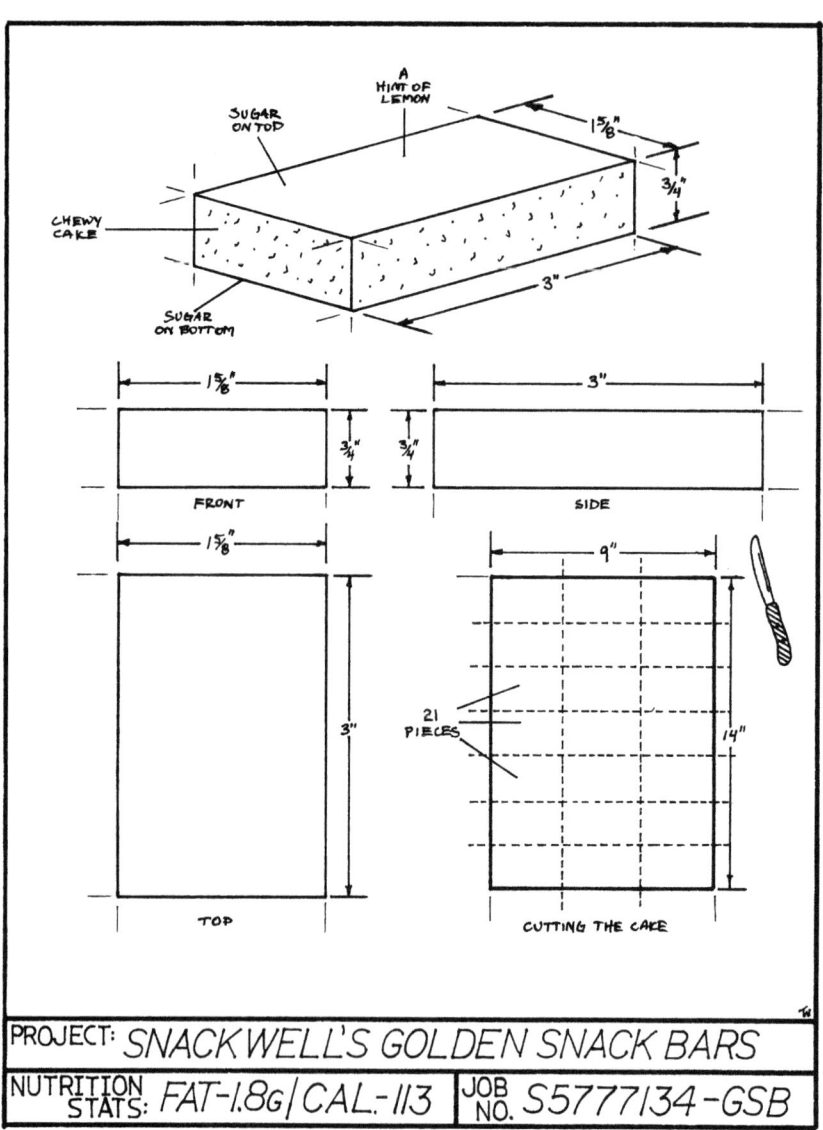

TOP SECRET RECIPES VERSION OF

RED LOBSTER LEMON-PEPPER GRILLED MAHI-MAHI

The Red Lobster menu describes this dish as: "A mild-tasting fillet sprinkled with lemon-pepper seasoning, plus rice." Simple enough. And, if you keep the butter to a minimum, this clone becomes a naturally low-fat meal. Most of the butter will melt away from the fish when grilling, and mahi-mahi has hardly any fat in it. The liquid smoke is here to give the fish a flavor similar to that served in the restaurant, and I find Jane's brand of lemon-pepper seasoning the best to use here, if you can find it. Add some rice on the side—either brown or converted—some steamed veggies, and you've got yourself an incredibly guilt-free meal.

You may also wish to serve this with the fat-free tartar sauce from page 212.

1 1/2 pounds mahi-mahi fillets, skinned
1 tablespoon water
2 to 3 drops liquid smoke

1 tablespoon butter, melted
1 teaspoon lemon-pepper seasoning (Jane's is best)

1. Preheat the barbecue or indoor grill to high heat.
2. Cut the mahi-mahi into four equal portions. Be sure to remove the skin.
3. Combine the water and liquid smoke in a small bowl. Brush this solution over the entire surface of each piece of fish.
4. Brush the melted butter over the entire surface of each piece of fish.

5. Sprinkle a generous portion of the lemon-pepper seasoning on the top of each piece of fish, then grill the fish with this side down on the grill. Sprinkle the remaining seasoning over the top of each piece.
6. Grill the fish for 5 to 6 minutes per side, then serve hot with rice.

- SERVES 2.

Nutrition Facts

SERVING SIZE—2 FILLETS	FAT (PER SERVING)—5G
TOTAL SERVINGS—2	CALORIES (PER SERVING)—340

• • • •

RED LOBSTER NANTUCKET BAKED COD

Here's another Red Lobster selection that is a simple, healthy choice for your next kitchen-cloned meal. The menu described it as: "A flaky, white fish, baked with fresh tomatoes & Parmesan, served with rice." Much of the butter will slip away from the fish, and you will get a very small amount of fat from the Parmesan cheese; but at a total of 6 grams of fat per serving, this is still a very low-fat choice for lunch or dinner. Serve this dish with rice and some steamed veggies, and save the fat grams for dessert.

You may also want to serve this with some of the fat-free tartar sauce from page 212.

SPICE BLEND

1/4 teaspoon salt
1/4 teaspoon paprika

dash black pepper
dash cayenne pepper

1 1/2 pounds fresh cod fillet
1 tablespoon butter, melted
lemon juice

2 small tomatoes, thinly sliced
2 tablespoons grated Parmesan cheese

1. Combine the spices in a small bowl and set aside.
2. Preheat the oven to 425 degrees. Cut the fish into 4 equal portions (2 per serving), and arrange the fillets in a 9 x 13-inch baking dish or pan.
3. Melt the butter in a small bowl in the microwave for 10 to 20 seconds. Brush the top of each fillet with butter, drizzle a little lemon juice on the fish, then sprinkle the spice blend evenly over the top of each fillet.

4. Arrange 2 to 3 tomato slices over the top of each fillet.
5. Sprinkle grated Parmesan cheese over each tomato slice. Each slice should be at least 50 percent covered with the cheese, and it's okay for some of the cheese to fall on the fish.
6. Bake the fish, uncovered, for 8 minutes, then turn the oven to a high broil and continue to cook for 6 to 8 minutes or until the cheese on the tomatoes begins to brown. Serve two pieces of fish together, with rice on the side.

- SERVES 2.

Nutrition Facts

SERVING SIZE—2 FILLETS   FAT (PER SERVING)—6G
TOTAL SERVINGS—2   CALORIES (PER SERVING)—370

• • • •

SWISS MISS FAT-FREE CHOCOLATE FUDGE PUDDING

TOP SECRET RECIPES VERSION OF

Hunt-Wesson first introduced a light variety of Swiss Miss Puddings in 1990, but three years later changed the formula to fat-free. This chocolaty clone of the rich pudding you find in the refrigerated section of the supermarket will satisfy your chocolate craving without contributing any of those nasty fat grams. You'll notice that the sweetened condensed milk helps to replace fat, and the cornstarch jumps in to keep the pudding thick and creamy. Add two types of chocolate and you've got an irresistible snack that tastes just like the real deal.

2½ cups fat-free milk
2 tablespoons unsweetened cocoa powder
3 tablespoons cornstarch
½ cup sweetened condensed skim milk
3 tablespoons Hershey's chocolate syrup
dash salt
½ teaspoon vanilla extract

1. In a saucepan, combine the fat-free milk with the cocoa powder and cornstarch and whisk thoroughly until the powders are dissolved.
2. Add the condensed milk, chocolate syrup, and salt to the saucepan. Set the pan over medium/low heat. Heat the mixture, stirring constantly, until it comes to a boil and then thickens. This will take about 6 minutes.

3. Remove the pan from the heat and let it sit, covered, for 5 minutes. Then add the vanilla.
4. Transfer the pudding to serving cups, cover each with plastic wrap, and chill for at least 2 to 3 hours before serving.

- Serves 4.

TIDBITS

Cover the pudding tightly when chilling and eat it within a few days or it may begin to thin.

Nutrition Facts

Serving size—¾ cup
Total servings—4
Fat (per serving)—0g
Calories (per serving)—170

• • • •

SWISS MISS FAT-FREE TAPIOCA PUDDING

TOP SECRET RECIPES VERSION OF

When the first instant hot cocoa mix was developed in the fifties, it was available only to the airlines in individual portions for passengers and was called Brown Swiss. This mix was so popular that the company packaged it for sale in the grocery stores and changed the name to Swiss Miss. In the seventies, the first Swiss Miss Puddings were introduced and quickly became the leader of dairy case puddings. When the fat-free versions of the puddings were introduced some 23 years later, they, too, would become a popular favorite.

No sugar needs to be added to this recipe that recreates one of the best-tasting brands of fat-free pudding on the market. The condensed milk is enough to sweeten the pudding; plus it provides a creamy consistency, which, along with the cornstarch, helps to replace the fat found in the full-fat version of this tasty tapioca treat. It's a simple recipe to make and you won't even "miss" the fat.

2 tablespoons cornstarch
2½ cups fat-free milk
½ cup sweetened condensed skim milk

dash salt
2½ tablespoons instant tapioca
½ teaspoon vanilla extract

1. Combine the cornstarch with the fat-free milk in a medium saucepan and whisk thoroughly to dissolve the cornstarch.
2. Add the condensed milk, salt, and tapioca to the pan. Stir until smooth and then set the pan aside for 5 minutes.
3. After 5 minutes, bring the mixture to a boil over medium/low

heat, stirring constantly until it thickens, then cover and remove from the heat. Let the pudding sit, covered, for 20 minutes.
4. Stir in the vanilla, then transfer the pudding to serving cups. Cover the cups with plastic wrap and let them chill for at least 2 to 3 hours before serving.

- Serves 4.

TIDBITS

Cover the pudding tightly when chilling and eat it within a few days or it may begin to thin.

Nutrition Facts
Serving size—¾ cup
Total servings—4
Fat (per serving)—0g
Calories (per serving)—140

• • • •

T.G.I. FRIDAY'S FAT-FREE CHEESECAKE

TOP SECRET RECIPES VERSION OF

For the last couple of years T.G.I. Friday's has been serving a delicious cheesecake drizzled with strawberry sauce. The cheesecake tastes like a decadent, fat-filled dessert; it's creamy and delicious. But the shocker comes when you realize that there is not one gram of fat in a single serving. Many recipes for fat-free cheesecakes produce a cheesecake with an unusual taste or one that is very hard on top. This clone recipe will solve those problems and produce a dessert that tastes like the popular cheesecake you can order at one of America's most successful restaurant chains.

You'll need a 9½-inch springform pan for this recipe, and be sure to let the cream cheese come to room temperature (keep it covered) before you use it. Serve this one to your friends and watch the surprise when you tell them it's 100 percent fat-free.

5 8-ounce pkgs. fat-free Philadelphia cream cheese
1¼ cups sugar
⅔ cup fat-free sour cream

2½ tablespoons flour
2 teaspoons vanilla
½ cup egg substitute

CRUST

1 tablespoon ground pecans
3 tablespoons graham cracker crumbs

1½ teaspoons sugar
nonstick cooking spray

STRAWBERRY SAUCE

8 ounces frozen strawberries
⅓ cup sugar

2 tablespoons water

1. Bring the cream cheese to room temperature. Preheat the oven to 325 degrees.
2. Using an electric mixer, whip the cream cheese in a large bowl until smooth. Add the sugar, sour cream, flour, and vanilla and beat until well incorporated.
3. Add the egg substitute and mix only until combined. Do not overmix once the egg substitute is added.
4. To make the crust, measure the pecans after grinding them up in a food processor or blender, then return them to the processor. Add the graham cracker crumbs and 1½ teaspoons of sugar to the pecans and pulse for about 15 seconds to form a fine meal. Spray the inside of a 9½-inch springform pan with a light coating of cooking spray. Wipe off any excess spray around the top rim of the pan. The spray should only coat the bottom and up about two inches on the sides. Anything sprayed above that can be wiped off. Dump the crumbs into the pan and swirl the pan so that the bottom and sides are coated with the crumbs. Lightly tap out any excess.
5. Pour the cream cheese mixture into the springform pan, being careful not to disturb the crumbs when pouring. Gently spread the cheese mixture close to the edge, but don't touch the sides or you may disturb the crumbs.
6. Bake the cheesecake for 50 to 60 minutes or until the top of the cheesecake is firm. The center may not entirely set until the cheesecake cools. Cover and cool for 2 hours at room temperature, and then refrigerate.
7. As the cheesecake cools, prepare the strawberry sauce by combining the strawberries, sugar, and water in a microwave-safe bowl. Cover, and microwave on 50 percent power for 2 minutes. If the strawberries are still frozen, you may have to heat the mixture for as long as 4 to 5 minutes. Stir to dissolve the sugar, then let stand for 10 to 15 minutes. Pour the mixture into the blender or food processor and puree until smooth. Strain and chill.
8. Cut the cheesecake into 12 slices. Serve each slice with about 1 tablespoon of the strawberry sauce poured over the top.

- Serves 12.

Nutrition Facts
   Serving size—1 slice   Fat (per serving)—0g
   Total servings—12   Calories (per serving)—223

• • • •

Drawing labels: 9", SLICE, FILLING, THIN CRUST, WHOLE CHEESECAKE, -INCH SPRINGFORM PAN, FAT-FREE CREAM CHEESE FILLING, 2", 1¾", 4½", THIN CRUST, ONE SLICE

PROJECT: T.G.I. FRIDAY'S FAT-FREE CHEESECAKE
NUTRITION STATS: FAT-0g/CAL.-223   **JOB NO.** TGIF 349756-FFC

T.G.I. FRIDAY'S JACK DANIEL'S GRILL SALMON

TOP SECRET RECIPES VERSION OF

The glaze that is brushed over this salmon is one of the most scrumptious sauces you will ever taste on fish, or just about any other meat. T.G.I. Friday's introduced the glaze in 1997 and it became the company's most successful new product launch. I was encouraged to figure out how to clone the stuff when the *Oprah Winfrey Show* requested a recreation of the glaze for an appearance. This recipe is the result of hard work, and darn accurate at that. Plus, when the glaze is brushed over salmon, it makes for a very healthy meal.

While the fat count here may seem high compared to other recipes in the book, don't be too concerned. That fat, which comes from the salmon, is called Omega-3 fatty acids, and it is a beneficial type of fat found in fish and nuts. Research has shown that Omega-3 fatty acids can actually prevent heart disease and lower cholesterol.

As for the sauce, you will find it is very versatile. You can brush it on almost any type of fish, as well as ribs, chicken, and beef. It also keeps very well for long periods of time if stored in the refrigerator in a sealed container.

GLAZE
- 1 head of garlic
- 1 tablespoon olive oil
- ⅔ cup water
- 1 cup pineapple juice
- ¼ cup teriyaki sauce
- 1 tablespoon soy sauce
- 1⅓ cups dark brown sugar
- 3 tablespoons lemon juice
- 3 tablespoons minced white onion
- 1 tablespoon Jack Daniel's whiskey
- 1 tablespoon crushed pineapple
- ¼ teaspoon cayenne pepper

- 4½-pound fresh Atlantic salmon fillets
- fat-free butter-flavored spray or spread
- salt
- pepper

1. Preheat the oven to 325 degrees.
2. To roast the garlic for the glaze, cut about ½-inch off the top of the garlic head. Cut the roots so that the garlic will sit flat. Remove most of the papery skin from the garlic, but leave enough so that the cloves stay together. Place the head of garlic in a small casserole dish or baking pan, drizzle the olive oil over it, and cover it with a lid or foil. Bake for 1 hour. Remove the garlic and let it cool until you can handle it.
3. Combine the water, pineapple juice, teriyaki sauce, soy sauce, and brown sugar in a medium saucepan over medium/high heat. Stir occasionally until the mixture boils, then reduce the heat until the mixture is just simmering.
4. Squeeze the sides of the head of garlic until the pasty roasted garlic is squeezed out. Measure 2 teaspoons into the saucepan and whisk to combine. Add the remaining glaze ingredients to the pan and stir.
5. Let the mixture simmer for 40 to 50 minutes or until the glaze has reduced by about one-third and is thick and syrupy. Make sure it doesn't boil over. When the glaze is done, cover the saucepan and set it aside until the fish is ready.
6. To cook the fish, preheat your barbecue or kitchen grill to medium/high heat. Remove any skin or bones from the fillets. Brush the entire surface of each fillet with a light coating of the

fat-free butter-flavored spread or spray. Lightly salt and pepper both sides of the fillets and place them on the hot grill at a slight angle, so that grill marks will be made at an angle on the fish. Cook each fillet for 2 to 4 minutes, then turn them over, placing them back on the grill at an angle once again. After 2 to 4 minutes, turn the fish over at a different angle so that the grill marks will criss-cross. Cook 2 to 4 minutes more, flip again, and cook until done. The entire cooking time should be somewhere between 8 to 15 minutes depending on the thickness of your fillets and the heat of the grill. Be careful not to burn the fish, and quickly move the fish away from any flare-ups.

7. When the fillets are done, remove them from the grill and spoon a generous portion of glaze over each one. Serve hot with a baked potato and vegetables, if desired.

- SERVES 4 AS AN ENTRÉE.

Nutrition Facts
SERVING SIZE—1 FILLET   FAT (PER SERVING)—16.5G
TOTAL SERVINGS—4   CALORIES (PER SERVING)—525

• • • •

WEIGHT WATCHERS SMART ONES CHOCOLATE ÉCLAIR

Weight Watchers was one of the first companies to introduce low-fat foods to the freezer section of your local supermarket. Those earlier items were mostly meals, such as dinners and lunch items. In 1980, the company began offering a selection of low-fat desserts, which quickly gained in popularity; probably because they didn't taste low-fat. But more recent favorites are these small chocolate-frosted, crème-filled eclairs, developed in 1993. The originals are bought and stored frozen, but they can be defrosted at room temperature within an hour and scarfed down, guilt-free.

The clone recipe here is designed so that you don't need a special pastry bag to make the shells, or to fill them with the delicious, custard-like combination of fat-free vanilla pudding and Dream Whip. It's an éclair recipe you won't find anywhere else, and it's guaranteed to satisfy your most fierce dessert craving.

FILLING
¼ cup instant vanilla pudding (½ of a 3.4-ounce package)
⅔ cup fat-free milk
1 envelope Dream Whip
dash salt

SHELLS
1½ cups cake flour, sifted
¼ teaspoon baking powder
1½ cups water
2½ tablespoons butter
¼ teaspoon vanilla
1 tablespoon sugar
dash salt
4 egg whites, slightly beaten

GLAZE
¾ cup powdered sugar
2 tablespoons cocoa powder
dash salt

scant ½ teaspoon vanilla
4 to 5 teaspoons water

1. First make the filling by combining the pudding mix with the milk and beating with an electric mixer on low speed for about 30 seconds.
2. Add the envelope of Dream Whip and mix again on low speed for about 30 seconds.
3. Turn the mixer speed to high and continue beating the mixture for about 2 minutes until it's light and fluffy. Cover and chill for at least an hour (while you are making the shells).
4. Preheat the oven to 400 degrees.
5. To make the shells, mix the flour and baking powder together in a medium bowl and set aside.
6. Combine the water, butter, vanilla, sugar, and salt in a medium saucepan and bring the mixture to a boil over high heat.
7. Turn the heat down to low and add the flour and baking powder mixture all at once. Stir vigorously with a wooden spoon until the mixture forms a ball and pulls away from the side of the pan. Remove the pan from the heat and immediately transfer the mixture to a medium mixing bowl.
8. Add the 4 egg whites to the bowl. Beat the mixture with a wooden spoon to incorporate the egg whites until it becomes smooth and forms a paste.
9. Make a pastry bag by cutting the corner off a plastic storage bag. Cut about ¾-inch in from the corner to create a hole that is about 1 inch in diameter. Fill the bag with the dough while it is still warm—you don't want the dough to cool.
10. Pipe 4½-inch strips of dough onto an ungreased baking sheet. You should be able to make 9 strips of dough.
11. Bake for 20 to 25 minutes, then reduce the heat to 325 degrees and bake for an additional 30 to 35 minutes until the shells are light brown. Let cool.
12. Cut the tip off one end of each shell and scrape out the soft doughy centers with a cocktail fork or handle end of a spoon.

13. When the inside of the shells have cooled completely, use another bag with a corner cut off (a little smaller hole this time) to fill each one with the chilled filling.
14. Make the chocolate glaze by combining the powdered sugar, cocoa, and salt in a medium bowl. Add the vanilla and 4 teaspoons of water and stir the mixture until it is smooth. If it is too thick, add an additional teaspoon of water.
15. Spread the glaze over the top of each éclair. Serve immediately, or you can freeze the éclairs. If frozen, the éclairs should thaw at room temperature for 1 hour before serving.

- MAKES 9 ÉCLAIRS.

Nutrition Facts

SERVING SIZE—1 ECLAIR FAT (PER SERVING)—4G
TOTAL SERVINGS—9 CALORIES (PER SERVING)—160

TOP SECRET RECIPES
LITE!
CONVERSIONS

TOP SECRET RECIPES REDUCED-FAT VERSION OF

APPLEBEE'S BAJA POTATO BOATS

This is Applebee's variation on the popular potato skins appetizer made famous by T.G.I. Friday's. Many seem to prefer these to regular potato skins because of their south-of-the-border flair. The only problem is, a serving of the version that you would order in the restaurant has around 12 grams of fat (even more if you glop on the sour cream). And that's for only three pieces. If you usually don't stop there, you may be interested in this TSR version of the delicious dish, which cuts the fat by 66 percent. Now you can eat three times as much of these Mexican-style potato skin wedges for the same amount of fat as the real deal, thanks to reduced-fat cheese and fat-free sour cream.

PICO DE GALLO
1 tomato, chopped (½ cup)
3 tablespoons chopped Spanish onion
1½ teaspoons minced fresh cilantro
1 tablespoon canned jalapeño slices (nacho slices), diced
dash salt
dash pepper

POTATO BOATS
3 medium russet potatoes
canola oil nonstick cooking spray
salt
⅓ cup reduced-fat shredded cheddar cheese
⅓ cup reduced-fat shredded mozzarella cheese
2 slices Canadian bacon, diced (about 2 tablespoons)

ON THE SIDE
fat-free sour cream
salsa

1. Make the pico de gallo by combining the ingredients in a small bowl. Cover and refrigerate until needed.
2. Bake the potatoes at 400 degrees for 1 hour, or until tender, and let cool.
3. When the potatoes are cool enough to handle, make two lengthwise cuts through each potato, resulting in three ½- to ¾-inch slices. Discard the middle slices or save them for a separate dish of mashed potatoes. This will leave you with two whole potato skins per potato.
4. Crank the oven up to 450 degrees.
5. With a spoon, scoop some of the potato out of each skin, being sure to leave about ¼ inch of potato inside of the skin.
6. Spray the entire surface of each potato skin, inside and out, with a light coating of the canola oil spray.
7. Place the skins on a baking sheet, cut side up, salt them, then bake them for 12 to 15 minutes, or until the edges are beginning to brown.
8. Combine the cheeses in a small bowl, then sprinkle about a tablespoon and a half of the cheese blend on each of the potato skins.
9. Sprinkle a teaspoon of Canadian bacon over the cheese on each skin.
10. Spread a heaping tablespoon of pico de gallo over the bacon on each skin.
11. Top off each potato skin with another pinch of the cheese blend.
12. Bake the skins once more for 2 to 4 minutes or until the cheese is melted. Remove the skins from the oven, let them sit for about a minute, then slice each one lengthwise. These are your "boats." Serve them hot with fat-free sour cream and salsa on the side.

- SERVES 4 AS AN APPETIZER.

Nutritional Facts (per serving)
SERVING SIZE—3 PIECES   TOTAL SERVINGS—4

	Lite	Original
Calories (est.)	246	390
Fat (approx.)	4g	12g

• • • •

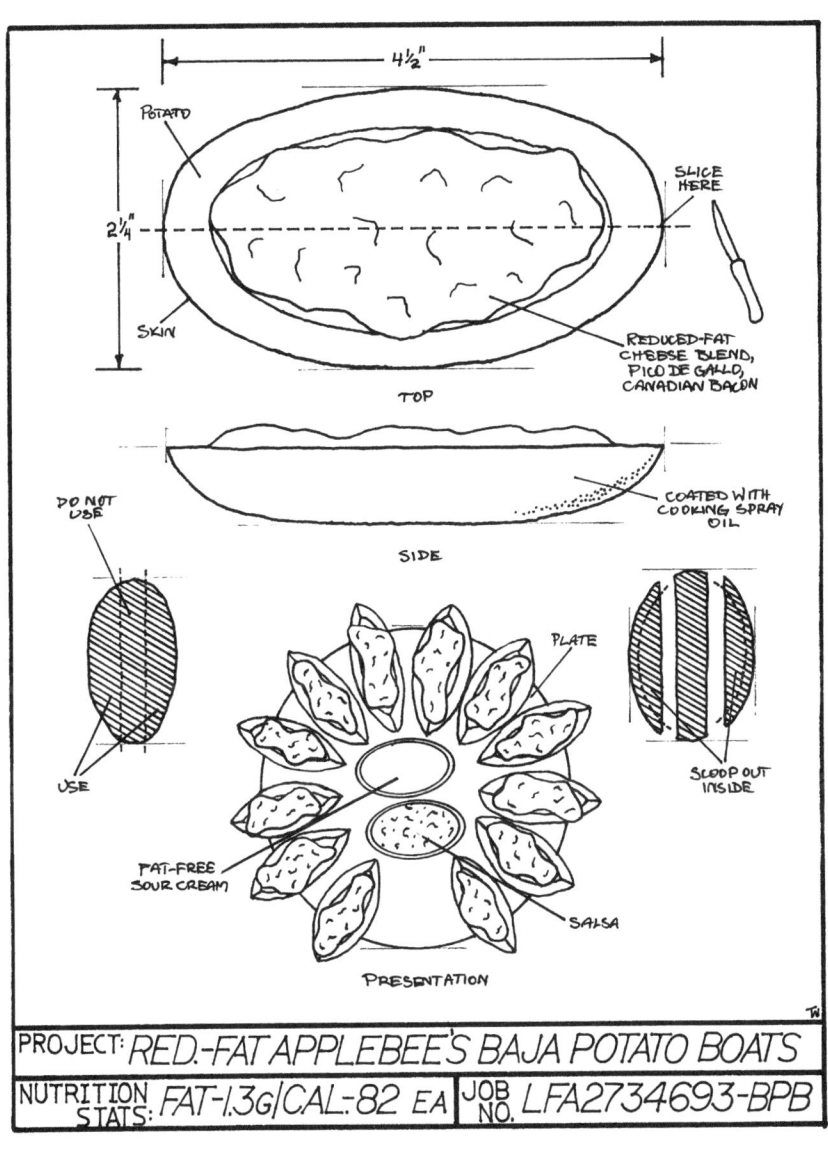

TOP SECRET RECIPES FAT-FREE VERSION OF

BOSTON MARKET BUTTERNUT SQUASH

In the biz, it's called home meal replacement. And Boston Market was one of the first companies out of the gate to enter into this recently very competitive sector of food service. The company was started in 1989 and offered its special recipe of marinated rotisserie chicken, along with several homestyle side dishes. The butternut squash was not one of the company's first side dish offerings, but has recently become one of the favorites. The light-tasting vegetable, seasoned with nutmeg and sweetened with sugar, is a healthy alternative to more fat-filled fare.

According to the nutrition sheet, the chain's version of this bright yellow side dish has some fat in it—probably from butter. We can make a great fat-free clone of Boston Market's butternut squash, using Butter Buds Sprinkles to replace any fat, along with the same type of spices that are found in the real thing.

1 butternut squash	¼ teaspoon salt
nonstick cooking spray	¼ teaspoon nutmeg
1 tablespoon sugar	¼ teaspoon allspice
2 teaspoons Butter Buds Sprinkles	dash pepper

1. Preheat the oven to 350 degrees.
2. Cut the butternut squash in half and scrape out the seeds and stringy stuff. Spray the cut surface of the squash with cooking spray and place the two halves facedown in a baking pan. Bake for 1 hour, or until tender.
3. Scoop out all of the tender squash and load it into a medium bowl. Use a potato masher to puree the squash. To make

it even smoother, like the original, you may want to run it through a food processor set to puree for about 30 seconds.
4. Add the remaining ingredients and mix well.
5. Reheat the squash in the microwave for 1 to 1½ minutes, or until hot, and serve.

- SERVES 4 AS A SIDE DISH.

Nutritional Facts *(per serving)*

SERVING SIZE—½ CUP   TOTAL SERVINGS—4

	LITE	ORIGINAL
CALORIES	74	160
FAT	0G	6G

• • • •

TOP SECRET RECIPES FAT-FREE VERSION OF

BOSTON MARKET CINNAMON APPLES

By the end of 1997, there were 1,166 Boston Market outlets in 38 states. It took only ten years for the company to reach this number of units—that's some pretty impressive growth. The cinnamon apple side dish has been on the menu since the company opened the doors to its first outlet. The dish from the chain is fairly low in fat—only 4.5 grams of fat per serving—but there is apparently some butter or oil in there. Using the right cooking techniques and some Butter Buds, we can easily take that fat all the way down to zippo, while still getting all of the same great flavors. The most work you'll do here is peeling the apples, a chore that's made easy by whipping out that peeler you use for carrots and potatoes.

3 Golden Delicious apples
⅔ cup water
½ tablespoon flour
1 teaspoon cornstarch

2 teaspoons Butter Buds Sprinkles
½ cup light brown sugar
¼ teaspoon cinnamon
dash salt

1. Preheat the oven to 350 degrees.
2. Peel and core the apples. Cut each one into 16 slices and arrange the slices in an 8 x 8-inch baking dish.
3. In a small bowl, combine the water with the flour, cornstarch, and Butter Buds and stir until the dry ingredients are dissolved and not lumpy. Add the brown sugar and cinnamon and stir until smooth.
4. Pour the cinnamon mixture over the apple slices, cover the

dish with foil, and bake for 40 minutes. Stir the apples every 10 minutes.

- Serves 4.

Nutritional Facts *(per serving)*
 Serving size—½ cup   Total servings—4

	Lite	Original
Calories	177	250
Fat	0g	4.5g

• • • •

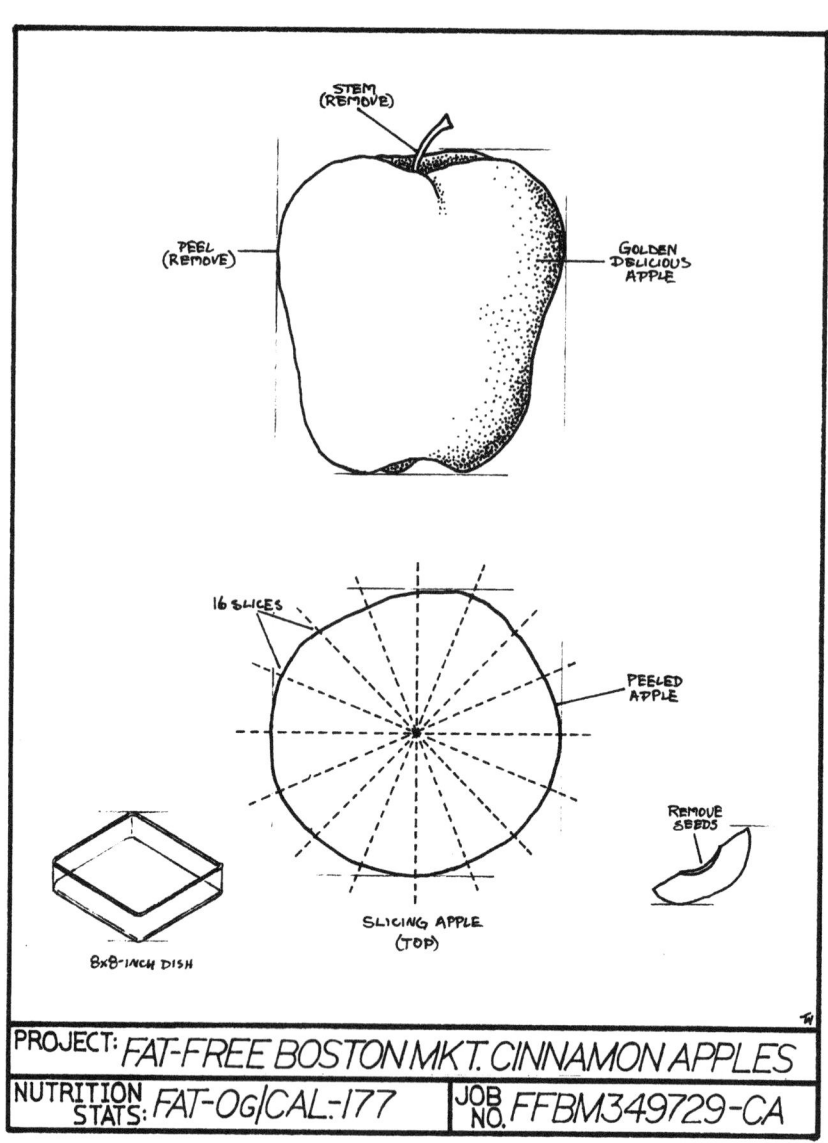

BOSTON MARKET CREAMED SPINACH

TOP SECRET RECIPES REDUCED-FAT VERSION OF

When Boston Market first opened in 1989, it was called Boston Chicken. That's because at that time chicken was the only meat served at the chain. But three years later, in 1992, the chain added meatloaf, turkey, and ham, and officially became Boston Market. Yes, a lot of signs had to be changed, at considerable expense.

This popular side dish, which contains three types of cheese, normally has 24 grams of fat per serving. So, for this clone recipe, we'll be using two fat-free cheeses along with regular Provolone, and we'll be able to re-create the taste of the real thing; but with only 25 percent of the fat in the original.

2 10-ounce packages chopped frozen spinach
2 tablespoons diced white onion
3 ounces provolone cheese, chopped
4 slices Kraft fat-free Swiss Cheese Singles, quartered
4 slices Kraft fat-free Mozzarella Singles, quartered
1 1/2 teaspoons white vinegar
1/4 heaping teaspoon salt

1. Thaw the spinach and place it in a medium saucepan over medium/low heat with the onion. Heat for 7 to 10 minutes or until the liquid begins to bubble. Drain.
2. Add the remaining ingredients to the saucepan and heat for an additional 5 to 7 minutes or until smooth and creamy.

- SERVES 4.

Nutritional Facts *(per serving)*
Serving size—½ cup   Total servings—4

	Lite	Original
Calories	180	300
Fat	6g	24g

• • • •

TOP SECRET RECIPES REDUCED-FAT VERSION OF

BURGER KING BK BROILER

Here's a clone for a sandwich that America's number-two burger chain introduced in 1990, and soon after the launch was selling over a million a day. This was the same year that Burger King switched from animal fat to vegetable oil to cook the fried items. But, even though the BK Broiler includes flame-broiled chicken, rather than fried, it still comes in with 29 grams. A big part of that comes from the mayonnaise. So, by replacing the regular mayonnaise with fat-free mayo and by not adding any additional fats, we can produce a sandwich that will taste like a BK Broiler, yet have less than one-quarter of the fat and fewer calories.

MARINADE
3/4 cup water
2 teaspoons ketchup
1 teaspoon salt
1/4 teaspoon liquid smoke
1/8 teaspoon pepper
1/8 teaspoon oregano
dash onion powder
dash parsley

2 chicken breast fillets
4 sesame seed hamburger buns
1 1/3 cups chopped lettuce
1/4 cup fat-free mayonnaise
8 tomato slices

1. Make the marinade by combining the ingredients in a medium bowl.
2. Prepare the chicken by cutting each breast in half. Fold a piece of plastic wrap around each piece of chicken and pound the meat with a tenderizing mallet until it is about 1/4-inch thick and

about the same diameter as the hamburger buns. Place the chicken in the marinade, cover it, and chill for at least four hours. Overnight is even better.
3. Preheat your barbecue or indoor grill to high heat. Grill the chicken for 3 to 4 minutes per side or until done.
4. Toast the faces of the hamburger buns in a pan or griddle, in a toaster oven, or facedown on the grill. Watch the buns closely to be certain that the faces turn only light brown and do not burn.
5. Build each sandwich from the top down by first spreading about a tablespoon of the fat-free mayonnaise on the toasted face of a top bun.
6. Spread about ⅓ cup of chopped lettuce over the mayonnaise.
7. Arrange two tomato slices on the lettuce.
8. Place a chicken breast on the toasted face of the bottom bun.
9. Flip the top part of the sandwich over onto the bottom and munch out.

- SERVES 4.

Nutritional Facts *(per serving)*
SERVING SIZE—1 SANDWICH   TOTAL SERVINGS—4

	LITE	ORIGINAL
CALORIES	335	550
FAT	6G	29G

• • • •

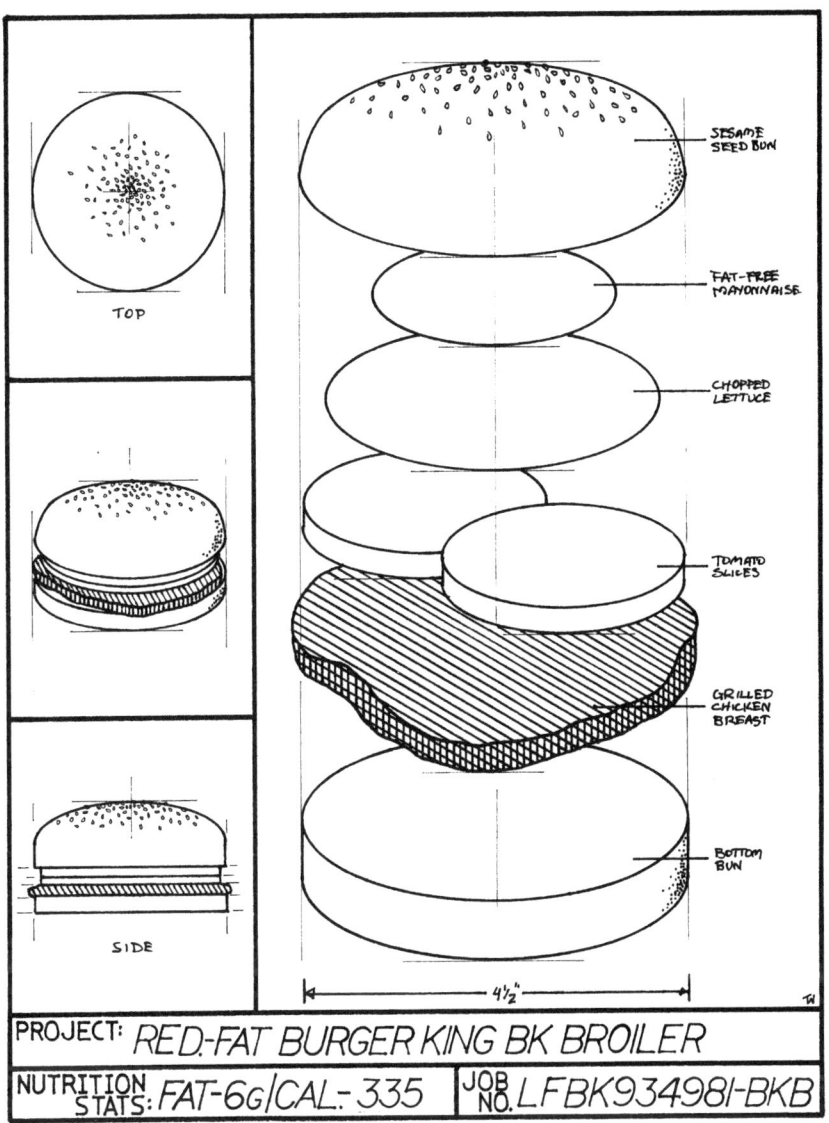

BURGER KING BIG KING

The burger wars are on and the battlefield is splattered with ketchup. Burger King stepped up first with this competitor of the Big Mac. Yes, it has two all-beef patties, special sauce, lettuce, cheese, pickles, onions on a sesame seed bun—although everything's arranged a bit differently, and there's no middle bun. The beef patties are also bigger than those found on a Big Mac. The other big difference? The Big King weighs in with 12 grams more fat than Mickey D's signature product, for a grand total of 43 grams. Now TSR enters into the fray. Check out this clone that re-creates the "secret" burger spread from scratch and includes super-lean ground beef. Add it all up and you've got a gram-zapping clone that comes in at around one-third the fat of the real thing.

SPREAD

1/4 cup fat-free mayonnaise
2 teaspoons fat-free French dressing
2 teaspoons sweet pickle relish
1 teaspoon white vinegar
1/2 teaspoon sugar
1/8 teaspoon paprika
1 1/2 pounds super-lean ground beef (7 percent fat)
dash salt
dash pepper
4 sesame seed hamburger buns
1 1/3 cups chopped lettuce
8 slices fat-free American cheese
1 to 2 slices white onion, separated
8 dill pickle slices

1. Prepare the spread by combining the ingredients in a small bowl. Set this aside until you are ready to use it.
2. Preheat your barbecue or indoor grill to high heat.
3. Divide the ground beef into 8 even portions (3 ounces each). Roll each portion into a ball, then press each ball flat to form a patty about the same diameter as the bun.
4. Grill the beef patties for 2 to 3 minutes per side, or until done. Lightly salt and pepper each side of the patties.
5. As the meat cooks, brown the faces of the buns in a hot skillet, toaster oven, or facedown on the grill. Watch the buns closely so that they do not burn.
6. Build each burger by first spreading a tablespoon of the spread on the face of the top bun. Arrange about ⅓ cup of lettuce evenly over the spread.
7. On the bottom bun, stack a patty, then a slice of American cheese, another patty, and another slice of cheese.
8. On the second slice of cheese, arrange 2 to 3 separated onion slices (rings), then 2 pickle slices.
9. Turn the top of the burger over onto the bottom and serve.

- SERVES 4.

Nutritional Facts *(per serving)*
SERVING SIZE—1 SANDWICH   TOTAL SERVINGS—4

	LITE	ORIGINAL
CALORIES	562	660
FAT	15G	43G

• • • •

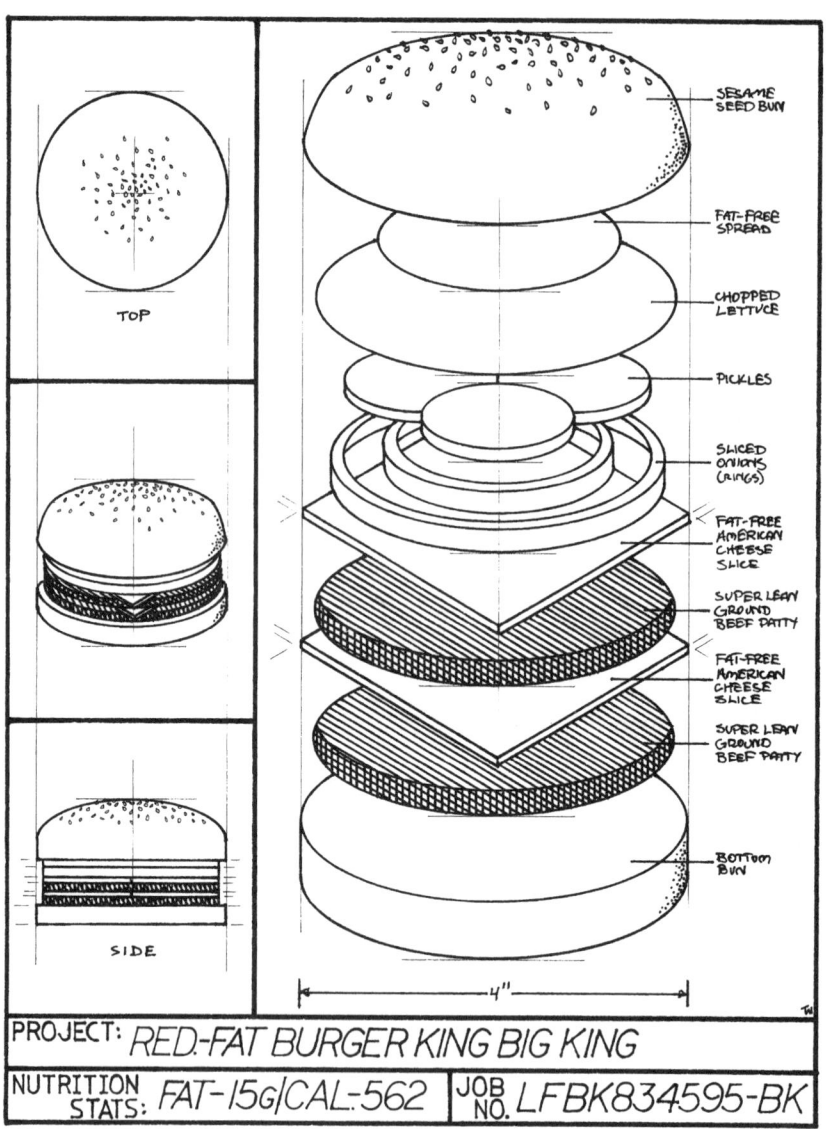

BURGER KING WHOPPER

TOP SECRET RECIPES REDUCED-FAT VERSION OF

Burger King's Whopper was an instant hit when it was first introduced in 1957 at a measly 37 cents each. And in more than 9,500 outlets dotting the globe, you can still have the burger "your way"—which comes to over 1,000 different combinations. But by using fat-free mayonnaise and super-lean ground beef, you can still have a sandwich with the taste of Burger King's most popular burger, but with almost 75 percent less in the fat column.

1 sesame seed hamburger bun
1/4-pound super-lean ground beef (7 percent fat)
dash salt
dash pepper
1 tablespoon fat-free mayonnaise
1/3 cup chopped lettuce
2 tomato slices
3 to 4 separated onion slices (rings)
3 dill pickle slices
1/2 tablespoon ketchup

1. Preheat your barbecue or indoor grill to high.
2. Toast the faces of the sesame seed bun in a hot pan or griddle set to medium heat, in a toaster oven, or facedown on the grill. Keep checking them so that they don't burn.
3. Roll the ground beef into a ball, then flatten it to form a patty about the same diameter as the bun. The patty should be around 1/4-inch thick.
4. Grill the meat on the hot grill for 2 to 3 minutes per side, or until it's done. Lightly salt and pepper each side of the meat.

5. To build the burger start at the top by spreading the mayonnaise onto the toasted face of the top bun.
6. Spread the lettuce on the mayo, then the tomatoes, and onions.
7. Stack the beef patty onto the toasted face of the bottom bun.
8. Arrange the pickles on the beef patty, then spread the ketchup over the pickles.
9. Turn the top of the sandwich over onto the bottom and serve.

- SERVES 1.

Nutritional Facts *(per serving)*
SERVING SIZE—1 SANDWICH   TOTAL SERVINGS—1

	LITE	ORIGINAL
CALORIES	430	640
FAT	11G	39G

• • • •

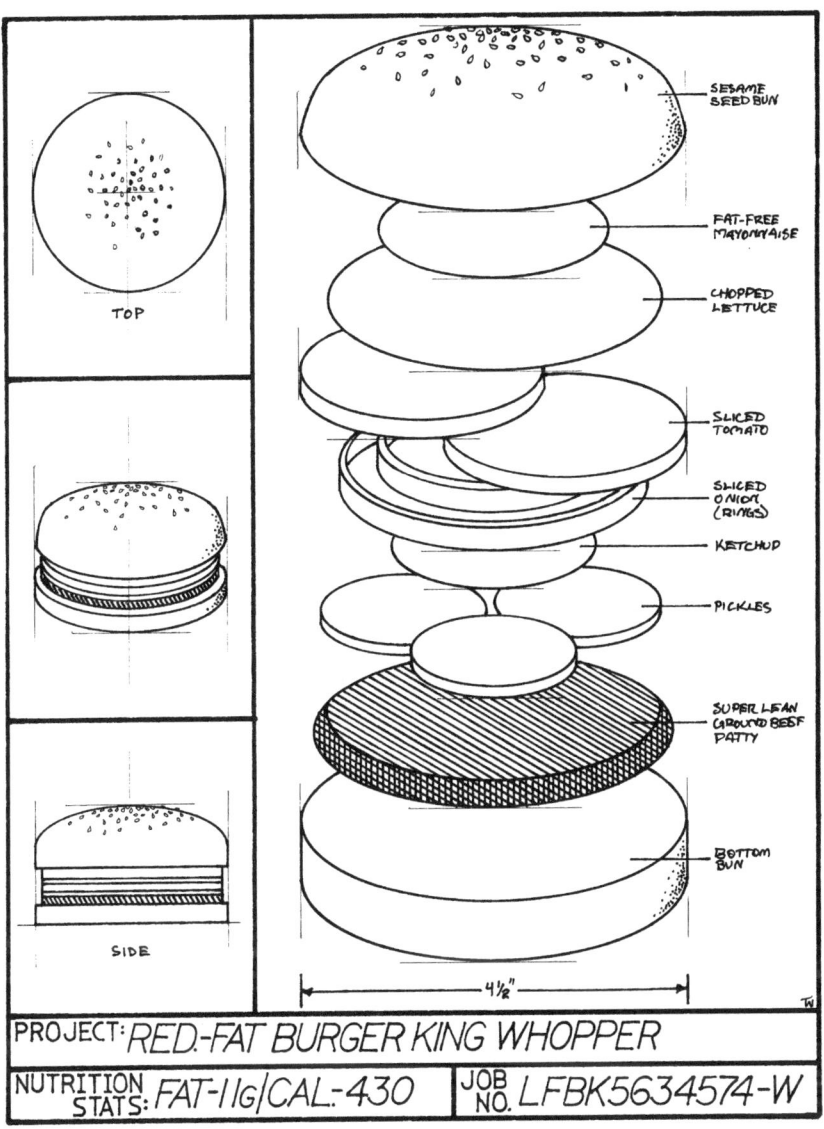

CHI-CHI'S MEXICAN "FRIED" ICE CREAM

TOP SECRET RECIPES REDUCED-FAT VERSION OF

At one time the ice cream in this popular dessert was actually fried. A scoop of ice cream was rolled in breading, then refrozen. Just before serving, the ice cream would be flash-fried in oil for a few seconds, and then served immediately, still frozen in the middle. Considering that the nonfried version served at the restaurant chain still has around 34 grams of fat per serving, we can assume the fried version would weigh in with even more fat.

Now we're going to take those grams down even further—by an amazing 80 percent! We'll do that by using fat-free ice cream and fat-free flour tortillas. We'll also cut way down on the fat by spraying the tortillas with a light coating of cooking spray and then baking them, rather than using the traditional frying method. Use a light touch on that whipped cream can, and you've got a very low-fat dessert that just has to be experienced.

2 6-inch fat-free flour tortillas
vegetable oil cooking spray
½ teaspoon cinnamon
2 tablespoons sugar
¼ cup cornflake crumbs

2 large scoops (about ¾ cup)
    fat-free vanilla ice cream
1 can whipped light cream
2 maraschino cherries,
    with stems

OPTIONAL TOPPINGS
Honey
Hershey's chocolate syrup
    (fat-free)

Strawberry topping

1. Preheat the oven to 375 degrees.
2. Spray both sides of each tortilla with a light coating of cooking spray. Place the tortillas on a baking sheet and bake for 10 to 12 minutes, or until the tortillas are golden brown and crispy. Turn the tortillas over halfway through the cooking time.
3. Combine the cinnamon and sugar in a small bowl.
4. Sprinkle half of the cinnamon mixture over both sides of each tortilla, coating evenly. Not all of the cinnamon/sugar will stick to the tortilla, and that's okay.
5. Combine the cornflake crumbs with the remaining cinnamon mixture. Pour this mixture into a large, shallow bowl or onto a plate.
6. Place a large scoop of the fat-free ice cream into the cornflake mixture, and, with your hands, roll the ice cream around until the entire surface of the ice cream is evenly coated.
7. Place the coated scoop of ice cream onto the center of a cinnamon/sugar-coated tortilla.
8. Spray a few small piles of whipped cream around the base of the ice cream, then spray an additional bit of whipped cream on top of the ice cream.
9. Place a cherry into the whipped cream on top. Repeat the process, using the second tortilla. Serve immediately, with a side dish of honey, fat-free chocolate syrup, or strawberry sauce, if desired.

- SERVES 2.

Nutritional Facts *(per serving)*
SERVING SIZE—1 DESSERT   TOTAL SERVINGS—2

	LITE	ORIGINAL
CALORIES (est.)	371	611
FAT (est.)	7G	34G

• • •

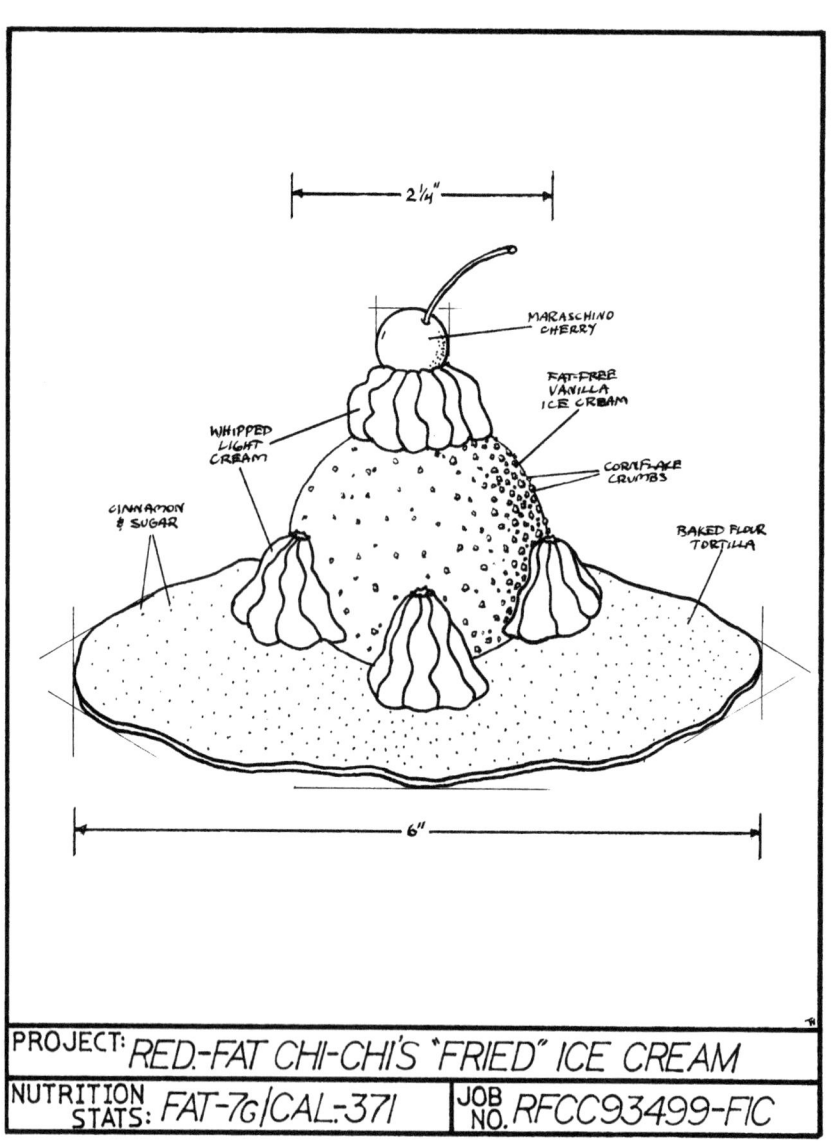

TOP SECRET RECIPES REDUCED-FAT VERSION OF

CHI-CHI'S SWEET CORN CAKE

A deserted Kroger grocery store in Richfield, Minnesota, was the site for the first Chi-Chi's in 1976. That was the year restaurateur Marno McDermott got together with ex-Green Bay Packer football player Max McGee to open the first of what would soon become a growing chain of Mexican food restaurants. Today, with around 100 restaurants found mostly in the Midwestern and Eastern states, Chi-Chi's has become famous for its large portions of food, and for the expression, "Don't touch the plate, it's very hot!"

Alongside many of the entrees served at the restaurant is this sweet side dish. It's sort of like a combination of custard and cornbread, with corn and cornmeal in it. But the original is loaded with butter. That means if you eat just a very small scoop of the tasty corn cake you'll be putting away around a dozen fat grams. By using light butter or margarine and substituting milk for the heavy cream, we knock those fat grams down to about half of the real thing served in the restaurant. Yet the flavor and texture is just as good.

½ cup (1 stick) light butter or margarine, softened
⅓ cup masa harina
¼ cup water
1 ½ cups frozen corn, thawed
¼ cup cornmeal
⅓ cup sugar
3 tablespoons whole milk
¼ teaspoon salt
½ teaspoon baking powder

1. Preheat the oven to 375 degrees.
2. Blend the butter or margarine in a medium bowl with an electric mixer until creamy. Add the masa harina and water to the butter and beat until well combined.
3. Put the defrosted corn into a blender or food processor and, with short pulses, coarsely chop the corn on low speed. You want to leave several whole kernels of corn. Stir the chopped corn into the butter and masa harina mixture. Add the cornmeal to the mixture. Combine.
4. In another medium bowl, mix together the sugar, milk, salt, and baking powder. When the ingredients are well blended, pour the mixture into the other bowl and stir everything together by hand.
5. Pour the corn batter into an ungreased 8 x 8-inch baking pan. Smooth the surface of the batter with a spatula. Cover the pan with aluminum foil. Place this pan into a 13 x 9-inch pan filled one-third of the way up with hot water. Bake for 50 to 60 minutes or until the corn cake is cooked through.
6. When the corn cake is done, remove the small pan from the larger pan and let it sit for at least 10 minutes. To serve, scoop out each portion with an ice cream scoop or rounded spoon.

- SERVES 8 AS A SIDE DISH.

Nutritional Facts *(per serving)*
SERVING SIZE—1 SCOOP   TOTAL SERVINGS—8

	LITE	ORIGINAL
CALORIES (est.)	125	185
FAT (est.)	6.5G	13G

• • • •

TOP SECRET RECIPES REDUCED-FAT VERSION OF

CINNABON CINNAMON ROLLS

How sinfully delicious are these cinnamon rolls? Their intoxicating aroma wafts through shopping malls and airports all over America, and at one time or another you've probably been a victim of that irresistible, gooey swirl of delight. Sometimes, though, for a treat this delicious, you just have to say "What the heck!" Right? There's a good chance that same thought has gone through the minds of millions since the first Cinnabon was served at Seattle's Sea-Tac Mall in 1985. But what if you could still get that marvelous Cinnabon taste with better than an 80 percent reduction in fat? Not possible, you say? Get out the rolling pin and prepare for an amazing reduced-fat conversion of America's favorite mall food.

ROLLS

1 1/4-ounce package active dry yeast
1 cup warm fat-free milk (105 to 110 degrees)
1/2 cup sugar
1/4 cup butter
6 tablespoons egg substitute
1 teaspoon salt
4 cups all-purpose flour

FILLING

1 cup dark brown sugar, packed
1/3 cup Wondra flour
2 1/2 tablespoons cinnamon
1/2 cup fat-free butter spread

ICING

1 8-ounce package fat-free cream cheese
1½ cups powdered sugar
1 tablespoon Butter Buds
½ teaspoon vanilla
⅛ teaspoon salt

1. Make the rolls by dissolving the yeast in the warm milk in a large bowl. Add the sugar and let the mixture sit for 5 minutes.
2. Melt the butter in the microwave or in a saucepan over low heat and add it to the mixture in the large bowl.
3. Add the egg substitute, salt, and flour to the large bowl, mix to incorporate the ingredients, then use flour-dusted hands to knead the dough into a large ball. Put the dough back into the bowl, cover it, and let it rise in a warm place for about 1 hour, or until it has doubled in size.
4. Make the filling by combining the brown sugar, Wondra flour, and cinnamon in a small bowl. Preheat the oven to 400 degrees.
5. Roll the dough out onto a lightly floured surface. Roll the dough into a flat rectangle until it is approximately 21 inches long and 16 inches wide. It should be about ¼-inch thick.
6. Spread ½ cup of the butter-flavored spread over the surface of the dough. Sprinkle the brown sugar and cinnamon mixture over the spread.
7. Working from the top (a 21-inch side), roll the dough down to the bottom edge.
8. Cut the rolled dough into 1¾-inch slices and place 6, evenly spaced, into each of two 9 x 13-inch lightly greased baking pans. Cover the baking pans and let the rolls rise for another 45 to 60 minutes, then bake for 15 to 22 minutes or until the rolls are light brown on top.
9. While the rolls bake, combine the icing ingredients in a medium bowl and beat well with an electric mixer at high speed until smooth and creamy.
10. Cool the rolls for 3 to 5 minutes after removing them from the oven, then spread icing over the top of each one.

- MAKES 1 DOZEN ROLLS.

Nutritional Facts *(per serving)*

Serving size—1 roll   Total servings—12

	Lite	Original
Calories	370	730
Fat	4g	24g

• • • •

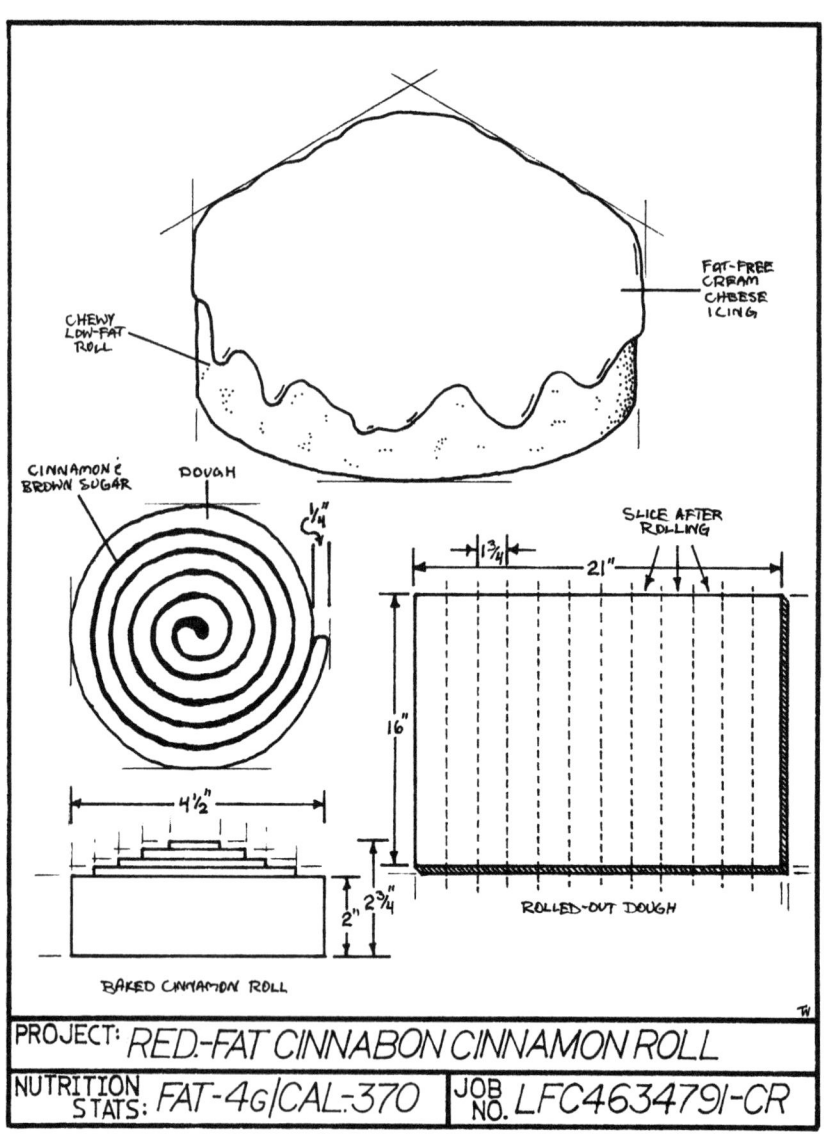

DENNY'S MOONS OVER MY HAMMY

TOP SECRET RECIPES LOW-FAT VERSION OF

It's got a goofy name and tons of fans. This is one of Denny's most popular sandwiches, and it has remained on Denny's menu since 1978. But whether you have it for breakfast, lunch, or dinner, you might like to know there's a way to enjoy the taste of this grilled sandwich for around 30 grams less fat than the real thing. This TSR version saves grams in several ways, but the most significant savings come from using fat-free cheese. Get some low-fat ham at your supermarket deli counter, or you can find it prepackaged near the luncheon meats. Start heating up a skillet and get ready to discover this delicious lower-fat treat.

½ cup egg substitute
salt
2 ounces low-fat deli-sliced ham
2 large slices sourdough bread

fat-free butter-flavored spray
2 slices Kraft Fat-Free Swiss Cheese Singles
2 slices Kraft Fat-Free American Cheese Singles

1. Preheat two skillets over medium heat. Lightly coat one skillet with cooking spray, then pour the egg substitute into the pan and scramble the egg, cooking it until done. Salt to taste. In the other skillet brown the stack of sliced ham without separating the slices.
2. When the stack of sliced ham has browned lightly on both sides, remove it from the pan. Spray one side of one slice of sourdough bread with the butter-flavored spray, and place it in the hot pan, sprayed side down, to grill.
3. Immediately place the two slices of Swiss cheese side-by-side onto the unbuttered side of the grilling sourdough bread slice.

4. Stack the browned ham on top of the Swiss cheese.
5. Scoop the scrambled egg substitute out of the other pan with a large spatula and slide it onto the ham.
6. Arrange the two slices of American cheese side-by-side onto the egg.
7. Top off the sandwich with the remaining slice of sourdough bread. Spray the top of the bread with a light coating of butter-flavored spray.
8. By this time the bottom surface of the bread in the pan will have browned. Carefully flip the sandwich over to grill the other side for about 2 minutes or until golden brown.
9. Slice the sandwich diagonally through the middle and serve hot.

- MAKES 1 SANDWICH.

Nutritional Facts *(per serving)*
SERVING SIZE—1 SANDWICH   TOTAL SERVINGS—1

	LITE	ORIGINAL
CALORIES (est.)	460	700
FAT (est.)	3G	33G

• • • •

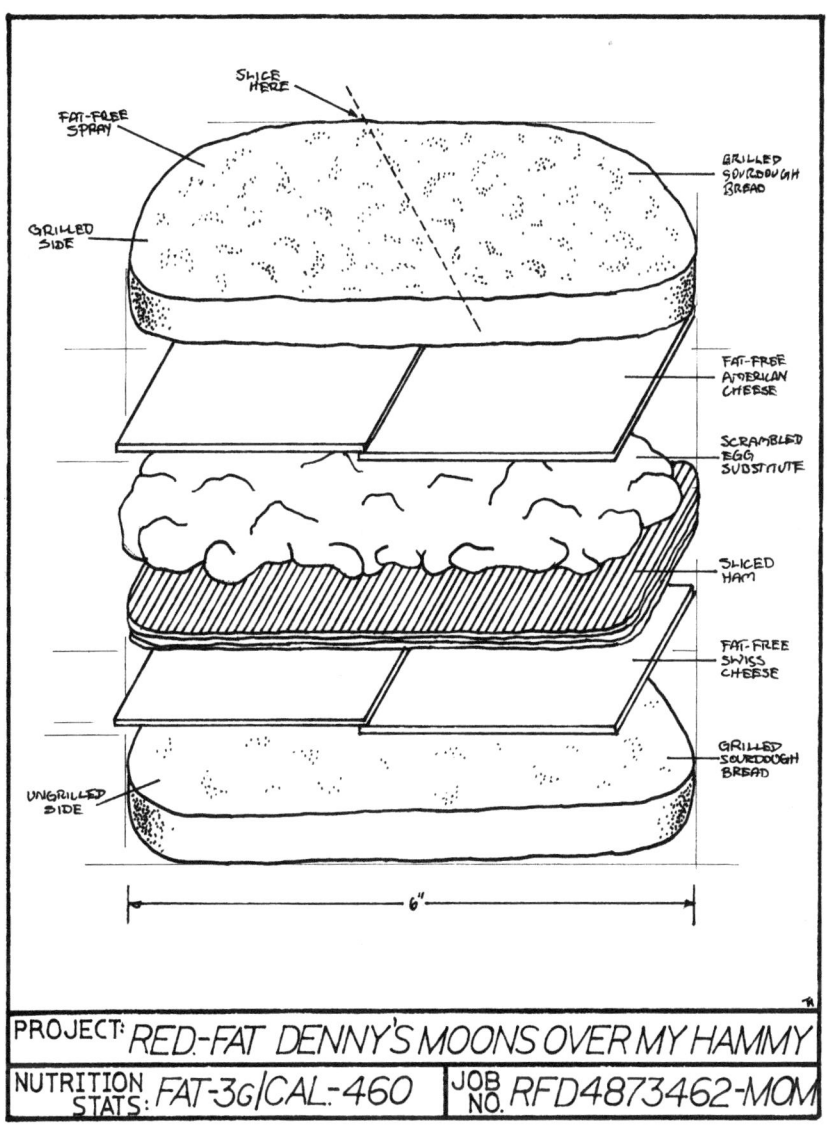

TOP SECRET RECIPES REDUCED-FAT VERSION OF

DENNY'S
THE SUPER BIRD

Here's another very popular Denny's creation. This 20-year-old menu item can be easily converted to a reduced-fat version by substituting fat-free cheese and turkey bacon. When shopping for that bacon, I've found that Butterball makes one of the best turkey bacons around—it tastes just like the real thing. Then get yourself some low-fat turkey breast from the supermarket deli counter or prepackaged near the other luncheon meats. A little butter-flavored spray and a hot skillet on the stove, and you're on your way to reducing the fat by around 60 percent, when compared to the sandwich you get from Denny's. Now that's super.

3 ounces low-fat deli-sliced turkey breast
2 large slices sourdough bread
fat-free butter-flavored spray
2 slices Kraft fat-free Swiss Cheese Singles
salt
2 slices turkey bacon, cooked (Butterball is best)
2 slices tomato

1. Heat a skillet or frying pan over medium heat. Grill the stack of turkey breast in the pan, without separating the stack, until the meat is light brown on both sides.
2. While the turkey is browning, lightly coat one side of a slice of bread with the butter-flavored spray. Place the bread, sprayed side down, in the pan next to the turkey to grill.
3. Arrange the slices of cheese on the face-up, unbuttered side of the bread in the pan.

4. When the turkey has browned, arrange it on top of the cheese. Salt the turkey to taste.
5. Arrange the cooked bacon side-by-side on top of the turkey.
6. Stack the tomato slices side-by-side on top of the bacon.
7. Top off the sandwich with the remaining slice of sourdough bread. Spray a light coating of butter-flavored spray over the surface of the top slice of bread.
8. When the surface of the bottom slice of bread has grilled to a light brown, flip the sandwich over to grill the top for about 2 minutes or until golden brown.
9. With a sharp knife, slice the sandwich twice at a slight angle, creating three equal-size slices. Serve hot.

- MAKES 1 SANDWICH.

Nutritional Facts *(per serving)*
SERVING SIZE—1 SANDWICH   TOTAL SERVINGS—1

	LITE	ORIGINAL
CALORIES (approx.)	425	565
FAT (approx.)	8.5G	22G

• • • •

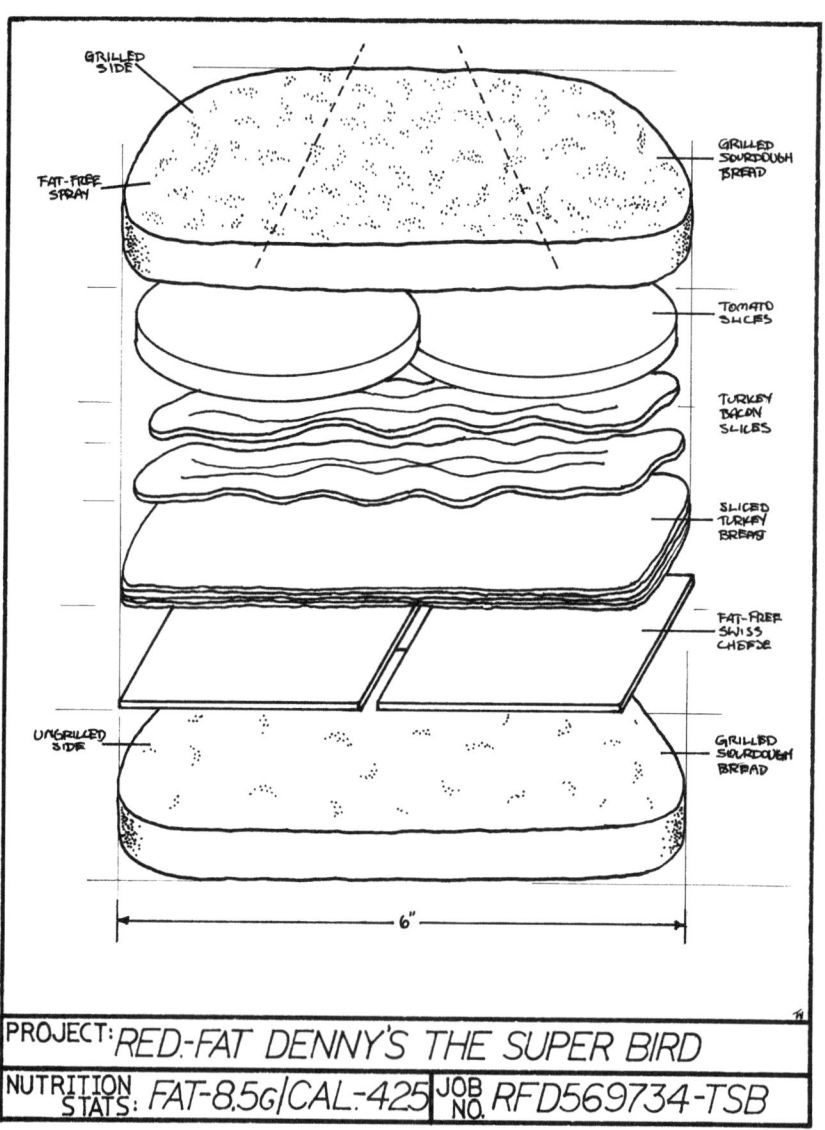

TOP SECRET RECIPES LOW-FAT VERSION OF

DOLLY MADISON BUTTERCRUMB CINNAMON

When Interstate Brands started the Dolly Madison line of baked goods that has today become the convenience store leader, it was known as Interstate Bakeries. Roy Nafziger started the bakery in 1927, and he could only have dreamed that one day his company would ring up more than one billion dollars in sales. One item that contributes to those impressive sales figures are these little brown sugar/cinnamon–topped cakes, which have become a popular addition to the Dolly Madison line of baked goods since the late eighties.

We can easily create a low-fat home clone of the real thing with only seven ingredients, thanks to white cake mix that can be found in practically all stores. Notice that the cake mix is not a reduced-fat variety. That's not necessary for the recipe to produce little cakes that taste just like the real thing, but still have less than one-third the fat. And even though the original is sort of square-shaped, we'll use a couple of 12-cup muffin pans to simplify the process. The shape will be different, but the flavor will be right on.

1 18.25-ounce box white cake mix
1 1/4 cups water
1/2 cup egg substitute
1 tablespoon Butter Buds Sprinkles

TOPPING
2/3 cup dark brown sugar
2 tablespoons sugar
1 tablespoon cinnamon

1. Preheat the oven to 350 degrees.
2. Combine the cake mix, water, egg substitute, and Butter Buds in a large bowl and mix with an electric mixer for 2 minutes.
3. Grease the cups of two 12-cup muffin tins (if you only have one, just be sure to clean it well after the first batch). Fill each cup about half full with batter.
4. Combine the ingredients for the topping in a small bowl and mix well.
5. Sprinkle about 2 teaspoons of the topping over the batter in each cup. Use a knife to slightly swirl the topping into the batter.
6. Bake the cakes for 20 to 25 minutes or until light brown on top. Store the cakes in a sealed container after they have cooled to keep them fresh.

- MAKES 24 CAKES.

Nutritional Facts (per serving)
SERVING SIZE—1 CAKE   TOTAL SERVINGS—24

	LITE	ORIGINAL
CALORIES	111	170
FAT	1.7G	6G

• • • •

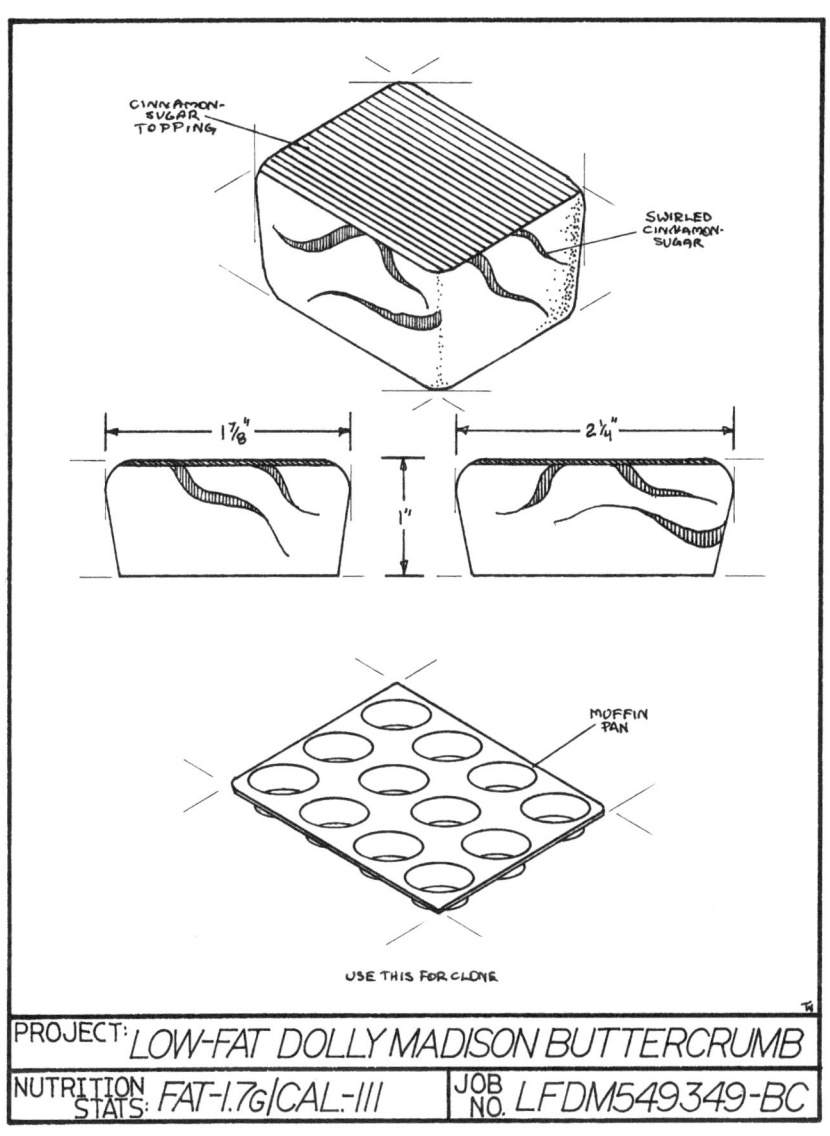

TOP SECRET RECIPES REDUCED-FAT VERSION OF

DOLLY MADISON CARROT CAKE

In the late thirties, as Roy Nafziger noodled through some names for his new line of baked goods for the Cakes Division of Interstate Bakeries, he decided on the name of former U.S. President James Madison's wife. Why her, you ask? Apparently the flamboyant first lady enjoyed entertaining guests with elaborate parties at the White House, and served those guests a fine selection of desserts and baked goods. Nafziger figured his company would create cakes "fine enough to serve in the White House." So, the name stuck, and today the company is a member of the Interstate Brands Corporation family, which also includes Hostess as part of a recent acquisition.

These carrot cakes have been produced and sold off and on through the years, but never as a reduced-fat version. So, with applesauce and egg substitute jumping in for some of the fat, here's a TSR version of the tasty carrot cake for the waistline-conscious. You'll swear it's the original, but each slice comes in at less than 4 grams. Even with butter in the icing, that's better than half the fat of the real thing.

1 1/3 cups sugar
2/3 cup unsweetened applesauce
1/3 cup egg substitute
1 tablespoon canola oil
1 teaspoon white vinegar
1/2 teaspoon salt
1/4 teaspoon vanilla
1/2 teaspoon cinnamon

1/4 teaspoon allspice
1/8 teaspoon ground clove
dash ground ginger
1 1/2 cups all-purpose flour
1/2 cup graham cracker crumbs
1 teaspoon baking soda
1 1/3 cups grated carrot

ICING

¼ cup fat-free cream cheese
  (⅓ of an 8-ounce package)
2 tablespoons butter, softened
½ teaspoon vanilla
⅛ teaspoon salt
3 cups powdered sugar

1. Preheat the oven to 325 degrees.
2. Combine the sugar, applesauce, egg substitute, oil, vinegar, salt, and vanilla in a large bowl and beat by hand.
3. Add the cinnamon, allspice, clove, and ginger and combine.
4. Add the flour, graham cracker crumbs, and baking soda and mix by hand for about 30 strokes.
5. Add the grated carrot and mix just until the carrot is well combined.
6. Pour the batter into a greased 9 x 13-inch baking pan, and bake for 30 to 35 minutes.
7. While the cake is baking, prepare the icing by creaming together the fat-free cream cheese, butter, vanilla, and salt with an electric mixer in a medium bowl. Add the powdered sugar, 1 cup at a time, to the mixture and continue to mix until smooth and creamy.
8. When the cake is done, turn it out of the pan onto a large piece of wax paper. Flip the cake over onto a cooling rack, and after it has cooled for about 15 minutes, peel away the wax paper. This will remove some of the top surface of the cake, allowing the icing to stick.
9. Slice the cake lengthwise down the middle, and then across five times, creating ten equal slices.

- SERVES 10.

Nutritional Facts *(per serving)*
  SERVING SIZE—1 SLICE   TOTAL SERVINGS—10

	LITE	ORIGINAL
CALORIES	520	360
FAT	3.5G	8G

• • • •

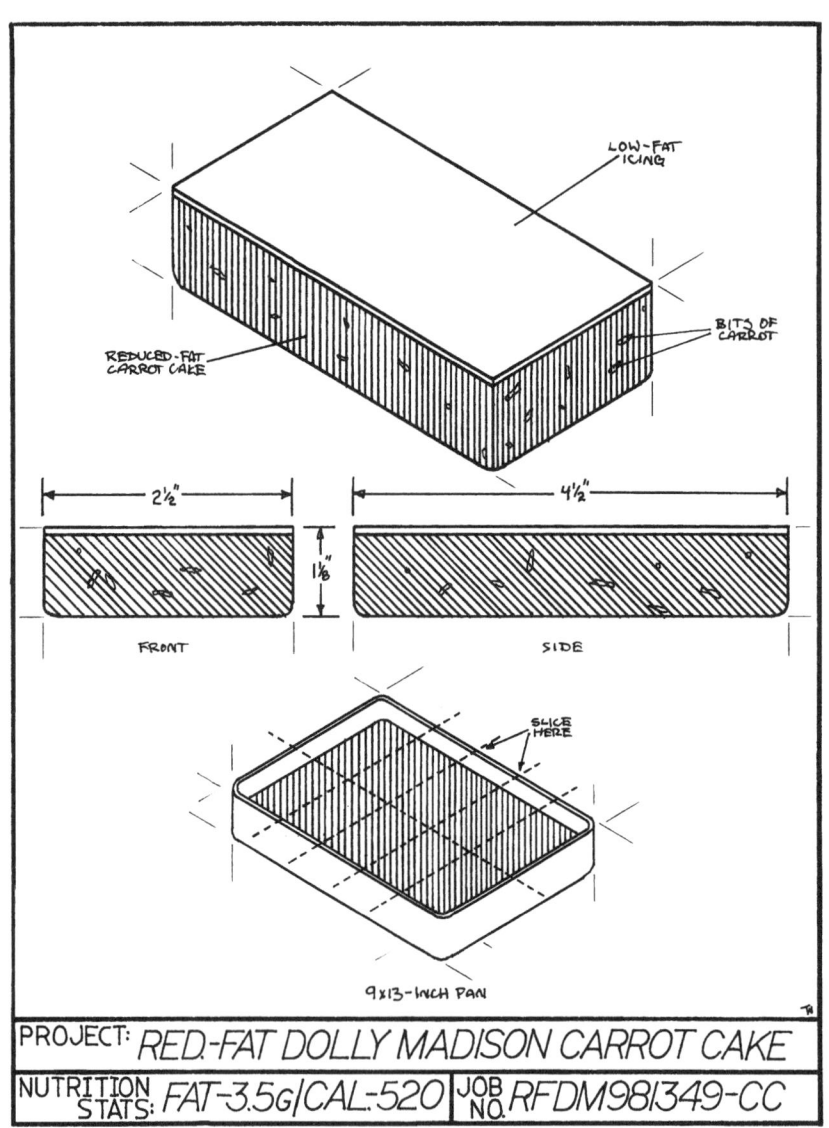

EINSTEIN BROS. CREAM CHEESE SHMEAR

TOP SECRET RECIPES FAT-FREE VERSION OF

The Einstein/Noah Bagel Corporation sold around 300 million bagels in 1997—around 6 million bagels a week. And on top of those bagels, customers will smear (or Shmear) more than 8 million pounds of the flavored cream cheeses created by the company. That's 11 tons of the stuff each day! The bagels themselves are reasonably low in fat—coming in at 1 to 3 grams each. But when you add just an ounce of cream cheese Shmear, you're quadrupling the fat, at the very least.

With fat-free cream cheese and a variety of different flavorings and ingredients, we can easily recreate Einstein Bros. Shmear, while reducing the fat to zero. These spreads are very easy to make, and if you would like yours to firm up more after mixing in the ingredients, just pop the finished spread in the microwave (in a microwave-safe bowl) for a minute or two, stir, cover, and chill completely. Use these spreads with bagels of your choice, or with those made in the clone recipes from pages 39 to 46.

ROASTED GARLIC

1 8-ounce tub Philadelphia fat-free cream cheese, softened
1 1/2 teaspoons Lawry's garlic spread concentrate
1/4 teaspoon dried parsley flakes
1/8 teaspoon salt
2 drops yellow food coloring

1. Whip the cream cheese until smooth.
2. Add the remaining ingredients and stir to combine. Cover and chill to firm.

- MAKES 1 CUP.

Nutritional Facts *(per serving)*
SERVING SIZE—2 TABLESPOONS   TOTAL SERVINGS—ABOUT 8

	LITE	ORIGINAL
CALORIES	35	100
FAT	0G	9G

STRAWBERRY

1 8-ounce tub Philadelphia fat-free cream cheese, softened
3 tablespoons sugar
¾ teaspoon strawberry extract
1 drop red food coloring

1. Whip the cream cheese until smooth.
2. Add the remaining ingredients and stir to combine. Let the mixture sit for about 5 minutes, then stir again. Cover and chill to firm.

- MAKES 1 CUP.

Nutritional Facts *(per serving)*
SERVING SIZE—2 TABLESPOONS   TOTAL SERVINGS—ABOUT 8

	LITE	ORIGINAL
CALORIES	35	100
FAT	0G	8G

JALAPEÑO SALSA

1 8-ounce tub Philadelphia fat-free cream cheese, softened
¼ cup Pace medium picante salsa
1 teaspoon minced jalapeño (nacho slices)
dash salt

1. Whip the cream cheese until smooth.
2. Add the remaining ingredients and mix to combine.
3. Heat the mixture in the microwave for 3 minutes in 1-minute intervals on full power, stirring after each minute. This will help the cream cheese to set up.

- MAKES APPROXIMATELY 1 ¼ CUPS.

Nutritional Facts (per serving)
SERVING SIZE—2 TABLESPOONS   TOTAL SERVINGS—ABOUT 10

	LITE	ORIGINAL
CALORIES	30	90
FAT	0G	8G

MAPLE WALNUT RAISIN

1 8-ounce tub Philadelphia fat-free cream cheese, softened
2 teaspoons chopped walnuts
2 teaspoons raisins
1 teaspoon water
3½ tablespoons dark brown sugar, packed
⅛ teaspoon maple flavoring
dash cinnamon

1. Whip the cream cheese until smooth.
2. Grind the walnuts into coarse pieces in a food processor. Remove and set aside.
3. Add the raisins and water to the food processor and chop on high speed until the raisins are cut into much smaller pieces.
4. Combine 1 teaspoon of the ground walnuts and 1 teaspoon of the chopped raisins to the cream cheese. Add the remaining ingredients and mix well. Cover and chill until firm.

- Makes 1 cup.

Nutritional Facts *(per serving)*
Serving size—2 tablespoons   Total servings—about 8

	Lite	Original
Calories	48	100
Fat	0g	9g

• • • •

EL POLLO LOCO FLAME-BROILED CHICKEN

TOP SECRET RECIPES REDUCED-FAT VERSION OF

This young chain of Mexican-style chicken outlets has had much success with its formula since the first store opened in the U.S. in 1980. Your order of chicken comes straight off of an open-flame grill, where it has been slowly roasting for around 45 minutes. The chicken is grilled whole, butterfly-style, and before it's boxed up for carry-out, cooks take a sharp hatchet to it in dramatic fashion. A couple of whacks and you're on your way with several pieces of very tasty and tender double-marinated chicken.

For this recipe, instead of butterflying the whole chicken, we will prepare precut pieces. Then, to save on fat grams, as soon as it's cooked, we'll remove the skin. At the restaurant, you're served flour or corn tortillas to wrap around chicken that you strip from the bone. You also get salsa and some side orders to put in the tortilla, if you choose, and I have included clone recipes for salsa, pinto beans, and rice as well (on pages 57, 161, and 162).

This recipe is improved from the version that appears in *More Top Secret Recipes*, so next time you want to clone El Pollo Loco, with or without skin, this is the recipe to use.

MARINADE
4 cups water
2 tablespoons salt
½ teaspoon pepper
2 teaspoons lemon juice
½ cup orange juice
1 large clove garlic, minced
¼ teaspoon yellow food coloring

½ roasting chicken, cut into pieces

1. Combine the marinade ingredients in a large bowl.
2. Add the chicken to the marinade, cover, and chill for 1 hour.
3. Preheat your barbecue or indoor grill to medium/high temperature. Cook the chicken on the grill. If the grill has a cover, leave it open. When the chicken has cooked for about 25 minutes, marinate the chicken once again for about 5 minutes. Place the chicken back on the grill and continue to cook for another 20 to 25 minutes or until done. Watch the chicken carefully so that it does not flare up and burn.
4. Before serving the chicken, remove the skin, and serve with steamed flour or corn tortillas—low-fat or fat-free, if you prefer—and with salsa from page 55. You may also wish to serve the chicken with side dishes of pinto beans (page 161) and rice (page 162). You can use this recipe in several of the burritos from pages 163 to 165.

Nutritional Facts *(per serving)*

SERVING SIZE—2 PIECES (4.5 OUNCES) TOTAL SERVINGS—2

	LITE	ORIGINAL
CALORIES	220	270
FAT	8.5G	14.5G

• • • •

EL POLLO LOCO PINTO BEANS

TOP SECRET RECIPES FAT-FREE VERSION OF

This is a simple little recipe that is healthy and delicious. Along with your chicken order from this fast-growing West Coast chain, comes your choice of side orders. Pinto beans is the most popular choice. But the real thing has some fat that you won't need to include in this light version. And this recipe will give you pintos that taste just like the original, down to the little zing in there from finely minced jalapeño pepper. Spoon some of these beans into a tortilla along with the chicken made from the recipe on page 159. Or you may just want to eat them on the side with that chicken recipe, or any other dish.

1 15-ounce can pinto beans, with liquid
dash salt
1 teaspoon finely minced fresh jalapeño

1. Combine all the ingredients in a small saucepan over medium heat.
2. Bring the beans to a boil, then reduce the heat and simmer for 5 minutes.

- SERVES 4.

Nutritional Facts (per serving)
SERVING SIZE—½ CUP   TOTAL SERVINGS—4

	LITE	ORIGINAL
CALORIES	96	145
FAT	0G	3G

• • • •

TOP SECRET RECIPES FAT-FREE VERSION OF

EL POLLO LOCO SPANISH RICE

Here's another clone for a dish served with your chicken from El Pollo Loco. We're gonna use our own culinary magic to cut the fat and create a delicious version of this Spanish rice that still has all of the flavor of the popular original side dish. Be sure that you get converted rice for this one—instant just won't cut it. Then you can use this side in the tortilla with your chicken from page 159, or in many of the burrito recipes on pages 163 to 165. It also makes a great side dish for any other Mexican meal.

1 1/2 cups water
1 cup converted rice (not instant)
1 cup tomato sauce
1 1/2 tablespoons finely minced onion
2 teaspoons finely minced green bell pepper
2 teaspoons finely minced red bell pepper
1/2 teaspoon salt
1/2 teaspoon chili powder
1/4 teaspoon oregano

1. Combine all the ingredients in a medium saucepan over high heat.
2. Bring the mixture to a boil, then reduce the heat and simmer the rice for 20 to 25 minutes, or until the rice is tender.

- SERVES 4.

Nutritional Facts (per serving)
SERVING SIZE—3/4 CUP   TOTAL SERVINGS—4

	LITE	ORIGINAL
CALORIES	187	155
FAT	0G	4G

TOP SECRET RECIPES LOW-FAT VERSION OF

EL POLLO LOCO BURRITOS

Here's where we tie it all together. In 1992, to meet the needs of its expanding customer base, El Pollo Loco added several different burrito selections to its menu. The burrito combinations were designed to be assembled with several prepared products the chain had been serving from the start. Here are TSR low-fat versions of four of the most popular burritos, using dishes that are made in the recipes from pages 159 through 162. The fat savings are significant, since the beans and rice are now fat-free, and the recipes use fat-free tortillas and fat-free shredded cheddar cheese. You may also want to add a salsa of your choice to these burritos, or you can use the El Pollo Loco clone recipe from page 57.

B.R.C. BURRITO

1 fat-free 12-inch flour tortilla
2 heaping tablespoons fat-free shredded cheddar cheese
1/3 cup Spanish rice (recipe from page 162)
1/3 cup pinto beans (recipe from page 161)

See preparation directions on page 165.

Nutritional Facts (per serving)
SERVING SIZE—1 BURRITO   TOTAL SERVINGS—1

	LITE	ORIGINAL
CALORIES	339	482
FAT	1G	15G

CLASSIC CHICKEN BURRITO

1 fat-free 12-inch flour tortilla
2 heaping tablespoons fat-free
   shredded cheddar cheese
⅓ cup Spanish rice
   (recipe from page 162)
⅓ cup pinto beans
   (recipe from page 161)
⅓ cup diced skinless chicken
   (recipe from page 159)

See preparation directions on page 165.

Nutritional Facts *(per serving)*
SERVING SIZE—1 BURRITO   TOTAL SERVINGS—1

	LITE	ORIGINAL
CALORIES	399	556
FAT	3G	22G

SPICY HOT CHICKEN BURRITO

1 fat-free 12-inch flour tortilla
2 heaping tablespoons
   fat-free shredded cheddar
   cheese
⅓ cup Spanish rice
   (recipe from page 162)
⅓ cup pinto beans
   (recipe from page 161)
⅓ cup diced skinless chicken
   (recipe from page 159)
½ tablespoon hot taco sauce
   (such as La Victoria brand)

See preparation directions on page 165.

Nutritional Facts *(per serving)*
SERVING SIZE—1 BURRITO   TOTAL SERVINGS—1

	LITE	ORIGINAL
CALORIES	402	559
FAT	3G	22G

LOCO GRANDE BURRITO

1 fat-free 12-inch flour tortilla
2 heaping tablespoons fat-free shredded cheddar cheese
⅓ cup Spanish rice (recipe from page 162)
⅓ cup pinto beans (recipe from page 161)
⅓ cup diced skinless chicken (recipe from page 159)
1 tablespoon guacamole
¼ cup chopped iceberg lettuce
¼ cup diced tomato
pinch chopped fresh cilantro

Nutritional Facts *(per serving)*
SERVING SIZE—1 BURRITO   TOTAL SERVINGS—1

	LITE	ORIGINAL
CALORIES	434	632
FAT	5G	26G

1. Steam the tortilla in a steamer, or in a moist towel in the microwave for 20 seconds on high.
2. Build the burrito of your choice by arranging the ingredients across the center of a tortilla in the order listed. Leave room at each end for folding.
3. To fold, turn the left and right ends of the tortilla over the filling. Fold the bottom of the tortilla up over the ingredients, then continue rolling the burrito up into a tight package.

- EACH RECIPE SERVES 1.

• • • •

HOOTERS BUFFALO CHICKEN WINGS

TOP SECRET RECIPES REDUCED-FAT VERSION OF

You probably don't need me to tell you that traditional chicken wings have significant fat and calories. In most cases, the wings deep-fried in hot oil, the skin is left on the chicken, and then they are smothered in spicy sauce that is usually about half butter. So then, how can we possibly reduce the fat in a clone recipe for what has become one of the most popular chicken wings around without compromising the flavor and everything else that makes the Hooters version so addicting?

First of all, we must bake them instead of using the traditional frying method. As the wings bake, we'll keep the skin on at first, so that the meat will not dry out, then we'll ditch the stuff and replace it with spiced breading and a light coating of cooking spray. We'll bake the wings a bit more until they're golden brown, smother them with a fat-free spicy sauce, and *voilà!*—a Hooters Buffalo Chicken Wing clone that weighs in at around one-third the fat of the original version.

10 chicken wings with skin
¼ cup Crystal Louisiana Hot Sauce or Frank's Red Hot Cayenne Sauce
¼ cup Fleischmann's Fat-Free Buttery Spread
1 tablespoon water
½ cup all-purpose flour
1 teaspoon salt
¼ teaspoon paprika
¼ teaspoon cayenne pepper
1 cup milk
canola oil nonstick spray

1. Preheat the oven on broil.
2. Line a cookie sheet or shallow baking pan with a sheet of aluminum foil. Spray the foil with nonstick spray.
3. Arrange the chicken wings on the foil with the side that has the most skin on it facing up. Broil the wings for 12 to 14 minutes, or until skin begins to dry.
4. Remove the wings from the oven, and set to 450 degrees. Allow the wings to cool for 10 to 15 minutes or just long enough so that they can be touched.
5. While the wings cool, prepare the sauce by combining the hot sauce, fat-free buttery spread, and water in a small saucepan over medium/low heat. Heat the mixture, stirring often, until it begins to boil. Immediately remove the sauce from the heat and cover the saucepan until the chicken wings are ready to coat.
6. Prepare the chicken breading by combining the flour with the salt, paprika, and cayenne pepper in a small bowl. Pour the milk into another small bowl.
7. When the wings are cool enough to touch, remove the skin from each of the chicken pieces, and discard it. Dip the wings, one at a time, in the breading, then into the milk and back in the breading, so that each one is well-coated.
8. Place the wings back on the baking sheet. Spray a coating of nonstick oil spray over each wing, so that the breading is moistened, and then bake the wings at 450 degrees for 12 minutes. Crank the oven up to broil for 3 to 5 minutes, or until the wings begin to brown and become crispy.
9. Remove the wings from the oven. Let them rest for about a minute, then put them into a plastic container (with a lid). Pour a generous amount of sauce over the wings, cover, and gently shake the wings so that they are all well coated with the sauce. Serve immediately.

- SERVES 2 AS AN APPETIZER.

Nutritional Facts *(per serving)*

Serving size—5 pieces   Total servings—2

	Lite	Original
Calories (est.)	210	471
Fat (est.)	10g	30g

• • • • •

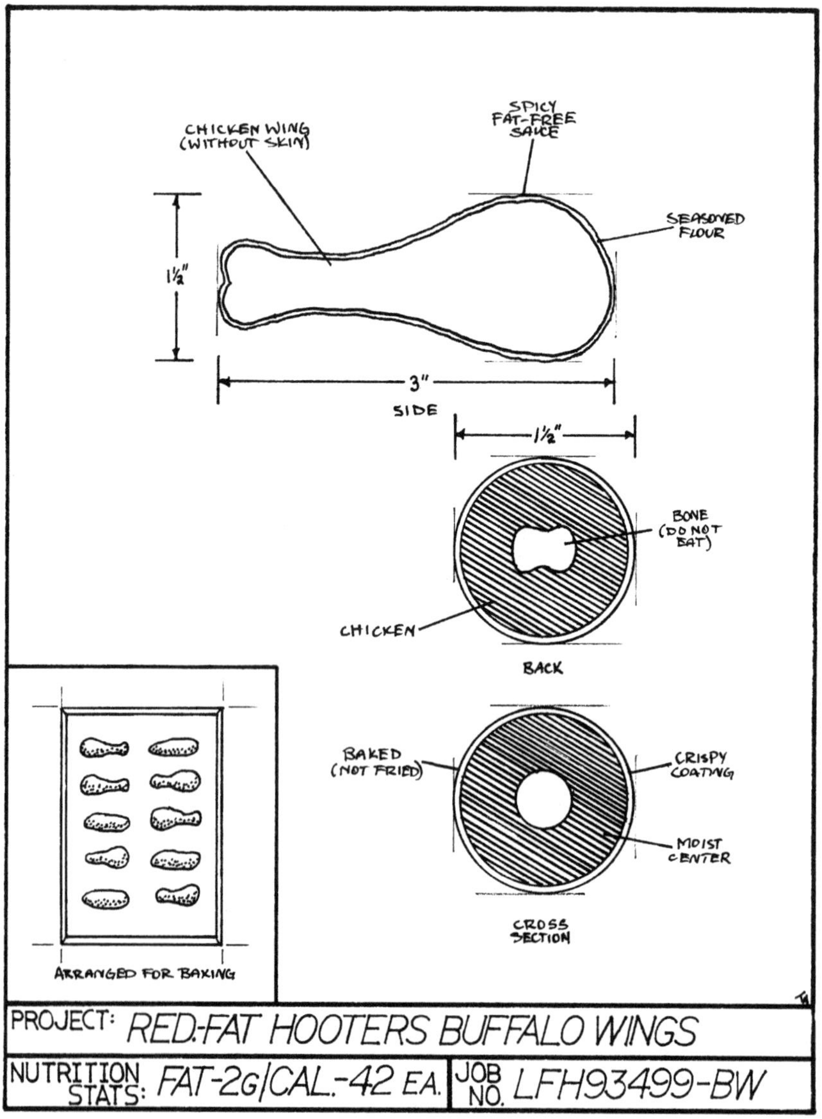

Diagram labels:

- Chicken wing (without skin)
- Spicy fat-free sauce
- Seasoned flour
- 1½"
- 3"
- SIDE
- 1½"
- Bone (do not eat)
- Chicken
- BACK
- Baked (not fried)
- Crispy coating
- Moist center
- CROSS SECTION
- ARRANGED FOR BAKING

PROJECT: RED-FAT HOOTERS BUFFALO WINGS
NUTRITION STATS: FAT-2G/CAL.-42 EA.
JOB NO. LFH93499-BW

HOOTERS BUFFALO SHRIMP

TOP SECRET RECIPES LOW-FAT VERSION OF

The Hooters chain continues its rapid expansion across the globe into 39 states and seven countries, including Taiwan, Aruba, Singapore, and Australia. In those 200 or so restaurants, this appetizer has become very popular since it was first introduced in 1995, as a variation on the Buffalo Chicken Wings recipe. Since this shrimp is fried, as are the chicken wings, we must resort to some tricks that will help bring the fat down. We'll bake the shrimp, rather than fry it, and prepare the sauce with a fat-free spread that adds flavor.

1/2 cup all-purpose flour
1 teaspoon salt
1/4 teaspoon paprika
1/4 teaspoon cayenne pepper
canola oil nonstick spray
12 large, uncooked (green) shrimp

1/4 cup Crystal Louisiana Hot Sauce or Frank's Red Hot Cayenne Sauce
1/4 cup Fleischmann's Fat-Free Buttery Spread
1 tablespoon water

1. Preheat the oven to 450 degrees.
2. Line a cookie sheet or shallow baking pan with a sheet of aluminum foil.
3. Make the breading by combining the flour, salt, paprika, and cayenne pepper in a small bowl.
4. Prepare the shrimp by cutting off the entire shell except the

last segment and the tailfins. Remove the vein from the back and clean the shrimp. Then, with a paring knife, cut a deeper slice where you removed the vein (down to the tail), so that you can spread the meat out. Be careful not to cut too deep. This will butterfly the shrimp.

5. Spray the foil on the baking sheet with nonstick spray. Roll each of the shrimp in the flour breading mixture. Then arrange them on the baking sheet. Place them on the spread-out, butterfly-cut, meaty part, with the tails sticking up. Spray each shrimp with a coating of nonstick spray, so that the breading is moistened.
6. Bake for 10 to 12 minutes or until the surface of the shrimp becomes light brown. Turn oven to broil for 4 to 5 minutes, or until the shrimp begin to brown and become crispy.
7. While the shrimp cooks, prepare the sauce by combining the hot sauce with the fat-free butter-flavored spread and a tablespoon of water in a small saucepan over medium/low heat. Cook it until the sauce starts to bubble, stirring occasionally, then reduce the heat to low and cover until the shrimp is ready.
8. When the shrimp is done, remove the pan from the oven, and let the shrimp sit for about a minute. Put all of the shrimp into a plastic container (with a lid), add a generous amount of the sauce, and cover. Gently shake the shrimp until each one is well coated with sauce. Pour the shrimp out onto a plate and serve hot.

- SERVES 2 AS AN APPETIZER.

Nutritional Facts *(per serving)*
SERVING SIZE—6 PIECES   TOTAL SERVINGS—2

	LITE	ORIGINAL
CALORIES (est.)	204	320
FAT (est.)	3G	10G

• • • •

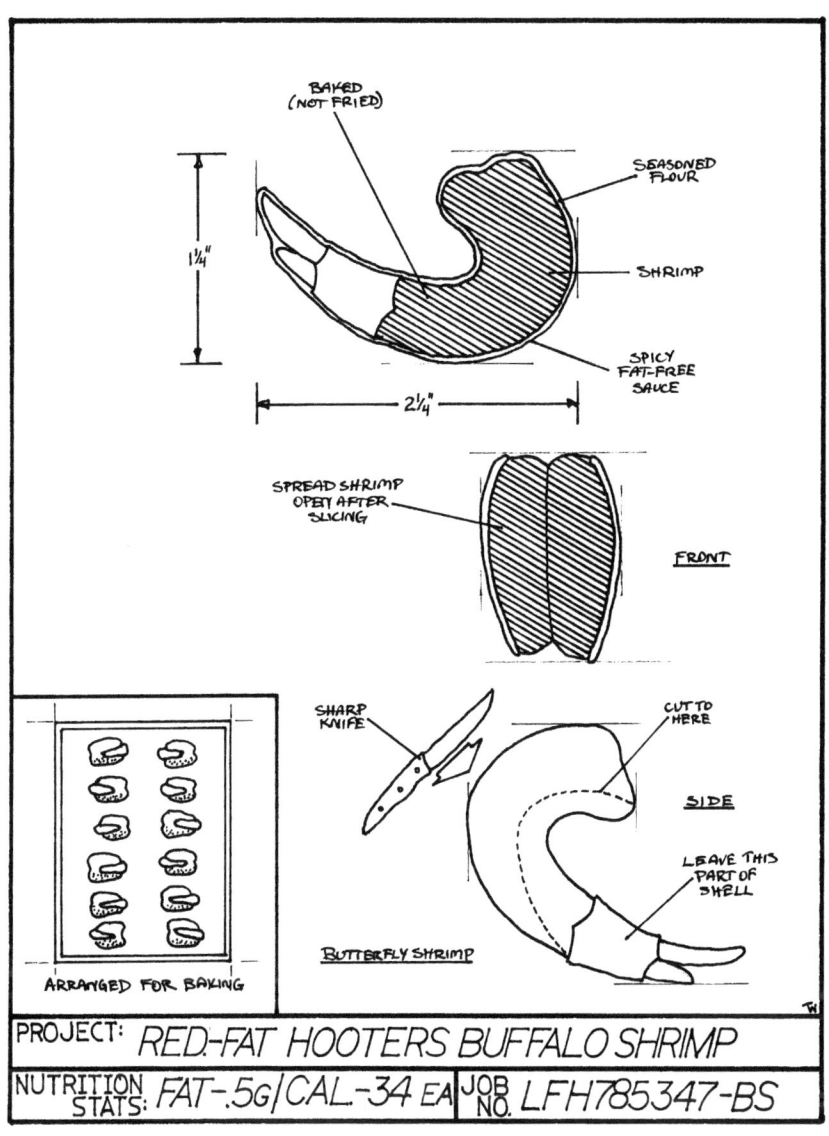

KELLOGG'S RICE KRISPIES TREATS

TOP SECRET RECIPES FAT-FREE VERSION OF

It wasn't long after the cereal's 1928 introduction that Kellogg Kitchens invented a way to mix Rice Krispies with melted marshmallows and butter to produce with an alternative, nonbreakfast use for the product. In the early forties the Rice Krispies Treats recipe was printed on boxes of Rice Krispies cereal and became a great recipe for kids since it was very easy to make, required no baking, and could be eaten almost immediately. The popularity of these treats inspired two additional cereals in the early nineties: Fruity Marshmallow Krispies, and Rice Krispies Treats Cereal. And at the same time, Kellogg came out with individually packaged Rice Krispies Treats, for those who wanted instant satisfaction without having to spend time in the kitchen. But that product, just like the popular recipe printed on the cereal box, contained 2 grams of fat. And since the packaged Treats are small, it's tough to eat just one (tell me about it).

By using Butter Buds Sprinkles and making some other important changes to the recipe, I have come up with a treat recipe for bars that taste like the packaged product, at considerably less cost (the recipe makes the equivalent of three boxes of the real thing), and with not one gram of fat.

nonstick cooking spray
7 cups miniature marshmallows
3 tablespoons Butter Buds Sprinkles

2 tablespoons water
¼ teaspoon vanilla
¼ teaspoon salt
6 cups Rice Krispies cereal

1. Lightly coat a large nonstick saucepan or pot with cooking spray.
2. Add the marshmallows, Butter Buds, water, vanilla, and salt to the pan and set over medium/low heat. Stir the mixture constantly while cooking until the marshmallows are completely melted. Turn off the heat.
3. Add the Rice Krispies and stir until the cereal is completely coated.
4. Spray a 9 x 13-inch baking pan with a light coating of the cooking spray. Pour the Rice Krispies mixture into the pan. Moisten your hands and press the mixture into the pan until flat.
5. When the mixture cools completely, cut four times down and four across, making 25 bars.

- MAKES 25 BARS.

Nutritional Facts *(per serving)*

SERVING SIZE—1 BAR   TOTAL SERVINGS—25

	LITE	ORIGINAL
CALORIES	90	90
FAT	0G	2G

• • •

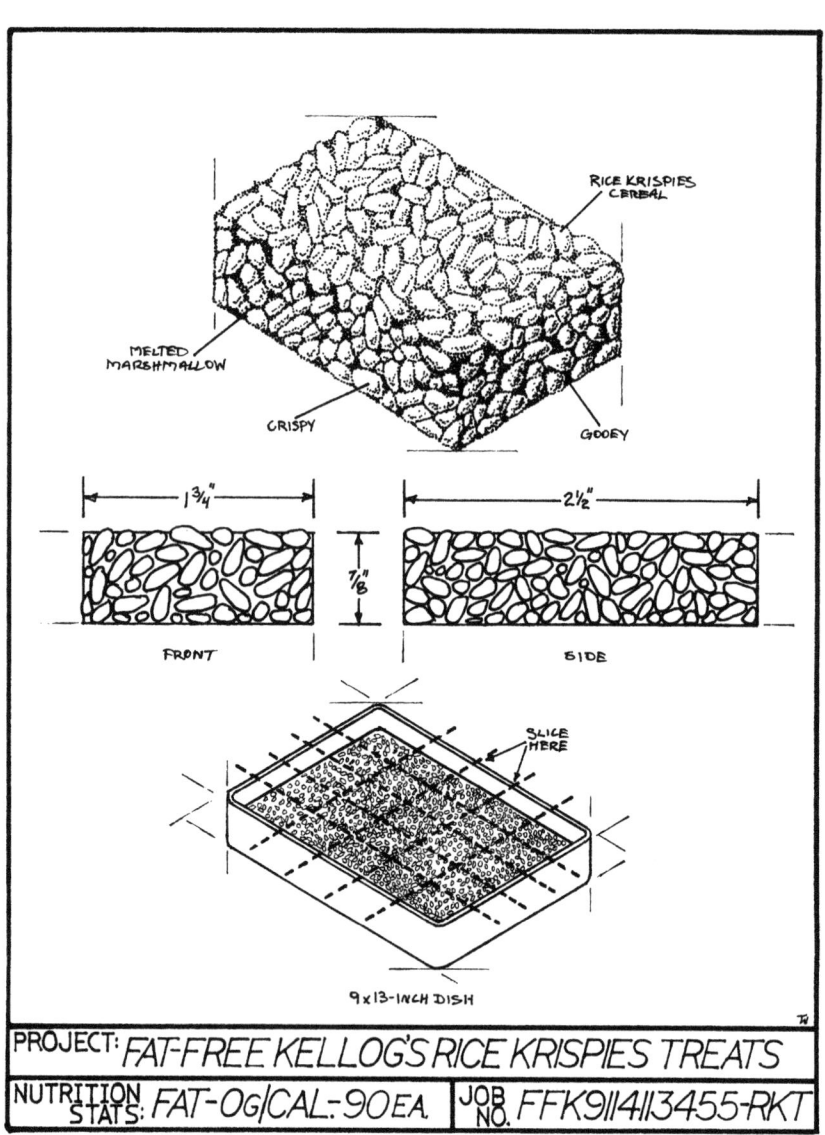

KFC BUTTERMILK BISCUITS

How would you like a killer biscuit recipe that has 75 percent less fat than typical biscuits, and tastes great? And what if I told you they would still taste like those introduced to the world in 1982 by the world's largest chicken chain? Here you go—a clone recipe for making a low-fat version of KFC's Buttermilk Biscuits. Reduced-fat Bisquick and Butter Buds Sprinkles are the secret ingredients that help make this TSR low-fat conversion of a fast food favorite.

2 cups reduced-fat Bisquick baking mix
¾ cup low-fat (1 percent) buttermilk
2 teaspoons Butter Buds Sprinkles
2 teaspoons sugar
¼ teaspoon salt
1 tablespoon margarine, melted

1. Preheat the oven to 450 degrees.
2. Combine the baking mix, buttermilk, Butter Buds, sugar, and salt in a medium bowl. Mix by hand until well blended.
3. Turn the dough out onto a floured surface and knead for about 30 seconds, or until the dough becomes elastic.
4. Roll the dough to about ¾-inch thick and punch out biscuits using a 3-inch cutter. Arrange the punched-out dough on an ungreased baking sheet, and bake for 10 to 12 minutes or until the biscuits are golden on top and have about doubled in height.
5. Remove the biscuits from the oven and immediately brush the top of each one with a light coating of the melted margarine. Serve warm.

- Makes 8 biscuits.

Nutritional Facts *(per serving)*

Serving size—1 biscuit   Total servings—8

	Lite	Original
Calories	115	180
Fat	2.5g	10g

• • •

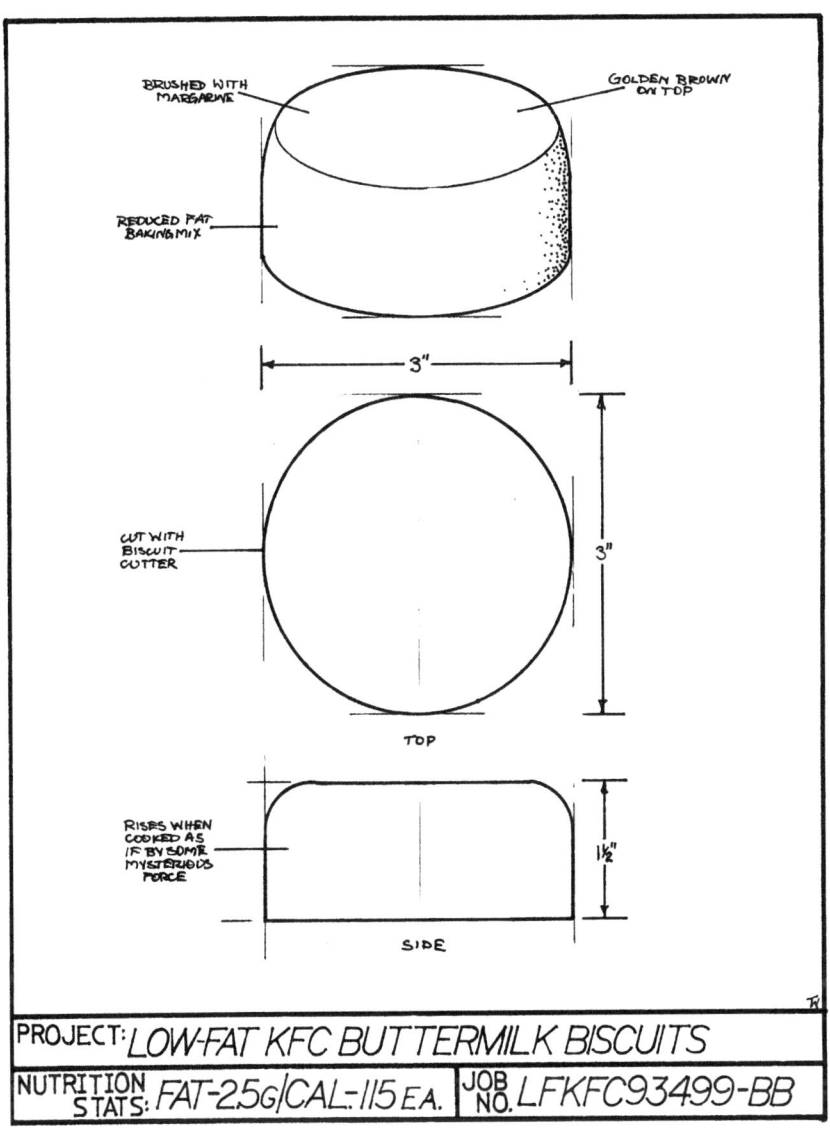

TOP SECRET RECIPES FAT-FREE VERSION OF

KFC COLE SLAW

How cool is this? A fat-free version of KFC's famous cole slaw with only five ingredients! As it turns out, fat-free Miracle Whip provides most of the necessary flavors and textures for this clone of the Colonel's beloved slaw, which he first created in the fifties. And there's nary a gram of fat in there to worry about. It just doesn't get much easier than this.

1 cup fat-free Miracle Whip
¼ cup sugar
8 cups cabbage, finely minced

2 tablespoons carrot, shredded then minced
2 tablespoons minced onion

1. Combine the Miracle Whip with the sugar in a large bowl. Mix well until the sugar is dissolved.
2. Add the cabbage, carrot, and onion, and toss well. Be sure the cabbage is chopped into very small pieces, about the size of rice.
3. Cover and chill for several hours.

- SERVES 8.

Nutritional Facts *(per serving)*
SERVING SIZE—
   APPROXIMATELY ¾ CUP
TOTAL SERVINGS—8

	LITE	ORIGINAL
CALORIES	57	210
FAT	0G	10.5G

• • • •

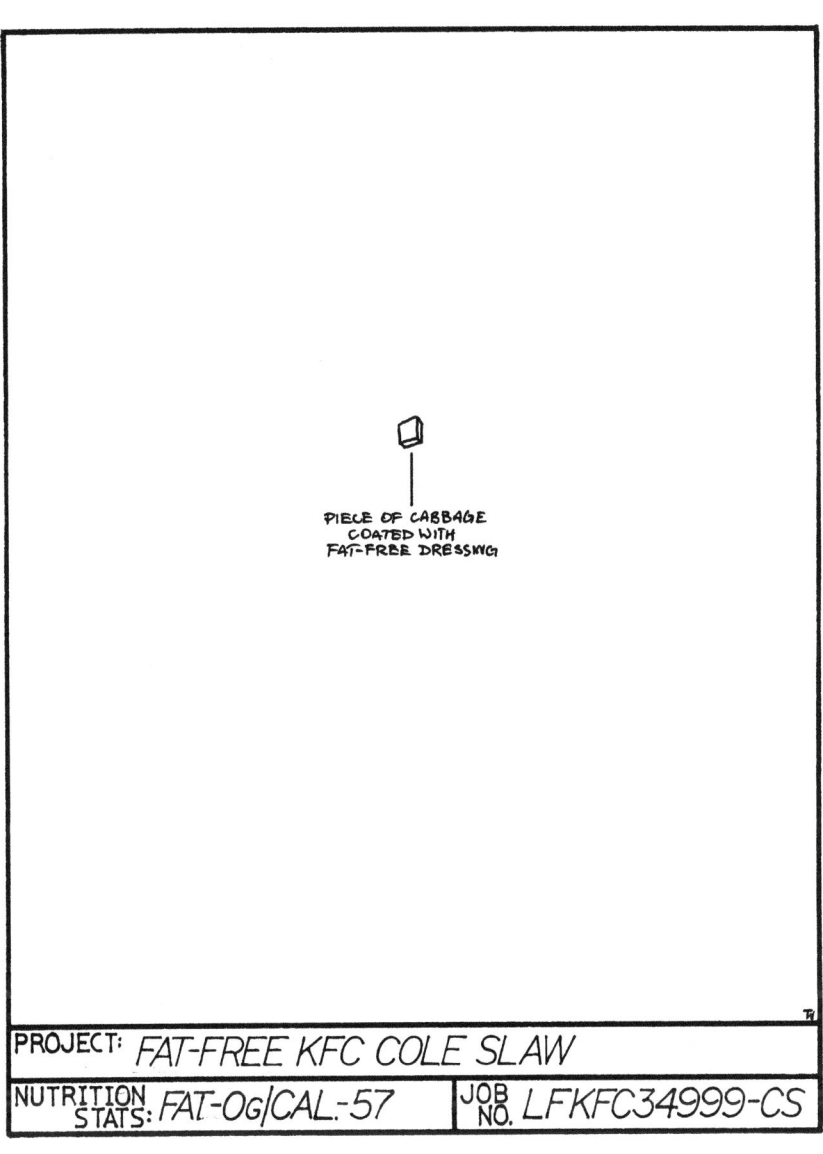

TOP SECRET RECIPES LOW-FAT VERSION OF

KFC MASHED POTATOES & GRAVY

The secret to cloning the Colonel's famous gravy at home is to first darken the chicken broth with a roux. Roux is a mixture of flour and oil that is cooked in a saucepan over low heat until it's browned, but not burned. This magical mixture not only colors the gravy for us, but also thickens it. The small amount of oil used here and no addition of drippings will give you gravy that tastes as good as the stuff from the world-famous chicken chain, but with significantly less fat.

And when you're done with the gravy, you can easily make mashed potatoes that taste just like KFC's with those popular Potato Buds. The taste of the real thing is imitated with fat-free butter-flavored spread that adds no fat. You're going to love this one.

GRAVY
1 tablespoon vegetable oil
5 tablespoons all-purpose flour
1 can Campbell's chicken broth
   (plus 1 can of water)
¼ teaspoon salt
⅛ teaspoon pepper

MASHED POTATOES
1½ cups water
⅓ cup reduced-fat (2 percent) milk
2½ tablespoons Fleischmann's
   Fat-Free Buttery Spread
½ teaspoon salt
1⅓ cups instant mashed potato
   flakes (Potato Buds)

1. Make the gravy by first preparing a roux: Combine the oil with 1½ tablespoons of flour in a medium saucepan. Cook over low heat for 20 to 30 minutes or until the mixture becomes a chocolate color.
2. Remove the pan from the heat and add the chicken broth, 1 can of water, the remaining flour, ¼ teaspoon of salt, and pepper. Put the pan back on the heat and bring the heat up to medium. When the mixture begins to boil, reduce the heat and simmer the gravy for 15 minutes or until thick.
3. As the gravy is reducing, prepare the potatoes by combining 1½ cups of water, ⅓ cup of milk, the fat-free buttery spread, and ½ teaspoon of salt in a medium saucepan over medium heat. Bring to a boil, add the potato flakes, and whip with a fork until smooth.
4. Serve the mashed potatoes with gravy poured over the top.

- MAKES 4 SERVINGS.

Nutritional Facts *(per serving)*
SERVING SIZE—½ CUP POTATOES   TOTAL SERVINGS—4
   AND 3 TABLESPOONS GRAVY

	LITE	ORIGINAL
CALORIES	120	120
FAT	2G	6G

• • • •

TOP SECRET RECIPES REDUCED-FAT VERSION OF

KFC TENDER ROAST CHICKEN

Tender Roast chicken was introduced in 1996 after KFC axed Rotisserie Gold, its short-lived, whole-roasted chicken product that was meant to compete with home meal replacement chains like Boston Market and Kenny Rogers Roasters. Although it's not fried, as are the other KFC chicken offerings, six ounces of Tender Roast still has approximately 7.6 grams of fat when the skin is left on. That's why we're going to strip it all off. But not so fast, amigos. We'll keep that skin on through most of the baking process, so that the meat stays nice and juicy. Then, once the skin is peeled away, we can simply sprinkle the tasty spice blend over the juicy chicken and let it finish baking.

Serve this one with some of the other reduced-fat KFC clone recipes and you won't even miss the dozens of grams of fat you're avoiding.

SPICE BLEND
½ teaspoon salt
½ teaspoon pepper
½ teaspoon lemon pepper
¼ teaspoon thyme
¼ teaspoon paprika

1 whole roasting chicken, cut into pieces

1. Preheat the oven to 375 degrees.
2. Prepare the spice blend by combining the ingredients in a small bowl.
3. Place the chicken pieces onto a baking sheet, skin side up. Bake

for 20 minutes, then remove the chicken from the oven and cool for 5 to 10 minutes.

4. When you can handle the chicken, remove the skin, sprinkle the entire surface of the chicken with a light coating of the spice blend (approximately ½ teaspoon for a big piece, ¼ teaspoon for a small piece), and replace on the baking sheet. Return the sheet to the oven for 10 more minutes or until the chicken is done.

- SERVES 4.

Nutritional Facts *(per serving)*

SERVING SIZE—6 OUNCES   TOTAL SERVINGS—4

	LITE	ORIGINAL
CALORIES	206	338
FAT	7.6G	17.4G

• • • •

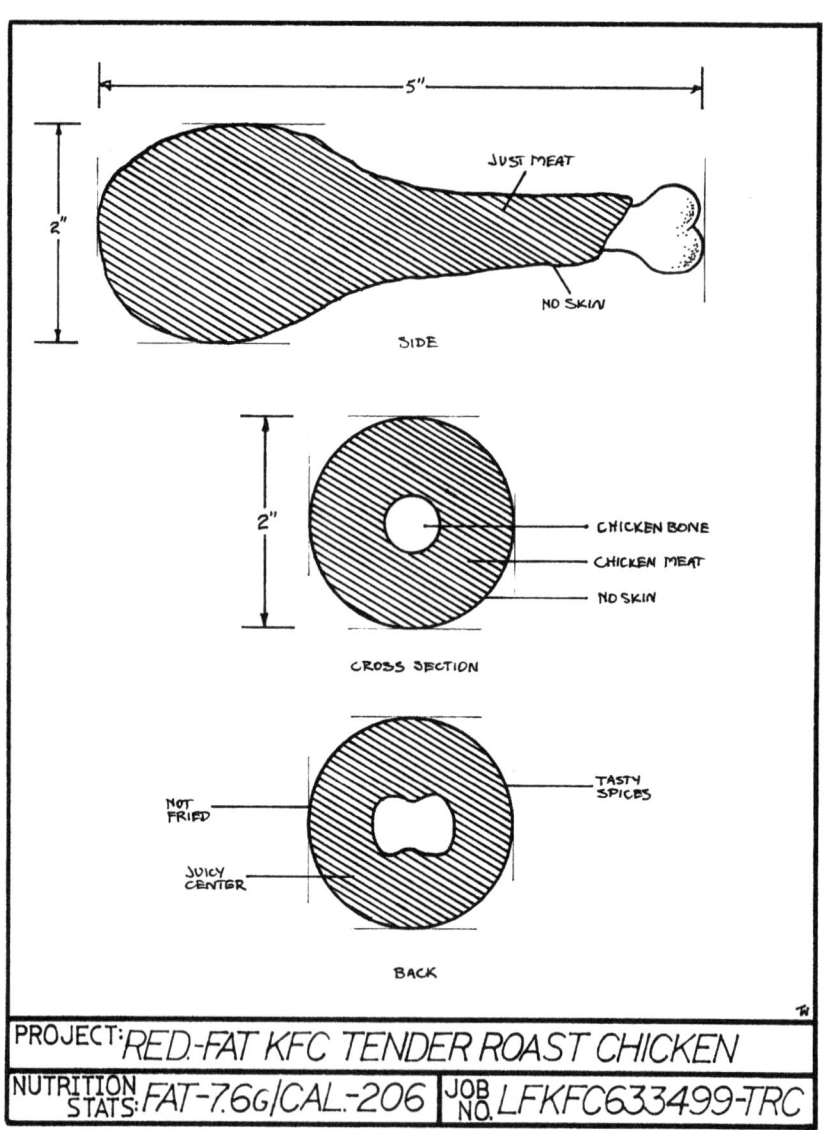

TOP SECRET RECIPES REDUCED-FAT VERSION OF

MCDONALD'S BIG MAC

When the first Big Mac was served by a McDonald's franchisee in 1968, it was a time when all food in America was prepared with little attention to the amount of fat. Some low-calorie products had been developed, but they were not hugely popular, and most Americans ate and prepared food using whatever ingredients made it taste the best. Around 27 years later, McDonald's responded to the public's rapidly changing, health-conscious eating habits with the McLean Deluxe, a burger with a significantly reduced amount of fat. But the McLean Deluxe was not a commercial success; it never even came close to selling as fast as the other McDonald's burgers. Soon, the McLean Deluxe was history. And today, as reduced-fat products in supermarkets are selling faster than ever, McDonald's has not replaced the McLean Deluxe on its menu. The Big Mac is still king, with its 31 grams of fat. Here's a clone to make a version of the Big Mac at home with less than half the fat of the original.

FAT-FREE "SPECIAL SAUCE"

¼ cup fat-free mayonnaise
1 tablespoon fat-free French dressing
2 teaspoons sweet pickle relish
1 ½ teaspoons finely minced white onion
½ teaspoon white vinegar
½ teaspoon sugar
dash salt

2 sesame seed hamburger buns
2 additional top buns
½ pound super-lean ground beef (7 percent fat)
dash salt
dash pepper
2 teaspoons finely diced white onion
1 cup chopped lettuce
2 slices fat-free American cheese
dill pickle slices

1. Prepare the sauce by combining all of the sauce ingredients in a small bowl and mixing well. Cover and chill until needed.
2. With a serrated knife, cut the top (the rounded part) off both of the extra top buns. This will create two double-faced middle buns for your double-decker hamburgers. The part you cut off—the part with the sesame seeds—can be tossed.
3. Brown the faces of all the buns—including both sides of the two middle buns—in a frying pan or griddle that has been preheated to medium heat. Keep the pan hot.
4. Divide the meat into four ⅛-pound portions. Roll each one into a ball and press down onto wax paper to approximately the same diameter as the bun. Peel the beef patties from the wax paper and cook them in the hot pan or on the griddle. Lightly salt and pepper each patty and cook them for 2 to 3 minutes per side.
5. While the meat cooks, prepare the rest of the sandwich by spreading about a tablespoon of the sauce onto the face of the bottom bun, and the same amount onto the top face of the middle bun.
6. Sprinkle about ½ teaspoon of white onion onto the sauce on each of the four buns.
7. Divide the lettuce into four even portions and spread it on the onions on each of the sauce-covered buns.

8. Place a slice of American cheese on the lettuce on each of the two bottom buns.
9. Place two dill pickle slices on the lettuce on each of the two middle buns.
10. When the meat is done, place the patties on each of the bottom and middle buns on top of the other ingredients, then assemble the burger by stacking the middle buns onto the bottom buns, and finish it off with the top bun. Microwave the burger for 10 to 15 seconds, if you would like it to have that just-out-of-the-wrapper heat.

- SERVES 2.

Nutritional Facts *(per serving)*

SERVING SIZE—1 BURGER   TOTAL SERVINGS—2

	LITE	ORIGINAL
CALORIES	500	560
FAT	13G	31G

• • • •

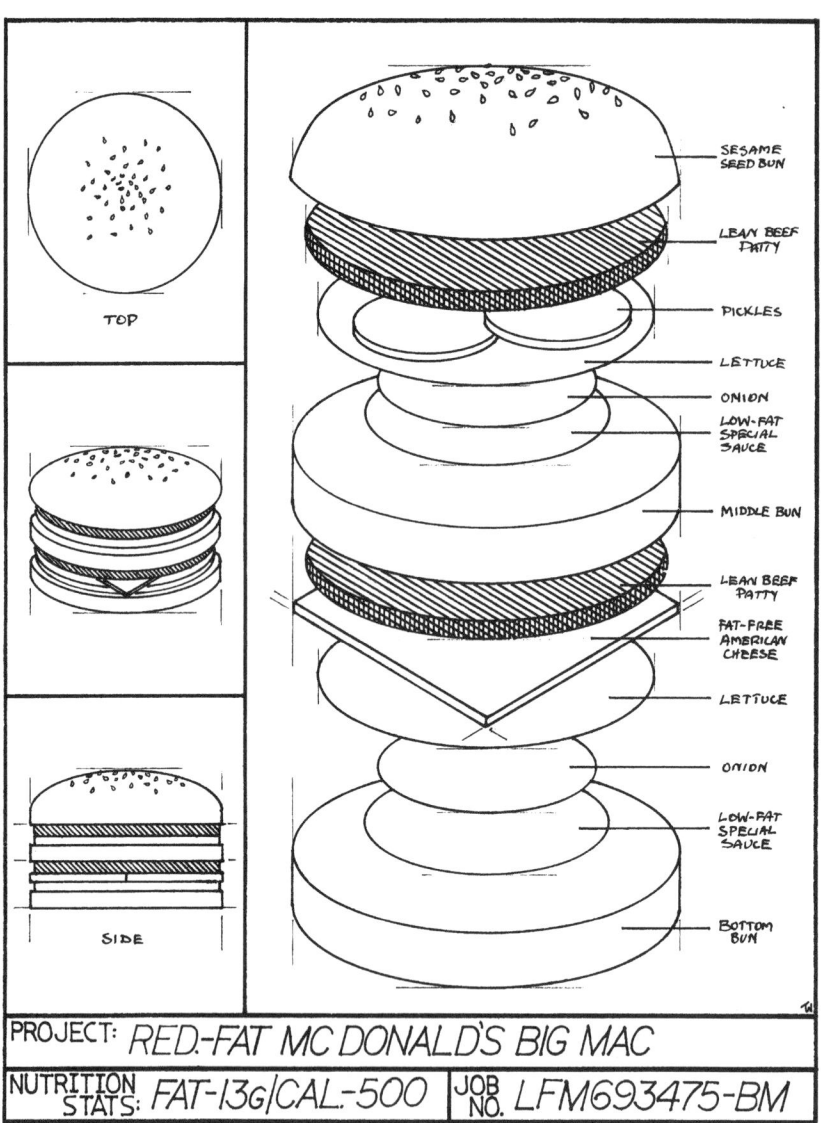

MCDONALD'S BREAKFAST BURRITO

TOP SECRET RECIPES LOW-FAT VERSION OF

It was in the late seventies, shortly after McDonald's had introduced the Egg McMuffin, that the food giant realized the potential of a quick, drive-thru breakfast. Soon, the company had developed several breakfast selections, including the Big Breakfast with eggs, hash browns, and sausage. Eventually one out of every four breakfasts served out of the home would be served at McDonald's—an impressive statistic indeed. The newest kid on the McBreakfast block is this morning meal in a tortilla, first offered on the menu in the summer of 1991. The Breakfast Burrito has 19 grams of fat. To keep the energy up for your busy day, try out this version of the tasty breakfast meal with significantly reduced fat. Ay-yi-yi!

4 ounces turkey sausage
1 tablespoon minced white onion
½ tablespoon minced mild green chilies
1 cup egg substitute
salt
pepper
4 8-inch fat-free flour tortillas
4 slices fat-free American cheese

ON THE SIDE
salsa

1. Preheat a skillet over medium heat. Crumble the sausage into the pan, then add the onion. Sauté the sausage and onion for 3 to 4 minutes, or until the sausage is browned.
2. Add the mild green chilies and continue to sauté for 1 minute.
3. Pour the egg substitute into the pan and scramble the eggs with the sausage and vegetables. Salt and pepper to taste.
4. Heat up the tortillas by steaming them in the microwave in moist paper towels or a tortilla steamer for 20 to 30 seconds.
5. Break each slice of cheese in half and position two halves end-to-end in the middle of each tortilla.
6. To make the burrito, spoon ¼ of the egg filling onto the cheese in a tortilla. Fold one side of the tortilla over the filling, then fold up about two inches of one end. Fold over the other side of the tortilla to complete the burrito. Serve hot with salsa on the side, if desired.

- MAKES 4 BURRITOS.

Nutritional Facts *(per serving)*

SERVING SIZE—1 BURRITO   TOTAL SERVINGS—4

	LITE	ORIGINAL
CALORIES	202	320
FAT	2.5G	19G

• • • •

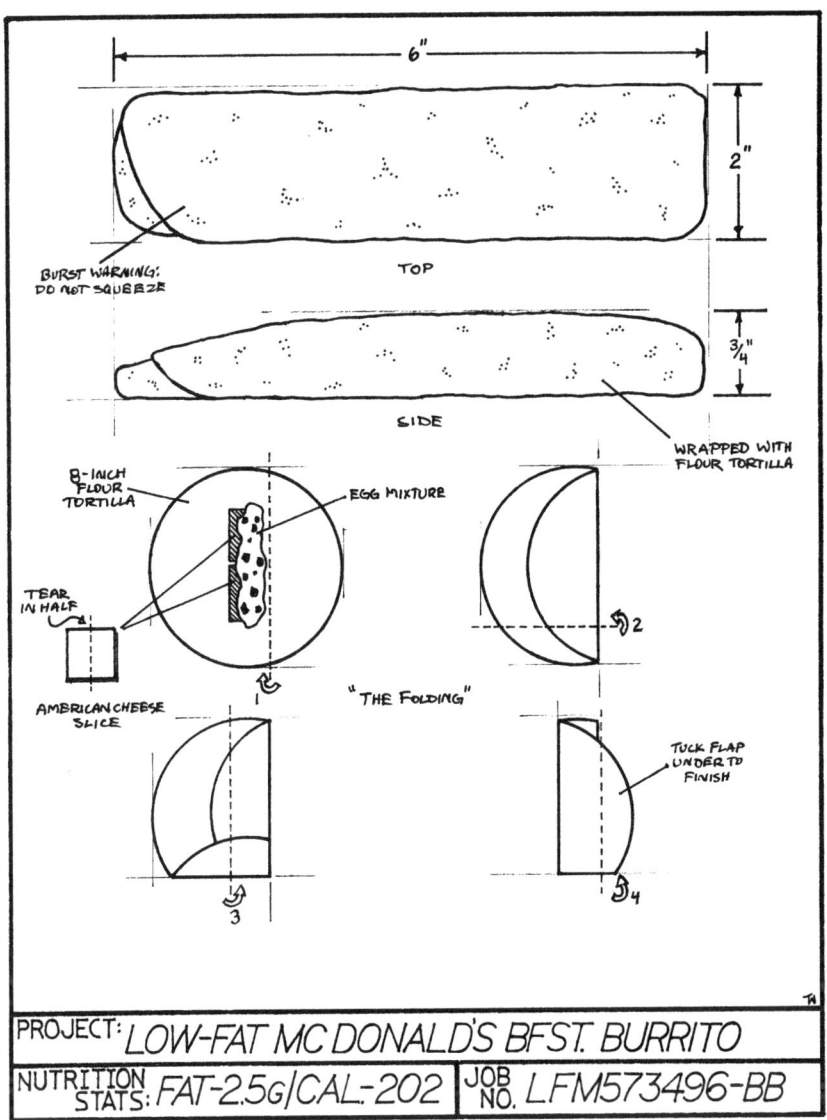

OLIVE GARDEN CHICKEN CAESAR SANDWICH

TOP SECRET RECIPES REDUCED-FAT VERSION OF

New to the lunch menu in 1995, this sandwich would normally have approximately 20.5 grams of fat because of the Caesar dressing. Ah, but if we use some low-fat and fat-free ingredients, we can reduce those fat grams by better than half of the original. And then we'll have a flavor-packed reduced-fat clone of the delicious Olive Garden creation that's great for lunch or dinner.

Keep in mind that the chicken will need to marinate for several hours, so start this one early, or even better, the day before you plan to eat it. This will ensure that your chicken is well marinated and the flavors in the dressing will have time to develop.

4 chicken breast fillets

CHICKEN MARINADE
1 cup water
1 cup pineapple juice
1 tablespoon lime juice
2 teaspoons soy sauce
1 teaspoon salt
¼ teaspoon liquid smoke
¼ teaspoon onion powder
¼ pepper
⅛ teaspoon garlic

CAESAR DRESSING
¼ cup fat-free mayonnaise
1 tablespoon egg substitute
1 teaspoon vinegar
1 ½ teaspoons grated Parmesan cheese
⅛ teaspoon coarse-ground pepper

⅛ teaspoon garlic powder
⅛ teaspoon salt

dash onion powder
3 drops Worcestershire sauce

4 Italian or sourdough sandwich rolls

2 cups chopped romaine lettuce

1. Cut each chicken breast in half. Fold a piece of plastic wrap around one piece of chicken and pound flat (to about ¼-inch thick) with a mallet. The chicken should be slightly larger in diameter than the sandwich rolls. Repeat with the remaining pieces.
2. Combine the ingredients for the marinade in a medium bowl. Add the chicken, cover, and chill for at least 4 hours. Overnight is best.
3. While the chicken marinates, combine all of the Caesar dressing ingredients in a small bowl. Cover and chill.
4. When the chicken has marinated, preheat your barbecue or indoor grill to high heat. Grill the chicken for 2 to 3 minutes per side, or until done.
5. Use the grill to brown the faces of each roll.
6. Build each sandwich by spreading about a half cup of lettuce on one of the bottom buns. Drizzle about a tablespoon of the dressing over the lettuce. Next, stack two pieces of chicken on the sandwich. Place one piece of the chicken slightly off to one side and then position the second piece off to the other side but overlapping the first piece.
7. Finish off the sandwich with the top half of the roll. Repeat the process to build the remaining sandwiches and serve.

- SERVES 4.

Nutritional Facts *(per serving)*
SERVING SIZE—1 SANDWICH   TOTAL SERVINGS—4

	LITE	ORIGINAL
CALORIES (est.)	450	543
FAT (est.)	9G	20.5G

• • • •

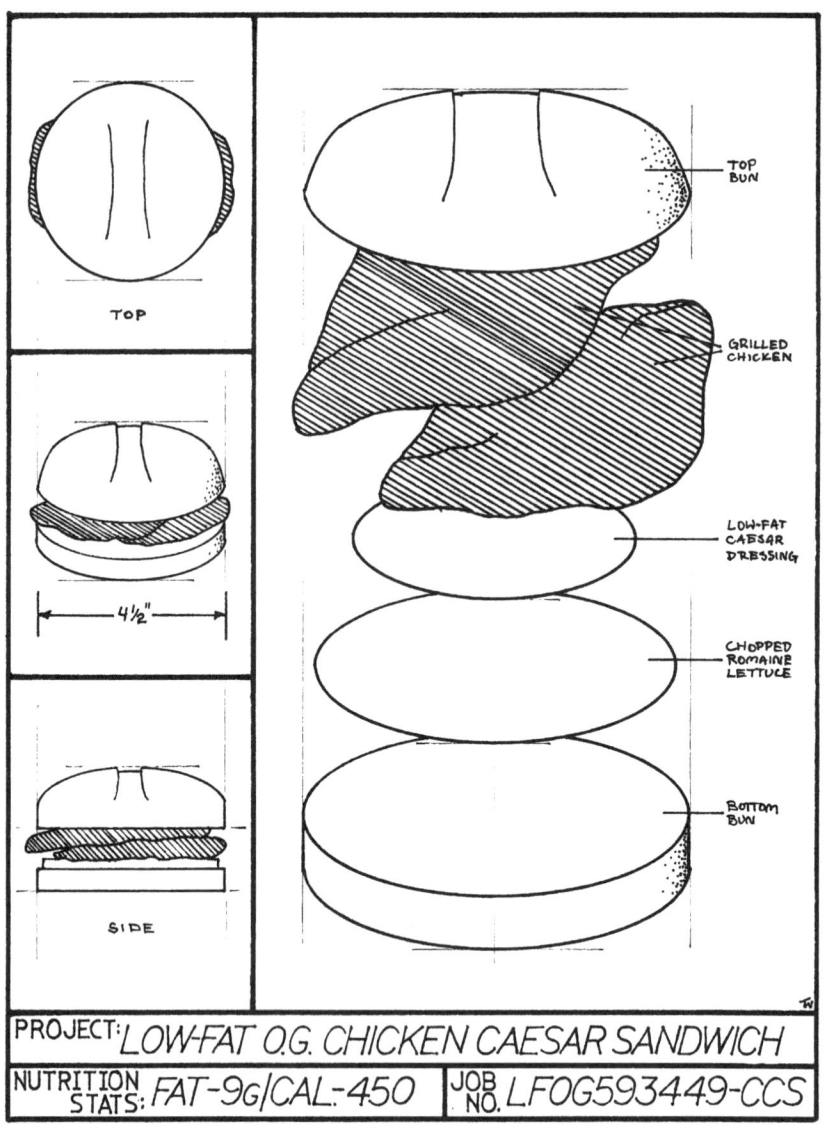

TOP SECRET RECIPES FAT-FREE VERSION OF

OLIVE GARDEN ITALIAN SALAD DRESSING

We love to eat salad because it seems so healthy—all those veggies wrestling around in there. But add just a couple tablespoons of salad dressing and you've gone from zero fat to quite a lot of grams of the stuff, before your main course has even hit the table. And if the salad dressing is as tasty and addicting as the dressing the Olive Garden serves, you might be pouring on a lot more than just a couple tablespoons. So now we just have to figure out a way to cut those fat grams and hold on to the flavor of the dressing that has become so popular you can buy it by the bottle at the Olive Garden restaurants.

Let's do this: We'll take out the oil, and add dry pectin to thicken the dressing, along with more water than would be used in the original version. We can even put a good amount of Romano cheese in there and still be sure that a single serving of the dressing has less than ½ gram of fat. Add some vinegar, a little corn syrup and lemon juice, some spices—bingo! Mission accomplished. This one's a keeper.

⅔ cup water
1 ½ tablespoons dry pectin
½ cup white vinegar
¼ cup corn syrup
1 ¼ teaspoons salt
1 teaspoon lemon juice
½ teaspoon minced garlic (1 clove)
¼ teaspoon dried parsley flakes
pinch of dried oregano
pinch of crushed red pepper flakes
¼ cup egg substitute
2 ½ tablespoons grated Romano cheese

1. In a small saucepan, combine the water and dry pectin and whisk until the pectin is mostly dissolved.
2. Add the remaining ingredients, except for the Romano cheese, and place the pan over medium heat. Stir often until the mixture begins to boil, then remove the pan from the heat. Cool for about 10 minutes.
3. Stir the Romano cheese into the thickened mixture.
4. Allow the mixture to cool thoroughly, then pour it into a sealed container and chill for at least 2 hours.

- MAKES 1 ⅓ CUPS

Nutritional Facts (per serving)
SERVING SIZE—2 TABLESPOONS   TOTAL SERVINGS—11

	LITE	ORIGINAL
CALORIES	42	90
FAT	0G	8G

• • • •

TOP SECRET RECIPES REDUCED-FAT VERSION OF

OLIVE GARDEN PASTA E FAGIOLI

One of the most popular and hard-to-pronounce items on the Olive Garden menu is found in the soup column. But it's more like a thick chili than a soup, really, with all those beans and veggies and ground beef in there. The reduced-fat grams in this clone are especially important when we consider that this dish makes an excellent meal by itself, and you may want to eat more than the 1½ cups serving size measured for the nutrition stats.

We'll keep the added fat to a minimum by sautéing the veggies in what little fat is not drained off from browning the super-lean ground beef. The soup will fill your mouth with so much flavor that it won't matter that we don't add any additional fat. You'll have a hard time distinguishing between this version and the original. Try it out, and you'll see what I mean.

This recipe makes about eight 1½-cup servings, so if you can't eat it all within a few days, it freezes well.

1 pound super-lean ground beef
   (7 percent fat)
1 small onion, diced (1 cup)
1 large carrot, julienned (1 cup)
3 stalks celery, chopped
   (1 cup)
2 cloves garlic, minced
2 14.5-ounce cans diced
   tomatoes
1 15-ounce can red kidney beans
   (with liquid)
1 15-ounce can great northern
   beans (with liquid)
1 15-ounce can tomato sauce
1 12-ounce can V-8 juice
1 tablespoon white vinegar
1½ teaspoons salt
1 teaspoon dried oregano
1 teaspoon dried basil
½ teaspoon pepper
½ teaspoon dried thyme
½ pound (½ package) ditali pasta

1. Brown the ground beef in a very large saucepan or soup pot over medium heat. Drain off the fat.
2. Add the onion, carrot, celery, and garlic and simmer for 10 minutes.
3. Add the remaining ingredients, except the pasta, and simmer for 1 hour.
4. About 50 minutes into the simmer time, cook pasta in 1½ to 2 quarts of boiling water over high heat. Cook for 10 minutes or just until pasta is *al dente*, or slightly tough. Drain.
5. Add the pasta to the large pot of soup. Simmer for 5 minutes and serve.

- SERVES 8 AS AN APPETIZER.

TIDBITS

Ditali pasta is small ¼-inch tubes of pasta—short, little hollow cylinders. They may also go by the name salad-roni.

Nutritional Facts *(per serving)*
   SERVING SIZE—1½ CUPS   TOTAL SERVINGS—8

	LITE	ORIGINAL
CALORIES (est.)	312	416
FAT (est.)	4G	17.5G

• • • •

OLIVE GARDEN TIRAMISU

You have now come to the most dramatic low-fat conversion recipe in this book, and one of the most unique. If you love tiramisu, but long for a lower-fat version, you should totally dig this one.

The Olive Garden chain offers a very popular and delicious tiramisu that is produced outside the restaurants and then delivered fresh to each outlet. The layers of fluffy mascarpone cheese and lady fingers soaked in a solution of strong coffee and coffee liqueur is a delicious and memorable combination. But mascarpone cheese has 13 grams of fat per ounce, and there's nothing that tastes quite like it.

However, there is one way to get very close; and it's a special combination of Dream Whip, gelatin, and fat-free cream cheese never before created and revealed in a cookbook. Entenmann's fat-free pound cake, sliced and brushed with a coffee/liqueur, will substitute nicely for the lady fingers. Layer it all into a square dish and you've got a "must try" TSR low-fat conversion clone that you won't forget.

FLUFFY CHEESE

1 cup low-fat milk (1 percent fat)
1 envelope unflavored gelatin
3 envelopes Dream Whip Mix
4 ounces Philadelphia fat-free cream cheese, softened
½ cup sugar

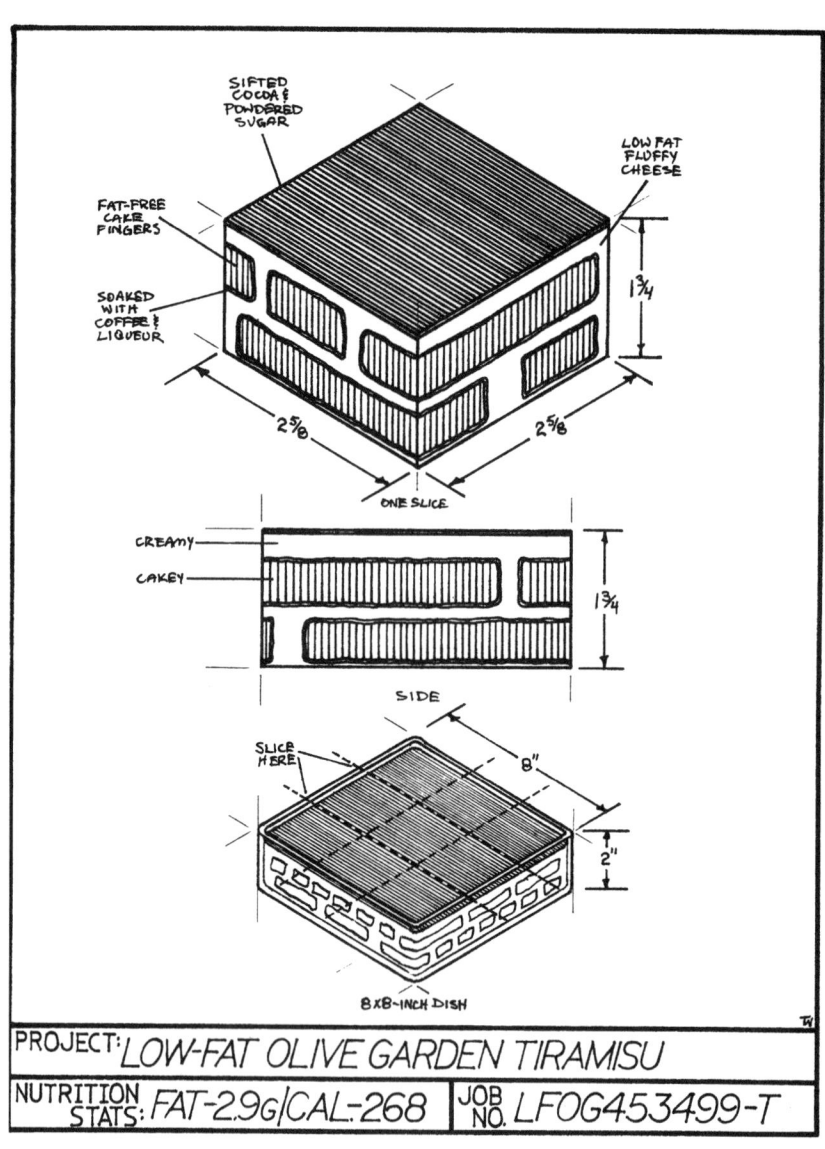

CAKE

1 Entenmann's fat-free
   Golden Loaf, or use recipe
   on p. 51
1 tablespoon instant coffee

¼ cup plus 2 tablespoons hot water
1 tablespoon sugar
2 tablespoons Kahlua Coffee
   Liqueur

FOR TOP
cocoa powder

1. For the fluffy cheese, measure 1 cup of milk, remove 3 tablespoons, and set the rest aside. In a small bowl, combine the 3 tablespoons of milk with the gelatin. Let the mixture sit for 5 to 10 minutes, then microwave on half power for 2 minutes, or until the gelatin dissolves. Set this mixture aside to cool for 15 minutes.
2. Pour the remaining milk into a large mixing bowl. Add one envelope of Dream Whip at a time to the milk and beat after each addition for about 2 minutes until the mixture is light and fluffy.
3. In a separate bowl, beat together the softened cream cheese and the sugar. Add the gelatin/milk mixture and beat until smooth.
4. While beating the Dream Whip on high speed, add $1/3$ of the cheese mixture at a time. Mix about 1 minute or until it is well-blended and smooth. Set aside while preparing the cake.
5. Cut the ends off the pound cake, then slice the remaining cake into 10 even slices. Discard the end pieces.
6. In a small bowl, mix the coffee with the hot water until the coffee dissolves. Add the sugar and stir until it dissolves as well. Add the Kahlua.
7. Cut each slice of cake into thirds (or in half, if using the recipe on p. 51), and arrange the slices on a wax paper–lined cookie sheet (rimmed to contain the liquid). Brush the coffee mixture generously over the top of each cake finger. Turn the fingers over and brush each once more with the coffee mixture.
8. To assemble the tiramisu, arrange the cake fingers side-by-side in an 8 x 8-inch baking dish. Leave about $1/4$-inch between the cake fingers. Cover the fingers with half of the fluffy cheese mixture and spread carefully with a spatula until smooth and flat. Arrange the remaining cake fingers on the cheese mixture the same way as the first layers. Cover the cake with the remaining cheese mixture and smooth.
9. Put a couple teaspoons of cocoa powder into a sieve and tap it

over the top of the tiramisu to dust it with a light, even coating of the cocoa. Cover the tiramisu and chill it for at least 3 hours so that it sets up. When you're ready to serve, slice it into 9 even squares.

- SERVES 9.

Nutritional Facts *(per serving)*

SERVING SIZE—1 SLICE   TOTAL SERVINGS—9 SLICES

	LITE	ORIGINAL
CALORIES (est.)	268	475
FAT (est.)	2.9G	38G

• • • •

TOP SECRET RECIPES REDUCED-FAT VERSION OF

OTIS SPUNKMEYER APPLE CINNAMON MUFFINS

So who is this Otis Spunkmeyer guy, anyway? Actually, it's no one at all. The character who flies around in the plane that's pictured on the product labels, searching the world for premium ingredients for his line of baked goods, is just a catchy name dreamed up by founder Ken Rawlings's 12-year-old daughter.

The company offers low-fat versions of many of its 11 varieties of muffins, but they are more difficult to track down than the original versions. So we've got a clone here that uses some tricks to replace a lot of the fat.

While this reduced-fat conversion clone recipe of the famous Texas-size muffins has 4 grams of fat per serving, or 8 grams total, it's still quite a saving compared to the original muffins, which have a total of 22 grams of fat each.

¾ cup sugar
⅔ cup unsweetened applesauce
¼ cup egg substitute
¼ cup vegetable oil
¾ teaspoon salt
½ teaspoon vanilla
1 teaspoon baking soda
½ cup low-fat buttermilk
   (1 percent fat)
2 cups all-purpose flour
2 teaspoons baking powder
2 teaspoons cinnamon
fat-free butter-flavored spray
⅓ cup brown sugar

1. Preheat the oven to 325 degrees.
2. In a large bowl, mix together the sugar, applesauce, egg substitute, oil, salt, vanilla, and baking soda. Add the buttermilk and blend.
3. In a separate bowl sift together the flour, baking powder, and cinnamon. Add the dry ingredients to the wet, and mix well with an electric mixer.
4. To bake the muffins, use a "Texas-size" muffin pan lined with large muffin cups. You may also bake the muffins without the cups, just be sure to grease the cups well with cooking spray. (If you use a regular-size muffin pan, which also works fine, your cooking time will be a few minutes less and your yield will double.) Fill the cups halfway with batter.
5. Spray a couple of squirts of fat-free butter-flavored spray over the top of each cup of batter. Follow that with a sprinkle of about 1 teaspoon of brown sugar.
6. Bake the muffins for 20 to 24 minutes or until brown on top (16 to 20 minutes for regular-size muffins). Remove the muffins from the oven and allow them to cool for about 30 minutes. Then put the muffins in a sealed container or resealable plastic bag.

- MAKES 8 TEXAS-SIZE MUFFINS (OR 16 REGULAR-SIZE MUFFINS).

Nutritional Facts (per serving)
SERVING SIZE—½ MUFFIN   TOTAL SERVINGS—16

	LITE	ORIGINAL
CALORIES	142	220
FAT	4G	11G

• • • •

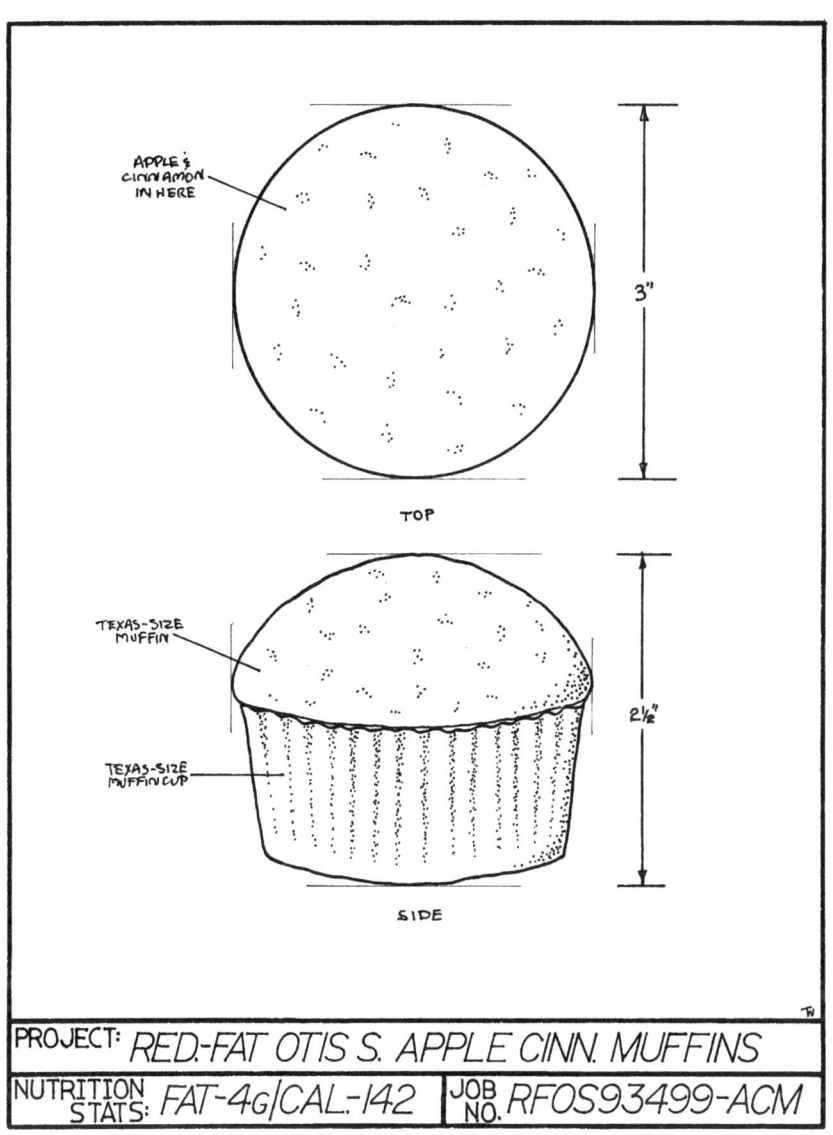

OTIS SPUNKMEYER BANANA NUT MUFFINS

TOP SECRET RECIPES REDUCED-FAT VERSION OF

Founder Ken Rawlings opened his first baked cookie store in San Francisco in 1977, and over the next five years the chain had grown to 22 stores throughout California. In 1990, after much success, Rawlings's Otis Spunkmeyer Company started selling Ready-to-Bake Cookie dough in grocery stores. That same year the company acquired a Modesto, California, muffin manufacturer, and Otis Spunkmeyer Muffins were born. Since then, the company has seen a 1200 percent increase in muffin sales, and today this is America's best-selling brand of muffins.

The banana-nut variety is my favorite, with 24 grams of fat per muffin. But we're in luck, because this product lends itself nicely to a reduced-fat clone. That banana is great for replacing the fat and helping to keep the muffin moist and flavorful. Even with a small amount of oil in there, and the walnuts on top, these tasty Texas-size dudes reduce the fat by more than one-half.

¾ cup sugar
⅔ cup mashed ripe banana
   (2 medium bananas)
¼ cup egg substitute
¼ cup vegetable oil
¾ teaspoon salt
½ teaspoon vanilla
¼ teaspoon banana extract

1 teaspoon baking soda
½ cup low-fat buttermilk
   (1 percent fat)
2 cups all-purpose flour
2 teaspoons baking powder
fat-free butter-flavored spray
¼ cup chopped walnuts

1. Preheat the oven to 325 degrees.
2. In a large bowl, mix together the sugar, mashed banana, egg substitute, oil, salt, vanilla, banana extract, and baking soda. Add the buttermilk and blend well.
3. In a separate bowl sift together the flour and baking powder. Add the dry ingredients to the wet and mix well with an electric mixer.
4. To bake the muffins, use a "Texas-size" muffin pan lined with large muffin cups. You may also bake the muffins without the cups, just be sure to grease the cups well with cooking spray. (If you use a regular size muffin pan, which also works fine, your cooking time will be a few minutes less and your yield will double.) Fill the cups halfway with batter.
5. Spray a couple of squirts of fat-free butter-flavored spray over the top of each cup of batter. Follow that with a sprinkle of about ½ tablespoon of chopped walnuts.
6. Bake the muffins for 20 to 24 minutes or until brown on top (16 to 20 minutes for regular-size muffins). Remove the muffins from the oven and allow them to cool for about 30 minutes. Then put the muffins in a sealed container or resealable plastic bag.

- MAKES 8 TEXAS-SIZE MUFFINS (OR 16 REGULAR-SIZE MUFFINS).

Nutritional Facts *(per serving)*
SERVING SIZE—½ MUFFIN   TOTAL SERVINGS—16

	LITE	ORIGINAL
CALORIES	147	240
FAT	5G	12G

• • • •

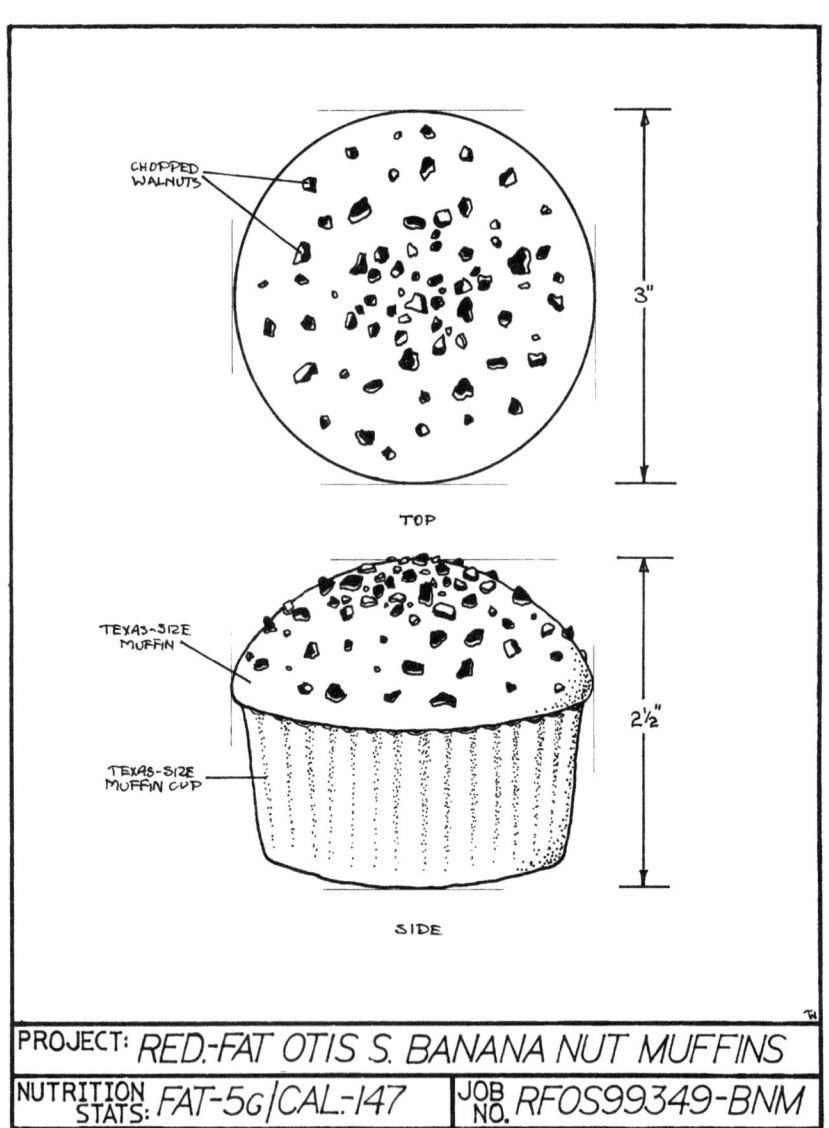

RED LOBSTER CHEDDAR BAY BISCUITS

The cheesy little biscuits that come with your meal at the country's largest seafood chain were first served in 1990 as a part of each entrée. According to a company spokesperson, it's the single item that the chain has now become best known for. It's estimated that in 1997 the chain served over 435 million of these puppies. And since it's the most requested recipe on the Internet and on the *topsecretrecipes.com* Web site, I figure it's time to satisfy those requests.

But, since this is a book of low-fat and reduced-fat recipes, and since each of those small biscuits has around 7 grams of fat, we're going to make this recipe unique. I'm going to show you how to make a delicious light version of this popular treat which tastes just as good as the original. The key is using reduced-fat Bisquick, as well as reduced-fat shredded cheddar cheese. This is an easy recipe to make, and these biscuits are scrumptious.

2 cups reduced-fat Bisquick baking mix
¾ cup low-fat buttermilk (1 percent fat)
1 cup reduced-fat shredded cheddar cheese
2 tablespoons Fleischmann's Fat-Free Buttery Spread
¼ teaspoon garlic powder
¼ teaspoon dried parsley flakes, crushed fine

1. Preheat the oven to 400 degrees.
2. Combine the baking mix, milk, and cheddar cheese in a medium bowl. Mix by hand until well combined.
3. Divide the dough into 12 equal portions (about 3 tablespoons each) and spoon onto a lightly greased or nonstick cookie sheet. Flatten each biscuit a bit with your fingers.
4. Bake for 18 to 20 minutes or until the tops of the biscuits begin to brown.
5. In a small bowl, combine the buttery spread with the garlic powder. Heat this mixture for 30 seconds in the microwave, then brush a light coating over the top of each biscuit immediately after removing them from the oven. Sprinkle a dash of parsley over the top of each biscuit.

- MAKES 12 BISCUITS

TIDBITS

To make fine parsley flakes, as can be found on the original, simply crush the flakes between your thumb and forefinger.

Nutritional Facts *(per serving)*
SERVING SIZE—1 BISCUIT   TOTAL SERVINGS—12

	LITE	ORIGINAL
CALORIES (est.)	112	130
FAT (est.)	3G	7G

• • • •

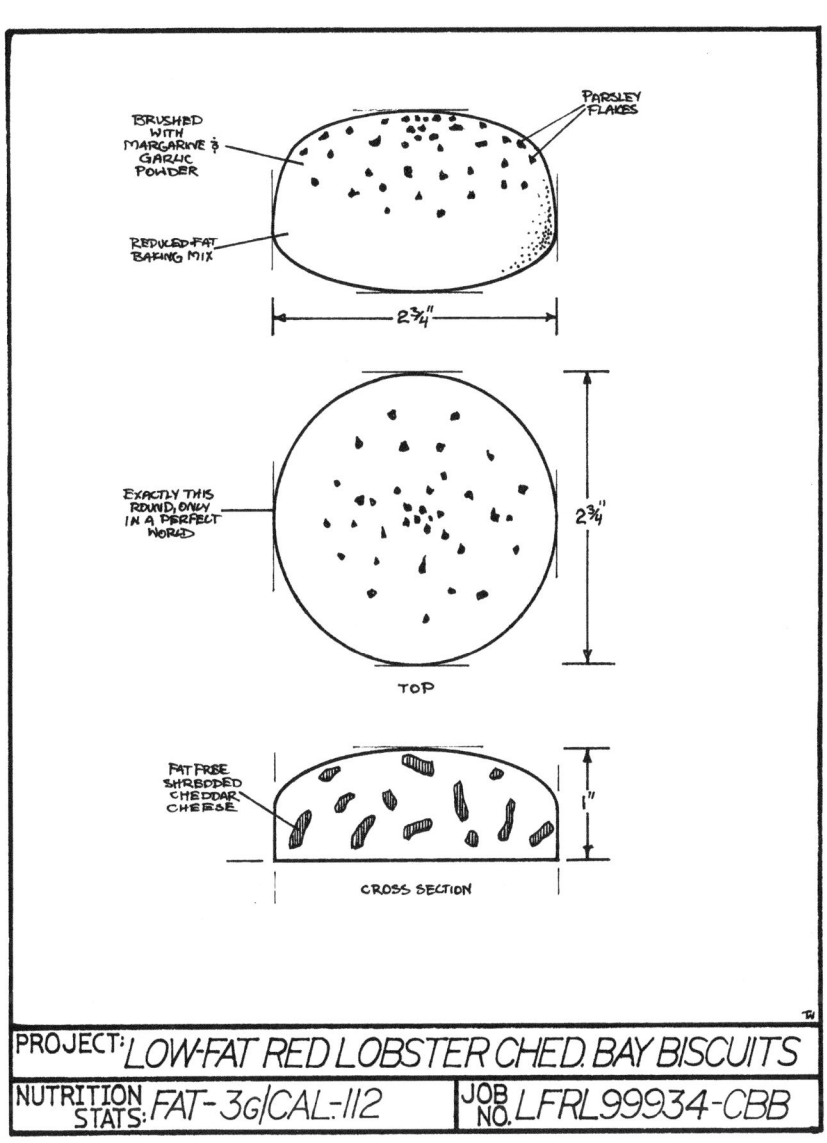

RED LOBSTER TARTAR SAUCE

Alongside your fish entrée served at this huge seafood chain, comes a dollop of delicious tartar sauce. But the sauce served at the restaurant has around 22 grams of fat per two tablespoons. This adds significant fat to an entrée that is otherwise so naturally light in fat and calories.

Using fat-free mayonnaise, we can easily eliminate every bit of the fat in this sauce. The finished product tastes just like the original.

½ cup fat-free mayonnaise
1 tablespoon finely minced onion
2 teaspoons shredded and chopped carrot (bits should be the size of rice)
2 teaspoons sweet pickle relish

Combine all the ingredients in a small bowl. Cover and chill until ready to serve.

- MAKES ½ CUP.

Nutritional Facts *(per serving)*
SERVING SIZE—2 TABLESPOONS   TOTAL SERVINGS—4

	LITE	ORIGINAL
CALORIES (est.)	25	200
FAT (est.)	0G	22G

• • • •

TOP SECRET RECIPES REDUCED-FAT VERSION OF

SHONEY'S HOT FUDGE CAKE

If you've ever laid your fork into one of these babies, you know how tough it is to take only a bite or two. Now you don't have to stop just as it's getting good. TSR drastically reduces the fat in this clone of the Shoney's creation with the help of reduced-fat devil's food cake mix and fat-free ice cream. Just be sure to get the type of ice cream that comes in a rectangular container, so that slicing and arranging the ice cream on the cake is made easier. Breyer's makes excellent fat-free vanilla ice cream and the container works well for this recipe. You may have some ice cream left over, which you can then eat with the small cake or cupcakes you can bake with the cup of leftover cake batter.

1 18.25-ounce box reduced-fat devil's food cake mix
1 1/3 cups water
2 tablespoons vegetable oil
3/4 cup egg substitute

1 half-gallon box fat-free ice cream (Breyer's is good)
1 16-ounce jar chocolate fudge topping
1 can whipped cream
12 maraschino cherries

1. Preheat the oven to 350 degrees.
2. Mix the batter for the cake as instructed on the box of the cake mix by combining the mix with the water, oil, and eggs in a large mixing bowl.
3. Remove a scant 1 cup of the batter from the bowl and set it aside, then add the remaining batter to a well-greased 9 x 13-inch baking pan. We won't be using the extra batter that

was set aside, so you can discard it or use it for another recipe, such as cupcakes.
4. Bake the cake according to the box instructions (about 30 minutes). Allow the cake to cool completely.
5. When the cake has cooled, carefully remove it from the pan and place it right side up onto a sheet of wax paper. With a long knife (a bread knife works great) slice the cake horizontally through the middle, and carefully remove the top. It helps to position the cake near the edge of your kitchen counter so that you can get a straight cut through the middle of the cake.
6. Pick up the wax paper with the bottom half of the cake still on it, and place it back into the baking pan.
7. Take the ice cream from the freezer and, working quickly, tear or cut the box open so that you can slice the ice cream like bread.
8. Make six ¾-inch slices of ice cream and arrange them side-by-side on the cake in the pan. Cover the entire surface of the cake with the ice cream slices. Fill in any gaps with additional ice cream. You may have about one-fifth of the ice cream left over in the box.
9. When you have covered the entire surface of the bottom cake half with ice cream slices, carefully place the top half of the cake, right side up, onto the ice cream in the pan. You should now have a layer of fat-free ice cream sandwiched between the two halves of reduced-fat cake. Cover the entire pan with plastic wrap or foil (trim the wax paper from the edges if necessary), and place the pan into your freezer for at least a couple of hours.
10. When you are ready to serve the dessert, slice the cake so that it will make 12 equal slices—that is, cut lengthwise twice and crosswise three times. If you will not be serving the entire desert, only slice what you will be using and save the rest, covered, in the freezer until you are ready to use it (it should keep for several weeks).
11. Heat up the fudge in the microwave or in a jar immersed in a saucepan of water over medium/low heat.

12. Pour about 2 tablespoons of fudge over the top of each slice of cake, and then add a small portion of whipped cream (about 2 tablespoons) on top of that.
13. Place a cherry onto the pile of whipped cream and serve immediately.

- SERVES 12.

Nutritional Facts *(per serving)*
SERVING SIZE—1 SLICE   TOTAL SERVINGS—12

	LITE	ORIGINAL
CALORIES	328	522
FAT	9.5G	20G

• • • •

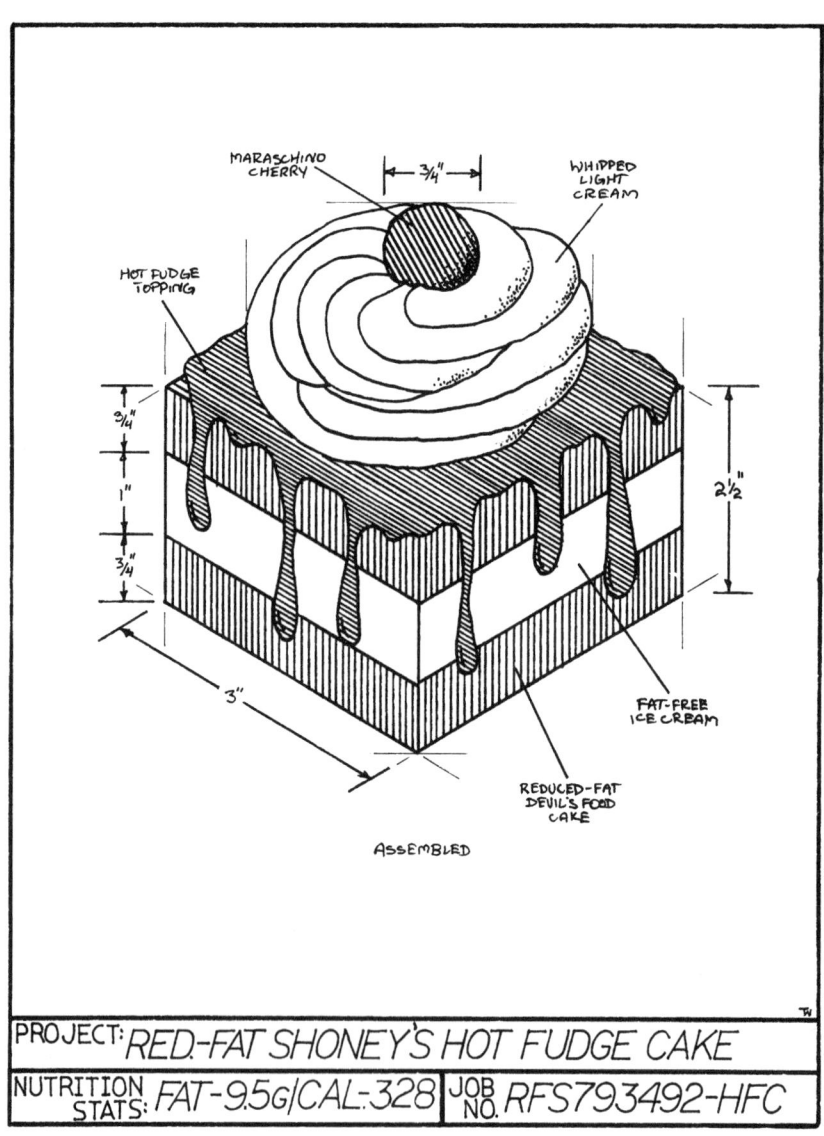

TOP SECRET RECIPES REDUCED-FAT VERSION OF

SHONEY'S COUNTRY FRIED STEAK

Okay, you got me. This TSR version of one of Shoney's most popular country-style items is not really fried. If it were, it surely wouldn't have nearly one-fourth the fat of the original, which you can order at any of the 900 restaurants that make up this mostly Southern U.S. chain. But you'll swear this version tastes like the original, because we still bread the steak, and then spray it with a light coating of cooking spray. Once it's baked, then broiled to a golden brown, the steak is smothered with very low-fat gravy. Check out how these low-fat cooking tricks used here make a country steak that's just as good as the fried version.

1 cup all-purpose flour
½ tablespoon salt
⅛ teaspoon pepper

1 cup fat-free milk
4 4-ounce cube steaks

LOW-FAT COUNTRY GRAVY
1 ½ tablespoons super-lean ground beef (7 percent fat)
heaping ⅓ cup all-purpose flour
2 cups fat-free chicken stock

2 cups fat-free milk
½ teaspoon salt
¼ teaspoon pepper

vegetable oil cooking spray

1. Preheat the oven to 425 degrees.
2. Combine the flour, salt, and pepper in a large shallow bowl.
3. Pour the milk into another shallow bowl.

4. Trim the cube steaks of any fat and press down firmly with the heel of your hand to flatten the steaks.
5. Coat each steak with the flour mixture, then put each into the bowl of milk, and back into the flour mixture, coating well. Arrange the steaks on a large plate and pop 'em into the refrigerator to chill for 10 minutes, while you begin the gravy.
6. Prepare the gravy by browning the 1½ tablespoons of super-lean ground beef in a small skillet over medium heat. Crumble the meat into tiny pieces as you cook it.
7. Transfer the browned meat into a medium saucepan. Add ¼ cup of flour to the pan and stir it in with the meat. Add the remaining ingredients for the gravy except the cooking spray, whisk to combine, turn the heat to high, and bring the mixture to a boil, stirring often. Reduce the heat and simmer the mixture for 15 to 20 minutes until thick. Turn the heat to low to keep the gravy hot as the steaks are prepared.
8. Spray a cooking sheet generously with the cooking spray and arrange the floured steaks side-by-side on the cooking sheet. Spray the top surface of the meat with a coating of the cooking spray and place the steaks into the oven to bake for 5 to 7 minutes.
9. Crank the oven up to broil and cook the steaks for 7 minutes, flip each one over, then broil for an additional 5 to 7 minutes or until the surface of the steaks is browned.
10. Serve the steaks with gravy poured over the top, with a side of mashed potatoes, grits, or steamed vegetables, if desired.

Nutritional Facts (per serving)

SERVING SIZE—1 STEAK   TOTAL SERVINGS—4

	LITE	ORIGINAL
CALORIES	260	563
FAT	10G	37G

• • • •

TOP SECRET RECIPES LOW-FAT VERSION OF

TACO BELL BEEF SOFT TACO

Yo quiero low-fat Taco Bell? Apparently not when faced with a choice. It took only one year for Taco Bell execs to cut the eight-item Border Lights selection from the Taco Bell menu in 1996. Those items, which featured several different taco and burrito selections, were made with reduced-fat ingredients. But, as other fast food companies discovered with their own discontinued light products, customers who roll into the drive-thrus aren't interested lower fat offerings. That is their time of the week to bite into something filled with flavor and just enjoy.

On the other hand, when we cook at home, and want to clone the flavor of food like that served at Taco Bell, it takes no extra effort to make the meal significantly lower in fat. So why not give this delicious recipe a go? And you'll soon find out these tacos will taste just like the soft tacos you get from the world's largest Mexican food chain, but with only one-quarter of the fat.

½ pound super-lean ground beef (7 percent fat)
2 tablespoons all-purpose flour
¾ teaspoon salt
¼ teaspoon dried minced onion
¼ teaspoon paprika
1 ½ teaspoons chili powder
dash garlic powder

dash onion powder
¼ cup water
5 6-inch fat-free flour tortillas
½ cup plus 2 tablespoons shredded iceberg lettuce
5 tablespoons fat-free shredded cheddar cheese

1. In a medium bowl combine the super-lean ground beef with the flour, salt, minced onion, paprika, chili powder, garlic powder, and onion powder. Use your hands to thoroughly incorporate everything into the ground beef.
2. Preheat a skillet over medium/low heat and add the ground beef mixture to the pan along with the water. Brown the beef mixture for 5 to 6 minutes, using a wooden spoon or spatula to break up the beef as it cooks.
3. Using the microwave, heat up the fat-free flour tortillas wrapped in a moist cloth or paper towels, or use a tortilla steamer. Heat for 25 to 30 seconds, or until hot.
4. Spoon about 3 tablespoons of the beef mixture into the center of one tortilla.
5. Place about 2 tablespoons of shredded lettuce on top of the beef.
6. Finish the soft taco by spreading about a tablespoon of shredded cheese over the lettuce and fold. Repeat for the remaining tacos.

- MAKES 5 SOFT TACOS.

Nutritional Facts *(per serving)*

SERVING SIZE—1 TACO   TOTAL SERVINGS—5

	LITE	ORIGINAL
CALORIES	170	225
FAT	3G	12G

• • • •

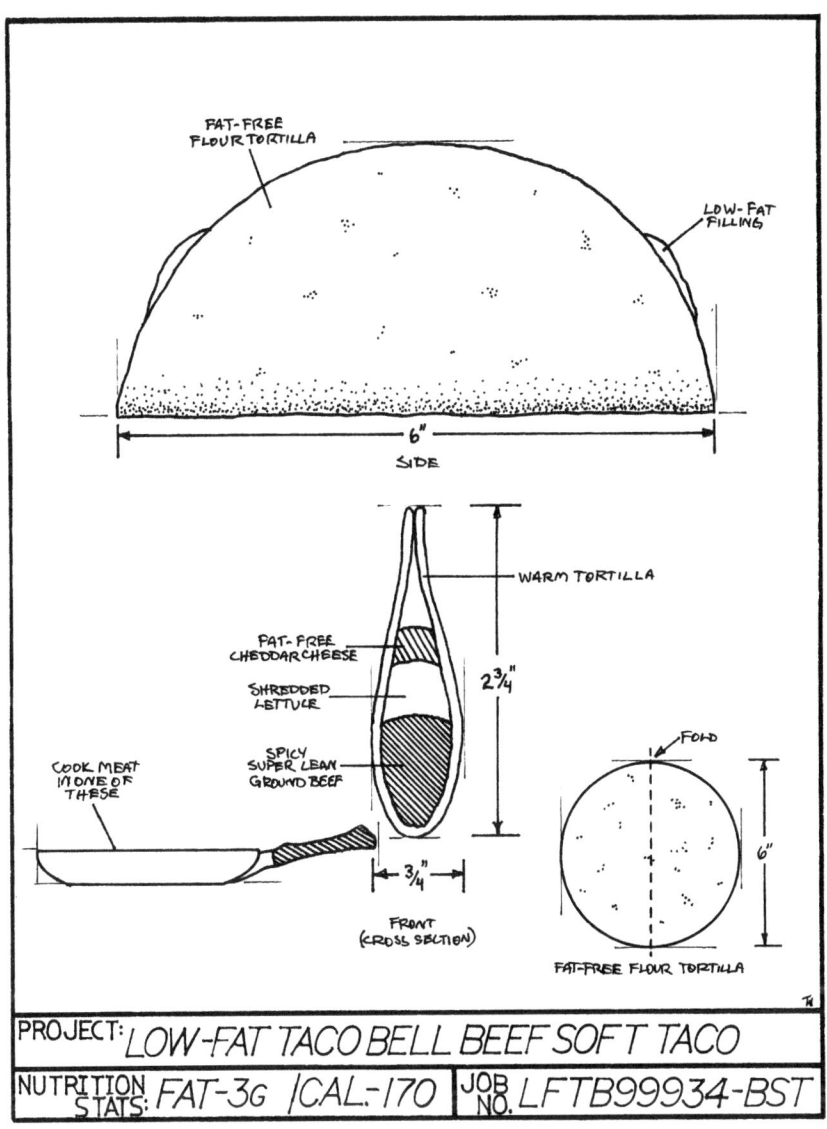

TOP SECRET RECIPES REDUCED-FAT VERSION OF

TACO BELL GRILLED CHICKEN BURRITO

When Glen Bell opened the first Taco Bell in 1962, he probably never envisioned that one day he would see his name on more than 10,000 locations serving his special brand of Americanized Mexican fast food. He probably also didn't expect there would one day be a book that would show you how to get significant fat savings when creating a low-fat kitchen clone of this popular menu item—around 80 percent less fat than the real thing!

You'll want to start this one several hours before, or even the day before you plan to eat it, so that the chicken can properly marinate.

MARINADE

½ cup water
1 teaspoon soy sauce
1 teaspoon salt
1 teaspoon brown sugar

½ teaspoon onion powder
¼ teaspoon liquid smoke
¼ teaspoon black pepper
¼ teaspoon chili powder

2 chicken breast fillets
1 cup instant rice
1 cup water
½ cup mild enchilada sauce
½ teaspoon salt

4 12-inch fat-free flour tortillas
⅓ cup fat-free shredded cheddar cheese
⅓ cup reduced-fat shredded Monterey Jack cheese

1. In a small bowl combine the ½ cup water, soy sauce, salt, brown sugar, onion powder, liquid smoke, black pepper, and chili powder. Pour the mixture over the chicken breasts and

marinate overnight. You can marinate for less time if you wish, but overnight is much better.
2. Cook the chicken on your barbecue or indoor grill over medium/high heat for 5 to 6 minutes per side, or until done. Slice the chicken into bite-size chunks.
3. While the chicken cooks, prepare the rice following the instructions on the box. It will probably tell you to bring the water to a boil, then add the rice, stir, cover, remove from the heat, and let it sit for 5 minutes.
4. When the rice is cooked, add the enchilada sauce and salt to the saucepan. Put the rice over low heat, uncovered, and cook until hot.
5. Heat the tortillas in a steamer, or wrap them in moist towels and heat on high for 25 to 30 seconds in the microwave.
6. Build a burrito by spreading ¼ of the chicken down the middle of one of the tortillas. Leave room at the ends for folding.
7. Spread ⅓ cup of rice over the chicken.
8. Sprinkle a heaping tablespoon of each of the cheeses over the rice.
9. Fold the left side of the tortilla over the filling, then fold up the bottom of the tortilla. Finish the burrito by folding the right side over and serve hot. Repeat for the remaining burritos. You may want to heat up each burrito in the microwave for 20 to 30 seconds to help the cheeses melt.

- MAKES 4 BURRITOS.

Nutritional Facts *(per serving)*
SERVING SIZE—1 BURRITO   TOTAL SERVINGS—4

	LITE	ORIGINAL
CALORIES	157	400
FAT	5G	16G

• • • •

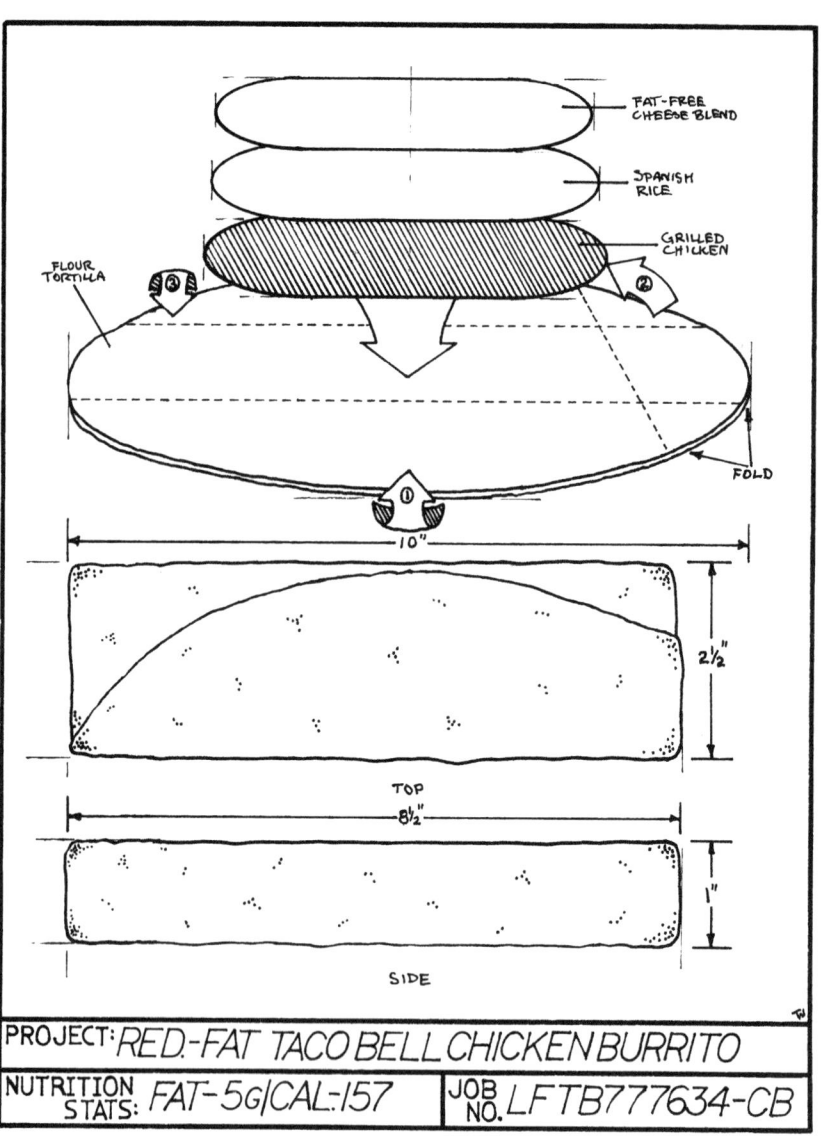

TOP SECRET RECIPES REDUCED-FAT VERSION OF

TACO BELL MEXICAN PIZZA

You probably didn't realize that these delicious pizzas you get from the world's largest Mexican food chain have 36 grams of fat. But they are good, and if you like 'em as much as I do, you'll be happy to know that you can make a version of your own at home with only 10 grams of fat.

The secret fat savings come from baking, rather than frying, the flour tortillas. You'll also adios much of the fat by using reduced-fat cheddar and jack cheeses. I picked reduced-fat for these, because the fat-free stuff does not melt well in the final baking step for the finished pizza.

½ pound super-lean ground beef (7 percent fat)
2 tablespoons all-purpose flour
¾ teaspoon salt
¼ teaspoon dried minced onion
¼ teaspoon paprika
1 ½ teaspoons chili powder
dash garlic powder
dash onion powder
¼ cup water
8 6-inch fat-free flour tortillas

vegetable oil nonstick cooking spray
1 ⅓ cups fat-free refried beans
⅔ cup mild Picante salsa
½ cup reduced-fat shredded cheddar cheese
½ cup reduced-fat shredded Monterey Jack cheese
1 medium tomato, diced
¼ cup chopped green onions

1. Preheat the oven to 375 degrees.
2. In a medium bowl combine the super-lean ground beef with

the flour, salt, minced onion, paprika, chili powder, garlic powder, and onion powder. Use your hands to thoroughly incorporate everything into the ground beef.
3. Preheat a skillet over medium/low heat and add the ground beef mixture to the pan along with the water. Brown the beef mixture for 5 to 6 minutes, using a wooden spoon or spatula to break up the meat as it cooks.
4. Spray both sides of each tortilla with a light coating of oil cooking spray. Place the tortillas onto baking sheets and bake for 10 to 12 minutes or until the tortillas are crispy and golden brown. Turn them over halfway through the cooking time, and pop any air bubbles if the tortillas begin to inflate. Keep the oven hot.
5. Heat up the refried beans in a small saucepan over medium/low heat, or in the microwave for 2 to 3 minutes, or until hot.
6. Assemble each pizza by first spreading about ⅓ cup of refried beans on the face of a tortilla.
7. Spread one-quarter of the meat over the beans.
8. Place on another tortilla, sandwiching the meat and beans between the two tortillas.
9. Coat the top tortilla with about two tablespoons of salsa.
10. Mix the two cheeses together and sprinkle about ½ cup over the top of the pizza.
11. Put a heaping tablespoon of diced tomato on next.
12. Garnish the pizza with green onion. Repeat the process with the remaining ingredients.
13. Bake the pizzas on a baking sheet for 8 to 12 minutes or until the cheese on top is melted.
14. Cut each pizza into quarters and serve hot.

- MAKES 4 PIZZAS.

Nutritional Facts (per serving)
SERVING SIZE—1 PIZZA   TOTAL SERVINGS—4

	LITE	ORIGINAL
CALORIES	427	570
FAT	10G	36G

• • • •

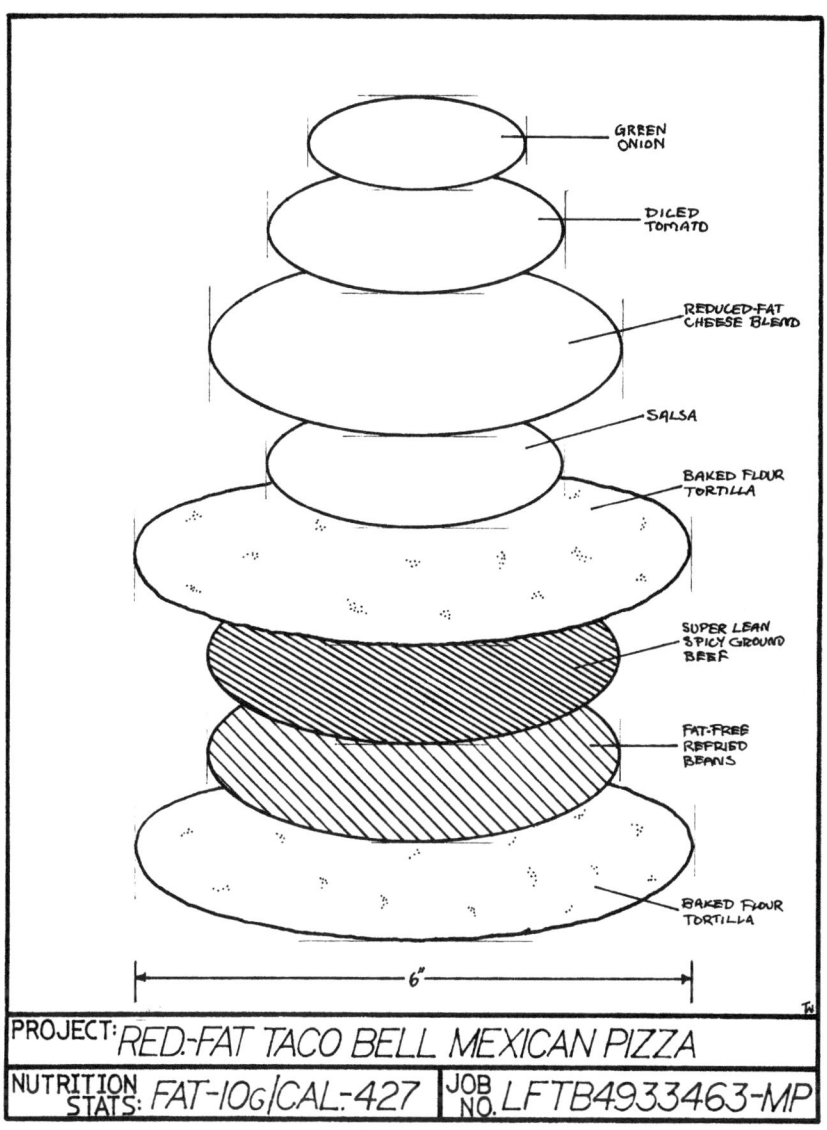

TOP SECRET RECIPES REDUCED-FAT VERSION OF

WENDY'S SINGLE WITH CHEESE

Over 5,000 Wendy's restaurants around the world serve the hamburger with the unique square patty that hangs over the edge of the bun. It's the burger that inspired the 1984 award-winning ad campaign that had a little old lady crying out, "Where's the beef?" With this secret recipe to create a lower-fat clone of the famous burger, the question is now, "Where's the fat?" By using super-lean ground beef, fat-free mayonnaise, and fat-free cheese, we have cut the fat to less than half of what is found in the original. Now you can have two cloned burgers for less than the fat found in one original.

1 plain hamburger bun
1/4 pound super-lean ground beef (7 percent fat)
salt
pepper
1 teaspoon ketchup
1/2 tablespoon fat-free mayonnaise
1 slice fat-free American cheese
1/2 teaspoon yellow mustard
1 lettuce leaf
2 to 3 separated onion slices
1 large tomato slice
3 dill pickle slices

1. Brown the faces of the bun in a large frying pan over medium heat. Keep the pan hot.
2. On wax paper, shape the ground beef into an approximately 4 x 4-inch square. You may find it easier to freeze the patty ahead of time, so that it doesn't fall apart when cooking. Don't defrost.
3. Cook the burger in the pan for 3 to 5 minutes per side, or until done. Salt and pepper both sides during the cooking.

4. Spread the ketchup and then the mayonnaise on the top bun.
5. Put the cooked patty on the bottom bun. On top of the meat, lay the slice of cheese.
6. Spread the mustard on the cheese, then place the lettuce, onion, tomato, and pickles on, in that order.
7. Complete the sandwich with the top bun and microwave the whole thing for 15 to 20 seconds to warm it up.

- SERVES 1.

Nutritional Facts *(per serving)*
SERVING SIZE—1 SANDWICH   TOTAL SERVINGS—1

	LITE	ORIGINAL
CALORIES (est.)	335	420
FAT (approx.)	10G	21G

• • • •

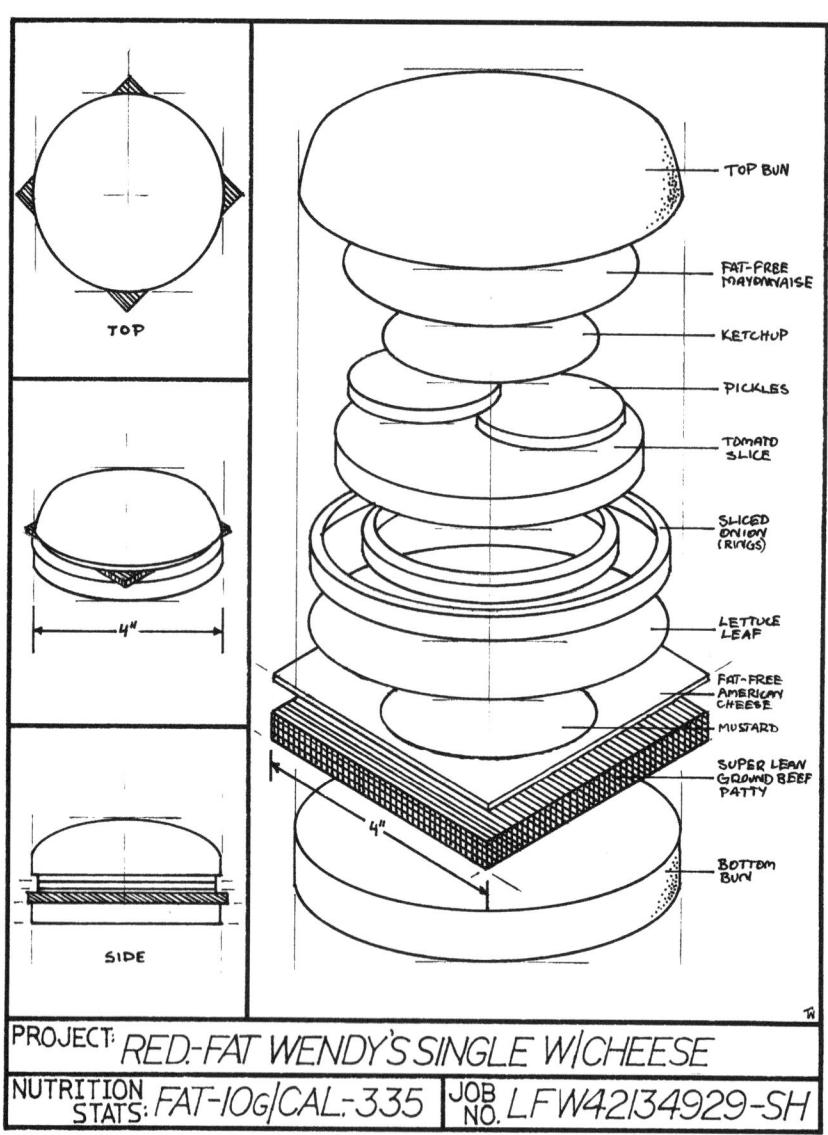

WENDY'S FROSTY

Over 22 million gallons of this frozen chocolate dessert are served at Wendy's each year.

To make a version of this tasty treat at home that reduces the fat by around 75 percent, you will just need some fat-free vanilla ice cream, Nestlé Quik, and low-fat milk. Oh yeah, and a blender.

¾ cup low-fat milk (2 percent)
3 tablespoons Nestlé Quik
4 cups fat-free vanilla ice cream

1. Combine all of the ingredients in a blender. Blend on medium speed until creamy. Stir if necessary.
2. If too thin, freeze the mixture in the blender or in cups until thicker.

- Makes 2 drinks.

Nutritional Facts (per serving)
Serving size—1 16-ounce dessert
Total servings—2

	Lite	Original
Calories	470	440
Fat	2g	11g

• • • •

TOP SECRET RECIPES REDUCED-FAT VERSION OF

WHITE CASTLE CHEESEBURGERS

Some may call them "whitey one-bites." They're also known as "sliders," "gut busters," and "belly bombers." This 300-unit Midwestern hamburger chain celebrated its 75th anniversary in 1996 without much of a peep, and the company continues to stay impressively profitable despite its low-key marketing. The cooking technique is unique to the chain, because it involves steaming the ground beef patties. The minced onions are placed on the grill, with a beef patty on top. The steam from the grilling onions rises up through the five holes in each thin, square patty, allowing thorough cooking without having to flip the meat over.

Now you can use the same method, but with reduced-fat ingredients, to cook a reduced-fat version of one of the country's oldest burger creations.

1 pound super-lean ground beef (7 percent fat)
16 dinner rolls
½ small onion, minced
salt
pepper
16 slices fat-free American cheese

1. Prepare the patties by separating the ground beef into 16 1-ounce portions. On a sheet of wax paper, form the portions into square, very thin, 2½-inch patties. Using a small, circular object, such as a straw or the tip of a clean pen cap, create five holes in each patty. Make one hole in the center of the patty,

and four holes surrounding the first one, with each about half an inch in from each corner. Freeze these patties, still on the wax paper, until firm.
2. Toast the faces of the dinner rolls, either in a hot frying pan over medium heat, or under the oven broiler.
3. In a hot frying pan or skillet preheated over medium heat, arrange tablespoon-size piles of onions, 3 inches apart. Salt and pepper each pile of onions.
4. Spread the onions flat, and then place a frozen beef patty on each pile of onions. Salt each patty.
5. Cook each burger for 4 to 6 minutes. If you made the patties thin enough, steam from the onions will rise around the meat and through the holes in the patty, cooking the meat thoroughly without having to flip it.
6. To build each burger, turn the bottom half of a dinner roll over onto a patty, then hold it down as you scoop a spatula under the meat and onions, and turn the sandwich over onto a plate.
7. Cut a slice of American cheese into 2-inch-square portions and place a square onto the onions on the beef patty.
8. Complete the burger with the top half of the roll. Repeat with the remaining burgers, and serve hot.

- MAKES 16 BURGERS.

Nutritional Facts *(per serving)*
SERVING SIZE—2 BURGERS   TOTAL SERVINGS—8

	LITE	ORIGINAL
CALORIES	310	310
FAT	5G	17G

• • • •

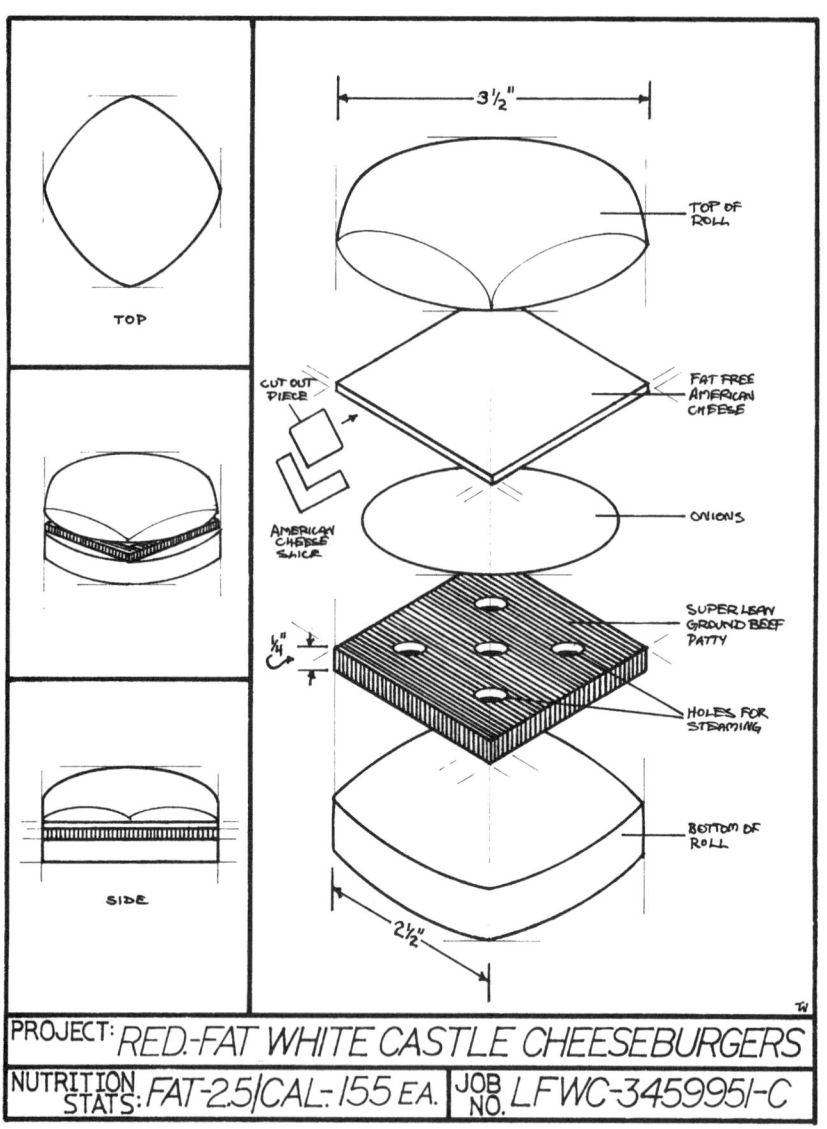

LOW-FAT TOP SECRET RECIPES

GUEST INTRODUCTION

A Word From Fat Gram Freddy

To all you beautiful people, I extend a greasy "hello," and my most heartfelt plea. My name is Fat Gram Freddy, and I am exactly one gram of pure, glistening fat. I slide onto these pages before you as the spokesfat for trillions and trillions of others just like me who can no longer congeal idly by as our kind succumb in great numbers to all the senseless digestion. For many years it appeared you were on the right track. But I'm afraid that a recent about-face is returning us to the days when a fat gram's existence is in a constant and tragic state of jeopardy.

Todd has been kind enough to allow me an open forum here in his new low-fat *Top Secret Recipes* cookbook to urge for a return to discretion in the consumption of my fatty brethren. He has allowed me to speak freely and has promised not to edit these thoughts—the first recorded words ever to be penned by a modestly handsome gram of fat—as long as I attempt to stay concise, reasonably polite, and off his new couch.

I assure you that I'm literate. I'm sincere. And, yes, I do wonders for fettucine alfredo and chicken wings. I'm told I make a lot of sense when I focus, so please read carefully these words I write.

Look, I know you like me ... you really like me. None of us can deny that fact. But just because I feel so good slipping over your tongue and down into the dark depths of your throat doesn't mean that my friends and I should be ingested in such massive amounts with every single snack and meal. Why not have an apple the next time that acid-filled torture chamber you people call a stomach begins its terrifying growl? I hear that the broccoli and tomatoes are fantastic this year. Heck, we've always stayed away from those wonderful foods unless you invite us. That's just how we are.

We fat grams have shared a lot of joy in the past decade as most of you worked hard to consume products created with little or none of us. We rejoiced in the early '90s as this trend encouraged manufacturers to go nuts creating entire product lines of scrumptious low-fat meals and fat-free snacks. It was beautiful! This helped many of us to survive, uneaten, for long periods of time.

But the dark clouds formed once again as the millennium came to a close. Toward the end of the '90s, low-fat food sales began to slump, and now my slippery amigos are once again disappearing at an alarming rate.

This tragic turn has left us all in a state of panic. I'm afraid that one day, very soon now, it'll be time for yours truly to take the one-way drive down Digestive Tract Highway. That is why I am now appealing to you for help ... by merely helping yourselves.

HOW IT ALL WENT DOWN

I remember like it was yesterday. Right after your second big war, I watched in terror as buddies of mine got slathered on toast, glopped over salads, smeared over pizza, and dolloped onto desserts in numbers that would make your fork spin.

Turns out you indulged in rich, creamy foods without any regard for content or consequence. Your average consumption of fat at this ghastly time reached 40 percent of calories. That's one of the highest percentages in history. It looked like you folks were on some kind of wild, self-destructive tear.

What you didn't realize was that all the fat grams you were sucking down couldn't just sit back and take the absorption without exacting a devious revenge with their dying breath. As you snarfed on my fellow fat boys, they went to work from the inside, raising your cholesterol, attacking your arteries, and making you all flabby and swollen. The deadly chain reaction that followed was devastating to your life support system. We were at war, and our troops were required to use cruel, desperate measures. With each choked artery and every seized heart we claimed another victory.

This battle raged on in your inner space for many years, until you were finally tipped off to our clandestine scheme.

In the '60s, the intelligence officers you call "doctors" detected our internal attack and sent out the alarm. You had no choice but to cut back on the massive consumption of my compadres by propagating a campaign to reduce the intake of fat in the American diet. Lower-fat dairy products were introduced and lean meat hit your grocery stores. For us, it was a glorious time; yet only a momentary victory.

Through the next several decades you worked hard to create edibles of all kinds, containing fewer of my kind. This trend escalated in the '90s as companies with names such as Nabisco, ConAgra, Quaker Oats, Keebler, Weight Watchers, Hostess, and Hershey had the heart to give you munchies that didn't rely on fat grams to appeal to that slimy, bud-covered muscle in your cavernous pie holes.

We thought that this change in your eating habits signaled the end of our fight for survival. What we failed to notice over the years, however, was the sedentary lifestyle you humans had been creating for yourselves. Homes were made to be more comfortable. Cars clogged up the roadways. Television, movies, and video games were developing into multibillion-dollar industries that required—even encouraged—an increasing amount of inactivity. Fat or no fat, this was the recipe for your doom. Yet you were still placing the blame on us.

Recently I took it upon my oily self to do a little research, and I found that in 1986 the census bureau determined that 52 percent of Americans were fat. This bloated condition—which you curiously named after us—would continue to spread through the years, even though record numbers of low-fat and fat-free products had been distributed amongst you.

As 1998 rolled around, the percentage was up. The bulges

affected an astounding 68 percent of you, with 22 percent referred to as "obese." Using a simple spreadsheet, I ran these figures through my laptop and came up with a shocking projection: If this rate continues, 100 percent of you will be obese by the year 2230!

So what's happening? Is it that you thought the low-fat and fat-free labels on all those products gave you the freedom to gorge? Your U.S. Department of Agriculture checked out the average American diet and found that even with the abundance of lower-fat products on store shelves the total amount of fat in most diets in the late 90s was the same as in the 60s, and in some cases even went up. And according to the USDA, total caloric intake was increasing, mostly from sugar and carbohydrates. Oh, and booze. Apparently eating lots of lower-fat food makes you want to get a buzz on.

I checked out Michael Fumento's book, *The Fat of the Land,* and he says the new lower-fat foods are so boring that many of you figure, like whales inhaling krill, that if you eat enough of it, somewhere in there might be a tasty morsel. You were often disappointed with what you fished out.

When you switched to lower-fat products and experienced no weight loss, you figured the food was to blame. You may have given no regard to the increased amount of low-fat foods you consumed or to the decrease in your weight-shedding activity. You decided that eating foods less appealing to the palate was pointless, so you happily returned back to mowing down the fat grams. Except now the food was chased with a good dose of guilt and regret.

Friends, this is no way for you to live. That is why Fat Gram Freddy has come to the rescue.

THE SOLUTION—
FROM A FAT GRAM WHO CARES

Yes indeed, 1998 was a dark year for fat grams everywhere. This was the year that food manufacturers attempted to revive sluggish sales of lower-fat products by putting more of us fat grams back in. Manufacturers realized that since you folks didn't see any weight-loss effects from eating the fat-free stuff, you started reevaluating your purchases. You figured if the weight loss never kicked in, you might as well return to a more stimulating eating experience.

The flavorlessness of many fat-free and low-fat products turned off consumers who decided that they would rather purchase products with moderate fat reduction or no fat reduction at all. Sure, I'll admit that some of that low-fat stuff tastes worse than the box it's packed in, but there are plenty of others out there that taste great. And improved products are still unveiled as manufacturers learn new, tasty, fat-saving tricks in the test kitchens.

But is it too late? My biggest fear is that most of you are tired of wasting money trying to figure out which lower-fat foods taste good and which don't. You aren't interested in playing the supermarket crapshoot, even when the food is not at the core of the problem.

The real problem, according to this other book I read called *The Skinny on Fat,* is that we have become a sedentary society. One-quarter of Americans are slugs. Too many of you make a habit of planting yourself in front of the television with salty snacks and plates of food, getting up only to replenish the rations or expel them.

In *The Skinny on Fat*, Shawna Vogel says, "Watching TV slows down a person's metabolism to the point where they expend less energy than if they were doing nothing at all. Television, through its advertisements, can also increase the amount people eat while they're watching. And if eating in front of the TV is common, then it can become a conditioned stimulus to eat."

According to *U.S. News & World Report*, only 15 percent of you get enough heart-strengthening aerobic exercise to live a long, healthy life. With work and family pressures and such easy access to engaging yet passive entertainment, you rarely make exercise a number-one priority.

Everyone in the know seems to be in agreement. When you exercise, or at least make an effort to participate in some sort of activity that hoists you off the posterior, you feel better about yourself and tend to eat better. Next time, perhaps you'll park your car a few blocks from your destination and walk, or maybe you can take the stairs once in while rather than the elevator. When you feel better about yourself, you'll be more likely to leave us fat grams alone.

And remember this: Diets rarely work. Don't even put that pressure on yourself. It's been shown over and over again that when dieters deny themselves the food they love to eat, it has a negative emotional impact. Sure, a few pounds may be shed early on, but there's usually a relapse on the horizon that will bring back those lost pounds and then some. A University of Toronto psychologist discovered that people rarely get fat from going on binges, but rather binge because they have been depriving themselves on a restrictive diet.

That cool Shawna Vogel book I mentioned earlier cites the fact that diet programs like Jenny Craig and Nutri/System have seen revenues plunge in recent years because "too much emphasis has been placed on restriction dieting and weight loss as the keys to health and not enough on activity, weight maintenance and metabolic fitness."

I realize I'm no picture of health—I'm made of pure fat for God's sake, so I think I have a pretty good excuse—but food and dieting is my business; it's all I know. And all I'm hearing lately is that you've got to get into a little activity each and every day. Or at least thirty minutes of exercise three or four times a week. Get over the obsession with dieting and thinness and have a burger once in a while if you like. It's not going to kill you. Then for other meals you can get back to fat-free and low-fat products, and eat those in moderation, too. Eat the kind of stuff made from this book, so that you will enjoy the experience. That's why Todd put it here.

WHY THIS BOOK ROCKS

From what Todd has shown me, this book proves that reduced-fat food doesn't have to taste like cardboard. The recipes here create the type of food you would love to eat with less fat and more taste. It's the kind of stuff that satisfies your taste buds by replacing fat with other carefully crafted ingredients. My buddies and I like that.

With this book you'll discover tricks for mixing up fat-free dressings using pectin and cornstarch. And a way to bake chicken so that it has a deep-fried texture and no skin. You'll also discover Todd's unique technique for using the microwave to make a fat-free cookie filling that looks and tastes just like the stuff inside an Oreo.

You'll notice that Todd's divided the book into two sections: "Clones," for re-creating kitchen copies of your favorite foods that are already low in fat grams, such as Nabisco Honey Maid Grahams, Gardenburgers, and SnackWell's products. And "Conversions," for creating reduced-fat clones of your normally fat-filled favorites, such as Chili's Southwestern Eggrolls, Wendy's Spicy Chicken Sandwich, and McDonald's Egg McMuffin. These conversions will let you enjoy the taste of your favorite products for which reduced-fat versions don't exist in stores. And just about all of these recipes cut fat from the real thing by at least half, sometimes by much more than that. To help you keep track, you'll find fat and calories counted at the bottom of each recipe.

I know that you can never entirely give up eating us fat grams. I understand that you need me and my kind in your diet to survive. Your huge bodies require the vitamins and fatty acids that we provide. But just because a package of cookies says "reduced fat" on the label doesn't mean you can eat a half a bag a day. There are still a lot of us little fellers in a quadruple-serving nosh fest. Not to mention a ton of those other guys, the calories.

Don't lose confidence that low-fat food can help you maintain a great physique when enjoyed in reasonable amounts. But remember that weight loss or maintenance cannot be realized in diet alone.

I speak for fat grams everywhere when I say that we will very much appreciate your efforts to return to eating lower-fat foods. When you're at the grocery store, please grab for the packages with the green "low-fat" labels again, and give those products another chance.

Better yet, when you have a craving for the oral sensation of a food that bursts with fat grams, open the pages of this fine book and satisfy your palate with some reduced-fat clones. The food will quell your craving, and your efforts will be rewarded. The process of cooking this food and shopping for the ingredients will keep you off the sofa. And that's a good thing.

Ladies and gentlemen, this is my message. It's a simple one. Eat more of the stuff on these pages ... and eat less of me. It's for your own good, and mine.

I'm a fat gram. I know what I'm talking about.

Thank you.

—Fat Gram Freddy

P.S. Todd wants me to remind you that you can find tons of additional secret clone recipes on his free Web site at:

http://www.topsecretrecipes.com

You can even contact him with suggestions for other recipes to clone at:

Todd@topsecretrecipes.com

Tell him Fat Gram Freddy sent you.

LOW-FAT TOP SECRET RECIPES CLONES

TOP SECRET RECIPES VERSION OF

APPLEBEE'S LOW-FAT ASIAN CHICKEN SALAD

My new diet plan is called the Chopsticks Diet. It requires that you use only chopsticks to eat everything: spaghetti, peas, hamburgers, cookies, ice cream, salads—whatever. As the food slips off the chopsticks, the pounds slip off of you. It's especially effective if you've never used chopsticks before. For those who can use them well, you've got to switch to the other hand. If you're Asian, you're only allowed to use one.

As the seasons change, so does the menu at this popular, casual, restaurant chain. You'll find this item in the "Low-Fat and Fabulous" column of the menu during the summer months where it's been a favorite since 1997. As with any salad, the waistline violator is the traditionally fat-filled dressing that is drizzled in gobs over the top of very healthy greens (a tablespoon of dressing usually contains around ten to twelve grams of fat). So if we can just figure out a cool way to make the dressing fat-free, we're well on our way to making a huge salad—four of them to be exact—with only twelve grams of fat on each plate. Most of those grams come from the chicken breast, and the crunchy chow mein noodles pick up the rest.

Just be sure to plan ahead when you make this one. The chicken should marinate for a few hours if you want it to taste like the original. Hope you're hungry.

1 cup teriyaki marinade   4 skinless chicken breast fillets

FAT-FREE ASIAN DRESSING

2 cups water
½ cup granulated sugar
3 tablespoons dry pectin
1 tablespoon white vinegar
½ teaspoon soy sauce

1 teaspoon salt
¼ teaspoon garlic powder
¼ teaspoon ground black pepper
¼ teaspoon paprika

8 cups chopped romaine lettuce
8 cups chopped iceberg lettuce
3 cups shredded red cabbage
3 cups shredded green cabbage
2 cups shredded carrots
1 cup chopped green onion
1 ⅓ cups crispy chow mein noodles

1. Combine teriyaki marinade and chicken breasts in a medium bowl or resealable plastic bag. Marinate chicken for 3 to 4 hours.
2. Prepare the dressing by combining all of the ingredients in a small saucepan over medium heat. Bring mixture to a rolling boil while stirring often with a whisk, then remove the pan from the heat to cool. When the dressing has cooled, pour it into a covered container and chill.
3. When chicken breasts have marinated, preheat barbecue grill to high heat. Grill chicken for 3 to 4 minutes per side or until done.
4. Combine the romaine and iceberg lettuce, red and green cabbage, and 1 cup of shredded carrots in a large bowl with the dressing. Toss well.
5. Divide the tossed greens among four plates. Sprinkle ¼ cup of green onions over each salad, followed by ⅓ cup of crispy chow mein noodles.
6. When the chicken breasts are done, slice each one, widthwise, into bite-size pieces. Sprinkle the sliced chicken breasts over each salad.
7. Place a ¼-cup pile of shredded carrots in the center of each salad.

- SERVES 4 AS AN ENTRÉE.

Nutrition Facts

SERVING SIZE—1 SALAD
TOTAL SERVINGS—4
FAT (PER SERVING)—12 G
CALORIES (PER SERVING)—575

• • • •

TOP SECRET RECIPES VERSION OF
APPLEBEE'S LOW-FAT & FABULOUS BROWNIE SUNDAE

The Applebee's chain is now the world's largest casual dining restaurant, with over one thousand units in seven countries and forty-eight states. In less than four years, the chain has doubled in size. That's great if you're a restaurant chain, but put enough fat-filled desserts in your belly, and you'll double in size, too.

That's why we're happy to see items like this one on the menu. It tastes like a decadent, guilty pleasure, but it actually contains only four grams of fat per serving. This is possible because the brownie "pie" is made in a special way using a combination of low-fat and fat-free chocolates, some egg whites, and just a bit of shortening. Grab yourself some fat-free frozen yogurt, and share this one with eight hungry friends.

LOW-FAT BROWNIE

2 egg whites
¾ cup granulated sugar
2 tablespoons shortening
½ cup Hershey's chocolate syrup
½ cup fudge topping
¼ cup warm water

1 teaspoon vanilla
1½ cups all-purpose flour
¼ cup cocoa
¾ teaspoon salt
¼ teaspoon baking soda
2 teaspoons chopped walnuts

9 scoops fat-free vanilla frozen yogurt

chocolate syrup, heated

1. Preheat oven to 350 degrees.
2. Make the brownie cake by whipping the egg whites in a large bowl (not plastic) with an electric mixer until they become thick.
3. Add the sugar to the egg whites and continue beating until the mixture forms soft peaks.
4. To the egg white and sugar mixture, add the shortening, chocolate syrup, fudge, water, and vanilla.
5. In a separate bowl, combine the flour, cocoa, salt, and baking soda.
6. While beating the wet mixture, slowly add the dry mixture and mix until smooth.
7. Lightly grease a 9-inch pie pan with shortening. Pour the brownie batter into the pan and sprinkle the chopped walnuts over the top. Bake for 35 minutes or until a toothpick poked into the center comes out clean.
8. When the brownie pie has cooled a bit, slice it into 9 equal pie-shaped portions.
9. Arrange a slice of the low-fat brownie pie on a plate next to a scoop of vanilla frozen yogurt.
10. Drizzle the warmed chocolate sauce over the top of the brownie and frozen yogurt, and serve.

- MAKES 9 DESSERTS.

Nutrition Facts

SERVING SIZE—1 DESSERT
TOTAL SERVINGS—9
FAT (PER SERVING)—4 G
CALORIES (PER SERVING)—424

• • • •

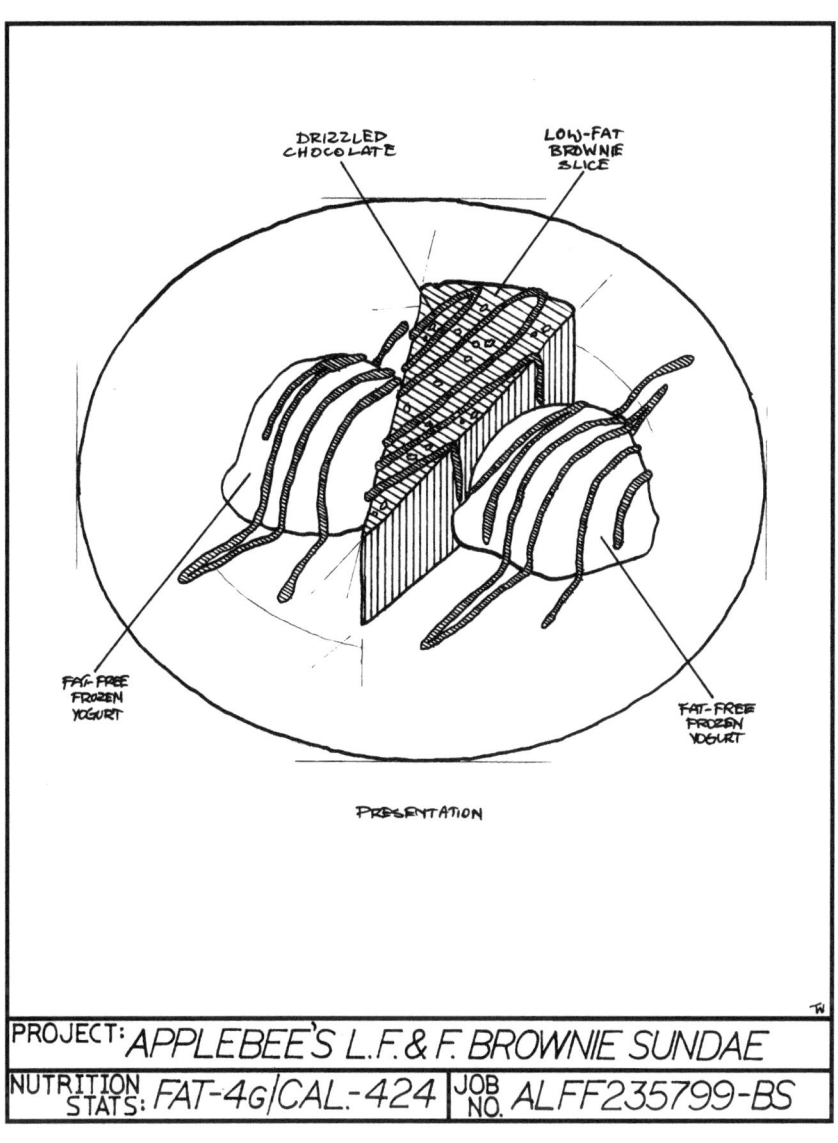

TOP SECRET RECIPES VERSION OF

CALIFORNIA PIZZA KITCHEN TUSCAN HUMMUS

Nowhere could I find the "Tuscan white bean," or any mention of it in research materials. But there it is in the California Pizza Kitchen menu description for this delicious hummus. Could this just be the chain's fancy way of describing garbanzo beans, otherwise known as chickpeas? After all, garbanzos are the only beans used for any traditional hummus recipe, and they seemed to work perfectly in this low-fat re-creation of the chain's tasty appetizer. Just be sure you have a good food processor to puree all the ingredients. If you have trouble finding sesame tahini in your supermarket, check out your local health food store. And while you're there, see if you can spot those Tuscan white beans.

1 15-ounce can garbanzo beans (strain and keep ¼ cup of liquid)
¼ cup liquid from the can
¼ cup fresh lemon juice
3 tablespoons sesame tahini
2 teaspoons minced garlic

1 teaspoon granulated sugar
¾ teaspoon white pepper
½ teaspoon salt
¼ teaspoon cumin
⅛ teaspoon cayenne pepper
⅛ teaspoon paprika

OPTIONAL GARNISH
2 tablespoons chopped Roma tomatoes
pinch fresh basil
pinch chopped fresh garlic

ON THE SIDE
warm pita bread slices

1. Dump the entire contents of the can of garbanzo beans into a strainer set over a bowl. Let the beans sit for a little while so that all of the liquid drips into the bowl.
2. Dump the beans and ¼ cup of the liquid from the bowl into a food processor.
3. Add the remaining ingredients to the food processor, and puree the mixture until completely smooth—about a minute or so.
4. Spoon the hummus into a covered container and chill for at least 2 hours so that the flavors can develop. When serving, you may wish to garnish the hummus with a couple tablespoons of chopped Roma tomatoes mixed with a dash of chopped fresh basil and garlic. Serve with warm, sliced pita bread or your choice of chips or crackers.

- MAKES 1¾ CUPS.

Nutrition Facts
SERVING SIZE—2 TABLESPOONS   FAT (PER SERVING)—2.5 G
TOTAL SERVINGS—14   CALORIES (PER SERVING)—48

• • • •

TOP SECRET RECIPES VERSION OF

CALIFORNIA PIZZA KITCHEN DAKOTA SMASHED PEA & BARLEY SOUP

Got one of those cool hand blenders? You know, the kind of gadget that used to be pitched on those annoying yet compelling late-night infomercials? It comes in handy for this recipe, which requires the split peas to be smashed into a smooth consistency, just like the original. If you don't have a hand mixer, a standard blender works just fine. This soup is very tasty and very low in fat. And the barley gives it a special chunky consistency and added flavor that aren't found in most pea soups. If you want to go even lower in fat, use fat-free chicken broth instead of the regular stuff, then run in place with a can in each hand to burn some extra calories.

2 cups split peas
6 cups water
2 14½-ounce cans chicken broth (4 cups)
⅓ cup minced onion
1 large clove garlic, minced
2 teaspoons lemon juice
1 teaspoon salt
1 teaspoon granulated sugar

¼ teaspoon dried parsley
⅛ teaspoon white pepper
dash dried thyme
½ cup barley
6 cups water
2 medium carrots, diced (about 1 cup)
½ stalk celery (¼ cup)

GARNISH
chopped green onion

1. Rinse and drain the split peas, then add them to a large pot with 6 cups of water, chicken broth, onion, garlic, lemon juice, salt, sugar, parsley, pepper, and thyme. Bring to a boil, then reduce heat and simmer for 75 to 90 minutes or until the peas are soft and the soup is thick.
2. While the peas are cooking, combine the barley with 6 cups of water, carrots, and celery in a saucepan. Bring to a boil, then reduce heat and also simmer for 75 to 90 minutes or until the barley is soft and most of the water has been absorbed.
3. When the split pea mixture has become a thick soup, use a handheld blender to puree the peas until the mixture is smooth. You may also use a standard blender or food processor for this step, pureeing the soup in batches. Alternately, if you like, you may skip this step, keeping the soup rather chunky. It's still good, just not as smooth as the real thing.
4. Drain the barley mixture in a sieve or colander and add it to the split pea mixture. Continue to simmer for about 15 minutes, stirring occasionally. Turn off the heat, cover the soup, and let it sit for 15 minutes before serving.

- MAKES 8 CUPS.

Nutrition Facts
SERVING SIZE—2 CUPS
TOTAL SERVINGS—4
FAT (PER SERVING)—3 G
CALORIES (PER SERVING)—450

TOP SECRET RECIPES VERSION OF

CALIFORNIA PIZZA KITCHEN GRILLED EGGPLANT CHEESELESS PIZZA

When PepsiCo shelled out $100 million for a 67 percent share of the trendy pizza chain back in 1992, founders Lawrence Flax and Richard Rosenfield thought they had it made. Unfortunately, the company behind Pizza Hut found expanding the more upscale eatery an unfamiliar struggle. The company expanded too quickly (Planet Hollywood, anyone?), and as costs began to dwarf sales figures, fresh ingredients were replaced with cheaper frozen products. Customers noticed, and sales took a nosedive. By 1996, PepsiCo decided to bail.

The following year, PepsiCo's share of the chain was picked up by New York investment firm Rosser, Sherrill & Co. Fresh ingredients returned to the kitchens, and the size of the pizzas was increased without adjusting the price. Sales once again blossomed, and the chain was on its way back to turning its first profit since 1991.

Here's a great pizza to clone if you need to take a little time off from delicious-yet-fat-filled mozzarella cheese. With the marinated, grilled eggplant and tasty honey-wheat dough, you won't even miss that gooey white stuff. Be sure to start this one a day before you plan to eat it. The dough needs that long to rise in the fridge for just the right California Pizza Kitchen–like consistency.

HONEY-WHEAT DOUGH

⅓ cup plus 1 tablespoon warm water (105 to 115 degrees F)
1 tablespoon honey
¾ teaspoon yeast
⅔ cup bread flour
⅓ cup whole wheat flour
½ teaspoon salt
½ tablespoon olive oil

TOPPING

1 ½ tablespoons soy sauce
1 tablespoon olive oil
⅛ teaspoon cayenne pepper
⅛ teaspoon garlic powder
⅛ teaspoon cumin
½ eggplant, sliced lengthwise ¼ inch thick
¼ medium red onion, sliced into thin rings (about ½ cup)
1 teaspoon minced fresh cilantro
1 ½ to 2 cups fresh spinach, chopped into thin strips
⅓ cup reconstituted sun-dried tomatoes,* sliced into strips

OPTIONAL

fat-free vinaigrette

1. Prepare the pizza dough by combining the water with the honey and yeast in a small bowl or measuring cup. Stir until the yeast is dissolved, then let the mixture sit for 5 minutes until the surface turns foamy. (If it doesn't foam, either the yeast was too old or the water was too hot. Try again.) Sift the flours and salt together in a medium bowl. Make a depression in the flour and pour the olive oil and yeast mixture into it. Use a fork or spoon to stir the liquid, gradually drawing in more flour as you stir, until all the ingredients are combined. At this point you will have to use your hands to blend the dough until it is smooth and to form it into a ball. Knead the dough with the heels of your hands on a lightly floured surface for 10 minutes or until the texture of the dough is smooth and elastic. Form the dough back into a ball, coat it lightly with oil, and place it into a clean bowl covered with plastic wrap. Keep the dough in a warm place for about 2 hours to allow the dough to double in size. Punch the dough

*Heat a couple cups of water to boiling in the microwave. Add 6 to 8 sun-dried tomato slices to the water and let them sit for about ½ hour. Remove the slices and drain on paper towels until you need them.

down and put it back into the covered bowl and back into the refrigerator overnight. Take the dough from the refrigerator 1 to 2 hours before you plan to build the pizza so that the dough can warm up to room temperature.
2. When you're ready to make your pizza, preheat the oven to 500 degrees. If you have a pizza stone, now's the time to use it.
3. Preheat barbecue grill to high temperature.
4. Combine the soy sauce with 1 tablespoon of olive oil, cayenne pepper, garlic powder, and cumin in a small bowl.
5. Brush the entire surface of each eggplant slice with this soy sauce mixture. Make sure you have some left over.
6. Grill the eggplant slices for 2 to 3 minutes per side, then remove them from the grill to cool.
7. On a lightly floured surface, form the pizza dough into a circle with an approximately 10-inch diameter. Be sure to form a lip around the edge.
8. Brush the top surface of the pizza dough with the remaining soy sauce mixture.
9. Arrange the red onion slices over the pizza dough.
10. The eggplant slices go on the pizza next, then toss the pizza into the oven on a pizza pan, or directly onto a pizza stone. Bake for 10 to 12 minutes or until the crust is light brown and crispy. Pop any bubbles in the crust that may form as the pizza bakes.
11. Remove the pizza from the oven and sprinkle cilantro over the top.
12. Slice the pizza into 6 even slices with a sharp pizza wheel.
13. Sprinkle the thinly chopped spinach over the top of the pizza.
14. Sprinkle the sun-dried tomato strips over the top.
15. Serve pizza with the optional vinaigrette on the side.

- MAKES 1 10-INCH PIZZA.

Nutrition Facts

SERVING SIZE—3 SLICES FAT (PER SERVING)—8 G
TOTAL SERVINGS—2 CALORIES (PER SERVING)—380

• • •

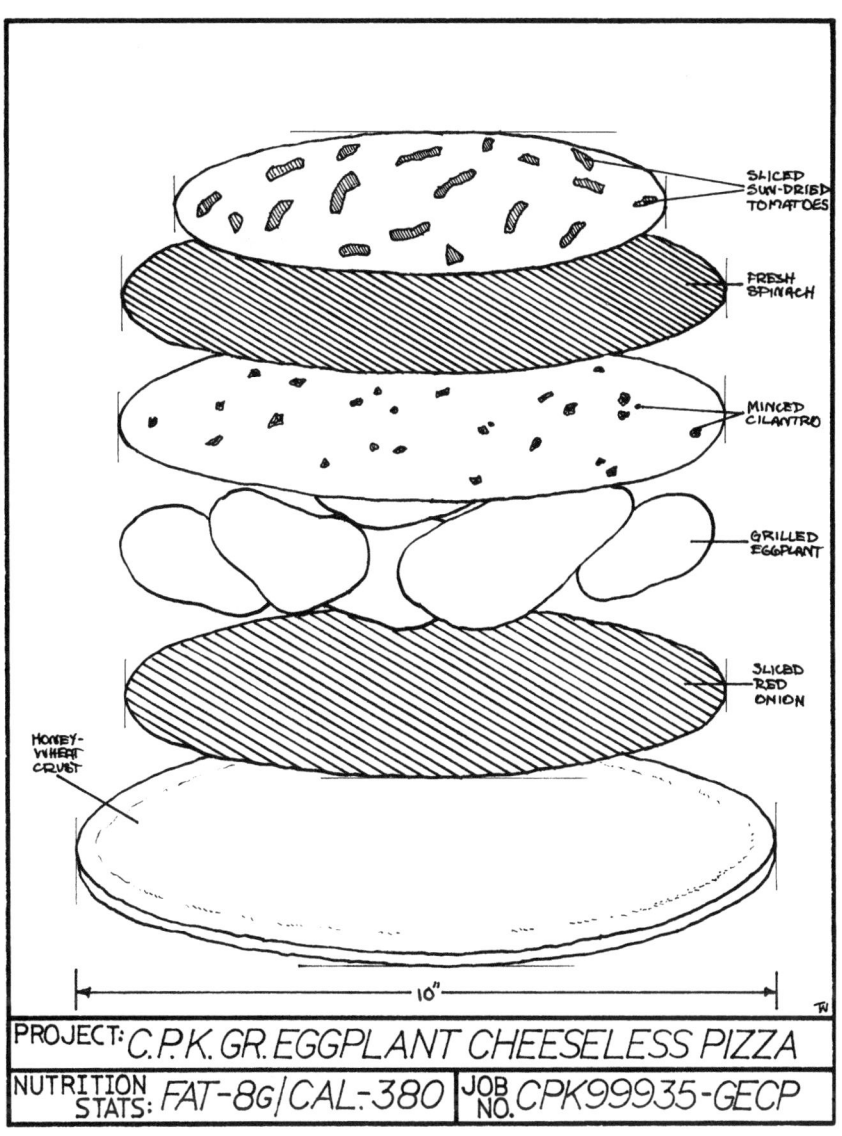

TOP SECRET RECIPES VERSION OF

CALIFORNIA PIZZA KITCHEN VEGETARIAN PIZZA

Who needs to cook with animal parts when you can make a pizza taste like this? It's grilled veggies and mozzarella cheese stacked on a great clone for the chain's tasty honey-wheat dough. With regular mozzarella cheese, the total fat for three slices comes in at around nineteen grams, which is still much less than you'd get from, say, the pepperoni-topped variety (tipping the scales at about fifteen grams *per slice*). Just remember to prepare your dough a day before you plan to make the pizza. This way you'll get the best consistency in the final product. And one heck of a better clone.

HONEY-WHEAT DOUGH

- 1/3 cup plus 1 tablespoon warm water (105 to 115 degrees F)
- 1 tablespoon honey
- 3/4 teaspoon yeast
- 2/3 cup bread flour
- 1/3 cup whole wheat flour
- 1/2 teaspoon salt
- 1/2 tablespoon olive oil

SAUCE

- 1 teaspoon olive oil
- 1 tablespoon minced white onion
- 1 clove garlic, minced
- 1 tomato, chopped
- 1 15-ounce can tomato sauce
- 2 teaspoons granulated sugar
- 1/4 teaspoon dried oregano
- 1/4 teaspoon dried basil
- 1/4 teaspoon salt
- 1/8 teaspoon dried thyme
- dash ground black pepper

1 ½ tablespoons soy sauce
1 tablespoon olive oil
⅛ teaspoon cayenne pepper
⅛ teaspoon garlic powder
⅛ teaspoon cumin
½ eggplant, sliced lengthwise ¼ inch thick
1 cup shredded mozzarella cheese

¾ cup mushrooms, sliced thin (2 to 3 mushrooms)
⅓ medium onion, sliced into thin rings (about ⅔ cup)
⅓ cup reconstituted sun-dried tomatoes,* sliced into strips
1 ½ cups steamed broccoli florets (bite-size)
1 teaspoon minced fresh oregano

1. Prepare the pizza dough by following step #1 from page 257.
2. When you are ready to make the pizza, preheat oven to 500 degrees. Use a pizza stone if you have one.
3. Prepare the sauce by first heating the olive oil over medium heat in a medium saucepan. Sauté the onion and garlic for 1 minute in the oil. Add the tomato and sauté for an additional minute before adding the remaining sauce ingredients to the pan. Bring the sauce to a boil, then reduce heat and simmer for 20 to 30 minutes, or until thicker. Cover the sauce until it is needed.
4. Preheat barbecue grill to high temperature.
5. Combine the soy sauce with 1 tablespoon olive oil, cayenne pepper, garlic powder, and cumin in a small bowl.
6. Brush the entire surface of the eggplant with the soy sauce mixture. Grill the eggplant slices for 2 to 3 minutes per side, then remove the slices from the heat and set them aside until they are needed.
7. On a lightly floured surface, form the pizza dough into a circle that is approximately 10 inches across.
8. Spread about ½ cup of the sauce evenly over the surface of the dough.
9. Arrange the grilled eggplant on the pizza, then sprinkle the cheese evenly over the top of the eggplant.

*Heat a couple cups of water to boiling in the microwave. Add 6 to 8 sun-dried tomato slices to the water and let them sit for about ½ hour. Remove and drain the slices on paper towels until you need them.

10. Next sprinkle the mushrooms onto the pizza, followed by the onion slices.
11. Sprinkle the sun-dried tomato slices on the pizza, followed by the broccoli florets.
12. Bake the pizza for 10 to 12 minutes or until the crust is light brown and the cheese begins to bubble. Pop any bubbles in the crust that may form as the pizza bakes.
13. Remove the pizza from the oven and sprinkle the fresh oregano over the top. Use a pizza wheel to slice the pizza into 6 pieces and serve.

- MAKES 1 10-INCH PIZZA.

Nutrition Facts

SERVING SIZE—3 SLICES
TOTAL SERVINGS—2
FAT (PER SERVING)—19 G
CALORIES (PER SERVING)—632

• • • •

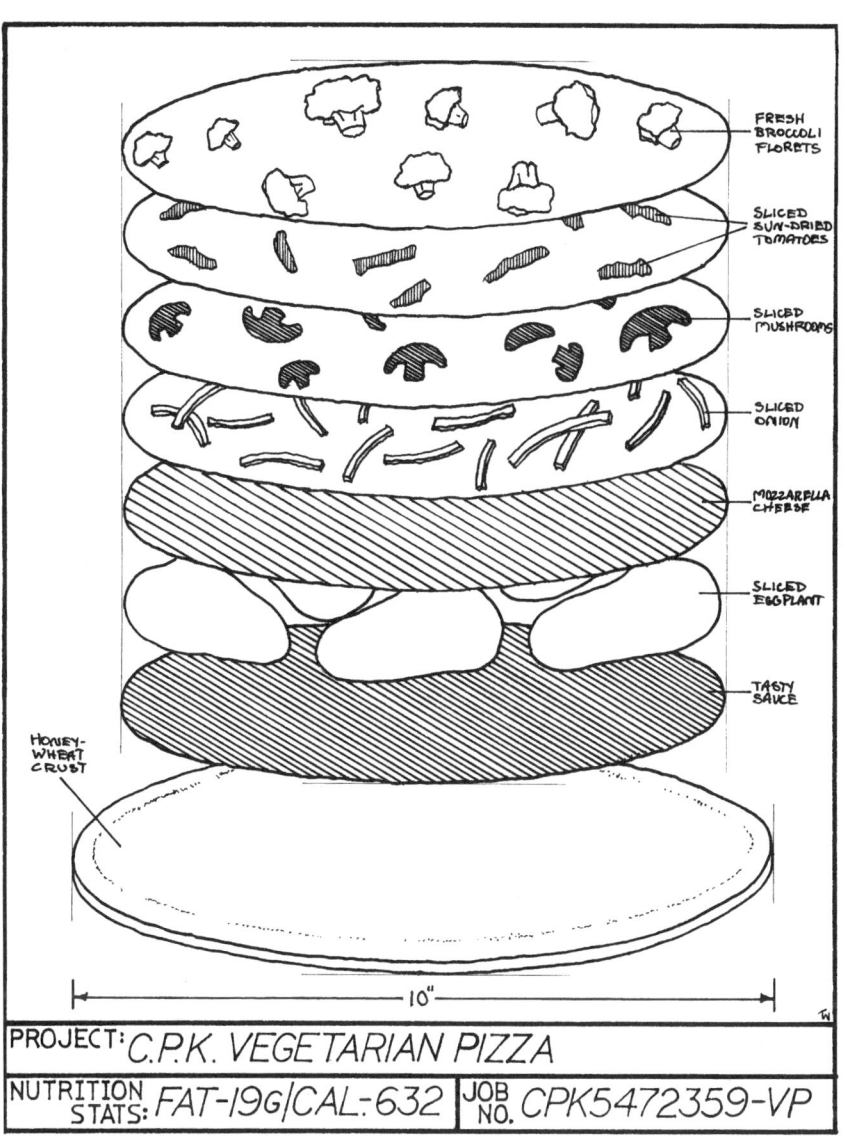

CHEVYS FRESH SALSA

TOP SECRET RECIPES VERSION OF

Chevys's concept of Fresh Mex® has made it one of the best Mexican restaurant chains in the country. You won't find any cans of food in the kitchen since every item on the menu is made daily with fresh ingredients. The restaurant claims it makes its heart-shaped tortillas each day, and this delicious, smoky salsa every hour. You can certainly taste that freshness in the salsa, along with the unique mesquite flavors that come from the restaurant's mesquite-fire grill.

For this clone you won't need a mesquite grill, just some mesquite liquid smoke flavoring and a hot barbecue grill. Oh, and you'll also need a food processor to get the right consistency. The original contains chipotle peppers, which is just another name for smoked red jalapeños. But if you get tired of hunting for the red jalapeños in your local supermarkets, just grab the green ones. They'll work fine. You'll need a total of ten peppers, which may seem like a lot, but their heat is tamed considerably when you grill 'em.

6 medium tomatoes
olive oil
10 jalapeños (red is best)
¼ medium Spanish
    onion
2 cloves garlic

2 tablespoons chopped fresh
    cilantro
2 teaspoons salt
2 tablespoons white vinegar
1 ½ teaspoons mesquite-flavored
    liquid smoke

1. Preheat your barbecue grill to high temperature.
2. Remove any stems from the tomatoes, then rub some oil

over each tomato. You can leave the stems on the jalapeños for now.
3. Place the tomatoes on the grill when it's hot. After about 10 minutes, place all of the jalapeños onto the grill. In about 10 minutes you can turn the tomatoes and the peppers. When nearly the entire surface of the peppers has charred black, you can remove them from the grill. The tomatoes will turn black partially, but when the skin begins to come off they're done. Put the peppers and tomatoes on a plate and let them cool.
4. When the tomatoes and peppers have cooled, remove most of the skin from the tomatoes and place them into a food processor. Pinch the stem off the end of the peppers and place them into the food processor as well. Don't include the liquid left on the plate. Toss that out.
5. Add the remaining ingredients to the food processor and puree on high speed for 5 to 10 seconds or until the mixture has a smooth consistency.
6. Place the salsa into a covered container and chill for several hours or overnight while the flavors develop.

- MAKES 2 CUPS.

Nutrition Facts
SERVING SIZE—2 TABLESPOONS   FAT (PER SERVING)—0 G
TOTAL SERVINGS—16   CALORIES (PER SERVING)—10

• • •

TOP SECRET RECIPES VERSION OF

ENTENMANN'S LIGHT LOW-FAT CINNAMON RAISIN SWEET ROLLS

Entenmann's was one of the first on the block to throw irresistible, low-fat versions of its delicious baked goods in front of us at the supermarket. The company's specialty is its low-fat sweet cinnamon rolls that taste as good as any of the full-fat varieties produced by other established brands. These rolls are so good that I'm presenting clones for two varieties. This recipe is for the smaller of the two and includes raisins for those of you who like shriveled grapes in your pastry. If you want bigger cinnamon rolls sans the mini prunes, check out the next recipe.

ROLLS
2 teaspoons yeast
1/2 cup warm water
1/4 cup granulated sugar
1 2/3 cups bread flour
1/2 teaspoon baking powder
1/4 teaspoon salt
2 tablespoons shortening, melted
3 tablespoons egg substitute

FILLING
1/4 cup fat-free butter-flavored spread
1/3 cup light brown sugar
2 tablespoons Wondra flour
2 teaspoons cinnamon
1/4 cup raisins

ICING
1/2 cup powdered sugar
2 tablespoons fat-free cream cheese
couple drops vanilla extract
dash salt

1. Dissolve the yeast in the warm water. When the yeast is dissolved, add the sugar and stir until it is dissolved as well. In about 5 minutes, foam will form on the surface. (If foam does not form, your yeast may be too old or the water may be too hot. Try again.)
2. In a large bowl, mix together the flour, baking powder, and salt.
3. Melt the shortening in the microwave, set on high, for about 1 minute. Add the melted shortening, egg substitute, and yeast mixture to the flour, and stir by hand until all ingredients are combined. Use your hands to knead the dough for about 5 minutes, then form it into a ball and put it into a covered bowl in a warm spot for 1 to 1½ hours or until it doubles in size.
4. Roll dough out onto a floured surface so that it is a rectangle measuring 12 inches wide and 18 inches long.
5. Use a spatula to spread the butter-flavored spread evenly over the surface of the dough. Combine the brown sugar, Wondra flour, and cinnamon in a small bowl. Spread this mixture evenly over the surface of the dough. Sprinkle the raisins evenly over the filling.
6. Starting from the top edge, roll the dough down until it forms a long roll. Cut off the ends, then slice the dough into 12 even slices and arrange them, cut side down, in an 9 × 13-inch greased baking pan or dish. Cover the pan with plastic wrap and let the rolls rise again for another 1 to 1½ hours in a warm place.
7. Preheat oven to 400 degrees.
8. Remove the plastic from the pan and bake the rolls for 18 to 22 minutes or until brown.
9. As rolls bake, combine the icing ingredients in a medium bowl with an electric mixer. Mix on high speed for about 1 minute.
10. When rolls are cool, spread icing over the top of each one. Cover the baking dish, and store the rolls at room temperature until you are ready to serve them.

- MAKES 12 ROLLS.

Nutrition Facts

Serving size—1 roll
Total servings—12

Fat (per serving)—2 g
Calories (per serving)—160

• • • •

Project: ENTENMANN'S L.F. CINN. RAIS. SWEET ROLL
Nutrition Stats: FAT-2g/CAL-160
Job No. ELF359972-CRSR

TOP SECRET RECIPES VERSION OF

ENTENMANN'S LIGHT LOW-FAT GOURMET CINNAMON ROLLS

You say you like your cinnamon rolls oversize? Then this is the clone recipe for you. You'll find this method is very similar to the previous recipe, but it makes rolls almost twice the size, and there ain't no raisins. Otherwise, the recipe still uses the same filling formula, with Wondra flour to keep it from liquefying. And like the other recipe, the icing here includes our good friend, fat-free cream cheese, to create a smooth consistency while keeping the goopy fat grams at bay.

ROLLS
2 teaspoons yeast
1/2 cup warm water
1/4 cup sugar
1 2/3 cups bread flour

1/2 teaspoon baking powder
1/4 teaspoon salt
2 tablespoons shortening, melted
3 tablespoons egg substitute

FILLING
1/4 cup fat-free butter-flavored spread
1/3 cup light brown sugar

2 tablespoons Wondra flour
2 teaspoons cinnamon

ICING
1/2 cup powdered sugar
2 tablespoons fat-free cream cheese

2 to 3 drops vanilla extract
dash salt

1. Dissolve the yeast in the warm water. When the yeast is dissolved, add the sugar and stir until it is dissolved as well. In about 5 minutes, foam will form on the surface. (If foam does not form, your yeast may be too old or the water may be too hot. Try again.)
2. In a large bowl, mix the flour, baking powder, and salt together.
3. Melt the shortening in the microwave, set on high, for about 1 minute. Add the melted shortening, egg substitute, and yeast mixture to the flour and stir by hand until all ingredients are combined. Use your hands to knead the dough for about 5 minutes, then form it into a ball and put it into a covered bowl in a warm spot for 1 to 1 1/2 hours or until it doubles in size.
4. Roll dough out onto a floured surface so that it is a rectangle measuring 18 inches long and 12 inches wide.
5. Use a spatula to spread the butter-flavored spread evenly over the surface of the dough. Combine the brown sugar, Wondra flour, and cinnamon in a small bowl. Spread this mixture evenly over the surface of the dough.
6. Starting from the top edge, roll the dough down until it forms a long roll. Cut off the ends, then slice the dough into 8 even slices and arrange them, cut side down, in a 9 x 13-inch greased baking pan or dish. Cover the pan with plastic wrap and let the rolls rise again for 1 to 1 1/2 hours in a warm place.
7. Preheat oven to 400 degrees.
8. Remove the plastic from the pan and bake the rolls for 18 to 22 minutes or until brown.
9. As rolls bake, combine the icing ingredients in a medium bowl with an electric mixer. Mix on high speed for about 1 minute.
10. When rolls are cool, spread icing over the top of each one. Cover the baking dish and store the rolls at room temperature until you are ready to serve them.

- MAKES 8 ROLLS.

Nutrition Facts
    Serving size—½ roll   Fat (per serving)—2 g
    Total servings—16   Calories (per serving)—160

• • • •

GARDENBURGER CLASSIC GREEK VEGGIE PATTY

In June of 1998, Gardenburger was on a roll. Bolstered by booming sales of its Original Veggie Burger, the company introduced three new varieties of its popular meatless patties: Classic Greek, Fire-Roasted Vegetable, and Savory Mushroom. Since all three sounded so good, I thought we'd just clone the lot of 'em right here in the following pages. The first one, the Classic Greek Veggie Patty, includes calamata olives, feta cheese, and spinach to give it a distinctively Mediterranean flavor, yet with only three grams of fat per serving.

2 tablespoons bulgur wheat
1 cup cooked brown rice
½ pound white button mushrooms, quartered
⅔ cup diced white onion
¼ cup diced red onion
½ cup rolled oats
¼ cup canned white beans, drained
⅔ cup reduced-fat mozzarella cheese (2% fat)
¼ cup crumbled feta cheese
2 tablespoons fat-free cottage cheese
2 tablespoons frozen chopped spinach, thawed
4 pitted calamata olives
1 teaspoon salt
½ teaspoon onion powder
½ teaspoon garlic powder
¼ teaspoon parsley
¼ teaspoon paprika
dash ground black pepper
3 egg whites
2 tablespoons cornstarch

1. Add ¼ cup of boiling water to the bulgur wheat in a small bowl or measuring cup and let it sit for about 1 hour. Now is a good time to prepare the brown rice according to the directions on the package.
2. Steam the quartered mushrooms for 10 minutes or until tender. Remove the mushrooms from your steamer, and replace them with the onions. Steam the diced onions for 10 minutes or until the pieces become translucent. Keep the steamed mushrooms and onions separate and set them aside.
3. Add ½ cup of water to the rolled oats and let them soak for at least 10 minutes, until soft.
4. Drain any excess water from the bulgur wheat and oats, then combine the grains with the steamed mushrooms, rice, beans, cheeses, spinach, olives, and spices in a food processor and pulse 3 to 4 times until the ingredients are chopped but not pureed. You want a coarse texture with some identifiable chunks of grain, mushrooms, beans, cheese, and olives.
5. Pour the mixture into a bowl with the remaining ingredients and mix well.
6. Preheat the oven to 300 degrees and set a large skillet over medium/low heat.
7. Spray the skillet with a light coating of olive oil cooking spray. Measure ½ cup at a time of the patty mixture into the pan and shape with a spoon into a 3¾-inch patty that is approximately ½ inch thick. Cook the patties in batches for 2 to 4 minutes per side, or until light brown on the surface.
8. When all of the patties have been cooked in the skillet, arrange them on a lightly sprayed baking sheet and bake for 20 to 25 minutes in the oven. Be sure to turn them over halfway through the cooking time. You can serve the patties immediately or freeze them, like the original, when they have cooled.
9. If you freeze the patties, you can reheat them several ways. Simply spray a light coating of olive oil cooking spray on each side and heat each patty in a pan over medium heat for 3 to 4 minutes per side until it is hot in the center. You can also use a grill to prepare the patties. Just be sure to spray each frozen patty with the oil, and be sure the flames are low. Cook for

3 to 4 minutes per side. Those are the best cooking methods; however, you can also prepare a frozen patty by microwaving it for 30 to 35 seconds, then turn the patty over and zap it for another 30 to 35 seconds. Finally, you can heat a frozen patty in the microwave for 30 to 35 seconds, then place the partially defrosted patty in a toaster or toaster oven and cook it on medium heat until it's hot in the center.

- MAKES 8 PATTIES.

Nutrition Facts

SERVING SIZE—1 PATTY   FAT (PER SERVING)—3 G
TOTAL SERVINGS—8   CALORIES (PER SERVING)—150

• • • •

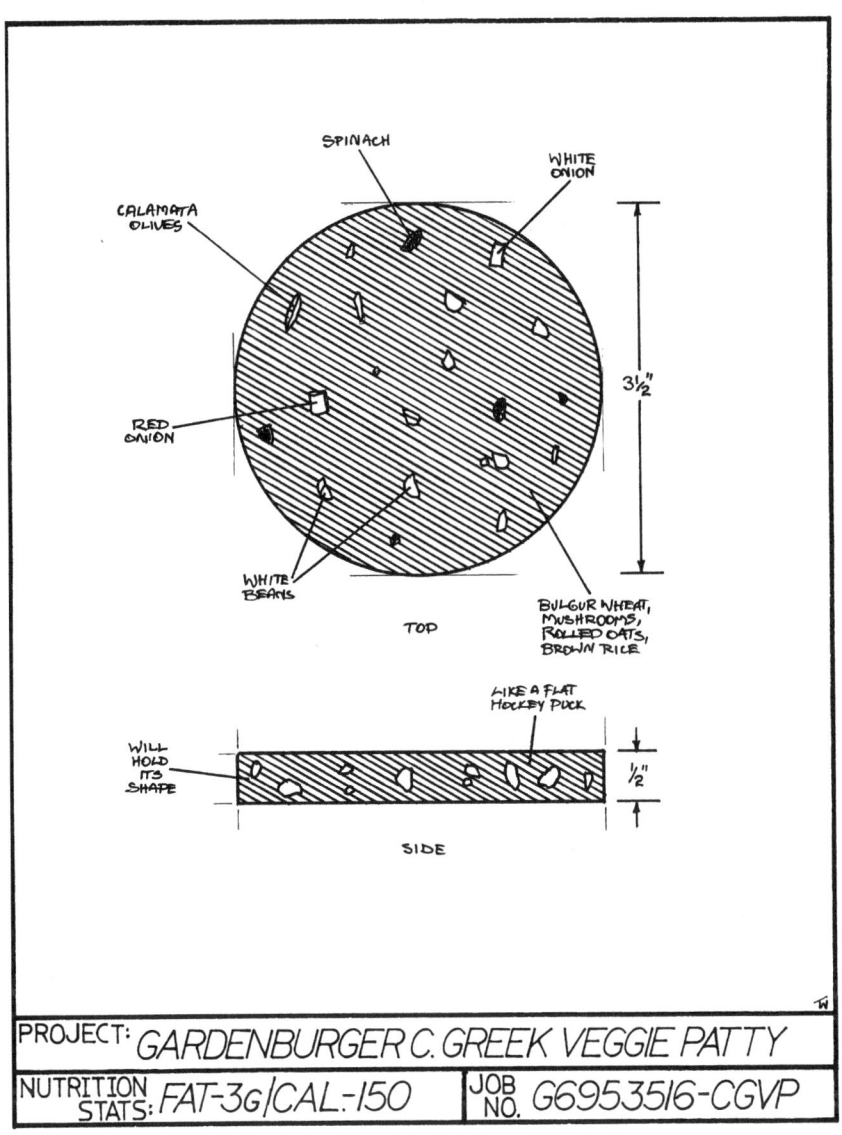

TOP SECRET RECIPES VERSION OF

GARDENBURGER FIRE-ROASTED VEGETABLE VEGGIE PATTY

Paul Wenner started his company in 1985 when he developed a meatless hamburger from leftovers at his vegetarian restaurant. Even though his Gardenburger was a hit, Paul was forced to close the restaurant due to dwindling sales. On the bright side, this gave Paul more free time to develop and sell his delicious puck-shaped plant patty. Today, Paul's Gardenburger brand is thriving, with an estimated fifty million patties served in restaurants, cafeterias, and concession stands in 1998 alone.

To make this clone, you'll need a food processor and a hot barbecue grill. And if you're looking for an interesting way to serve it, the manufacturer suggests you slap the veggie patty onto some focaccia bread and top it off with marinara sauce, grilled squash, and a little Parmesan cheese.

1 head garlic
olive oil
2 tablespoons bulgur wheat
2/3 cup cooked brown rice
1/4 red bell pepper
1 ear yellow sweet corn
1/4 red onion
1/2 small tomato
1 pound white button mushrooms, quartered
1 cup diced white onion
1/2 cup rolled oats
2/3 cup reduced-fat mozzarella cheese (2% fat)
1/4 cup Kraft Parmesan cheese
2 tablespoons fat-free cottage cheese
1 1/4 teaspoons salt
1/2 teaspoon garlic powder
1/2 teaspoon paprika
1/2 teaspoon onion powder
dash ground black pepper

2 egg whites
3 tablespoons cornstarch
2 tablespoons cornmeal
2 teaspoons minced sun-dried tomatoes (marinated and drained)

2 teaspoons lemon juice
2 teaspoons juice from canned jalapeños (nacho slices)

1. Preheat your oven to 325 degrees.
2. To roast the garlic, cut about ½ inch off the top of the garlic head. Cut the roots so that the garlic will sit flat. Remove most of the papery skin from the garlic, but leave enough so that the cloves stay together. Place the head of garlic in a small casserole dish or baking pan, drizzle about a tablespoon of olive oil over it, and cover it with a lid or foil. Bake for 1 hour. Remove the garlic from the oven and let it cool until you can handle it.
3. Add ¼ cup of boiling water to the bulgur wheat in a small bowl or measuring cup and let it sit for about 1 hour. Prepare the brown rice according to the directions on the package.
4. To fire-roast the vegetables, use a barbecue grill preheated to medium. Rub olive oil on ¼ of a red bell pepper, an ear of corn, ¼ of a red onion, and ½ of a small tomato. Place the vegetables on the hot grill with the skin of the pepper and tomato facing toward the flame. Turn the corn and red onion as they cook. Grill for 30 minutes or until vegetables are tender. The skin of the red bell pepper should turn black so that it can be quickly peeled off. Also remove the skin from the tomato. (If you don't have a grill, you can roast the vegetables in your oven set to high broil for around 15 to 20 minutes. Face the skin of the tomato and pepper toward the heat and be sure to turn the corn and red onion as they cook.) Dice the pepper, onion, and tomato when cool. Keep separate.
5. Steam the quartered mushrooms for 10 minutes or until tender. Remove the mushrooms from your steamer and replace them with the white onion. Steam the diced onion for 10 minutes or until the pieces become translucent. Keep these two ingredients separate and set aside.

6. Add ½ cup of water to the rolled oats and let them soak for at least 10 minutes, until soft.
7. Drain any excess water from the bulgur wheat and oats, then combine the grains with the steamed mushrooms, rice, cheeses, corn, and spices in a food processor and pulse 4 or 5 times until the ingredients are chopped but not pureed. You want a coarse texture with some identifiable chunks of grain, mushrooms, corn, and cheese.
8. Pour the mixture into a bowl with the remaining ingredients and mix well.
9. Preheat the oven to 300 degrees and set a large skillet over medium/low heat.
10. Spray the skillet with a light coating of olive oil cooking spray. Measure ½ cup at a time of the patty mixture into the pan and shape with a spoon into a 3¾-inch patty that is approximately ½ inch thick. Cook the patties in batches for 2 to 4 minutes per side, or until light brown on the surface.
11. When all of the patties have been cooked in the skillet, arrange them on a lightly sprayed baking sheet and bake for 20 to 25 minutes in the oven. Be sure to turn them over halfway through the cooking time. You can serve the patties immediately or freeze them, like the originals, when they have cooled.
12. If you freeze the patties like the originals, you can reheat them several ways. Refer to step #9 on page 273 for heating instructions.

- MAKES 8 PATTIES.

Nutrition Facts

SERVING SIZE—1 PATTY   FAT (PER SERVING)—3 G
TOTAL SERVINGS—8   CALORIES (PER SERVING)—150

• • • •

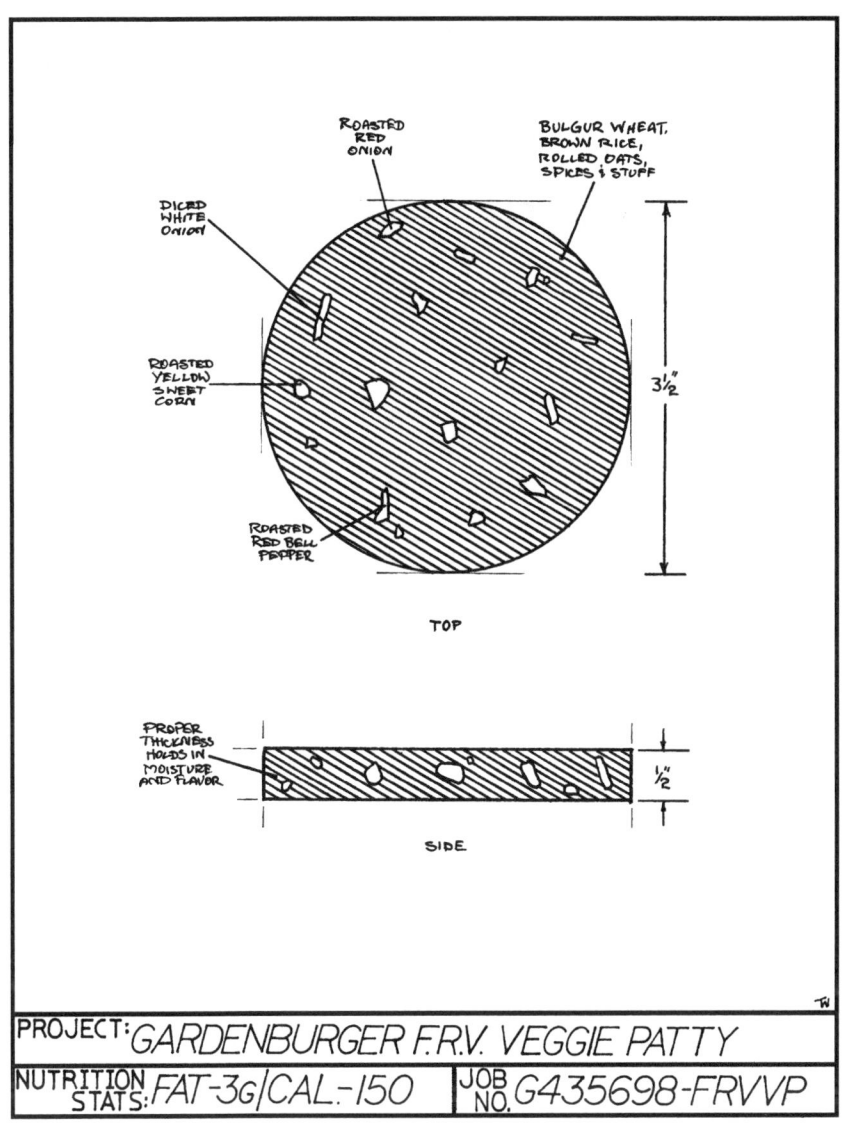

TOP SECRET RECIPES VERSION OF

GARDENBURGER SAVORY MUSHROOM VEGGIE PATTY

Chef Paul Wenner fathered a hot product when he ground up those leftover vegetables at his restaurant and formed them into the shape of a hamburger patty. When Paul got out of the restaurant business, he peddled the meatless patties out of his van under the name Wholesome & Hearty Foods. In 1992, when his company went public, the stock shot up to $30 from $3 on rumors that McDonald's was planning to sell the veggie patties under the golden arches. When those rumors proved to be false, the stock came crashing down quicker than sales figures for the McLean Deluxe. Later, the name of the company was changed to Gardenburger, and new products, such as the Savory Mushroom Veggie Patty, were developed.

For this clone, you'll need to track down three types of mushrooms: the common white button, brown (or crimini), and portobello. You'll also need a food processor to mash everything up real good.

2 tablespoons bulgur wheat
⅔ cup cooked brown rice
6 ounces white button mushrooms, quartered
6 ounces brown Italian mushrooms (crimini), quartered
4 ounces portobello mushroom (1 small cap), quartered
1 cup diced white onion (about ½ cup steamed)
½ cup rolled oats
⅔ cup reduced-fat mozzarella cheese (2% fat)
2 tablespoons shredded Gorgonzola cheese

2 tablespoons fat-free cottage cheese	2 egg whites
1¼ teaspoons salt	3 tablespoons cornstarch
1 teaspoon onion powder	1 tablespoon all-purpose flour
½ teaspoon garlic powder	2 teaspoons soy sauce
dash ground black pepper	2 teaspoons brown sugar
	2 teaspoons molasses

1. Add ¼ cup of boiling water to the bulgur wheat in a small bowl or measuring cup and let it sit for about 1 hour. Prepare the brown rice according to the directions on the package.
2. Steam the quartered mushrooms for 10 minutes or until tender. Remove the mushrooms from your steamer and replace them with the onion. Steam the diced onion for 10 minutes or until the pieces become translucent. Keep the mushrooms separate from the onions and set them aside.
3. Add ½ cup of water to the rolled oats and let them soak for at least 10 minutes, until soft.
4. Drain any excess water from the bulgur wheat and oats, then combine the grains with the steamed mushrooms, rice, cheeses, and spices in a food processor and pulse 4 or 5 times until the ingredients are chopped but not pureed. You want a coarse texture with some identifiable chunks of grain, mushrooms, and cheese.
5. Pour the mixture into a bowl with the remaining ingredients and mix well.
6. Preheat the oven to 300 degrees and set a large skillet over medium/low heat.
7. Spray the skillet with a light coating of olive oil cooking spray. Measure ½ cup of the patty mixture at a time into the pan and shape with a spoon into a 3¾-inch patty that is approximately ½ inch thick. Cook the patties in batches for 2 to 4 minutes per side or until light brown on the surface.
8. When all of the patties have been cooked in the skillet, arrange them on a lightly sprayed baking sheet and bake for 20 to 25 minutes in the oven. Be sure to turn them over halfway through the cooking time. You can serve the patties immediately or freeze them, like the originals, when they have cooled.

9. If you freeze the patties, you can reheat them several ways. Refer to step #9 on page 273 for heating instructions.

- MAKES 8 PATTIES.

Nutrition Facts
    SERVING SIZE—1 PATTY   FAT (PER SERVING)—3 G
    TOTAL SERVINGS—8   CALORIES (PER SERVING)—140

• • • •

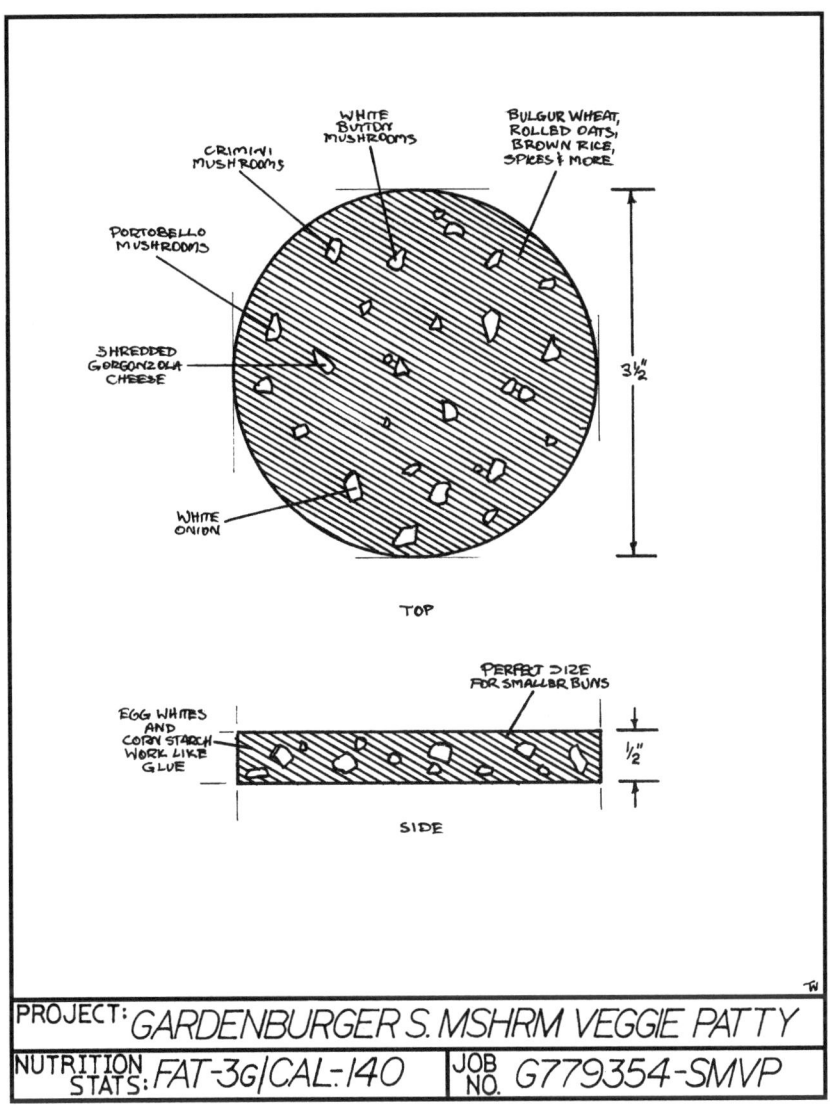

GIRL SCOUT COOKIES REDUCED-FAT LEMON PASTRY CREMES

TOP SECRET RECIPES VERSION OF

How can you resist the cute little girls smiling up at you with two missing front teeth, in those adorable green outfits—and a change machine around their waists? If you can't, then at least it's good to know that less than one-third of the sales price of each box of Girl Scout Cookies goes to the manufacturer. That's much less than the wholesale price food retailers pay for similar products. In fact, most of the money raised from each sale goes to support the Girl Scouts. But how do we get our Girl Scout Cookie fix during those off times when the cookies aren't being sold? That's when we can turn to a clone recipe such as this one for the reduced-fat cookie with the lemony tang. Included here is the custom Top Secret Recipes technique for making a delicious filling, entirely fat-free.

⅓ cup shortening
⅓ cup granulated sugar
½ cup powdered sugar
¼ cup egg substitute
½ teaspoon salt
½ teaspoon lemon extract

¾ teaspoon baking soda
⅓ cup plus 1 tablespoon buttermilk (1% fat)
3 cups all-purpose flour (plus about ¼ cup reserved for rolling the dough)

GLAZE
½ cup powdered sugar
2½ teaspoons water

FILLING
1 cup granulated sugar
¼ cup very hot water
¼ teaspoon lemon extract
⅛ teaspoon salt
2 drops yellow food coloring
1 cup sifted powdered sugar

1. To make the cookies, cream together the first 7 ingredients (shortening through baking soda) in a large bowl with an electric mixer. Add the buttermilk and mix until incorporated.
2. Add the 3 cups of flour to the wet mixture, 1 cup at a time. Use your hands to form the dough into a ball, then cover it with plastic wrap and chill for 1 hour.
3. Preheat oven to 325 degrees.
4. Roll dough out onto a lightly floured surface to about 1/16 inch thick. Punch out cookies with a 1½-inch cutter and arrange them on an ungreased cookie sheet. Bake for 8 to 12 minutes or until just turning light brown around the edges. Turn pan around halfway through cooking time to help the cookies bake evenly.
5. As cookies bake, prepare glaze by combining powdered sugar and water in a small bowl. Mix until smooth. Cover and set aside.
6. When cookies have cooled, dip a brush in the glaze, wipe off excess, and brush a very, very light coating of the glaze over the top of each cookie.
7. Prepare the filling by combining the granulated sugar, hot water, lemon extract, salt, and yellow food coloring in a microwave-safe medium bowl (glass or ceramic works the best). Stir the mixture for at least 30 seconds to begin dissolving the sugar.
8. Cover the bowl with plastic wrap, and then microwave mixture for 2 minutes at 50% power. Remove mixture from microwave and stir very gently to help dissolve the sugar crystals around the sides and bottom of the bowl. Cover the bowl again, then microwave mixture at full power for 2 more minutes. Remove the bowl from the microwave. Poke holes in the plastic wrap to let the steam escape. Let mixture cool for 15 minutes. Do not let mixture sit longer than this or

a hardened skin may develop and new sugar crystals may form.
9. After mixture has cooled for 15 minutes, stir it again very gently to dissolve any additional crystals that may have formed, and then add 1 cup of powdered sugar. Stir very gently to incorporate the sugar until mixture is smooth. Cover mixture again until it can be handled.
10. Roll filling into ½-inch balls and flatten between two cookies, with the frosted sides facing out. Repeat with the remaining filling.

- MAKES 42 SANDWICH COOKIES.

Nutrition Facts
SERVING SIZE—3 COOKIES   FAT (PER SERVING)—4.5 G
TOTAL SERVINGS—14   CALORIES (PER SERVING)—150

HEALTHY CHOICE TRADITIONAL PASTA SAUCE

TOP SECRET RECIPES VERSION OF

It was a heart attack that inspired Charles M. Harper of ConAgra Foods to come up with a new product line. In 1988, the Healthy Choice brand introduced frozen dinners with reduced fat, sodium, and cholesterol. Hundreds of other products followed through the '90s, including this fat-free pasta sauce, which hit stores in 1992. It's a cinch to make and goes great on any pasta, pizza, or meatball sandwich. If it's a chunky sauce you're looking for, check out the next recipe.

2 10¾-ounce cans tomato puree
1 cup water
½ teaspoon dried minced garlic
1 teaspoon dried minced onion
5 teaspoons granulated sugar
½ teaspoon salt

1 tablespoon lemon juice
¼ teaspoon dried parsley
⅛ teaspoon dried thyme
¼ teaspoon dried basil
¼ teaspoon dried oregano
dash ground black pepper

1. Combine all of the ingredients in a medium saucepan over medium/high heat and bring to a boil.
2. Reduce heat to low and simmer for 1 to 1½ hours or until sauce is thick.

- MAKES 2½ CUPS.

Nutrition Facts
SERVING SIZE—½ CUP
TOTAL SERVINGS—5
FAT (PER SERVING)—0 G
CALORIES (PER SERVING)—50

HEALTHY CHOICE CHUNKY TOMATO, MUSHROOM & GARLIC PASTA SAUCE

Healthy Choice was one of the first low-fat brands to hit the stores. The *Wall Street Journal* reported in 1993, "When Healthy Choice dinners first arrived in stores, big competitors were caught off guard: nothing quite like it had ever been marketed on a large scale." But nowadays the competition ain't so lean. You'll find more than a dozen brands devoted to the same low-fat, healthy claims in stores, all fighting it out for shelf space and market share.

If you like your marinara sauce with big chunks of veggies in it, then this is the one you'll want to make. The canned tomatoes, plus fresh mushrooms, onion, and garlic make for a thicker sauce that works great over your favorite pasta creation.

2 10¾-ounce cans tomato puree
1 cup water
1 cup chopped canned tomatoes
¾ cup sliced white button mushrooms
2 teaspoons minced garlic
¼ cup minced white onion
5 teaspoons granulated sugar
½ teaspoon salt
4 teaspoons lemon juice
¼ teaspoon dried parsley
⅛ teaspoon dried thyme
¼ teaspoon dried basil
¼ teaspoon dried oregano
dash ground black pepper

1. Combine all of the ingredients in a medium saucepan over medium/high heat and bring to a boil.
2. Reduce heat to low and simmer for 1 to 1½ hours or until sauce is thick.

- Makes 2½ cups.

Nutrition Facts
Serving size—½ cup
Total servings—5
Fat (per serving)—0 g
Calories (per serving)—45

• • • •

KEEBLER REDUCED-FAT PECAN SANDIES

The full-fat version of these delicious discs are the top-selling shortbread cookies in the United States. It's no wonder the baked-goods giant elected to introduce a reduced-fat version in 1994. You'll find this clone as easy to make as any other cookie recipe, but with much less fat in the crispy finished product.

1/3 cup shortening
1 cup powdered sugar
1/2 teaspoon baking soda
1/2 teaspoon vanilla
1/4 teaspoon salt

1/8 teaspoon coconut extract
2 tablespoons buttermilk
1 1/2 cups sifted all-purpose flour
1/4 teaspoon baking powder
1/4 cup finely chopped pecans

1. Preheat oven to 325 degrees.
2. With an electric mixer, cream together the shortening, sugar, baking soda, vanilla, salt, coconut extract, and buttermilk in a large bowl.
3. Combine flour and baking powder in another bowl.
4. Pour the dry ingredients into the wet ingredients and mix well.
5. Add pecans and mix until incorporated.
6. Roll dough into 1-inch balls and press them down onto an ungreased cookie sheet. Flatten the dough slightly with your fingers, and bake for 15 to 18 minutes or until cookies are light brown.

- MAKES 30 COOKIES.

Nutrition Facts

SERVING SIZE—1 COOKIE FAT (PER SERVING)—3 G
TOTAL SERVINGS—30 CALORIES (PER SERVING)—80

• • • •

2¼"

CRUNCHY

½"

CROSS SECTION

REDUCED-FAT SHORTBREAD COOKIE

2¼"

PECAN BITS

TOP

PROJECT: KEEBLER RED.-FAT PECAN SANDIES
NUTRITION STATS: FAT-3G/CAL-80   JOB NO. KRF587357-PS

TOP SECRET RECIPES VERSION OF

KOO KOO ROO ORIGINAL SKINLESS FLAME-BROILED CHICKEN

This fast-growing West Coast chain is another popular contender in the home meal replacement biz, which includes Boston Market and Kenny Rogers' Roasters. In 1990, shortly after Kenneth Berg sold his mortgage banking business for $125 million, he came across a little two-unit chicken chain in Los Angeles that seemed to attract clientele from an income bracket above that of typical burger chain customers. Kenneth discovered that the chicken served in these stores was not only delicious but also prepared with a secret marinade and baste that allowed the chicken to be cooked in a more health-conscious way—without skin. The owners of the restaurants, brothers Michael and Raymond Badalian, had created a marinade of juices and spices that kept the chicken moist and juicy inside. The company claims the chicken is marinated for up to seventy-two hours in this secret concoction and then brushed with a tangy orange baste when grilling. Just three months later, Kenneth purchased the chain for $2.5 million—ten times what it was earning each year—and expanded into other Western states, growing the restaurant to around forty units strong. That's about the time the company merged with Family Restaurants, the corporation behind the El Torito and Chi-Chi's Mexican food chains.

MARINADE

1 cup water
1 cup apple juice
1 cup V-8 juice
1 tablespoon lemon juice

½ cup pineapple juice
1 cup chopped onion
2 teaspoons salt
2 teaspoons ground black pepper

1 whole chicken, skinned and cut into 8 pieces (legs, thighs, breasts, and wings)

BASTE

2 tablespoons plus 1 teaspoon vegetable oil
½ cup thinly sliced onions
1 10¾-ounce can tomato puree
¼ cup water

1 tablespoon white vinegar
1 tablespoon lemon juice
¼ teaspoon salt
dash ground black pepper
dash garlic powder

1. Combine all of the ingredients for the marinade in a medium bowl. Mix well.
2. Add chicken to the marinade and leave it for at least 24 hours. It is even better if you let the chicken marinate longer, for as much as 48 to 72 hours.
3. Sometime before the chicken is done marinating, prepare the basting sauce by heating 1 teaspoon of the oil in a medium skillet. Sauté the sliced onions until they begin to blacken a bit. Pour the onions into a medium saucepan with the other baste ingredients. Bring mixture to a full boil, then reduce heat and simmer for 5 to 7 minutes. Remove from heat. When cool, cover the baste and chill it until it's needed.
4. When you are ready to cook the chicken, fire up your grill to medium heat. Grill the chicken for 5 to 6 minutes, then turn it over and grill for another 5 to 6 minutes. Turn chicken over once more and brush the top with the baste. Grill for another 5 to 6 minutes, then turn the chicken over again, baste the other side, and cook it until it's done—around 25 to 35 min-

utes total cooking time. You should see a few charred black spots on the surface of the chicken, but don't let it burn.

- SERVES 4.

Nutrition Facts

SERVING SIZE—2 PIECES FAT (PER SERVING)—8 G
TOTAL SERVINGS—4 CALORIES (PER SERVING)—195

• • • •

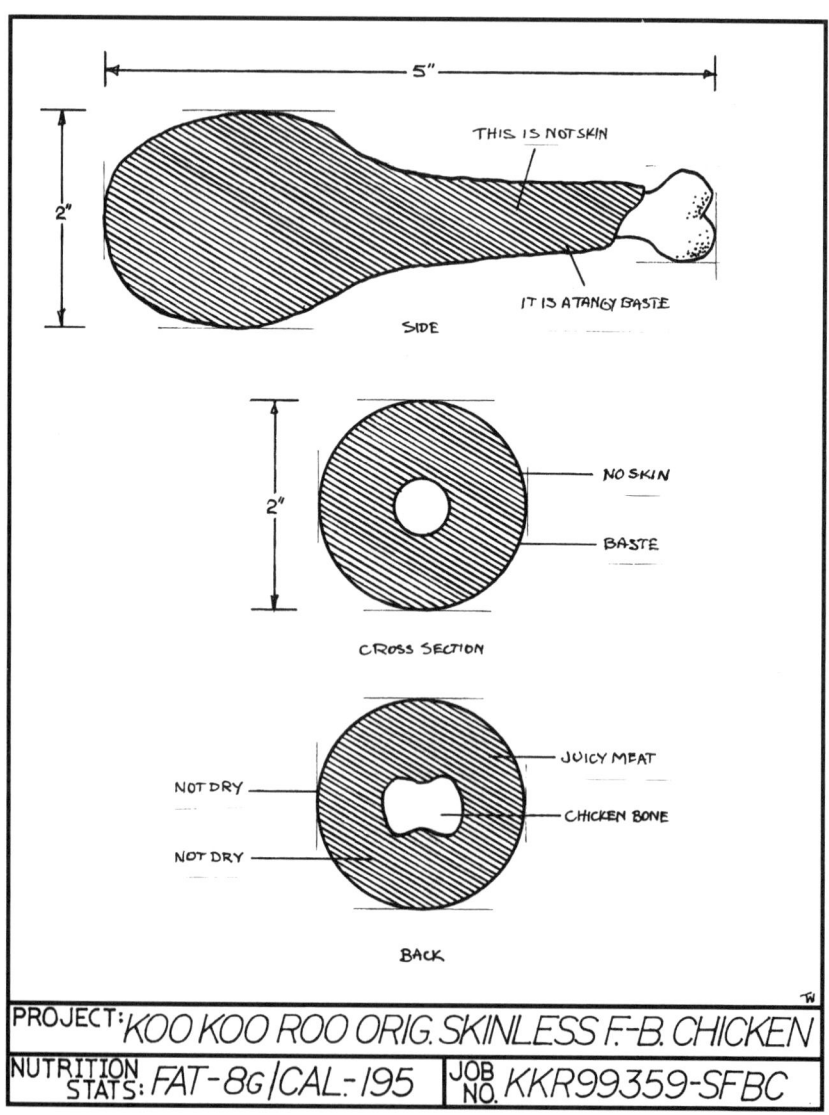

KOO KOO ROO SANTA FE PASTA

TOP SECRET RECIPES VERSION OF

In 1998, ex–Chrysler chairman Lee Iacocca took the reins at the struggling chicken chain. Lee had been an investor in the company since 1995, so when increasing competition from chains like Boston Market and Kenny Rogers' Roasters caused the Koo Koo Roo bottom line to sag, he was called in to rescue it. Can Lee perform the same comeback magic as he did with Chrysler's historic turnaround in the early '80s? While we wait to find out, let's make some pasta. This one goes great with the chicken from the previous recipe or with just about any other meal. The Southwestern-style dressing includes a small amount of oil, but the total fat grams per six-ounce serving stays quite modest.

1 16-ounce package rotini pasta
4 to 5 quarts water

DRESSING
1 cup V-8 juice
2 tablespoons olive oil
4 teaspoons red wine vinegar
1 teaspoon chili powder

½ teaspoon paprika
¾ teaspoon salt
¼ teaspoon ground black pepper
⅛ teaspoon garlic powder

⅔ cup grated Parmesan cheese
½ cup cooked yellow corn kernels
¼ cup chopped fresh cilantro
¼ cup chopped green onion

2 tablespoons diced red bell pepper
2 tablespoons diced green bell pepper

1 boneless chicken breast fillet, cooked and diced (best to use chicken breast meat from page 292)

1. Prepare the pasta by bringing 4 to 5 quarts of water to a rolling boil in a large saucepan. Add pasta to the pan, and when water begins to boil again, cook for 8 to 11 minutes. Pasta should be *al dente*, or mostly tender but with a slight toughness in the middle.
2. Whisk all of the dressing ingredients together in a small bowl. Cover and chill the dressing until you're ready to use it.
3. When pasta is done, drain it and pour it into a large bowl to cool. Add the dressing, then toss.
4. Add the remaining ingredients to the pasta and toss until pasta is well coated. Cover and chill for several hours before serving.

- SERVES 10 AS A SIDE DISH.

Nutrition Facts

SERVING SIZE—6 OUNCES FAT (PER SERVING)—5 G
TOTAL SERVINGS—10 CALORIES (PER SERVING)—230

• • • •

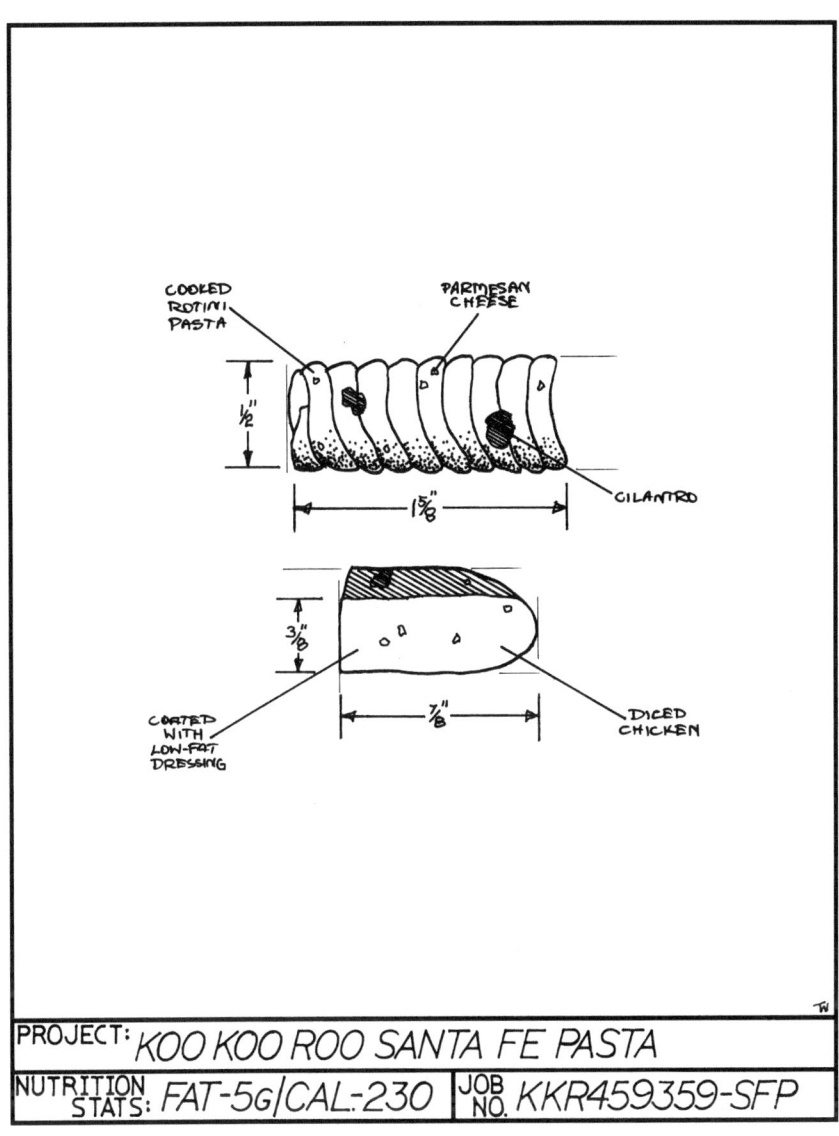

LITTLE DEBBIE OATMEAL LIGHTS

TOP SECRET RECIPES VERSION OF

These soft, creme-filled cookies are one of the most drooled-over goodies in the popular line of Little Debbie snacks. Good thing they're wrapped in plastic. The secret to cloning the light version of these mouthwatering sandwich cookies is in re-creating the soft, chewy consistency of the oatmeal cookies. To duplicate the texture, the cookies are slightly underbaked. For the filling, we just use marshmallow creme straight out of the jar. I found that this is the best way to get the taste and texture of the original's fat-free filling. Just be sure to eat these within a day or two of filling them, since the filling will begin to slowly creep from between the cookies. Also, keep these sandwich cookies wrapped in plastic or sealed in an airtight container so that they'll stay moist and chewy.

COOKIES

3½ tablespoons softened margarine
¾ cup dark brown sugar
¼ cup granulated sugar
1 tablespoon molasses
1 teaspoon vanilla
½ cup egg substitute
1½ cups all-purpose flour
1¼ cups 1-minute Quaker Oats
¾ teaspoon salt
½ teaspoon baking soda
¼ teaspoon cinnamon

1 7-ounce jar marshmallow creme

1. Preheat oven to 350 degrees.
2. In a large bowl, cream together margarine, sugars, molasses, vanilla, and egg substitute with an electric mixer.

3. In a separate bowl, combine the flour, oats, salt, baking soda, and cinnamon.
4. Combine the dry ingredients with the wet ingredients and mix by hand.
5. Drop the dough by tablespoonfuls onto a well-greased baking sheet. The dough will be very tacky, so you may wish to moisten your fingers so that the dough does not stick. With moistened fingers, press down on the dough and form it into circles about ⅛ inch thick. The circles should be about 2 inches in diameter before baking. Bake for 6 to 8 minutes or until a couple of the cookies start to darken around the edges. They will still be very tender in the center until cool. Be careful not to overcook. When cooled, the cookies should be about ¼ inch thick and very soft and chewy.
6. When the cookies have completely cooled, assemble each creme pie by spreading about 1½ tablespoons of marshmallow creme over the flat side of a cookie and press another cookie on top, making a sandwich. Repeat for the remaining cookies and filling.

- MAKES 20 SANDWICH COOKIES.

Nutrition Facts
SERVING SIZE—1 SANDWICH COOKIE
TOTAL SERVINGS—20
FAT (PER SERVING)—2.5 G
CALORIES (PER SERVING)—146

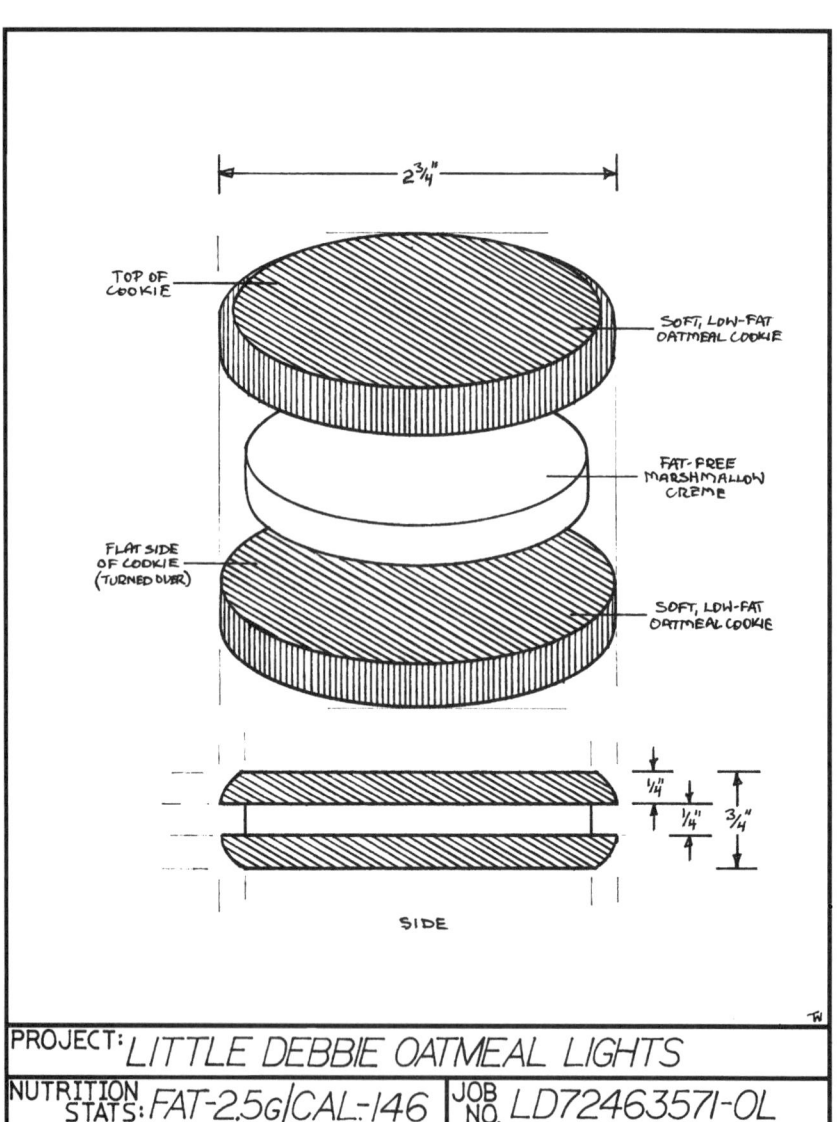

TOP SECRET RECIPES VERSION OF NABISCO HONEY MAID GRAHAMS

The beginning of the graham cracker goes back to the early 1800s when Sylvester Graham thought his new invention was the secret to a lifetime of perfect health, even sexual prowess—certainly extraordinary claims for a cracker. But this came from the man thought to be quite a whacko in his time, since he had earlier claimed that eating ketchup could ruin your brain. So, while his crispy whole wheat creation was not the cure for every known ailment, the sweet crackers still became quite a fad, first in New England around the 1830s and then spreading across the country. Today, graham crackers remain popular as a low-fat, snack time munchable, and they're the main ingredient in s'mores.

You don't need to use graham flour for this recipe, since it's similar to the whole wheat flour you find in your local supermarket. Just pick your favorite variety among these three clones of Nabisco's most popular crackers, and be sure to roll out the dough paper thin.

HONEY (ORIGINAL)

1/3 cup shortening
3/4 cup plus 1 tablespoon granulated sugar
3 tablespoons honey, warmed
1 1/2 teaspoons vanilla
1 3/4 cups whole wheat flour

1 1/4 cups all-purpose flour
1 1/4 teaspoons salt
1 teaspoon baking powder
1/2 teaspoon baking soda
1/2 cup plus 2 tablespoons water

1. Preheat oven to 300 degrees.
2. Combine shortening with sugar, honey (warmed for 20 to 30 seconds in the microwave), and vanilla in a large bowl. Blend with an electric mixer until smooth.
3. Combine flours, salt, baking powder, and baking soda in another large bowl, and then add the dry mixture to the wet ingredients and blend well with an electric mixer.
4. Slowly add the water to the mixture while beating. You may have to mix by hand until the mixture forms a large ball of dough.
5. Divide the dough in thirds and roll 1/3 out in the shape of a rectangle that is at least 1/16 inch thick on wax paper. This dough should be paper thin! It will double when cooked to the desired 1/8-inch thickness. Use a knife to trim the dough so that it has straight edges in the shape of a rectangle slightly smaller than the size of the baking sheet you are using.
6. Grease the baking sheet with a light coating of shortening. Turn the dough over onto the baking sheet, and carefully peel away the wax paper.
7. Use a knife to score the dough in 5 × 2⅜-inch rectangles. Use a toothpick to poke holes that are 1/4 inch apart across the entire surface of the dough.
8. Bake for 22 to 24 minutes or until the dough begins to turn light brown around the edges. Be sure to turn the baking sheet around about halfway through the cooking time.
9. Cool the graham cracker sheets before breaking them apart along the scored lines. Repeat the process with the remaining dough.

- MAKES 44 CRACKERS.

CINNAMON

1/3 cup shortening
3/4 cup plus 1 tablespoon granulated sugar
2 tablespoons honey, warmed
1 tablespoon molasses
1 1/2 teaspoons vanilla

1 3/4 cups whole wheat flour
1 1/4 cups all-purpose flour
1 1/4 teaspoons salt
1 teaspoon baking powder
1/2 teaspoon baking soda
1/2 cup plus 2 tablespoons water

TOPPING

1½ teaspoons cinnamon   2 tablespoons sugar

1. Preheat oven to 300 degrees.
2. Combine shortening with sugar, honey (warmed for 20 to 30 seconds in the microwave), molasses, and vanilla in a large bowl. Blend with an electric mixer until smooth.
3. Combine flours, salt, baking powder, and baking soda in another large bowl, and then add the dry mixture to the wet ingredients and blend well with an electric mixer.
4. Slowly add the water to the mixture while beating. You may have to mix by hand until the mixture forms a large ball of dough.
5. Divide the dough in thirds and roll ⅓ out in the shape of a rectangle that is at least 1/16 inch thick on wax paper. This dough should be paper thin! It will double when cooked to the desired ⅛-inch thickness. Use a knife to trim the dough so that it has straight edges in the shape of a rectangle slightly smaller than the size of the baking sheet you are using.
6. Grease the baking sheet with a light coating of shortening. Turn the dough over onto the baking sheet, and carefully peel away the wax paper.
7. Use a knife to score the dough in 5 × 2⅜-inch rectangles. Use a toothpick to poke holes that are ¼ inch apart across the entire surface of the dough.
8. Sprinkle a light coating of the cinnamon/sugar over the top surface of the dough. Shake the baking sheet around gently to evenly distribute the cinnamon/sugar topping.
9. Bake for 22 to 24 minutes or until the dough begins to turn light brown around the edges. Be sure to turn the baking sheet around about halfway through the cooking time.
10. Cool the graham cracker sheets before breaking them apart along the scored lines. Repeat the process with the remaining dough.

- MAKES 44 CRACKERS.

CHOCOLATE

⅓ cup shortening
¾ cup plus 1 tablespoon granulated sugar
3 tablespoons honey, warmed
1 tablespoon chocolate syrup
1 ½ teaspoons vanilla
1 ½ cups whole wheat flour
1 ¼ cups all-purpose flour

⅓ cup cocoa
1 ¼ teaspoons salt
1 teaspoon baking powder
½ teaspoon baking soda
¼ cup water
¼ cup fat-free milk
2 tablespoons whole milk

TOPPING
2 tablespoons granulated sugar

1. Preheat oven to 300 degrees.
2. Combine shortening with sugar, honey (warmed for 20 to 30 seconds in the microwave), chocolate syrup, and vanilla in a large bowl. Blend with an electric mixer until smooth.
3. Combine flours, cocoa, salt, baking powder, and baking soda in another large bowl, and then add the dry mixture to the wet ingredients and blend well with an electric mixer.
4. Slowly add the water and milk to the mixture while beating. You may have to mix by hand until the mixture forms a large ball of dough.
5. Divide the dough in thirds and roll ⅓ out in the shape of a rectangle that is at least 1/16 inch thick on wax paper. This dough should be paper thin! It will double in thickness when cooked to the desired ⅛-inch thickness. Use a knife to trim the dough so that it has straight edges in the shape of a rectangle slightly smaller than the size of the baking sheet you are using.
6. Grease the baking sheet with a light coating of shortening. Turn the dough over onto the baking sheet and carefully peel away the wax paper.
7. Use a knife to score the dough in 5 × 2⅜-inch rectangles. Use a toothpick to poke holes that are ¼ inch apart across the entire surface of the dough.

8. Sprinkle a light coating of granulated sugar over the top surface of the dough. Gently shake the baking sheet around to help evenly distribute the sugar.
9. Bake for 22 to 24 minutes or until the dough begins to turn light brown around the edges. Be sure to turn the baking sheet around about halfway through the cooking time.
10. Cool the graham cracker sheets before breaking them apart along the scored lines. Repeat the process with the remaining dough.

- MAKES 44 CRACKERS.

Nutrition Facts
SERVING SIZE—2 CRACKERS   FAT (PER SERVING)—3 G
TOTAL SERVINGS—22   CALORIES (PER SERVING)—120

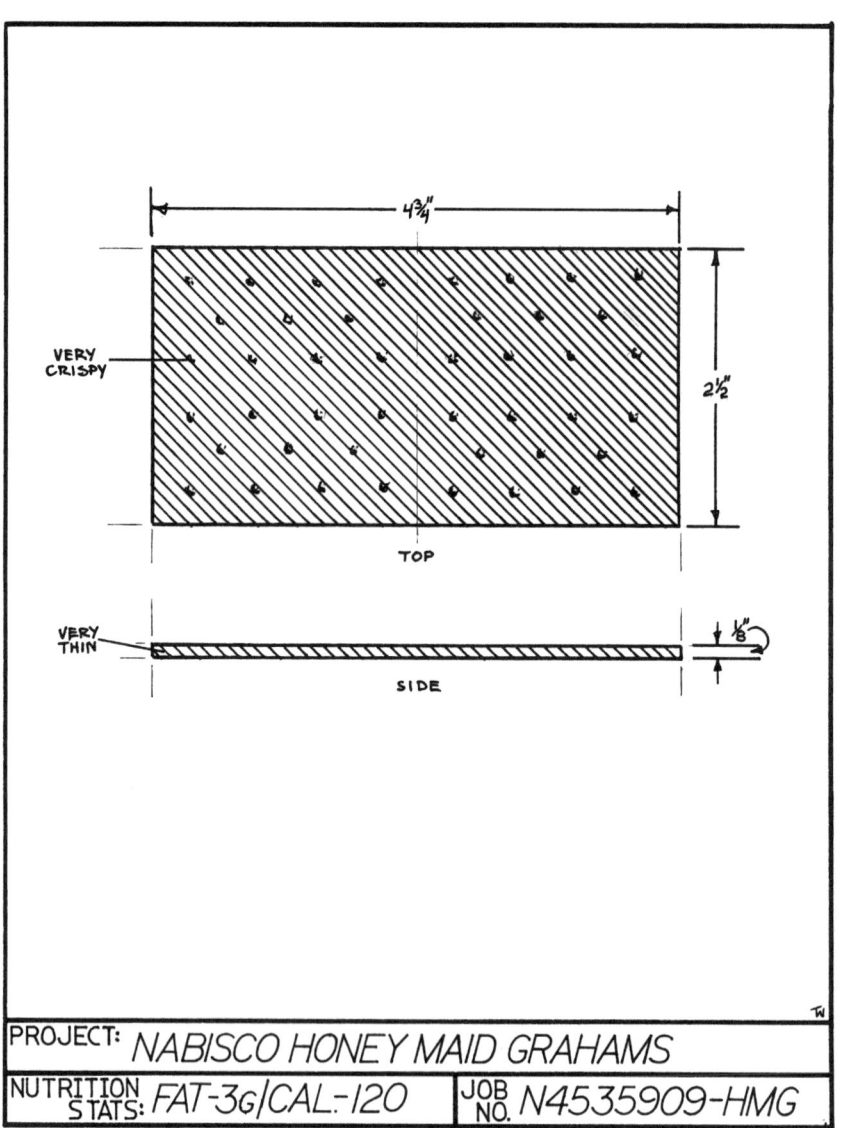

NABISCO OLD FASHION GINGER SNAPS

TOP SECRET RECIPES VERSION OF

According to legend, if you place a ginger snap in the palm of your hand and press down on the middle, and it breaks into three pieces, good luck will follow. Though you'll wish a broom would follow, since you just got crumbs all over your clean floor.

1 cup packed dark brown sugar
¾ cup granulated sugar
6 tablespoons shortening
¼ cup molasses
¼ cup egg substitute
½ teaspoon vanilla
2½ cups all-purpose flour

2 teaspoons baking soda
2 teaspoons ground ginger
1 teaspoon salt
1 teaspoon ground cinnamon
½ teaspoon ground cloves
¼ cup water

1. Preheat oven to 300 degrees.
2. Cream together the sugars, shortening, molasses, egg substitute, and vanilla in a large bowl. Beat with an electric mixer until smooth.
3. In another large bowl, combine the flour, baking soda, ginger, salt, cinnamon, and cloves.
4. Pour the dry mixture into the wet mixture and beat while adding the water. Continue to mix until ingredients are incorporated.
5. Measure 1 rounded teaspoon of dough at a time. Roll the dough into a sphere between the palms of your hands, then press the dough onto a lightly greased cookie sheet. Flatten to about ¼ inch thick, and leave at least ½ inch between the cookies

since they will spread out a bit when baking. Use flour or water on your fingers if the dough sticks.
6. Bake cookies for 12 to 14 minutes or until edges begin to turn light brown. Cookies should be crispy, not soft, when cool.

- MAKES 120 COOKIES.

Nutrition Facts

SERVING SIZE—4 COOKIES FAT (PER SERVING)—2.5 G
TOTAL SERVINGS—30 CALORIES (PER SERVING)—110

• • • •

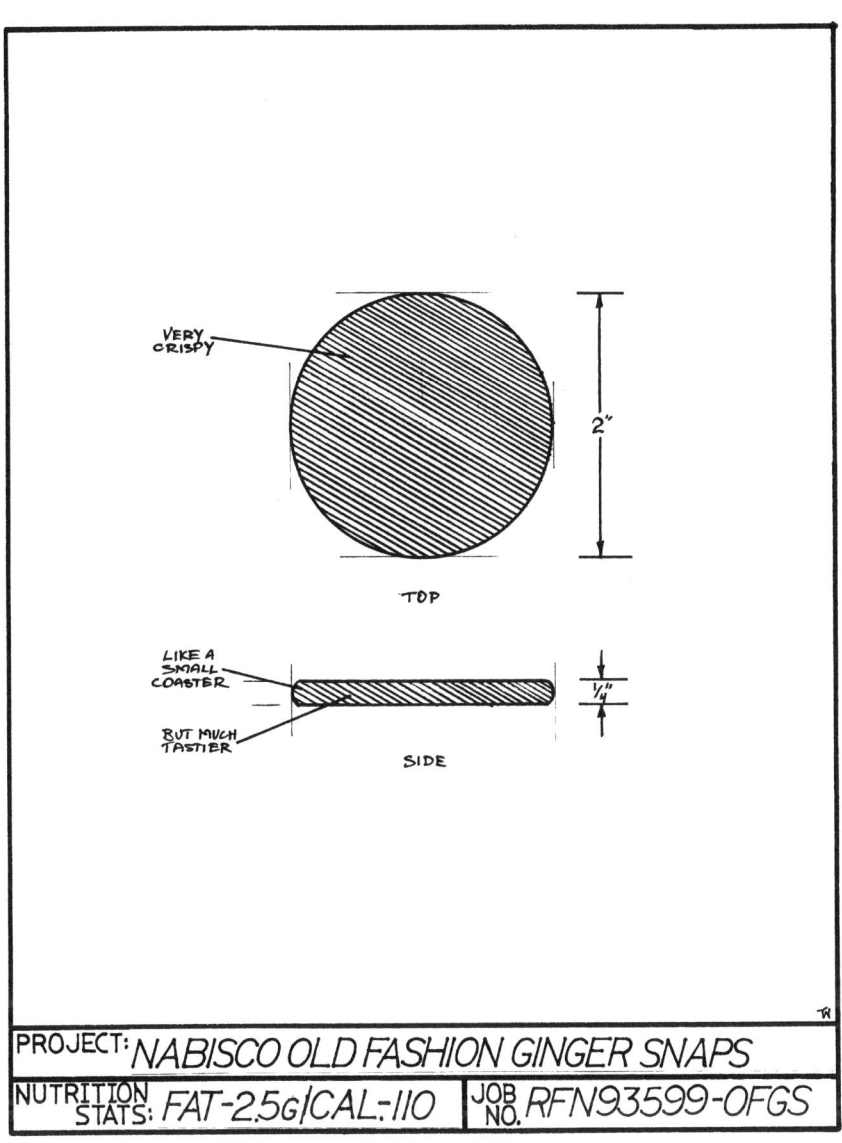

NABISCO REDUCED-FAT OREO COOKIES

TOP SECRET RECIPES VERSION OF

I've been researching the King of All Cookies for years now, and I've still not found anyone who is sure where the name *Oreo* came from. One of the most interesting and obscure explanations I've heard is that the two o's from the word *chocolate* were placed on both sides of *re* from the word *creme*. This way the name seems to mimic the construction of the famed sandwich cookie.

That may not be true, but I do know this for sure: Nabisco introduced a reduced-fat version of its popular cookie in 1994. With only half the fat, it manages to taste just as good as the original version invented way back in 1912. We cut back on the fat for our clone here by re-creating the creme filling without any of the shortening you'd find in the original full-fat version. We do this with a special technique developed in the secret underground Top Secret Recipes test kitchen that allows you to create a delicious, fat-free filling in your microwave. If you want the cookies as dark as the original, include the optional brown paste food coloring in your recipe.

COOKIES

1 18¼-ounce package reduced-fat devil's food cake mix (Betty Crocker Sweet Rewards is best)
¼ cup shortening, melted
½ cup all-purpose flour, measured then sifted
¼ cup egg substitute
3 tablespoons brown paste food coloring (2 1-ounce containers)*
3 tablespoons water

*This addition of brown paste food coloring is an optional step to help re-create the color of the original cookie. If you do not use the paste food coloring, be sure to change the amount of water added to the wafer cookies from 3 tablespoons to ⅓ cup. The food coloring gives the cookies the dark brown, almost black color. The coloring can be found with cake decorating supplies at art supply and craft stores.

FILLING

1 cup granulated sugar
¼ cup hot water
½ teaspoon vanilla (clear is best)*

dash salt
1 ⅓ cups powdered sugar

1. Combine the cookie ingredients in a large bowl. Add the water a bit at a time until the dough forms. (You may need as much as ¼ cup of water to create a dough ball that is pliable and easy to roll but not sticky.) Cover and chill for 2 hours.
2. Preheat oven to 350 degrees.
3. On a floured surface, roll out a portion of the dough to just under 1/16 inch thick. To cut, use a cutter or lid from a spice container with a 1½-inch diameter (Schilling brand is good). Arrange the cut dough on a cookie sheet that is sprayed with a light coating of nonstick spray. Bake for 10 minutes. Remove the chocolate wafers from the oven and cool completely.
4. As the wafers bake, make the filling by combining the granulated sugar, hot water, vanilla, and salt in a medium bowl. Stir mixture for about 30 seconds to begin dissolving the sugar.
5. Cover bowl with plastic wrap and microwave on 50% power for 2 minutes. Remove the bowl from the microwave. Stir very gently to help dissolve the sugar crystals around the sides and bottom of the bowl. Cover bowl again and microwave at full power for 2 more minutes. Remove the bowl from the microwave, and poke holes in the plastic wrap to let the steam escape. Let the mixture cool for 15 minutes. Do not let the mixture stand for longer than this or sugar crystals may begin to form.
6. After mixture has cooled for 15 minutes, stir it very gently once again to dissolve any additional crystals that may have formed, then add the 1⅓ cups of powdered sugar. Stir gently to incorporate the sugar, until mixture is smooth. Cover mixture again until it can be handled.

*This clear vanilla can also be found with cake decorating supplies in craft stores. The clear vanilla will give you a much whiter filling like the original, although the brown vanilla works fine for taste, if that's all you've got on hand.

7. When the cookies have cooled, roll a small portion (rounded ¼ teaspoon) of the filling into a ball (just over ¼ inch in diameter), and press it between two of the cookies. Repeat with the remaining cookies.

- MAKES 54 SANDWICH COOKIES.

TIDBITS

If the dough for the wafers seems too sticky, you can work in as much as ¼ cup of additional flour as you pat out and roll the dough. Use just enough flour to make the dough workable but not tough.

Nutrition Facts

SERVING SIZE—3 COOKIES   FAT (PER SERVING)—3.5 G
TOTAL SERVINGS—18   CALORIES (PER SERVING)—150

• • • •

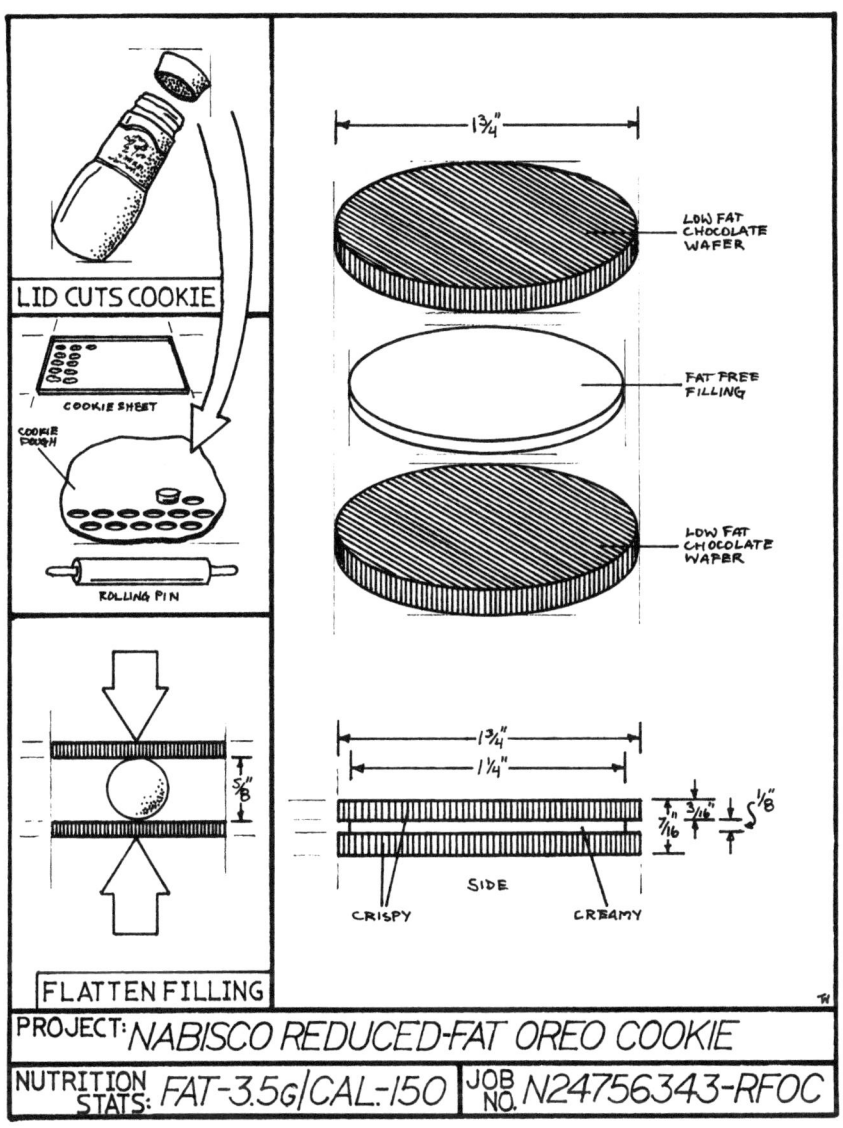

NABISCO SNACKWELL'S APPLE RAISIN SNACK BARS

Nabisco unveiled a line of reduced-fat products in 1992 with the introduction of SnackWell's Devil's Food cookie cakes. The product was an instant hit with demand quickly outstripping the supply, leaving store shelves empty. The company poked fun at the situation with a series of humorous TV spots, showing the dweebish "Cookie Man" hounded by pushy shoppers trying to get their hands on his cookies. The successful product launch was followed up with the introduction of dozens of new SnackWell's products through the years, including Apple Raisin Snack Bars. Our clone uses a secret combination of unsweetened applesauce along with molasses and apple juice to keep the cake moist and tasty.

2 egg whites
1 cup plus 5 tablespoons
   granulated sugar
2 tablespoons brown sugar
1 tablespoon molasses
1 tablespoon dark corn syrup
½ cup unsweetened applesauce
¼ cup apple juice concentrate

3 tablespoons shortening
½ teaspoon vanilla
1½ cups all-purpose flour
¾ teaspoon salt
½ teaspoon cinnamon
¼ teaspoon baking soda
½ cup raisins

1. Preheat oven to 350 degrees.
2. In a large bowl, whip the egg whites with an electric mixer until they become thick. Do not use a plastic bowl for this.
3. Add the granulated sugar to the egg whites and continue to beat until the mixture forms soft peaks.

4. Add the brown sugar, molasses, dark corn syrup, applesauce, apple juice concentrate, shortening, and vanilla to the mixture while beating.
5. In a separate bowl, combine the remaining ingredients, except raisins.
6. While beating the wet mixture, slowly add the dry mixture.
7. Add the raisins, and combine by hand.
8. Lightly grease a 9 × 14-inch pan with a light coating of nonstick cooking spray. Be sure to coat the sides as well as the bottom of the pan. Dump about 3 tablespoons of sugar into the pan, then tilt and shake it so that a light layer of sugar coats the entire bottom of the pan and about halfway up the sides. Pour out the excess sugar.
9. Pour the batter into the pan and spread it evenly around the inside. Sprinkle a light coating of sugar—about 2 tablespoons—over the entire top surface of the batter. Gently shake the pan from side to side to evenly distribute the sugar over the batter. Bake for 25 to 28 minutes or until the cake begins to pull away from the sides of the pan.
10. Remove the cake from the oven and turn it out onto a cooling rack. When the cake has cooled, place it onto a sheet of wax paper on a cutting board and slice across the cake 6 times, creating 7 even slices. Next cut the cake lengthwise twice, into thirds, creating a total of 21 snack bars. When the bars have completely cooled, store them in a resealable plastic bag or an airtight container.

- MAKES 21 BARS.

Nutrition Facts

SERVING SIZE—1 BAR	TOTAL FAT (PER SERVING)—1.7 G
SERVINGS—21	CALORIES (PER SERVING)—120

• • • •

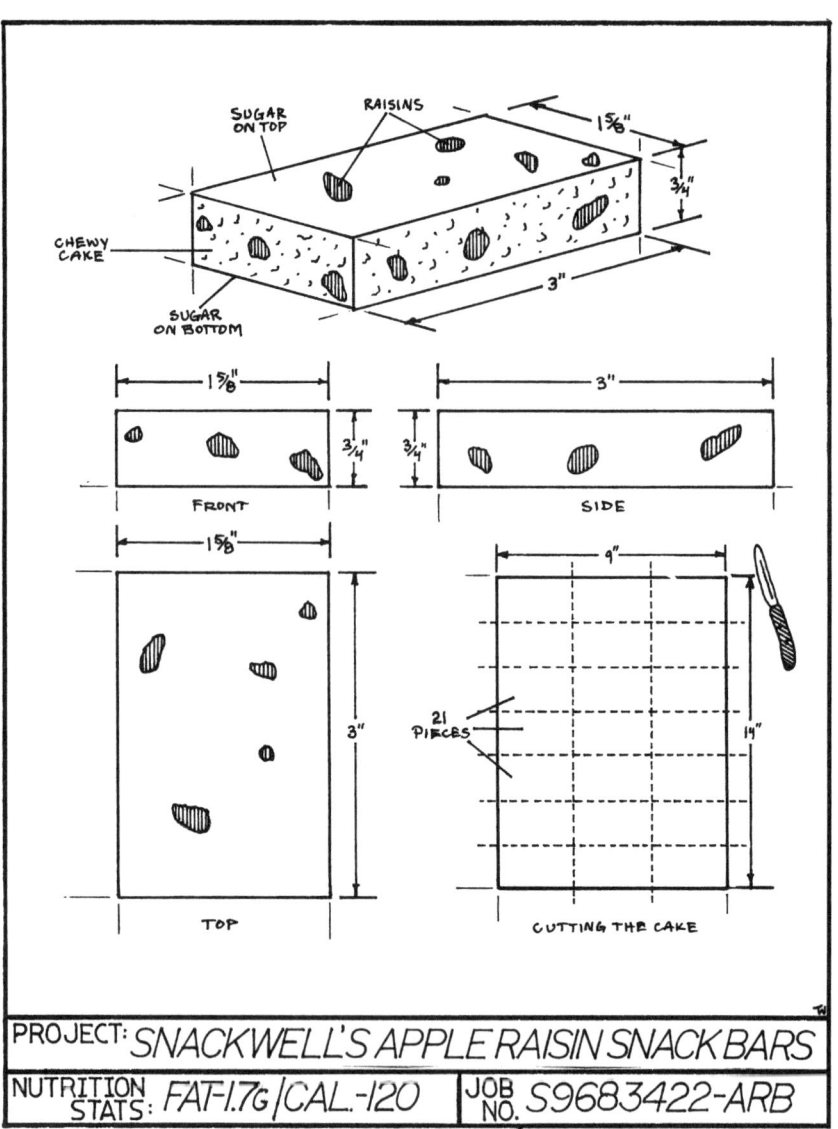

NABISCO SNACKWELL'S BANANA SNACK BARS

TOP SECRET RECIPES VERSION OF

In 1996, Nabisco built up its growing line of SnackWell's baked products with the introduction of low-fat snack bars in several varieties, including fudge brownie, golden cake, apple raisin (see previous recipe), and the chewy banana variety cloned here.

The secret to keeping the fat grams down in this recipe is the use of egg whites, molasses, and just a little shortening. But it's the banana puree that really slips in there to replace most of the fat while giving the cake real banana flavor and helping to keep it very moist.

2 egg whites
1 cup plus 5 tablespoons granulated sugar
2 tablespoons brown sugar
2 tablespoons molasses
1 ½ cups banana puree*
3 tablespoons shortening

¼ cup whole milk
½ teaspoon vanilla butter nut extract
1 ½ cups all-purpose flour
½ teaspoon salt
¼ teaspoon baking soda

1. Preheat oven to 350 degrees.
2. In a large bowl, whip the egg whites with an electric mixer until they become thick. Do not use a plastic bowl for this.
3. Add the sugar to the egg whites and continue to beat until the mixture forms soft peaks.
4. Add the brown sugar, molasses, banana puree, shortening,

---

*Puree whole bananas (approximately 3) in a food processor or blender until smooth and creamy.

milk, and vanilla butter nut flavoring to the mixture, beating after each addition.
5. In a separate bowl, combine the remaining ingredients.
6. While beating the wet mixture, slowly add the bowl of dry ingredients.
7. Lightly grease a 9 × 14-inch pan with a light coating of nonstick cooking spray. Be sure to coat the sides as well as the bottom of the pan. Dump about 3 tablespoons of sugar into the pan, then tilt and shake it so that a light layer of sugar coats the entire bottom of the pan and about halfway up the sides. Pour out the excess sugar.
8. Pour the batter into the pan and spread it evenly around the inside of the pan. Sprinkle a light coating of sugar—about 2 tablespoons—over the entire top surface of the batter. Gently shake the pan from side to side to evenly distribute the sugar over the batter. Bake for 25 to 28 minutes or until the cake begins to pull away from the sides of the pan.
9. Remove the cake from the oven and turn it out onto a cooling rack. When cake has cooled, place it onto a sheet of wax paper on a cutting board and slice across the cake 6 times, creating 7 even slices. Next cut the cake lengthwise twice, into thirds, creating a total of 21 snack bars. When the bars have completely cooled, store them in a resealable plastic bag or an airtight container.

- MAKES 21 BARS.

Nutrition Facts

SERVING SIZE—1 BAR   TOTAL FAT (PER SERVING)—1.8 G
SERVINGS—21   CALORIES (PER SERVING)—118

• • •

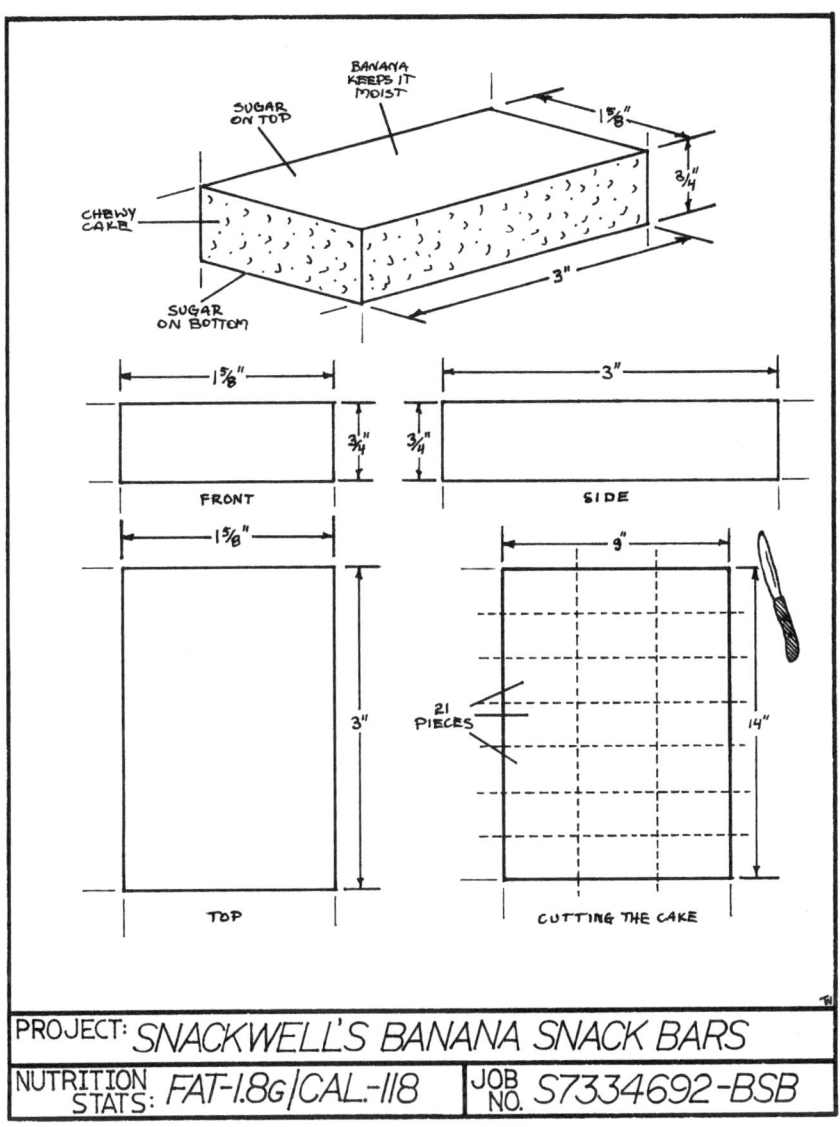

TOP SECRET RECIPES VERSION OF

PLANTERS FAT-FREE FIDDLE FADDLE

For many years now, the monocled Mr. Peanut has been Planters' nutty pitchman. The character was created in 1916 by a Virginia schoolboy, Anthony Gentile, who won $5 in a contest for drawing a "little peanut person." A commercial artist later added the top hat, cane, and monocle to make Mr. Peanut the stuffy socialite that he is today. But the character has not always been in the limelight. Planters' adman Bill McDonough says, "Though Mr. Peanut has always been identified with the brand, over the years he has been dialed up or down to different degrees." In 1999, the company dialed up the polite-and-proper legume to capitalize on nostalgia for the older folks and the young buyers' craving for retro chic.

Even though we think of Planters as the "nut company," you won't find a single nut, with or without monocle, in the fat-free version of Planters' popular Fiddle Faddle. All you need to whip together this clone is a good low-fat microwave popcorn and a few other common ingredients. This recipe requires your microwave to help coat the popcorn with a thin, crunchy coating of the tasty candy mixture.

1 teaspoon vegetable oil
1/2 cup light corn syrup
3/4 cup light brown sugar
1/4 cup water
1/2 teaspoon salt
1/4 teaspoon vanilla extract
1 bag 94% fat-free microwave popcorn

1. Combine the oil, corn syrup, brown sugar, water, and salt in a small saucepan over medium heat. Stir while bringing mixture

to a boil, then use a candy thermometer to bring mixture to 300 degrees (also known as the hard crack stage to candy makers).
2. When the candy reaches about 275 degrees, start cooking the popcorn by following the directions on the package. You want to time it so that the popcorn is done at approximately the same time as the candy. This way, the popcorn will be hot when you pour the candy over it.
3. When the candy has reached the right temperature, add the vanilla, then remove it from the heat. Pour the hot popcorn into a large plastic or glass bowl and quickly pour the candy over the top. Stir the popcorn so that the candy coats all of the pieces. To better help the candy coat the popcorn, place the bowl into the microwave and zap it for about 30 seconds on high. Stir the popcorn, and then, if necessary, microwave it for another 30 seconds. Stir it once more. By this time, the popcorn should be very well coated with a thin layer of the candy.
4. Quickly pour the popcorn out onto wax paper and spread it around to cool it.
5. When candy is cool, break it into bite-size pieces. Store it in a sealed container.

- MAKES 12 CUPS.

Nutrition Facts
SERVING SIZE—1 CUP
TOTAL SERVINGS—12
FAT (PER SERVING)—0 G
CALORIES (PER SERVING)—114

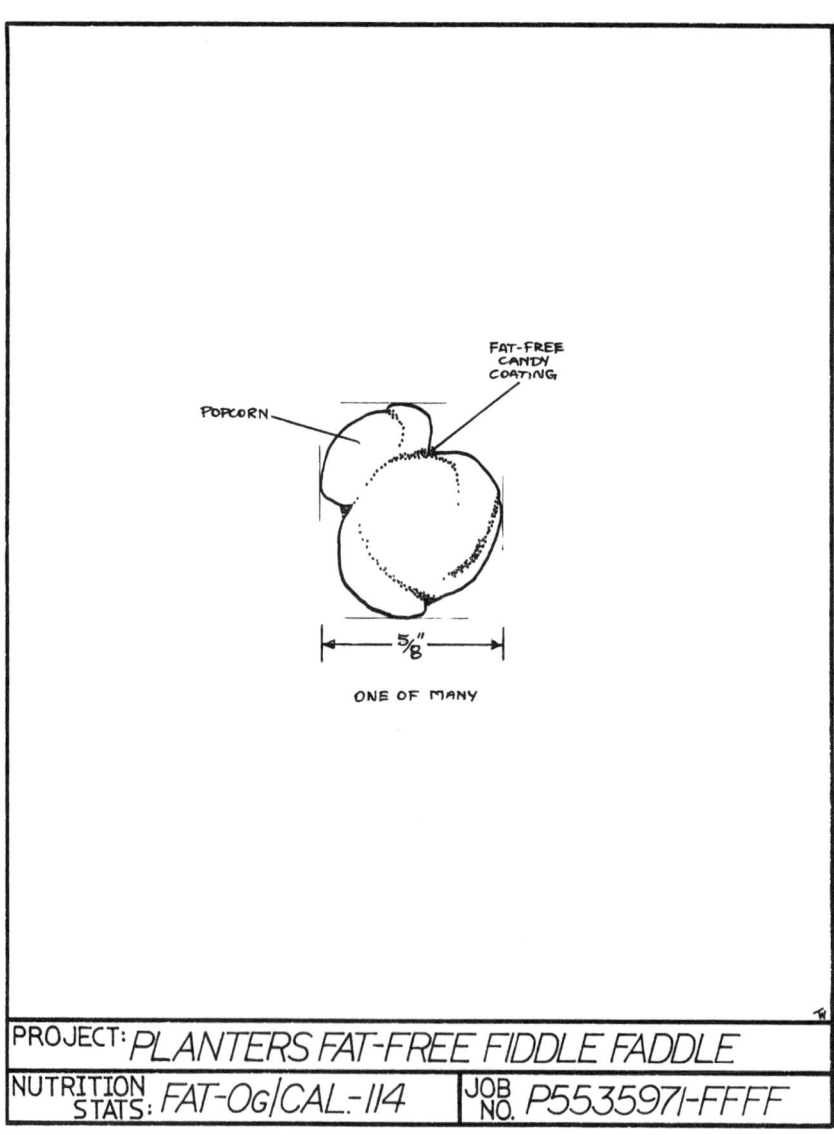

RAINFOREST CAFE REGGAE BEAT SEASONING

TOP SECRET RECIPES VERSION OF

Walk inside Steve Schussler's house in Minneapolis, Minnesota, and you'd think you had stepped into a jungle. That's because seventeen years of research and seven years of construction went into re-creating a working rain forest inside the doors of his not-exactly-humble abode. This is how Steve presented the idea for his theme restaurant chain to the numerous potential investors. One of them, Lyle Berman, liked the idea and helped to provide the financing to open the first Rainforest Cafe in Minneapolis's Mall of America in 1994.

The popular chain has always used the Reggae Beat Seasoning in several of its recipes, including the Tropical Chicken Quartet (for which a conversion can be found on page 425). In 1998, Rainforest Cafe decided to bottle the spice and sell it in the gift shops attached to each of its thirty-three units around the world.

2 teaspoons minced dried onion
1 teaspoon minced dried garlic
1 teaspoon granulated sugar
¾ teaspoon salt
½ teaspoon crushed red pepper
½ teaspoon cayenne pepper
½ teaspoon ground black pepper
½ teaspoon allspice
¼ teaspoon cinnamon
¼ teaspoon ground clove
dash cornstarch
dash dried savory
dash dried thyme

1. Combine all ingredients in a small cup or bowl.
2. Crush with the back of a spoon until finer in texture. Store in a covered container.

- MAKES ABOUT 3 TABLESPOONS.

• • • •

RAINFOREST CAFE
THE PLANT SANDWICH

Inside each Rainforest Cafe, customers are immersed in a thunder and lightning storm every twenty minutes. But don't worry, you don't have to bring your umbrella, since the rain only falls over specially designed troughs that recycle the water and ready it for the next downpour.

This sandwich was introduced in 1998 and uses Rainforest Cafe's delicious balsamic vinaigrette to marinate the mushrooms, making it one of the most delicious portobellos you've ever munched on. For this clone, prepare the vinaigrette and marinate the mushrooms a couple hours before you plan to assemble the sandwich.

BALSAMIC VINAIGRETTE
1/2 cup mayonnaise
5 teaspoons balsamic vinegar
1 tablespoon water
1/2 teaspoon cracked black pepper
1/4 teaspoon garlic powder
1/8 teaspoon onion powder
1/8 teaspoon lemon juice
dash ground black pepper
dash salt

SANDWICH
4 portobello mushroom caps
1 medium zucchini, sliced thinly lengthwise
1 red bell pepper, seeded and quartered
4 large romaine lettuce leaves, chopped
2 tablespoons Caesar salad dressing
fat-free butter-flavored spray
a handful fresh spinach leaves
8 slices 7- or 9-grain bread

1. Prepare the balsamic vinaigrette by mixing the ingredients in a small bowl until smooth.
2. Place the mushroom caps into a large resealable plastic bag. Pour the balsamic vinaigrette into the bag, seal it up, and chill for an hour or two.
3. When the mushrooms have marinated, preheat your barbecue or indoor grill to high temperature.
4. Place the mushroom caps on the grill along with the zucchini and quartered bell pepper with the skin side down. Cook the zucchini for 3 to 4 minutes per side, and the mushrooms for 5 to 7 minutes per side. Leave the bell pepper with the skin side facing the heat for the entire time, until the skin is well charred.
5. In a medium bowl, toss the chopped lettuce with the Caesar dressing until well coated.
6. Preheat a large skillet over medium heat.
7. When you are ready to build the sandwiches, spray a light coating of butter spray over the face of each slice of bread. Grill the faces of the bread in the hot skillet until light brown.
8. Build each sandwich by first arranging a few spinach leaves on the face of one slice of bread, followed by about ¼ of the tossed romaine lettuce.
9. Place a grilled portobello mushroom cap on the lettuce.
10. Remove the charred skin from one of the bell pepper quarters and then slice the pepper in half, lengthwise. Place the two slices on the sandwich.
11. Cut one grilled zucchini slice in half, across the middle, and arrange the slices on the sandwich.
12. Top the sandwich with a grilled slice of bread. Cut the sandwich diagonally and stick a toothpick in each half. Repeat for the remaining sandwiches.

- MAKES 4 SANDWICHES.

Nutrition Facts

SERVING SIZE—1 SANDWICH   FAT (PER SERVING)—11 G
TOTAL SERVINGS—4   CALORIES (PER SERVING)—335

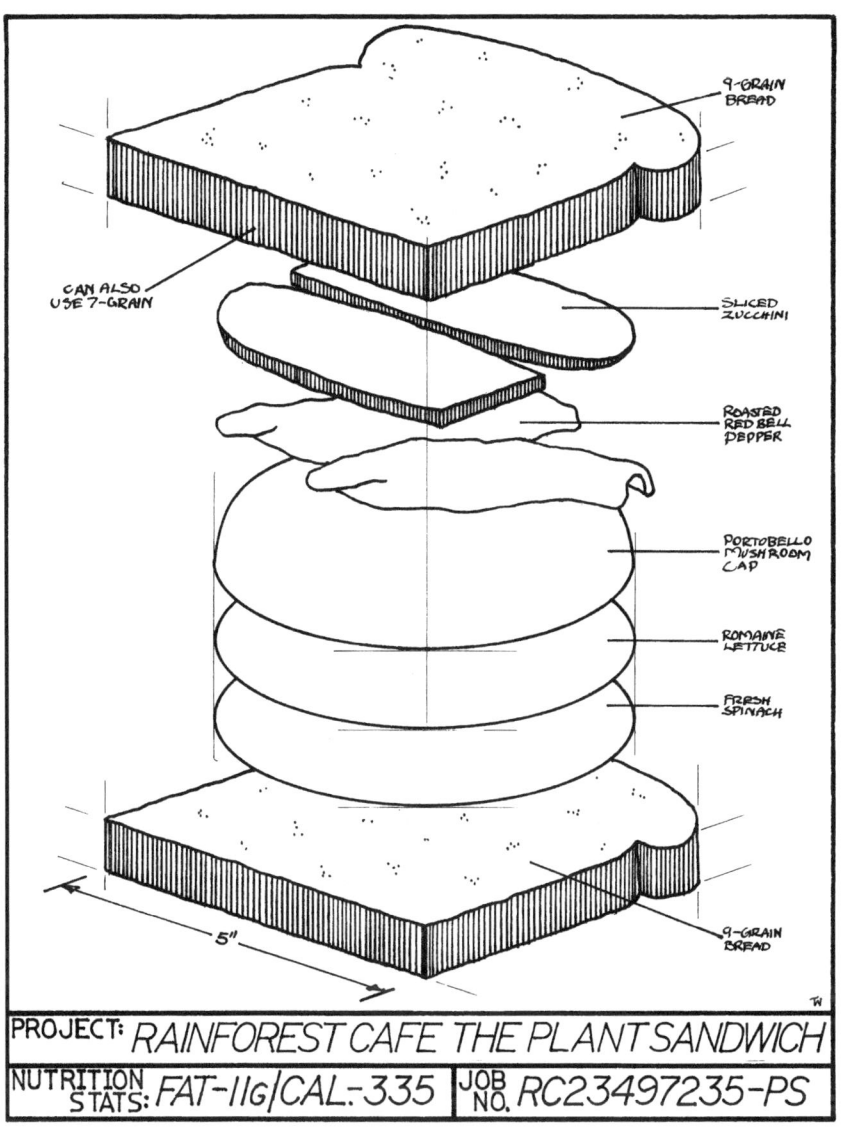

RAINFOREST CAFE RUMBLE IN THE JUNGLE TURKEY PITA

TOP SECRET RECIPES VERSION OF

No two Rainforest Cafes are the same. While they all include plant-covered walls and ceilings, waterfalls, starry skies, and live birds, you will find many unique features in each of the restaurants. The Las Vegas store includes an aquarium archway under which you must walk to enter the restaurant, and the original store in the Mall of America features a talking banyan tree spouting ecological messages twice a minute.

The turkey pita sandwich has been on the menu since the first restaurant opened in 1994, and our clone is a great way to use up your leftover Thanksgiving turkey and cranberry sauce. We can use full-fat Caesar dressing for our clone, just like the restaurant uses, and still keep the fat reasonably low. But if you find a tasty lower-fat substitute, you can knock those fat grams down even further.

CRANBERRY RELISH (OPTIONAL)
1 16-ounce can whole berry cranberry relish
½ cup orange juice
¼ cup raisins
¼ cup gold raisins

PITA
10 large leaves romaine lettuce, chopped (5 to 6 cups)
¼ cup Caesar dressing
4 large pita breads
2 Roma tomatoes, sliced (16 slices)
1 cooked turkey breast, chilled (about 12 ounces)
½ cup French's french fried onions

1. Prepare the cranberry relish, if you plan to use it, by combining all of the ingredients in a medium saucepan over medium/high heat. Bring mixture to a boil, then reduce heat and simmer for 5 to 7 minutes. Remove mixture from heat, and cool. Pour mixture into a covered container and chill until cold.
2. Toss the lettuce with the Caesar dressing in a large bowl.
3. Wrap the pitas in a moist towel and heat in the microwave on high for about 1 minute or until all of the pitas are hot.
4. To make a sandwich, fold a pita like a taco and fill it with about ¼ the romaine lettuce.
5. Arrange four of the Roma tomato slices along one side of the pita.
6. Spoon 3 ounces (about ¾ cup) of the turkey over the lettuce and tomato slices, then sprinkle 2 tablespoons of fried onions on top. Serve with cranberry relish on the side, if desired. Repeat for the remaining sandwiches.
- MAKES 4 SANDWICHES.

Nutrition Facts
SERVING SIZE—1 SANDWICH FAT (PER SERVING)—13 G
TOTAL SERVINGS—4 CALORIES (PER SERVING)—350

• • • •

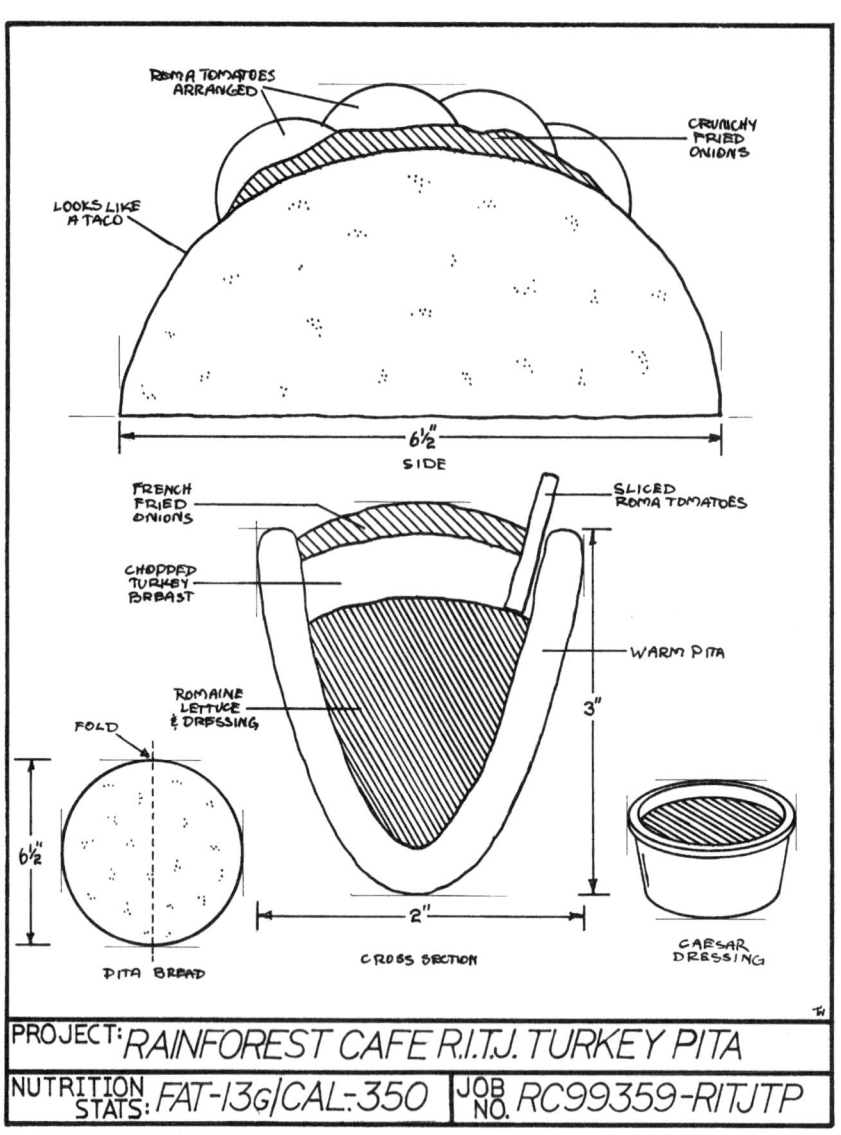

TOP SECRET RECIPES VERSION OF

SEVEN SEAS FREE RED WINE VINEGAR FAT-FREE DRESSING

The original version of this bright red dressing is made with a generous amount of oil and is filled with gobs of greasy fat grams. The trend toward fat-free foods was in its infancy when Seven Seas went to work on a nonfat variety of the Red Wine Vinegar Dressing that would taste as good as the original. They did a pretty darn good job, too. Just by tasting the Seven Seas version of this clone, it's hard to believe there's not a speck of fat in the bottle.

We can replace the oil by thickening the dressing with a top secret combination of water, cornstarch, and a little gelatin. A couple drops of food coloring will give your clone the bright, beet-red hue of the original. Of course, you can leave the coloring out of the recipe if you like, but when you see the color without the red, you'll understand why it's in there.

1 1/3 cups water
1/4 cup granulated sugar
2 teaspoons cornstarch
1/8 teaspoon Knox unflavored gelatin
1 1/2 teaspoons dried minced onion
1 teaspoon salt
1/2 cup red wine vinegar
7 drops red food coloring

1. Combine water, sugar, cornstarch, gelatin, onion, and salt in a small saucepan. Whisk to dissolve cornstarch, then set pan over medium/low heat.
2. Heat mixture until boiling, stirring often. When mixture begins

to boil, cook for 2 additional minutes, stirring constantly, then remove from heat. Let mixture cool for 5 minutes.
3. Add vinegar and food coloring to saucepan and stir. Transfer dressing to a covered container and refrigerate—preferably overnight—before serving.

- MAKES 1 ½ CUPS.

Nutrition Facts
SERVING SIZE—2 TABLESPOONS   FAT (PER SERVING)—0 G
TOTAL SERVINGS—12   CALORIES (PER SERVING)—15

• • • •

SEVEN SEAS FREE VIVA ITALIAN FAT-FREE DRESSING

Seven Seas dressings were first introduced by Anderson Clayton Foods back in 1964. Kraft Foods later picked up the brand, and Seven Seas today ranks number four in sales of salad dressings in the United States.

If it's a spice-filled Italian dressing you prefer, here's the secret technique to creating a clone of Seven Seas fat-free Italian dressing, using a combination of water, cornstarch, and gelatin.

1 ⅓ cups water
1 ½ tablespoons granulated sugar
2 teaspoons cornstarch
1 teaspoon salt
½ teaspoon dried minced onion
½ teaspoon dried minced garlic
½ teaspoon finely minced red bell pepper
½ teaspoon Italian seasoning
¼ teaspoon gelatin
½ cup white vinegar
1 teaspoon dry nonfat buttermilk

1. Combine water, sugar, cornstarch, salt, onion, garlic, bell pepper, Italian seasoning, and gelatin in a small saucepan. Whisk to dissolve cornstarch, then set pan over medium/low heat.
2. Heat mixture until boiling, stirring often. When mixture begins to boil, cook for 1 additional minute, stirring constantly, then remove from heat.
3. Add vinegar and dry buttermilk to saucepan and stir. Transfer dressing to a covered container and refrigerate—preferably overnight—before serving.

- MAKES 1 ½ CUPS.

TIDBITS

If you can't find dry buttermilk, you can substitute it with low-fat buttermilk—you know, the wet stuff. Measure 1 tablespoon into the dressing after you add the vinegar.

Nutrition Facts
    SERVING SIZE—2 TABLESPOONS   FAT (PER SERVING)—0 G
    TOTAL SERVINGS—12   CALORIES (PER SERVING)—10

• • • •

TOOTSIE ROLL MIDGEES

How would you react if your dentist suddenly whipped out a giant Tootsie Roll for you to bite down on so that he could make a mold of your teeth? Ask patients of a dentist in Philadelphia who does just that. This is just one of many facts that you learn researching the history of the Tootsie Roll, which, by the way, was named after the inventor's five-year-old daughter. Leo Hirschfield created the chewy brown candy in his small store in New York in 1896. In those days, the candy was hand rolled and delivered to customers by horse-drawn carriage. Over one hundred years later, more than forty-nine million Tootsie Rolls are produced each day from operations all over the world. And that's not counting the sixty bite-size clones—Tootsie Roll calls them "Midgees"—you'll make with this secret recipe.

1 cup granulated sugar
½ cup light corn syrup
2½ tablespoons shortening
4 teaspoons cocoa

2 tablespoons condensed skim milk
½ teaspoon vanilla

1. Combine sugar, corn syrup, shortening, and cocoa in a medium saucepan over medium/high heat.
2. Bring mixture to a boil, then reduce heat to medium, and simmer candy until temperature comes to 275 degrees on a candy thermometer.
3. Remove pan from heat. When bubbling stops, add condensed milk and beat in pan with electric mixer for about 30 seconds.

4. Add vanilla, then continue to beat candy until it begins to firm up and you can no longer beat it.
5. Pour candy out onto wax paper. When it is cool, divide candy into several portions and roll into long ropes that are approximately ½ inch thick.
6. Use a sharp knife to slice candy into 1 ⅛-inch-long portions.
7. Arrange the candy on a plate and let it sit out overnight so that it firms up.

- MAKES 60 PIECES.

Nutrition Facts

SERVING SIZE—6 PIECES   FAT (PER SERVING)—3 G
TOTAL SERVINGS—10   CALORIES (PER SERVING)—180

• • • •

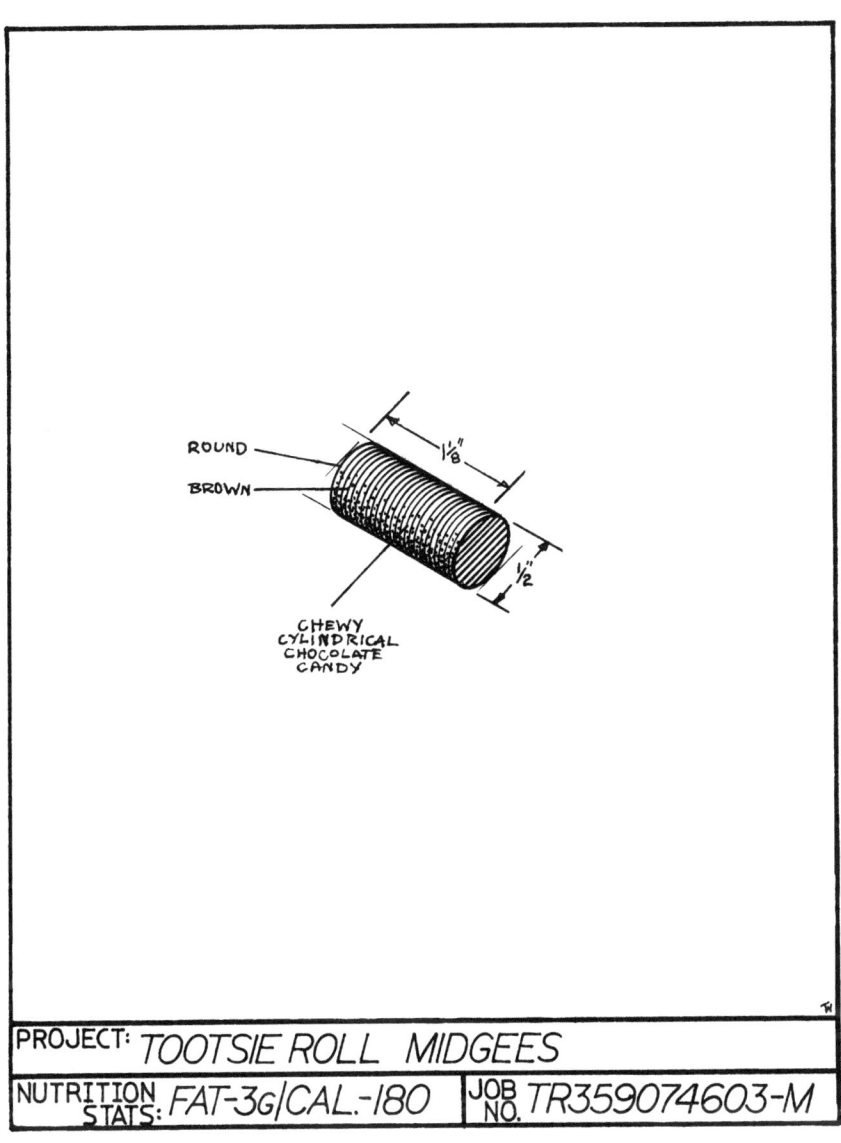

LOW-FAT TOP SECRET RECIPES CONVERSIONS

TOP SECRET RECIPES REDUCED-FAT VERSION OF

APPLEBEE'S TEQUILA LIME CHICKEN

This item has been a huge best-seller since it was first added to Applebee's menu in 1993 as promotional summer chow. The original version of this chicken dish is topped with an oil-based Mexi-ranch dressing, plus a melted cheddar and Monterey Jack cheese blend, making it every shade of tasty, yet brutal on the midriff. And customers freak over the marinade, which adds an addictive tang to the chicken breast that blends nicely with the other mellower ingredients. You'll need only a small amount of tequila to make this taste like the original—we're not making a margarita here! I learned the hard way that if you add more than the seemingly minuscule ¼ teaspoon of tequila to your chicken, it'll taste like it just got back from a bachelor party in Tijuana.

MARINADE

- 1 cup water
- ⅓ cup teriyaki sauce
- 2 tablespoons lime juice
- 2 teaspoons minced garlic
- 1 teaspoon mesquite liquid smoke flavoring
- ½ teaspoon salt
- ¼ teaspoon ground ginger
- ¼ teaspoon tequila

4 skinless chicken breast fillets

FAT-FREE MEXI-RANCH DRESSING

- ¼ cup fat-free mayonnaise
- ¼ cup fat-free sour cream
- 2 tablespoons reduced-fat milk
- 2 tablespoons water
- 2 teaspoons minced tomato
- 1 teaspoon minced canned jalapeño slices (nacho rings)
- 1 teaspoon minced onion

1 teaspoon white vinegar
¼ teaspoon dried parsley
¼ teaspoon salt
¼ teaspoon Tabasco pepper sauce
⅛ teaspoon dried dillweed

⅛ teaspoon paprika
⅛ teaspoon cayenne pepper
⅛ teaspoon cumin
⅛ teaspoon chili powder
dash garlic powder
dash ground black pepper

1 cup reduced-fat shredded cheddar/Monterey Jack cheese blend

2 cups crumbled baked corn tortilla chips

1. Prepare the marinade by combining the ingredients in a medium bowl. Add the chicken to the bowl, cover, and chill for 2 to 3 hours.
2. Make the Mexi-ranch dressing by combining all of the ingredients in a medium bowl. Mix well until smooth, then cover the dressing and chill it until needed.
3. When you are ready to prepare the entrée, preheat the oven to high broil. Also preheat barbecue grill to high heat. When the barbie is hot, grill the marinated chicken breasts for 3 to 5 minutes per side, or until they're cooked all the way through.
4. Arrange the cooked chicken in a baking pan. Spread a layer of Mexi-ranch dressing over each piece of chicken followed by ¼ cup of the shredded cheese blend. Broil the chicken for 1 to 2 minutes or just until the cheese melts.
5. Spread a bed of ½ cup of the crumbled tortilla chips on each of 4 plates. Slide a chicken breast onto the crumbled chips on each plate, and serve with your choice of rice and pico de gallo or salsa.

- SERVES 4 AS AN ENTRÉE.

Nutrition Facts *(per serving)*
SERVING SIZE—1 ENTRÉE   TOTAL SERVINGS—4

	LOW-FAT	ORIGINAL
CALORIES (APPROX.)	495	580
FAT (APPROX.)	15G	30G

• • • •

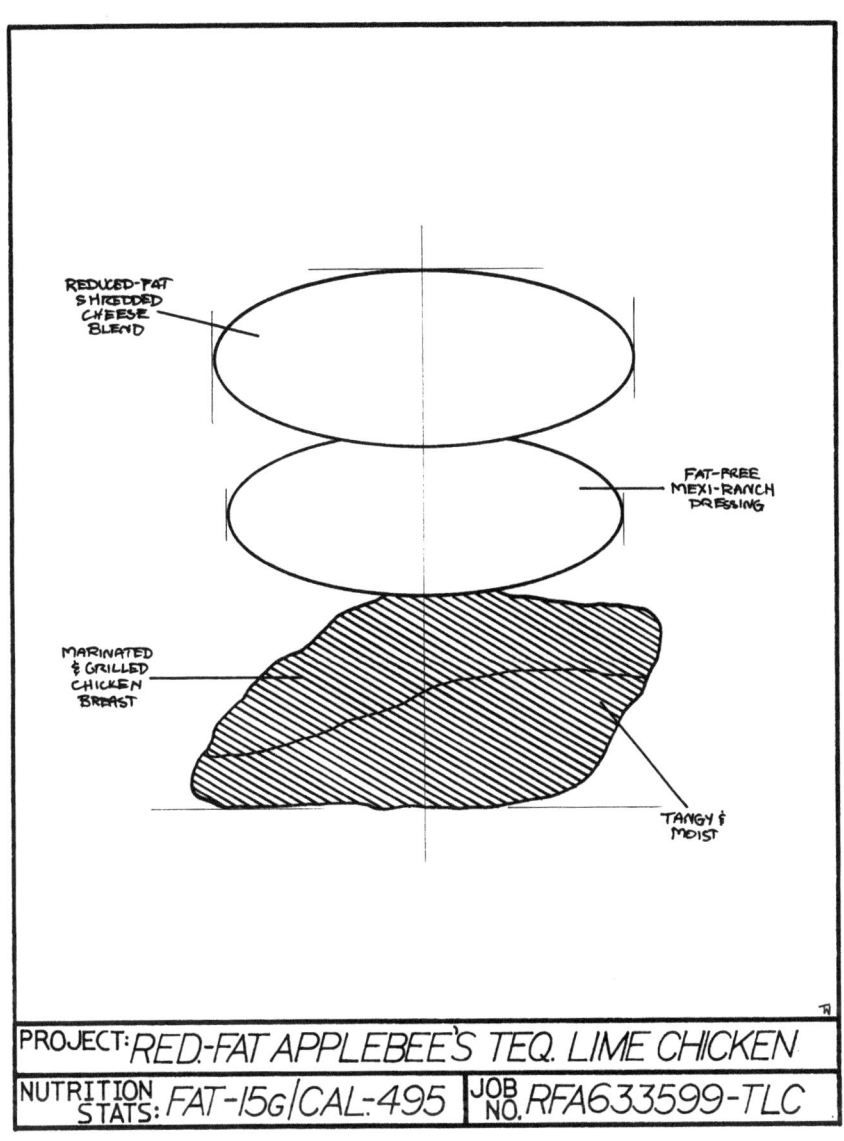

TOP SECRET RECIPES REDUCED-FAT VERSION OF

BENNIGAN'S BUFFALO CHICKEN SANDWICH

Visit the Bennigan's Web site and you'll find out that in the early 1900s, Irishman D. Bennigan came to the United States to work as a bartender with the dream of one day opening his own tavern. During the depression, Bennigan got his wish when he purchased an old, foreclosed bar, redecorated it, and opened the original Bennigan's Irish American Grill & Tavern. The "Our Story" page also explains that today all Bennigan's restaurants still use elements from that original location such as the brass rails, period pictures, and memorabilia hanging from the walls. What the Web page won't tell you is that this history is entirely made up. You'll have to dig a little deeper to find out that Bennigan's actually started in Atlanta, Georgia, in 1976, and was, at that time, owned by Pillsbury.

For this clone, we'll use a special technique developed in the secret underground test kitchens to prepare the chicken without frying. This will knock that fat down to just around one-third of the original.

1 skinless chicken breast fillet
½ cup all-purpose flour
½ teaspoon salt
½ cup egg substitute
    (or ½ cup milk)
nonstick cooking spray
2 tablespoons Louisiana hot sauce
    or Frank's Red Hot

1 tablespoon fat-free
    butter-flavored spread
1 hamburger bun
2 tomato slices
1 leaf green leaf lettuce
2 to 3 red onion rings
    (separated slices)

1. Wrap the chicken breast in plastic wrap and pound with a mallet until it is somewhere between ½ to ¼ inch thick and about the same size as the diameter of the bun.
2. Combine the flour and salt in a small bowl. Pour the egg substitute into another bowl. Drop the chicken breast into the bowl of flour and coat well. Coat the chicken with the egg substitute, and then put it back into the flour. When chicken is well coated, place it into the refrigerator to sit for 10 to 15 minutes. This is a good time to preheat the oven to 450 degrees.
3. Coat a baking pan with nonstick spray and place the chicken breast in it. Coat the top of the chicken breast with the cooking spray and bake it for 20 minutes or until it begins to brown.
4. Combine the hot sauce and fat-free spread in a plastic container big enough to hold the chicken. Be sure the container has a lid. When the chicken is done, place it into the plastic container with the spicy coating, cover, and gently shake the container until the chicken is well covered with the sauce.
5. Toast the face of the top and bottom bun and build the sandwich by turning the top bun over and arranging the lettuce on it. Stack the tomato slices, side by side, on the lettuce, then arrange 2 or 3 separated rings of onion on the sliced tomato.
6. Place the chicken breast on the face of the bottom bun, then turn the top half of the sandwich over onto the bottom. Serve immediately.

- MAKES 1 SANDWICH.

Nutrition Facts (per serving)
SERVING SIZE—1 SANDWICH   TOTAL SERVINGS—1

	LOW-FAT	ORIGINAL
CALORIES (APPROX.)	512	1038
FAT (APPROX.)	9G	27G

• • • •

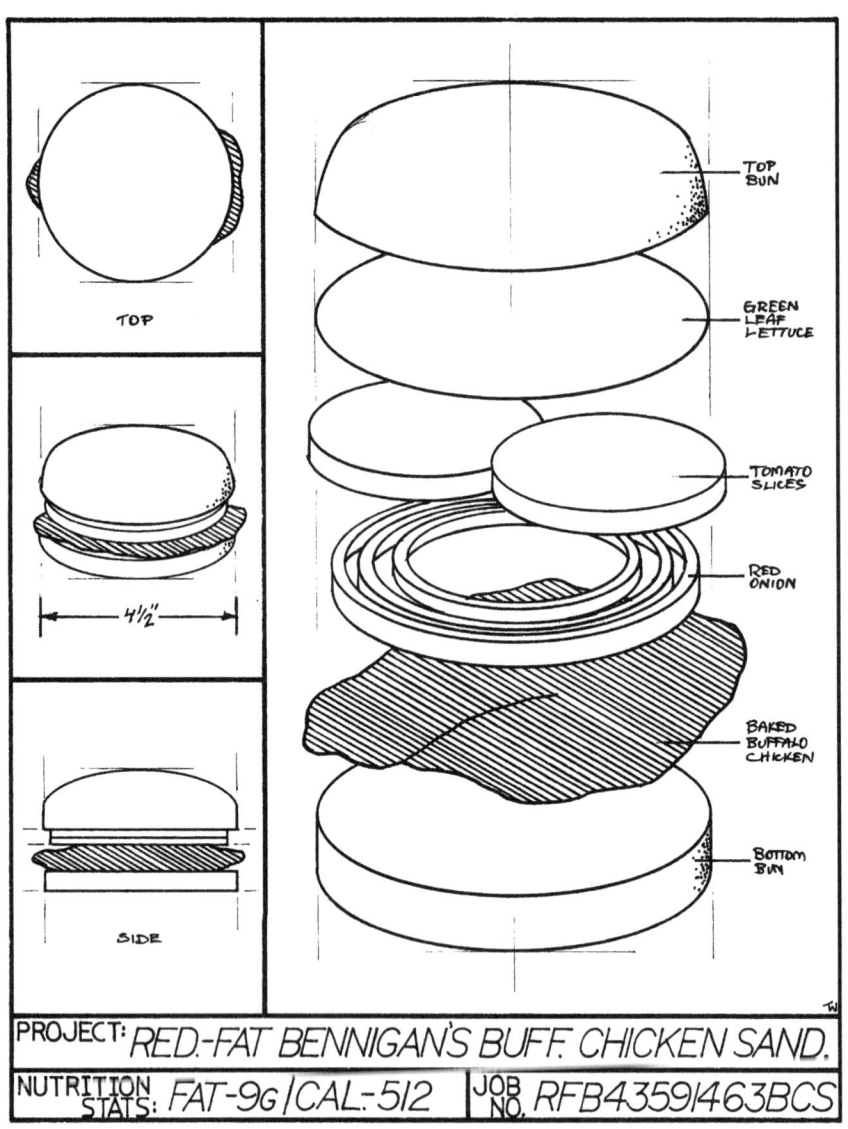

CALIFORNIA PIZZA KITCHEN SEDONA WHITE CORN TORTILLA SOUP

TOP SECRET RECIPES LOW-FAT VERSION OF

When you get a steaming bowl of good tortilla soup plopped in front of you, it's tough to stop slurping until you hit bottom. California Pizza Kitchen has just such a soup, but the oil and fried tortilla chips put it a bit too far on the fat side. Never fear; we can make this delicious white corn tortilla soup taste just as good as the original without most of the oil and fat. Fat-free chicken broth stands in well for the regular stuff, and baked corn tortilla chips give the soup its traditional taste and texture. You'll want to use a hand blender for this one, if you've got one. If not, a regular blender or food processor will work fine to puree the soup so that it has the smooth consistency of the original but with only a minuscule two grams of fat per serving.

1 teaspoon olive oil
1/4 cup minced white onion
2 cloves garlic, minced
3 cups frozen white corn, thawed
3 medium tomatoes, chopped (about 3 cups)
1 cup tomato sauce
2 tablespoons granulated sugar
1 teaspoon ground cumin
1 teaspoon salt
1/4 teaspoon crushed red pepper flakes
1/8 teaspoon white pepper
1/2 teaspoon chili powder
2 14 1/2-ounce cans fat-free chicken broth (4 cups)
1 1/2 cups crumbled baked corn tortilla chips

OPTIONAL GARNISH

½ cup crumbled baked tortilla chips
½ cup fat-free shredded cheddar cheese
1 tablespoon minced cilantro

1. Preheat 1 teaspoon of oil in a large saucepan over medium heat.
2. Sauté the onion and garlic in the oil for a couple minutes or until the onions begin to turn translucent.
3. Add half of the corn and the remaining ingredients to the saucepan, then bring mixture to a boil. Reduce heat and simmer for 20 minutes.
4. Using an electric handheld blender, puree the soup until it is smooth. You may also puree the soup with a standard blender or food processor in batches.
5. Add the remaining corn to the soup, and simmer for an additional 20 minutes or until the soup is thick.
6. If desired, add some of the crumbled baked tortilla chips, cheddar cheese, and cilantro as a garnish and serve hot.

- SERVES 4.

Nutrition Facts *(per serving)*

SERVING SIZE—1 ½ CUPS   TOTAL SERVINGS—4

	LOW-FAT	ORIGINAL
CALORIES (APPROX.)	260	305
FAT (APPROX.)	2G	14G

• • • •

TOP SECRET RECIPES REDUCED-FAT VERSION OF

CARL'S JR. RANCH CRISPY CHICKEN SANDWICH

The 1980s were the beginning of tough times for one of the world's largest burger chains. Carl Karcher had built the little hot-dog cart he purchased for $311 in 1941 into a successful West Coast hamburger chain 600 units strong; but his luck was about to change. Carl took his company public, then opened several Carl's Jr. restaurants in Texas. The bottom line for the Texas stores fell way below expectations, and the stock began to skid. In 1988, Carl was charged with insider trading for selling stock just before its price fell, and he paid almost $1 million in fines. When poor Southern California real estate investments left him millions of dollars in debt, Carl was desperate to find a way out of the hole. He proposed to the board of directors that Carl's Jr. should sell Mexican food. The board rejected the plan, so Carl tried to fire its members. In 1993, the board voted to fire Carl instead, and the man with the vision was ousted from the very company he had founded.

For this reduced-fat clone of an excellent chicken sandwich, we'll make the ranch dressing from scratch with fat-free ingredients. Then we'll use a special Top Secret Recipes baking technique cooked up in the underground test kitchen that eliminates much of the fat we can't avoid when frying.

FAT-FREE RANCH DRESSING

1/3 cup fat-free mayonnaise
2 tablespoons fat-free sour cream
1 tablespoon reduced-fat buttermilk
1 1/2 teaspoons white vinegar
1 teaspoon granulated sugar
1/4 teaspoon lemon
1/8 teaspoon salt
1/8 teaspoon dried parsley
1/8 teaspoon onion powder
1/16 teaspoon dried dillweed
dash garlic
dash ground black pepper
1/2 teaspoon unflavored gelatin
2 teaspoons hot water

SANDWICH

1/4 cup egg substitute
1 cup water
1 cup flour
2 1/2 teaspoons salt
1 teaspoon paprika
1 teaspoon onion powder
1/8 teaspoon garlic powder
2 skinless chicken breast fillets
vegetable oil cooking spray
4 sesame seed hamburger buns
4 lettuce leaves
4 tomato slices

1. Prepare the ranch dressing by combining all ingredients except the gelatin and hot water in a medium bowl. Combine the gelatin with the hot water in a small bowl and stir to dissolve all of the gelatin. Add this to the other ingredients and stir well. Cover and chill (best to chill for at least a couple hours).
2. Preheat oven to 475 degrees.
3. Combine the egg substitute and water in a large, shallow bowl.
4. Combine the flour, salt, paprika, onion powder, and garlic powder in another shallow bowl.
5. Cut each chicken breast in half across the middle. Wrap each half in plastic wrap and pound it to about 1/4 inch thick. Trim each piece so that it is round.
6. Working with one fillet at a time, coat each with the flour, then dredge it in the egg and water mixture. Coat the chicken once again with the flour and set it aside until all of the fillets have been breaded.
7. Line a large baking sheet with aluminum foil. Spray the foil

with a generous coating of cooking oil. Place the chicken fillets on the baking sheet, then coat each one with a light layer of cooking spray.
8. Bake the fillets for 12 minutes, then crank the oven up to broil for 4 to 5 minutes, then flip the chicken over and broil for another 2 to 4 minutes or until the chicken is browned and crispy on both sides.
9. As chicken is cooking, prepare each sandwich by grilling the faces of the hamburger buns on a hot skillet over medium heat. Spread about 1½ teaspoons of the ranch dressing on the face of the top and bottom buns.
10. On the bottom bun, stack a leaf of lettuce and a tomato slice.
11. When the chicken is done cooking, stack a fillet over the tomato onto the bottom of the sandwich, then top off the sandwich with the top bun. Repeat for the remaining sandwiches.

- MAKES 4 SANDWICHES.

Nutrition Facts *(per serving)*
SERVING SIZE—1 SANDWICH   TOTAL SERVINGS—4

	LOW-FAT	ORIGINAL
CALORIES	580	620
FAT	11G	29G

• • • •

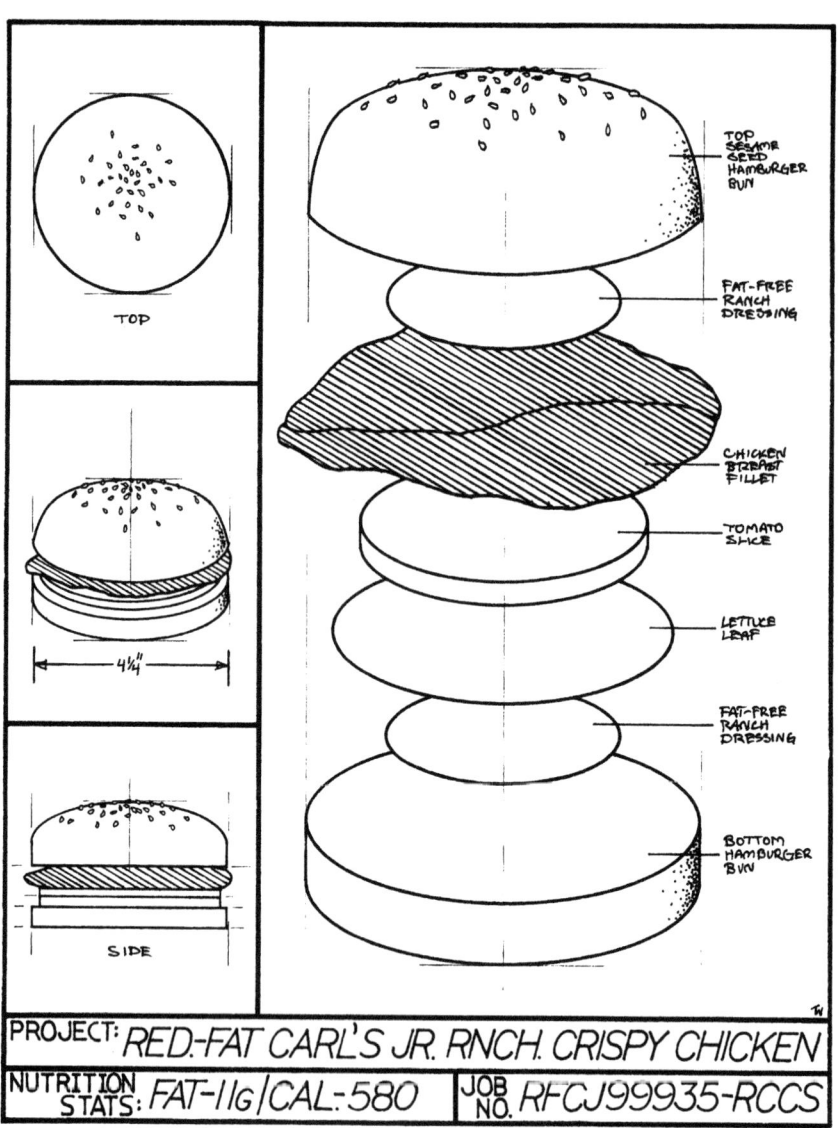

CARL'S JR. CHARBROILED CHICKEN CLUB SANDWICH

TOP SECRET RECIPES REDUCED-FAT VERSION OF

Eight weeks after the board of directors locked seventy-six-year-old Carl Karcher out of his office in 1993, he was engineering a takeover of the "Happy Star" company that he had built over five decades. Crafty Carl found financier William P. Foley to assume his debts in exchange for stock and take control of the company as the new chairman of the board. Carl was named chairman emeritus and finally got his desk back. His plan to sell Mexican food at Carl's Jr. restaurants was later adopted and became a huge success for the chain, and almost all of the executives who had fired him have since left the company.

Here's one of Carl's delicious sandwiches that we can clone with much fewer fat grams by using turkey bacon, fat-free mayonnaise, and fat-free Swiss cheese. These substitutions for full-fat ingredients can bring the fat down from twenty-nine grams to just over ten without compromising that distinctive Carl's Jr. taste.

2 skinless chicken breast fillets
½ cup teriyaki marinade (thick style)
4 whole wheat hamburger buns
8 slices turkey bacon
¼ cup fat-free mayonnaise
1 cup alfalfa sprouts
4 lettuce leaves
4 large tomato slices
4 slices fat-free Swiss cheese slices

1. Cut each chicken breast in half across the middle, then wrap the halves, one at a time, in plastic wrap. Pound each one with a mallet until it is about ¼ inch thick.

2. Pour the teriyaki marinade over the meat. Cover and chill the meat and let it marinate for at least two hours. Marinating them overnight is even better.
3. When the chicken is well marinated, heat up a skillet and toast the face of each of the buns. Keep the pan hot. Preheat your barbecue or indoor grill to medium heat.
4. Fry the turkey bacon in the skillet for 5 to 6 minutes or until it's crispy, turning each slice over halfway through the cooking time.
5. As the bacon is frying, cook the chicken on the grill for 3 to 4 minutes per side or until done.
6. Build the sandwiches by first spreading ½ tablespoon of fat-free mayo on each toasted face of the buns.
7. Divide the sprouts into four even portions and stack a mound on each of the bottom buns.
8. On the sprouts, stack a lettuce leaf, and then a slice of tomato.
9. Place a piece of chicken on the tomato slice on each of the sandwiches.
10. Next, place a slice of Swiss cheese on the chicken, and then two pieces of bacon, crossed over each other.
11. Finish building the sandwiches by adding the top bun.
12. Microwave each sandwich for 15 seconds on high, and serve.

- MAKES 4 SANDWICHES.

Nutrition Facts (per serving)
SERVING SIZE—1 SANDWICH   TOTAL SERVINGS—4

	LOW-FAT	ORIGINAL
CALORIES	366	570
FAT	10.5G	29G

• • • •

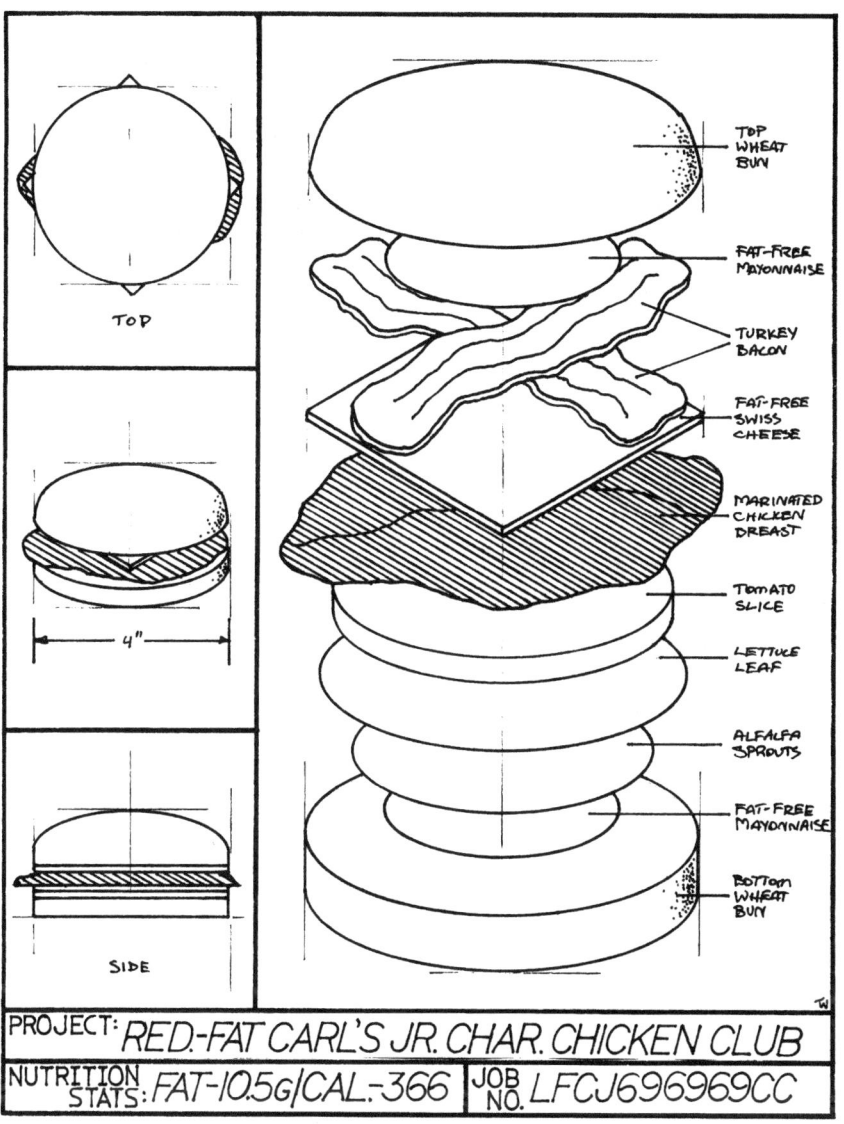

TOP SECRET RECIPES REDUCED-FAT VERSION OF

CARL'S JR. CHARBROILED SANTA FE CHICKEN SANDWICH

In the last few years, Carl's Jr. has become one of the fastest-growing fast-food chains in the country. In 1997, the burger joint grew from 930 restaurants in nine states to nearly 3,900 in forty-four states with its purchase of Hardee's hamburger outlets. This makes Carl's Jr. the fourth-largest burger chain in the country, behind McDonald's, Burger King, and Wendy's.

One of the unique sandwiches that makes Carl's a popular stop for the lunch crowd is this Charbroiled Santa Fe Chicken Sandwich with the delicious spicy sauce. It's that tasty sauce that gives the real thing much of its fat, so by cloning it with nonfat ingredients, we can cut the grease on this sandwich to one-fifth of that of the original, while keeping all of the zing.

SANTA FE SAUCE

1/3 cup fat-free mayonnaise
1/4 teaspoon paprika
1/4 teaspoon curry powder
1/8 teaspoon cayenne pepper
1/8 teaspoon salt

SANDWICH

2 skinless chicken breast fillets
1/2 cup teriyaki marinade (thick style)
4 whole wheat hamburger buns
4 lettuce leaves
2 large canned mild green chili peppers, halved
4 slices fat-free American cheese

1. Make the sauce by combining all of the ingredients in a small bowl, and stir well. Cover and chill until needed.
2. Cut each chicken breast in half across the middle, and then wrap the halves, one at a time, in plastic wrap. Pound each one with a mallet until it is about ¼ inch thick.
3. Pour the teriyaki marinade over the chicken. Cover and chill the chicken and let it marinate for at least two hours. Marinating it overnight is even better.
4. When the chicken is well marinated, heat up a skillet and toast the face of each of the buns. You may also toast the buns in a toaster oven.
5. Cook the chicken on the grill for 3 to 4 minutes per side or until done.
6. Build the sandwiches by first spreading ½ tablespoon of the Santa Fe sauce on each toasted face of the buns.
7. Stack the lettuce on next.
8. Spread out a pepper half and place it on top of the lettuce on each sandwich. Depending on the size of the pepper, you may have to trim the pepper or add more. You want to have just enough to fit on the sandwich without too much excess falling over the side.
9. Place a piece of chicken on the pepper on each of the sandwiches.
10. Next, place a slice of American cheese on the chicken.
11. Finish building the sandwiches by adding the top bun.
12. Microwave each sandwich for 15 seconds on high.

- MAKES 4 SANDWICHES.

Nutrition Facts (per serving)
SERVING SIZE—1 SANDWICH   TOTAL SERVINGS—4

	LOW-FAT	ORIGINAL
CALORIES	305	530
FAT	5.5G	29G

• • • •

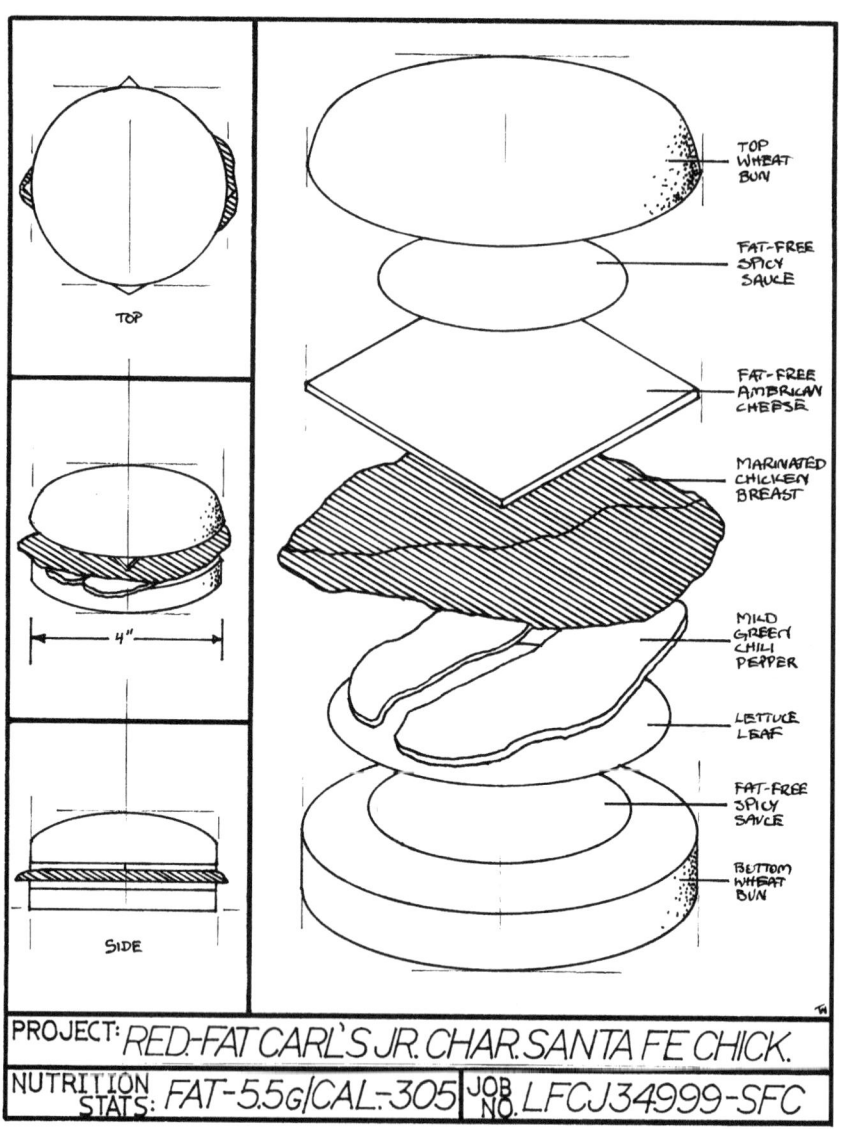

CARL'S JR. BACON SWISS CRISPY CHICKEN SANDWICH

TOP SECRET RECIPES REDUCED-FAT VERSION OF

Helping Carl's Jr. rebound from its sales slump was a series of TV commercials featuring oversauced sandwiches that splattered ketchup and mayo onto floors, clothes, and shoes. The tag line, "If it doesn't get all over the place, it doesn't belong in your face," made sloppy synonymous with tasty.

If you look forward to messing up your clean clothes but don't need all the saturated fat that usually comes with this drippy fare, you'll want to give this clone a try. The fat-free ranch dressing saves you from oodles of nasty fat grams, and then the special baking technique that clones the taste and texture of deep frying eliminates a bunch more.

FAT-FREE RANCH DRESSING

1/3 cup fat-free mayonnaise
2 tablespoons fat-free sour cream
1 tablespoon reduced-fat buttermilk
1 1/2 teaspoons white vinegar
1 teaspoon granulated sugar
1/4 teaspoon lemon juice
1/8 teaspoon salt
1/8 teaspoon dried parsley
1/8 teaspoon onion powder
1/16 teaspoon dried dillweed
dash garlic
dash ground black pepper
2 teaspoons hot water
1/2 teaspoon unflavored gelatin

SANDWICH

8 slices lean turkey bacon, cooked
1/4 cup egg substitute
1 cup water
1 cup flour

2½ teaspoons salt
1 teaspoon paprika
1 teaspoon onion powder
⅛ teaspoon garlic powder
2 skinless chicken breast fillets

vegetable oil cooking spray
4 sesame seed hamburger buns
4 lettuce leaves
4 tomato slices
4 Kraft fat-free Swiss cheese singles

1. Prepare the ranch dressing by combining the ingredients in a small bowl. Cover and chill.
2. Preheat oven to 475 degrees.
3. Cook bacon following directions on package. Drain on paper towels and set aside.
4. Combine the egg substitute and water in a large, shallow bowl.
5. Combine the flour, salt, paprika, onion powder, and garlic powder in another shallow bowl.
6. Cut each chicken breast in half across the middle, and then wrap the halves, one at a time, in plastic wrap. Pound each one with a mallet until it is about ¼ inch thick. Trim each fillet until it is round.
7. Working with one fillet at a time, first coat each fillet with the flour, then dredge it in the egg and water mixture. Coat the chicken once again in the flour, and set it aside until all of the fillets have been breaded.
8. Line a large baking sheet with aluminum foil. Spray the foil with a generous coating of cooking oil. Place the chicken fillets on the baking sheet, then coat each one with a coating of cooking spray.
9. Bake the fillets for 12 minutes, then crank the oven up to broil for 4 to 5 minutes, then flip the chicken over and broil for another 2 to 4 minutes or until the chicken is browned and crispy on both sides.
10. As chicken is cooking, prepare each sandwich by grilling the face of the hamburger buns on a hot skillet over medium heat. Spread about 1½ teaspoons of the ranch dressing on the face of the top and bottom buns.
11. On the bottom bun, stack a leaf of lettuce and a tomato slice.
12. When the chicken is done cooking, place a fillet over the

tomato onto the bottom of the sandwich, then stack a slice of the fat-free Swiss cheese onto the chicken.
13. Arrange the bacon, crosswise, on top of the Swiss cheese, then top off the sandwich with the top bun. Repeat the stacking process for each of the remaining sandwiches.

- MAKES 4 SANDWICHES.

Nutrition Facts *(per serving)*
SERVING SIZE—1 SANDWICH   TOTAL SERVINGS—4

	LOW-FAT	ORIGINAL
CALORIES	660	720
FAT	19G	36G

• • • •

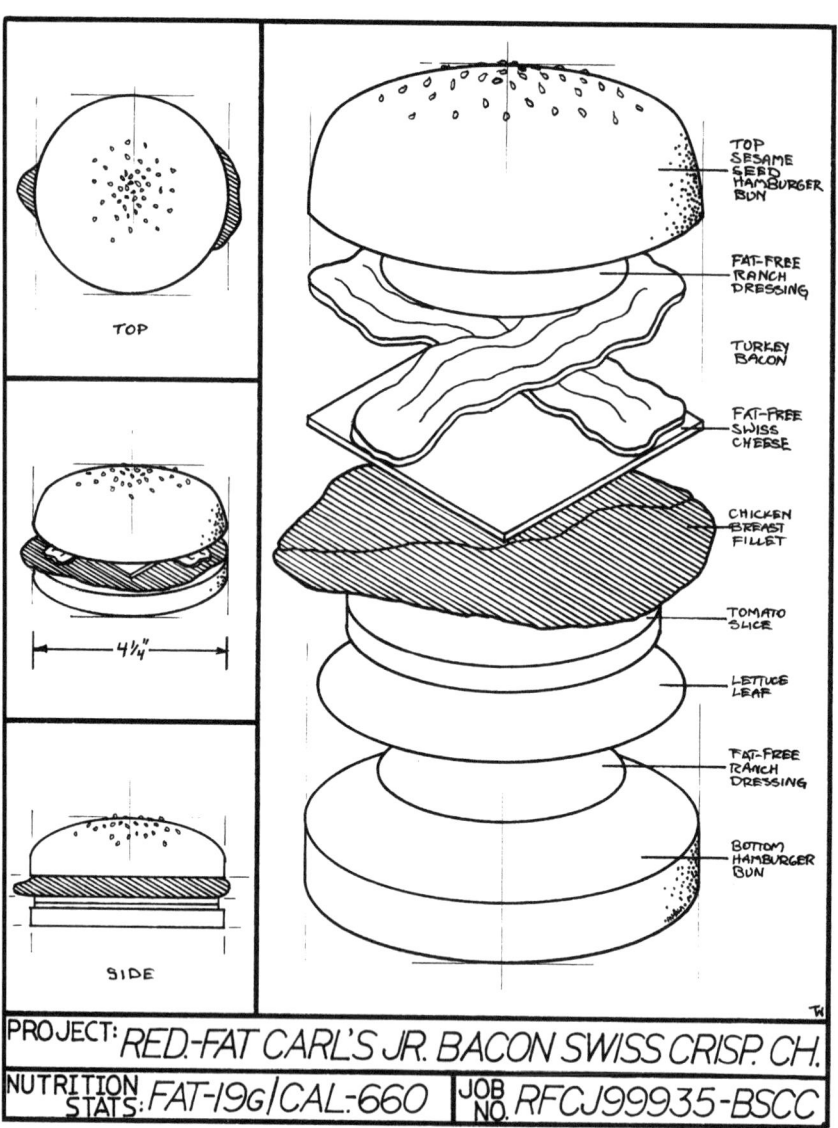

CHEVYS GARLIC MASHED POTATOES

TOP SECRET RECIPES FAT-FREE VERSION OF

Everyone seems to love these delicious mashed potatoes at the "Fresh Mex" Mexican Food chain. Sure, mashed potatoes may seem like a healthy side dish, but when the traditional recipe includes cream and butter, it's easy to whip up quite a few fat grams in one small serving.

This recipe proves that mashed potatoes don't have to include fat to taste good. Use this recipe by itself or as part of the next tasty clone from this popular chain, Chevys Texas BBQ Wrap.

- 4 medium russet potatoes
- 1 tablespoon fat-free butter-flavored spread
- 1 tablespoon minced fresh garlic (3 to 4 cloves)
- 1 1/4 cups fat-free milk
- 3/4 teaspoon salt
- 1/8 teaspoon ground black pepper

1. Preheat oven to 400 degrees.
2. Bake the potatoes by first spraying them with oil cooking spray and then baking them in the preheated oven for 1 hour or until they are tender. Cool.
3. Remove about half of the skin and mash the potatoes. Leave the rest of the skin in.
4. Melt the butter in a large saucepan over medium heat, then add the garlic and sauté for 5 minutes.
5. Add the potatoes and remaining ingredients to the pan and cook for 5 to 10 minutes while stirring often until mashed potatoes are very hot.

- SERVES 4.

Nutrition Facts *(per serving)*
SERVING SIZE—1 ¼ CUPS   TOTAL SERVINGS—4

	LOW-FAT	ORIGINAL
CALORIES (APPROX.)	285	338
FAT (APPROX.)	0G	9G

• • •

CHEVYS TEXAS BBQ WRAP

TOP SECRET RECIPES REDUCED-FAT VERSION OF

Here's a great recipe that uses the previous Chevys clone recipe along with some cool new elements. In the restaurant, these are made with red chili tortillas. Since that sort of thing can be hard to find in the real world, especially in fat-free versions, we'll use plain flour fat-free tortillas. Except for the color, you can hardly tell the difference. You'll want to prepare several elements of this recipe ahead of time. The relish and slaw is best when made the day before, and the chicken will have to marinate for an hour or so before you grill it. Be sure to prepare the garlic mashed potatoes well ahead of time, following the instructions on page 363. And be real hungry.

CORN AND PEPPER RELISH
uncooked corn cut from 1 ear of corn (about ½ cup)
2 tablespoons diced red bell pepper
2 tablespoons diced green bell pepper
2 tablespoons diced Spanish onion
pinch minced fresh cilantro
dash salt

DRESSING
1 tablespoon white vinegar
1 tablespoon water
½ teaspoon granulated sugar
⅛ teaspoon cayenne pepper
⅛ teaspoon plus a pinch cumin
1 teaspoon light mayonnaise

CHIPOTLE SLAW
1¼ cups shredded red cabbage
¼ cup green cabbage

MESQUITE MARINADE
1 cup water
2 teaspoons mesquite-flavored liquid smoke
1 teaspoon salt
dash ground black pepper

2 skinless chicken breast fillets

BEANS
1 15-ounce can black beans, with liquid
1/4 teaspoon chili powder
1/8 teaspoon salt
dash garlic powder

4 large fat-free flour tortillas
4 cups garlic mashed potatoes (from page 363)
1/2 cup spicy BBQ sauce (from page 369)

1. Prepare the corn and pepper relish by combining the ingredients in a medium bowl.
2. Prepare the dressing for the relish and chipotle slaw by mixing the vinegar, water, sugar, cayenne pepper, and cumin in a small bowl. Stir to dissolve the sugar. Measure 1 tablespoon of this mixture and add it to the corn and pepper relish. Cover the relish and chill it until needed. This relish is best when made the day before.
3. Add a teaspoon of light mayonnaise and an additional pinch of cumin to the small bowl of dressing. Whisk the mixture to help the mayonnaise blend in. Add this remaining dressing to the shredded cabbage in a medium bowl. Stir well, then cover and chill until needed. This slaw is also best when chilled overnight.
4. One hour before you are ready to make the dish, prepare the mesquite marinade by mixing the ingredients in a medium bowl. Add the chicken breast fillets to the marinade, cover, and chill for 1 hour.
5. If you haven't already done so, prepare the garlic mashed potatoes from page 363 and the spicy BBQ sauce from page 369.

6. When chicken has marinated, preheat grill on high temperature.
7. Prepare the black beans by combining the beans (with liquid), chili powder, salt, and garlic powder in a small saucepan over low heat. Simmer for 15 to 20 minutes or until beans boil and mixture becomes thicker.
8. Spray each side of the chicken with a light coating of nonstick oil cooking spray. Lightly salt and pepper each side of each chicken breast and grill for 4 to 5 minutes per side or until done. After removing the chicken from the grill, chop it into bite-size pieces. Remove about ⅓ of the spicy barbecue sauce and mix it in with the diced chicken in a medium bowl.
9. Wrap the tortillas in moist paper towels (or place them in a tortilla steamer) and microwave on high temperature for 30 to 45 seconds or until tortillas are hot and pliable.
10. Build each wrap by first spooning about ½ cup of the garlic mashed potatoes into the center of a hot tortilla. Spoon ¼ of the black beans onto the potatoes, followed by ¼ of the chicken. Spread ¼ of the slaw onto the chicken and then ¼ of the corn and pepper relish. Fold in the ends of the tortilla and then roll it up from the bottom into a tight package. Drizzle some of the leftover spicy BBQ sauce over the top of the wrap, slice it through the middle, and serve. Repeat for the remaining ingredients.

- SERVES 4 AS AN ENTRÉE.

Nutrition Facts *(per serving)*
SERVING SIZE—1 WRAP   TOTAL SERVINGS—4

	LOW-FAT	ORIGINAL
CALORIES (APPROX.)	515	644
FAT (APPROX.)	5G	15G

• • • •

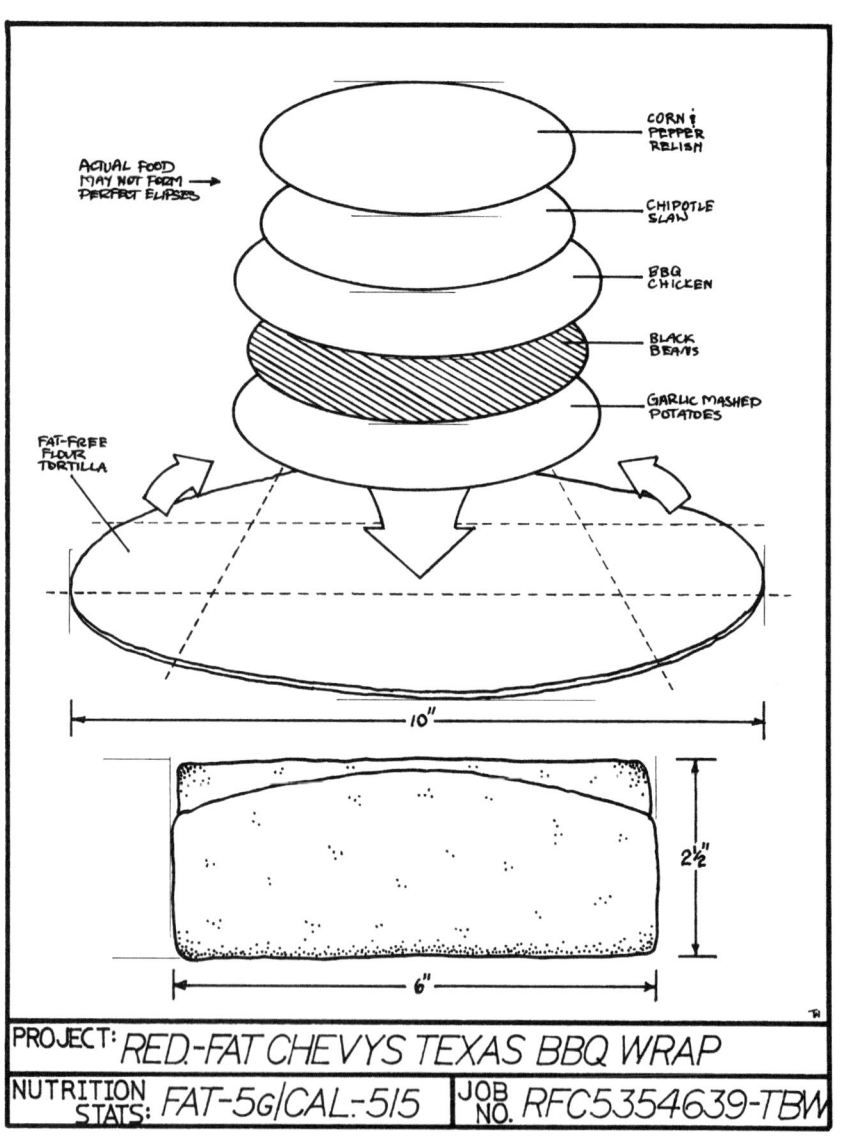

CHEVYS MESQUITE-GRILLED BBQ CHICKEN QUESADILLA

With this secret recipe it isn't necessary to cook the chicken over a mesquite grill as they do in the restaurant chain. Sure, you could get some mesquite wood chips and throw 'em on your barbecue or you can use that charcoal that has mesquite in it. But an easier way to get the flavor of mesquite—especially if all you've got is a gas grill—is to soak the chicken in a marinade made with mesquite-flavored liquid smoke. Again, in the restaurant these quesadillas are made with red chili tortillas. Since these can be a drag to track down, especially in fat-free versions, we will use plain fat-free flour tortillas.

MESQUITE MARINADE
- 1/2 cup water
- 1 teaspoon mesquite-flavored liquid smoke
- 1/2 teaspoon salt
- dash ground black pepper

1 skinless chicken breast fillet

SPICY BBQ SAUCE
- 1/2 cup Bull's-Eye Original BBQ sauce
- 1/4 teaspoon cayenne pepper
- dash chili powder

- 1/3 cup sliced red bell pepper
- 1/3 cup sliced green bell pepper
- 1/3 cup sliced Spanish onion
- 2 large (12-inch) fat-free flour tortillas
- 1 1/3 cups shredded Monterey Jack cheese

1. Prepare the marinade by combining the ingredients in a medium bowl. Add chicken breast fillet to the bowl, cover, and chill for one hour.
2. When the chicken is finished marinating, preheat your grill to high temperature.
3. As grill is heating, prepare the spicy BBQ sauce by mixing the ingredients in a small bowl.
4. Throw the chicken on the grill and cook it for 4 to 5 minutes per side or until it's done. When the chicken is done cooking, chop it into bite-size pieces.
5. Spray a light coating of nonstick cooking spray on a medium skillet over medium heat. Sauté the sliced peppers and onion in the pan for 4 or 5 minutes or until the veggies start to brown.
6. Set a large skillet over medium/low heat.
7. Put one flour tortilla in the skillet and sprinkle ⅓ cup of cheese over half of the tortilla. Spoon half of the vegetables over the cheese, followed by half of the chicken.
8. Spoon a generous portion of the spicy BBQ sauce over the chicken, followed by another ⅓ cup of cheese.
9. Fold the other side of the tortilla over the filling, and press down so that it stays in place.
10. By this time, the cheese on the bottom should be melted. If not, wait another minute or so, then flip the quesadilla over and heat for another couple minutes or until all of the cheese has melted.
11. Slide the quesadilla onto a plate and slice it into 4 pieces. Repeat for the second quesadilla and serve immediately with salsa from page 264.

- SERVES 4 AS AN APPETIZER.

Nutrition Facts *(per serving)*

Serving size—2 pieces   Total servings—4

	Low-Fat	Original
Calories (approx.)	278	400
Fat (approx.)	10g	20g

• • • •

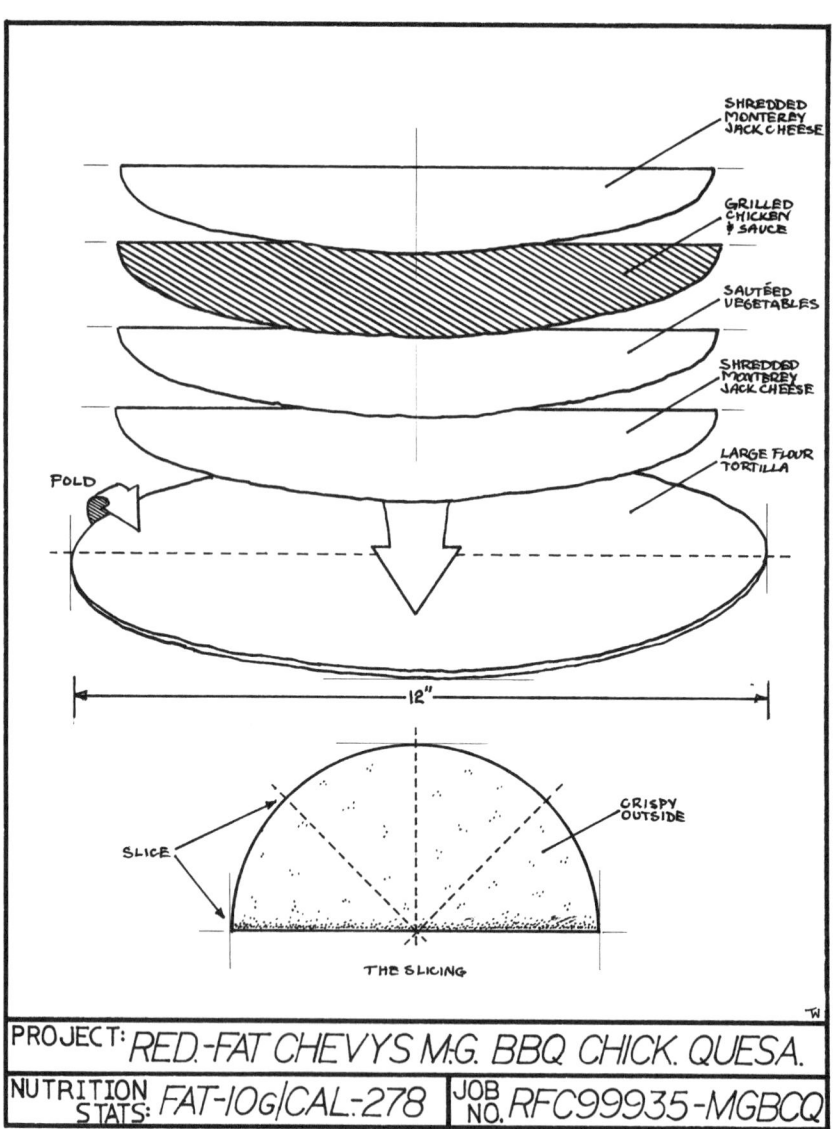

TOP SECRET RECIPES REDUCED-FAT VERSION OF

CHILI'S BONELESS BUFFALO WINGS

Not only does this conversion for Chili's new appetizer give us the zesty flavor of traditional Buffalo chicken wings without the bones or fatty skin, but I've come up with a way to bake the chicken, rather than fry it, so that we eliminate even more of those pesky fat grams. These "wings" are actually nuggets sliced from chicken breast fillets that have been breaded and fried and smothered with the same type of spicy wing sauce used on typical wings, but without the butter. If you like Buffalo wings, you'll love this reduced-fat clone, which can be served up with some celery sticks and fat-free bleu cheese dressing on the side for dipping. Party down.

1 cup all-purpose flour
2 teaspoons salt
1/4 teaspoon ground black pepper
1/4 teaspoon cayenne pepper
1/4 teaspoon paprika
1/4 cup egg substitute
1 cup reduced-fat (2%) milk

2 skinless chicken breast fillets
oil cooking spray
1/4 cup Frank's or Crystal Louisiana hot sauce
2 tablespoons fat-free butter-flavored spread
2 tablespoons water

ON THE SIDE
Fat-free bleu cheese dressing (for dipping)
celery sticks

1. Preheat oven to 475 degrees.
2. Combine flour, salt, peppers, and paprika in a medium bowl.
3. Whisk egg and milk together in a small bowl.

4. Slice each chicken breast into 5 or 6 pieces.
5. Working with one or two pieces of chicken at a time, dip each piece into the egg mixture, then into the breading blend; then repeat the process so that each piece of chicken is double-coated.
6. Coat a baking sheet with a generous portion of the oil cooking spray. Arrange the chicken on the baking sheet and then spray a light coating over the top of each piece.
7. Bake the chicken for 10 to 12 minutes or until it begins to brown. Crank the heat up to broil, and continue to cook the chicken for 2 to 4 more minutes or until the surface begins to become golden brown and crispy.
8. As the chicken cooks, combine the hot sauce, butter-flavored spread, and water in a small saucepan over medium/low heat. Cook just until the mixture begins to bubble, then remove the sauce from the heat and cover it until it's needed.
9. When the chicken pieces are cooked, remove them from the oven and let them cool for a couple minutes. Place the chicken into a covered container such as Tupperware or a large jar with a lid. Pour the sauce over the chicken in the container, cover, and then shake gently until each piece of chicken is coated with sauce. Pour the chicken onto a plate and serve the dish with fat-free bleu cheese dressing and sliced celery sticks on the side.

- SERVES 4 AS AN APPETIZER.

Nutrition Facts (per serving)
SERVING SIZE—3 PIECES   TOTAL SERVINGS—4

	LOW-FAT	ORIGINAL
CALORIES (APPROX.)	200	280
FAT (APPROX.)	5.5G	15G

• • • •

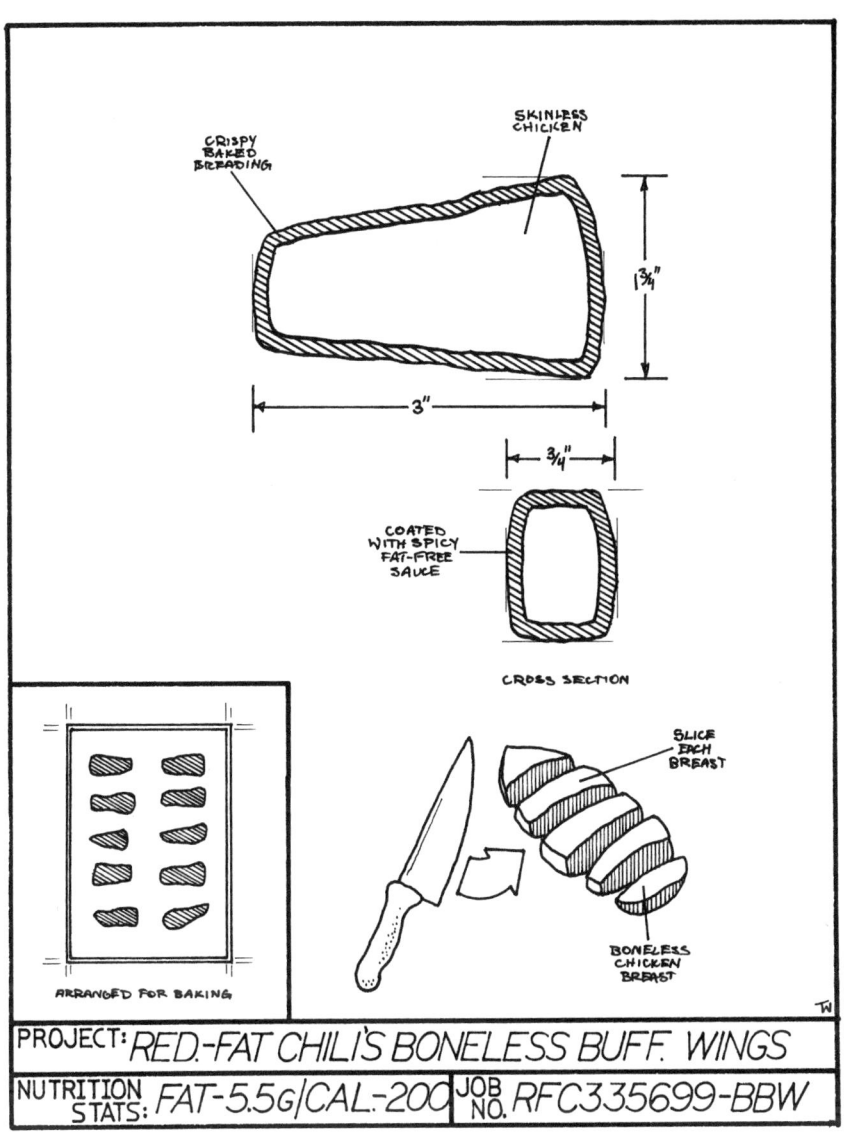

TOP SECRET RECIPES REDUCED-FAT VERSION OF

CHILI'S FAJITA SALAD

This big salad of mixed greens, fajita steak, pico de gallo, black beans, bell peppers, corn and guacamole comes slathered with two types of salad dressings plus fried tortilla chips, making the restaurant version a fat-filled fiesta.

When made from scratch with this secret Top Secret Recipes formula, the two dressings are made fat-free, knocking the fat grams down to around a third of what you munch down in the original. There are several components here in this conversion, but this recipe makes four of the huge entrée-size salads, and the results are worth the effort. This recipe clones the steak version of the salad, but you can also replace the beef with chicken.

MARINADE
2/3 cup water
1 tablespoon vegetable oil
2 tablespoons soy sauce
1 large clove garlic, pressed
1 tablespoon granulated sugar
1 teaspoon liquid smoke
1 teaspoon chili powder
1/2 teaspoon salt
1/2 teaspoon cayenne pepper
1/2 teaspoon ground black pepper
1/2 teaspoon onion powder

4 sirloin steaks (approximately 4 ounces each)

FAT-FREE CHIPOTLE RANCH DRESSING
1/4 cup fat-free mayonnaise
1/4 cup fat-free sour cream
3 tablespoons buttermilk
1 tablespoon water
1 1/2 teaspoons white vinegar
1/4 teaspoon plus 1/8 teaspoon salt

⅛ teaspoon dried parsley
⅛ teaspoon onion powder
dash dried dillweed

dash garlic powder
dash ground black pepper

FAT-FREE SANTA FE DRESSING
⅓ cup fat-free Catalina dressing
1 tablespoon stone ground mustard
1 tablespoon water
½ teaspoon lemon juice

½ teaspoon white vinegar
¼ teaspoon cumin
¼ teaspoon cayenne pepper
⅛ teaspoon ground black pepper
⅛ teaspoon dried thyme

PICO DE GALLO
2 medium tomatoes, chopped
½ cup chopped Spanish onion
1 jalapeño, seeded and diced (about 2 tablespoons)

2 teaspoons finely chopped cilantro
⅛ teaspoon salt

SOUTHWESTERN GARNISH
1 cup frozen corn, thawed
⅔ cup canned black beans, drained and rinsed

¼ cup diced red bell pepper
¼ cup diced green bell pepper
⅛ teaspoon salt

MIXED GREENS
1 head iceberg lettuce, chopped
1 head romaine lettuce, chopped

1 carrot, shredded
1 cup shredded red cabbage

2 cups crumbled baked corn tortilla chips

1 cup guacamole

1. Prepare the marinade by combining all of the ingredients in a small bowl. Stir well. Add meat to marinade, cover, and chill for at least 4 hours. Marinating overnight is even better.
2. While meat marinates, prepare the dressings and garnishes. Combine the ingredients for each of the dressings in separate small bowls. Stir well, then cover and chill. Hope you have some more small, clean bowls, because you're going to need a few more for the garnishes. Combine the ingredients for

each of the garnishes in separate bowls, then cover and chill these as well.
3. If you have some more room in the fridge, you may want to prepare your greens now by combining the lettuces with the carrot and cabbage in a large salad bowl. Cover this bowl and chill it until you are ready to assemble the salads. You may choose to save this step until you are ready to grill the meat.
4. When the meat has marinated, preheat your barbecue grill to high heat.
5. Grill the steaks for 5 to 7 minutes per side or until done.
6. While the meat is grilling, prepare the salad by tossing the mixed greens with the Santa Fe dressing in a large bowl.
7. Spoon approximately ⅛ of the greens onto each of four plates.
8. Sprinkle ¼ of the pico de gallo onto the greens on each plate, followed by ¼ of the Southwestern garnish.
9. Spoon ¼ of the remaining greens onto the salad on each plate.
10. Sprinkle ¼ of the tortilla chips over the greens on each plate.
11. Drizzle the ranch dressing over the salads with a sweeping motion. If you have an empty squirt bottle, such as an empty mustard or honey bottle, fill that with the dressing and use it to drizzle the dressing across the salad.
12. When the meat is done grilling, slice each steak into bite-size strips and arrange it over the top of each salad.
13. Spoon the guacamole onto the top of each of the sliced steaks and serve.

- SERVES 4 AS AN ENTRÉE.

Nutrition Facts *(per serving)*
SERVING SIZE—1 SALAD   TOTAL SERVINGS—4

	LOW-FAT	ORIGINAL
CALORIES (APPROX.)	591	784
FAT (APPROX.)	15G	45G

• • • •

TOP SECRET RECIPES REDUCED-FAT VERSION OF

CHILI'S MARGARITA GRILLED TUNA

A plateful of rice and black beans are topped with a corn tortilla, garlic aioli, lettuce, pico de gallo and a fresh tuna steak smothered with chipotle ranch dressing.

There are many opportunities to obliterate fat in this one, most easily in the garlic aioli and chipotle ranch dressing. The tuna you purchase may come in thick eight-ounce steaks. If so, slice the tuna through the center, making two thinner four-ounce pieces. With the rice, black beans, and toppings, this dish is an entire meal on its own. And, oh my, what an impressive presentation.

GARLIC AIOLI
1 head garlic
1 teaspoon olive oil
2 tablespoons fat-free mayonnaise
½ teaspoon lemon juice
¼ teaspoon vinegar
dash salt

FAT-FREE SANTA FE DRESSING
⅓ cup fat-free Catalina dressing
1 tablespoon stone ground mustard
1 tablespoon water
½ teaspoon lemon juice
½ teaspoon white vinegar
¼ teaspoon cumin
¼ teaspoon cayenne pepper
⅛ teaspoon ground black pepper
⅛ teaspoon dried thyme

PICO DE GALLO
2 medium tomatoes, chopped
½ cup chopped Spanish onion
1 jalapeño, seeded and diced (about 2 tablespoons)
2 teaspoons finely chopped cilantro
⅛ teaspoon salt

MARGARITA MARINADE

1 cup sweet and sour mix
2 teaspoons tequila
1 teaspoon lime juice

SEARING SPICE

¼ cup olive oil
2 tablespoons chopped onion
2 cloves garlic
1 teaspoon cayenne pepper
1½ teaspoons Schilling poultry seasoning
1½ teaspoons salt
½ teaspoon paprika
½ teaspoon lemon juice
¼ teaspoon ground black pepper

RICE

2⅓ cups chicken stock
1 tablespoon butter
1 cup converted or long-grain white rice (not instant rice)
¼ cup frozen corn
2 tablespoons diced carrots
2 tablespoons diced red bell pepper
2 tablespoons diced celery
1 tablespoon diced white onion
½ teaspoon salt
½ teaspoon dried parsley
dash ground black pepper

BLACK BEANS

1 teaspoon olive oil
⅓ cup diced white onion
¼ cup diced red bell pepper
2 15-ounce cans black beans with liquid

4 4-ounce tuna fillets (2 8-ounce fillets cut through the center)
4 corn tostada shells
1⅓ cups shredded iceberg lettuce

1. Preheat the oven to 325 degrees.
2. Prepare the garlic aioli by roasting the garlic: Cut ½ inch off the top of the papery skin from the garlic, but leave enough so that the cloves stay together. Place the head of garlic in a small casserole dish or baking pan, drizzle the olive oil over it, and cover it with a lid or foil. Bake for 1 hour. Remove the garlic and let it cool until you can handle it.
3. Prepare the dressing, pico de gallo, and margarita marinade

by combining the ingredients in small bowls. Cover and chill these mixtures until later.
4. Pour the searing spice ingredients into a blender or food processor and puree until you have a smooth mixture with the consistency of pesto. Set this aside.
5. Prepare the rice by bringing chicken stock and butter to a boil over medium/high heat. Add the remaining ingredients to the pan, stir, and cover. Reduce heat to low and simmer for 20 to 25 minutes or until liquid has been absorbed and the rice is cooked.
6. Prepare black beans by pouring a teaspoon of olive oil into a saucepan. Use a paper towel to wipe the oil around the pan and then set it over medium heat. Sauté the diced onion and red bell pepper in the oil for a minute or two and then add the cans of black beans, along with the liquid, to the pan. Reduce heat to medium/low, and simmer until needed. Stir occasionally.
7. Preheat a large skillet over medium heat.
8. Place your tuna fillets into the margarita marinade. Marinate for only 15 minutes and then dry the tuna on paper towels. Be sure not to marinate the tuna for more than 15 minutes or the lime juice will begin to toughen the fish.
9. Place the four tostada shells into an oven preheated to 350 degrees. Turn off the heat after 5 minutes and let the shells sit in the oven until they are needed.
10. Brush the top of each of the fillets with the searing spice blend and turn them with the spice side down onto the hot skillet. Brush additional searing spice over the top of each fillet. Cook the fish for about 2 minutes per side or until the fish is browned on both sides and cooked through.
11. Build each dish by spooning about ¾ cup of rice into the center of a dinner plate. Encircle the rice with a portion of the black beans. Spread a thin layer of garlic aioli onto a tostada shell and place it on the rice. Sprinkle about ⅓ cup of lettuce onto the shell next. Place a tuna fillet on top of the lettuce. Drizzle the Santa Fe dressing over the entire dish with a sweeping motion. Finally, pile about ⅓ cup of the pico

de gallo on top of the tuna. Repeat for the remaining plates and serve immediately.

- SERVES 4 AS AN ENTRÉE.

Nutrition Facts *(per serving)*

SERVING SIZE—1 ENTRÉE   TOTAL SERVINGS—4

	LOW-FAT	ORIGINAL
CALORIES (APPROX.)	691	899
FAT (APPROX.)	16G	38G

• • • •

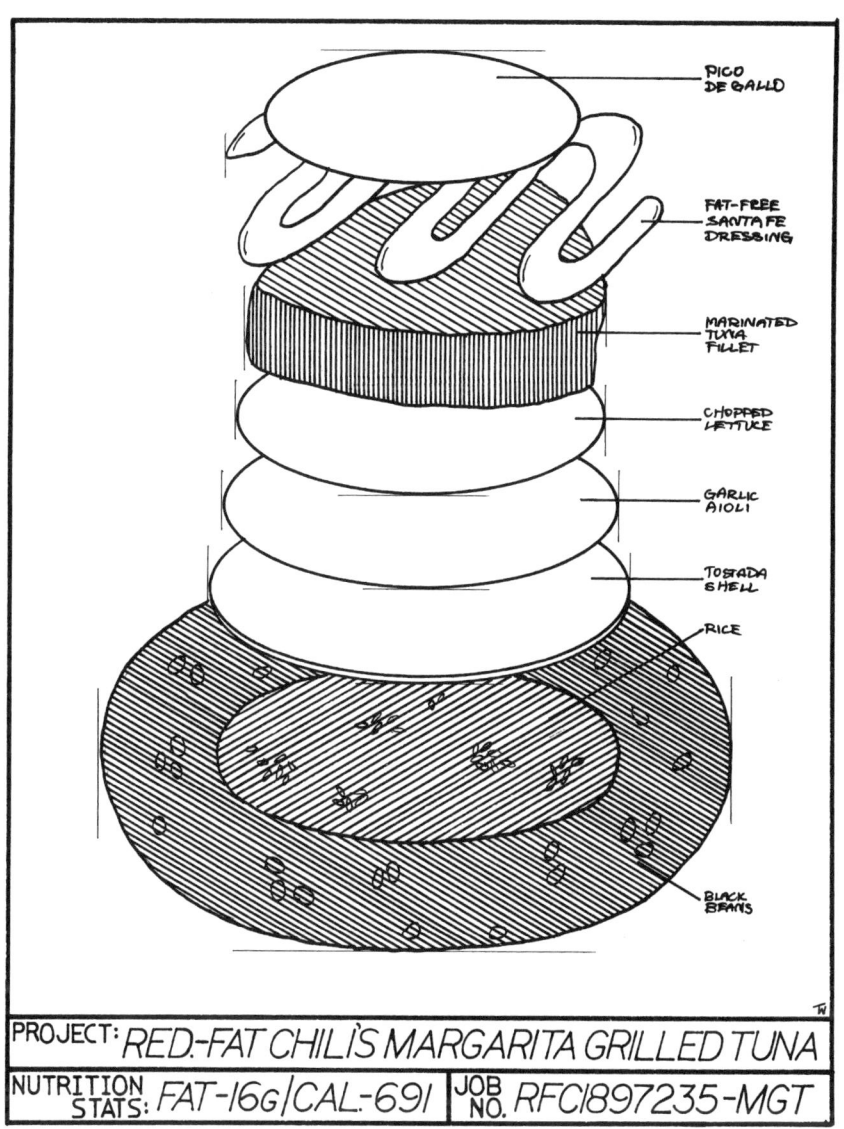

TOP SECRET RECIPES REDUCED-FAT VERSION OF

CHILI'S SOUTHWESTERN EGGROLLS

Spend some time on the message boards at the Top Secret Recipes Web site (*www.topsecretrecipes.com*), and you'll find out that this is one of the most requested conversion recipes. Here now is our reduced-fat version of the tastiest appetizer on Chili's menu. Unlike the real thing that's fried, this amazing clone is baked. Inside is a delicious mixture of corn, green onions, black beans, spinach, jalapeño peppers, reduced-fat Monterey Jack cheese, and spices. Once these babies come out of the oven hot and crispy, just slice 'em in half and serve 'em surrounding a killer low-fat version of the tasty avocado ranch dressing. It's a taste bud party, and your tongue's invited!

1 skinless chicken breast fillet
salt
ground black pepper
1 teaspoon vegetable oil
2 tablespoons minced red bell pepper
2 tablespoons minced green onion
1/3 cup frozen corn
1/4 cup canned black beans, rinsed and drained
2 tablespoons frozen spinach, thawed and drained
2 tablespoons diced, canned jalapeño peppers
1/2 tablespoon minced fresh parsley
1/2 teaspoon cumin
1/2 teaspoon chili powder
1/4 teaspoon salt
dash cayenne pepper
3/4 cup shredded reduced-fat (2%) Monterey Jack cheese
5 7-inch flour tortillas

LOW-FAT AVOCADO-RANCH DIPPING SAUCE

¼ cup smashed, fresh avocado
  (about ½ avocado)
¼ cup fat-free mayonnaise
¼ cup fat-free sour cream
1 tablespoon buttermilk
1 ½ teaspoons white vinegar
⅛ teaspoon salt
⅛ teaspoon dried parsley
⅛ teaspoon onion powder
dash dried dillweed
dash garlic powder
dash ground black pepper

oil cooking spray

GARNISH

2 tablespoons chopped tomato   1 tablespoon chopped onion

1. Preheat barbecue grill to high heat.
2. Rub the chicken breast with some vegetable oil, then grill it on the barbecue for 4 to 5 minutes per side or until done. Lightly salt and pepper each side of the chicken while it cooks. Set chicken aside until it cools down enough to handle.
3. Preheat 1 teaspoon of vegetable oil in a medium-size skillet over medium/high heat.
4. Add the red pepper and green onion to the pan and sauté for a couple minutes until tender.
5. Dice the cooked chicken into small cubes and add it to the pan. Add the corn, black beans, spinach, jalapeño peppers, parsley, cumin, chili powder, salt, and cayenne pepper to the pan. Cook for another 4 minutes. Stir well so that the spinach begins to fall apart and is incorporated into the mixture.
6. Remove the pan from the heat and add the cheese. Stir the mixture until the cheese is melted.
7. Wrap the tortillas in a moist cloth and microwave on high temperature for 1 ½ minutes or until hot.
8. Spoon approximately ⅕ of the mixture into the center of a tortilla. Fold in the ends and then roll the tortilla over the mixture. Roll the tortilla very tightly, then pierce it with a toothpick to hold it together. Repeat with the remaining ingredients until you have five eggrolls. Cover the plate with

plastic wrap and chill for an hour or two. You may chill the eggrolls overnight if you wish.
9. When you are ready to cook the eggrolls, preheat the oven to 425 degrees.
10. Prepare the low-fat avocado-ranch dipping sauce by combining all of the ingredients in a small bowl. Cover and chill this until needed.
11. Spray the entire surface of each of the eggrolls with the oil cooking spray. Arrange the eggrolls on a baking sheet and bake for 17 to 20 minutes or until surface browns and becomes crispy. Turn the eggrolls over about halfway through cooking time.
12. Let the eggrolls cool for a few minutes and then slice each one diagonally lengthwise and arrange on a plate around a small bowl of the dipping sauce. Garnish the dipping sauce with the chopped tomato and onion.

- SERVES 3 OR 4 AS AN APPETIZER.

Nutrition Facts (per serving)
SERVING SIZE—3 HALVES   TOTAL SERVINGS—3.3

	LOW-FAT	ORIGINAL
CALORIES (APPROX.)	480	725
FAT (APPROX.)	12G	42G

• • • •

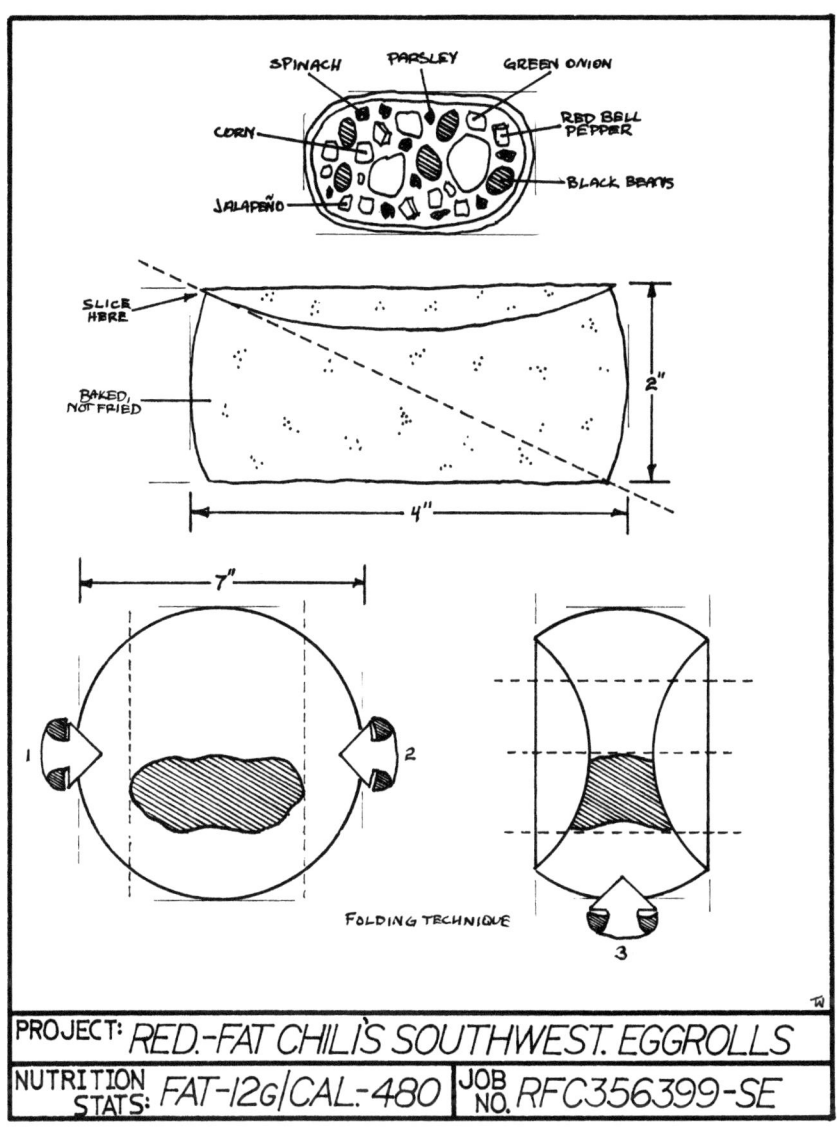

KFC MACARONI & CHEESE

TOP SECRET RECIPES REDUCED-FAT VERSION OF

In 1991, the world's largest chicken chain introduced a new logo to better reflect the addition of non–fried chicken products. Kentucky Fried Chicken morphed into KFC.

One of the chain's classic side dishes is the tasty macaroni and cheese, which has been on the menu for years. Using the light version of Velveeta cheese and some reduced-fat cheddar, we easily duplicate the taste while cutting the fat grams in half here in our cheesy conversion.

6 cups water
2 cups elbow macaroni
4 ounces Velveeta Light cheese
½ cup reduced-fat shredded cheddar cheese (2% fat)
2 tablespoons fat-free milk
¼ teaspoon salt

1. Bring water to a boil over high heat in a medium saucepan. Add the elbow macaroni to the water and cook it for 10 to 12 minutes or until tender, stirring occasionally.
2. While the macaroni is boiling, prepare the cheese sauce by combining the remaining ingredients in a small saucepan and cooking over low heat. Stir often as the cheese melts into a smooth consistency.
3. When the macaroni is done, turn off the heat, then use a colander or sieve to strain off the water. Pour the macaroni back into the pan without the water.
4. Pour the cheese sauce over the macaroni and stir until it is well coated. Serve immediately.

- Serves 6 as a side dish.

Nutrition Facts *(per serving)*
Serving size—5.4 ounces   Total servings—6

	Low-Fat	Original
Calories	95	180
Fat	4g	8g

• • •

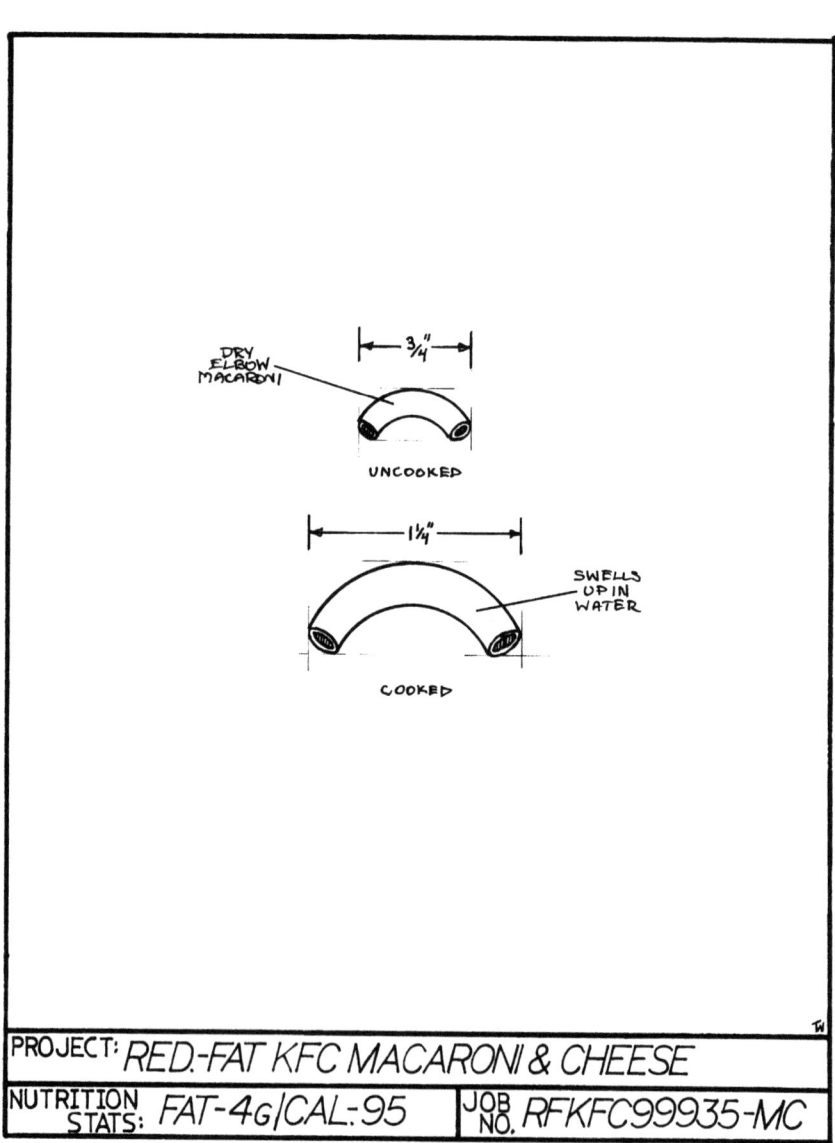

TOP SECRET RECIPES FAT-FREE VERSION OF

KFC POTATO SALAD

Sure, KFC's potato salad is good, but have you ever wondered why they don't sell a fat-free version? It really wouldn't be so tough to substitute fat-free mayo for the regular stuff, then just sweeten it up with some sweet pickle relish and sugar. Throw a few spices in there, some bits of veggies, and the recipe might look something like this:

2 pounds russet potatoes, diced
6 cups water
salt
1 cup fat-free mayonnaise
4 teaspoons sweet pickle relish
4 teaspoons granulated sugar
2 teaspoons minced white onion
2 teaspoons prepared mustard
1 teaspoon vinegar
1 teaspoon minced celery
1 teaspoon diced pimentos
½ teaspoon shredded carrot
¼ teaspoon dried parsley
¼ teaspoon ground black pepper
dash salt

1. Lightly peel the potatoes (you don't have to get all of the skin off) then chop them into bite-size pieces (approximately ½-inch cubes) and boil the pieces in 6 cups of boiling, salted water for 7 to 10 minutes. The potato chunks should be tender, yet slightly tough in the middle when done. Drain and rinse the potatoes with cold water.
2. In a medium bowl, combine the remaining ingredients and whisk until smooth.
3. Pour the drained potatoes into a large bowl. Pour the dressing

over the potatoes and mix until all of the potato pieces are well coated.
4. Cover and chill for at least 4 hours. Overnight is best.

- SERVES 8 AS A SIDE DISH.

Nutrition Facts *(per serving)*
SERVING SIZE—5.6 OUNCES   TOTAL SERVINGS—8

	LOW-FAT	ORIGINAL
CALORIES	90	230
FAT	0G	14G

• • • •

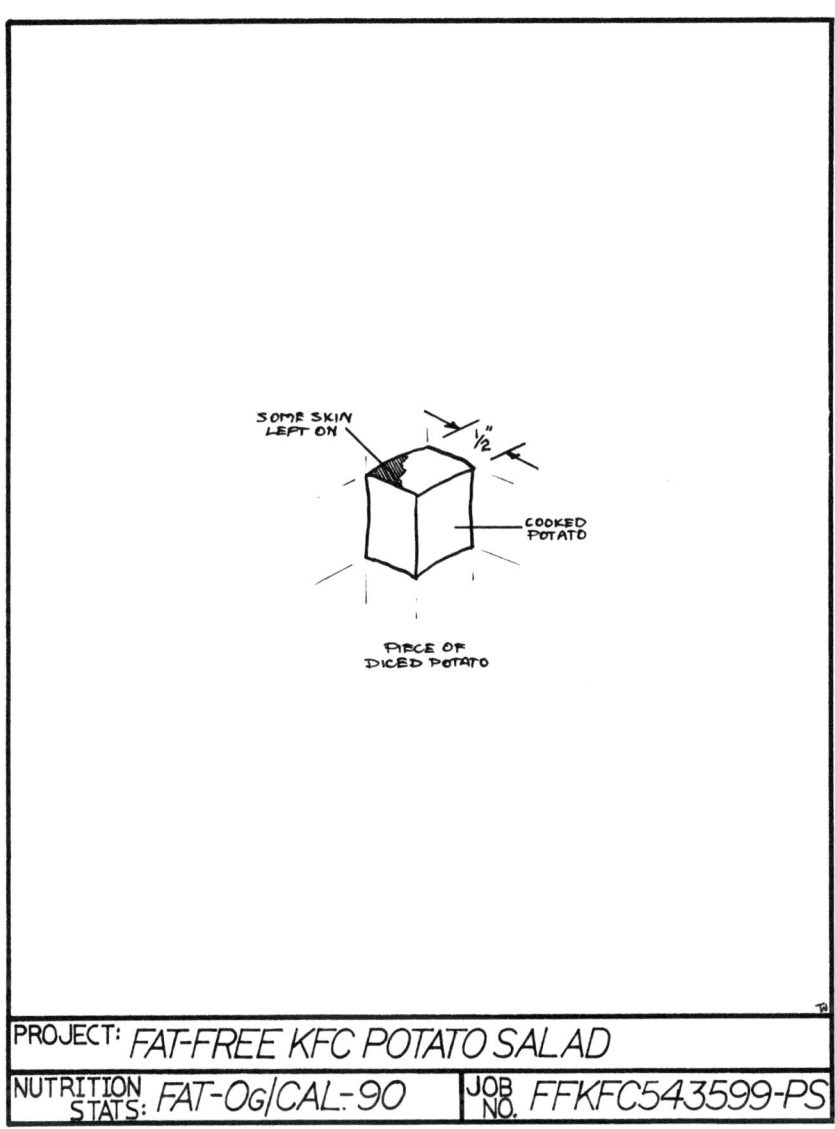

PROJECT:	*FAT-FREE KFC POTATO SALAD*
NUTRITION STATS: *FAT-0G/CAL:-90*	JOB NO. *FFKFC543599-PS*

TOP SECRET RECIPES REDUCED-FAT VERSION OF

MCDONALD'S ARCH DELUXE

McDonald's introduced its new sandwich in 1996 with a $200 million marketing blitz aimed at winning over grown-ups. We watched Ronald McDonald golf, dance, and hang out with sophisticated human beings, rather than his usual gang of creepy dancing puppets. These messages were supposed to tug at the adult market lost to more inspired sandwich creations from chains like Wendy's and Arby's and Carl's Jr.

Did the campaign work? So far, the sales figures have been less than stellar for the burger with even more fat in it than a Big Mac. But the sandwich, with its specially developed Dijon mustard–mayo sauce, does have its share of devoted fans. Perhaps even more of us would get on the Arch Deluxe team if we could make a clone using reduced-fat ingredients to knock the fat down to nearly one-third that of the original, as I have here.

1 tablespoon fat-free mayonnaise
½ teaspoon brown mustard
   (French's Hearty Deli is good)
1 sesame seed hamburger bun
¼ pound super lean ground beef
   (7% fat)

salt and pepper
1 slice fat-free American cheese
1 large tomato slice
1 to 2 lettuce leaves, chopped
½ tablespoon ketchup
2 tablespoons chopped onion

1. In a small bowl, mix together the mayonnaise and the brown mustard. Set this mixture aside.
2. Grill the face of each of the buns on a griddle or frying pan over medium heat.
3. Roll the ground beef into a ball and pat it out until it's approxi-

mately the same diameter as the bun. You can freeze this patty before you cook it just like the restaurant chain does. This will also make it stay together better when it cooks.

4. Cook the meat on a hot griddle or frying pan for about 5 minutes per side until done. Be sure to lightly salt and pepper each side of the patty.
5. Build the burger in the following order, from the bottom up:

ON BOTTOM BUN
beef patty
American cheese slice

tomato slice
lettuce

ON TOP BUN
mayo/mustard
ketchup

onion

6. Slap the top of the sandwich onto the bottom and serve. Microwave sandwich on high for 15 seconds if you like the sandwich hotter.

- Makes 1 sandwich.

TIDBITS

If you'd like to add bacon to the sandwich, as you can order with the original, just cook a piece of turkey bacon sprinkled with coarsely ground black pepper. Break the bacon in half and place each half of the bacon side by side onto the bottom bun before stacking on the beef patty.

Nutrition Facts *(per serving)*
Serving size—1 burger   Total servings—1

	Low-Fat	Original
Calories	430	550
Fat	11g	31g

WITH BACON:

Nutrition Facts *(per serving)*
Serving size—1 sandwich   Total servings—1

	Low-Fat	Original
Calories	450	590
Fat	13.5g	34g

• • • •

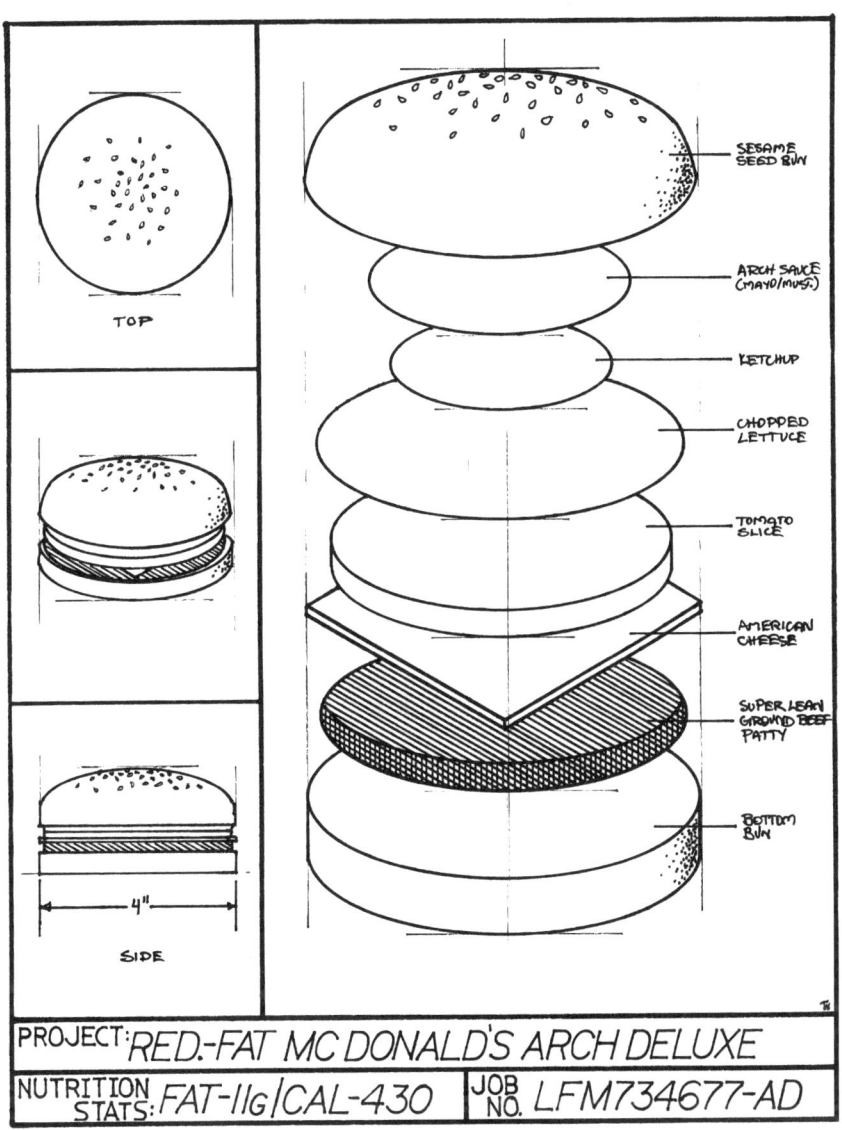

TOP SECRET RECIPES LOW-FAT VERSION OF

MCDONALD'S EGG MCMUFFIN

Like the Big Mac, the idea for this breakfast product came from an inspired McDonald's franchisee goofing around with ingredients in the kitchen—in this case, English muffins and a cylindrical egg mold. It was in 1977 that the world's largest burger chain unveiled the Egg McMuffin to a ravenous America on the go: the eat-breakfast-while-driving, morning rush hour workforce with the spill-proof coffee mugs.

Back then, concerns with fat intake were not big on our minds or in the news, so the 12 grams of fat per Egg McMuffin was disregarded. But if you've had your share of greasy breakfast sandwiches over the years and have a little extra time one morning, give this cool clone a test. Using egg substitute (egg whites) and fat-free American cheese, you can still create that signature Mickey D's taste while cutting the fat down to just 2.5 grams per sandwich. Now when you eat two of these you won't make such a dent in your daily fat allotment before the sun is barely up.

1 English muffin
¼ cup egg substitute
salt

1 slice Canadian bacon
1 slice fat-free American cheese

1. Split the English muffin and toast it or grill the faces until brown in a hot pan set over medium heat. Keep the pan hot.
2. Find a shallow can—such as an 8-ounce sliced pineapple can—that has the same diameter as the English muffin. Cut off both ends of the can and thoroughly clean it. Spray a

coating of nonstick spray on the inside of the can, and place it into the hot pan so that it heats up.
3. When the can is hot, spray more nonstick spray over the surface of the pan, and pour the egg substitute into the can. Salt the egg.
4. Place the slice of Canadian bacon into the same pan to heat up while the egg cooks.
5. When the egg seems to be firming up on top, use a knife to scrape around the edge of the can to help release the egg. Carefully pull the can off the egg, then flip the egg over and cook it for an additional minute or so.
6. Build the sandwich by first placing the slice of American cheese on the bottom half of the English muffin.
7. Place the egg on top of the cheese.
8. Stack the Canadian bacon on the egg.
9. Top the sandwich off with the top half of the English muffin.
10. Microwave the sandwich for 10 to 15 seconds until warm, and serve immediately.

- MAKES 1 SANDWICH.

TIDBITS

You can also purchase a device similar to what McDonald's uses to cook the eggs. It is a handle that has 2 to 4 circular molds at the end to hold the egg while it cooks. This can be used instead of a can, but it ain't as cheap!

Nutrition Facts (per serving)
SERVING SIZE—1 SANDWICH   TOTAL SERVINGS—1

	LOW-FAT	ORIGINAL
CALORIES	217	290
FAT	2.5G	12G

• • • •

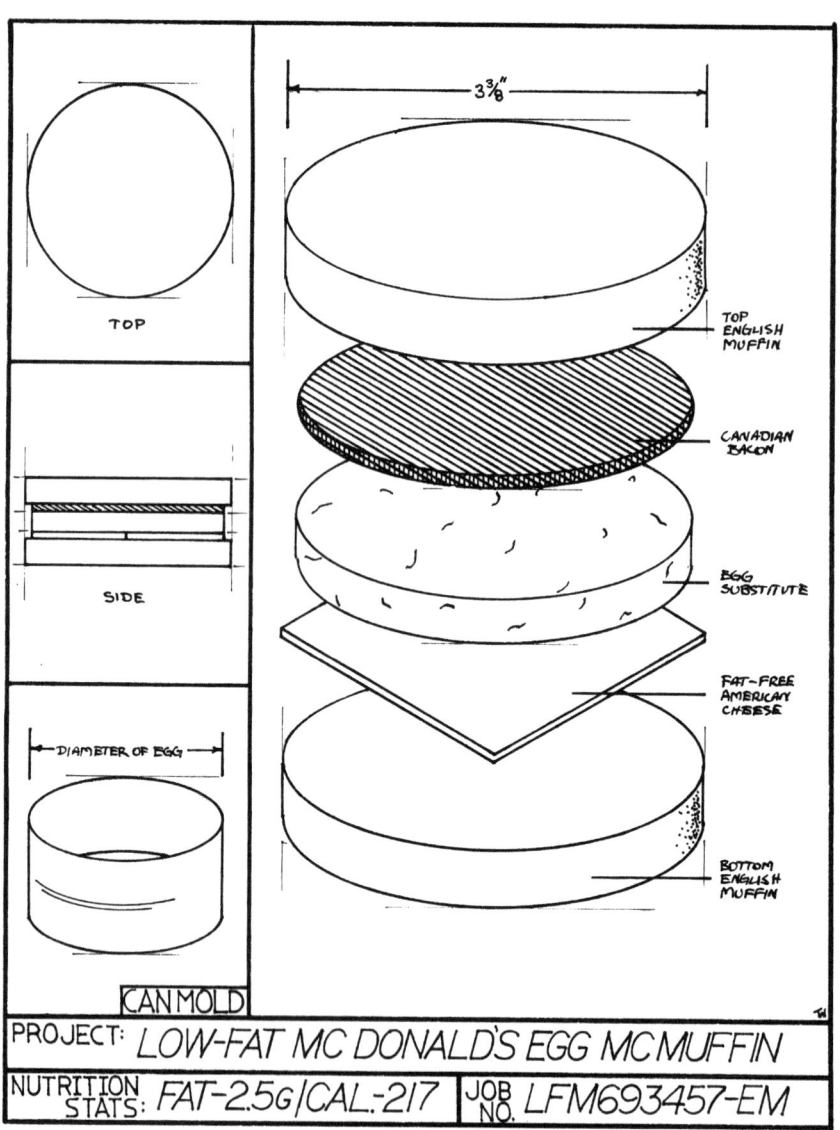

OLIVE GARDEN CHICKEN PARMIGIANA SANDWICH

TOP SECRET RECIPES REDUCED-FAT VERSION OF

Chicken parmigiana is delicious, but who needs all the fat that comes from the traditional process of breading and panfrying the chicken breast in hot oil? Olive Garden's delicious chicken parmigiana sandwich was the perfect product for a reduced-fat clone using a special baking technique for the chicken to replace the greasy frying. Even when we use regular provolone cheese in this recipe, our conversion comes out to around half the fat of the original, which has been filling the bellies of Olive Garden customers since 1995. And there won't be any hot oil splattering your arm.

MARINARA SAUCE

1 1/4 cups tomato puree (1 10 1/2-ounce can)
1 teaspoon granulated sugar
1 small clove garlic, minced
1/2 cup canned, diced tomatoes
1/4 teaspoon salt
1/4 teaspoon dried oregano
1/4 teaspoon dried basil
1/8 teaspoon pepper
1/4 teaspoon lemon juice

4 skinless chicken breast fillets
1/2 cup all-purpose flour
1/2 cup egg substitute
1/2 cup Italian-style bread crumbs
olive oil cooking spray

4 Italian or sourdough sandwich rolls
1/2 cup shredded provolone cheese

1. Combine the ingredients for the marinara sauce in a small or medium saucepan over high heat. When mixture begins to boil, reduce heat to low and simmer for 45 minutes.
2. Prepare chicken by first cutting each breast in half. Fold a piece of plastic wrap around one piece of chicken and pound flat (to about ¼ inch thick) with a mallet. The chicken should be slightly larger in diameter than the sandwich rolls. Repeat with the remaining pieces of chicken.
3. Put the flour, egg substitute, and bread crumbs into 3 separate small bowls. Drop each piece of chicken, 1 at a time, first into the flour, then into the egg, and then coat each thoroughly with the bread crumbs.
4. Preheat oven to 450 degrees.
5. Spray a baking sheet with a generous coating of cooking spray. Place each piece of chicken on the coated baking sheet, then spray the surface of each piece with the cooking spray. Bake for 20 minutes or until the chicken begins to brown.
6. Toast or grill the faces of each roll until light brown.
7. Build each sandwich by first placing one piece of chicken on the bottom half of a roll. Position the chicken slightly off to one side on the roll. Spoon about 1½ tablespoons marinara sauce onto the chicken. Sprinkle a couple teaspoons of the provolone over the sauce. Stack another piece of chicken on the first, with this piece stacked over to the other side of the roll, but also slightly overlapping the first piece. Spread sauce and cheese on this piece as well.
8. Top off the sandwich with the top half of the roll, and serve. Repeat the process to build the remaining sandwiches.

- MAKES 4 SANDWICHES.

Nutrition Facts *(per serving)*

SERVING SIZE—1 SANDWICH   TOTAL SERVINGS—4

	LOW-FAT	ORIGINAL
CALORIES (APPROX.)	553	631
FAT (APPROX.)	11G	21G

• • • •

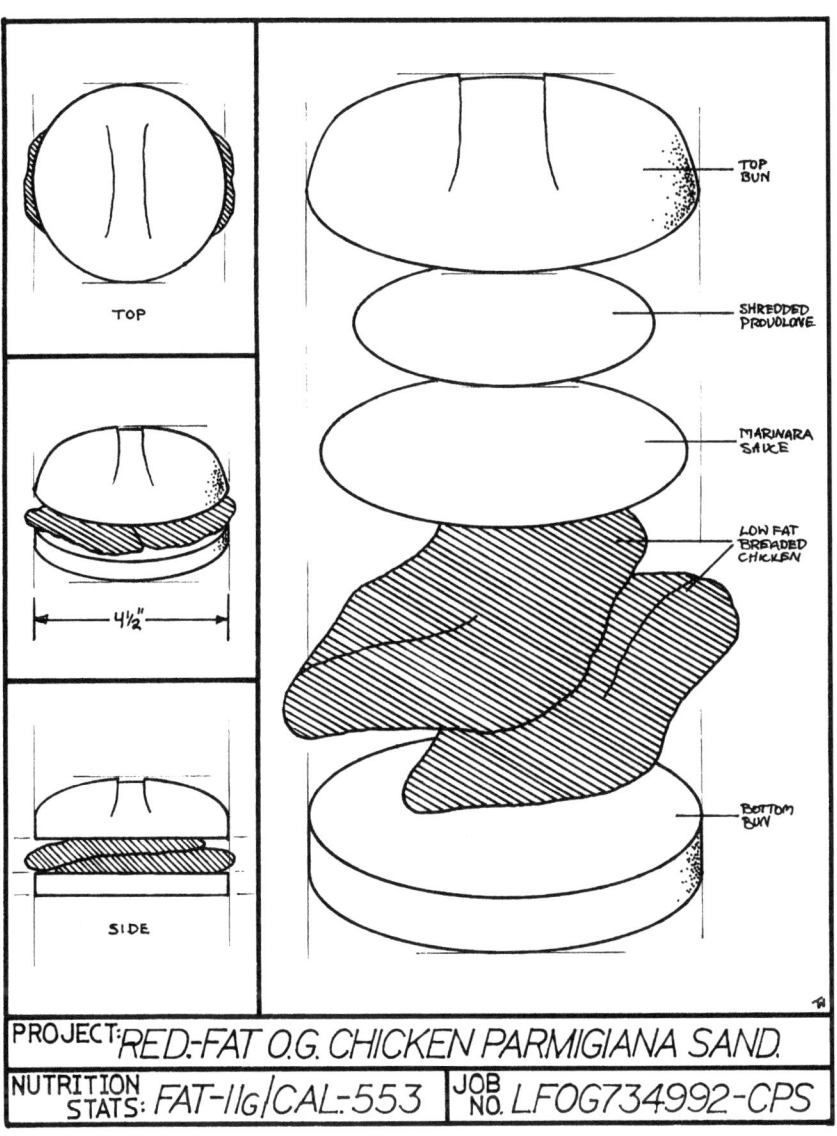

OLIVE GARDEN FETTUCINE ALFREDO

TOP SECRET RECIPES REDUCED-FAT VERSION OF

This is a classic Italian dish, but with cheese and cream and butter in the traditional version, you can get a whopping seventy grams of fat in a single plateful. For this conversion, we'll replace those fatty ingredients with substitutes such as evaporated skim milk, fat-free milk, Butter Buds, and a great cheeselike substance made from straining yogurt with a coffee filter.

To easily prepare this useful ingredient, we'll use a technique that I picked up from watching Graham Kerr, the once–galloping gourmet. Graham loves to use this yogurt cheese in many of his low-fat dishes that require a creamy white sauce, traditionally made with fatty foodstuffs. This fat-free substitute is made by straining the whey from the yogurt with a coffee filter. You simply place a filter into a large strainer or metal steamer basket in a covered saucepan. Pour the yogurt into the filter, and let this sit covered overnight in the refrigerator. As the hours tick by, the whey slowly drips from the yogurt, leaving a thick, creamy substance in the filter. The liquid in the bottom of the pan is chucked out, and you measure the yogurt cheese left in the coffee filter for the recipe.

Using this technique, we can shave something like forty-nine grams of fat off the traditional recipe for fettucine alfredo presented at the country's largest Italian restaurant chain. This recipe makes two way-huge dinner-size entrées like they serve at the restaurant, though you might rather divide this up as four more modestly portioned servings.

1 cup strained yogurt (see above)
2 tablespoons cornstarch
1 cup evaporated skim milk
½ teaspoon olive oil
1 large clove garlic, minced
½ cup grated Parmesan cheese
½ cup fat-free milk
1 tablespoon Butter Buds Sprinkles
¼ teaspoon salt
⅛ teaspoon ground black pepper
4 to 5 quarts water
12-ounce box fettucine pasta

1. Combine the strained yogurt with the cornstarch in a medium bowl. Stir until smooth. Add the evaporated skim milk. Set aside.
2. Heat the oil in a medium saucepan over medium heat. When the oil is hot, add the garlic and sauté for about a minute. Don't cook the garlic long enough that it begins to brown.
3. Add the yogurt mixture to the saucepan and stir. Add remaining ingredients, except the water and pasta, to the saucepan and continue to heat over medium/low heat. If it begins to boil, turn heat to low and simmer, stirring often.
4. As the sauce heats, bring 5 to 6 quarts of water to a rolling boil in a large pot or saucepan. Add the pasta to the boiling water and stir. Return water to a boil, and cook uncovered for 12 to 15 minutes or until pasta is mostly tender but slightly tough (*al dente*). Strain.
5. Toss pasta and sauce together in a large bowl and serve.

- SERVES 2 AS A LARGE, RESTAURANT-SIZE PORTION (OR SERVES 4 AS A STANDARD-SIZE ENTRÉE).

Nutrition Facts *(per serving)*
SERVING SIZE—4 CUPS   TOTAL SERVINGS—2

	LOW-FAT	ORIGINAL
CALORIES (APPROX.)	1035	1236
FAT (APPROX.)	18G	67G

• • • •

OLIVE GARDEN ZUPPA TOSCANA

TOP SECRET RECIPES REDUCED-FAT VERSION OF

It's the white, creamy broth in the original version of this delicious soup that adds unnecessary fat grams. By replacing the fat-filled dairy ingredients from the original with fat-free milk and chicken broth, and by using lean Italian turkey sausage, we can whack around fifteen grams off the original version.

½ pound hot Italian lean turkey sausage (2 large links)
3 cups fat-free chicken broth
3 cups fat-free milk
2 tablespoons minced onion
1 tablespoon Hormel Real Bacon Pieces
¼ teaspoon salt
dash of crushed red pepper flakes
1 medium russet potato
2 cups chopped kale

1. Grill or sauté the sausage until cooked.
2. Combine the chicken broth, milk, onion, bacon pieces, salt, and pepper flakes in a medium saucepan over medium/high heat.
3. Quarter the potato lengthwise, then cut into ¼-inch slices. Add to the saucepan. When mixture begins to boil, reduce heat and simmer for 30 minutes.
4. Cut the sausage at an angle into ¼-inch-thick slices. Add the sausage to the saucepan. Simmer for 1 hour or until potato slices begin to soften.
5. Add the kale to the soup and simmer for an additional 10 to 15 minutes or until potatoes are soft.

- SERVES 3.

Nutrition Facts *(per serving)*
Serving size—1 ½ cups   Total servings—3

	Low-Fat	Original
Calories (approx.)	196	275
Fat (approx.)	4.5g	19g

• • • •

OTIS SPUNKMEYER CHOCOLATE CHIP MUFFINS

TOP SECRET RECIPES REDUCED-FAT VERSION OF

In Cayce, South Carolina, Otis Spunkmeyer muffins are manufactured with state-of-the-art robotic equipment that would make R2-D2 jealous. The amazing machines do everything from packaging 130 muffins per minute to sealing up the cartons ready for a quick shipment to stores across the country.

This custom Top Secret Recipes reduced-fat clone version uses unsweetened applesauce to keep the muffin moist and to help replace unnecessary fat.

¾ cup granulated sugar
⅔ cup unsweetened applesauce
¼ cup egg substitute
¼ cup vegetable oil
½ teaspoon salt
¾ teaspoon vanilla

1 teaspoon baking soda
½ cup low-fat buttermilk
2 cups all-purpose flour
2 teaspoons baking powder
½ cup mini chocolate chips

1. Preheat oven to 325 degrees.
2. In a large bowl, mix together sugar, applesauce, egg substitute, oil, salt, vanilla, and baking soda. Add buttermilk and blend well.
3. In a separate bowl, sift together the flour and baking powder. Add the dry ingredients to the wet, and mix well with an electric mixer. Add half of the chocolate chips to the batter, and fold them in by hand.
4. To bake the muffins, use a "Texas-size" muffin pan lined with large muffin cups. You may also bake the muffins without the cups; just be sure to grease the pan well with cooking spray. (If you use a regular-size muffin pan, which also works fine, your

cooking time will be a few minutes less and your yield will double.) Fill the cups halfway with batter.
5. Sprinkle the remaining chocolate chips over the tops of each cup of batter. That will be about ½ tablespoon of chips per muffin (or a scant teaspoon of chips if you make the regular-size muffins).
6. Bake the muffins for 20 to 24 minutes or until brown on top (16 to 20 minutes for regular-size muffins). Remove the muffins from the oven and allow them to cool for about 30 minutes. Then put the muffins in a sealed container or resealable plastic bag.

- MAKES 8 "TEXAS-SIZE" MUFFINS (OR 16 REGULAR-SIZE MUFFINS).

Nutrition Facts *(per serving)*
SERVING SIZE—½ MUFFIN   TOTAL SERVINGS—16

	LOW-FAT	ORIGINAL
CALORIES	160	240
FAT	5.5G	13G

• • • •

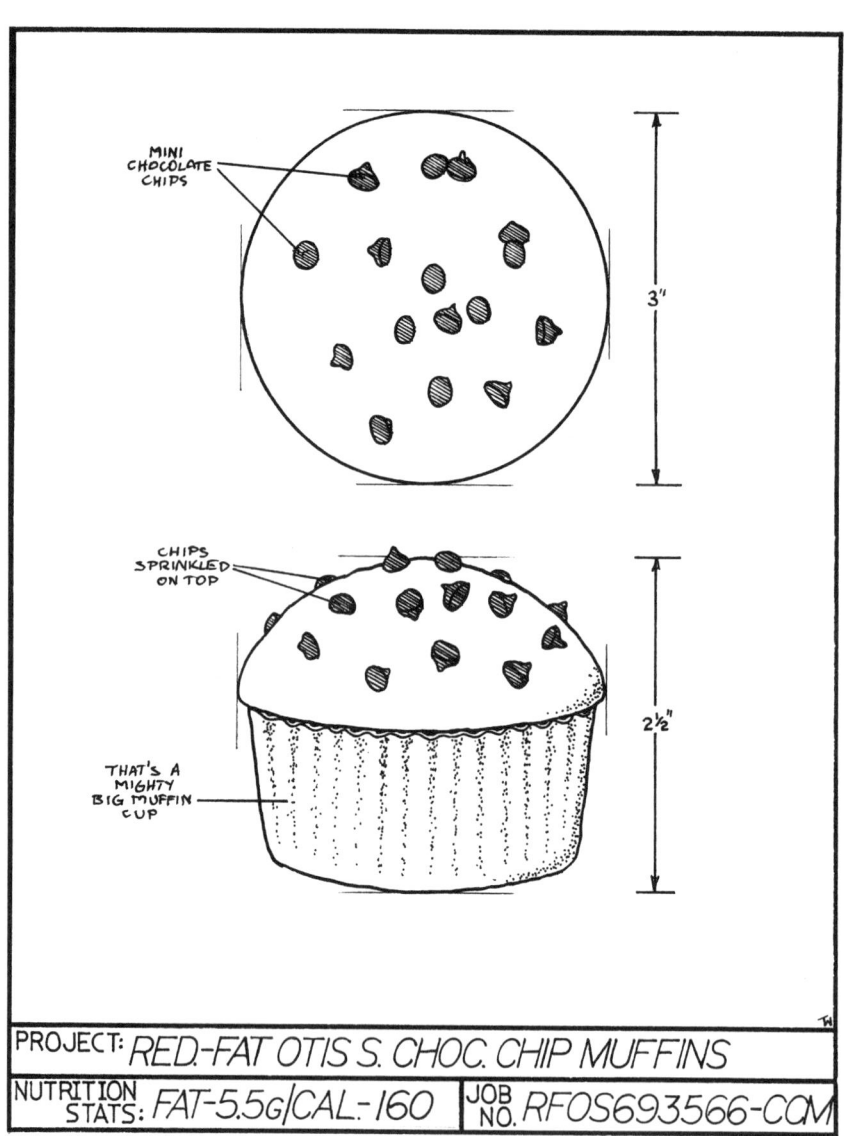

TOP SECRET RECIPES REDUCED-FAT VERSION OF

OTIS SPUNKMEYER WILD BLUEBERRY MUFFINS

After baking the big 'ol muffins, Otis Spunkmeyer freezes them so that they stay fresh on the way to the stores. Vendors thaw out the tasty baked goodies before displaying them on their shelves. Even after the muffins reach room temperature, they still have a very impressive shelf life of twenty-one days.

You can also freeze the muffins you make with this reduced-fat clone recipe. Just wait until they cool, then wrap the muffins in plastic wrap, and toss them in the freezer. And remember, the shelf life of your version without preservatives will be much less than that of the real McCoy, so dive into those muffins post haste.

1 cup dried blueberries
¼ cup water
¾ cup plus 1 tablespoon granulated sugar
⅔ cup unsweetened applesauce
¼ cup egg substitute
¼ cup vegetable oil
¾ teaspoon salt
½ teaspoon vanilla
1 teaspoon baking soda
½ cup low-fat buttermilk
2 cups all-purpose flour
2 teaspoons baking powder
fat-free butter-flavored spray

1. Combine blueberries with ¼ cup water in a small, microwave-safe bowl. Zap blueberries in the microwave on 50% power for 2 minutes, stir, cover with plastic wrap, then set aside.
2. Preheat oven to 325 degrees.
3. In a large bowl, mix together ¾ cup of sugar, applesauce, egg substitute, oil, salt, vanilla, and baking soda. Add buttermilk and blend well.
4. In a separate bowl, sift together the flour and baking powder.

Add the dry ingredients to the wet, and mix well with an electric mixer.
5. Add 1 tablespoon of sugar to the blueberries, then add them to the batter and fold in by hand with as few strokes as possible.
6. To bake the muffins, use a "Texas-size" muffin pan lined with large muffin cups. You may also bake the muffins without the cups; just be sure to grease the pan well with cooking spray. (If you use a regular-size muffin pan, which also works fine, your cooking time will be a few minutes less, and your yield will double.) Fill the cups halfway with batter.
7. Spray a couple of squirts of fat-free butter-flavored spray over the top of each portion of batter.
8. Bake the muffins for 20 to 24 minutes or until brown on top (16 to 20 minutes for regular-size muffins). Remove the muffins from the oven, and allow them to cool for about 30 minutes. Then put the muffins in a sealed container or resealable plastic bag.

- MAKES 8 "TEXAS-SIZE" MUFFINS (OR 16 REGULAR-SIZE MUFFINS).

Nutrition Facts *(per serving)*
SERVING SIZE—½ MUFFIN   TOTAL SERVINGS—16

	LOW-FAT	ORIGINAL
CALORIES	165	210
FAT	4G	11G

• • • •

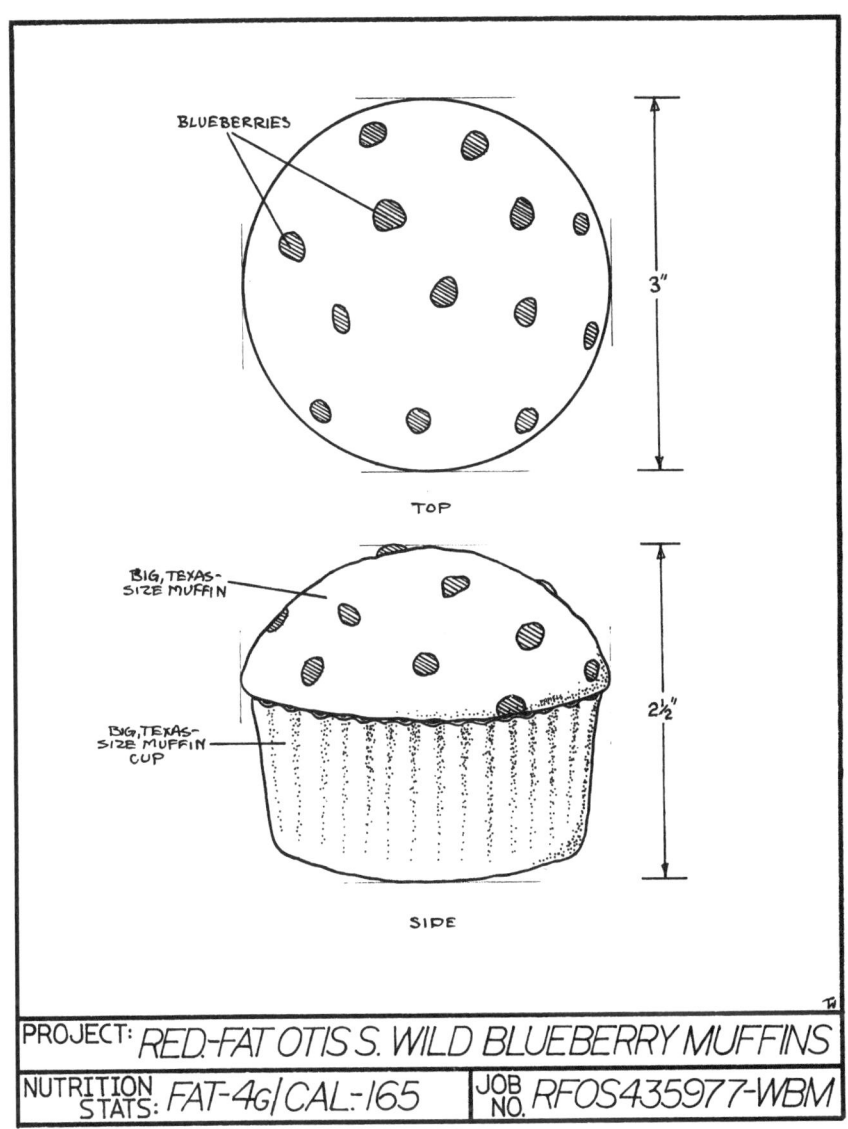

OUTBACK STEAKHOUSE WALKABOUT SOUP

TOP SECRET RECIPES REDUCED-FAT VERSION OF

Restaurateurs Chris Sullivan, Robert Basham, and Timothy Gannon knew they wanted an Australian theme for their new steakhouse and hunkered down to come up with a name. Robert's wife Beth pulled out her lipstick and started writing names on a mirror. "Outback" jumped out as the best name among the choices. When looking for Windex, the group later wondered if it wouldn't have been too much trouble to have just used a pen and a piece of paper.

This creamy onion soup has become a favorite item on the Outback menu. With this formula, you'll get all the flavor of the original with only one-third of the fat.

7 cups water
5 beef bouillon cubes
3 medium-size white onions
2 cups reduced-fat milk (2%)
1½ tablespoons sugar

1 teaspoon salt
½ teaspoon pepper
¾ cup all-purpose flour
1 cup reduced-fat shredded
    cheddar cheese

GARNISH

¼ cup reduced-fat shredded
    cheddar cheese

¼ cup Hormel Real Bacon Pieces
1 to 2 green onions, sliced

1. Combine 6 cups of water with the 5 beef bouillon cubes in a large saucepan over medium/high heat. Heat until bouillon cubes have dissolved.
2. Cut the onions into thin slices, then quarter the slices.

3. Add the onions to the broth, reduce heat, and simmer for 15 minutes.
4. Add milk to the pan. Add sugar, salt, and pepper.
5. Combine flour with 1 cup of water in a small bowl or cup, and stir until smooth. Stir the soup while adding this mixture to the pan.
6. Crank heat back up to high, add the reduced-fat cheddar cheese to the pan, and stir. Bring mixture back to boiling. Once the soup begins to boil, reduce heat and simmer for 15 to 20 minutes or until very thick.
7. Spoon 1 cup of soup into a bowl, and garnish with about ½ tablespoon each of cheddar cheese, bacon pieces, and chopped green onion.

- MAKES 8 SERVINGS.

Nutrition Facts (per serving)

SERVING SIZE—1 CUP   TOTAL SERVINGS—8

	LOW-FAT	ORIGINAL
CALORIES (APPROX.)	144	230
FAT (APPROX.)	5.8G	17G

• • • •

OUTBACK STEAKHOUSE CAESAR SALAD DRESSING

TOP SECRET RECIPES LOW-FAT VERSION OF

The salad dressings are made fresh in each Outback Steakhouse from authentic ingredients, including olive oil from Italy's Tuscany region and Parmesan cheese that comes from eighty-pound wheels rolled in from Parma, Italy.

Salad dressings are usually one of the most fat-contributing components in your meal, but with a few tricks, we can clone Outback's delicious salad dressing with only two grams of fat per serving.

1 cup fat-free mayonnaise
1/3 cup water
1/4 cup egg substitute
1/4 cup grated Parmesan cheese
1 1/2 tablespoons lemon juice
1 tablespoon anchovy paste
2 cloves garlic, pressed
1/2 teaspoon salt
1/2 teaspoon coarsely ground pepper
1/4 teaspoon dried parsley flakes, crushed fine

1. Combine all ingredients in a medium bowl. Use an electric mixer to beat ingredients for about 1 minute.
2. Cover the dressing and chill it for several hours so that flavors can develop.

- MAKES 1 1/2 CUPS.

Nutrition Facts *(per serving)*
Serving size—¼ cup   Total servings—6

	Low-Fat	Original
Calories (approx.)	51	331
Fat (approx.)	2g	35g

• • • •

TOP SECRET RECIPES REDUCED-FAT VERSION OF

OUTBACK STEAKHOUSE ALICE SPRINGS CHICKEN

Always a popular choice since the very beginning of this 517-unit steakhouse chain in 1988, the Alice Springs Chicken entrée would not likely be part of any low-fat diet. This marinated chicken breast is covered with honey mustard and bacon. Then the entrée is baked until the cheese on top is all melted and drippy. Add it up, and you've got yourself around forty-four grams of fat in just one serving.

We can cut the fat by more than half using fat-free and low-fat ingredients, plus some delicious-yet-low-fat turkey bacon (I recommend Butterball brand). Tastes just like the original without the guilt. Or the tip.

MARINADE
2 cups water
1 1/2 teaspoons salt
1/2 teaspoon liquid smoke
1/4 teaspoon ground black pepper
1/4 teaspoon onion powder
1/4 teaspoon garlic powder
1/4 teaspoon paprika

4 skinless chicken breast fillets

FAT-FREE HONEY MUSTARD SAUCE
1/2 cup fat-free mayonnaise
1/2 cup honey
2 tablespoons Grey Poupon Dijon mustard
2 teaspoons white vinegar

8 slices turkey bacon
salt
ground black pepper
paprika
2 cups sliced mushrooms
   (10 to 12 mushrooms)
1 tablespoon butter
2 cups reduced-fat shredded
   Colby and Monterey Jack
   cheese
2 teaspoons minced fresh
   parsley

1. Combine the marinade ingredients in a medium bowl. Add all 4 chicken breasts to the marinade in a covered container or resealable plastic bag, and chill for 3 to 4 hours.
2. Combine the mayonnaise, honey, Dijon mustard, and vinegar in a small bowl. Stir well until smooth. Chill.
3. When chicken has marinated, preheat barbecue grill to high heat.
4. As barbecue preheats, prepare turkey bacon by frying it in a skillet over medium heat until done. Remove the bacon from the skillet to a plate lined with paper, which helps soak up excess fat. The bacon can sit here until it is time to assemble the dish.
5. Spray a light coating of nonstick oil cooking spray over the surface of each chicken breast. Sprinkle both sides of each chicken breast with salt, pepper, and paprika, and then grill for 7 to 10 minutes on each side. Preheat oven to 375 degrees.
6. As chicken grills, prepare mushrooms by heating up a medium skillet over medium/high heat. Add 1 tablespoon of butter to the pan. When the butter has melted, add the mushrooms, along with a little salt and pepper. Sauté the mushrooms for 10 to 15 minutes or until they become cooked through and light brown. If the mushrooms finish before the chicken, just turn the heat to the lowest setting until you are ready to assemble the dish.
7. When chicken is cooked, transfer the chicken breast fillets to a large baking dish. Slather the top surface of each breast with a generous portion of the honey mustard sauce. Stack two slices of bacon, crosswise, on top of each breast.
8. Quarter the mushrooms and stack a portion on top of the

bacon on each chicken breast. Carefully pour about ½ cup of the Colby/Monterey Jack cheese blend over each of the chicken breasts.
9. Bake chicken in the preheated oven for 7 to 12 minutes or until cheese is melted.
10. Sprinkle each with about ½ teaspoon of fresh minced parsley. Serve with additional honey mustard sauce on the side.

- SERVES 4 AS AN ENTRÉE.

Nutrition Facts *(per serving)*
SERVING SIZE—1 PORTION   TOTAL SERVINGS—4

	LOW-FAT	ORIGINAL
CALORIES (APPROX.)	603	838
FAT (APPROX.)	19G	44G

• • • •

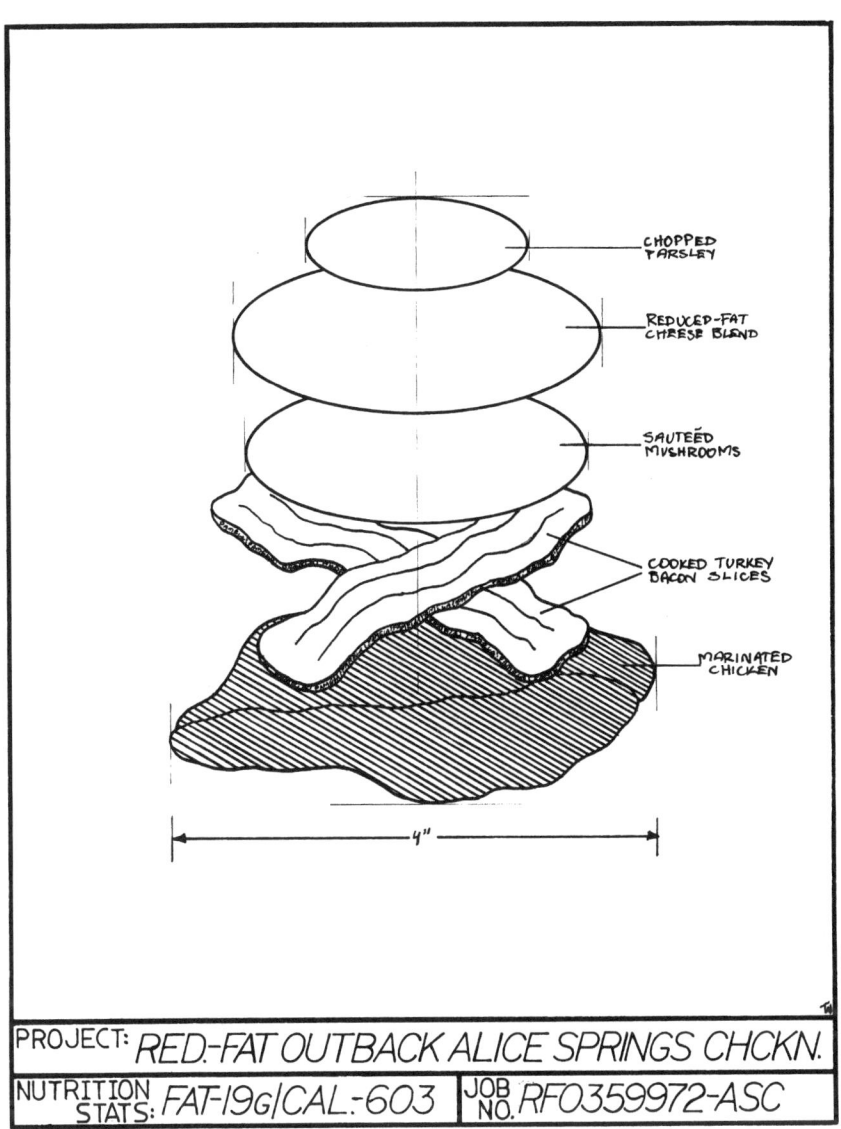

TOP SECRET RECIPES REDUCED-FAT VERSION OF

PANDA EXPRESS ORANGE-FLAVORED CHICKEN

Andrew J. C. Cherng had lived in China, Taiwan, and Japan before he came to the United States to study mathematics at Baker University. After graduation in 1973, this brainiac used his extensive education and business savvy to open an Asian restaurant in Pasadena with his father, Master Chef Ming Tsai Cherng. Southern Californians went crazy for the Panda Inn and its cutting-edge menu that blended the styles of Szechwan and Mandarin cooking.

Today, the chain includes more than 320 units in thirty-two states and Japan and is famous for the addictive fried chicken dish with the tangy orange sauce. We can re-create this dish using a special baking technique to avoid the fat that's unavoidable when frying.

SAUCE

- 1½ cups water
- 2 tablespoons orange juice
- 1 cup packed dark brown sugar
- ⅓ cup rice vinegar
- 2½ tablespoons soy sauce
- ¼ cup plus 1 teaspoon lemon juice
- 1 teaspoon minced water chestnuts
- ½ teaspoon minced fresh ginger
- ¼ teaspoon minced garlic
- 1 rounded teaspoon chopped green onion
- ¼ teaspoon crushed red pepper flakes
- 5 teaspoons cornstarch
- 2 teaspoons arrowroot

CHICKEN

4 skinless chicken breast fillets
½ cup ice water
¼ cup egg substitute
1 cup self-rising flour
¼ teaspoon salt

vegetable oil cooking spray

1. Combine all of the sauce ingredients—except the cornstarch and arrowroot—in a small saucepan over high heat. Stir often while bringing mixture to a boil. When sauce reaches a boil, remove it from heat and allow it to cool a bit, uncovered.
2. Slice chicken breasts into bite-size chunks. Remove exactly 1 cup of the marinade from the pan and pour it over the chicken in a large resealable plastic bag or other container that allows the chicken to be completely covered with the marinade. Chicken should marinate for at least a couple hours. Cover remaining sauce and leave it to cool until the chicken is ready.
3. When chicken has marinated, preheat your oven to 475 degrees.
4. Combine cornstarch with arrowroot in a small bowl, then add 3 tablespoons of water. Stir until cornstarch and arrowroot have dissolved. Pour this mixture into the sauce, and set the pan over high heat. When sauce begins to bubble and thicken, cover and remove from heat.
5. Beat the ice water and egg together in a medium bowl. In another medium bowl, combine the flour and salt.
6. Line a baking sheet with foil. Spray foil with a generous coating of oil cooking spray.
7. First dip each piece of chicken into the flour, then into the egg mixture, and finally back into the flour. Arrange the coated chicken pieces on the baking sheet. When all of the chicken is positioned on the baking sheet, spray a coating of the oil cooking spray over the top of the chicken.
8. Bake the chicken for 4 to 6 minutes or until it begins to brown on top. Turn the oven up to high broil for 2 to 3 minutes or until chicken has browned and has a crispy coating.

9. As the chicken cooks, reheat the sauce left covered on the stove. Stir it occasionally.
10. Pour the chicken into a large serving dish. Cover it with the thickened sauce. Stir gently until all of the pieces are well coated.

- SERVES 4.

Nutrition Facts *(per serving)*

SERVING SIZE—1 SLICED CHICKEN BREAST   TOTAL SERVINGS—4

	LOW-FAT	ORIGINAL
CALORIES (APPROX.)	400	580
FAT (APPROX.)	12G	30G

• • • •

TOP SECRET RECIPES REDUCED-FAT VERSION OF

RAINFOREST CAFE TROPICAL CHICKEN QUARTET

This item has been on the theme eatery's menu since the first restaurant opened back in 1994. It was called Tortuga Tidbits back then, but as a restaurant spokesperson explains, "No one knew what a Tortuga Tidbit was ... neither did we. So last year we changed the name to make it more descriptive of the menu item."

For this low-fat conversion, we'll need to use the Top Secret Recipes version of Rainforest Cafe Reggae spice blend from page 323. The recipe is designed to make a rather unusual yield total of three sandwiches, since the dinner rolls come in packages of twelve.

SPICY REMOULADE SAUCE

¼ cup fat-free mayonnaise
2 teaspoons finely minced fresh parsley
1 teaspoon prepared horseradish
1 teaspoon French dressing
1 teaspoon finely minced onion
½ teaspoon finely minced garlic
½ teaspoon Tabasco pepper sauce
½ teaspoon Grey Poupon Dijon mustard
¼ teaspoon white vinegar

3 skinless chicken breast fillets
oil cooking spray
TSR version of Reggae Beat Seasoning (from page 323)
6 canned pineapple slices
1 package of 12 homestyle dinner rolls
fat-free butter-flavored spray

1 ½ cups shredded lettuce
2 Roma tomatoes, sliced

4 slices fat-free Kraft mozzarella cheese singles

1. Prepare the spicy remoulade sauce by combining the ingredients in a small bowl. Cover and chill until needed.
2. Preheat barbecue grill to high temperature.
3. Pound the chicken breasts lightly until about ½ inch thick. Spray each breast with a light coating of oil cooking spray. Sprinkle a generous portion of Reggae Beat Seasoning clone over one side of each chicken breast. Place each breast, seasoned side down, onto the grill. Sprinkle additional seasoning over the top of each chicken breast. Arrange the pineapple slices on the grill with the chicken. Grill the pineapple slices and chicken for 2 to 3 minutes per side or until done.
4. While chicken cooks, heat up a large skillet over medium heat. Separate the dinner rolls into groups of four.
5. Keeping the rolls attached in groups of four, spray the face of each group of rolls with a light coating of butter-flavored spray, and then grill the faces until golden brown in the hot skillet. Arrange the rolls on three separate plates for assembly.
6. Spread 1 teaspoon of the remoulade sauce onto the faces of the bottom buns. Sprinkle some shredded lettuce onto the sauce, and then place a slice of tomato on each of the 4 rolls per sandwich.
7. When the chicken is done, cut each breast into 4 equal-size pieces. Arrange the chicken onto the lettuce on each sandwich.
8. Cut each slice of cheese into quarters. Arrange a quarter-slice of cheese over the chicken on each sandwich.
9. Cut each pineapple slice in half and position the half on the cheese on each sandwich. That's 4 pineapple halves per 4-roll sandwich.
10. Finish off the sandwich by placing the top half of the group of 4 rolls on each sandwich and serve.

- SERVES 3 AS AN ENTRÉE.

Nutrition Facts *(per serving)*
SERVING SIZE—1 4-ROLL SANDWICH   TOTAL SERVINGS—3

	LOW-FAT	ORIGINAL
CALORIES (APPROX.)	768	863
FAT (APPROX.)	14G	27G

• • • •

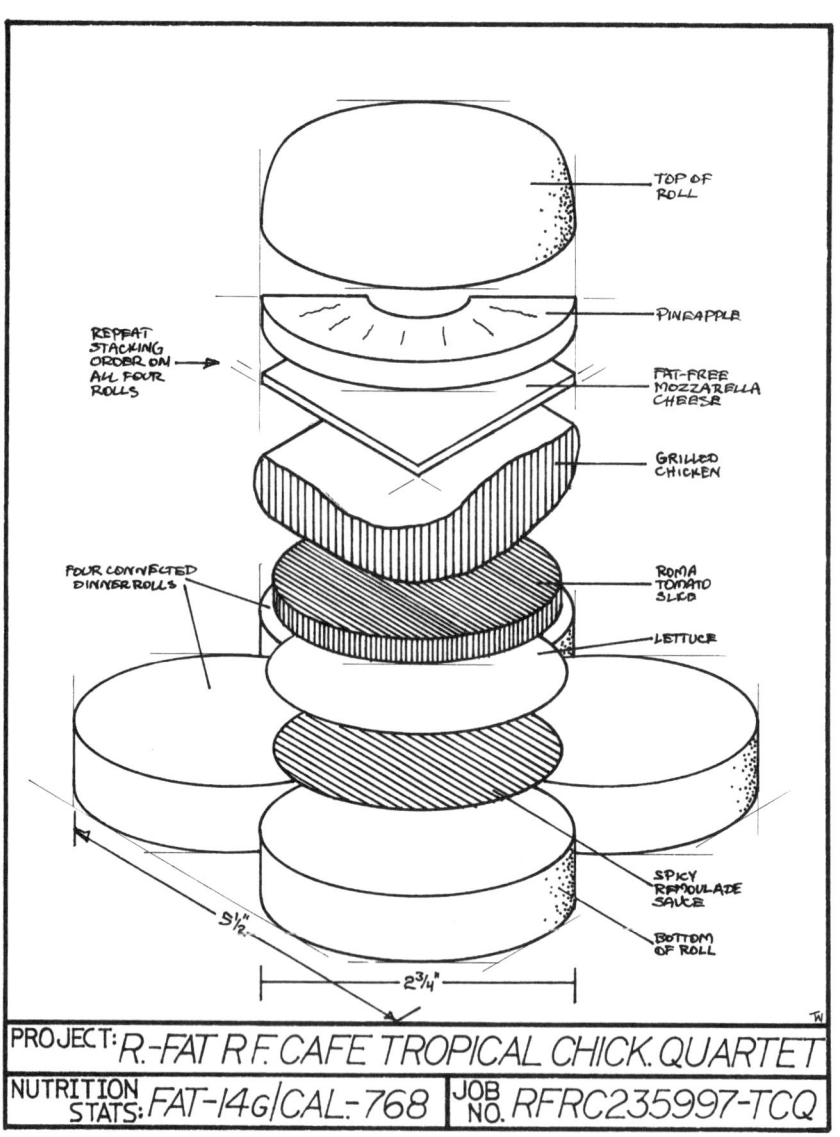

TOP SECRET RECIPES LOW-FAT VERSION OF

SCREAMING YELLOW ZONKERS

This oddly named popcorn confection gets its yellow color from the butter-flavored popcorn beneath the nearly clear candy coating. We'll use microwave popcorn for this low-fat version, and we'll throw in some real butter and butter flavoring for just the right touch. With this secret formula, we can duplicate the taste of the original with only half the fat.

½ cup light corn syrup
½ cup granulated sugar
¼ cup water
2 tablespoons butter
¾ teaspoon salt

½ teaspoon butter flavoring
¼ teaspoon vanilla extract
1 bag of 94% fat-free microwave butter popcorn

1. Combine the corn syrup, sugar, water, butter, and salt in a small saucepan over medium heat. Stir while bringing mixture to a boil, then use a candy thermometer to bring mixture to 300 degrees (in candy making this is known as the hard crack stage).
2. When the candy reaches about 275 degrees, start cooking the popcorn following the directions on the package. You want to time it so that the popcorn is done at approximately the same time as the candy. This way the popcorn will be hot when you pour the candy over it.
3. When the candy has reached the right temperature, remove it from the heat, then add the butter flavoring and vanilla extract. Pour the hot popcorn into a large plastic or glass bowl and quickly pour the candy over it. Stir the popcorn around a bit,

then microwave the bowl on high temperature for 30 seconds. Stir the popcorn again; then, if necessary, microwave it once more for an additional 30 seconds. Stir again. By this time, the popcorn should be very well coated with the candy.
4. Quickly pour the popcorn out onto wax paper and spread it around to cool it.
5. When candy is cool, break it into bite-size pieces. Store it in a sealed container.

- MAKES 12 CUPS.

Nutrition Facts *(per serving)*
SERVING SIZE—1 CUP   TOTAL SERVINGS—12

	LOW-FAT	ORIGINAL
CALORIES	107	140
FAT	2G	4G

• • • •

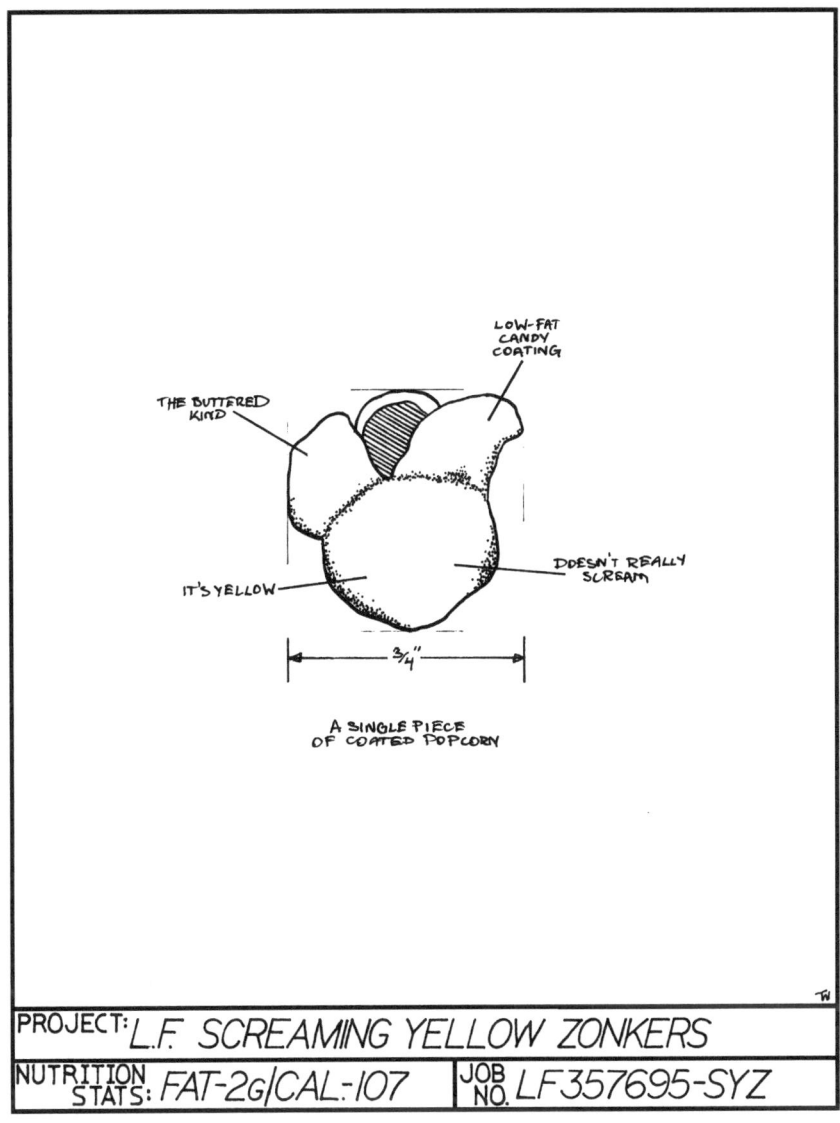

TOP SECRET RECIPES REDUCED-FAT VERSION OF

SONIC DRIVE-IN NO. 1 BURGER

The Sonic story starts back in 1953, when Troy Smith traded in his failing fried chicken stand in Shawnee, Oklahoma, for a parcel of land that had a steakhouse and a root beer stand on it. Troy thought he'd make the steakhouse his primary operation, but as it turned out, patrons preferred the hot dogs and cold drinks at the root beer stand. Troy dumped the steakhouse and focused on offering additional items at the stand, such as hamburgers. Those hamburgers became the big seller at this revised restaurant, which Troy had dubbed the Top Hat. But that name would soon change when the Top Hat sign was replaced by one that read Sonic Drive-In.

This is a lower-fat clone of that first hamburger, which has been on the menu since the beginning. We'll substitute lean ground beef and fat-free mayonnaise to shear off more than sixteen grams of fat.

¼-pound super lean ground beef (7% fat)
1 large plain white hamburger bun
fat-free butter-flavored spray
salt
ground black pepper
2 teaspoons fat-free mayonnaise
3 dill pickle slices (hamburger slices)
1 tablespoon chopped white onion
⅓ cup chopped lettuce
2 tomato slices

1. Pound the ground beef into a thin circle the same diameter as the bun. Cover with wax paper and freeze.
2. When ready to prepare the burger, preheat a large skillet over medium heat.

3. Spray a light coating of the butter spray over the face of the top and bottom bun. Brown the faces of the bun in the skillet, then remove them and set them aside.
4. Place the beef patty into the skillet, and lightly sprinkle it with salt and pepper. Cook for 3 to 4 minutes per side until done.
5. As the patty cooks, build the burger by first spreading the mayonnaise over the face of the bottom bun.
6. Arrange the pickle slices on the mayonnaise.
7. Sprinkle the chopped onion over the pickles.
8. Arrange the lettuce on the sandwich next.
9. Stack the tomato slices on the lettuce.
10. When the beef is ready, stack it on top of the other condiments, and top off the sandwich with the top bun. If you'd like the sandwich hotter, microwave on high for 10 to 15 seconds.

- MAKES 1 SANDWICH.

Nutrition Facts *(per serving)*
SERVING SIZE—1 SANDWICH   TOTAL SERVINGS—1

	LOW-FAT	ORIGINAL
CALORIES	400	409
FAT	10.5G	26.6G

• • • •

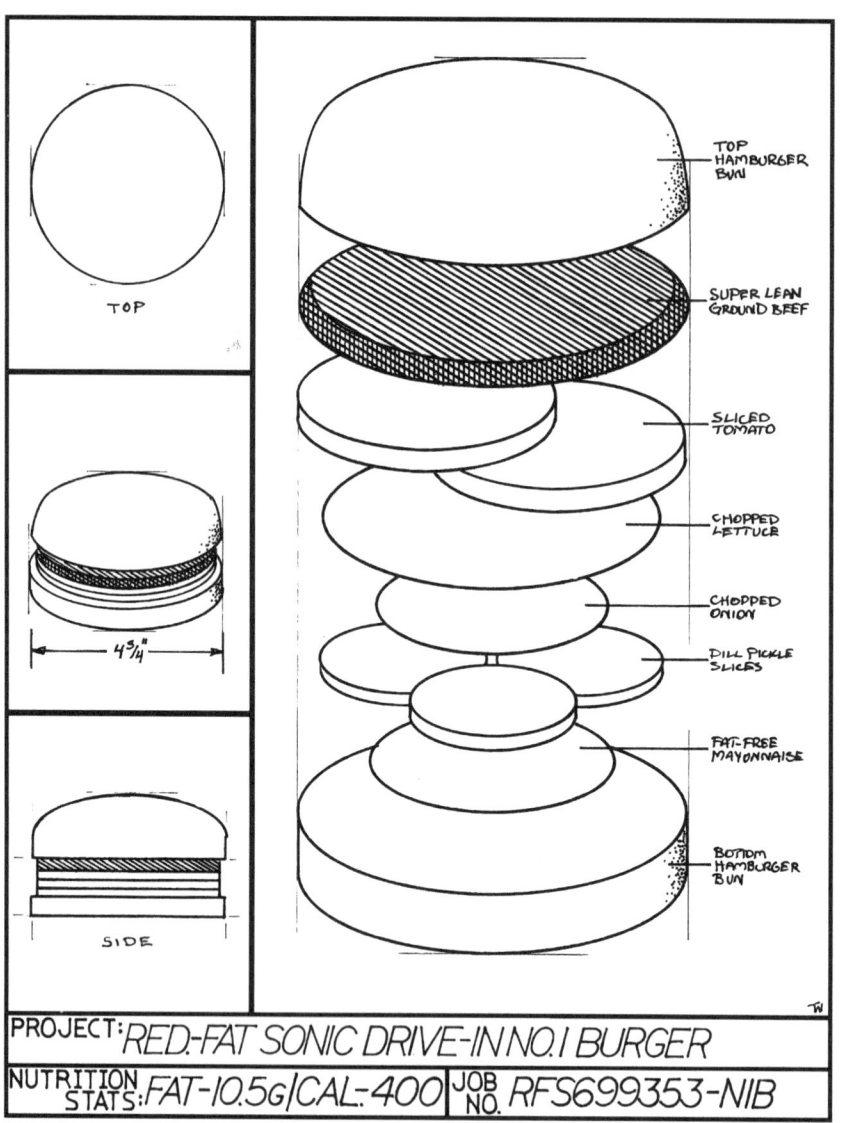

TOP SECRET RECIPES REDUCED-FAT VERSION OF

SONIC DRIVE-IN HICKORY BURGER

Driving through Louisiana in 1953, Troy Smith happened upon a cozy hamburger stand that had installed an intercom system to speed up ordering. Troy adapted the idea for his small chain of burger joints and hired nimble servers to bring the food out to customers quickly. The concept was a smash, with revenues for the chain doubling during the first week. Sonic was cashing in on the growing popularity of the automobile. Customers parked their cars in a stall, rolled down the window, and ordered from a speaker. The food was then brought to the car on a tray by a roller-skating carhop with extraordinary balance.

Today, Sonic has rejuvenated the carhop concept by serving customers the same way as in the '50s; with individual car stalls, speakers, and waitresses on wheels. The company is America's largest drive-in hamburger chain with more than two thousand units rolling in 1999.

¼ pound super lean ground beef (7% fat)
1 large plain white hamburger bun
fat-free butter-flavored spray
salt
ground black pepper
1 tablespoon Kraft Hickory BBQ Sauce
1 tablespoon chopped white onion
⅓ cup chopped lettuce

1. Pound the ground beef into a circle the same diameter as the bun. Cover the meat with wax paper and freeze it.
2. When ready to prepare the burger, preheat a large skillet over medium heat.

3. Spray a light coating of the butter-flavored spray over the face of the top and bottom bun. Brown the faces of the bun in the skillet, then remove it and set it aside.
4. Place the beef patty into the skillet, and lightly sprinkle it with salt and pepper. Cook for 3 to 4 minutes per side until done.
5. As patty cooks, build the burger by first spreading the BBQ sauce over the face of the bottom bun.
6. Sprinkle the chopped onion over the sauce.
7. Arrange the lettuce on the sandwich next.
8. When the beef is ready, stack it on top of the other condiments and top off the sandwich with the top bun. If you'd like the sandwich hotter, microwave on high for 10 to 15 seconds.

- MAKES 1 SANDWICH.

Nutrition Facts *(per serving)*
SERVING SIZE—1 SANDWICH   TOTAL SERVINGS—1

	LOW-FAT	ORIGINAL
CALORIES	400	314
FAT	10.5G	15.7G

• • • •

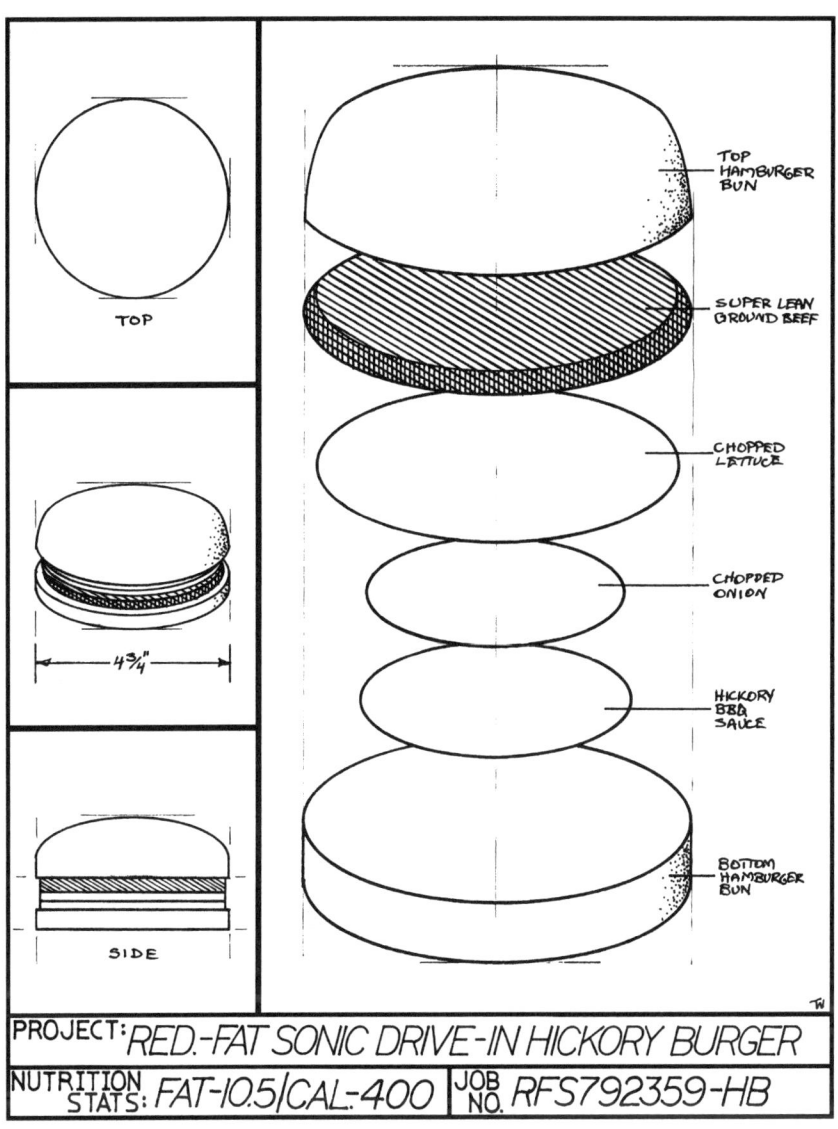

TOP SECRET RECIPES REDUCED-FAT VERSION OF

SONIC DRIVE-IN JALAPEÑO BURGER

One day in 1958, when Top Hat chains were operating in several Oklahoma cities, lawyers informed founder Troy Smith that *Top Hat* was already a copyrighted name and that he would have to make some hasty changes. The chain's partners searched for a name that summed up the company motto: "Service at the Speed of Sound." They decided that the name *Sonic* had a spiffy ring to it.

Sonic is now the country's fifth-largest hamburger chain, boasting some amazing statistics. For example, if you were to take all of the hamburger patties Sonic served last year and stack them up, they would be as tall as 2,576 Empire State Buildings stacked one on top of the other. Which guy with too much free time figured that one out?

If you like your burgers with a spicy kick and dig mustard, try this reduced-fat clone for one of Sonic's tastiest creations.

¼ pound super lean ground beef (7% fat)
1 large plain white hamburger bun
fat-free butter-flavored spray
salt
ground black pepper
1 ½ teaspoons prepared yellow mustard
6 to 10 canned jalapeño slices (nacho rings)
⅓ cup chopped lettuce

1. Pound the ground beef into a circle the same diameter as the bun. Cover the meat with wax paper and freeze it.
2. When ready to prepare the burger, preheat a large skillet over medium heat.

3. Spray a light coating of the butter spray over the face of the top and bottom bun. Brown the faces of the bun in the skillet, then remove it and set it aside.
4. Place the beef patty into the skillet, and lightly sprinkle it with salt and pepper. Cook for 3 to 4 minutes per side until done.
5. As the patty cooks, build the burger by first spreading the mustard over the face of the bottom bun.
6. Arrange the jalapeño slices on the mustard.
7. Arrange the lettuce on the sandwich next.
8. When the beef is ready, stack it on top of the other condiments and top off the sandwich with the top bun. If you'd like the sandwich hotter, microwave on high for 10 to 15 seconds.

- Makes 1 sandwich.

Nutrition Facts *(per serving)*
Serving size—1 sandwich   Total servings—1

	Low-Fat	Original
Calories (approx.)	400	380
Fat (approx.)	10.5g	16g

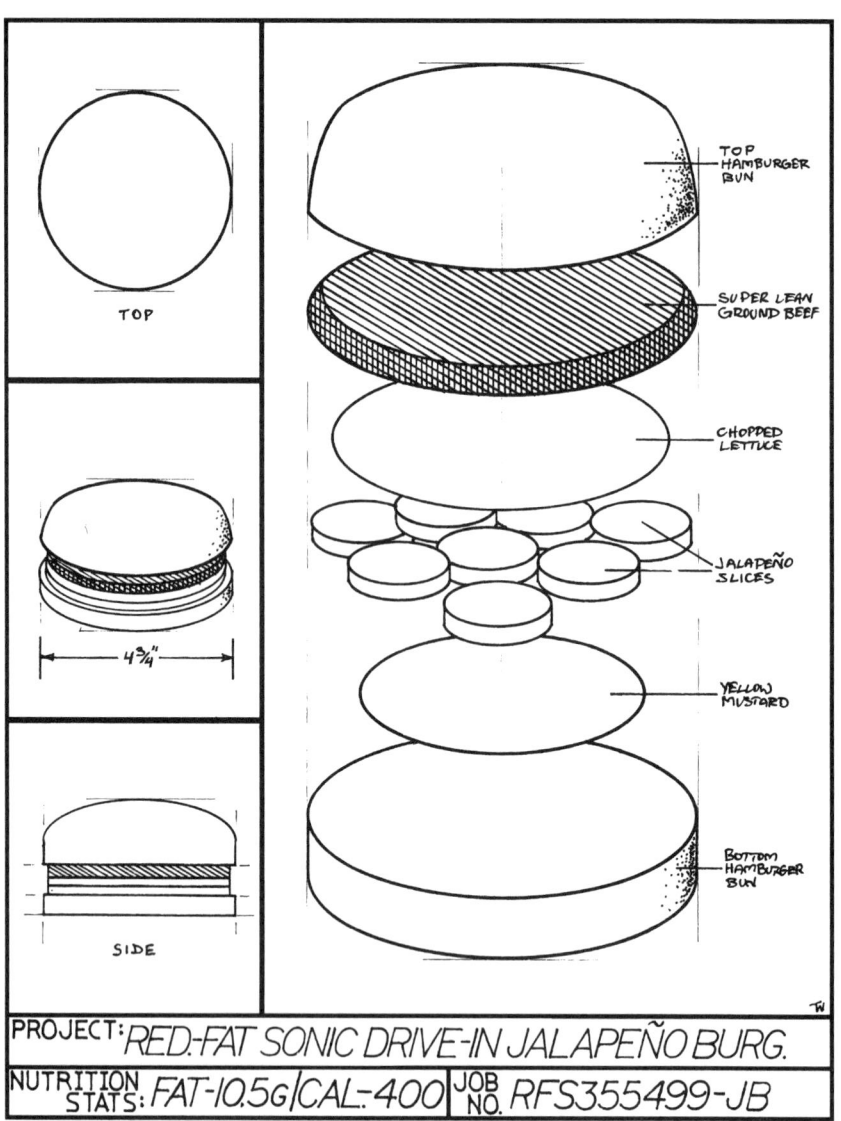

TOP SECRET RECIPES REDUCED-FAT VERSION OF

TACO BELL BEEF BURRITO SUPREME

How's this for coincidence: Both McDonald's and Taco Bell got their start in San Bernardino, California, in the early '50s. Glen Bell opened a hamburger and hot dog stand called Bell's Drive-In, while the McDonald brothers, Dick and Mac, were just around the corner with their golden arches and speedy drive-up service. "The appearance of another hamburger stand worried me then," says Glen. "I just didn't think there was enough room in town for both of us." Turns out there was enough room—at least for a little while.

In 1962, Glen decided that it was time to offer an alternative to the hamburger stands that were saturating the area, so he opened the first Taco Bell and changed his menu to Mexican food.

Ten years and hundreds of new Taco Bell openings later, the Burrito Supreme hit the menu and became an instant hit. By making this clone version at home, we can reduce the fat to less than one-fifth that of the original.

½ pound super lean ground beef (7% fat)
2 tablespoons all-purpose flour
¾ teaspoon salt
¼ teaspoon dried, minced onion
¼ teaspoon paprika
1 ½ teaspoons chili powder
dash garlic powder
dash onion powder

¼ cup water
1 cup fat-free refried beans
4 10-inch fat-free flour tortillas
1 cup shredded iceberg lettuce
½ cup fat-free shredded cheddar cheese
1 medium tomato, diced
¼ cup fat-free sour cream

1. In a medium bowl, combine the super lean ground beef with the flour, salt, minced onion, paprika, chili powder, garlic powder, and onion powder. Use your hands to thoroughly incorporate everything into the ground beef.
2. Preheat a skillet over medium/low heat, and add the ground beef mixture to the pan along with the water. Brown the beef mixture for 5 to 6 minutes, using a wooden spoon or spatula to break up the meat as it cooks.
3. Put the refried beans into a microwave-safe container and cover. Heat on high for 2 to 3 minutes or until hot. You may also heat the beans in a small saucepan on the stove over medium/low heat. Stir occasionally, and heat until hot.
4. Using the microwave, heat up 4 10-inch fat-free flour tortillas in a tortilla steamer (or wrapped in a moist cloth or paper towels) for 25 to 30 seconds or until hot.
5. Spread about ¼ cup of refried beans in a 2-inch-wide strip down the center of one tortilla. Don't spread the beans all the way to the edge of the tortilla. Leave a margin of a couple inches so that you can later fold the tortilla.
6. Spread ¼ cup of the beef over the refried beans.
7. Sprinkle ¼ cup of lettuce onto the beef.
8. Sprinkle 2 tablespoons of the fat-free cheese onto the lettuce.
9. Sprinkle 2 tablespoons of diced tomato over the cheese.
10. Finish the burrito by dropping a tablespoon of fat-free sour cream over the other fillings.
11. Fold the left side of the tortilla over the fillings. Fold up the bottom, then fold the right side over, and serve hot. Repeat with the remaining ingredients.

- MAKES 4 BURRITOS.

Nutrition Facts *(per serving)*
SERVING SIZE—1 BURRITO   TOTAL SERVINGS—4

	LOW-FAT	ORIGINAL
CALORIES	325	503
FAT	4G	22G

• • • •

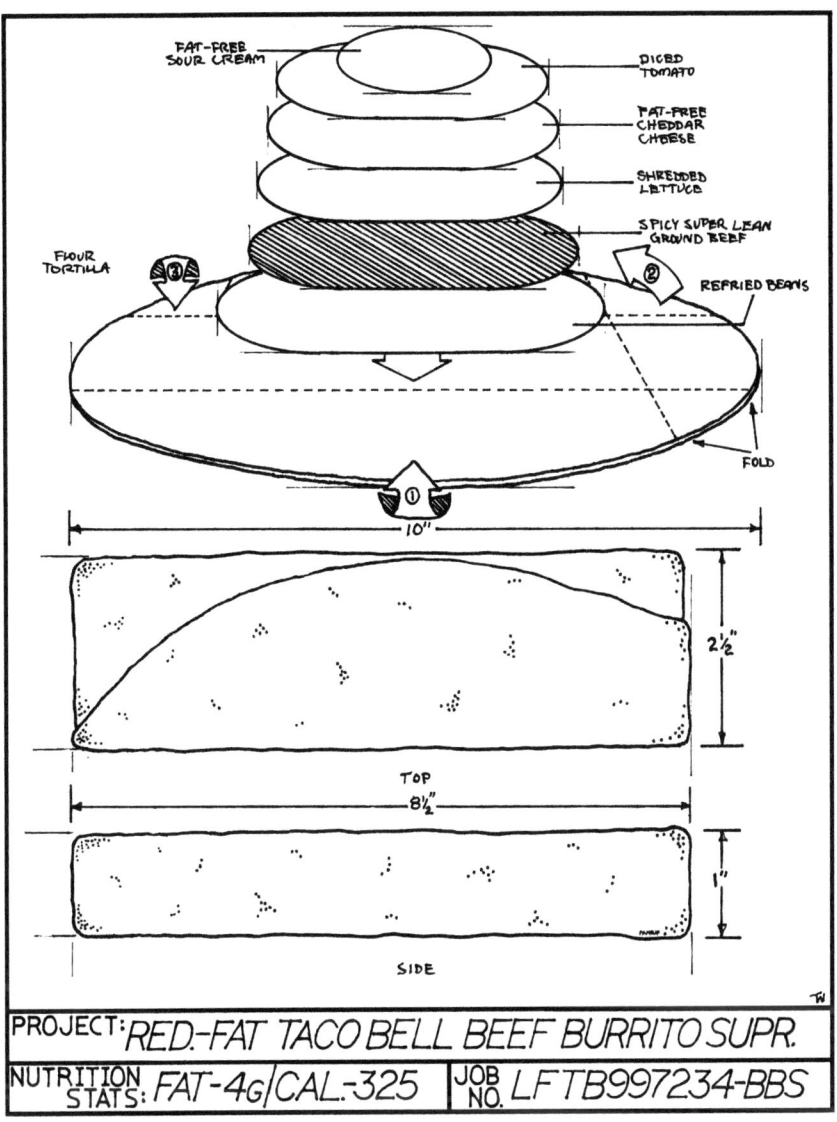

TOP SECRET RECIPES
LOW-FAT VERSION OF

TACO BELL CHICKEN SOFT TACO

Taco Bell had very little luck with light menu items over the years. In 1983, the Mexican fast-food chain introduced Taco Light, a taco with a fried flour tortilla shell. But the fried flour tortilla that replaced the traditional corn tortilla only made the taco light in weight and color, not in fat or calories. The item was quickly discontinued. In 1995, the chain tried again with Light Line, a selection of several lower-fat menu items that also took a sales digger. Customers who frequented the drive-thru weren't there to lose weight; they were there to ingest some greasy taco meat and handfuls of shredded cheddar.

When we cook at home, though, we'd like to do what we can to make a meal better on the waistline, especially if it takes no extra effort and the food still tastes good. This recipe will show that you can do just that: knock the fat way down—from ten grams to just two grams—without compromising flavor. Check it out.

1/2 cup water
1 teaspoon soy sauce
1 teaspoon salt
1 teaspoon brown sugar
1/2 teaspoon onion powder
1/4 teaspoon liquid smoke
1/4 teaspoon ground black pepper

1/4 teaspoon chili powder
2 skinless chicken breast fillets
6 6-inch fat-free flour tortillas
3/4 cups shredded iceberg lettuce
1/2 cup fat-free shredded cheddar cheese
1 medium tomato, diced

1. In a small bowl combine water, soy sauce, salt, brown sugar, onion powder, liquid smoke, black pepper, and chili powder in

a small bowl. Pour the mixture over the chicken breasts and marinate overnight. You can marinate for less time if you wish, but overnight is best.
2. Cook chicken on barbecue or indoor grill over medium/high heat for 5 to 6 minutes per side or until done. Slice chicken into bite-size chunks.
3. Heat the tortillas in a steamer, or wrap them in a moist towel and heat for about 30 seconds in the microwave.
4. Spread about ¼ cup of chicken down the middle of one of the flour tortillas.
5. Sprinkle about 2 tablespoons of lettuce over the chicken.
6. Sprinkle a heaping tablespoon of cheese over the lettuce.
7. Finish the taco by stacking a heaping tablespoon of diced tomato on the cheese, then fold up the edges of the taco, and serve immediately. Repeat with the remaining ingredients.

- MAKES 6 TACOS.

Nutrition Facts (per serving)
SERVING SIZE—1 TACO   TOTAL SERVINGS—6

	LOW-FAT	ORIGINAL
CALORIES	172	213
FAT	2G	10G

• • • •

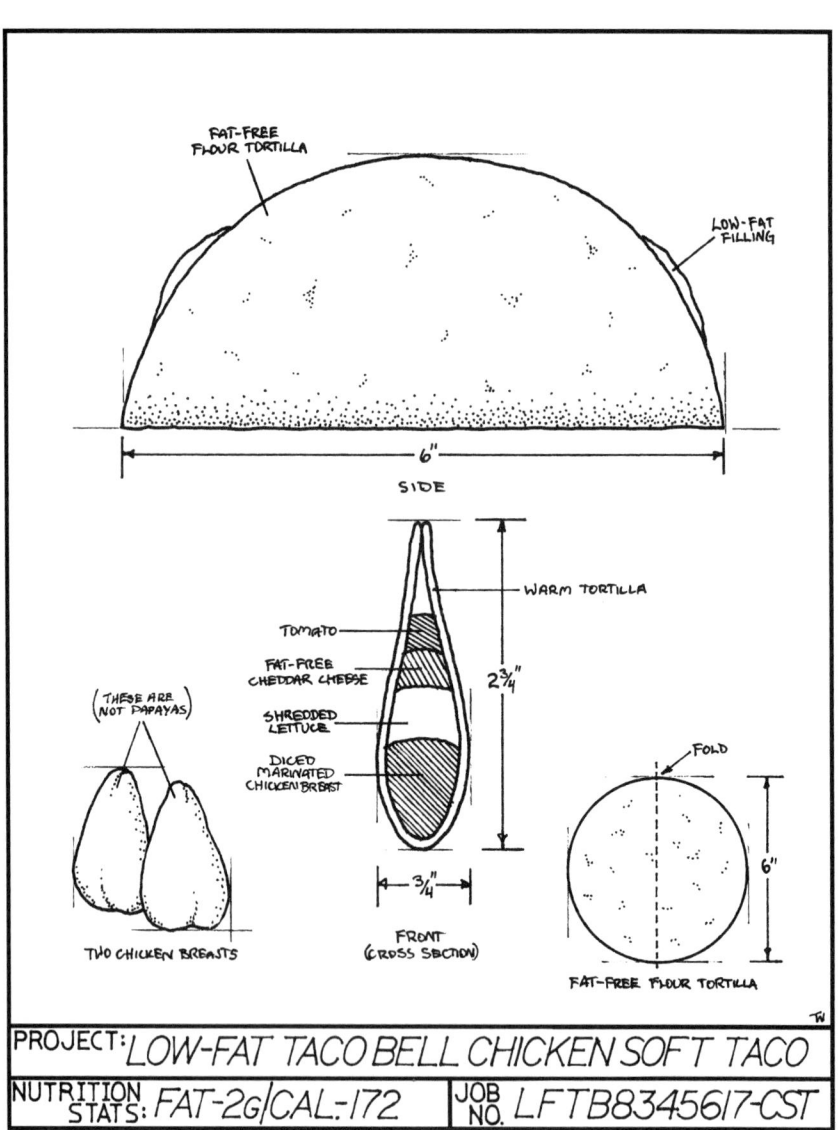

TOP SECRET RECIPES REDUCED-FAT VERSION OF

T.G.I. FRIDAY'S BBQ CHICKEN WINGS

You've got to hand it to him. Alan Stillman thought that if he opened his own restaurant, it might be a great way to meet the flight attendants who lived in his New York City neighborhood. Not only did the dude follow through on his plan in 1965 with the first T.G.I. Friday's, but today the company is 387 units strong, Alan's rich, and his inspiration is still a popular casual dining spot for delicious finger foods, drinks, lunches, and dinners in an upbeat, festive atmosphere. Nowadays, the chain goes through more than five million chicken wings in a year, serving buffalo wings as well as this variation of the tasty appetizer.

Friday's kitchen came up with a delicious blend of barbecue sauce and apple butter to coat the deep-fried chicken wings. For our reduced-fat clone, we'll re-create the exact taste of the barbecue sauce, but we'll strip the skin from the chicken wings and use a cool baking process that'll cut the fat way down. By the way, I hear flight attendants love wings.

oil nonstick cooking spray
12 chicken wings with skin
½ cup Bull's-Eye or K.C. Masterpiece Barbecue Sauce (original flavor only)
2 tablespoons apple butter
½ cup flour
1 teaspoon salt
½ teaspoon ground pepper
1 cup milk

1. Preheat the oven on broil.
2. Line a cookie sheet or shallow baking pan with a sheet of aluminum foil. Spray the foil with nonstick spray.
3. Arrange each chicken wing on the foil with the side that has

the most skin on it facing up. Broil the wings for 12 to 14 minutes or until the skin begins to turn light brown and becomes crispy. Remove wings from the oven and let them cool. Turn the oven to 450 degrees.
4. While the wings are broiling, combine the barbecue sauce with the apple butter in a small bowl. Chill the sauce until the wings are ready.
5. Prepare the breading by combining the flour, salt, and pepper in a small bowl. Pour the milk into another small bowl.
6. When you can handle the chicken wings, remove the skin from each one. Throw the skin out.
7. Dip the wings, one at a time, into the breading, then into the milk, and finally back in the breading, so that each one is well coated.
8. Place the wings back onto the baking sheet. Spray a coating of oil spray over each wing so that the breading is completely moistened, and then bake the wings at 450 degrees for 12 minutes. Crank the oven up to broil for 3 to 5 minutes or until the wings begin to brown and become crispy.
9. Remove the wings from the oven. Let them rest for about a minute, then put them into a large plastic container or jar with a lid. Pour a generous amount of sauce over the wings, cover, and gently shake the wings up so that they are all well coated with the sauce. Be careful not to shake too hard or the breading may fall off. Serve immediately.

- SERVES 4 AS AN APPETIZER.

Nutrition Facts (per serving)

SERVING SIZE—3 PIECES   TOTAL SERVINGS—4

	LOW-FAT	ORIGINAL
CALORIES (APPROX.)	150	235
FAT (APPROX.)	6G	16G

• • •

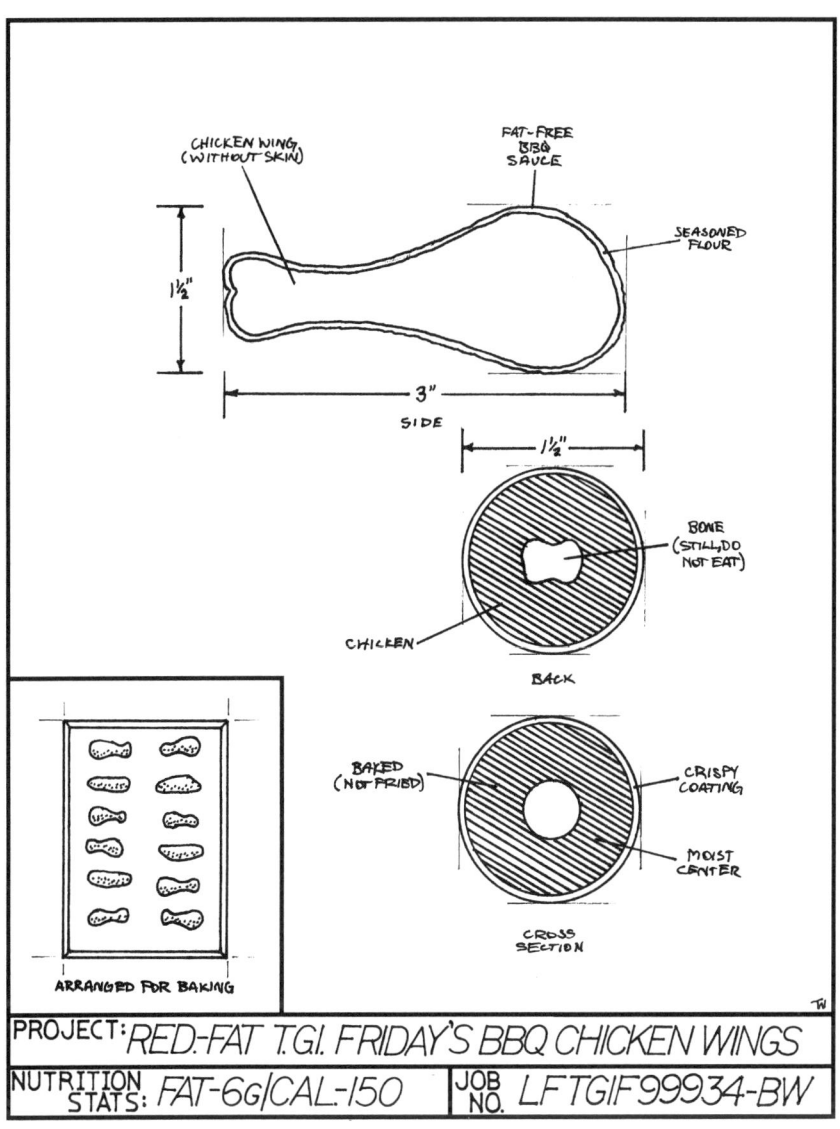

T.G.I. FRIDAY'S DIJON CHICKEN PASTA

TOP SECRET RECIPES REDUCED-FAT VERSION OF

That creamy, white Dijon sauce that smothers the original version of this delicious pasta is luscious indeed but cursed by oodles of flabby fat grams. This can be fixed in our reduced-fat clone by using strained fat-free yogurt—an ingredient apparently inspired by the ancient Mediterranean technique of straining yogurt through a cheesecloth—that adds a thick, creamy consistency to our sauce without adding fat.

DIJON PASTA SAUCE

1 clove garlic, pressed
1/2 teaspoon olive oil
1 cup strained fat-free yogurt*
2 tablespoons cornstarch
1 cup evaporated skim milk
1/4 cup fat-free milk
2 teaspoons Grey Poupon Dijon mustard
2 tablespoons grated Parmesan cheese
1/4 teaspoon salt
dash ground black pepper
1 1/2 tablespoons fresh parsley, chopped

CHICKEN SPICE BLEND

2 teaspoons salt
1 teaspoon paprika
1/2 teaspoon dried thyme
dash or two ground black pepper

fat-free butter-flavored spread or spray
4 skinless chicken breast fillets
1-pound package penne pasta
3 to 4 quarts water

*Make the strained yogurt by pouring a large container of plain yogurt into a coffee filter placed in a metal steamer basket or strainer. Overnight, the liquid whey will drain from the yogurt, leaving a thick, cheeselike substance in the strainer. Measure this thick stuff for the recipe and toss out the liquid.

GARNISH
1 small tomato, diced   *fresh parsley, chopped*

1. Preheat barbecue or stovetop grill to medium/high heat.
2. Prepare pasta sauce by first sautéing the pressed garlic in the olive oil in a medium saucepan. Sauté only for a minute or two over medium heat. Do not let the garlic brown or it will become bitter. Remove pan from heat.
3. Combine strained yogurt with cornstarch in a medium bowl. Add evaporated milk, fat-free milk, and mustard, and mix. Pour mixture into saucepan and place it back over heat. Add Parmesan cheese, salt, and pepper, and stir.
4. When sauce thickens, add parsley and turn heat to low, stirring often.
5. As sauce cooks, prepare the chicken by combining all of the spice blend ingredients in a small bowl. Rub a light coating of butter-flavored spread or spray over each breast, and sprinkle some of the spice blend over both sides of each chicken breast. Cook the chicken on the grill for 4 to 5 minutes per side. Turn the chicken at a 45-degree angle halfway through the cooking time on each side, so that you get crisscrossed grill marks on the surface.
6. While chicken is grilling, prepare pasta by bringing 3 to 4 cups of water to a boil in a large pan. Add pasta to the water and cook for 12 to 15 minutes or until pasta is tender. Strain.
7. Divide strained pasta into four portions on four plates, and pour a generous portion of the sauce over the pasta. Sprinkle some diced tomato over the pasta on each plate. Sprinkle some additional fresh parsley over the pasta.
8. Slice each chicken breast across the grain, and arrange each sliced breast on top of the pasta on each plate, being careful to retain the shape of the chicken breast as you position it.

- SERVES 4 AS AN ENTRÉE.

Nutrition Facts *(per serving)*

SERVING SIZE—1 ENTRÉE   TOTAL SERVINGS—4

	LOW-FAT	ORIGINAL
CALORIES (APPROX.)	730	930
FAT (APPROX.)	8G	45G

• • • •

TOP SECRET RECIPES REDUCED-FAT VERSION OF

T.G.I. FRIDAY'S POTATO SKINS

Thousands of restaurants all over the world now serve this tasty finger food on their appetizer menu, but T.G.I. Friday's is the potato skin king. The restaurant introduced America to the little cheese- and bacon-covered spud boats back in 1974, and the dish quickly took off. As this recipe demonstrates, potato skins can be a great choice for the munchies and don't have to be filled with even half of the traditional fourteen grams of fat per serving.

4 medium russet potatoes
canola oil nonstick cooking spray
salt
1 cup reduced-fat cheddar cheese

8 teaspoons Hormel Real Bacon Pieces
1 tablespoon snipped fresh chives
1/3 cup sour cream

1. Preheat oven to 400 degrees.
2. Bake the potatoes for 1 hour or until tender.
3. When potatoes have cooled enough so that you can handle them, make two lengthwise cuts through each potato, resulting in three 1/2- to 3/4-inch slices. Discard the middle slices or save them for a separate dish of mashed potatoes. This will leave you with two potato skins per potato.
4. With a spoon, scoop some of the potato out of each skin, being sure to leave about 1/4 inch of potato inside of the skin.
5. Pop oven temperature up to 450 degrees.
6. Spray the entire surface of each potato skin, inside and out, with a light coating of the canola oil spray.
7. Place the skins on a baking sheet, open side up, salt each one,

and then bake them for 12 to 15 minutes or until the edges begin to brown.
8. Spread about two tablespoons of cheese on each of the potato skins.
9. Sprinkle a teaspoon of bacon pieces on top of the cheese on each potato skin.
10. Bake the skins for another 2 to 4 minutes or until cheese is melted. Remove the skins from the oven and transfer them to a serving plate.
11. Combine the chives with the sour cream and serve in a small sauce cup in the center of the plate, with the skins arranged around the sour cream, like spokes on a wheel.

- SERVES 4 AS AN APPETIZER.

Nutrition Facts (per serving)
SERVING SIZE—3 PIECES   TOTAL SERVINGS—4

	LOW-FAT	ORIGINAL
CALORIES (APPROX.)	302	420
FAT (APPROX.)	5G	14G

• • • •

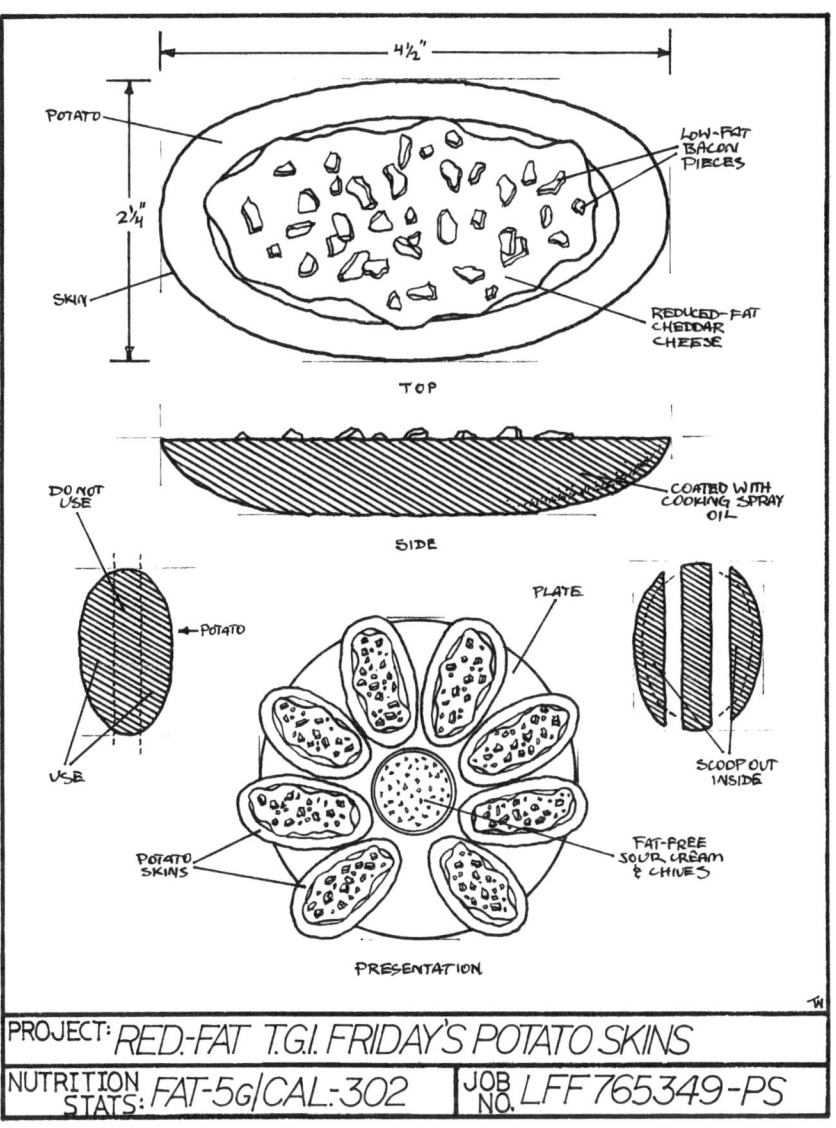

TOP SECRET RECIPES REDUCED-FAT VERSION OF

WENDY'S CHICKEN CAESAR FRESH STUFFED PITA

Publicity stunt alert! For one day in 1997, St. Petersburg, Florida, became "St. Pitas-burg" to celebrate the introduction of Wendy's Fresh Stuffed Pita sandwiches. Over 40,000 balloons formed a giant pita sandwich on a local Wendy's restaurant, while local residents and Wendy's staff learned the "art of eating a pita" from pita eating experts. (I hear that next time, they'll be showing us how to drink water.)

The Chicken Caesar Fresh Stuffed Pita was one of those pitas introduced on that glorious day. See if you can figure how to eat this clone version, made with much less fat, on your own.

DRESSING

2 teaspoons arrowroot
1/2 cup water
3 tablespoons white vinegar
2 teaspoons lemon juice
1/4 teaspoon finely minced red bell pepper
1/2 teaspoon salt
1/2 teaspoon granulated sugar
1/8 teaspoon garlic powder

1/8 teaspoon coarsely ground black pepper
dash dried parsley
dash dried oregano
dash dried thyme
1 tablespoon grated Romano cheese
1 tablespoon egg substitute

oil cooking spray
2 skinless chicken breast fillets
salt

ground black pepper
6 cups romaine lettuce, chopped
1/4 cup red cabbage, shredded

¼ cup carrot, shredded
4 large pita breads

4 teaspoons shredded, fresh Parmesan

1. Make the dressing by dissolving the arrowroot in the water. Heat the water in the microwave for 1 to 1½ minutes or until it begins to boil. Add the remaining ingredients except the Romano cheese and egg substitute, and let the mixture cool. When the mixture has reached room temperature, add the cheese and egg substitute. Cover and chill this dressing until it's thick.
2. Preheat a barbecue or indoor grill to medium heat. Spray a little oil cooking spray on each chicken breast. Salt and pepper the chicken, then grill it for 5 minutes per side or until done. Remove the chicken from the grill and dice it.
3. While chicken cooks, prepare the salad by combining the romaine lettuce, red cabbage, and shredded carrot in a large bowl and toss.
4. Prepare the sandwiches by first microwaving each pita for 20 seconds. Fold each pita in half like a taco, then fill them with 1 to 1½ cups of romaine salad each.
5. Add about ⅓ cup of diced chicken on top of the salad in the pita.
6. Pour about a tablespoon of dressing over each sandwich.
7. Sprinkle about a teaspoon of shredded fresh Parmesan on top of each sandwich, and serve.

- MAKES 4 SANDWICHES.

Nutrition Facts *(per serving)*
SERVING SIZE—1 SANDWICH   TOTAL SERVINGS—4

	LOW-FAT	ORIGINAL
CALORIES (APPROX.)	283	490
FAT (APPROX.)	5G	18G

• • • •

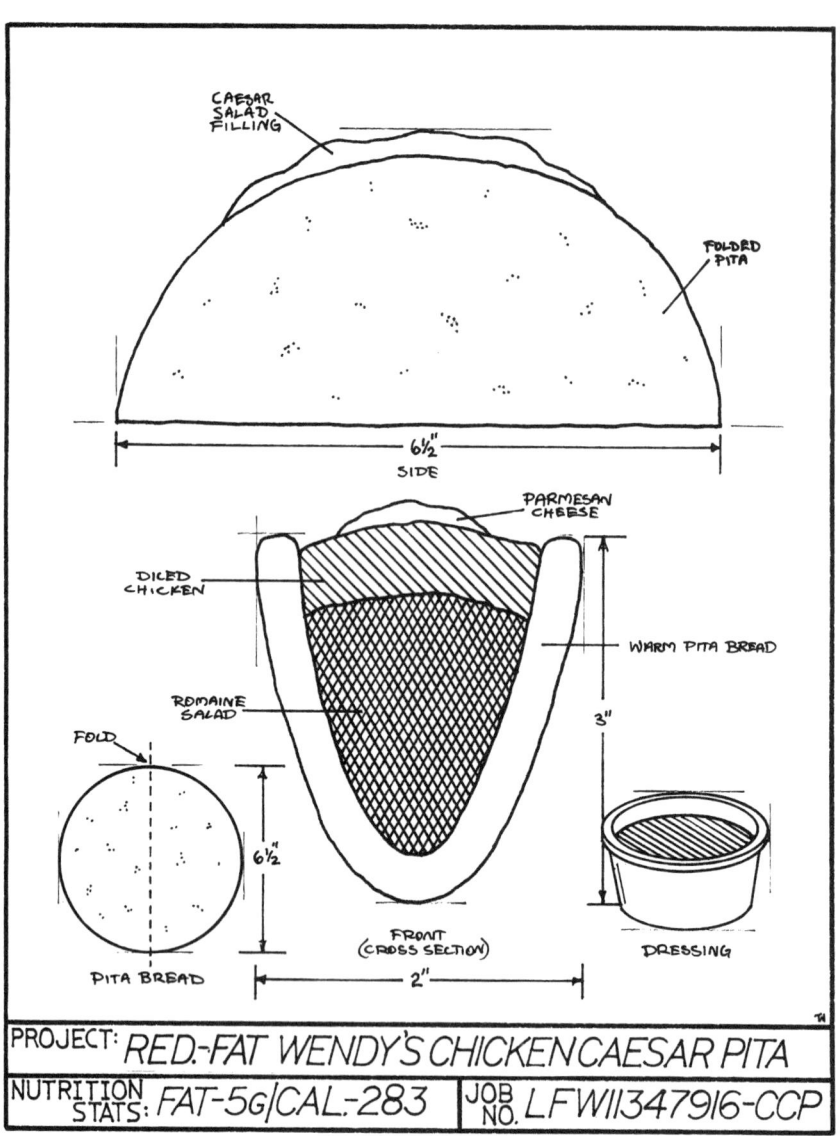

TOP SECRET RECIPES LOW-FAT VERSION OF

WENDY'S CLASSIC GREEK FRESH STUFFED PITA

Publicity stunt alert number two! In 1997, Wendy's announced its IPO—otherwise known as the Initial Pita Offering—on the floor of the New York Stock Exchange. Wendy's CEO Gordon Teter rang the bell to open the day of trading while Wendy's stock traders on the floor munched out on four varieties of the pita sandwiches, including this one, the Classic Greek Fresh Stuffed Pita.

For our low-fat clone, we'll save a gaggle of grams by making the dressing fat-free, and then we'll use low-fat feta cheese. Following this secret formula below, you can turn what is normally a 20-fat-gram sandwich into one that weighs in with only 2.5 grams.

FAT-FREE DRESSING

2 teaspoons arrowroot
½ cup water
3 tablespoons white vinegar
2 teaspoons lemon juice
¼ teaspoon finely minced red bell pepper
½ teaspoon salt
½ teaspoon granulated sugar
⅛ teaspoon garlic powder
⅛ teaspoon coarsely ground black pepper
dash dried parsley
dash dried oregano
dash dried thyme
1 tablespoon grated Romano cheese
1 tablespoon egg substitute

1 cup crumbled low-fat feta cheese
½ cup tomato, seeded and diced
¼ cup cucumber, thinly sliced and chopped
¼ cup red onion, diced
6 cups romaine lettuce, chopped
¼ cup red cabbage, shredded
¼ cup carrot, shredded
4 large pita breads

1. Make the dressing by dissolving the arrowroot in the water. Heat the water in the microwave for 1 to 1½ minutes or until it begins to boil. Add the remaining ingredients except the Romano cheese and egg substitute, and let the mixture cool. When the mixture has reached room temperature, add the cheese and egg substitute. Cover and chill until thick.
2. Make the Greek topping for the sandwich by combining the crumbled feta cheese, tomato, cucumber, and red onion in a small bowl.
3. Prepare the salad by combining the romaine lettuce, red cabbage, and carrot in a large bowl and toss.
4. Prepare the sandwiches by first microwaving each pita for 20 seconds. Fold each pita in half like a taco, then fill them with 1 to 1½ cups of romaine salad each.
5. Add ½ to ⅓ cup of the Greek topping to each sandwich.
6. Pour about a tablespoon of the dressing over each sandwich, and serve.

- MAKES 4 SANDWICHES.

Nutrition Facts (per serving)
SERVING SIZE—1 SANDWICH   TOTAL SERVINGS—4

	LOW-FAT	ORIGINAL
CALORIES (APPROX.)	240	440
FAT (APPROX.)	2.5G	20G

• • •

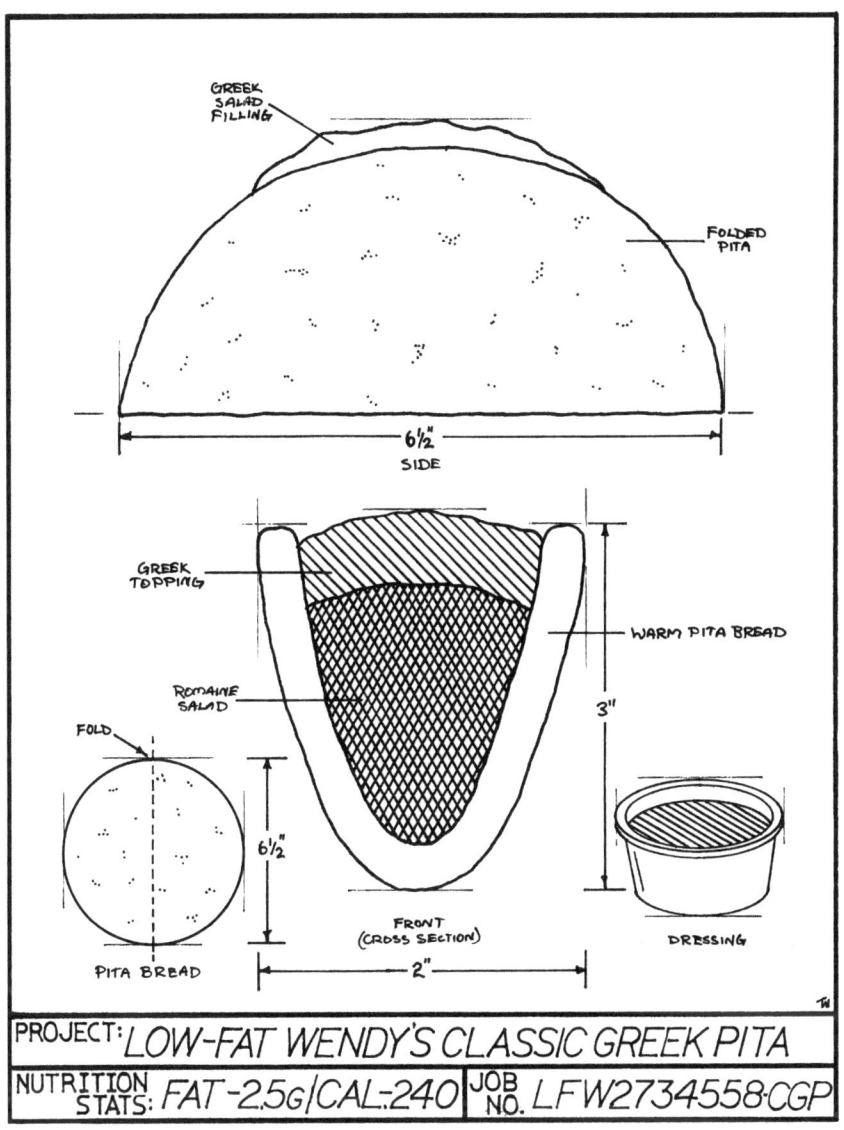

TOP SECRET RECIPES REDUCED-FAT VERSION OF

WENDY'S JUNIOR BACON CHEESEBURGER

Did you know that Dave Thomas, the spokesman and founder of the country's third-largest hamburger chain, got his start in fried chicken with a famous Kentucky colonel? That's right, kiddies! In 1962, Dave had an opportunity to turn around four failing KFC carryouts for an ownership stake in the lot of 'em. Dave worked hard and was eventually successful. He then parlayed his new ownership into four more KFC restaurants. In 1968, he sold them all and was handed $1.5 million. Dave was suddenly a millionaire at age thirty-five.

Not one to sit still, just a year later, Dave opened his first Wendy's restaurant, and today the chain is nearly 5000 units strong. Pretty good for a guy who didn't even finish high school, eh?

Here's my conversion of one of the best items on Wendy's bargain ninety-nine-cents menu, but at twenty-five grams (hey, that's four cents per fat gram!), it's just got too much fat, don't you think? Let's knock this one down to just eleven grams, using lean ground beef, fat-free mayo, and turkey bacon.

1 plain hamburger bun
⅛ pound super lean ground beef (7% fat)
salt
ground black pepper

½ tablespoon fat-free mayonnaise
1 slice fat-free American cheese
2 strips turkey bacon
1 lettuce leaf
1 tomato slice

1. Brown the faces of the bun in a hot frying pan over medium heat. Keep the pan hot.
2. Form the ground beef into a square patty approximately 4 × 4 inches.
3. Cook the patty in the pan for 3 to 4 minutes per side or until done. Salt and pepper each side while cooking.
4. Spread the fat-free mayonnaise on the face of the top bun.
5. Place the cooked patty on the bottom bun.
6. Stack the cheese on the meat.
7. Place the bacon on the cheese.
8. Put the lettuce on next, then the tomato.
9. Top off the sandwich with the top bun. Microwave for 15 seconds on high to warm, if necessary.

- MAKES 1 SANDWICH.

Nutrition Facts (per serving)
SERVING SIZE—1 SANDWICH   TOTAL SERVINGS—1

	LOW-FAT	ORIGINAL
CALORIES (APPROX.)	310	430
FAT (APPROX.)	11G	25G

• • • •

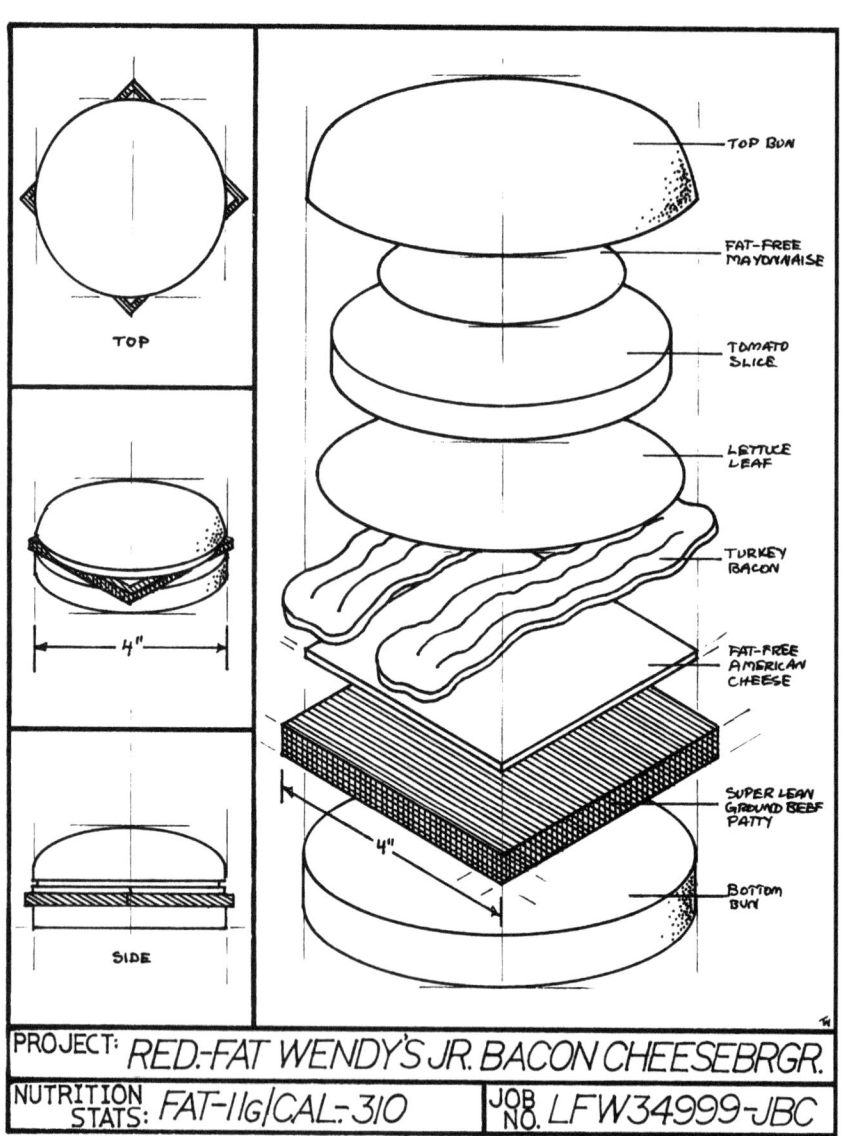

WENDY'S SPICY CHICKEN FILLET SANDWICH

TOP SECRET RECIPES REDUCED-FAT VERSION OF

Wendy's kicked it up a notch in 1996 when the burger chain introduced the Spicy Chicken Fillet Sandwich. The deep-fried chicken fillet in the middle of this puppy is breaded with a secret coating containing just a bit of zing for those who like their food with some heat. It's not exactly the knock-your-socks-off kind of hot, but the spice gives the chicken a great flavor that's got customers coming back for more.

In this Top Secret Recipes reduced-fat conversion, you'll learn how to get that heat in the chicken, and then how to use a special baking technique that will give the cluck meat a breaded-and-fried consistency without too much oil.

1/3 cup Frank's Original Red Hot Pepper Sauce
2/3 cup water
1 cup all-purpose flour
2 1/2 teaspoons salt
4 teaspoons cayenne pepper
1 teaspoon coarsely ground black pepper
1 teaspoon onion powder
1/2 teaspoon paprika
1/8 teaspoon garlic powder
2 skinless chicken breast fillets
oil cooking spray
8 teaspoons fat-free mayonnaise
4 plain hamburger buns
4 tomato slices
4 lettuce leaves

1. Preheat oven to 475 degrees.
2. Combine the pepper sauce and water in a small bowl.

3. Combine the flour, salt, cayenne pepper, black pepper, onion powder, paprika, and garlic powder in another shallow bowl.
4. Slice each of the breast fillets in half across the middle. Wrap each piece of chicken in plastic wrap and pound it with a mallet to about ¼ inch thick. If necessary, trim each breast fillet to help it fit on the bun.
5. Working with one slice of chicken at a time, coat each piece with the flour mixture, then dredge it in the diluted pepper sauce. Coat the chicken once again in the flour mixture, and set it aside until the rest of the chicken is breaded.
6. Line a large baking sheet with aluminum foil. Spray foil with a generous coat of oil cooking spray. Arrange all of the breaded chicken onto the sprayed foil. Spray a light coat of the oil spray over the entire surface of each slice of chicken.
7. Bake chicken for 8 to 12 minutes or until it begins to brown. Crank oven up to a high broil and broil for 3 to 5 minutes per side or until the surface begins to become crispy. (Be careful not to cook too long, or chicken may dry out.)
8. As chicken bakes, spread about 2 teaspoons of mayonnaise on the face of each of the inverted top buns.
9. Place a tomato slice onto the mayonnaise, and a leaf of lettuce on top of the tomato.
10. When the chicken is done, stack one piece onto each of the bottom buns.
11. Flip the top half of each sandwich onto the bottom half, and serve hot.

- MAKES 4 SANDWICHES.

Nutrition Facts (per serving)
SERVING SIZE—1 SANDWICH   TOTAL SERVINGS—4

	LOW-FAT	ORIGINAL
CALORIES (APPROX.)	380	410
FAT (APPROX.)	8G	15G

• • • •

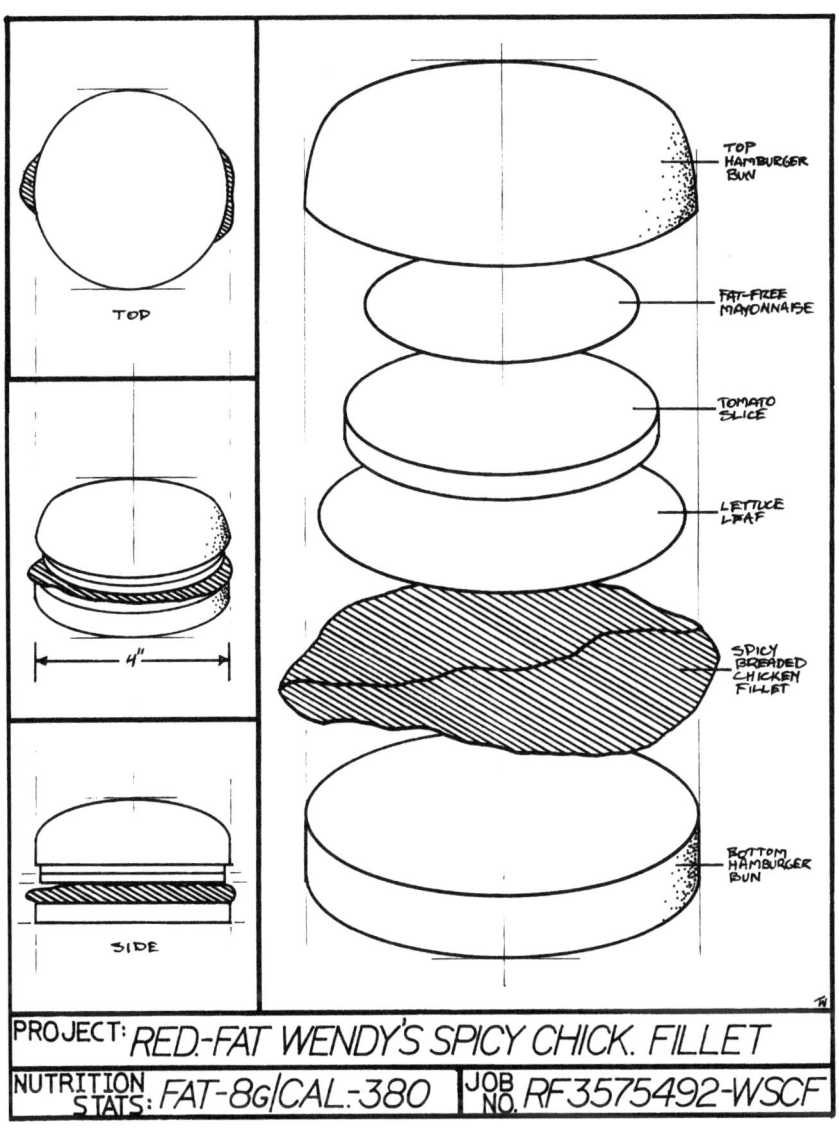

TOP SECRET RECIPES

SODAS, SMOOTHIES, SPIRITS, & SHAKES

INTRODUCTION

Today I've been drinking the world's number one beverage but I can't give you the recipe. Unless you already know how to combine two hydrogen atoms with one oxygen atom in abundance, you'll have to settle for drinking it out of a bottle or straight off the tap.

What I can give you, though, is a bunch of recipes to duplicate the taste of the other drinks we hold dear, including several iced versions for the second most popular beverage in the world: tea. You'll recognize many of these products, because it would be nearly impossible to exist in civilization on this planet without being reminded several times each day that you absolutely must drink these wonderful drinks. And that you will enjoy them. And that when you are thirsty again you will come back for more.

It's true that this book includes clone recipes for some of the most successful products in the world—those drinks you've enjoyed since birth—with long, remarkable histories and huge profits. But a collection such as this would not be complete without also including copycat formulas for the newer, trendier drinks that have garnered more recent worship.

Sure, I've got recipes in here for sodas, milk shakes, smoothies, lemonades, coffee drinks, and punches, but this book isn't just for the teetotalers. If you, uh, "total" more than "tee," I've got some of the coolest cocktail, mixer and liqueur-making recipes ever assembled. Spirits were around a long time before fizzy flavored sodas and grande Frappuccinos, and this book recognizes that delicious cocktail recipes are just as fun to re-create at home as are recipes for famous foodstuffs found in previous *Top Secret Recipes* volumes.

    This book is divided into two major sections, with the first half consisting of clone recipes for famous sodas, milk shakes, and smoothies, plus a section for drinks that don't fit into those three categories. This is where you learn how to re-create your favorite sodas using the old soda fountain technique: adding flavored syrup to cold soda water. This is also where you get the secret to mixing a Dairy Queen Blizzard clone of your own at home so that the ice cream won't get too runny when you stir in all the chunks. If you like coffee, you'll find out what secret ingredients will copy a Starbucks Frappuccino and the instant General Foods International Coffees. You'll find out how to make the perfect lemonade from scratch and how to duplicate the taste of Sunny Delight using more fruit juice than the real thing's got in it.

    The second half of the book is devoted to spirits. This is where you find clone recipes for famous brands such as Kahlúa, Bailey's Irish Cream, and Grand Marnier. You'll find out how to add flavorings and fruit to inexpensive vodka to create a variety of delicious liqueurs. In this section you'll also get dozens and dozens of recipes for the most popular cocktails from America's largest restaurant chains. If you've ever been to Applebee's, Chili's, T.G.I. Friday's, Planet Hollywood, or Outback Steakhouse and have seen the glossy table cards with beautiful photos of delicious and colorful cocktails on them and wished you could make drinks that good at home, this is where you learn how. And right at the end you'll get the secrets to making the delicious mixers that go into those awesome drinks, all from scratch.

    So grab a straw and dive on in. As with all the other *Top Secret Recipes* books, measure carefully and follow the directions precisely. In no time at all you'll soon be downing a duplicate of your favorite drink, from your favorite glass, while sitting in your favorite chair.

✳ ✳ ✳

If you'd like to try some clone recipes for solid food, check out the other books in the *Top Secret Recipes* series or come to the web site at www.TopSecretRecipes.com.

If you have suggestions for other drinks to clone, drop me some e-mail at Todd@topsecretrecipes.com.

I'll be back again to uncover more of your most requested clone cuisine secrets in the next book, *Even More Top Secret Recipes*, coming soon. Until then, cheers to you.

—Todd Wilbur

SODAS

When America figured out how to mix carbon dioxide gas with water in the early 1800s a monumental industry was born. The fizzy fluid, invented to clone carbonated water found in natural springs, was originally thought to be a magical curative for a variety of ailments ranging from indigestion to arthritis. Ambitious pharmacists looking to strike it rich with their own new "patent medicines" added custom mixtures of herbs, flowers, fruits, berries, and bark to the soda water, creating a wide range of flavors with a variety of claimed health benefits. Their background in medicine and chemistry made these pharmacists perfectly suited for such a task, despite the many dubious claims of miracle cures provided by the new formulas. It is these pharmacists who are responsible for launching today's monumental soft drink industry.

Since alcoholic drinks are called "hard drinks," the new beverages became "soft drinks." But they were more than just bubbling thirst quenchers, since soft drinks in this era had some potent medicinal ingredients: Coca-Cola contained cocaine extracted from coca leaves to provide energy; Pepsi-Cola contained pepsin, an enzyme to aid in digestion; and 7UP came packed with lithium, used today to treat depression and mental illness.

Through the end of the 1800s and into the twentieth century, customers stopped in at soda fountains at their local pharmacies for a dose of chat, refreshment, and remedy, and walked out with a great big smile. It's no wonder these stores became the central attraction in town. At the soda fountain, when a soft drink was ordered, sweetened syrup was added to cold soda water, it was stirred up a bit and served ready to drink. In the early days of these soda fountains ice cream sodas were hugely popular, as were root beer, ginger ale, and a whole mess of different cola drinks.

Still, the soda business was limited by the fact that customers needed access to a pharmacy. For soda pioneers to make their products fly high they had to figure out how to go from getting the people to the soda, to getting the soda to the people. At first, glass bottles blown by hand were filled with the drink and capped with corks. But pressure from the carbonation was too much for the early stoppers, and many bottles blew their tops before arriving at their destinations. Inventors racked their brains for years to figure out a design for the perfect stopper until, 1500 patents later, the crown bottle cap was invented in 1892. The glass bottle–blowing machine followed the crown cap a few years after that, and the soda distribution industry popped into high gear.

When Prohibition made it illegal to drink the hard stuff, soda sales skyrocketed. Bars that used to serve real beer had to substitute root beer when liquor-free drinks became the legal alternative to booze. As an added bonus, many of the soda brands were used as underground mixers in illegal drinking parties. Ginger ale was a very fashionable mixer in the 20s, as was 7UP, which was invented during Prohibition. So popular in cocktails was that particular lemon-lime soda that when Prohibition was repealed in 1933, 7UP was heavily marketed as a mixer.

During Prohibition convenience drove the soda industry. Vending machines were created that dispensed sodas into a cup so that workers could get their brand-name refreshment on the job, and six-pack cartons made it easy to carry home several bottles of soda at once. Thirsty consumers were bombarded with a variety of new flavors, and as the country was about to go to war, metal cans were introduced. Metal cans were lighter and more durable than bottles, but at that time the metal was more costly than glass, plus it made the drinks taste funny.

The can problems were fixed after the war, and in 1957 the first lightweight aluminum cans were used to package sodas. It took old customers some time to adjust to the new metal containers, but today more sodas are sold in cans than any other way. The plastic bottles introduced in the 70s are now the second most common package for sodas, with glass bottles practically fading into obscurity.

These days the cocaine is gone from Coke, Pepsi is pepsin-free, and 7UP comes without the attitude-adjusting benefits of lithium. When we drink these drinks today it's usually because we're thirsty. Or we need to get kicked up a notch by the caffeine that's still added to several brands. Whatever the motivation, Joe Average American will knock back over 50 gallons of soda this year, all by himself. With more than 450 different varieties now competing for attention, it's no wonder soft drink ads are everywhere we turn.

Choosing which of the most popular sodas to clone for this book was fairly easy: I picked the most successful brand of the most popular flavors (in other words, Coke instead of Pepsi). I would have preferred to create these recipes using the original product's syrup without dilution, since it's really the syrup that we're cloning. But that wasn't always possible. Most of the time, I had to use the original product right out of the bottle or can, as you find it in any store. Then I worked backward, concentrating the flavors, to develop thick, sweet syrup that could be made from scratch.

When the syrup's done, the soda's done. When you've cooled off your syrup and are ready to have a drink, simply add the proper amount of flavored syrup to cold soda water, just as the jerks did (c'mon, that's what they were called) at the soda fountains of yesteryear. Give the drink a little stir, add some ice, and you've just used an old-fashioned technique to re-create one of today's most popular beverages.

A&W CREAM SODA

TOP SECRET RECIPES VERSION OF

Sure, Roy Allen and Frank Wright are better known for their exquisite root beer concoction sold first from California drive-up stands under the A&W brand name. But these days the company makes a darn good vanilla cream soda as well. And the formula is one that we can easily clone at home just by combining a few simple ingredients. Most of the flavor comes from vanilla, but you'll also need a little lemonade flavor Kool-Aid unsweetened drink mix powder. This mix comes in .23-ounce packets and provides the essential citric acid that gives this soda clone the necessary tang of the real thing. Once you make the syrup, let it cool down in the fridge, then just combine the syrup with cold soda water in a 1 to 4 ratio, add a little ice, and get sipping.

1⅓ cups granulated sugar
⅛ teaspoon Kool-Aid lemonade unsweetened drink mix
1 cup very hot water
1 cup corn syrup

½ teaspoon plus ¼ teaspoon vanilla extract

10 cups cold soda water

1. Dissolve the sugar and Kool-Aid drink mix in the hot water in a small pitcher.
2. Add the corn syrup and vanilla extract and stir well. Cover and chill syrup until cold.
3. When the syrup is cold, pour ¼ cup syrup into 1 cup cold soda water. Stir gently, add ice, and serve.

- MAKES 10 10-OUNCE SERVINGS.

A&W ROOT BEER

TOP SECRET RECIPES VERSION OF

In 1919, when Roy Allen and Frank Wright started selling their new root beer beverage to a thirsty America, national Prohibition was taking its grip on the country. Their timing couldn't have been better. No longer able to legally drink real beer, thirsty patriots had to settle for this sweet, foamy concoction derived from roots, herbs, and berries. Roy and Frank had thirteen years of Prohibition to make their mark and their fortune from this refreshing drink. By 1933, when Prohibition came to a screeching halt, Roy and Frank had 171 stands in various shapes and sizes, each with the familiar A&W logo on them, all across the country. These drive-up stands with their tray boys and tray girls bringing cold drinks out to the cars were an inspiration for many other roadside stands and diners, and the prelude to the popular fast food drive-thrus of today. You can still get a foamy mug of A&W root beer at outlets across the country, or just enjoy some from a 12-ounce can.

But if it's some home cloning you'd like to get into, check out this improved version of A&W Root Beer that was first printed in *More Top Secret Recipes*. The beauty is you won't have to worry about collecting roots, herbs, and berries like the pros do. Instead you just need to get some root beer extract, manufactured by McCormick, that you'll find near the vanilla in your local supermarket. Make up some root beer syrup, let it cool off in the fridge, and you can whip up 10 servings by combining the syrup with cold soda water whenever you're ready to drink. Cool, eh?

1 ⅓ cups granulated sugar
1 cup very hot water
1 cup corn syrup

1 teaspoon McCormick root beer concentrate

10 cups cold soda water

1. Dissolve the sugar in the hot water in a small pitcher.
2. Add the corn syrup and root beer concentrate and stir well. Cover and chill syrup until cold.
3. When the syrup is cold, pour ¼ cup syrup into 1 cup of cold soda water. Stir gently, add ice, and serve.

- MAKES 10 10-OUNCE SERVINGS.

TOP SECRET RECIPES VERSION OF COCA-COLA

When Atlanta pharmacist John Pemberton whipped up his first cocaine-laced drink he was actually cloning Vin Mariani, a coca leaf–infused red wine that had been selling successfully in Europe since 1863. John's version—called "Pemberton's French wine coca"—had cocaine and wine in it too, but John added kola nut extract to give the drink additional kick (as if it needed it) from the stimulant alkaloid caffeine. Shortly after John had perfected his new drink, local Prohibition hit Atlanta in 1886, and the booze had to come out. The wine was replaced with sugar syrup to make it sweet along with some citric acid for tang, and the name of the new drink was changed to "Coca-Cola," representing the beverage's two very stimulating ingredients. As enthusiasm for cocaine-based tonics waned toward the end of the century, Coca-Cola manufacturers were again forced to ditch another key ingredient. By 1903, the cocaine in Coca-Cola had to come out too.

Although it was a major change to the recipe, removing cocaine from Coca-Cola didn't alter the beverage enough to keep it from becoming the world's number one fountain and bottled soft drink over the years. People enjoyed the drink for its refreshing taste. And, the drink did, after all, still contain enough caffeine to provide a sufficient spring to the step. The drink's success spawned many clones from competitors with only slight variations on the formula's top secret taste, but none, including Pepsi, would become as big a phenomenon as Coke. Many recipes were floating around at the time. It is well documented that John sold several copies of the original recipe along with shares in his company to help him through the morphine addiction and poverty that plagued his later years. John died at age 57 in 1888 from stomach cancer before knowing the enormous success of his creation.

Although the drink is 99 percent sugar water, that other 1 percent is the key to the drink's unique taste. The tangy citrus flavors, from lime juice, citrus oils, and citric acid (today the citric acid has been replaced with phosphoric acid), was used by John to overcome the inherent unpleasant bitterness of cocaine and caffeine. Even after removing the coca from the drink, it was still necessary to conceal the ghastly flavor of kola nut caffeine from the taste buds with the sweet, tangy syrup.

To make an accurate clone of Coca-Cola at home I started with the medicinal ingredient, probably just as John did. But rather than harvesting kola nuts, we have the luxury of access to caffeine pills found in any grocery store or pharmacy. One such brand is Vivarin, but it is yellow in color with a thick coating and it tastes much too bitter. NoDoz, however, is white and less bitter, with a thinner coating. Each NoDoz tablet contains 200 milligrams of caffeine, and a 12-ounce serving of Coke has 46 milligrams in it. So if we use 8 NoDoz tablets that have been crushed to powder with a mortar and pestle (or in a bowl using the back of a spoon) we get 44 milligrams of caffeine in a 12-ounce serving, or 36 milligrams in each of the 10-ounce servings we make with this recipe.

Finding and adding the caffeine is the easy part. You'll probably have more trouble obtaining Coke's crucial flavoring ingredient: cassia oil. I was hoping to leave such a hard-to-get ingredient out of this recipe, but I found it impossible. The unique flavor of Coke absolutely requires the inclusion of this Vietnamese cinnamon oil (usually sold for aromatherapy), but only a very small amount. You'll find the cassia oil in a health food store (I used the brand Oshadhi), along with the lemon oil and orange oil. The yield of this recipe had to be cranked up to 44 10-ounce servings since these oils are so strong—just one drop of each is all you'll need. Find them in bottles that allow you to measure exactly one drop if you can. If the oils don't come in such a bottle, buy eyedroppers at a drug store. Before you leave the health food store, don't forget the citric acid.

This recipe, because of the old-fashioned technique of adding the syrup to soda water, creates a clone of Coke as it would taste coming out of a fountain machine. That Coke is usually not as fizzy as the bottled stuff. But if you add some ice to a glass of bottled Coke, and then some to this cloned version, the bubbles will settle down and you'll discover how close the two are.

Because subtle difference in flavor can affect the finished product, be sure to measure your ingredients very carefully. Use the flat top edge of a butter knife to scrape away the excess sugar and citric acid from the top of the measuring cup and teaspoon, and don't estimate on any of the liquid ingredients.

6 cups granulated sugar

2 cups (one 16-ounce bottle) light corn syrup
8 NoDoz tablets, crushed to powder
2 teaspoons citric acid
7 cups boiling water
1 tablespoon lime juice
½ teaspoon vanilla
1 drop lemon oil
1 drop orange oil
1 drop cinnamon (cassia) oil

COLOR
1 tablespoon red food coloring
1½ teaspoons yellow food coloring
½ teaspoon blue food coloring
18 drops green food coloring

44 cups cold soda water

1. Combine sugar, corn syrup, powdered NoDoz, and citric acid in a large pitcher or bowl. Add the boiling water, and stir until the sugar has dissolved and the solution is clear. Strain the syrup through a paper towel–lined strainer to remove the NoDoz sediment.
2. Add the lime juice, vanilla, lemon oil, orange oil, and cassia oil to the syrup and stir.
3. Add the colors to the syrup, then cover it and chill it for several hours until cold.
4. To make the soda, add ¼ cup of cold syrup to 1 cup of cold soda water. Stir gently, drop in some ice, and serve.

- MAKES 44 10-OUNCE SERVINGS.

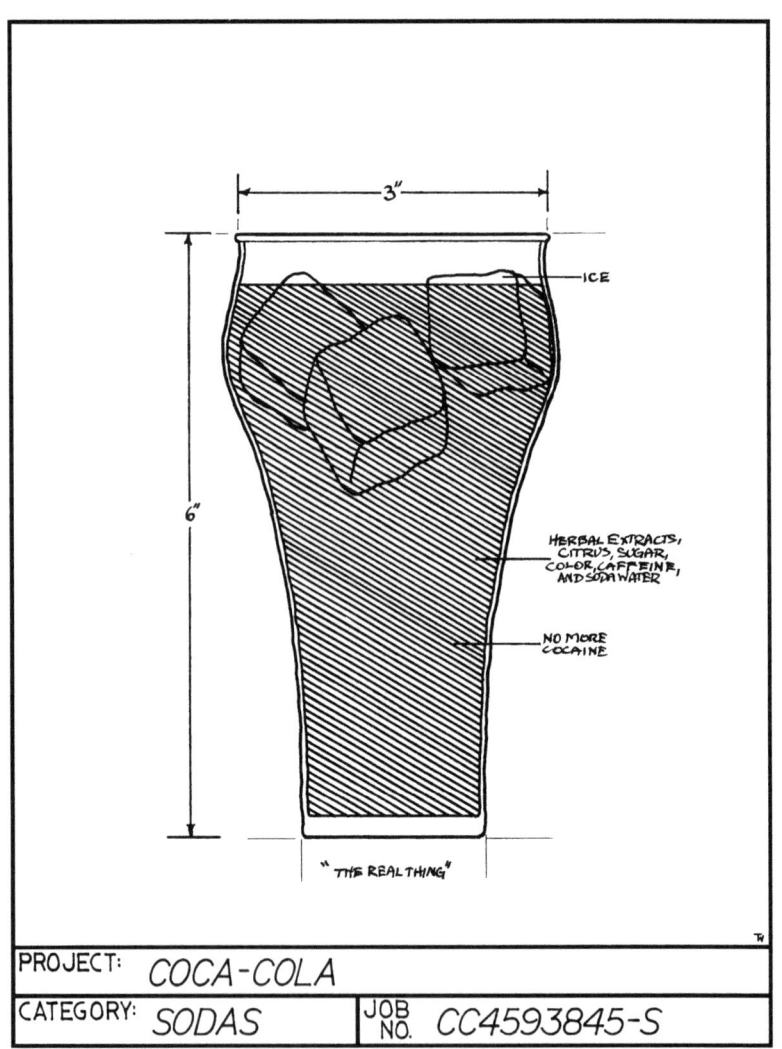

TOP SECRET RECIPES VERSION OF ORANGE SLICE

To make your own version of the syrup for this orange soda that comes to us from the Pepsi-Cola Company, you need to combine a simple syrup recipe with two popular versions of dry orange drink mix: Kool-Aid orange unsweetened drink mix and Tang. But unlike the real thing that "contains no juice," your homemade version includes a bit of real orange juice solids that come powdered into every scoop of Tang mix. After you make the syrup, be sure to let it cool in the refrigerator before you combine it with cold soda water to make a perfect finished product.

1 cup granulated sugar
1 cup corn syrup
1 0.15-ounce package Kool-Aid orange unsweetened drink mix
1 tablespoon Tang orange drink mix
1 ¼ cups boiling water

8 cups cold soda water

1. Combine sugar, corn syrup, and drink mix powders in a medium pitcher or bowl. Add boiling water and stir until sugar has dissolved and syrup is clear. Cover and chill this syrup for several hours until cold.
2. To make the soda, add ⅓ cup of cold syrup to 1 cup of cold soda water (1 to 3 ratio). Stir gently, drop in some ice, and serve.

- MAKES 8 13-OUNCE SERVINGS.

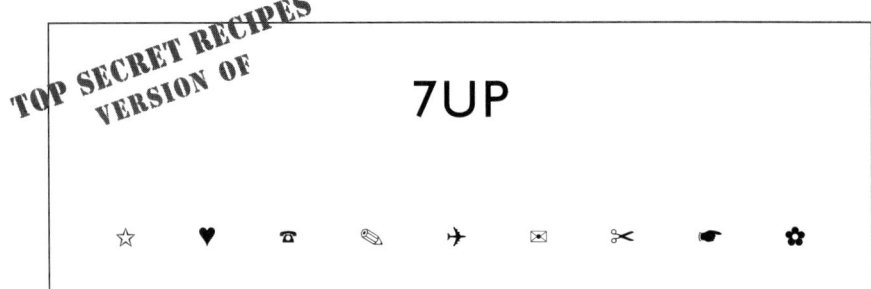

7UP

It was the perfect drink for a Great Depression. In 1929, the United States slipped into a giant economic slump, and a new lemon-lime soda with an attitude-adjusting additive was rolled out. The drink's slogan, "Takes the Ouch Out of the Grouch," referred to lithium, a powerful drug used to treat manic depression and prevent mood swings. Lithium was added to every serving of 7UP until the mid-1940s.

The soda wasn't called 7UP at first. The drink, created by Charles Leiper Grigg, was originally called Bib-Labeled Lithiated Lemon-Lime Soda, but that name, and even the abbreviated version, BLLLLS, was too long.

Today, no one can agree on the origin of the name 7UP. Some theorize that it came from the number of ingredients in the soda, while others say it came from the size of the 7-ounce bottles in which the drink was first sold. There are even theories that the name came from a popular card game at the time called 7UP, or from a cattle brand Charlie Grigg saw one day.

During the sugar rationing of World War II, 7UP was especially popular with bottlers since it used less sugar than other soft drinks. In 1967, the company introduced the famous "uncola" ads, with an image of the drink served in an upside-down bell-shaped cola glass. That campaign continued through the 70s with deep-throated actor Geoffrey Holder explaining the secret of the drink to be the "uncola nut."

The slogan "follow the liter" was later developed to announce 7UP's new packaging in 1-liter bottles. Soon afterward, every major soft drink label was selling their sodas in metric bottles.

In 1986, the Seven Up Company merged with the Dr Pepper Company, creating the world's third-largest soft drink company behind Coca-Cola and Pepsi.

Now you can make a home clone for this refreshing citrus beverage in no time at all. Just add lemon and lime juice to a syrup solution, along with a little Kool-Aid lemonade drink mix for that special tang (thanks to included citric acid), and you're almost there. When the syrup has cooled, you just mix it into some cold soda water in a 1 to 4 ratio. And that's it. You've just made this clone of 7UP yours.

1 cup plus 1 tablespoon granulated sugar
1 cup corn syrup
½ teaspoon Kool-Aid lemonade unsweetened drink mix

1¼ cups very hot water
1 tablespoon bottled lime juice
2 teaspoons bottled lemon juice

11 cups cold soda water

1. Combine sugar, corn syrup, and lemonade drink mix in a medium pitcher or bowl. Add hot water and stir until sugar has dissolved and syrup is clear.
2. Add lime juice and lemon juice and stir. Cover and chill for several hours until cold.
3. To make the soda, add ¼ cup of cold syrup to 1 cup of cold soda water (1 to 4 ratio). Stir gently, drop in some ice, and serve.

- MAKES 11 10-OUNCE SERVINGS.

SONIC DRIVE-IN CHERRY LIMEADE

TOP SECRET RECIPES VERSION OF

Here's the signature drink from the chain that's reviving the drive-in burger joint, just like a scene out of *American Graffiti* or *Happy Days*.

It was in 1953 that Troy Smith obtained the parcel of land in Shawnee, Oklahoma, that was big enough to fit the new steakhouse and root beer stand that was his dream. Troy thought he'd make the steakhouse his primary operation, but as it turned out folks preferred the hot dogs and cold drinks over at the root beer stand. So Troy did the smart thing and ditched the steakhouse to focus all his efforts on the other joint. At first he called the root beer stand "Top Hat," but when Troy found out later that name was already being used, he came up with "Sonic" to signify "service at the speed of sound." Today the chain is the sixth-largest hamburger outlet in the country.

This recipe makes a simple, old-fashioned drink by combining Sprite with cherry juice and some lime wedges. Use cherry juice made by Libby under the brand name Juicy Juice for the best clone.

12 ounces cold Sprite (1 can)
3 lime wedges (⅛ of a lime each)
¼ cup cherry juice (Libby's Juicy Juice is best)

1. Fill a 16-ounce glass ⅔ full with ice.
2. Pour Sprite over the ice.
3. Add the juice of three lime wedges and drop them into the drink.
4. Add the cherry juice and serve with a straw.

- MAKES 1 16-OUNCE DRINK (MEDIUM SIZE).

SONIC DRIVE-IN STRAWBERRY LIMEADE

TOP SECRET RECIPES VERSION OF

Troy Smith isn't the one who came up with the idea to use an intercom system in the parking lot so that customers could pull up to order, and then eat while still in their cars. He was inspired by another hamburger stand he saw while driving through Louisiana, and had the same system designed for his place. Troy's borrowed concept survived the generations thanks to a menu of food with wide appeal. Today Sonic is the only major fast food chain still incorporating the nearly 50-year-old service concept. And just as in the 50s, roller-skating carhops still bring the food right to the car window so diners can stay comfortably seated behind the wheel.

This is a flavor variation of Sonic's signature Cherry Limeade. This version is just as good, even with the minor inconvenience of little chunks of strawberry clogging up the straw.

12 ounces cold Sprite (1 can)
3 lime wedges (⅛ of a lime each)

2 tablespoons frozen sweetened sliced strawberries, thawed

1. Fill a 16-ounce glass ⅔ full with ice.
2. Pour Sprite over the ice.
3. Add the juice of three lime wedges.
4. Add two tablespoons of strawberries with the syrup. Serve with a straw.

- MAKES 1 16-OUNCE DRINK (MEDIUM SIZE).

TOP SECRET RECIPES VERSION OF SONIC DRIVE-IN OCEAN WATER

Any Sonic Drive-In regular knows the four or five unique fountain drink favorites on the menu. There's the Limeade, the Diet Limeade, Strawberry Limeade, and, of course, the Cherry Limeade. But that bright blue stuff called Ocean Water has become a recent favorite for anyone who digs the taste of coconut—it's like a pina colada soda. The server simply squirts a bit of blue coconut-flavored syrup into a cup of cold Sprite. The big secret to duplicating this one at home is re-creating that syrup, so that's the first step. After that's done, you make the drink as they do at the restaurant in less time than it takes to say, "Does my blue tongue clash with what I'm wearing?"

3 tablespoons water
2 tablespoons sugar
1 teaspoon imitation coconut extract
2 drops blue food coloring
2 12-ounce cans cold Sprite
ice

1. Combine the water and the sugar in a small bowl. Microwave for 30 to 45 seconds, and then stir to dissolve all of the sugar. Allow this syrup to cool.
2. Add coconut extract and food coloring to the cooled syrup. Stir well.
3. Combine the syrup with two 12-ounce cans of cold Sprite. Divide and pour over ice. Add straws and serve.

- MAKES 2 12-OUNCE SERVINGS.

TOP SECRET RECIPES VERSION OF SQUIRT

Soda and citrus flavors were combined in 1938 to create a grapefruit-lemon soft drink that would later inspire Coke to make Fresca. Fresca was popular when it was introduced in the 60s since it was artificially sweetened and contained no calories. That was back when diet drinks were just catching on. Nowadays just about every soda comes in a diet version, and Fresca sales have slipped, despite a tweaking of the formula in the early 90s.

Squirt continues to hold on to a loyal cult following, with many who claim the soda is the only true cure for a hangover. To clone it, just add real bottled white grapefruit juice, along with a little Kool-Aid mix for a lemony tang, to the simple syrup recipe. Chill the syrup and soda water until cold and get ready to make a dozen cups' worth of citrus soda at home.

1 1/2 cups granulated sugar
1/8 teaspoon Kool-Aid lemonade unsweetened drink mix
1/4 cup boiling water

1 cup corn syrup
1 1/2 cups white grapefruit juice

12 cups cold soda water

1. Combine sugar and Kool-Aid mix with the boiling water in a medium pitcher or bowl. Stir well. Add corn syrup and stir.
2. Add grapefruit juice and stir until sugar crystals are dissolved. Cover and chill for several hours until cold.
3. To make the soda, stir the syrup first, then add 1/4 cup of cold syrup to 1 cup of cold soda water (1 to 4 ratio). Stir gently, drop in some ice, and serve.

- MAKES 12 10-OUNCE SERVINGS.

TOP SECRET RECIPES VERSION OF T.G.I. FRIDAY'S NOVEMBER SEA BREEZE FLING

Not only does the restaurant still serve some of the tastiest cocktails and mixed drinks, but Friday's also has one of the best darn selections of custom non-alcoholic drinks in the business. The smoothies and shakes at Friday's are all excellent, as are the designer sodas called "Flings." These are hand-mixed soda beverages made in a fashion reminiscent of old-time soda fountains. Juices and sweeteners are mixed with cold soda water and served elegantly over ice—you can't go wrong with one of these. The Fling cloned here uses cranberry juice, apple juice, simple syrup, and sweet & sour mix. If you've got the time, make the sweet & sour from scratch using the recipe at the back of the book.

1½ ounces cranberry juice
1½ ounces apple juice
1½ ounces sweet & sour mix (bottled or use the recipe from page 705)
½ ounce simple syrup (from page 700)
1½ ounces club soda

GARNISH
lime wedge

1. Fill a 14-ounce glass with ice.
2. Pour juices, sweet & sour mix, and simple syrup into a shaker and shake well.
3. Pour drink over the ice, add a lime wedge and the club soda on top, and serve with a straw.

- MAKES 1 DRINK.

TOP SECRET RECIPES VERSION OF T.G.I. FRIDAY'S STRAWBERRY SURPRISE FLING

This version of a Friday's Fling is more tropical than the preceding recipe and doesn't require simple syrup. When you're ready to be flung, get some of the sweetened sliced strawberries out of the freezer and start thawing.

2 tablespoons frozen sweetened sliced strawberries, thawed
1 1/2 ounces pineapple juice
1 1/2 ounces papaya juice
1 1/2 ounces apple juice

1 1/2 ounces club soda

GARNISH
1 fresh strawberry

1. Fill a 14-ounce glass with ice.
2. Pour strawberries, with syrup, and juices into a shaker and shake well.
3. Pour drink over the ice, and add a fresh strawberry to the rim of the glass. Splash the club soda over the top and serve with a straw.

- MAKES 1 DRINK.

SMOOTHIES

Frozen blended fruit drinks weren't called "smoothies" back in the 20s when Orange Julius first made them popular. That name, and the many different ingredients used in the drinks today, didn't catch on until the 1990s.

The trend toward smoothies as we know them these days may have started in health club shake bars where a wide variety of juices and fruits were mixed with ice, protein powders, and vitamins in a blender. Sometimes ice cream, frozen yogurt, or sorbet was added to the mix to give the drink a smooth texture.

These juice bars would eventually break away from the health clubs and become independently run outlets or large chains, such as Jamba Juice. Soon, established ice cream chains such as Baskin-Robbins and Dairy Queen were offering their own versions of smoothies, and today the drink is everywhere.

You can make smoothies very easily at home with the same type of ingredients the pros use, as long as you have a blender. Professional smoothie makers have blenders designed specifically for the job. Industrial-strength models speed up and slow down automatically and stop on cue when the drink is just right. These machines make the job much easier for the cats behind the counter when multiple orders are flying in.

You can use a regular home blender, though, to create perfect smoothies like those you get at a chain. You may have to stop your machine once in a while to stir things up a bit with a long-handled spoon, but when the ice is all crushed and the drink is smooth, you will have re-created the refreshing smoothie experience without waiting in any pesky lines.

APPLEBEE'S BANANABERRY FREEZE

TOP SECRET RECIPES VERSION OF

Ah, if only kitchen cloning were an exact science. While researching this one I saw the same bartender make the drink two different ways on two different days. Only after a firm grilling did I get her to admit to her personal "improvement" to the chain's secret recipe. The official clone includes the ingredients found below. But if you want to add a little pineapple juice—as some independent-thinking bartenders are apt to do—you might discover you have indeed created a tastier version of this refreshing smoothie. On that day the cloning gods shall be looking the other way.

But, for heaven's sake, be sure your banana is soft and ripe. This is a detail the gods won't ignore.

1 10-ounce box frozen sweetened sliced strawberries, thawed
1/3 cup pina colada mix (from recipe on page 704)
2 cups ice

2 ripe bananas

GARNISH
whipped cream
2 fresh strawberries

1. Use a blender to puree the entire contents of the thawed box of frozen strawberries.
2. Add 1/3 cup pina colada mix and 2 cups of ice to the blender.
3. Cut the end off each banana—set these pieces aside to use later as a garnish—then put the bananas into the blender.
4. Blend on high speed until the ice is crushed and the drink is smooth. Pour into two tall stemmed glasses, such as daiquiri glasses.

5. Slice each strawberry halfway up through the middle and add one to the rim of each glass.
6. Cut each banana slice halfway through the middle and add one to the rim of each glass next to the strawberry. Top with whipped cream and serve with a straw.

- MAKES 2 DRINKS.

TOP SECRET RECIPES VERSION OF BASKINS-ROBBINS PEACH SMOOTHIE

Dairy Queen's got twice as many stores, but Baskin-Robbins is still the country's second-largest ice cream chain with around 2,500 outlets spread across the nation. And, naturally, when the chain known for its 31 flavors of ice cream noticed the smoothie craze building in 1997, it hopped right on board with its own selection made from sherbet or vanilla fat-free frozen yogurt. In the stores, servers use a pineapple juice concentrate for this smoothie, but we can still get a great clone by using the more popular canned pineapple juice found in any supermarket. As for the peaches, you may want to let them thaw a bit and then chop them up so you can get a more accurate measure.

1 cup pineapple juice
¾ cup frozen peaches, sliced

1 scoop fat-free vanilla frozen yogurt
3 or 4 ice cubes

Combine all ingredients in a blender and blend on high speed until all the ice is crushed and the drink is smooth.

- MAKES 1 16-OUNCE DRINK.

TOP SECRET RECIPES VERSION OF BASKIN-ROBBINS STRAWBERRY SMOOTHIE

When Irv Robbins was discharged from the army in 1945, he hooked up with his brother-in-law Burt Baskin and the two opened an ice cream parlor in Glendale, California. A simple coin flip determined whose name would go first on the sign. By 1948 six Baskin-Robbins stores had opened their doors and the concept of franchising in the ice cream industry was born.

As in the previous recipe, you may want to let the fruit thaw out a bit here so that you can chop up the strawberries and get a more accurate measure. The word on the street is that some of those frozen whole strawberries can be quite big. Chopping them up first also helps you get a smoother blend going.

1 cup Kern's strawberry nectar
¾ cup frozen whole strawberries, chopped
1 scoop fat-free vanilla frozen yogurt
3 or 4 ice cubes

Combine all ingredients in a blender and blend on high speed until all the ice is crushed and the drink is smooth.

- MAKES 1 16-OUNCE DRINK.

TOP SECRET RECIPES VERSION OF BASKIN-ROBBINS STRAWBERRY BANANA SMOOTHIE

It was in 1953 that the now-famous "31 Flavors" sign was introduced, burdening customers with the dilemma of having to decide which of so many great ice cream flavors they would choose. The number 31 was picked to suggest that a new flavor could be selected every day of the month. The company has come up with around one thousand flavors so far. And as with their most famous flavor, Rocky Road, many other Baskin-Robbins flavor creations would be often imitated—among them Pralines and Cream and Jamoca Almond Fudge.

This recipe for a smoothie is very similar to the previous clone, the only difference being a reduction in strawberries and the addition of half of a ripe banana. You may want to chop up those frozen strawberries (especially the big 'uns) to make measuring easier and more accurate.

1 cup Kern's strawberry nectar
½ cup frozen whole strawberries, chopped
1 scoop fat-free vanilla frozen yogurt
½ ripe banana
3 or 4 ice cubes

Combine all ingredients in a blender and blend on high speed until all the ice is crushed and the drink is smooth.

- MAKES 1 16-OUNCE DRINK.

TOP SECRET RECIPES VERSION OF BASKIN-ROBBINS WILD BERRY BANANA SMOOTHIE

Baskin-Robbins has become known for creating flavors representing the events of the day. When the Brooklyn Dodgers moved to Los Angeles, the chain introduced "Baseball Nut." When James Bond films were popular in the 60s, the chain rolled out "0031 Secret Bonded Flavor." When the TV show *Laugh-In* became a big hit, the company created "Here Comes the Fudge." And when Americans landed on the moon, Baskin-Robbins celebrated with "Lunar Cheesecake."

This smoothie clone is the only one of the four represented here to use some raspberry sherbet along with the vanilla frozen yogurt. It's the most complex of Baskin-Robbins' smoothie selections, but worth every bit of extra effort.

1 cup pineapple juice
½ cup frozen blueberries
½ scoop fat-free vanilla frozen yogurt
½ scoop raspberry sherbet
½ ripe banana
3 or 4 ice cubes

Combine all ingredients in a blender and blend on high speed until all the ice is crushed and the drink is smooth.

- MAKES 1 16-OUNCE DRINK.

JAMBA JUICE BANANA BERRY

TOP SECRET RECIPES VERSION OF

Jamba Juice has become America's favorite smoothie chain, with tasty fruit-filled blends served up in giant 24-ounce cups at over 325 stores. Appreciate the ease with which you are able to suck down your next Jamba Juice smoothie, since the wide straws at the chain have been through rigorous "suckability factor" testing to ensure that the good stuff gets all the way through to your gullet.

¾ cup apple juice
¾ cup Kern's strawberry nectar
⅔ cup frozen blueberries
1 sliced banana
1 scoop raspberry sherbet
1 scoop fat-free vanilla frozen yogurt
1 cup ice

Combine all ingredients in a blender and blend on high speed until all the ice is crushed and the drink is smooth.

- Makes 1 24-ounce drink.

TOP SECRET RECIPES VERSION OF JAMBA JUICE CITRUS SQUEEZE

This smoothie is a very popular choice among the more than 16 varieties of smoothies made fresh at this smoothie chain. If your blender stalls out on you from the thickness of the drink, stop it and stir with a long spoon. That should get things going again. For the perfect clone, you want to be sure all the ice is crushed so that the drink is smooth-a-licious.

1 cup fresh orange juice
½ cup pineapple juice
⅔ cup frozen whole strawberries
1 sliced banana

2 scoops orange sherbet
1 cup ice

Combine all ingredients in a blender and blend on high speed until all the ice is crushed and the drink is smooth.

- Makes 1 24-ounce drink.

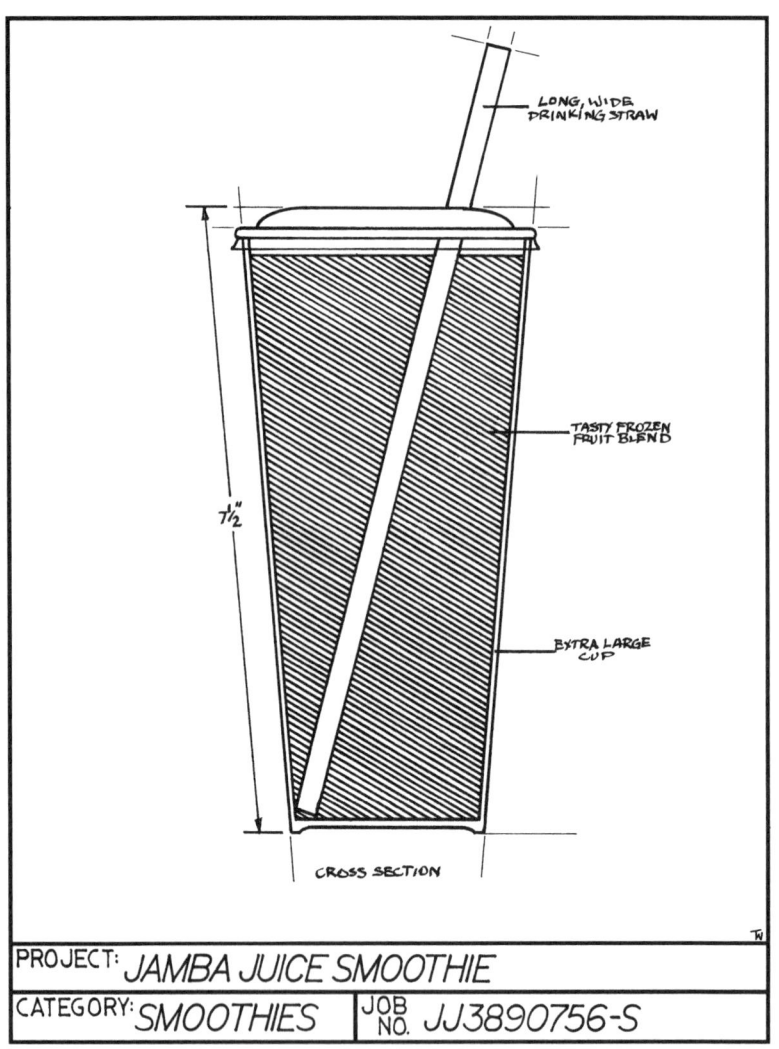

TOP SECRET RECIPES VERSION OF JAMBA JUICE CRANBERRY CRAZE

The menu description says that this drink includes plain nonfat yogurt (not the frozen kind), but I noticed that the server at the store I visited didn't put it in. When I asked her if she forgot the ingredient, she told me they don't include the yogurt anymore, even if the board says otherwise. Okay, right. So, while the menu might insist that this smoothie includes plain yogurt, today we make our clone without it.

1 1/2 cups cranberry juice
1/2 cup frozen whole strawberries
1/4 cup frozen blueberries
2 scoops raspberry sherbet
1 cup ice

Combine all ingredients in a blender and blend on high speed until all the ice is crushed and the drink is smooth.

- MAKES 1 24-OUNCE DRINK.

JAMBA JUICE ORANGE-A-PEEL

Pick your juice wisely. For this smoothie Jamba Juice squeezes whole oranges with a handy orange squeezing machine in each store. So if it's the addicting taste of the real thing you're shooting for, be sure to get your orange juice freshly squeezed or squish some out yourself.

1 1/2 cups fresh orange juice
2/3 cup frozen whole strawberries
1 sliced banana
2 scoops fat-free vanilla frozen yogurt
1 cup ice

Combine all ingredients in a blender and blend on high speed until all the ice is crushed and the drink is smooth.

- MAKES 1 24-OUNCE DRINK.

TOP SECRET RECIPES VERSION OF JAMBA JUICE PEACH PLEASURE

Jamba Juice got its start as "Juice Club" in San Luis Obispo, California. Early success with healthy food and juice blends led to quick growth with more stores and eventually a name change in 1995. The company claims "Jamba" means "to celebrate," just as your tastebuds do when they get a load of a smoothie like the one this recipe clones. It uses an entire can of Kern's peach nectar plus frozen peaches, banana, and some orange sherbet. Tastebuds, party on.

12 ounces Kern's peach nectar (1 can)
1 cup frozen peaches
½ ripe banana
2 scoops orange sherbet
1 cup ice

Combine all ingredients in a blender and blend on high speed until all the ice is crushed and the drink is smooth.

- MAKES 1 24-OUNCE DRINK.

JAMBA JUICE STRAWBERRIES WILD

TOP SECRET RECIPES VERSION OF

One of the most popular smoothie combinations around is strawberry-banana. This clone imitates Jamba's version, which adds apple juice and vanilla frozen yogurt to the mix. Look for the strawberry nectar in the juice aisle and warm up the blender.

¾ cup apple juice
¾ cup Kern's strawberry nectar
⅔ cup frozen whole strawberries
1 sliced banana
2 scoops fat-free vanilla frozen yogurt
1 cup ice

Combine all ingredients in a blender and blend on high speed until all the ice is crushed and the drink is smooth.

- MAKES 1 24-OUNCE DRINK.

TOP SECRET RECIPES VERSION OF ORANGE JULIUS, PINEAPPLE JULIUS, & STRAWBERRY JULIUS

Coffeehouses have replaced many of the old Orange Julius stands, but there's still a nostalgic group of us who long for the frothy juice drinks invented decades ago by Julius Freed. Today Orange Julius has tailored its business to meet the changing demands of customers by including several varieties of fruit drinks and updated smoothies on its menu. But it's the foamy fruit juice creation developed in the late twenties that made the company famous, and that's what I've cloned here in improved versions of the recipes found in *Top Secret Recipes* and *More Top Secret Recipes*. The flavor and consistency are better now, plus we use the blender to dissolve the sugar before adding the ice. Use pasteurized egg whites found packaged in your local supermarket or just use egg substitute, which is also made from pasteurized egg whites.

ORANGE JULIUS

1 1/4 cups orange juice
1 cup water
3 tablespoons egg white or egg substitute
1 teaspoon vanilla extract
1/4 cup granulated sugar
1 1/2 cups ice

Combine all of the ingredients except ice in a blender and blend on high speed for 15 to 20 seconds or until the sugar is dissolved. Add the ice and blend for another 10 to 15 seconds or so, until ice is mostly crushed yet still a bit coarse.

- MAKES 2 16-OUNCE DRINKS.

PINEAPPLE JULIUS

1 8-ounce can crushed pineapple in juice
1 cup water
3 tablespoons egg white or egg substitute
1 teaspoon vanilla extract
¼ cup granulated sugar
1½ cups ice

Combine all of the ingredients except ice in a blender and blend on high speed for 15 to 20 seconds or until the sugar is dissolved. Add the ice and blend for another 10 to 15 seconds or so, until ice is mostly crushed yet still a bit coarse.

- MAKES 2 16-OUNCE DRINKS.

STRAWBERRY JULIUS

1 cup frozen sliced strawberries, thawed (1 10-ounce box)
1 cup water
3 tablespoons egg white or egg substitute
1 teaspoon vanilla extract
¼ cup granulated sugar
1½ cups ice

Combine all of the ingredients except ice in a blender and blend on high speed for 15 to 20 seconds or until the sugar is dissolved. Add the ice and blend for another 10 to 15 seconds or so, until ice is mostly crushed yet still a bit coarse.

- MAKES 2 16-OUNCE DRINKS.

TOP SECRET RECIPES VERSION OF RED ROBIN CHILLIN' MANGO SMOOTHIE

Masterful mixologists make this drink as a special limited-time-only summer refresher at the popular eatery. The chain uses a special pureed mango fruit mix made by Torani, the same company that makes the flavoring syrups used in coffeehouses. But since this special ingredient can be hard to come by, we'll substitute with canned mango chunks that you'll find in jars in the produce section.

¾ cup canned mango, with juice
¾ ounce grenadine
¼ cup orange juice
1 cup ice

GARNISH
orange wedge
maraschino cherry

1. Combine all ingredients in a blender on high speed and mix until smooth.
2. Pour into a 12-ounce glass, then add an orange wedge and maraschino cherry speared on a toothpick. Serve with a straw.

- MAKES 1 DRINK.

RED ROBIN GROOVY SMOOTHIE

TOP SECRET RECIPES VERSION OF

The strawberries used for this drink come in 10-ounce boxes in the freezer section of your local supermarket. These berries work great because when thawed they wind up swimming in a juicy sweet syrup that's perfect for this clone recipe. The restaurant adds a special blend of apple, raspberry, and blackberry juices called "Groovy Mix" to the drink, but we can still create an excellent carbon copy using a blend of apple and berry juices made by Langer's. If you can't find that brand, use any berry juice blend you can get your hands on and you'll still have an extremely groovy drink.

⅓ cup frozen sweetened sliced strawberries, thawed
½ ripe banana
⅓ cup Langer's berry juice (a blend of berry and apple juices)
¼ cup Kern's peach nectar
½ cup ice
½ cup vanilla ice cream

GARNISH
orange wedge
maraschino cherry

1. Combine all ingredients in a blender and blend on high speed until smooth. Pour into a 16-ounce glass.
2. Add an orange wedge and a maraschino cherry speared on a toothpick. Serve with a straw.

- MAKES 1 DRINK.

STARBUCKS TAZOBERRY TEA

TOP SECRET RECIPES VERSION OF

Check out the menu board at any Starbucks and you'll find this frozen drink described as a blend of raspberry and other fruit juices plus Starbucks' own Tazo brand tea. We've discovered that those other fruit juices include white grape juice, aroniaberry, cranberry, and blackberry. Since aroniaberry juice is next to impossible to track down in a local supermarket, we'll have to make a taste-alike drink with a combination of just the other, more important flavors. Grab the raspberry syrup and a jar of seedless blackberry jam made by Knott's Berry Farm, and brew up a little tea. Starbucks uses Tazo black tea for the drink, but you can use the more common Lipton tea bags. You will only use ⅓ cup of the tea for this 1-serving recipe, so you'll have plenty left over for additional servings, or for a quick iced tea fix.

4 cups water
1 tea bag
¼ cup Ocean Spray cranberry/raspberry juice
2 tablespoons concentrated white grape juice, thawed
2 tablespoons Knott's Berry Farm raspberry syrup
1 tablespoon Knott's Berry Farm seedless blackberry jam
1 teaspoon lemon juice
2 cups ice

1. First brew the tea by bringing 4 cups of water to a rapid boil. Turn off the heat, drop in the tea bag, and let the tea steep for an hour or so. Remove the tea bag and put the tea into the refrigerator to chill.
2. When the tea is cold, make your drink by pouring juices, raspberry syrup, blackberry jam, and ⅓ cup of tea into a blender.

3. Add 2 cups of ice and blend on high speed for 20 to 30 seconds or until the drink is smooth and all ice has been crushed.
- MAKES 1 16-OUNCE SERVING.

TAZOBERRY & CREAM

Some folks like their Tazoberry a little creamier. It's an easy variation that includes adding just 2 tablespoons of cream to the blender with the other ingredients in the recipe above. Blend as described in Step 3, and top the drink off with whipped cream if you've got it.

T.G.I. FRIDAY'S TROPICAL OASIS SMOOTHIE

I remember when the menu at T.G.I. Friday's used to include over half a dozen smoothies, but in many Friday's restaurants today the list has been trimmed to just the top few sellers. This is a clone for one of those three favorites. The other two—Gold Medalist and Tropical Runner—are cloned in *Top Secret Restaurant Recipes*.

¼ cup pineapple juice
¼ cup papaya juice
½ cup canned peaches
1 scoop orange sherbet
½ cup ice

GARNISH
orange slice
maraschino cherry

1. Combine all ingredients in a blender and mix on high speed until smooth.
2. Pour into a 14-ounce glass, add an orange slice and maraschino cherry on a toothpick. Serve with a straw.

- MAKES 1 DRINK.

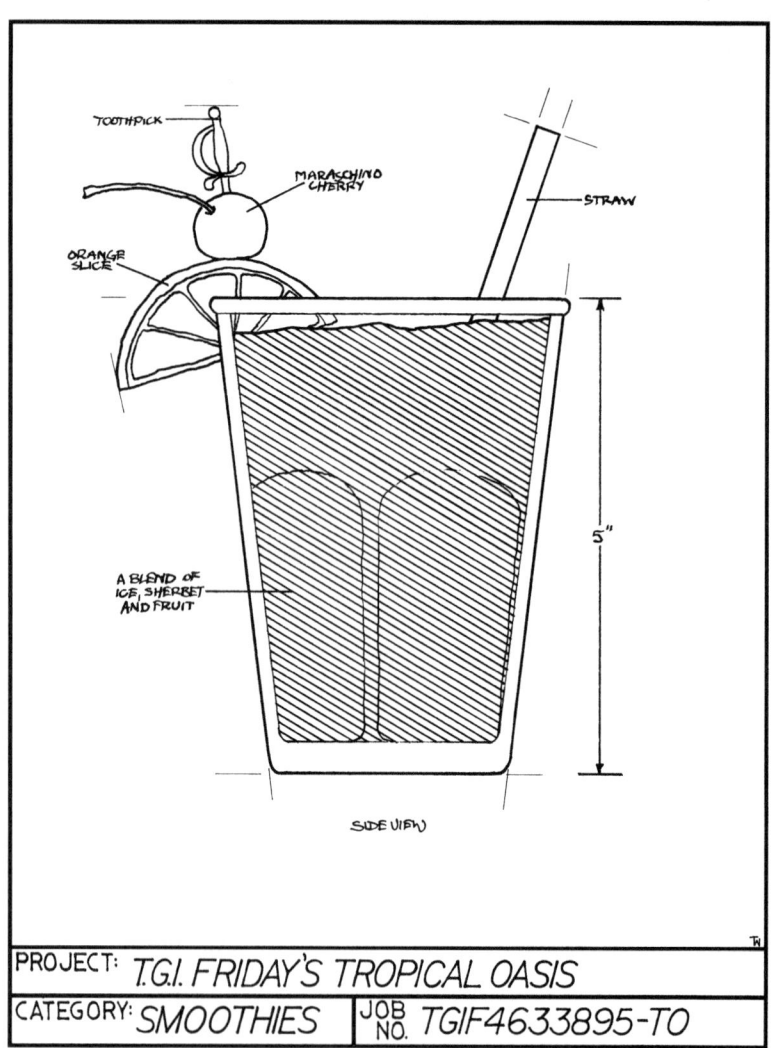

SHAKES

To make a milk shake you must use ice cream. I don't care what they say in Rhode Island and parts of Massachusetts where a milk shake is just milk shaken up with flavored syrup. To those folks, when you add ice cream it's called a *cabinet*. And I don't care what they say in other parts of New England where milk shakes are called *velvets* or *frappes*. A milk shake, according to the ultimate food reference guide, *Food Lover's Companion*, "consists of a blended combination of milk, ice cream, and flavored syrup, fruit or other flavorings."

Milk shakes became very popular in the 40s and 50s when machines were developed to dispense a perfectly frozen creamy product. Busy soda fountains and drive-in restaurants welcomed the extra convenience and consistency offered by these handy machines. Ray Kroc, the man who made McDonald's a household name, was once the exclusive distributor of a milk shake machine called the Multimixer. While on his route he heard about a thriving hamburger stand in San Bernardino, California, that was using a row of eight Multimixers at a time to serve lines of people. His initial pitch to the McDonald brothers for franchise rights was motivated by his dream of selling each new store a bunch of these milk shake machines.

In the last decade or so the most popular milk shakes are more than just thin, lightly colored desserts served with a straw. With the success of Dairy Queen's Blizzard, milk shakes have become much thicker and chunkier. Bits of fruit, candy, cookies, and cereal are added to the mix, making for a treat that can no longer be sucked through a straw without collapsing a lung.

The beauty of all these excellent desserts-in-a-cup is that they can be re-created at home without having to go out and get a Multimixer. For most of them, just get out the blender. For the thicker, chunkier shakes (such as the Blizzard and McFlurry clones), you won't even need a blender. Instead you'll use a custom technique developed for this book that incorporates a frozen glass or ceramic bowl. When the ice cream is mixed with milk and other ingredients in the frozen bowl, the ice cream won't melt, creating a thick and creamy finished product that will hold up a spoon.

TOP SECRET RECIPES VERSION OF ARBY'S JAMOCHA SHAKE

Okay, wash out the blender; this one's been begging to be cloned for years now. Arby's famous Jamocha Shake was one of the first frozen coffee drinks to gain popularity, even before Starbucks pummeled us with Frappuccinos. This thick drink is actually more milk shake than coffee drink, but if you like the original, you'll love this easy-to-make clone that serves two.

1 cup cold coffee
1 cup low-fat milk
3 tablespoons granulated sugar

3 cups vanilla ice cream
3 tablespoons chocolate syrup

1. Combine the coffee, milk, and sugar in a blender and mix on medium speed for 15 seconds to dissolve the sugar.
2. Add the ice cream and chocolate syrup, then blend on high speed until smooth and creamy. Stop blender and stir mixture with a spoon if necessary to help blend ingredients.
3. Pour drink into two 16-ounce glasses and serve.

- MAKES 2 LARGE DRINKS.

BASKIN-ROBBINS B.R. BLAST

TOP SECRET RECIPES VERSION OF

Burt Baskin and Irv Robbins' idea to franchise their ice cream stores for rapid growth was so inspired that the company's former milk shake machine salesman, Ray Kroc, adopted the technique to successfully expand his new chain of McDonald's hamburger outlets.

Ice cream is this chain's staple. So this coffee drink, unlike the Frappuccino made famous by Starbucks, requires adding ice cream for a creamy texture and rich taste. If you've got a blender you can clone either of the two varieties of this refreshing coffee beverage. For chocoholics bent on everything mocha, just add some chocolate syrup to the mix.

CAPPUCCINO

1 cup cold espresso or double-strength coffee (see Tidbits)
1 cup milk
1/3 cup granulated sugar
1 heaping cup vanilla ice cream

2 cups crushed ice or ice cubes

GARNISH
whipped cream
cinnamon

1. Combine the espresso, milk, and sugar in a blender and mix on medium speed for 15 seconds to dissolve sugar.
2. Add ice cream and ice, then blend on high speed until smooth and creamy.
3. Pour drink into two 16-ounce glasses. If desired, add whipped cream to the top of each drink followed by a sprinkle of cinnamon.

- MAKES 2 LARGE DRINKS.

MOCHA

For this version, add 2 tablespoons of chocolate syrup to the recipe above and prepare as described.

TIDBITS

Make double-strength coffee in your coffee maker by adding half the water suggested by the manufacturer. Allow coffee to chill in the refrigerator before using it in this recipe.

CINNABON ICESCAPE

In a blender, Cinnabon adds concentrated flavoring, some ice and a curious secret ingredient referred to only as a "dairy product." When blended smooth, out come these thick, refreshing drinks that look and taste like they were made with ice cream. For this clone we just need a little half-and-half to give our version the exact same creamy consistency as the original with that custom "dairy" ingredient. Strawberry is the most popular of the flavors, but the other two are tasty as well. The Mochalatta version uses the *TSR* clone of the Mochalatta Chill (following this recipe on page 530) and produces a thicker blended version of the drink, similar to Starbucks' popular frozen Frappuccino.

STRAWBERRY

1 cup water
1/4 cup granulated sugar
3 cups crushed ice
1/2 cup frozen whole strawberries (4 large strawberries)
1/2 cup half-and-half
1/4 cup lemon juice
1/4 cup Hershey's strawberry syrup

1. Combine the water and sugar in a cup and stir until the sugar is dissolved.
2. Combine this sugar syrup with remaining ingredients in a blender. Blend on high speed until the drink is smooth. Serve in two 16-ounce glasses.

- MAKES 2 LARGE DRINKS.

ORANGE

3 cups crushed ice
1 cup water
⅔ cup orange juice
½ cup half-and-half
3 tablespoons Tang orange drink mix

Mix all ingredients in a blender set on high speed until smooth and creamy. Serve in two 16-ounce glasses.

- MAKES 2 LARGE DRINKS.

MOCHALATTA

3 cups crushed ice
1½ cups TSR version of Mochalatta Chill (found on page 530)
½ cup half-and-half
2 tablespoons chocolate syrup

Mix all ingredients in a blender set on high speed until smooth and creamy. Serve in two 16-ounce glasses.

- MAKES 2 LARGE DRINKS.

CINNABON MOCHALATTA CHILL

If you want your refreshing caffeine buzz kicked up with a nice chocolate rush, try this clone for Cinnabon's Mochalatta Chill. Brew some strong coffee and let it cool off, then get out the half-and-half and chocolate syrup. The real thing from Cinnabon is made with Ghirardelli chocolate syrup, but Hershey's syrup, which can be found everywhere, works great for this delicious duplicate.

1 cup double-strength coffee, cold (see Tidbits)
1 cup half-and-half
½ cup Hershey's chocolate syrup

GARNISH
whipped cream

Combine all ingredients in a small pitcher. Stir well or cover and shake. Pour over ice in two 16-ounce glasses, and top with whipped cream.

- MAKES 2 LARGE DRINKS.

TIDBITS

Make double-strength coffee in your coffee maker by adding half the water suggested by the manufacturer. Allow coffee to chill in the refrigerator before using it in this recipe.

TOP SECRET RECIPES VERSION OF DAIRY QUEEN BLIZZARD

It's Dairy Queen's most successful product ever. Over 175 million Blizzards were sold in the year following the product's debut in 1985. Such a sales phenomenon was the new creation that other fast food chains invented their own versions of the soft-serve ice cream treats with mixed in chunks of cookies and candies and fruit. McDonald's McFlurry is one popular example. Today there are over a dozen varieties of the frozen treat to choose from at Dairy Queen, and I've got all of the most creative and tasty versions cloned right here. Even though Oreo Cookie, Reese's Peanut Butter Cup, Butterfinger, and M&M's are four of the top five most-requested varieties at Dairy Queen, I've left those versions out of this section, and included them instead in the McFlurry clones on pages 539–541.

The biggest challenge we face when making our Blizzard replicas at home is keeping the ice cream from going all soft and runny on us when the other ingredients are stirred in. To solve that problem, we'll use a special technique inspired by marble slab ice cream stores. These outfits mix your choice of chunky ingredients with your choice of ice cream on a slab of frozen stone. This method keeps the ice cream cold and firm while mixing, until it's served to a drooling you.

To incorporate this technique at home you need to put a glass or ceramic bowl in the freezer for at least 30 minutes (while you're at it you may also want to freeze the glass you're going to serve the thing in). An hour or more is even better. Then, we simply mix our ingredients in the icy bowl, while the ice cream stays frosty cold. Just be sure to use plain vanilla ice cream (not French vanilla) for these clones, if you have a choice.

BABY RUTH

1 Baby Ruth candy bar
2½ cups vanilla ice cream
¼ cup milk
3 tablespoons caramel topping

1. Before you start to make this clone, freeze a medium glass or ceramic bowl in the freezer for at least 30 minutes.
2. When the bowl is frozen, mince the Baby Ruth into small bits with a big knife.
3. Measure the ice cream into the bowl, and add the milk. Stir the ice cream and milk together until smooth and creamy. Add the candy bar pieces and caramel and stir to combine. Pour into a 20-ounce glass and serve with a long spoon.

- MAKES 1 20-OUNCE SERVING.

BANANA PUDDING

Amaze everybody with this one that tastes just like homemade banana pudding with Nilla Wafers in it.

1 ripe banana
8 Nilla Wafers
2½ cups vanilla ice cream
¼ cup milk

1. Before you start to make this clone, freeze a medium glass or ceramic bowl in the freezer for at least 30 minutes.
2. Mash the banana in a separate small bowl.
3. Crumble the Nilla Wafers into small pieces.
4. Measure the ice cream and milk into the frozen bowl. Stir with a spoon until smooth and creamy.
5. Add the banana and Nilla Wafers to the ice cream and stir to combine.
6. Pour into a 20-ounce glass and serve with a long spoon.

- MAKES 1 20-OUNCE SERVING.

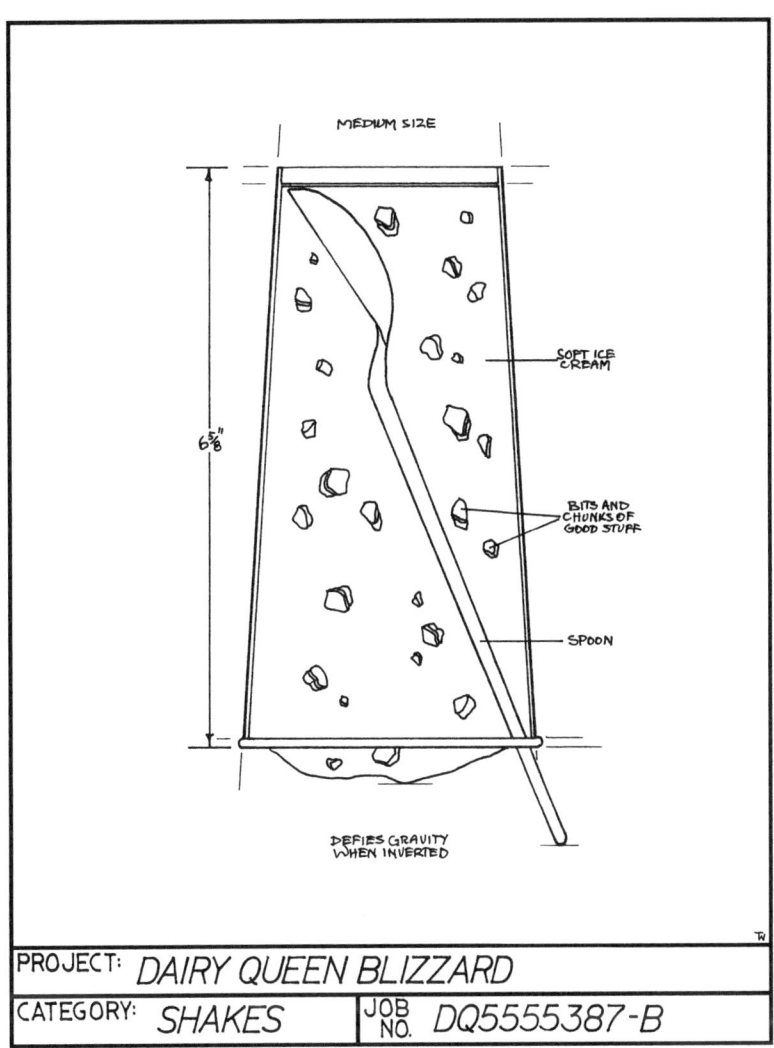

BANANA SPLIT

Tastes like a banana split with all the toppings. Yum city.

1 ripe banana	*3 tablespoons strawberry topping*
2½ cups vanilla ice cream	*3 tablespoons pineapple topping*
¼ cup milk	*2 tablespoons chocolate syrup*

1. Before you start to make this clone, freeze a medium glass or ceramic bowl in the freezer for at least 30 minutes.
2. Mash the banana in a separate small bowl.
3. Measure the ice cream and milk into the frozen bowl. Stir with a spoon until smooth and creamy.
4. Add the banana, strawberry topping, pineapple topping, and chocolate syrup and stir to combine.
5. Pour into a 20-ounce glass and serve with a long spoon.

- MAKES 1 20-OUNCE SERVING.

BERRY BANANA

With strawberry ice cream topping, banana, and crumbled Vienna Fingers you can't go wrong.

1 ripe banana	*¼ cup milk*
2 Vienna Fingers cookies	*¼ cup strawberry topping*
2½ cups vanilla ice cream	

1. Before you start to make this clone, freeze a medium glass or ceramic bowl in the freezer for at least 30 minutes.
2. Mash the banana in a separate small bowl.
3. Crumble the Vienna Fingers into small pieces.
4. Measure the ice cream and milk into the frozen bowl. Stir with a spoon until smooth and creamy.
5. Add the banana, Vienna Fingers, and strawberries to the ice cream and stir to combine.
6. Pour into a 20-ounce glass and serve with a long spoon.

- MAKES 1 20-OUNCE SERVING.

CHOCOLATE CHIP

Use Magic Shell topping here, which will harden into little bits while mixing to create chocolate chips.

2½ cups vanilla ice cream
¼ cup milk

3 tablespoons chocolate Magic Shell topping

1. Before you start to make this clone, freeze a medium glass or ceramic bowl in the freezer for at least 30 minutes.
2. Measure the ice cream and milk into the frozen bowl. Stir with a spoon until smooth and creamy.
3. Add the chocolate Magic Shell and stir gently to combine.
4. Pour into a 20-ounce glass and serve with a long spoon.

- MAKES 1 20-OUNCE SERVING.

CHOCOLATE CHIP COOKIE DOUGH

The dough comes from a tube of Pillsbury cookie dough. It's simple and sinfully good.

¼ cup Pillsbury cookie dough
2½ cups vanilla ice cream

¼ cup milk
¼ cup fudge topping

1. Before you start to make this clone, freeze a medium glass or ceramic bowl in the freezer for at least 30 minutes.
2. While the bowl is freezing, separate the cookie dough into pea-sized pieces and keep the dough pieces in the refrigerator.
3. Measure the ice cream and milk into the frozen bowl. Stir with a spoon until smooth and creamy.
4. Add the cookie dough and fudge topping and stir to combine.
5. Pour into a 20-ounce glass and serve with a long spoon.

- MAKES 1 20-OUNCE SERVING.

HAWAIIAN

If you like riding a wave of tropical flavors, you'll love this blend of pineapple ice cream topping and shredded coconut. Aloha, baby.

1 ripe banana
2½ cups vanilla ice cream
¼ cup milk

3 tablespoons pineapple topping
3 tablespoons shredded coconut

1. Before you start to make this clone, freeze a medium glass or ceramic bowl in the freezer for at least 30 minutes.
2. Mash the banana in a separate small bowl.
3. Measure the ice cream and milk into the frozen bowl. Stir with a spoon until smooth and creamy.
4. Add the mashed banana, pineapple topping, and coconut and stir to combine.
5. Pour into a 20-ounce glass and serve with a long spoon.

- MAKES 1 20-OUNCE SERVING.

WHOPP'N'WILD

You can't go wrong with a blend of Whoppers and ice cream. The flavor of malted milk ball candy is accentuated with the addition of extra malted milk powder and chocolate sauce.

16 Whoppers malted milk balls
2½ cups vanilla ice cream
¼ cup milk

2 tablespoons malted milk powder
3 tablespoons chocolate sauce

1. Before you start to make this clone, freeze a medium glass or ceramic bowl in the freezer for at least 30 minutes. While you're at it, put the Whoppers in a small plastic bag and put them in the freezer too.
2. When the bowl is frozen, remove the Whoppers from the freezer and, while they are still in the bag, smash them into pieces with your fist or the handle of a knife.
3. Measure the ice cream and milk into the frozen bowl. Stir with a spoon until smooth and creamy.

4. Add the Whoppers, malted milk powder, and chocolate sauce to the ice cream and stir to combine.
5. Pour into a 20-ounce glass and serve with a long spoon.

- MAKES 1 20-OUNCE SERVING.

YUKON CRUNCHER

Just like eating s'mores, except you use a spoon and this version is cold.

2½ cups vanilla ice cream
¼ cup milk
3 tablespoons fudge topping
3 tablespoons marshmallow crème
¼ cup Rice Krispies cereal

1. Before you start to make this clone, freeze a medium glass or ceramic bowl in the freezer for at least 30 minutes.
2. Measure the ice cream and milk into the frozen bowl. Stir with a spoon until smooth and creamy.
3. Add the fudge, marshmallow crème, and Rice Krispies to the ice cream and stir to combine.
4. Pour into a 20-ounce glass and serve with a long spoon.

- MAKES 1 20-OUNCE SERVING.

TIDBITS

If your Blizzard clone is not as thick as the real thing, just put the whole glass into the freezer for 5 to 10 minutes, or until it's thick.

TOP SECRET RECIPES VERSION OF JACK IN THE BOX OREO COOKIE SHAKE

If you live in one of the 15 Western states served by Jack in the Box, you have no doubt cracked a gut from the hilarious TV ads produced by this popular hamburger chain. In the spots a suit-wearing "Jack" runs the company, even though he's got a bulbous antenna ball for a head with a smiley-face painted on it. He has a private jet, he plays golf, and he even has kids with mini antenna-ball heads.

Jack also has a featured shake flavor that, as it turns out, is very easy to make at home with a blender, ice cream, milk, and a handful of Oreo cookies. Sure, the drive-thru is convenient and easy. But if you don't feel like getting out, now you can enjoy this clone at home from the first fast food chain in the country to use a drive-thru window way back when.

3 cups vanilla ice cream
1 ½ cups milk

8 Oreo cookies

1. Combine the ice cream and milk in a blender and mix on low speed until smooth. Stir the shake with a spoon to mix, if necessary.
2. Break Oreo cookies while adding them to the blender. Mix on low speed for 5 to 10 seconds or until cookies are mostly pureed into the shake, but a few larger pieces remain. Stir with a spoon to help combine the cookies, if necessary.
3. Pour shake into two 12-ounce glasses.

- SERVES 2.

TOP SECRET RECIPES VERSION OF MCDONALD'S MCFLURRY

These 16-ounce desserts-in-a-cup are made with McDonald's soft-serve ice cream and one of several crumbled sweet additives. Duplicating soft-serve ice cream at home comes easy using regular vanilla ice cream (not French vanilla), a little whole milk, and a frozen bowl to do the mixing. You might also want to freeze the glass that you plan to serve this in to ensure the ice cream is served up creamy yet firm, rather than melted and soupy.

BUTTERFINGER

2 cups vanilla ice cream
1/4 cup milk

2/3 Butterfinger candy bar

1. Freeze a medium glass or ceramic bowl in the freezer for at least 30 minutes. Freeze the Butterfinger candy bar (in a plastic bag) as well, along with the 16-ounce glass you plan to use.
2. When the bowl is frozen, first break your candy bar (while it's still in the bag) into little pieces with the handle of a butter knife.
3. Pour the ice cream and milk into the frozen bowl and stir well until smooth and creamy.
4. Add the candy bar pieces and stir, then pour into the frozen 16-ounce glass and serve with a spoon.

- MAKES 1 16-OUNCE DESSERT.

M&M'S

2 cups vanilla ice cream
¼ cup milk

¼ cup (1 mega-tube) M&M's Minis

1. Freeze a medium glass or ceramic bowl in the freezer for at least 30 minutes. While you're at it put the 16-ounce glass you plan to use in there as well.
2. When the bowl is frozen, pour the ice cream and milk into the frozen bowl and stir well until smooth and creamy.
3. Add the M&M's and stir, then pour it all into the frozen 16-ounce glass and serve with a spoon.

- MAKES 1 16-OUNCE DESSERT.

OREO COOKIE

2 cups vanilla ice cream
¼ cup milk

3 Oreo cookies

1. Freeze a medium glass or ceramic bowl in the freezer for at least 30 minutes. While you're at it put the 16-ounce glass you plan to use in there as well.
2. When the bowl is frozen, crumble the cookies (in a plastic bag) into little pieces with your fist or the handle of a butter knife.
3. Pour the ice cream and milk into the frozen bowl and stir well until smooth and creamy.
4. Add the Oreo cookie pieces and stir, then pour it all into the frozen 16-ounce glass and serve with a spoon.

- MAKES 1 16-OUNCE DESSERT.

REESE'S

2 cups vanilla ice cream
¼ cup milk

2 Reese's Peanut Butter Cups (1 package)

1. Freeze a medium glass or ceramic bowl in the freezer for at least 30 minutes. Freeze the peanut butter cups in a plastic

bag, and while you're at it put the 16-ounce glass you plan to use in there as well.
2. When the bowl is frozen, break the peanut butter cups (while still in the bag) into little pieces with the handle of a butter knife.
3. Pour the ice cream and milk into the frozen bowl and stir well until smooth and creamy.
4. Add the candy pieces and stir, then pour into the frozen 16-ounce glass and serve with a spoon.

- MAKES 1 16-OUNCE DESSERT.

TOP SECRET RECIPES VERSION OF MCDONALD'S SHAKES

Forty million customers get a dose of Mickey D's fast food every day. That also happens to be the exact same number of Americans who snore every night. Coincidence? But seriously, with all those daily McDonald's fans, you have to figure that at least a million or so go for one of the chain's three standard flavors of thick shakes: vanilla, chocolate, or strawberry (as for the special Shamrock Shake, we'll talk about that one in the next recipe). The clone recipes here are quick since each one requires just three simple ingredients and a blender to mix it all up. How McEasy is that? Throw everything in a blender and press a button—the one on the right. And if you want your shake thicker, just stash it in the freezer for a while.

CHOCOLATE SHAKE

2 cups vanilla ice cream
1 1/4 cups low-fat milk

2 tablespoons chocolate flavor Nesquik mix

STRAWBERRY SHAKE

2 cups vanilla ice cream
1 1/4 cups low-fat milk

3 tablespoons strawberry flavor Nesquik mix

VANILLA SHAKE

2 cups vanilla ice cream
1 1/4 cups low-fat milk

3 tablespoons sugar

1. Combine all ingredients for the shake flavor of your choice in a blender and mix on high speed until smooth. Stop blender, stir if necessary, and blend again to help combine the ingredients.
2. Pour into two 12-ounce cups.

- Serves 2.

TOP SECRET RECIPES VERSION OF MCDONALD'S SHAMROCK SHAKE

You'll find it very easy to re-create the flavors of McDonald's perennial St. Patrick's Day shake using only four ingredients. The two that make this holiday shake unique are the mint extract and green food coloring. Make sure your extract says "mint" and not "peppermint." And if you don't want shakes that are green like the real ones, you can certainly leave out the food coloring. After all, it's only for looks. Now you can sip on a Shamrock any time of the year. Blarney!

2 cups vanilla ice cream
1 1/4 cups low-fat milk

1/4 teaspoon mint extract (not peppermint)
8 drops green food coloring

1. Combine all ingredients in a blender and blend on high speed until smooth. Stop blender to stir with a spoon if necessary to help blend ice cream.
2. Pour into two 12-ounce cups and serve each with a straw.

- SERVES 2.

TOP SECRET RECIPES VERSION OF SONIC DRIVE-IN CREAM PIE SHAKES

If you placed all the cups end to end that Sonic uses in a year, they would circle the earth twice. That's including the detour the cups would make to avoid passing through downtown Detroit.

These awesome shakes are unique for the graham cracker crumbs in the mix that make them taste as if you're slurping up a creamy chilled pie. You can either crumble up your own graham crackers or use the already ground stuff in a box that's used most often to make graham cracker pie crusts.

BANANA

If you love banana cream pies, you'll love this shake. Just be sure your banana is ripe.

2½ cups vanilla ice cream
½ cup milk
1 ripe banana
2 tablespoons graham cracker crumbs

GARNISH
whipped cream
graham cracker crumbs

1. Put all ingredients in a blender and mix until smooth. You may have to stop the blender and stir the shake with a spoon so that it blends evenly.
2. Pour the shake into two 12-ounce glasses. Garnish each serving with a dollop of whipped cream, and shake some graham cracker crumbs over the top. Serve with a straw.

- MAKES 2 12-OUNCE SHAKES.

CHOCOLATE

Simply add a little chocolate syrup to the shake if chocolate is your thing. This recipe makes two medium shakes or one big one for real chocoholics.

2½ cups vanilla ice cream
½ cup milk
2 tablespoons Hershey's chocolate syrup
2 tablespoons graham cracker crumbs

GARNISH
whipped cream
graham cracker crumbs

1. Put all ingredients in a blender and mix until smooth. You may have to stop the blender and stir the shake with a spoon so that it blends evenly.
2. Pour the shake into two 12-ounce glasses. Garnish each serving with a dollop of whipped cream, and shake some graham cracker crumbs over the top. Serve with a straw.

- MAKES 2 12-OUNCE SHAKES.

COCONUT

This shake uses cream of coconut for flavoring. This is the canned ingredient used most often to make pina coladas, and can be found near the bar mixers in your supermarket.

2½ cups vanilla ice cream
½ cup milk
¼ cup cream of coconut
2 tablespoons graham cracker crumbs

GARNISH
whipped cream
graham cracker crumbs

1. Put all ingredients in a blender and mix until smooth. You may have to stop the blender and stir the shake with a spoon so that it blends evenly.
2. Pour the shake into two 12-ounce glasses. Garnish each serv-

ing with a dollop of whipped cream, and shake some graham cracker crumbs over the top. Serve with a straw.

- MAKES 2 12-OUNCE SHAKES.

STRAWBERRY

This flavor uses the frozen sliced strawberries that are found in boxes in the freezer section with the other frozen fruit. Thaw out a box and measure the berries along with the syrup into the blender.

2½ cups vanilla ice cream
½ cup milk
¼ cup frozen sweetened sliced strawberries, thawed
2 tablespoons graham cracker crumbs

GARNISH
whipped cream
graham cracker crumbs

1. Put all ingredients in a blender and mix until smooth. You may have to stop the blender and stir the shake with a spoon so that it blends evenly.
2. Pour the shake into two 12-ounce glasses. Garnish each serving with a dollop of whipped cream, and shake some graham cracker crumbs over the top. Serve with a straw.

- MAKES 2 12-OUNCE SHAKES.

STARBUCKS FROZEN FRAPPUCCINO

TOP SECRET RECIPES VERSION OF

It was in 1995 that Starbucks stores started selling this frozen drink, one of the company's most successful new products. The Frappuccino is blended with strong coffee, sugar, a dairy base, and ice. Each one is made to order and each one is guaranteed to give you a throbbing brain freeze if you sip too hard. The drinks come in several different varieties, the most popular of which I've cloned here for your frontal lobe—pounding, caffeine-buzzing pleasure.

Make double-strength coffee by measuring 2 tablespoons of ground coffee per cup (serving) in your coffee maker. The drink will be even more authentic if you use Starbucks beans and grind them yourself just before brewing.

COFFEE

¾ cup double-strength coffee, cold
1 cup low-fat milk
3 tablespoons granulated sugar
2 cups ice

1. Make double-strength coffee by brewing with twice the coffee required by your coffee maker. That should be 2 tablespoons of ground coffee per each cup of coffee. Chill before using.
2. To make drink, combine all ingredients in a blender and blend on high speed until ice is crushed and drink is smooth. Pour into two 16-ounce glasses, and serve with a straw.

- MAKES 2 "GRANDE" DRINKS.

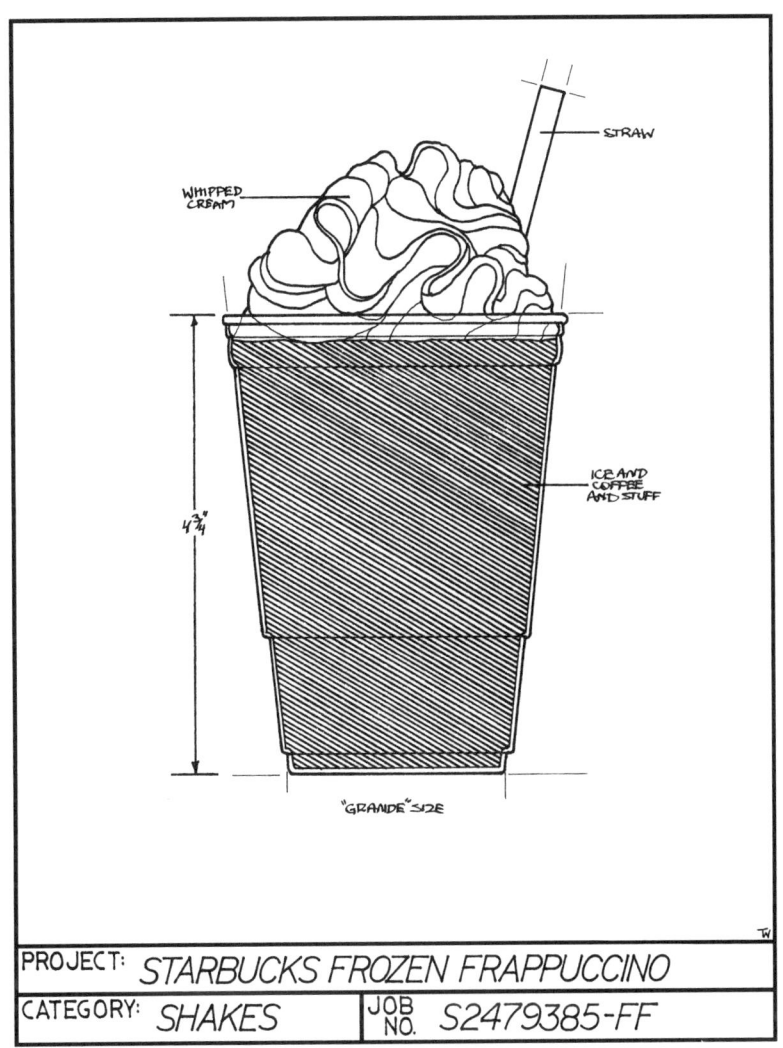

CARAMEL

For this version, add 3 tablespoons of caramel topping to the original recipe and prepare as described. Top each glass with whipped cream and drizzle additional caramel over the whipped cream.

MOCHA

For this version, add 3 tablespoons Hershey's chocolate syrup to the original recipe and prepare as described. Top each glass with whipped cream, if desired.

WENDY'S FROSTY

First served at Wendy's in 1969, the Frosty continues as a favorite in fast food shakes, even if it only comes in chocolate flavor. This clone recipe is an improved version of the recipe that appears in the first book, *Top Secret Recipes*. I've designed this for just a one-person serving and have reduced the chocolate in the shake so that it's more like the real thing served today. I find the smaller yield also helps to make the thing blend better.

½ cup milk
4 teaspoons Nesquik chocolate drink mix

2 cups vanilla ice cream

Combine all of the ingredients in a blender. Blend on medium speed, stopping to stir several times with a long spoon, if necessary, to help the ingredients blend well.

- MAKES 1 SERVING.

OTHER SIPS

TOP SECRET RECIPES VERSION OF ARIZONA GREEN TEA WITH GINSENG AND HONEY

Hard to believe it takes only one regular-sized green tea bag to make an entire 2-quart clone of the popular iced tea in the foam green bottles. Ah, but it's true. Find the liquid ginseng for this recipe in your local health food store, and try to get American ginseng if you can because the Chinese stuff tastes kinda nasty.

2 quarts (8 cups) water
1 Lipton green tea bag
½ cup sugar
2 tablespoons honey

3 tablespoons lemon juice
¼ teaspoon ginseng extract
  (American ginseng)

1. Heat water in a large saucepan until it boils. Turn off heat, put the teabag in the water, then cover the pan and let the tea steep for 1 hour.
2. Pour the sugar and honey into a 2-quart pitcher. Pour the tea into the pitcher and stir to dissolve sugar.
3. Add lemon juice and ginseng and stir. Cool and serve.

- MAKES 2 QUARTS.

ARIZONA ICED TEA WITH GINSENG

TOP SECRET RECIPES VERSION OF

When John Ferolito and Don Vultaggio pondered a name for a new line of canned iced teas, all they had to do was look at a map of the United States. They wanted to name their iced tea after a hot place where a cold can of iced tea was worshipped. Originally they picked "Santa Fe," but soon ditched the name of the city and settled on a state: AriZona, complete with an uppercase "Z" in the middle for kicks. The secret to the duo's early success was largely in their creative packaging decisions. If you think the tea's great chilled, the company claims you can also sip it hot by simply zapping a cupful in the microwave.

2 quarts (8 cups) water
1 Lipton tea bag (black tea)
⅔ cup sugar

2 tablespoons lemon juice
¼ teaspoon ginseng extract
(American ginseng)

1. Heat water in a large saucepan until it boils. Turn off heat, put the teabag in the water, then cover the pan and let the tea steep for 1 hour.
2. Pour the sugar into a 2-quart pitcher. Pour the tea into the pitcher and stir to dissolve sugar.
3. Add lemon juice and ginseng and stir. Cool and serve.

- MAKES 2 QUARTS.

You can find liquid ginseng, usually in dropper bottles, in your local health food store. Be sure to get American ginseng if you have a choice. Some of the Chinese ginseng tastes too bitter for this tea.

TOP SECRET RECIPES VERSION OF

CINNABON STRAWBERRY LEMONADE

Cinnabon, the 470-unit chain famous for its gooey cinnamon rolls, gives lemonade a twist by adding strawberry syrup. It's a simple clone when you snag some Hershey's strawberry syrup (near the chocolate syrup in your supermarket), and a few juicy lemons. While you're at it, toss in a straw.

½ cup lemon juice (from 3 or 4 fresh lemons)
¼ cup sugar
2 cups water
2 tablespoons Hershey's strawberry syrup

Mix ingredients together in a pitcher. Serve over ice with a straw, if you've got one.

- MAKES 2 DRINKS.

GENERAL FOODS INTERNATIONAL COFFEES

TOP SECRET RECIPES VERSION OF

With just a few simple ingredients you can re-create the European-style coffees that come in rectangular tins at a fraction of the cost. Since these famous instant coffee blends are created by Maxwell House, it's best to use Maxwell House instant coffee, although I've tried them all with Folgers and Taster's Choice, and the recipes still work out fine. You'll also need a coffee bean grinder to grind the instant coffee into powder. When you're finished making the mix, you can store it for as long as you like in a sealed container, until you're ready for a hot coffee drink. At that point, simply measure some of the mix into a cup with boiling water. Stir it all up and enjoy while watching shows about Europe on the Travel Channel to enhance the experience.

CAFÉ VIENNA

A creamy coffee with a hint of cinnamon.

¼ cup instant coffee
¼ cup plus 3 tablespoons granulated sugar
½ cup plus 1 tablespoon Coffee-mate creamer
⅛ teaspoon cinnamon

1. Grind the instant coffee into powder using a coffee grinder.
2. Mix all ingredients together in a small bowl. Store in a sealed container.
3. To make coffee, measure 2 tablespoons of the powdered mix into a coffee cup. Add 8 ounces (1 cup) of boiling water and stir.

- MAKES 9 SERVINGS.

FRENCH VANILLA CAFÉ

This one gets its subtle vanilla flavor from a little French Vanilla Coffee-mate creamer.

¼ cup instant coffee
¼ cup plus 3 tablespoons granulated sugar
½ cup Coffee-mate creamer (plain)
¼ cup French Vanilla Coffee-mate creamer

1. Grind the instant coffee into powder using a coffee grinder.
2. Mix all ingredients together in a small bowl. Store in a sealed container.
3. To make coffee, measure 2 tablespoons of the powdered mix into a coffee cup. Add 8 ounces (1 cup) of boiling water and stir.

- MAKES 10 SERVINGS.

HAZELNUT BELGIAN CAFÉ

As in the above recipe, you'll need to use flavored creamer along with the plain stuff to hit the right note.

¼ cup instant coffee
¼ cup plus 3 tablespoons granulated sugar
¼ cup plus 3 tablespoons Coffee-mate creamer (plain)
2 tablespoons Hazelnut Coffee-mate creamer

1. Grind the instant coffee into powder using a coffee grinder.
2. Mix all ingredients together in a small bowl. Store in a sealed container.
3. To make coffee, measure 2 tablespoons of the powdered mix into a coffee cup. Add 8 ounces (1 cup) of boiling water and stir.

- MAKES 9 SERVINGS.

SUISSE MOCHA

It takes just a couple tablespoons of cocoa to give this version its chocolate accent. When making the coffee in a cup, notice that this is the only recipe of the bunch requiring a measurement of 4 teaspoons of mix to 1 cup of boiling water.

¼ cup instant coffee
½ cup plus 2 tablespoons granulated sugar
½ cup plus 1 tablespoon Coffee-mate creamer
2 tablespoons cocoa

1. Grind the instant coffee into powder using a coffee grinder.
2. Mix all ingredients together in a small bowl. Store in a sealed container.
3. To make coffee, measure 4 teaspoons of the powdered mix into a coffee cup. Add 8 ounces (1 cup) of boiling water and stir.

- MAKES 16 SERVINGS.

VIENNESE CHOCOLATE CAFÉ

Vanilla *and* chocolate go great together in this one.

¼ cup instant coffee
¼ cup plus 3 tablespoons granulated sugar
½ cup Coffee-mate creamer (plain)
2 tablespoons French Vanilla Coffee-mate creamer
2 teaspoons cocoa

1. Grind the instant coffee into powder using a coffee grinder.
2. Mix all ingredients together in a small bowl. Store in a sealed container.
3. To make coffee, measure 2 tablespoons of the powdered mix into a coffee cup. Add 8 ounces (1 cup) of boiling water and stir.

- MAKES 10 SERVINGS.

TOP SECRET RECIPES VERSION OF HAWAIIAN PUNCH FRUIT JUICY RED

Real Hawaiian Punch contains only 5 percent fruit juice. Even though some of the ingredients in our clone are not pure fruit juice, and we're adding additional water and sugar, this *Top Secret Recipes* version still contains a lot more tasty real fruit juice than the real thing. Plus, you can leave the food coloring out, if you like. It's only for looks, in a traditionally punchy way.

1 ½ cups water
1 cup pineapple juice
¾ cup Mauna Lai Paradise Passion guava/passion fruit blend
¼ tablespoon orange juice
¼ cup apple juice
¼ cup Kern's papaya nectar
¼ tablespoon Kern's apricot nectar
3 tablespoons granulated sugar
¼ teaspoon red food coloring

Combine all ingredients in a pitcher and stir until sugar is dissolved.

- MAKES 1 LITER.

HOT DOG ON A STICK MUSCLE BEACH LEMONADE

Entrepreneur Dave Barham opened the first Hot Dog on a Stick location in Santa Monica, California, near famed Muscle Beach. That was in 1946, and today the chain has blossomed into a total of more than 100 outlets located in shopping malls across America. You've probably seen the bright red, white, blue, and yellow go-go outfits and those cylindrical fez-style bucket hats on the girls behind the counter.

In giant clear plastic vats at the front of each store floats ice, fresh lemon rinds, and what is probably the world's most thirst-quenching substance—Muscle Beach Lemonade. Our clone is a simple concoction really, with only three ingredients. And with this *TSR* formula, you'll have your own version of the lemonade in the comfort of your own home at a fraction of the price.

1 cup fresh-squeezed lemon juice (about 5 lemons)
7 cups water
1 cup granulated sugar

1. Combine the lemon juice with the water and sugar in a 2-quart pitcher. Stir or shake vigorously until all the sugar is dissolved.
2. Slice the remaining lemon rind halves into fourths, then add the rinds to the pitcher. Add ice to the top of the pitcher and chill.
3. Serve the lemonade over ice in a 12-ounce glass and add a couple of lemon rind slices to each glass.

- MAKES 2 QUARTS, OR 8 SERVINGS.

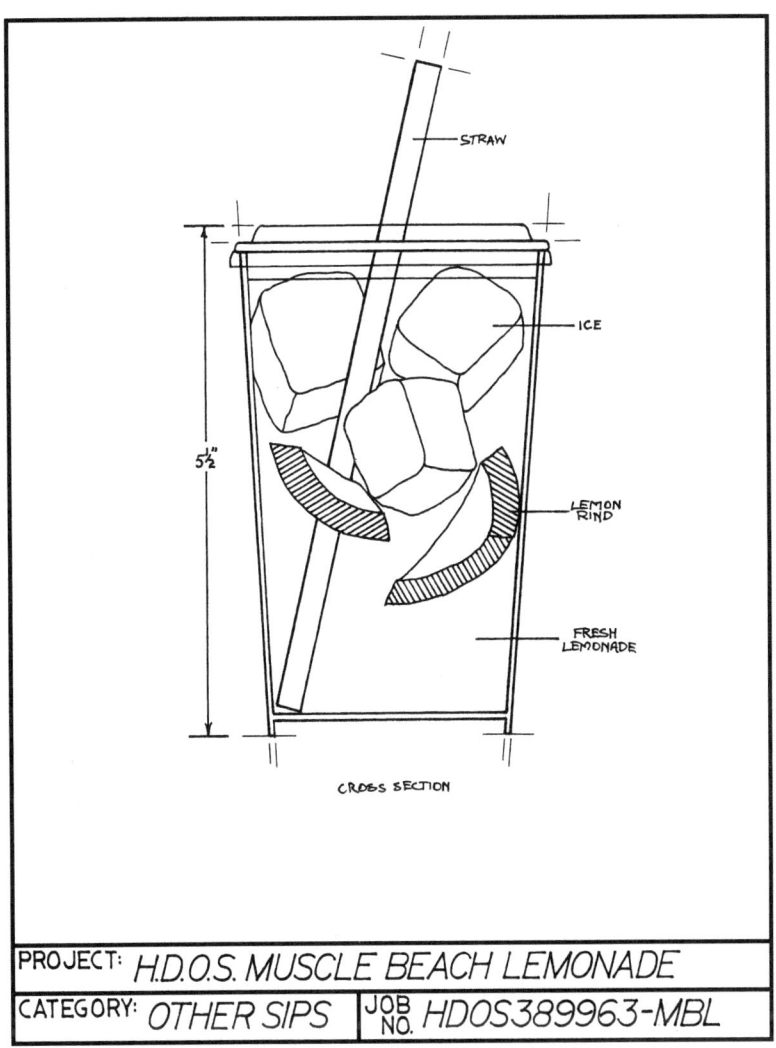

MINUTE MAID ALL NATURAL LEMONADE

Minute Maid is credited with creating the modern orange juice industry by marketing the first frozen concentrated orange juice in 1946. Today the company is owned by The Coca-Cola Company and sells juices, punches, and fruit drinks in countries all over the world. Minute Maid also sells one of the most recognized brands of lemonade, made from lemon concentrate. You can easily duplicate the taste of the drink at home, but since this *TSR* version is made with fresh lemons, it might just edge out the real thing in a side-by-side taste test.

½ cup fresh-squeezed lemon juice (from 2 to 3 lemons)
3¼ cups water

¼ cup plus 3 tablespoons granulated sugar

Combine the lemon juice with the water and sugar in a 1-quart pitcher. Stir or shake the pitcher vigorously until all the sugar is dissolved. Cover and chill.

- MAKES 1 QUART.

NESTEA NATURAL LEMON FLAVORED ICED TEA

TOP SECRET RECIPES VERSION OF

For five thousand years tea was served hot. But when a heat wave hit the World's Fair in St. Louis in 1904, tea plantation owner Richard Blechynden couldn't give the steamy stuff away. So he poured it over ice, creating the first iced tea, and the drink became the hit of the fair. Today Nestle's drink division, which markets Nestea, produces somewhere in the area of 50 percent of the world's processed tea. That's huge business when you consider that tea is second only to water in worldwide consumption.

2 quarts (8 cups) water
2 Lipton tea bags

¾ cup plus 2 tablespoons granulated sugar
¼ cup bottled lemon juice

1. Bring 2 quarts of water to a boil. Add tea bags and let the tea steep for 1 to 2 hours.
2. Remove the tea bags and pour the tea into a 2-quart pitcher. Add sugar and lemon juice. Cover and chill.

- MAKES 2 QUARTS.

RED ROBIN FRECKLED LEMONADE

TOP SECRET RECIPES VERSION OF

This is Red Robin's signature non-alcoholic drink, and is simple to make with pre-made lemonade (unless you want to use one of the fresh lemonade recipes from page 562 or 564) and the strawberries that come frozen in sweet syrup. When added to the top of the ice-filled lemonade glass the strawberries and syrup speckle the drink. Serve this one without stirring it up, or the freckles will be gone.

⅓ cup frozen sweetened sliced strawberries, thawed
1 cup lemonade

GARNISH
lemon wedge

1. Fill a 16-ounce glass with ice.
2. Ladle strawberries with syrup over the top of the ice.
3. Fill the glass with lemonade. Add a lemon wedge and serve with a straw.

- MAKES 1 DRINK.

RED ROBIN STRAWBERRY ECSTACY

After adding the juices to the blender the restaurant does a "flash blend." That means you use just a couple of pulses on high speed so that the ice is broken up into small pieces, without being completely crushed to a slushy consistency.

½ cup orange juice
⅓ cup pineapple juice
½ ounce grenadine

1 cup ice
⅓ cup frozen sweetened sliced strawberries, thawed

1. Add orange juice, pineapple juice, grenadine, and ice to a blender. Blend the drink with just a couple pulses on high speed so that the ice is still a bit chunky.
2. Pour into a 16-ounce glass and ladle strawberries with the syrup into the drink.
3. Add a wedge of orange and a maraschino cherry speared on a toothpick. Serve with a straw.

- MAKES 1 DRINK.

TOP SECRET RECIPES VERSION OF 7-ELEVEN CHERRY SLURPEE

Put on a big red smile. Now you can make your own version of the popular convenience store slush we know by the excruciating brain throb that follows a big ol' gulp. You must have a blender to make this clone of 7-Eleven's Slurpee, and enough room to stick that blender into your freezer to get it nice and thick. This recipe gets close to the original with Kool-Aid mix and a little help from cherry extract, but you can make this drink with any flavor Kool-Aid mix (if you decide to make some variations, don't worry about adding extract). This recipe makes enough to fill one of those giant 32-ounce cups you find at the convenience store. Now if we could just figure out how to make those funky spoon-straws.

2 cups cold club soda
1/2 cup sugar
1/4 teaspoon plus 1/8 teaspoon Kool-Aid cherry-flavored unsweetened drink mix

1/2 teaspoon cherry extract
2 1/2 cups crushed ice

1. Pour 1 cup of the club soda into a blender. Add the sugar, Kool-Aid mix, and cherry extract. Blend this until all of the sugar is dissolved.
2. Add the crushed ice and blend on high speed until the drink is a slushy, smooth consistency, with no remaining chunks of ice.
3. Add the remaining club soda and blend briefly until mixed. You may have to stop the blender and use a long spoon to stir up the contents.
4. If necessary, put the blender into your freezer for 1/2 hour. This

will help thicken it up. After ½ hour remove blender from freezer and, again, blend briefly to mix.

- MAKES 1 32-OUNCE DRINK (OR 2 16-OUNCERS).

Snapple was selling juices for five years—since 1982—before the fruity line of teas was rolled out. Just five years after that, Snapple was selling more tea in the U.S. than Lipton or Nestea. Today, even though Snapple sells over 50 different bottled beverages, the iced teas are still the most successful products in the line. But not all the fruity flavors of tea were hits. Cranberry, strawberry, and orange are now extinct, so those flavors can only be enjoyed by making versions of your own at home with these simple formulas. I've also got lemon and peach flavors here, Snapple's two top-selling products, plus raspberry, another big seller.

Included here are improved versions of iced tea clones printed in the book *More Top Secret Recipes*.

CRANBERRY ICED TEA

2 quarts (8 cups) water
2 Lipton tea bags
¾ cup granulated sugar

⅓ cup plus 2 tablespoons bottled
  lemon juice
2 tablespoons Ocean Spray
  cranberry juice cocktail
  concentrate

DIET LEMON ICED TEA

2 quarts (8 cups) water
2 Lipton tea bags

16 1-gram packages Equal
  sweetener
⅓ cup bottled lemon juice

LEMON ICED TEA

2 quarts (8 cups) water
2 Lipton tea bags

¾ cup granulated sugar
⅓ cup bottled lemon juice

ORANGE ICED TEA

2 quarts (8 cups) water
2 Lipton tea bags
¾ cup granulated sugar

⅓ cup bottled lemon juice
⅛ teaspoon orange extract

PEACH ICED TEA

2 quarts (8 cups) water
2 Lipton tea bags
¾ cup granulated sugar

¼ cup plus 1 tablespoon bottled lemon juice
3 tablespoons Torani peach flavoring syrup

Alternate clone: Rather than Torani peach flavoring use one 12-ounce can Kern's peach nectar, and 3 tablespoons lemon juice instead of ¼ cup plus 1 tablespoon lemon juice.

RASPBERRY ICED TEA

2 quarts (8 cups) water
2 Lipton tea bags
¾ cup granulated sugar

¼ cup plus 1 tablespoon lemon juice
2 tablespoons Torani raspberry flavoring syrup

STRAWBERRY ICED TEA

2 quarts (8 cups) water
2 Lipton tea bags
¾ cup granulated sugar

⅓ cup lemon juice
1 tablespoon strawberry extract

1. Bring water to a rapid boil in a large saucepan.
2. Turn off heat, add tea bags, cover saucepan and let the tea steep for 1 to 2 hours.
3. Pour the sugar into a 2-quart pitcher, and then add the tea. The water will still be warm and the sugar (or sweetener if making the diet tea) should dissolve easily.
4. Add the lemon juice and fruit flavoring ingredients. Stir, cover and chill.

- MAKES 2 QUARTS.

TOP SECRET RECIPES VERSION OF

SUNNY DELIGHT

If you love the taste of Sunny D but wish it was made with more than just 5 percent real fruit juice, this is the recipe for you. Rustle up some frozen juice concentrates and let them thaw out before measuring. Since tangerine juice concentrate is tough to find on its own I designed the recipe to use the orange tangerine blend concentrate from Minute Maid.

6 cups water
1 cup corn syrup
1 1/3 cups frozen concentrated Minute Maid orange tangerine juice, thawed
6 tablespoons frozen concentrated apple juice, thawed
2 tablespoons frozen concentrated limeade, thawed
4 teaspoons frozen concentrated grapefruit juice, thawed
1 teaspoon Kool-Aid lemonade unsweetened drink mix

1. Combine all ingredients in a 2-quart pitcher. Stir well.
2. Chill for several hours before serving.

- MAKES 2 QUARTS.

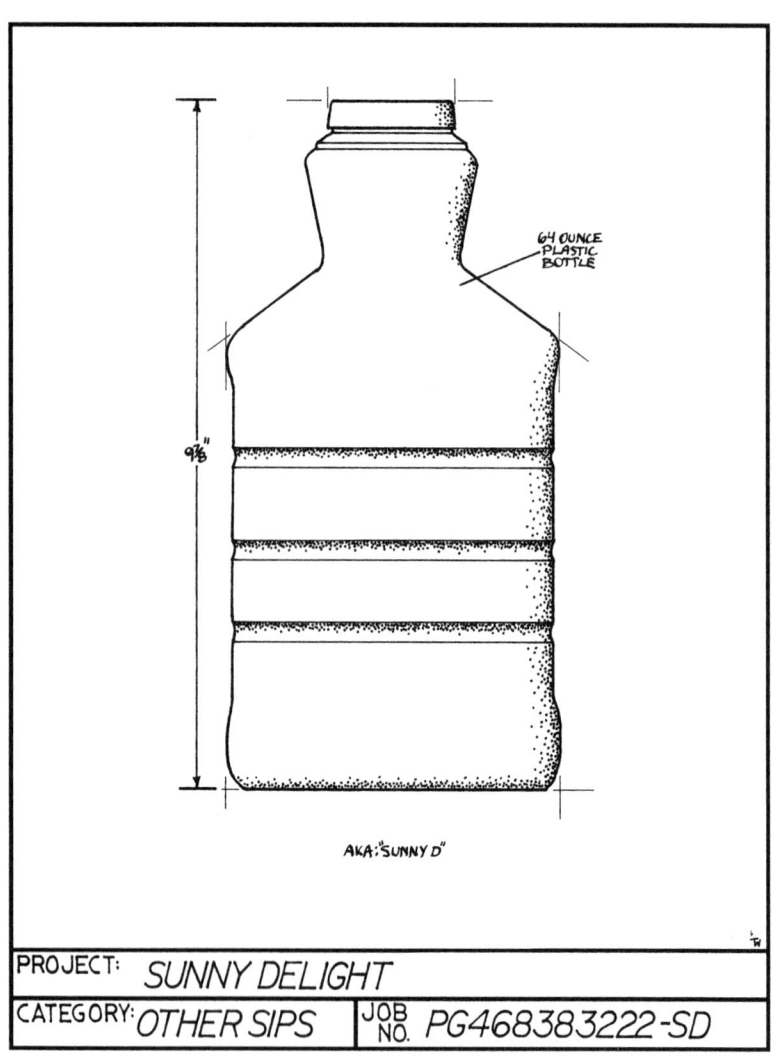

TOP SECRET RECIPES VERSION OF YOO-HOO CHOCOLATE DRINK

Watching his wife can tomatoes inspired Natale Olivieri to create a bottled chocolate drink with a long shelf life back in the early 1920s. When New York Yankee great Yogi Berra later met Natale and tasted his drink, he was an instant fan, and went on to help raise the funds that helped make Yoo-hoo a national success.

I cloned this drink in the first book, *Top Secret Recipes*, but have since discovered an improved technique. Using a blender to mix the drink, as instructed in that version, adds too much unnecessary foam. So here now is a revised recipe that you shake to mix, that could fool even the most devoted Yoo-hoo fanatics.

¾ cup nonfat dry milk
3 tablespoons Nesquik chocolate drink mix

1 ½ cups cold water

Combine all ingredients in a container or jar with a lid. Shake until dry milk is dissolved. Drink immediately or chill in refrigerator.

- MAKES 1 14-OUNCE DRINK.

YOO-HOO MIX-UPS

A while back when I was rummaging through my pantry I came upon several bottles of flavored Yoo-hoo that I'd scored from Wal-Mart and tucked away for over a year. Each of the bottles was covered with a little dust and needed a pretty fierce shaking, but the contents were very well preserved and quite tasty. After some web browsing of a few unofficial Yoo-hoo web sites, I discovered these previously worshipped "Mix-Ups" varieties of the famous chocolate drink had since been put to rest. Now, after a little work in the top secret underground lab, I've come up with a way to clone the flavor of this "dead product" that's no longer obtainable outside of the ethereal food-world afterlife.

CHOCOLATE-BANANA

¾ cup nonfat dry milk
3 tablespoons Nesquik chocolate drink mix
1½ cups cold water
1½ teaspoons sugar
½ teaspoon banana extract

CHOCOLATE-MINT

¾ cup nonfat dry milk
3 tablespoons Nesquik chocolate drink mix
1½ cups cold water
1 teaspoon sugar
dash mint extract (less than ⅛ teaspoon)

CHOCOLATE-STRAWBERRY

¾ cup nonfat dry milk
3 tablespoons Nesquik chocolate drink mix

1 ½ cups cold water
1 tablespoon sugar
1 ½ teaspoons strawberry extract

Combine all ingredients for flavor of your choice in a container or jar with a lid. Shake until dry milk is dissolved. Drink immediately or chill in refrigerator.

- MAKES 1 14-OUNCE DRINK.

SPIRITS:
SCHNAPPS & LIQUEURS

Liqueur-making dates back to somewhere around 900 A.D., when Arabs and European monks had to do something to break up the boredom of living in 900 A.D. Think about it: no DVDs, no video games, no extreme sports on ESPN2. These guys had nothing better to do than spend their time crafting the perfect beverage on which to get wasted. I respectfully toast their devotion.

    Luckily for us, creating liqueurs at home today is a much simpler task than in those days thanks to the availability of a variety of extracts and flavorings, and pre-distilled spirits. This leaves us plenty of time in one day to both make liqueur *and* watch a DVD.

    These clone recipes are very easy. For most of them it's a simple matter of creating a simple syrup, then adding 80-proof vodka and the correct flavoring. Vodka works well because of its neutral flavor. You can use any inexpensive vodka you like, but I recommend Smirnoff. That's the brand I used to make these clones, since it tastes good without being too expensive. For the flavorings and extracts, try to use Schilling or McCormick brand.

    Each of the recipes has been designed to create a finished product with the same approximate alcohol content as the original.

    For the liqueurs with fruit additives or cocoa you will want to strain the liqueur to remove the sediment. For this, use a wire strainer that has been lined with a coffee filter or two, or a paper towel. Moisten the filters with a bit of water first, then, after the liqueur has aged a while, pour it in and let it drip through the filter. If the liqueur has settled for several days the sediment will be on the bottom of your bottle or jar, so if you pour carefully most of the solid material will stay behind. It may take several hours for all of the liqueur to drip through the filter.

Store your finished product in a tightly sealed bottle in a cool, dry place. Except for the Irish cream clone, your finished product will store indefinitely, and even improve with age.

Then go watch that DVD.

TOP SECRET RECIPES VERSION OF
BAILEY'S ORIGINAL IRISH CREAM

Bailey's uses a special process to combine two otherwise incompatible ingredients: cream and whiskey. This secret process keeps the cream from clumping and separating from the whiskey, and allows the liqueur to go for two years unrefrigerated without spoiling. Since we can't use the same process, we'll replace cream with canned evaporated milk in our recipe. This gives us a finished product with the taste and texture of the deliciously famous Irish cream. Here now is an improved version of the Bailey's clone recipe that appears in *More Top Secret Recipes*. This version has fewer ingredients, is easier to make, and tastes amazing.

1 ½ cups evaporated milk (1 12-ounce can)
1 cup Irish whiskey
⅔ cup granulated sugar
1 tablespoon Hershey's chocolate syrup
1 teaspoon vanilla extract
½ teaspoon instant coffee

Combine all ingredients in a pitcher and mix well or shake until sugar is dissolved. Store in the refrigerator in a sealed container. Shake before serving.

- MAKES 3 CUPS.

DEKUYPER THRILLA VANILLA FRENCH VANILLA LIQUEUR

Just as with the real thing, this clone of the unique vanilla liqueur from DeKuyper can be mixed with cola over ice, or with 1 part vanilla liqueur to 2 parts raspberry liqueur for another tasty tipple. Also try splashing some of it into the shaker with your favorite vodka for a sweet vanilla-tini.

1 1/4 cups very hot water
3/4 cup granulated sugar
1 cup 80-proof vodka
1 teaspoon McCormick vanilla butter & nut flavoring

1. Dissolve sugar in the hot water.
2. Add vodka and flavoring, and stir well. Store in a sealed container.

- Makes 2 2/3 cups.

TOP SECRET RECIPES VERSION OF DISARONNO AMARETTO

The story behind this one is that for several months artist Bernardino Luini worked closely with a model to help him paint a fresco of the Madonna in Saronno, Italy. As the months passed the girl, whose name has since been forgotten, fell in love with Bernardino. To show her feelings for him, the girl gave Bernardino a gift of sweet almond-flavored liqueur she made from the trees growing in her garden. The year was 1525, and that bottle is said to have been the first DiSaronno Amaretto. The recipe was passed down through the ages, until late in the eighteenth century when the liqueur went into commercial production.

Reenact the legend by giving someone a bottle of your own version of the famous liqueur, whether they paint you on a wall or not.

½ cup granulated sugar
¼ cup dark brown sugar
¾ cup very hot water
½ cup corn syrup

1 ½ cups 80-proof vodka
1 tablespoon almond extract
1 teaspoon vanilla extract

1. Combine the water with the sugars in a medium glass pitcher or bowl. Stir until the sugar is dissolved. Add corn syrup and stir well.
2. Add vodka and flavorings and stir well. Store in a sealed container.

- MAKES 3 CUPS.

TOP SECRET RECIPES VERSION OF

GRAND MARNIER LIQUEUR

In 1880s France, oranges were quite rare and exotic. So when Louis Alexandre Marnier-Lopostolle traveled to the Caribbean in search of ingredients, he came back with bitter oranges to combine with his family's fine cognac. While other orange-flavored liqueurs such as triple sec and curaçao are mixed with a neutral alcohol base, Grand Marnier took it to the next level with a more complex flavor that makes it today's top-selling French liqueur.

Now you too can combine cognac with real orange to make a home version of this tasty (and pricey) stuff. By using an inexpensive cognac that costs around 18 to 20 dollars a bottle, you can create a clone cousin of the real thing that normally sells for 28 to 32 dollars a bottle. All you need, in addition to the cognac, is some sugar, an orange, and a little patience.

2 cups cognac
1 medium orange

⅔ cup granulated sugar

1. Pour the cognac into a 2-cup jar with a lid.
2. Peel and section the orange, then slice each of the orange sections in half lengthwise, and add them to the jar along with the sugar.
3. Cover jar and shake until the sugar is dissolved.
4. Store the jar at room temperature for at least 2 weeks, then strain the orange slices and pulp from the liquid. Use as you would the real thing, for sipping or in mixed drinks.

- MAKES 2 CUPS.

HIRAM WALKER ANISETTE LIQUEUR

TOP SECRET RECIPES VERSION OF

For centuries anise has been a key ingredient in distilled spirits, and it is the most widely used flavor for drinks in countries surrounding the Mediterranean. Today it's used as the key flavoring ingredient in ouzo, sambuca, raki, Pernod, and a host of other international aperitifs and liqueurs. The availability of anise extract (found near the vanilla in most supermarkets) makes home cloning this popular brand of anisette liqueur an easy project.

½ cup very hot water
⅔ cup granulated sugar

1 cup 80-proof vodka
¼ teaspoon anise extract

1. Dissolve sugar in the hot water.
2. Add vodka and anise extract. Store in sealed container.

- MAKES 2 CUPS.

TOP SECRET RECIPES VERSION OF HIRAM WALKER CRÈME DE BANANA LIQUEUR

In the Cocktails section you'll find many recipes that require banana-flavored liqueur, a very common ingredient at the bars these days. Here's how to make some from scratch for your top secret concoctions if you don't feel like fetching the real thing.

¾ cup very hot water
¾ cup granulated sugar
1 cup 80-proof vodka

¼ teaspoon imitation banana extract
1 drop yellow food coloring

1. Combine the hot water with the sugar in a small pitcher. Stir until sugar is dissolved.
2. Add vodka, banana extract, and food coloring and stir well. Cool to room temperature before using. Store in a sealed container.

- MAKES 2 CUPS.

TOP SECRET RECIPES VERSION OF HIRAM WALKER CRÈME DE CACAO LIQUEUR

The chocolate taste in this liqueur comes from cocoa most commonly used for baking. After storing this liqueur for a week or so, we'll strain it through a coffee filter or a wire strainer that's been lined with paper towels to remove most of the cocoa. Sediment is not cool in liqueurs. Our finished product won't be quite as clear as the real thing, but the taste should be right there.

¾ cup very hot water
¾ cup plus 1 tablespoon granulated sugar
1 cup 80-proof vodka
2 tablespoons cocoa
½ teaspoon vanilla extract

1. Dissolve the sugar in the hot water.
2. Add the vodka, cocoa, and vanilla. Stir well. Store in a covered container for at least a week. Shake the liqueur every day or two.
3. Strain the liqueur through a coffee filter or paper towel–lined strainer into a bowl or pitcher. Store in a covered container.

- MAKES 2 CUPS.

HIRAM WALKER CRÈME DE MENTHE LIQUEUR

TOP SECRET RECIPES VERSION OF

The popular mint liqueur is quick to make at home, and we'll even make it a deep, dark green like the real thing with 45 drops (or ½ teaspoon) of green food coloring. As for the mint flavoring, be sure to get "peppermint" extract, not "mint" extract.

½ cup very hot water
⅔ cup plus 1 tablespoon granulated sugar
1 cup 80-proof vodka
¾ teaspoon peppermint extract
45 drops green food coloring (½ teaspoon)

1. Dissolve the sugar in the hot water.
2. Add the vodka, peppermint extract, and food coloring. Store in a sealed container.

- MAKES 2 CUPS.

HIRAM WALKER CRÈME DE STRAWBERRY LIQUEUR

TOP SECRET RECIPES VERSION OF

If you want to try a couple of good cocktails that use this fruity liqueur, check out the clone recipe for T.G.I. Friday's Banana Split Blender Blaster on page 687, or for Bahama Breeze Verry Berry Good on page 609.

1 cup very hot water
2/3 cup granulated sugar
1 cup 80-proof vodka

3/4 teaspoon imitation strawberry extract

1. Dissolve the sugar in the hot water.
2. Add the vodka and strawberry extract. Stir well and store in a sealed container.

- MAKES 2½ CUPS.

TOP SECRET RECIPES VERSION OF

HIRAM WALKER RAZZ ATTACK RASPBERRY SCHNAPPS

To make this delicious raspberry schnapps you'll need to track down the raspberry flavoring syrup used in coffeehouses with the brand name Torani. A few of the more popular flavors, raspberry included, are now available in most supermarkets.

1 cup very hot water
1/3 cup sugar
1 cup 80-proof vodka

1/2 cup Torani raspberry flavoring syrup

1. Dissolve the sugar in the hot water.
2. Add vodka and flavoring syrup and stir well. Store in a covered container.

- MAKES 2 2/3 CUPS.

HIRAM WALKER ROOT BEER SCHNAPPS

TOP SECRET RECIPES VERSION OF

You could use this liqueur to make a teddy bear shooter: Layer ½ ounce of vodka over ½ ounce of root beer schnapps in a shot glass. Or you could make a root beer float as described on the bottle of the real Hiram Walker Root Beer Schnapps by adding 1 part Root Beer Schnapps to 2 parts milk or cream, and 4 parts 7UP or Sprite, then combining it all in a blender with ice until smooth. Or you could just pour it over some ice cream and dive in.

1 cup very hot water
¾ cup granulated sugar
1 cup 80-proof vodka

¼ teaspoon root beer concentrate

1. Dissolve the sugar in the hot water.
2. Add the vodka and root beer concentrate. Store in a sealed container.

- MAKES 2½ CUPS.

KAHLÚA COFFEE LIQUEUR

Kahlúa may market itself as the coffee liqueur developed in Mexico, but many believe the brand originated in Turkey. Looking at the label, we can still see an Arabic archway under which a sombrero-wearing man rests. Old labels of the brand show this man wearing a turban and smoking a pipe. Even the name *Kahlúa* is of Arabic origin. Regardless of where the drink came from, it dominates all other coffee liqueurs out there, including the very popular Tia Maria.

Here's a greatly improved version of the clone recipe that appears in *Top Secret Recipes*. You'll find this recipe is easier to make, tastes better, and, just as with the first recipe, improves with age.

1 cup light corn syrup
½ cup granulated sugar
5 teaspoons instant coffee
½ cup hot water
1 ⅓ cups vodka
1 ½ teaspoons vanilla extract

1. Combine corn syrup, sugar, and instant coffee with hot water in a medium pitcher or large jar. Stir or shake until sugar has dissolved.
2. Add vodka and vanilla extract and stir well. Store in a covered container.

- MAKES 3 CUPS.

MARIE BRIZARD WATERMELON LIQUEUR

TOP SECRET RECIPES VERSION OF

This delicious brand of watermelon liqueur is easy to duplicate by pureeing fresh watermelon. You'll need a cup of pureed melon that comes from about ⅛ of a medium watermelon. I suggest you get the seedless kind.

1 cup pureed watermelon (no seeds)	½ cup plus 1 tablespoon granulated sugar
	1 cup 80-proof vodka

1. Make pureed watermelon by removing the seeds and rind from about ⅛ of a medium watermelon (seedless watermelon is the easiest to use). Use a large fork or potato masher to mash the watermelon in a large bowl. You don't need to puree it in the bowl, just mash it up enough to create some liquid so that the fruit will puree well in the blender. Pour the melon and sugar into your blender and blend for 15 seconds or so, or until the sugar has dissolved.
2. Pour the watermelon puree into a container with a lid, add the vodka, and cover. Store at room temperature for a week.
3. Strain the melon pulp from the liquid by pouring it through a paper towel–lined strainer. Store in a sealed container.

- MAKES 2½ CUPS.

MIDORI MELON LIQUEUR

The world's most famous melon liqueur can be imitated at home by pureeing fresh honeydew melon. After the liqueur sits for a week or so, strain out the melon, put on your drinking cap, and enjoy thoroughly.

1 cup pureed honeydew melon
¾ cup granulated sugar
1 cup 80-proof vodka

4 drops green food coloring
3 drops yellow food coloring

1. Puree the honeydew melon by first slicing ¼ of the melon away from the rind. Remove the seeds and then slice the melon into big chunks. Put the chunks into a medium bowl and mash with a potato masher to create some juice. Pour the mashed melon and juice into a blender and blend on medium speed for 10 to 15 seconds or until pureed. Measure 1 cup of melon into a jar with a lid.
2. Add sugar, vodka, and food coloring to the jar. Cover and shake until sugar is dissolved.
3. Store liqueur at room temperature for a week, then strain the melon pulp from the liquid by pouring it through a paper towel–lined strainer.

- MAKES 2 CUPS.

SPIRITS:
Cocktails

I'm fascinated by Prohibition. There's something intriguing about the way drinking alcoholic beverages in the United States reached a new level of hip when the federal government took away the right in 1920. Forever chiseled into history will be clear proof that when people are told too often how to live their lives, it has the reverse effect. Sure, you can take the cocaine out of their Coca-Cola, but stay the heck away from their whiskey.

Before Prohibition drinking was mostly a man's sport. The drinks were pretty dull, and they were usually made with whiskey. When the cocktail parties went underground as fancy private shindigs and secret speakeasies, women got into the party full swing, and many of the mixed drinks that are still around today were invented at those gatherings using creative new ingredients.

At that time, gangs ran the liquor industry. Bootleggers imported alcohol into the country and got filthy rich. Murders, beatings, and bribery were commonplace. Shipments of booze were smuggled secretly into the U.S. from Canada and the Caribbean, and homemade distilleries were built in darkened cellars and on backwoods riverbanks. Many local governments and law enforcement officials got on the gangs' payroll and looked the other way. Some joined in on the party because even they thought the law was lame.

The United States lost somewhere around 500 million dollars in whiskey taxes every year during Prohibition and the economy skidded into a deep depression. When the government realized that Prohibition was causing more harm than good, the Eighteenth Amendment was repealed by the Twenty-first in 1933, and the bars reopened for business. By then, though, the damage was done.

Since American distilleries had shut down, European booze-makers captured the U.S. market by immediately flooding the country with their own brands. Some domestic distillers struggled to start from scratch again, only to be forced to shut down during World War II to produce industrial alcohol for the war effort.

After the war, the distilling industry finally got back on its feet. A wider variety of spirits were in demand and the market's taste shifted from the old standards of whiskey, rum, and gin. Vodka became the number one spirit in the later decades of the twentieth century as a new generation of drinkers enjoyed festive happy hours with fancy designer libations that edged out old cocktail formulations their parents used to drink.

Newsweek and *The Saturday Evening Post* reported that the beginning of the "singles age" started when the first T.G.I. Friday's opened in New York City in 1965. Bars in growing casual restaurant chains became hot spots every night of the week where the professional crowd gathered after a hard day's work.

The ability to quickly serve up a well-mixed cocktail with flair from an expanding number of combinations had grown into a welcomed and appreciated social art form, even overcoming a slight setback in 1988 as the subject of a really bad Tom Cruise flick.

HOW TO USE THIS SECTION

In this section I'll show you how to use your home bar to re-create the most popular drinks from the country's biggest and fastest-growing casual restaurant chains. For years now companies have been bottling mixers to make home bartending a simpler task. But you should know that many of the restaurant chains make their own mixers from scratch at the beginning of each business day. So to create the tastiest cocktails at home, you should take the extra time to make all your mixers—sweet & sour, pina colada mix, and mai tai mix—using the simple recipes in the last section of the book. It's definitely worth the extra effort, especially if you're hosting a little bash.

You'll also need some jiggers if you want to mix good drinks from this book. As with any proper cocktail guide, I've listed the ingredients in ounces. A two-sided metal jigger is easy to find at liquor stores and supermarkets, and it's cheap. First find one with 1 ounce on one side and 1½ ounces on the other side. Then you might also get one with ¾ ounce and 1¼-ounce measurements.

In case you don't have a jigger and want to get on with the mixing, never fear. I've got a chart here that converts ounces so that you can mix your drinks using tablespoons and cups. Also, I've conveniently included cup equivalents in the recipes (in parentheses) for all measurements of 2 ounces or more.

½ ounce = 1 tablespoon
¾ ounce = 1½ tablespoons
1 ounce = 2 tablespoons
1¼ ounces = 2½ tablespoons
1½ ounces = 3 tablespoons
2 ounces = ¼ cup
3 ounces = approx. ⅓ cup
4 ounces = ½ cup
6 ounces = ¾ cup
8 ounces = 1 cup

You'll notice that brand names for spirits and sodas are specified in many of the recipes. Usually it's because the restaurant has marketed the drink with those particular ingredients. For an exact clone, you should use the same brands. But, as a general rule, your drinks won't suffer if you replace the Smirnoff vodka, for example, with whatever vodka you've got in the bar. As well, you can use any cola where Coke is specified (such as Pepsi), and any lemon-lime soda where 7UP is listed (such as Sprite), and vice-versa. But try to use Kern's nectars for recipes that require it, and when you shop for cranberry juice cocktail, always go with Ocean Spray.

TOP SECRET RECIPES VERSION OF APPLEBEE'S BANANABERRY SPLIT

The secret to re-creating many of Applebee's drinks is to stay away from the bottled cocktail mixers and make your own from scratch. The recipe for the pina colada mix is a simple 2-to-1 ratio of pineapple juice to cream of coconut and can be found on page 704. You'll be making two drinks here, so have a companion ready.

2 ripe bananas
1 10-ounce box frozen sweetened sliced strawberries, thawed
3 ounces Captain Morgan spiced rum
2 cups ice

1/3 cup pina colada mix (from page 704)

GARNISH
2 fresh whole strawberries
whipped cream

1. Cut an end off each banana—set these smaller pieces aside to use as a garnish later—then put the rest of the bananas into a blender.
2. Add the remaining ingredients to the blender and blend until the ice is crushed and the drink is smooth.
3. Pour the drinks into two stemmed drink glasses—such as daiquiri glasses—and add a banana piece and fresh strawberry to the rim of each glass. Add a dollop of whipped cream on top of each drink and serve with a straw.

- MAKES 2 DRINKS.

APPLEBEE'S BLUE SKIES

TOP SECRET RECIPES VERSION OF

Check this out. The blue curaçao is drizzled over the top of the white frozen pina colada–like drink, then it slides down the inside of the glass with groovy lava lamp flair.

1 cup ice
6 ounces (¾ cup) pina colada
   mix (from page 704)
1½ ounces peach schnapps
½ ounce blue curaçao liqueur

GARNISH
1 pineapple slice
1 pineapple leaf

1. Combine one cup of ice with pina colada mix and peach schnapps in a blender. Blend on high speed until ice is crushed and the drink is smooth.
2. Pour the drink into a white wine glass.
3. Invert the bowl of a spoon just over the rim of the drink. Carefully pour ½ ounce of blue curaçao over the back of the spoon so that it rests on top of the drink. The blue stuff will slowly fall down around the edge of the drink. You can trip out on this for a while, but don't go too long since we still need to garnish.
4. Slice halfway into a fresh pineapple slice and display it on the rim of the glass. Add a pineapple leaf into the top of the drink, if you've got it, then add a straw and serve.

- MAKES 1 DRINK.

APPLEBEE'S PERFECT MARGARITA

TOP SECRET RECIPES VERSION OF

You'll need a cocktail shaker for this one. And if you want to serve it up the same way as in the restaurant you also need a small martini glass. This recipe involves making sweet & sour mix from scratch with fresh lemons and limes following the recipe on page 705. You'll also need some simple syrup to sweeten the drink. That's a basic common recipe requiring two parts sugar to one part boiling water. You'll have some leftover ingredients for an additional serving if you like. And once you taste this, you'll like.

1 cup ice
1¼ ounces Cuervo 1800 Añejo tequila
¾ ounce Cointreau liqueur
¾ ounce Grand Marnier liqueur
1 ounce fresh lime juice
1 ounce simple syrup (from page 700)

6 ounces (¾ cup) sweet & sour mix (from page 705)

GARNISH
margarita salt
lime wedge
olive

1. Put ice in a shaker, followed by the tequila, Cointreau, Grand Marnier, and 1 ounce of fresh lime juice. Add 1 ounce of simple syrup and 6 ounces (¾ cup) of sweet & sour mix to the shaker. Shake well.
2. Salt the rim of a martini glass if you'd like. Spear a lime wedge and olive with a toothpick and drop it in the glass. Pour the drink into the glass through a strainer, and serve the cocktail with the rest of the drink in the shaker on the side.

- SERVES 1.

APPLEBEE'S SUMMER SQUEEZE

For this drink, make the lemonade from scratch to re-create that familiar Applebee's barstool experience. Okay, so maybe it's just familiar to me, and I probably shouldn't go around announcing it. This recipe makes two drinks.

LEMONADE
4 ounces (½ cup) fresh lemon juice (from 2 to 3 lemons)
¼ cup granulated sugar
2 cups water
3 ounces Bacardi Limon rum
6 lemon wedges

1. Prepare lemonade by combining the fresh lemon juice, sugar, and water in a small pitcher. Stir until sugar dissolves.
2. Make drinks by filling each of two 16-ounce glasses with ice. Add 1½ ounces of Bacardi Limon to each glass and fill to the top with lemonade. Squeeze two lemon wedges into each glass, and then drop the wedges into the drink. Put a slice in each of the remaining two lemon wedges and add one to the rim of each glass. Serve 'em up with straws and a smile.

- MAKES 2 DRINKS.

TOP SECRET RECIPES VERSION OF BAHAMA BREEZE BAHAMA MAMA

Be sure to use freshly squeezed orange juice if you want this to be a true cocktail replica. Bahama Breeze bartenders not only squeeze fresh orange juice for these famous drinks, but they also operate a sugar cane juice extractor to produce sweet nectar for other tasty libations and non-alcoholic sips.

½ ounce Malibu rum
½ ounce Myers's dark rum
½ ounce Bacardi light rum
½ ounce banana liqueur
2 ounces (¼ cup) pineapple juice
2 ounces (¼ cup) freshly squeezed orange juice (about ½ of a large orange)
splash Sprite

GARNISH
pineapple slice

1. Fill a 14-ounce glass with ice.
2. Pour all ingredients, except Sprite, into a shaker. Shake well and pour over ice.
3. Add a splash of Sprite on top. Garnish with a pineapple slice on the rim of the glass, add a straw, and serve.

- MAKES 1 DRINK.

BAHAMA BREEZE CARIBBEAN MAGIC

TOP SECRET RECIPES VERSION OF

Prepare to clone another Bahama Breeze favorite. Use fresh orange juice to properly re-create the magic.

1 ounce vodka
½ ounce amaretto liqueur
½ ounce Southern Comfort
1 ½ ounces sweet & sour mix (from page 705)
1 ½ ounces pineapple juice

2 ounces (¼ cup) freshly squeezed orange juice
splash cranberry juice

GARNISH

pineapple slice

1. Fill a 14-ounce glass with ice.
2. Combine all ingredients, except cranberry juice, in a shaker and shake well. Pour over ice.
3. Add a splash of cranberry juice, garnish with a pineapple slice, and serve with a straw.

- MAKES 1 DRINK.

TOP SECRET RECIPES VERSION OF BAHAMA BREEZE MALIMBO BREEZE

A tropical wind of flavors blows over your tongue and soothes like a cool island... ah, just drink it.

1¼ ounces Malibu rum
¾ ounce triple sec liqueur
2 ounces (¼ cup) pineapple juice
2 ounces (¼ cup) freshly squeezed orange juice

splash Rose's lime juice
splash cranberry juice

GARNISH
pineapple slice

1. Fill a 14-ounce glass with ice.
2. Combine all ingredients, except lime juice and cranberry juice, in a shaker and shake well. Pour over ice.
3. Add a splash of Rose's lime juice and cranberry juice, garnish with a pineapple slice on the rim, and serve with a straw.

- MAKES 1 DRINK.

TOP SECRET RECIPES VERSION OF BAHAMA BREEZE VERRY BERRY GOOD

A delicious frozen berry drink that'll make you a verry bad speller.

1 ounce strawberry schnapps
½ ounce DeKuyper Razzmatazz schnapps
½ ounce blueberry schnapps
⅓ cup frozen raspberries

3 ounces sweet & sour mix (from page 702)
½ cup ice

GARNISH
pineapple slice

1. Combine all ingredients in a blender. Blend until ice is crushed and drink is smooth.
2. Pour into a 12-ounce glass, and garnish with a pineapple slice on the rim. Serve with a straw.

- MAKES 1 DRINK.

BENNIGAN'S EMERALD ISLE ICED TEA

Here's a great version of Long Island Iced Tea with an Irish twist that's loved by all twisted Irish.

½ ounce Cointreau liqueur
½ ounce Skyy vodka
½ ounce Captain Morgan spiced rum
½ ounce Jameson Irish whiskey

4 ounces (½ cup) sweet & sour mix (from page 705)
1 ounce Coca-Cola

GARNISH
lemon wedge

1. Fill a 14-ounce glass with ice. Add all ingredients in the order listed.
2. Garnish with a lemon wedge and serve with a straw.

- MAKES 1 DRINK.

BENNIGAN'S IRISH COFFEE

TOP SECRET RECIPES VERSION OF

Time for the ultimate Irish coffee clone recipe from the country's favorite Irish-themed chain restaurant. It wakes you up, takes you down, kicks you around, and looks great with green crème de menthe drizzled over the whipped cream and a nice little cherry hat.

1 ounce Jameson Irish whiskey
½ ounce Kahlúa liqueur
10 ounces hot coffee
whipped cream

splash crème de menthe

GARNISH
maraschino cherry

1. Pour the whiskey and Kahlúa into a coffee cup.
2. Add coffee to the top of the cup.
3. Squirt a big pile of whipped cream on top of the coffee.
4. Drizzle crème de menthe over the whipped cream.
5. Garnish with a cherry on top of the whipped cream and serve.

- MAKES 1 DRINK.

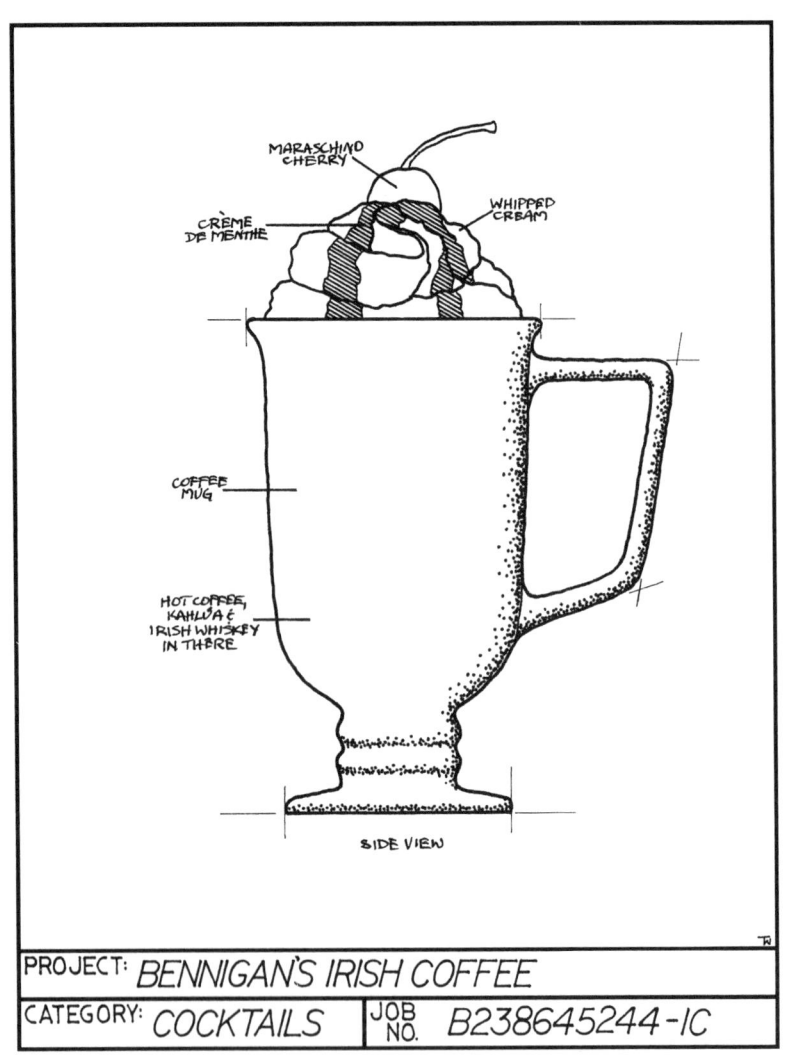

TOP SECRET RECIPES VERSION OF BENNIGAN'S O'MALLEY'S ORANGE COOLER

This drink is an overdue improvement on the old-school screwdriver. Mix this with orange-flavored vodka, add a little sugar and Sprite, and you've got a tastier new twist on a tired old favorite.

1 ½ ounces Absolut Mandrin vodka
4 ounces (½ cup) orange juice
1 packet (1 teaspoon) sugar or sweetener
1 ounce Sprite

GARNISH
orange wedge
maraschino cherry

1. Fill a 14-ounce glass with ice.
2. Combine the vodka, orange juice, and sugar in a shaker. Shake well and pour over ice.
3. Add Sprite on top of drink, garnish with an orange wedge and maraschino cherry speared on a toothpick. Serve with a straw.

- MAKES 1 DRINK.

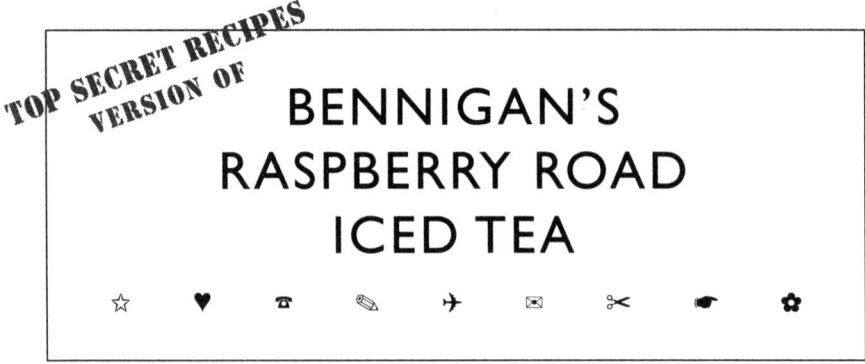

BENNIGAN'S RASPBERRY ROAD ICED TEA

Bennigan's tweaks the Long Island Iced Tea with this Chambord-laced beauty.

½ ounce Skyy vodka
½ ounce Beefeater gin
½ ounce triple sec liqueur
½ ounce Chambord raspberry
   liqueur

4 ounces (½ cup) sweet & sour
   mix (from page 705)
1 ounce Coca-Cola

GARNISH
1 lemon wedge

1. Fill a 14-ounce glass with ice.
2. Pour all ingredients over ice in the order listed.
3. Garnish with a lemon wedge and serve with a straw.

- MAKES 1 DRINK.

TOP SECRET RECIPES VERSION OF THE CHEESECAKE FACTORY CARIBBEAN COOLER

This recipe clones a delicious smoothie-type cocktail using strawberry puree that you make from a thawed box of the frozen sliced strawberries. One ounce of puree goes into the glass first before you add the drink. Check out the cool layering effect.

1 cup ice
¾ ounce white rum
¾ ounce Malibu rum
1¼ ounces cream of coconut
1¼ ounces half-and-half
2 ounces (¼ cup) mango juice
2 ounces (¼ cup) pineapple juice
2 ounces (¼ cup) strawberry puree

GARNISH
whole strawberry
orange slice
pineapple slice

1. Make the strawberry puree by thawing frozen sweetened sliced strawberries. Blend until smooth.
2. Combine ice, rums, coconut, half-and-half, mango juice, pineapple juice, and half (1 ounce) of the strawberry puree in a blender and blend on high speed until the ice is crushed and the drink is smooth.
3. Pour the remaining 1 ounce of strawberry puree into the bottom of a 14-ounce wine glass.
4. Pour the drink into the glass over the strawberry puree. Add the strawberry, orange slice, and pineapple slice to the rim of the glass. Add a straw and serve.

- MAKES 1 DRINK.

TOP SECRET RECIPES VERSION OF THE CHEESECAKE FACTORY KEY LIME MARTINI

It's like eating a key lime pie, except there's no crust, it looks like a martini, and you're drinking it. For the whipped cream in this recipe be sure to use the canned kind with a nozzle top. Estimate about a cup's worth into the shaker with everything else and shake it up real good.

1½ ounces Vox vodka
½ ounce Midori liqueur
½ ounce white crème de cacao liqueur
juice of ½ lime
1 ounce simple syrup (from page 700)
1 cup canned whipped cream (nozzle top)

GARNISH
sugar for rim
whole lime slice

1. Chill a martini glass by filling it with ice and water.
2. Add all the ingredients into a shaker, along with a handful of ice, and shake well.
3. Remove ice and water from the martini glass, then moisten just half of the rim of the glass and dip it into sugar.
4. Strain drink into the glass, and add a lime slice to the sugared side of the rim (so that the drink is sipped from the unsugared edge), and serve.

- MAKES 1 DRINK.

TOP SECRET RECIPES VERSION OF

THE CHEESECAKE FACTORY J.W. PINK LEMONADE

This drink is named after the bartender who invented it over nine years ago: Mr. Jeff Wiley, of the Redondo Beach, California, Cheesecake Factory. He's still there inventing killer drinks, but none have been as successful as this cocktail, which is currently one of the top five best-selling drinks at the chain.

If you don't want to make lemonade from scratch and want something that tastes similar to the stuff used at the Factory, pick up Country Time lemonade. If you've got time to take the fresh-squeezed route, check out the fresh lemonade recipes on pages 562–564.

1½ ounces Absolut Citron vodka
½ ounce Chambord liqueur
6 ounces (¾ cup) Country Time lemonade

GARNISH
sugar for rim
lemon wedge

1. Moisten the rim of a 16-ounce glass. Dip the rim in sugar then fill it with ice.
2. Add the ingredients in the order listed, garnish with a lemon wedge, and serve with a straw.

- MAKES 1 DRINK.

TOP SECRET RECIPES VERSION OF THE CHEESECAKE FACTORY TWILIGHT ZONE

Next stop...this crazy drink. Looking at this list of ingredients, you just know it's going to end with an ironic, thought-provoking twist.

½ ounce Bacardi light rum
½ ounce Myers's dark rum
½ ounce crème de cacao liqueur
¼ ounce Bacardi 151 rum
¼ ounce triple sec liqueur
¼ ounce amaretto liqueur
2 ounces (¼ cup) mango juice

2 ounces (¼ cup) orange juice
2 ounces (¼ cup) pineapple juice
splash grenadine

GARNISH
lime wedge
orange slice
maraschino cherry

1. Fill a 16-ounce glass with ice.
2. Add all the ingredients in the order listed.
3. Drop in lime wedge, orange slice, and maraschino cherry. Serve with a straw.

- MAKES 1 DRINK.

TOP SECRET RECIPES VERSION OF THE CHEESECAKE FACTORY TROPICAL MARTINI

This drink weaves together the sophistication of a martini with the loose fruity fun of a tasty tropical number. If you can't find straight passion fruit juice, pick up a passion fruit blend, such as Mauna Lai Paradise Passion guava/passion fruit blend, and make one of these immediately.

2 ounces vodka
2 ounces passion fruit juice
1 ounce mango juice
1 ounce pineapple juice
½ ounce simple syrup (from page 700)

splash grenadine

GARNISH
sugar for rim
whole strawberry
pineapple slice

1. Chill a martini glass by filling it with ice and water.
2. Add all the ingredients into a shaker, along with some ice, and shake well.
3. Remove ice and water from martini glass, then moisten half of the rim of the glass and dip it into sugar.
4. Strain drink into the glass, add a strawberry and pineapple slice to the sugared side of the rim (so that the drink is sipped from the unsugared edge), and serve.

- MAKES 1 DRINK.

CHEVYS 100% BLUE AGAVE MARGARITA

TOP SECRET RECIPES VERSION OF

If you want to enjoy a really good margarita get to a Mexican food chain and order it "on the rocks." The rocks versions are usually made with top shelf tequilas, rather than the cheaper stuff found in the slushy blended kind. Create your next margarita masterpiece with this bright blue dazzler, or with one of the other happy Chevys clone recipes that follow.

1 ½ ounces Herradura silver tequila
½ ounce triple sec liqueur
½ ounce blue curaçao liqueur
½ cup sweet & sour mix (from page 705)

OPTIONAL
salt around the rim

GARNISH
lime wedge

1. Put a handful of ice into a shaker.
2. Add all ingredients and shake. Pour the drink into a 12-ounce margarita glass (salt the rim first, if you want it).
3. Garnish with a lime wedge on a toothpick, add a straw, and serve.

- MAKES 1 DRINK.

CHEVYS HOUSE ROCKS MARGARITA

This formula re-creates the chain's basic rocks margarita. Nothing fancy, but still good when you use freshly made sweet & sour.

1 ½ ounces El Jimador silver tequila
½ ounce triple sec liqueur
½ cup sweet & sour mix (from page 705)

OPTIONAL
salt around the rim

GARNISH
lime wedge

1. Put a handful of ice into a shaker.
2. Add all ingredients and shake. Pour the drink into a 12-ounce margarita glass (salt the rim first, if you want it).
3. Garnish with a lime wedge on a toothpick, add a straw, and serve.

- MAKES 1 DRINK.

CHEVYS LAVA LAMP MARGARITA

This one gets its name from the look of the Chambord that's added to the glass after the drink is mixed. Drizzled on top of the drink, the tasty raspberry liqueur serpentines in slow-mo to the bottom of the glass. Since the drink is served layered, instruct your designated drinker to stir before sipping, or get a mouthful of lava.

1 ½ ounces Sauza
  Conmemorativo tequila añejo
½ ounce triple sec liqueur
½ cup sweet & sour mix (from page 705)
½ ounce Chambord liqueur

OPTIONAL
salt around the rim

GARNISH
lime wedge

1. Put a handful of ice into a shaker.
2. Add tequila, triple sec, and sweet & sour mix to the shaker, shake, then pour the drink into a 12-ounce margarita glass (add salt around the rim of the glass first if you want it).
3. Drizzle Chambord into the glass, add a lime wedge on a toothpick, add a straw, and serve.

- MAKES 1 DRINK.

CHEVYS THE SUNBURN MARGARITA

TOP SECRET RECIPES VERSION OF

Here's a sweeter margarita for tequila lovers with a cranberry fetish.

1 1/2 ounces El Jimador silver tequila
1/2 ounce triple sec liqueur
1/4 cup sweet & sour mix (from page 705)
1/4 cup cranberry juice

OPTIONAL
salt around the rim

GARNISH
lime wedge

1. Put a handful of ice into a shaker.
2. Add all ingredients, shake, and pour the drink into a 12-ounce margarita glass (salt the rim first, if you want it).
3. Garnish with a lime wedge on a toothpick, add a straw, and serve.

- MAKES 1 DRINK.

TOP SECRET RECIPES VERSION OF CHEVYS ULTIMATE ORANGE MARGARITA

If by delicious you mean Herradura tequila, Cointreau, orange juice, and homemade sweet & sour mix, then, yes, this margarita is quite delicious.

1 1/2 ounces Herradura reposado tequila
1/2 ounce Cointreau liqueur
2 ounces (1/4 cup) orange juice
2 ounces (1/4 cup) sweet & sour mix (from page 705)

OPTIONAL
salt around the rim

GARNISH
lime wedge

1. Put a handful of ice into a shaker.
2. Add all ingredients and shake. Pour the drink into a 12-ounce margarita glass (salt the rim first, if you want it).
3. Garnish with a lime wedge on a toothpick, add a straw, and serve.

- MAKES 1 DRINK.

TOP SECRET RECIPES VERSION OF CHEVYS WATERMELON FRESH FRUIT MARGARITA (ON THE ROCKS)

Chevys is famous for margaritas made with fresh, pureed fruits. While these drinks usually come in blended form combined with house margarita mix right out of a machine, they are much better when ordered on the rocks. Here now is a clone of the most popular flavor, watermelon, made by simply pureeing some fresh melon in your blender. First cut some ripe seedless watermelon from the rind, and then coarsely smash it in a bowl with a potato masher or large fork (this gives the blender something to grab on to). Pour the melon from the bowl into a blender and blend on high speed for 10 seconds or until the watermelon is pureed.

1 ½ ounces El Jimador silver tequila
½ ounce triple sec liqueur
2 ounces (¼ cup) sweet & sour mix (from page 705)
2 ounces (½ cup) pureed watermelon (seedless)

GARNISH
lime wedge

1. Put a handful of ice into a shaker.
2. Add all ingredients and shake. Pour the drink over ice in a 10-ounce margarita glass.
3. Garnish with a lime wedge on a toothpick and serve.

- MAKES 1 DRINK.

CHILI'S CALYPSO COOLER

Ever order one of those expensive specialty drinks off the shiny, full-color restaurant table-stand cards and wish you had a clone recipe? This is one of those drinks, off one of those cards. And here's the clone recipe.

1 1/4 ounces Captain Morgan spiced rum
1/2 ounce peach schnapps
4 ounces (1/2 cup) orange juice
splash Rose's lime juice

1/2 ounce grenadine

GARNISH
orange wedge
maraschino cherry

1. Fill a 16-ounce glass with ice.
2. Pour all ingredients over ice in order listed. Don't stir.
3. Garnish with an orange wedge and cherry on a toothpick. Serve with a straw.

- MAKES 1 DRINK.

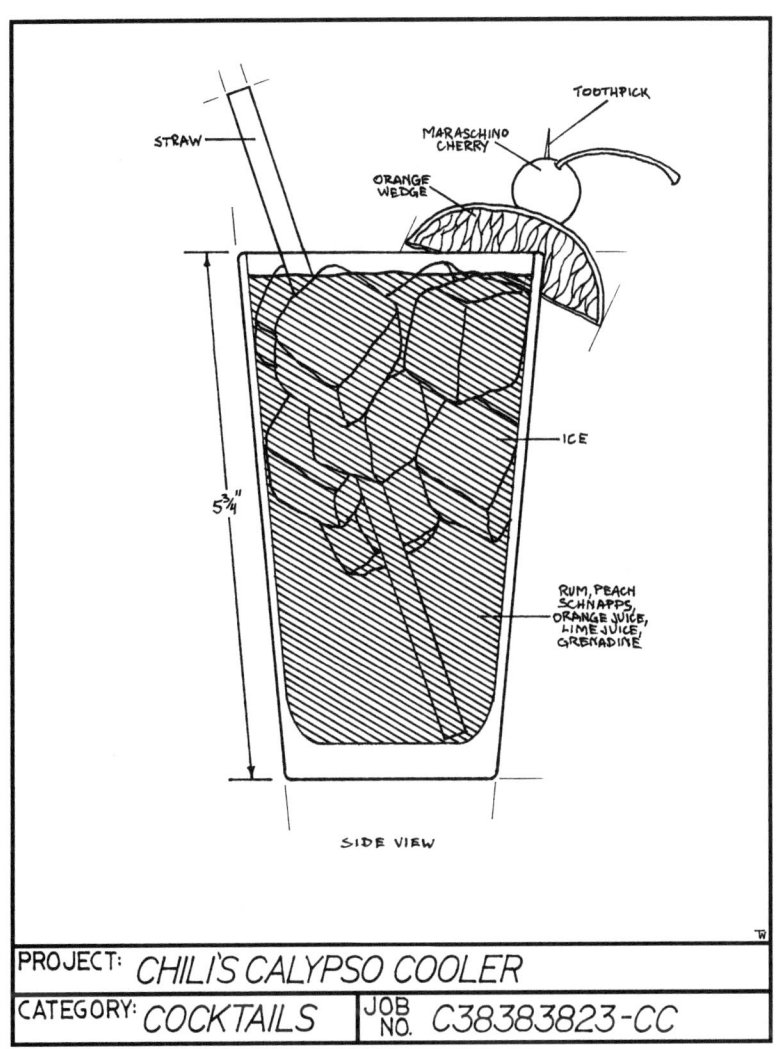

CHILI'S CHAMBORD 1800 MARGARITA

TOP SECRET RECIPES VERSION OF

Meet the drink that comes in a giant 21-ounce "schooner" glass at Chili's. Now go find something big enough to hold it.

2½ ounces Cuervo 1800 Añejo tequila
¾ ounce Cointreau liqueur
1 ounce Chambord liqueur

4 ounces (½ cup) sweet & sour mix (from page 705)
splash Rose's lime juice

GARNISH
lime wedge

1. Prepare a 21-ounce glass by salting the rim if desired. Fill the glass with ice.
2. Combine all ingredients in a shaker, shake, and pour over ice.
3. Garnish with a lime wedge on the rim and serve with a straw.

- MAKES 1 21-OUNCE DRINK.

CHILI'S JAMAICAN PARADISE

TOP SECRET RECIPES VERSION OF

Thanks to Chili's you can catch a Jamaica-style buzz without leaving the States.

1 1/4 ounces Malibu rum
1/2 ounce Sauza gold tequila
1/2 ounce Midori liqueur
1/2 ounce blue curaçao liqueur
2 ounces (1/4 cup) sweet & sour mix (from page 705)

splash Rose's lime juice

GARNISH
orange wedge
maraschino cherry

1. Fill a 16-ounce mug with ice.
2. Combine all ingredients in a shaker, shake, and pour over ice.
3. Add an orange wedge and maraschino cherry on a toothpick. Serve with a straw.

- MAKES 1 DRINK.

CHILI'S MANDRIN BLUSH

The subtle orange flavor combines well with the cranberry juice and Sprite. The vodka combines well with you.

1 ½ ounces Absolut Mandrin vodka
2 ounces (¼ cup) cranberry juice
4 ounces (½ cup) Sprite

GARNISH
orange wedge

1. Combine all ingredients in a shaker, shake, and pour into an ice-filled 16-ounce glass.
2. Garnish with an orange wedge on the rim and serve with a straw.

- MAKES 1 DRINK.

CHILI'S MARGARITA PRESIDENTE

TOP SECRET RECIPES VERSION OF

The Margarita Presidente is Chili's fancy designer libation made from Sauza Conmemorativo, Cointreau, and Presidente brandy. It's served up in a salt-rimmed martini glass along with additional servings in a shaker on the side. The drink comes highly recommended by the dozens of placards and signs dangling from rafters overhead in Chili's bar. I do concur.

This clone recipe should fill your glass around three times, and your head with many happy thoughts.

1 ¼ ounces Sauza Conmemorativo tequila añejo
½ ounce Cointreau liqueur
½ ounce Presidente brandy
4 ounces (½ cup) sweet & sour mix (from page 705)

splash Rose's lime juice

GARNISH
lime wedge

1. Combine all ingredients in a shaker with crushed ice. Shake.
2. Pour drink into an ice-filled martini glass rimmed with salt. Add a lime wedge and serve the remainder of the drink in the shaker on the side.

- SERVES 1.

CHILI'S TROPICAL SUNBURN

TOP SECRET RECIPES VERSION OF

The rums, Cointreau, and juices create an island flavor that anyone will love. This drink is named after its tendency to leave you passed out on the beach before applying sunscreen.

1¼ ounces Captain Morgan spiced rum
¾ ounce Myers's dark rum
¾ ounce Cointreau liqueur
2 ounces (¼ cup) cranberry juice
2 ounces (¼ cup) pineapple juice
2 ounces (¼ cup) sweet & sour mix (from page 705)

GARNISH
maraschino cherry

1. Combine all ingredients in a shaker, shake, and pour into an ice-filled 16-ounce glass or mug.
2. Garnish with a maraschino cherry, add a straw, and serve.

- MAKES 1 DRINK.

CHILI'S TWISTED LEMONADE

TOP SECRET RECIPES VERSION OF

Bars across the country are finding clever new ways to use the growing number of flavor-infused vodkas. Here's one simple, delicious example.

1¼ ounces Smirnoff Citrus Twist vodka
¾ ounce triple sec liqueur
3 ounces sweet & sour mix (from page 705)

GARNISH
lemon wedge

1. Fill a 14-ounce glass with crushed ice. Add vodka and triple sec.
2. Top off the drink with sweet & sour mix.
3. Add a lemon wedge garnish and serve with a straw.

- MAKES 1 DRINK.

TIDBITS

You can also add a splash of cranberry juice to make this a pink lemonade twist.

TOP SECRET RECIPES VERSION OF CLAIM JUMPER ABSOLUTELY ELECTRIC LEMONADE

Tastes like lemonade, buzzes like booze. Use one of the fresh lemonade clones from pages 562–564 for this one, or a pre-made lemonade when on time-sensitive missions.

2 ounces Absolut Citron vodka
1 ounce blue curaçao liqueur
6 ounces (¾ cup) fresh lemonade
    (from pages 562–564)

GARNISH
1 lemon slice

1. Fill a 16-ounce glass with ice.
2. Pour all ingredients in the order listed over the ice.
3. Garnish the rim with a lemon slice that has been slit with a knife to the middle. Add a straw and serve.

- MAKES 1 DRINK.

CLAIM JUMPER BERMUDA SUNSET

TOP SECRET RECIPES VERSION OF

Tropical drinks are everywhere, with nearly every chain restaurant offering at least a few variations. If you're a single guy, though, you might want to drink them at home. Tall, fruity drinks like this one taste great and hit hard, but it's tough to look cool sipping a towering pink cocktail sporting a paper umbrella fruit garnish.

½ ounce Absolut vodka
½ ounce Bacardi Limon rum
½ ounce Midori liqueur
½ ounce peach schnapps
2 ounces (¼ cup) pineapple juice
2 ounces (¼ cup) orange juice
2 ounces (¼ cup) cranberry juice

splash Bacardi 151 rum

GARNISH
pineapple slice
maraschino cherry
paper umbrella

1. Fill a 16-ounce glass with ice.
2. Pour all ingredients over ice in the order listed.
3. Add a garnish of pineapple slice and maraschino cherry on a paper umbrella. Serve with a straw.

- MAKES 1 DRINK.

CLAIM JUMPER HAWAIIAN PUNCH

TOP SECRET RECIPES VERSION OF

It tastes just like Hawaiian Punch. Except this one can really punch.

½ ounce Southern Comfort
½ ounce sloe gin
½ ounce amaretto liqueur
3 ounces pineapple juice
3 ounces orange juice
splash Bacardi 151 Rum

GARNISH
pineapple juice
maraschino cherry
paper umbrella

1. Fill a 16-ounce glass with ice.
2. Pour all ingredients over ice in the order listed. Do not stir.
3. Garnish with a pineapple slice and maraschino cherry speared on a paper umbrella. Serve with a straw.

- MAKES 1 DRINK.

CLAIM JUMPER MAI TAI

TOP SECRET RECIPES VERSION OF

This cocktail requires the homemade mai tai mix from page 703, which should tell you from the start that it's going to be good. Of course you can go the lazy route and use a pre-made mixer, like the one made by Mr & Mrs T. But I've got to say, there's nothing like the smooth, fruity taste that comes from the homemade fresh stuff. If you want to serve your guests a masterful mai tai, take the time to really make it rock.

2 ounces Bacardi light rum
6 ounces (¾ cup) mai tai mix (from page 703)
splash Myers's dark rum
splash Bacardi 151 rum

GARNISH
pineapple slice
maraschino cherry
whole lime slice
½ orange slice

1. Fill a 16-ounce glass with ice.
2. Pour light rum and mai tai mix over the ice.
3. Carefully add a splash of Myers's rum and Bacardi 151 to the top of the drink. These are floaters—do not stir.
4. Garnish with a pineapple slice and a cherry slice speared on a paper umbrella. Cut a slit in a whole lime slice and put it on the rim of the glass along with half an orange slice. Serve with a straw.

- MAKES 1 DRINK.

TOP SECRET RECIPES VERSION OF
CLAIM JUMPER OTTER POP

Relive the taste of blue Otter Pops with your very first sip from this ingenious concoction. If you ever sucked on an Otter Pop as a kid, you'll have a cool flashback when tasting this one.

1 ounce vodka
½ ounce DeKuyper Wilderberry schnapps
½ ounce blue curaçao liqueur
4 ounces (½ cup) sweet & sour mix (from page 705)

splash Sprite

GARNISH
lemon slice

1. Fill a 16-ounce glass with ice.
2. Pour all ingredients over ice in the order listed. Do not stir.
3. Cut a slit in a lemon slice and use as a garnish on the rim of the glass. Add a straw and serve.

- MAKES 1 DRINK.

CLAIM JUMPER ROOT BEER FLOAT

TOP SECRET RECIPES VERSION OF

Kahlúa and Galliano combine to duplicate the flavor of a root beer float. You must try it to believe it.

1 ounce Kahlúa liqueur
½ ounce Galliano liqueur

⅓ cup half-and-half
splash Coca-Cola

1. Fill a 14-ounce glass with ice.
2. Add all ingredients in the order listed. Do not stir.
3. Serve with a straw.

- MAKES 1 DRINK.

CLAIM JUMPER SHARK ON THE BEACH

The fruity layered drink with a bite. Much better than that other drink "on the beach."

1 ½ ounces Smirnoff vodka
1 ounce Midori liqueur
1 ounce Chambord liqueur
3 ounces orange juice
3 ounces pineapple juice

splash cranberry juice

GARNISH
pineapple slice
lime slice

1. Fill a 16-ounce glass with ice.
2. Pour all ingredients over ice in the order listed. Do not stir.
3. Cut a slit in a pineapple slice and a lime slice and add the fruit as a garnish to the rim of the glass. Serve with a straw.

- MAKES 1 DRINK.

TOP SECRET RECIPES VERSION OF CLAIM JUMPER TROPICAL STORM

Board up the windows and tie down the patio furniture, then lay the grenadine and passion fruit juice into the bottom of your glass before adding the ice to clone a Tropical Storm. This is how to make a layered drink that absolutely does not suck.

1 ounce passion fruit juice
1 ounce grenadine
1 ounce Malibu rum
1 ounce Myers's dark rum
1 ounce Bacardi light rum
2 ounces (¼ cup) sweet & sour mix (from page 705)
2 ounces (¼ cup) orange juice
splash Bacardi 151 rum

GARNISH
orange slice
maraschino cherry

1. Pour the passion fruit juice and grenadine into a 16-ounce glass. Add ice.
2. Pour the rums over the glass in the order listed. Add sweet & sour mix and orange juice. Do not stir.
3. Float a splash of Bacardi 151 over the top of the drink.
4. Garnish with an orange slice and maraschino cherry speared on a toothpick. Serve with a straw.

- MAKES 1 DRINK.

TOP SECRET RECIPES VERSION OF HARD ROCK CAFE THE HARD ROCK HURRICANE

This rock-and-roll theme chain's signature drink comes in a tall souvenir glass that you pay extra for, then take home and never use again. If you don't already have one of the tall glasses covered with dust somewhere in the back of a cupboard, you'll have to find another goblet suitable for 23 ounces of fruity, brain-tingling, theme-chain goodness.

1 1/2 ounces Bacardi light rum
6 ounces (3/4 cup) mai tai mix
   (from page 703)
3/4 ounce Myers's dark rum
3/4 ounce amaretto liqueur

GARNISH
lemon wedge
maraschino cherry

1. Fill a 23-ounce glass with ice.
2. Pour all ingredients in the order listed over the ice. Do not stir.
3. Garnish with a lemon wedge and a cherry, and serve with a straw.

- MAKES 1 DRINK.

TOP SECRET RECIPES VERSION OF
HARD ROCK CAFE LYNCHBURG LO-RIDER

Ever try a Lynchburg lemonade? Good stuff, right? This drink is like one of those, but even better, with the addition of Southern Comfort and a splash of Coke.

¾ ounce Jack Daniel's whiskey
¾ ounce Southern Comfort
½ ounce triple sec liqueur
2 ounces (¼ cup) sweet & sour mix (from page 705)

2 ounces (¼ cup) Sprite
splash Coca-Cola

GARNISH
lemon wedge

1. Fill a 12-ounce glass with ice.
2. Pour all ingredients over ice in order listed. Do not stir.
3. Garnish with a lemon wedge and serve with a straw.

- MAKES 1 DRINK.

TOP SECRET RECIPES VERSION OF HARD ROCK CAFE SHOOTERS

When someone at your party yells out that it's time for shooters, you'd better be ready with some good recipes. Here's how the Hard Rock handles a couple of the most popular shooters making the circuit these days. Then turn to pages 674–675 and check out some even more creative and memorable shooter clone recipes from Planet Hollywood that will get your guests grinning.

LEMON DROP

1 ounce Absolut Citron vodka
¾ ounce triple sec liqueur
1½ ounces sweet & sour mix
  (from page 705)
juice of 1 lemon wedge
1 teaspoon sugar

1. Combine all ingredients in a shaker with a handful of ice, shake.
2. Strain into a rocks glass and serve.

- MAKES 1 SHOOTER.

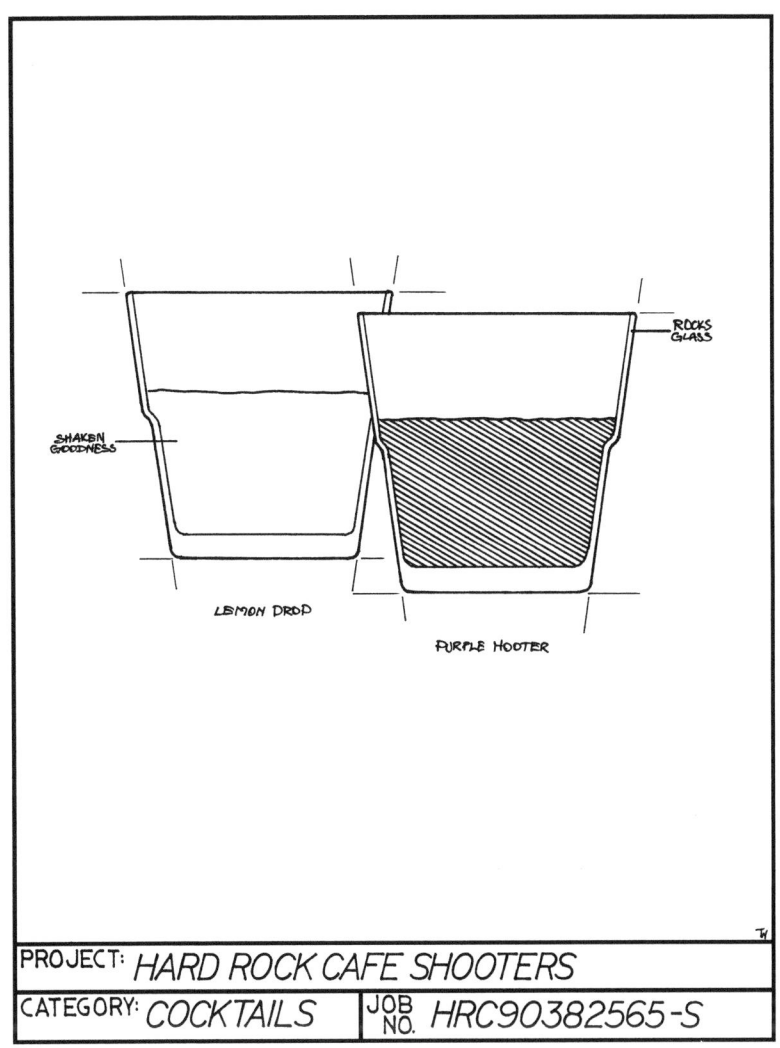

PURPLE HOOTER

1 ounce vodka
¾ ounce Chambord liqueur
splash cranberry juice
splash sweet & sour mix
 (from page 705)
splash Rose's lime juice
splash Sprite

1. Combine all ingredients in a shaker with a handful of ice, shake.
2. Strain into a rocks glass and serve.

- MAKES 1 SHOOTER.

TOP SECRET RECIPES VERSION OF HOUSE OF BLUES EVE'S REVENGE MARTINI

Sour apple martinis are big-time right now. Every bartender's got a version. Most of the time it's just straight vodka shaken up with sour apple schnapps and ice. With a super-smooth, high-end vodka this is a cherished cocktail. Add a couple other ingredients in there, like sweet & sour mix and lemon-lime soda, and you experience the House of Blues.

1 1/4 ounces Absolut vodka
3/4 ounce DeKuyper Pucker sour apple schnapps
1 ounce sweet & sour mix (from page 705)
1 ounce Sprite

1. Put a handful of ice in a martini glass so that it chills while you mix.
2. Add another handful of ice to a shaker.
3. Add the vodka, schnapps, sweet & sour mix, and Sprite to the shaker and give it a good shake.
4. Dump the ice out of the martini glass, pour in the cocktail, and serve.

- MAKES 1 DRINK.

HOUSE OF BLUES HOB BLUE MARTINI

TOP SECRET RECIPES VERSION OF

When making any martini always fill the glass with ice and water and let it sit while you make the drink in a shaker. A glass with a good chill on it is key, whether serving a connoisseur or carefree party animal.

1 1/4 ounces Absolut Citron vodka
1/4 ounce blue curaçao liqueur

1 1/4 ounces sweet & sour mix
(from page 705)

1. Put a handful of ice and some water in a martini glass so that it chills while you mix.
2. Add another handful of ice to a shaker.
3. Add the vodka, blue curaçao, and sweet & sour mix to the shaker and give it a good shake.
4. Dump the ice water out of the martini glass, pour in the cocktail, and serve.

- MAKES 1 DRINK.

TOP SECRET RECIPES VERSION OF HOUSE OF BLUES HOB CRUISER

Here's a tasty blue concoction for those who like the sweeter libations, especially the blended kind with tropical flair.

1 cup ice
1 ounce Malibu rum
½ ounce Midori liqueur
½ ounce blue curaçao liqueur
½ cup pina colada mix (from page 704)

1. Combine all ingredients in a blender.
2. Blend on high speed until smooth.
3. Pour into a 12-ounce glass and serve with a straw.

- MAKES 1 DRINK.

TOP SECRET RECIPES VERSION OF HOUSE OF BLUES MO' BETTA BLUES

If you're into trying tasty new margarita variations, you're into this. It's got lemonade in it.

1 ounce Sauza Conmemorativo tequila añejo
½ ounce white rum
½ ounce blue curaçao liqueur

2 ounces (¼ cup) lemonade
2 ounces (¼ cup) sweet & sour mix (from page 705)

1. Fill a 14-ounce glass with ice.
2. Put all ingredients into a shaker and shake well.
3. Pour the drink over the ice and serve.

- MAKES 1 DRINK.

TOP SECRET RECIPES VERSION OF JOE'S CRAB SHACK JOE MAKIN' ME JAVA

Here's one of Joe's "coffee specialties." It's perfect after your meal, or, for the early crowd, as a morning pick-me-up.

½ ounce Kahlúa liqueur
½ ounce Bailey's Irish Cream
½ ounce amaretto liqueur
1 cup hot coffee

1. Pour Kahlúa, Bailey's, and amaretto into a coffee cup.
2. Add coffee and serve.

- MAKES 1 DRINK.

JOE'S CRAB SHACK
JOE'S YA YA

Silly name, delicious drink.

1 ounce vodka
½ ounce peach schnapps
½ ounce Malibu rum
1½ ounces orange juice
1½ ounces pineapple juice
1½ ounces cranberry juice

1 ounce grenadine

GARNISH
orange slice
maraschino cherry

1. Fill a 14-ounce glass with ice.
2. Add all ingredients and shake or stir.
3. Garnish with an orange slice and maraschino cherry on a toothpick. Serve with a straw.

- MAKES 1 DRINK.

TOP SECRET RECIPES VERSION OF JOE'S CRAB SHACK RED SNAPPER

How about a shooter for whiskey lovers? Whiskey usually isn't my thing, but the amaretto and juice in this one got me all the way through without a shiver.

1 ounce Crown Royal whiskey
1 ounce amaretto liqueur
2 ounces (¼ cup) cranberry juice

1. Add a handful of ice to a shaker.
2. Add Crown Royal, amaretto, and cranberry juice to shaker, shake thoroughly, and strain into a 6-ounce rocks glass.

- MAKES 1 DRINK.

TOP SECRET RECIPES VERSION OF JOE'S CRAB SHACK SECRET PASSION PUNCH

If you have a choice, use DeKuyper Razzmatazz raspberry schnapps or Hiram Walker Razz Attack for the raspberry liqueur required in this recipe. You'll get a better clone than using Chambord.

1 ounce light rum
½ ounce raspberry liqueur
½ ounce banana liqueur
3 ounces pineapple juice
3 ounces cranberry juice

GARNISH
orange slice
maraschino cherry

1. Fill a 14-ounce glass with ice.
2. Add all ingredients and shake or stir until well blended.
3. Garnish with an orange slice and maraschino cherry on a toothpick. Serve with a straw.

- MAKES 1 DRINK.

JOE'S CRAB SHACK SHARK TOOTH

TOP SECRET RECIPES VERSION OF

At Joe's they use Whaler's Great White Rum in this drink, but any white rum you have in the cabinet will work fine in this sweet sipper.

1 ounce Whaler's Great White Rum
½ ounce Midori liqueur
½ ounce banana liqueur
3 ounces pineapple juice

3 ounces sweet & sour mix (from page 705)
½ ounce grenadine

GARNISH
orange slice
maraschino cherry

1. Fill a 16-ounce glass with ice.
2. Add all ingredients, then shake or stir until well blended.
3. Garnish with an orange wedge and maraschino cherry on a toothpick.

- Makes 1 drink.

TOP SECRET RECIPES VERSION OF JOE'S CRAB SHACK SWAMP MOSS

Appropriately named, this green concoction tastes a lot better than it looks.

1 ounce Southern Comfort
½ ounce Midori liqueur
½ ounce Malibu rum
6 ounces pineapple juice

GARNISH
lime wedge

1. Fill a 14-ounce glass with ice.
2. Add all ingredients and shake or stir until well blended.
3. Garnish with a lime wedge and serve with a straw.

- MAKES 1 DRINK.

TOP SECRET RECIPES VERSION OF OLIVE GARDEN CHOCOLATE ALMOND AMORÉ

To make this scrumptious dessert drink the famous Italian chain combines liquid ice cream base with shaved ice to produce a creamy milk shake–like cocktail. We'll just use real ice cream in our secret formula to get this one all up and cloned.

¾ ounce Kahlúa liqueur
¾ ounce Bailey's Irish Cream
¾ ounce amaretto liqueur
¼ teaspoon almond extract
1 scoop vanilla ice cream

6 or 7 ice cubes

GARNISH
Hershey's chocolate syrup
whipped cream

1. Combine all ingredients in a blender and blend on high speed until ice is crushed and drink is smooth.
2. Drizzle chocolate syrup around the inside of a 14-ounce glass.
3. Pour drink into glass, add whipped cream on top, and serve with a straw.

- MAKES 1 DRINK.

TOP SECRET RECIPES VERSION OF OLIVE GARDEN ITALIAN MARGARITA

This is like a traditional Mexican margarita, except there's a shot of amaretto served on the side for added pleasure. Also, the rim of the glass on the real thing is dipped in green sugar crystals usually used for cake decorating. Looks nice. But it's an optional garnish that's skipped if you don't have any green sugar crystals lying around. And, quite frankly, who does?

1 1/4 ounces Jose Cuervo gold tequila
1/2 ounce triple sec liqueur
4 ounces (1/2 cup) sweet & sour mix (from page 705)

1 1/4 ounces amaretto liqueur

GARNISH
lime wedge
orange wedge

1. Moisten the rim of a margarita glass and dip it in green sugar crystals.
2. Fill the glass with ice. Add tequila, triple sec, and sweet & sour mix.
3. Serve with a shot of amaretto on the side, and garnish with a lime wedge and orange wedge on the rim.

- MAKES 1 DRINK.

TOP SECRET RECIPES VERSION OF OLIVE GARDEN STRAWBERRY SICILIANO

Hop aboard this creamy strawberry shake, 'cause Captain Morgan's at the helm.

1½ ounces Captain Morgan spiced rum
1 ounce banana liqueur
¼ cup frozen sweetened sliced strawberries, thawed
1 scoop vanilla ice cream

6 to 7 ice cubes

GARNISH
whole strawberry
pineapple slice

1. Combine all ingredients in a blender and blend until ice is crushed and drink is smooth.
2. Pour into a 14-ounce glass and garnish with a whole strawberry and pineapple slice on the rim of the glass. Serve with a straw.

- MAKES 1 DRINK.

OLIVE GARDEN VENETIAN SUNSET

TOP SECRET RECIPES VERSION OF

This is a great way to use up the sweet sparkling wine sitting on the shelf, and it's better than a mimosa. Olive Garden uses Martini & Rossi Asti, but you can use whatever you want.

6 ounces (¾ cup) Martini & Rossi Asti sparkling wine
3 ounces (approx. ⅓ cup) pineapple juice
splash grenadine

GARNISH
pineapple slice
maraschino cherry

1. Fill a 14-ounce glass with ice.
2. Add sparkling wine until the glass is about ⅔ full.
3. Fill to the top with pineapple juice.
4. Add a splash of grenadine, then garnish with a pineapple slice on the rim and drop in a cherry. Serve with a straw.

- MAKES 1 DRINK.

TOP SECRET RECIPES VERSION OF
OUTBACK STEAKHOUSE CORAL REEF 'RITA

This Outback margarita selection will handily quench, soothe, and ring the bell in your clock tower. A mildly fruity on-the-rocks margarita is powerful ammunition in any home bartender's arsenal of party cocktails. I like tequila. Tequila is my friend. But get to the bottom of too many of these tasty pink drinks and you'll feel like a used piñata in the morning.

1 1/4 ounces Margaritaville gold tequila
3/4 ounce triple sec liqueur
3 ounces (approx. 1/3 cup) sweet & sour mix (from page 705)
3 ounces (approx. 1/3 cup) cranberry juice
3/4 ounce Grand Marnier liqueur

GARNISH
wedge of lime

OPTIONAL
margarita salt (for rim of glass)

1. If you want salt on the rim of your glass, moisten the rim of a 16-ounce mug (or glass) and dip it in margarita salt.
2. To make the drink, fill the glass with ice.
3. Add the tequila, triple sec, then some sweet & sour mix and cranberry juice (in equal amounts—about 1/3 cup each should do it) to within a half-inch of the top of the glass. Stir.
4. Splash a half shot of Grand Marnier over the top of the drink.
5. Add a wedge of lime and serve with a straw.

- MAKES 1 DRINK.

TOP SECRET RECIPES VERSION OF

OUTBACK STEAKHOUSE DON'T KOALA ME, I'LL KOALA YOU COOLER

To make this long-winded cocktail clone correctly you must squeeze the juice from a fresh grapefruit. Bottled juice still works, but this cocktail is at its best when you make it the way the big boys do.

1 1/2 ounces vodka
4 ounces (1/2 cup) fresh squeezed grapefruit juice
2 ounces (1/4 cup) sweet & sour mix (from page 705)

splash cranberry juice
splash Sprite

GARNISH
lime wedge

1. Fill a 12-ounce frozen mug (or glass) with ice.
2. Pour all ingredients, except Sprite, over ice.
3. Pour drink into a mixer cup and then back into the mug, to mix.
4. Add a splash of Sprite, and garnish with a lime wedge on the rim. Serve with a straw.

- MAKES 1 DRINK.

OUTBACK STEAKHOUSE GREAT BARRIER PUNCH

TOP SECRET RECIPES VERSION OF

Get out the citrus juicer and start cranking out the o.j. That's what Outback bartenders do, and what you must do as well to become the cocktail clone master.

1 ½ ounces Malibu rum
¾ ounce Midori liqueur
3 ounces (approx. ⅓ cup) fresh squeezed orange juice

3 ounces (approx. ⅓ cup) Ocean Spray cranberry juice

GARNISH
orange wedge

1. Fill a 12-ounce frozen mug (or glass) with ice.
2. Pour all ingredients over ice.
3. Pour drink into a mixer cup and then back into the mug, to mix.
4. Garnish with an orange wedge on the rim, and serve with a straw.

- MAKES 1 DRINK.

OUTBACK STEAKHOUSE MELBOURNE COOLER

To juice or not to juice? Sure, you could use a chilled orange juice brand and still make this drink tasty. But if you want big giggles and tips, slap on some elbow grease and juice your own fruit, man. That's how Outback makes this great cocktail, and you, I sense, are no less resourceful. I see it in your eyes.

1½ ounces Bacardi Limon rum
2 ounces (¼ cup) sweet & sour mix (from page 705)
2 ounces (¼ cup) fresh squeezed orange juice
2 ounces (¼ cup) cranberry juice

GARNISH
orange wedge

1. Fill a 12-ounce frozen mug (or glass) with ice.
2. Pour all ingredients over ice.
3. Pour drink into a mixer cup and then back into the mug, to mix.
4. Garnish with an orange wedge on the rim.

- MAKES 1 DRINK.

OUTBACK STEAKHOUSE WALLABY DARNED

The menu describes this steakhouse chain's popular fruity drink as a "down under frozen wonder with peaches, DeKuyper Peachtree schnapps, champagne, Smirnoff vodka, and secret mixers." While you don't need to use the same brand-name booze the chain does, you will need to find a can of Kern's peach nectar to re-create the same secret mixer magic.

1 cup frozen sliced peaches
2 ounces champagne
1 ounce peach schnapps
1 ounce vodka

4 ounces (½ cup) Kern's peach nectar
2 or 3 ice cubes

1. Combine all of the ingredients in a blender. Blend on high speed for approximately 30 seconds or until ice is completely crushed and the drink is smooth.
2. Pour into a 12-ounce glass and serve with a straw.

- MAKES 1 DRINK.

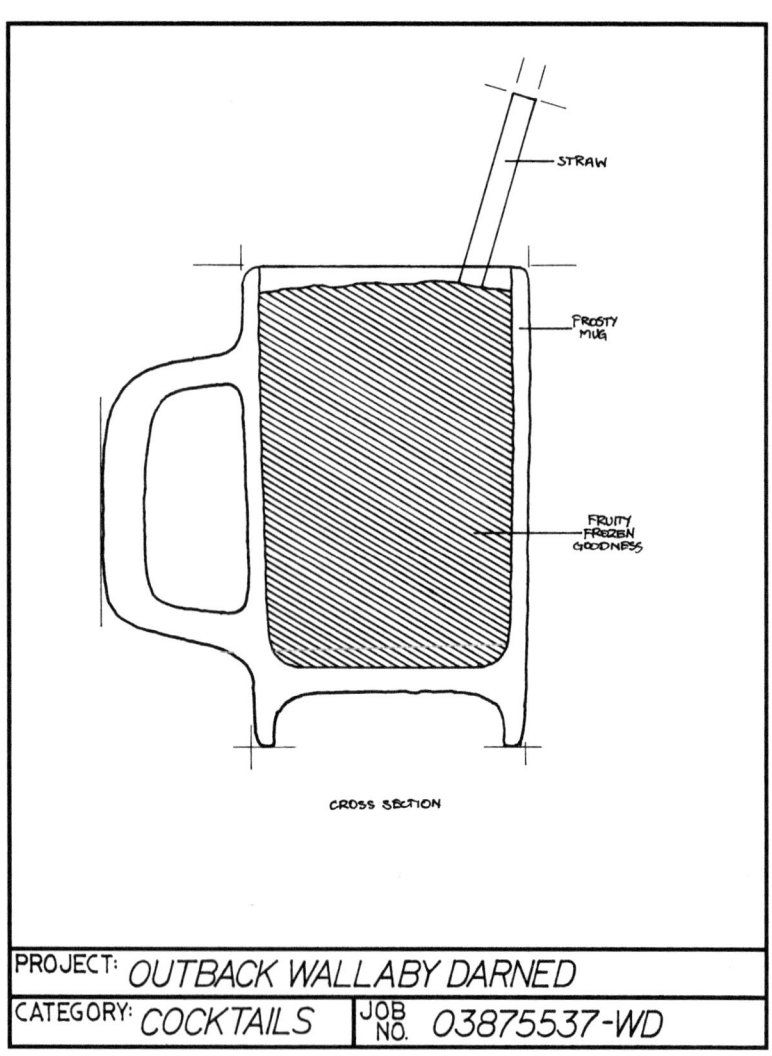

P.F. CHANG'S BUDDHA'S DREAM

TOP SECRET RECIPES VERSION OF

Even though bartenders are instructed to make this creamy drink without adding ice, go ahead and thicken yours up by adding a few cubes to the blender for more of a shake-like drink with the perfect richness level.

¾ ounce Malibu rum
½ ounce Bacardi light rum
½ ounce Myers's dark rum
¾ ripe banana
4 ounces (½ cup) pineapple juice

1 large scoop vanilla ice cream
dash grenadine

GARNISH
maraschino cherry

1. Combine all ingredients except grenadine in a blender. Blend until smooth.
2. Drizzle grenadine around the inside of a 14-ounce stemmed glass.
3. Pour the drink into the glass, add a maraschino cherry on a toothpick, and serve with a straw.

- MAKES 1 DRINK.

P.F. CHANG'S HEAT WAVE

Go from zero to hero in seconds with this easy-to-make, and always refreshing, light rum drink.

1 1/4 ounces Bacardi light rum
1 1/4 ounces peach schnapps
4 ounces (1/2 cup) pineapple juice
splash grenadine

GARNISH
pineapple slice
maraschino cherry
paper umbrella

1. Fill a 16-ounce glass with ice.
2. Combine all ingredients in glass over ice. Shake or stir and garnish with a pineapple wedge and maraschino cherry speared on a paper umbrella. Add a straw and serve.

- MAKES 1 DRINK.

P.F. CHANG'S NUTTY UNCLE CHANG'S FAVORITE

TOP SECRET RECIPES VERSION OF

You will thaw out a box of frozen strawberries, Grasshopper, to make this most delicious drink in a blender, with rums and juice and amaretto. Ah, yes, you have learned much, my son.

1 ounce Malibu rum
1 ounce Bacardi light rum
½ ounce amaretto liqueur
1½ ounces (3 tablespoons) frozen sweetened sliced strawberries, thawed
2 ounces (¼ cup) pineapple juice

½ cup ice

GARNISH
pineapple slice
maraschino cherry
paper umbrella

1. Combine all ingredients in a blender until ice is crushed.
2. Pour into a 14-ounce stemmed glass. Add a pineapple slice and maraschino cherry speared on a paper umbrella. Serve with a straw.

- MAKES 1 DRINK.

P.F. CHANG'S THE POOLSIDE

Got pool? Make drink.

1¼ ounces Captain Morgan's spiced rum
1¼ ounces Malibu rum
2 ounces (¼ cup) orange juice
2 ounces (¼ cup) pineapple juice

splash Sprite

GARNISH
lemon wedge
lime wedge

1. Fill a 16-ounce glass with ice.
2. Combine the rums and juices in the glass, and stir.
3. Add a splash of Sprite, then garnish the drink with a lemon wedge and lime wedge on the rim of the glass. Toss in a straw and serve.

- MAKES 1 DRINK.

TOP SECRET RECIPES VERSION OF

PLANET HOLLYWOOD THE COMET

Arnie, Bruce, Sly, where are you guys going? What's that? To cash in all of your Planet Hollywood stock to buy a dirt bike? Why so gloomy? You still get to share a cool dirt bike. Here, better have a drink. This one's perfect because it's the chain's signature drink and it's really big. It comes in one of those 22-ounce souvenir glasses. You guys probably have a few of those lying around the house, right? Go ask your wives. Oops, sorry, Bruce.

1 ounce vodka
1 ounce Captain Morgan spiced rum
1 ounce Myers's rum
3 ounces (approx. 1/3 cup) pineapple juice
3 ounces (approx. 1/3 cup) sweet & sour mix (from page 705)
3 ounces (approx. 1/3 cup) cranberry juice
3/4 ounce DeKuyper Razzmatazz raspberry schnapps

GARNISH
orange wedge
maraschino cherry

1. Fill a 22-ounce glass with ice.
2. Combine all ingredients, except Razzmatazz, in a shaker and shake well.
3. Pour over ice and add Razzmatazz as a floater to the top of the drink.
4. Garnish with an orange wedge on the rim of the glass, drop in a cherry, add a straw, and serve.

- MAKES 1 DRINK.

PLANET HOLLYWOOD COOL RUNNING

TOP SECRET RECIPES VERSION OF

The impressive ingredients list makes for an equally impressive cocktail. Serve this with a 7-dollar cheeseburger, crank up some clips of bad Stallone movies, and it's almost like you're at a famous Hollywood-themed eatery.

¾ ounce Captain Morgan spiced rum
¾ ounce Malibu rum
¾ ounce Bacardi Limon rum
2 ounces (¼ cup) pineapple juice
1 ounce cranberry juice
1 ounce orange juice

splash grenadine
splash Rose's lime juice
splash Bacardi 151 rum

GARNISH
orange wedge
maraschino cherry

1. Fill a 16-ounce glass with ice.
2. Combine all ingredients, except Bacardi 151, in a shaker. Shake, shake, shake.
3. Pour over ice.
4. Pour a splash of Bacardi 151 on top, garnish with an orange wedge on the rim of the glass, drop in a cherry, and serve with a straw.

- MAKES 1 DRINK.

PLANET HOLLYWOOD MEET JACK BLACK

No, you don't have to love Jack Daniel's to enjoy this drink. But man, it really helps.

1 1/4 ounces Jack Daniel's whiskey
3/4 ounce amaretto liqueur
4 ounces (1/2 cup) sweet & sour mix (from page 705)

splash cola

GARNISH
orange wedge

1. Fill a 16-ounce glass with ice.
2. Combine all ingredients, except cola, in a shaker and shake well.
3. Pour over ice and add a splash of cola.
4. Garnish with an orange wedge, add a straw, and serve.

- MAKES 1 DRINK.

TOP SECRET RECIPES VERSION OF PLANET HOLLYWOOD SHOOTERS

The pressure's on. It's time for shooters and you haven't a clue what to make. Don't worry, I've got your back. Pick any one of these clone recipes for shooters from Planet Hollywood and you'll be tonight's big hero. By the way, it's best to start at the top of the list (Blue Hawaii). See, I told you, I've got your back.

BLUE HAWAII

¾ ounce Malibu Rum
¾ ounce blue curaçao liqueur
splash pineapple juice
splash sweet & sour mix (from page 705)

BUBBLE GUM

¾ ounce vodka
¾ ounce banana liqueur
splash cranberry juice
splash grenadine

GRAPE CRUSH

¾ ounce vodka
¾ ounce DeKuyper Pucker Grape Liqueur
splash sweet & sour mix (from page 705)
splash Chambord liqueur

1. Combine all ingredients for your choice of shooter in a shaker with a handful of ice, and shake.
2. Strain into a 2-ounce shot glass and serve.

- MAKES 1 SHOOTER.

PEANUT BUTTER & JELLY

½ ounce Frangelico liqueur
¾ ounce Chambord liqueur

½ ounce Bailey's Irish Cream

1. Combine Frangelico and Chambord in a shaker with a handful of ice and shake well.
2. Strain into a 2-ounce shot glass.
3. Gently pour the Bailey's into the shot glass. It will first sink, then rise to the top as a floater.

- MAKES 1 SHOOTER.

PLANET HOLLYWOOD SWEET DEATH BECOMES HER

With a name like Sweet Death Becomes Her this drink's got to be good. With four different rums in there, you won't care what it's called.

½ ounce light rum
½ ounce Malibu rum
½ ounce Bacardi 151 Rum
½ ounce Captain Morgan spiced rum

4 ounces (½ cup) pineapple juice
splash 7UP

GARNISH
pineapple slice
maraschino cherry

1. Fill a 16-ounce glass with ice.
2. Combine all ingredients, except 7UP, in a shaker and shake well.
3. Pour over the ice and add a splash of 7UP on top.
4. Garnish with a pineapple slice on the rim, drop in a maraschino cherry, and serve with a straw.

- MAKES 1 DRINK.

PLANET HOLLYWOOD TERMINATOR

Terminator is right. Look at all the different liquors that go into this one: vodka, rum, gin, Grand Marnier, Kahlúa. Be sure to paint the ceiling before you start drinking these so that later you'll have something nice to look at.

¾ ounce vodka
¾ ounce white rum
¾ ounce gin
¾ ounce Grand Marnier liqueur
¾ ounce Kahlúa liqueur

2 ounces (¼ cup) sweet & sour mix (from page 705)
1 ounce cranberry juice
splash beer

GARNISH
orange wedge

1. Fill a 16-ounce glass with ice.
2. Mix all ingredients, except beer, in a shaker and shake well.
3. Pour over ice.
4. Pour a splash of beer over the top, garnish with an orange wedge, and serve with a straw.

- MAKES 1 DRINK.

TOP SECRET RECIPES VERSION OF RED LOBSTER BAHAMA MAMA

If you're going to clone a cocktail from Red Lobster you have to include the chain's signature drink, don't you think?

1 ounce Captain Morgan spiced rum
1 ounce Bacardi light rum
3 ounces (approx. 1/3 cup) pineapple juice
3 ounces (approx. 1/3 cup) orange juice
3/4 ounce grenadine
1 cup ice

GARNISH
orange wedge

1. Combine all ingredients in a blender. Blend until ice is crushed and drink is smooth.
2. Pour into a 16-ounce glass and garnish with an orange wedge on the rim. Serve with a straw.

- MAKES 1 DRINK.

RED LOBSTER BUTTER-TINI FUNTINI

A creamy white martini that's buttery, rich, and smooth. Plus it's a cinch to make.

1 ½ ounces butterscotch schnapps
1 ounce Bailey's Irish Cream
2 ounces (¼ cup) half-and-half

1. Chill a martini glass by filling it with ice and water.
2. Combine all ingredients in a shaker with a handful of ice. Shake well.
3. Dump ice water out of martini glass and pour in drink.

- MAKES 1 DRINK.

TOP SECRET RECIPES VERSION OF RED LOBSTER THE HAWAIIAN FUNTINI

If it's a "Funtini" is it still a martini? Think about that as you're sipping this simple combination of Malibu rum and homemade pina colada mix served up in a trendy martini glass.

1 ½ ounces Malibu rum
3 ounces (approx. ⅓ cup) pina colada mix (from page 704)

1. Chill a martini glass by filling it with ice and water.
2. Combine all ingredients in a shaker with a handful of ice. Shake well.
3. Dump ice water out of martini glass and pour in drink.

- MAKES 1 DRINK.

TOP SECRET RECIPES VERSION OF RED LOBSTER RED PASSION COLADA

Ah, Alizé. The chilled blend of cognac and fruit makes magic with pina colada mix in this take on a chain specialty.

3 ounces Alizé Red Passion
4 ounces (½ cup) pina colada mix (from page 704)
1 cup ice

GARNISH
pineapple slice

1. Combine all ingredients in a blender and blend until ice is crushed and drink is smooth.
2. Pour into 14-ounce glass. Add a splash of Alizé to the top of the drink.
3. Garnish with a pineapple slice on the rim of the glass, and serve with a straw.

- MAKES 1 DRINK.

RED ROBIN ABSOLUT LEMONADE

TOP SECRET RECIPES VERSION OF

Amaretto works its nutty magic to set this drink apart from other cloned lemonade cocktails in this book. Use pre-made lemonade or get up the gumption to make it yourself from fresh-squeezed lemons as described in the clone recipes on pages 562–564.

1 ounce Absolut Citron vodka
½ ounce amaretto liqueur
8 ounces (1 cup) lemonade

GARNISH
lemon wedge

1. Fill a 16-ounce glass with ice.
2. Add Absolut Citron and amaretto.
3. Fill with lemonade, add a lemon wedge and a straw, and serve.

- MAKES 1 DRINK.

RED ROBIN JAMAICAN SHAKE

TOP SECRET RECIPES VERSION OF

More like dessert than a cocktail, really. You won't hear me complain.

½ cup ice
½ ounce amaretto liqueur
½ ounce Grand Marnier liqueur
½ ounce Kahlúa liqueur
2 ounces (¼ cup) milk

1 ½ cups vanilla ice cream

GARNISH
whipped cream

1. Add ½ cup of ice to a blender.
2. Add amaretto, Grand Marnier, Kahlúa, milk, and ice cream to the blender.
3. Blend for 15 to 20 seconds or until the ice is crushed and the drink is smooth.
4. Pour the shake into a large glass, add whipped cream to the top, add a straw, and serve.

- MAKES 1 DRINK.

RED ROBIN SAND IN YOUR SHORTS

To make this layered drink, Chambord is poured into the glass even before the ice is added. Stirring it before serving is not an option.

½ ounce Chambord raspberry liqueur
½ ounce vodka
½ ounce peach schnapps
½ ounce Midori liqueur
½ ounce triple sec liqueur
3 ounces (approx. ⅓ cup) orange juice
1 ounce sweet & sour mix (from page 702)
1 ounce cranberry juice

GARNISH
orange wedge
maraschino cherry

1. Pour the Chambord into the bottom of a 16-ounce glass.
2. Fill the glass with ice, then add the vodka, peach schnapps, Midori, and triple sec.
3. Without stirring the drink, add the orange juice and sweet & sour mix.
4. Top the drink off with the cranberry juice. Serve the drink, unstirred, with a garnish of orange wedge and maraschino cherry speared on a toothpick, plus a straw.

- MAKES 1 DRINK.

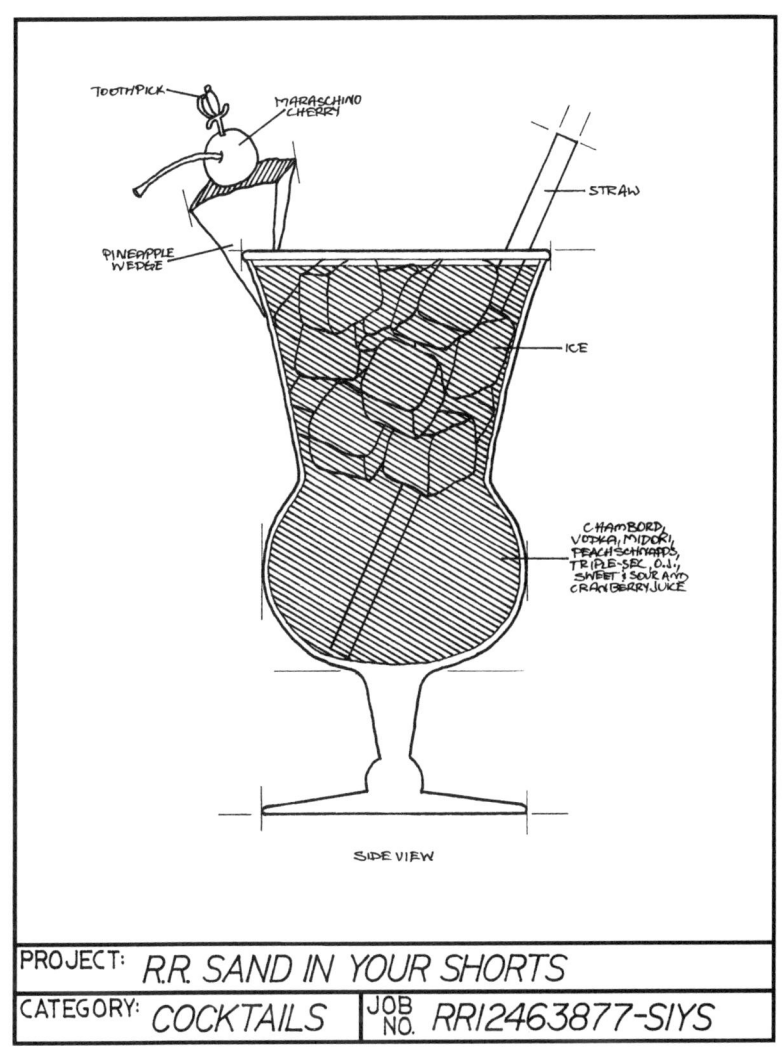

TOP SECRET RECIPES VERSION OF RED ROBIN T.N.T.

This one's a variation on the old-time potent favorite, Long Island Iced Tea. While the restaurant has another version of this drink made with the less-expensive "well" alcohol, this concoction is whipped up with top shelf stuff comprising—as the menu says—"a powder keg of ingredients ... and a blasting cap full of cola." Still, you can use your favorite liquors or whatever you have on the shelf, be it on the top, middle, or bottom.

½ ounce Beefeater gin
½ ounce Smirnoff vodka
½ ounce Bacardi light rum
½ ounce triple sec liqueur

1 ounce sweet & sour mix (from page 705)
3 to 4 ounces (⅓ to ½ cup) cola

GARNISH
lemon wedge

1. Add ice to a 16-ounce glass.
2. Add the ingredients in the order listed, topping the drink off with Pepsi or Coke to the top of the glass.
3. Add a wedge of lemon and a straw, and serve.

- MAKES 1 DRINK.

TOP SECRET RECIPES VERSION OF T.G.I FRIDAY'S BANANA SPLIT BLENDER BLASTER

If you ever crave a banana split, but don't have all the ingredients, mosey over to your well-stocked bar and make one of these drinks from Friday's Blender Blaster selections. It's like drinking the traditional version you usually consume with a spoon.

½ ounce banana liqueur
½ ounce strawberry liqueur
½ ounce crème de cacao liqueur
2 scoops vanilla ice cream
2 ounces (¼ cup) frozen sweetened sliced strawberries, thawed
½ ripe banana
3 ounces (approx. ⅓ cup) milk
½ cup ice

GARNISH

whipped cream
banana slice
maraschino cherry

1. Put all ingredients in a blender and blend on high speed until smooth. You may have to stop the blender to stir the drink with a spoon to help it blend better.
2. Pour drink into a 14-ounce glass. Add a dollop of whipped cream on top of the drink, then add a banana slice to the edge of the glass.
3. Put a maraschino cherry on the side of the whipped cream and serve with a straw.

- MAKES 1 DRINK.

T.G.I. FRIDAY'S ELECTRIC LEMONADE

TOP SECRET RECIPES VERSION OF

Good thing you're wearing aqua blue so this drink won't show up when Dexter over there spills one on you. Fortunately, or unfortunately, this version of Friday's bright blue lemonade cocktail goes down real fast, be it into your gullet or onto a cosmic jumpsuit.

1 ¼ ounces vodka
1 ounce blue curaçao liqueur
4 ounces (½ cup) sweet & sour mix (from page 705)

splash Sprite

GARNISH
lemon wedge

1. Fill 14-ounce glass with ice.
2. Add vodka, blue curaçao, and sweet & sour mix to a shaker and shake it up.
3. Pour the drink over the ice, add a splash of Sprite followed by a squeezed lemon wedge and a straw.

- MAKES 1 DRINK.

T.G.I. FRIDAY'S HAWAIIAN VOLCANO

TOP SECRET RECIPES VERSION OF

Behold, the eruption of sweet, fruity flavors. Okay, that was bad. But the drink's great.

1 ounce vodka
1 ounce amaretto liqueur
¾ ounce Southern Comfort
2 ounces (¼ cup) pineapple juice
2 ounces (¼ cup) orange juice
½ ounce lime juice
¾ ounce grenadine

GARNISH
orange slice
lemon wedge
lime wedge
maraschino cherry

1. Fill a 14-ounce glass with ice.
2. Shake up all liquid ingredients in a shaker. Pour over the ice.
3. Add an orange slice to the rim of the glass, then add a wedge of lemon and a wedge of lime into the glass. Finish it off with a maraschino cherry and a straw.

- MAKES 1 DRINK.

T.G.I. FRIDAY'S JUNE BUG

I know candy. I like candy. And this drink, senator, tastes just like candy.

1 ounce Midori liqueur
¾ ounce Malibu rum
¾ ounce banana liqueur
2 ounces (¼ cup) pineapple juice

2 ounces (¼ cup) sweet & sour mix (from page 705)

GARNISH
maraschino cherry

1. Fill a 14-ounce glass with ice.
2. Shake all liquid ingredients in a shaker and pour over the ice.
3. Add a maraschino cherry and a straw.

- MAKES 1 DRINK.

T.G.I. FRIDAY'S LIGHTS OF HAVANA

TOP SECRET RECIPES VERSION OF

Just because it's tropical doesn't mean it's typical. There's a lot of Malibu rum flowing out there these days, and when it's mixed with Midori and fruit juices you've got a drink only those without a single sweet tooth in them could turn down.

1 1/4 ounces Malibu rum
1 1/4 ounces Midori liqueur
2 ounces (1/4 cup) orange juice
2 ounces (1/4 cup) pineapple juice
splash soda

GARNISH
orange slice
lime slice

1. Fill a 14-ounce glass with ice.
2. Add liquid ingredients to a shaker and shake well. Pour over ice.
3. Cut a bit into a slice of orange and a slice of lime and add them to the rim of the glass. Throw in a straw and serve.

- MAKES 1 DRINK.

T.G.I FRIDAY'S STRAWBERRY SHORTCAKE BLENDER BLASTER

TOP SECRET RECIPES VERSION OF

Friday's gave its selection of ice cream cocktails the spiffy name "Blender Blasters," otherwise known as milk shakes with an attitude. Shock 'em all with this one when amaretto pitches in to help re-create the taste of a real strawberry shortcake.

1 ½ ounces amaretto liqueur
2 scoops vanilla ice cream
2 ounces (¼ cup) milk
2 ounces (¼ cup) frozen
   sweetened sliced strawberries,
   thawed

½ cup ice

GARNISH
whipped cream
1 fresh strawberry

1. Put all ingredients in a blender and blend on high speed until smooth. You may have to stop the blender to stir the drink with a spoon to help it blend better.
2. Pour drink into a 14-ounce glass. Add a dollop of whipped cream on top of the drink, then add a fresh strawberry to the edge of the glass. Serve with a straw.

- MAKES 1 DRINK.

TOP SECRET RECIPES VERSION OF Z'TEJAS Z' BIG STICK MARGARITA

In the southwestern cities where Z'Tejas serves these incredible margaritas, they are truly legendary. The secret mixture is made fresh every day in a freezing dispenser machine with a dirt-cheap brand of tequila and custom-made sweet & sour mix. Perhaps that's the beauty of this drink. It's one of the most potent margaritas around, but with the addition of sweet liqueurs, its strength is well hidden. Even though the chain uses a special machine to make this one, preparing your own clone doesn't require any special equipment. It does take patience, however. Most good things do. But before long you'll be enjoying either a clone of Z' Big Stick with three layers of liqueurs, or a copy of the Famous Chambord Raspberry Margarita, the drink that earns "Best Margarita in Town" awards for the chain on a regular basis. That recipe follows this one.

You can, of course, drink the basic margarita base without the liqueurs, but the added liqueurs give the drink its charm. To create the margarita, you just mix all the ingredients in a pitcher and put it in the freezer for at least 4 hours, even overnight if you can. The cocktail won't freeze solid since there's tequila in there. When it's frozen, you take it out, and give it a little stir until it's the perfect slushy consistency.

This recipe clones the tall, 14-ounce drink served in a pilsner glass with layers of Chambord, Midori, and blue curaçao. The restaurant limits customers to just two of these drinks per visit. Try it and you'll find out why.

2 cups warm water
½ cup granulated sugar
⅓ cup fresh lime juice
⅓ cup fresh lemon juice
5 ounces Montezuma gold tequila
2½ ounces triple sec liqueur

1 ounce Midori liqueur
1 ounce Chambord liqueur
1 ounce blue curaçao liqueur

GARNISH
2 lime wedges

1. Combine sugar with warm water in a pitcher and stir or shake until sugar is dissolved. Add lime juice, lemon juice, tequila, and triple sec and put pitcher in the freezer for several hours, until drink is frozen.
2. When drink is frozen, use a long spoon to mix up the drink so that it is slushy and smooth. The alcohol in the drink will prevent it from freezing solid so that you can easily break it up by stirring.
3. To make the drink, pour ½ ounce of Midori into the bottom of 2 14-ounce pilsner glasses. Add about ¼ cup of the frozen margarita on top of the liqueur. Pour ½ ounce of Chambord into each glass, then add another ¼ cup of frozen margarita. Add ½ ounce blue curaçao to each glass and top off the drink with the remaining frozen margarita.
4. Add a straw and lime wedge to each drink and serve.

- MAKES 2 14-OUNCE DRINKS.

TOP SECRET RECIPES VERSION OF

Z'TEJAS FAMOUS CHAMBORD RASPBERRY MARGARITA

At only 10½ ounces per serving you might think this drink a bit wee. But I assure you, just one of these packs a wallop, and two will get you speaking in haiku. This delicious raspberry margarita, along with an incredible southwestern cuisine, is making this small chain a growing success story.

2 cups warm water
½ cup granulated sugar
⅓ cup fresh lime juice
⅓ cup fresh lemon juice
5 ounces Montezuma gold tequila
2½ ounces triple sec liqueur

1½ ounces Chambord raspberry liqueur

GARNISH
3 lime wedges

1. Combine sugar with warm water in a pitcher and stir or shake until sugar is dissolved. Add lime juice, lemon juice, tequila, and triple sec and put the pitcher in the freezer for several hours, until the drink is frozen. This is the straight margarita.
2. When drink is frozen, use a long spoon to mix it up so it's slushy and smooth. The alcohol in the drink will prevent it from freezing solid so that you can easily break it up by stirring.
3. To make each drink, pour ½ ounce of Chambord into the bottom of 3 10½-ounce glasses—large martini glasses work well for this. Pour the frozen margarita over the liqueur and it will swirl itself into the drink.
4. Add a straw to each drink plus a lime wedge and serve.

- MAKES 3 10.5-OUNCE DRINKS.

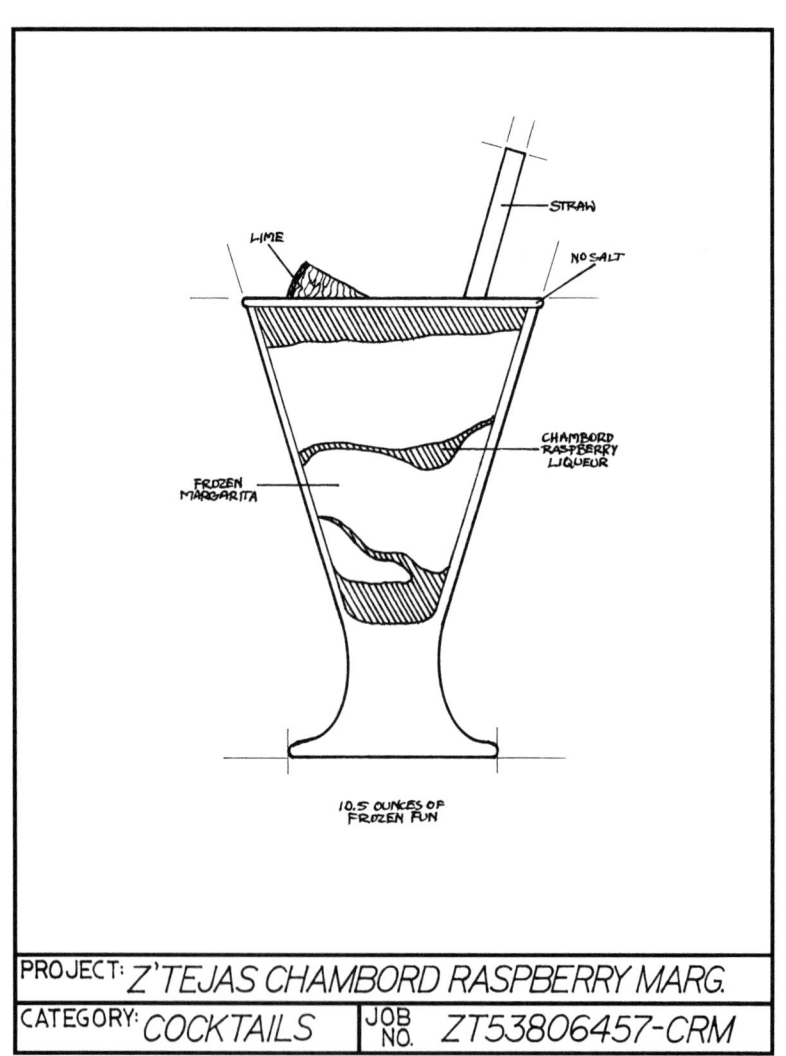

SPIRITS:
MIXERS

BEAU RIVAGE BLOODY MARY MIX

Why make a clone recipe for an obscure bloody mary mix from a Biloxi, Mississippi, casino? Because I've had every major bloody mary mix brand on the market and none can compare to this one. With other mixes I find myself doctoring up the drink with additional Tabasco or salt or Worcestershire sauce. That's sure not the case here. This mix tastes great right out of the bottle, and it doesn't even contain horseradish, which is commonly found in good bloody marys. Make this one soon and keep it handy.

- 1 6-ounce can tomato paste
- 2 cups water
- 1 12-ounce can V-8 vegetable juice
- 1/3 cup distilled white vinegar
- 1/4 cup Worcestershire sauce
- 2 teaspoons Lawry's seasoned salt
- 1 1/4 teaspoons ground black pepper
- 1/2 teaspoon Tabasco

Combine all ingredients in a pitcher and stir well. Combine with vodka to make bloody mary cocktails.

- MAKES 1 QUART.

MARA SIMPLE SYRUP

Simple syrup will sometimes be needed to mix great-tasting drinks that require additional sweetening. Use enough of the clone recipes for cocktails in this book and you'll eventually need to use some simple syrup.

½ cup hot water
½ cup sugar

Stir ingredients together until sugar is dissolved.

- MAKES APPROX. 7 OUNCES.

TOP SECRET RECIPES VERSION OF MR & MRS T BLOODY MARY MIX

Here's a way to clone the famous and very popular bloody mary mix from that couple with a letter for a last name. It's a simple-to-make blend of tomato juice and spices with some prepared horseradish and canned jalapeño juice thrown in for a "spicier, zestier" drink. Mix this with vodka over ice and you've got a delicious cocktail. But if you're not in the mood to get zoinked, this clone recipe is also a great way to kick up your tomato juice, just for drinking straight.

1 46-ounce can tomato juice
4 tablespoons lime juice
3 tablespoons juice from canned jalapeños (nacho slices)
3 tablespoons vinegar
2 tablespoons sugar
2 teaspoons prepared horseradish
¼ teaspoon salt
¼ teaspoon pepper
⅛ teaspoon onion powder
dash garlic

1. Combine all ingredients in a 2-quart pitcher. Store covered in the refrigerator.
2. Directions for mixing a drink, as per the original mix: "Add 3 parts Mr & Mrs T Rich & Spicy Bloody Mary Mix to 1 part vodka, gin, rum or tequila, over ice. Mr & Mrs T Rich & Spicy Bloody Mary Mix is also delicious by itself. Simply pour over ice and serve."

- MAKES 52 OUNCES.

MR & MRS T SWEET & SOUR MIX

This clone recipe makes a little more of the popular sweet & sour mixer than you'll get in the 34-ounce plastic bottles at the store. So now when you crave that frosty margarita or snappy whiskey sour and don't have any sweet & sour mix on hand, you can whip together a batch of your own. Just mix this stuff, as you would the brand-name sweet & sour mix, in your favorite cocktails and party libations.

3 cups hot water
¾ cup bottled lime juice
½ cup corn syrup
¼ cup granulated sugar
¼ cup bottled lemon juice
1 drop yellow food coloring

Combine all ingredients in a 2-quart pitcher and mix until sugar is dissolved. Store covered in refrigerator.

- MAKES 40 OUNCES.

RESTAURANT-STYLE MAI TAI MIX

TOP SECRET RECIPES VERSION OF

Use this in restaurant drink clones that require fresh mai tai mix. To make it you'll need passion fruit nectar, which can be hard to find in some stores. In that case use passion fruit juice that's blended with another juice, such as Mauna Lai Paradise Passion guava/passion fruit blend.

¼ cup orange juice
¼ cup pineapple juice
¼ cup passion fruit juice
2 tablespoons maraschino cherry juice
1½ tablespoons simple syrup (from page 700)

Combine ingredients in a pitcher. Cover and refrigerate until needed.

- MAKES APPROX. 1 CUP.

TOP SECRET RECIPES VERSION OF RESTAURANT-STYLE PINA COLADA MIX

Use this in restaurant drink clones that require fresh pina colada mix. This tastes exactly five-and-a-half times better than any pina colada mix you get out of a bottle.

1 1/3 cups cream of coconut (one 15-ounce can)

3 1/2 cups pineapple juice

Combine ingredients in a pitcher. Cover and refrigerate until needed.

- Makes approx. 4 3/4 cups.

TOP SECRET RECIPES VERSION OF RESTAURANT-STYLE SWEET & SOUR MIX

This is a versatile, fresh recipe for restaurant drinks that require sweet & sour mix. It's so good you'll want to drink it straight.

1 cup hot water
¼ cup granulated sugar
3 tablespoons fresh lime juice

3 tablespoons fresh lemon juice
1 drop yellow food coloring

1. Combine the hot water with the sugar and stir until sugar dissolves.
2. Add lime juice and lemon juice and food coloring. Chill.

- Makes 1 ½ cups.

BIBLIOGRAPHY

Broom, David. *Spirits & Cocktails.* London: Carlton Books, 1998.

Cresswell, Stephen. *Homemade Root Beer, Soda & Pop.* Pownal, VT: Storey Communications, 1998.

Herbst, Sharon Tyler. *Food Lover's Companion.* Hauppauge, NY: Barron's Educational Series, Inc., 1990.

Pendergrast, Mark. *For God, Country and Coca-Cola.* New York, NY: Collier Books, 1993.

Witzel, Michael Karl & Young-Witzel, Gyvel. *Soda Pop!* Stillwater, MN: Voyageur Press, Inc., 1998.

World Book, Inc. *The World Book Encyclopedia.* Chicago, IL: World Book, Inc., 1986.

Wyman, Carolyn. *I'm a Spam Fan.* Stamford, CT: Longmeadow Press, 1993.

TRADEMARKS

A&W, Dr Pepper, 7UP, Squirt, and Hawaiian Punch are registered trademarks of Dr Pepper/Seven Up, Inc.
Applebee's and Low Fat & Fabulous are registered trademarks of Applebee's International, Inc.
Arby's is a registered trademark of Arby's, Inc.
AriZona is a registered trademark of AriZona Beverage Co.
Baby Ruth, Butterfinger, and Nestea are registered trademarks of Nestlé USA.
Bahama Breeze, Olive Garden, and Red Lobster are registered trademarks of Darden Restaurants, Inc.
Bailey's is a registered trademark of R & A Bailey & Co.
Baskin-Robbins and BR Blast are registered trademarks of Baskin-Robbins, Inc.
Bennigan's is a registered trademark of Metromedia Co.
Boston Market is a registered trademark of Boston Chicken, Inc.
Burger King, B.K. Broiler, and Whopper are registered trademarks of Burger King Corp.
California Pizza Kitchen is a registered trademark of California Pizza Kitchen, Inc.
Carl's Jr., Charbroiled Santa Fe Chicken Sandwich, and Ranch Crispy Chicken Sandwich are registered trademarks of Carl Karcher Enterprises, Inc.
The Cheesecake Factory is a registered trademark of The Cheesecake Factory, Inc.
Chevys and Fresh Mex are registered trademarks of Chevys, Inc.
Chi-Chi's and Mexican "Fried" Ice Cream are registered trademarks of Family Restaurants, Inc.
Chili's and Chili's Guiltless Grill are registered trademarks of Brinker International.
Cinnabon is a registered trademark of Cinnabon World Famous Cinnamon Rolls.
Cinnabon, Icescape, and Mochalatta Chill are registered trademarks of AFC Enterprises.
Claim Jumper is a registered trademark of Claim Jumper Enterprises.
Coca-Cola, Fresca, and Minute Maid are registered trademarks of The Coca-Cola Company.
DeKuyper and Thrilla Vanilla are registered trademarks of John DeKuyper & Son, Inc.
DiSaronno is a registered trademark of Illva Saronno S.p.a.
Einstein Bros. and Shmear are registered trademarks of Einstein Noah Bagel Corp.

El Pollo Loco, B.R.C., Denny's, The Super Bird, and Moons Over My Hammy are registered trademarks of Flagstar Cos., Inc.
Entenmann's and Entenmann's Light are registered trademarks of Entenmann's, Inc.
Gardenburger is a registered trademark of Gardenburger, Inc.
Girl Scout Cookies is a registered trademark of Girl Scouts U.S.A.
Grand Marnier is a registered trademark of Marnier-Lapostolle Co.
Hard Rock Café is a registered trademark of Rank Organisation, PLC.
Healthy Choice is a registered trademark of ConAgra, Inc.
Hiram Walker and Razz Attack are registered trademarks of Hiram Walker & Sons, Inc.
Hooters is a registered trademark of Hooters of America.
Hostess Lights, Twinkie, Dolly Madison, and Buttercrumb Cinnamon are registered trademarks of Interstate Brands, Inc.
Hot Dog on a Stick and Muscle Beach Lemonade are registered trademarks of HDOS Enterprises.
House of Blues is a registered trademark of House of Blues, Inc.
Jack in the Box is a registered trademark of Jack in the Box, Inc.
Jamba Juice is a registered trademark of Jamba Juice Company.
Joe's Crab Shack is a registered trademark of Landry's Seafood Restaurants, Inc.
Kahlúa is a registered trademark of Kahlúa, S.A.
Keebler and Pecan Sandies are registered trademarks of Keebler Company.
Kellogg's, Pop-Tarts, Rice Krispies, and Rice Krispies Treats are registered trademarks of Kellogg Company.
KFC, Tender Roast, and Mexican Pizza are registered trademarks of Kentucky Fried Chicken Corporation.
Koo Koo Roo and Original Skinless Flame-Broiled Chicken are registered trademarks of Koo Koo Roo, Inc.
Kraft, Kraft Free, and Catalina are registered trademarks of Kraft Foods, Inc.
Little Debbie and Oatmeal Lights are registered trademarks of McKee Foods Corporation.
M&M's is a registered trademark of Mars, Inc.
Marie Brizard is a registered trademark of Marie Brizard, USA.
McDonald's, Big Mac, Breakfast Burrito, McFlurry, Shamrock Shake, Egg McMuffin, and Arch Deluxe are registered trademarks of McDonald's Corporation.
Midori is a registered trademark of Suntory International Corp.
Mr & Mrs T is a registered trademark of Mott's, Inc.
Nabisco, SnackWell's, Golden Snack Bars, Fudge Brownie Bars, HoneyMaid Grahams, Apple Raisin Snack Bars, Banana Snack Bars, Oreo, and General Foods International Coffees are registered trademarks of Kraft Foods Holdings, Inc.
Orange Julius, Dairy Queen, and Blizzard are registered trademarks of American Dairy Queen Corp.
Otis Spunkmeyer is a registered trademark of Otis Spunkmeyer, Inc.
Outback Steakhouse, Walkabout Soup, and Alice Springs Chicken are registered trademarks of Outback Steakhouses, Inc.

Panda Express is a registered trademark of Panda Management Company, Inc.
P.F. Chang's is a registered trademark of P.F. Chang's China Bistro, Inc.
Planet Hollywood is a registered trademark of Planet Hollywood International.
Planters, Fiddle Faddle, and Screaming Yellow Zonkers are registered trademarks of Planters, Inc.
Rainforest Cafe, Reggae Beat Seasoning, Rumble in the Jungle Turkey Pita, and Chicken Quartet are registered trademarks of Rainforest Cafe, Inc.
Red Lobster, The Olive Garden, and Cheddar Bay Biscuits are registered trademarks of Darden Restaurants, Inc.
Red Robin is a registered trademark of Red Robin Gourmet Burgers, Inc.
Reese's is a registered trademark of Hershey Foods, Inc.
7-Eleven and Slurpee are registered trademarks of Southland Corporation.
Seven Seas is a registered trademark of Kraft Foods, Inc.
Shoney's is a registered trademark of Shoney's, Inc.
Slice is a registered trademark of Pepsi-Cola Company.
Snapple is a registered trademark of Quaker Oats.
Sonic Drive-In and Ocean Water are registered trademarks of America's Drive-In Trust.
Starbucks, Tazoberry, Tazo, and Frappuccino are registered trademarks of Starbucks Corporation.
Sunny Delight is a registered trademark of Procter & Gamble.
Swiss Miss is a registered trademark of Hunt-Wesson Foods, Inc.
Taco Bell and Beef Burrito Supreme are registered trademarks of Taco Bell Corp.
T.G.I. Friday's, Flings, and Jack Daniel's Grill are registered trademarks of T.G.I. Friday's, Inc.
Tootsie Roll is a registered trademark of Tootsie Roll Industries.
Weight Watchers and Smart Ones are registered trademarks of Weight Watchers International.
Wendy's, Chicken Caesar Fresh Stuffed Pita, Classic Greek Fresh Stuffed Pita, and Frosty are registered trademarks of Wendy's International, Inc.
White Castle is a registered trademark of White Castle System, Inc.
Yoo-hoo and Mix-Ups are registered trademarks of Yoo-hoo Chocolate Beverage Corporation.
Z'Tejas is a registered trademark of Z'Tejas Southwestern Grill.

INDEX

Page numbers in *italics* refer to illustrations.

Absolutely Electric Lemonade, Claim Jumper, 634
Absolut Lemonade, Red Robin, 682
Alice Springs Chicken, Outback Steakhouse, 418–20, *421*
All Natural Lemonade, Minute Maid, 564
Almond, Chocolate, Amoré, Olive Garden, 657
Amaretto, Disaronno, 585
American cheese, *See* Cheese, American
Anisette Liqueur, Hiram Walker, 587
Appetizers
    Applebee's
        Baja Potato Boats, 115–17, *117*
        Veggie Quesadilla, 22–23, *24*
    California Pizza Kitchen Tuscan Hummus, 252–53
    Chili's
        Boneless Buffalo Wings, 373–74, *375*
        Southwestern Eggrolls, 384–86, *387*
    Hooters
        Buffalo Chicken Wings, 166–68, *168*
        Buffalo Shrimp, 169–70, *171*
    T.G.I. Friday's
        BBQ Chicken Wings, 447–48, *449*
        Potato Skins, 453–54, *455*
Applebee's
    Asian Chicken Salad, 247–48
    Baja Potato Boats, 115–17, *117*
    Bananaberry Freeze, 500–501
    Bananaberry Split, 602
    Blackened Chicken Salad, 19–21
    Blue Skies, 603
    Brownie Sundae, 249–50, *251*
    Perfect Margarita, 604
    Summer Squeeze, 605
    Tequila Lime Chicken, 341–42, *343*
    Veggie Quesadilla, 22–23, *24*
Apple(s)
    Cinnamon, Boston Market, 120–21, *122*
    Cinnamon Muffins, Otis Spunkmeyer, 203–4, *205*
    Raisin Snack Bars, Nabisco Snackwell's, 314–15, *316*
Arby's
    Jamocha Shake, 525
    Roast Chicken Deluxe, 25–26, *27*
    Roast Turkey Deluxe, 28–29, *29*
Arizona
    Green Tea with Ginseng and Honey, 555
    Iced Tea with Ginseng, 556
Asian Chicken Salad, Applebee's, 247–48
A&W
    Cream Soda, 480
    Root Beer, 481–82
Baby Ruth Blizzard, Dairy Queen, 532
Bacon
    Alice Springs Chicken, Outback Steakhouse, 418–20, *421*
    Baja Potato Boats, Applebee's, 115–17, *117*
    Charbroiled Chicken Club Sandwich, Carl's Jr., 353–54, *355*
    Egg McMuffin, McDonald's, 398–99, *400*
    Junior Cheeseburger, Wendy's, 462–63, *464*
    Potato Skins, T.G.I. Friday's, 453–54, *455*
    Super Bird, The, Denny's, 146–47, *148*
    Swiss Crispy Chicken Sandwich, Carl's Jr., 359–61, *362*

Bagels, Einstein Bros., 39, *40*
  Chopped Garlic, 44
  Chopped Onion, 45
  Cinnamon Sugar, 42–43
  Everything, 45–46
  Jalapeño, 43–44
  Plain, 41–42
Bahama Breeze
  Bahama Mama, 606
  Caribbean Magic, 607
  Malimbo Breeze, 608
  Verry Berry Good, 609
Bahama Mama
  Bahama Breeze, 606
  Red Lobster, 678
Bailey's Original Irish Cream, 583
Baja Potato Boats, Applebee's, 115–17, *117*
Banana
  Bananaberry Split, Applebee's, 602
  Blizzard, Dairy Queen
    Pudding, 532
    Split, 534
  -Chocolate Yoo-hoo Mix-Up, 576
  Cream Pie Shake, Sonic Drive-In, 545
  Crème de, Liqueur, Hiram Walker, 588
  Nut Muffins, Otis Spunkmeyer, 206–7, *208*
  Smoothie(s)
    Bananaberry Freeze, Applebee's, 500–501
    Berry, Jamba Juice, 506
    Strawberry, Baskin-Robbins, 504
    Snack Bars, Nabisco Snackwell's, 317–18, *319*
    Split Blender Blaster, T.G.I. Friday's, 687
Bananaberry
  Freeze, Applebee's, 500–501
  Split, Applebee's, 602
Barley & Pea Soup, Smashed, Dakota, California Pizza Kitchen, 254–55
Baskin-Robbins
  B.R. Blast, 526–27
  Peach Smoothie, 502
  Strawberry Banana Smoothie, 504
  Strawberry Smoothie, 503
  Wild Berry Banana Smoothie, 505
BBQ
  Chicken Wings, T.G.I. Friday's, 447–48, *449*
  Mesquite-Grilled Chicken Quesadilla, Chevys, 369–71, *372*
  Texas Wrap, Chevys, 365–67, *368*

Beans
  Chili's Southwestern Eggrolls, 384–86, *387*
  Margarita Grilled Tuna, Chili's, 379–82, *383*
  Pasta e Fagioli, Olive Garden, 197–98
  Pinto, El Pollo Loco, 161
  Tuscan Hummus, California Pizza Kitchen, 252–53
Beau Rivage Bloody Mary Mix, 699
Beef
  Chili's Fajita Salad, 376–78
  Olive Garden Pasta e Fagioli, 197–98
  Shoney's Country Fried Steak, 217–18
  Taco Bell
    Burrito Supreme, 441–42, *443*
    Mexican Pizza, Taco Bell, 225–26, *227*
    Soft Taco, 219–20, *221*
  See also Cheeseburgers; Hamburgers
Belgian Café, Hazelnut, General Foods International Coffees, 559
Bennigan's
  Buffalo Chicken Sandwich, 344–45, *346*
  Emerald Isle Iced Tea, 610
  Irish Coffee, 611, *612*
  O'Malley's Orange Cooler, 613
  Raspberry Road Iced Tea, 614
Bermuda Sunset, Claim Jumper, 635
Berry
  Bananaberry Freeze, Applebee's, 500–501
  Bananaberry Split, Applebee's, 500–501
  Banana Blizzard, Dairy Queen, 534
  Tazoberry Tea, Starbucks, 517–18
  Verry Berry Good, Bahama Breeze, 609
  Wild, Banana Smoothie, Baskin-Robbins, 505
  See also names of specific berries
Beverages
  7-Eleven Cherry Slurpee, 568–69
  spirits, See Cocktails; Liqueurs; Mixers; Schnapps
  Yoo-hoo Chocolate Drink, 575
    Chocolate-Banana Mix-Up, 576
    Chocolate-Mint Mix-Up, 576
    Chocolate-Strawberry Mix-Up, 577
  See also Coffee(s); Fruit juice drinks; Lemonade; Limeade; Shakes; Smoothies; Sodas; Tea, Iced

Big King, Burger King, 128–29, *130*
Big Mac, McDonald's, 185–87, *188*
Biscuits
    Buttermilk, KFC, 175–76, *177*
    Cheddar Bay, Red Lobster, 209–19, *211*
BK Broiler, Burger King, 125–26, *127*
Blizzard, Dairy Queen, 531–37, *533*
    Baby Ruth, 532
    Banana
        Berry, 534
        Pudding, 532
        Split, 534
    Chocolate Chip, 535
        Cookie Dough, 535
    Hawaiian, 536
    Whopp'N'Wild, 536–37
    Yukon Cruncher, 537
Bloody Mary Mix
    Beau Rivage, 699
    Mr & Mrs T, 701
Blueberry(ies)
    Banana Berry, Jamba Juice, 506
    Cranberry Craze, Jamba Juice, 509
    Wild, Muffins, Otis Spunkmeyer, 411–12, *413*
    Wild Berry Banana Smoothie, Baskin-Robbins, 505
Blue Hawaii Shooter, Planet Hollywood, 674
Blue Skies, Applebee's, 603
Boneless Buffalo Wings, Chili's, 373–74, *375*
Boston Market
    Butternut Squash, 118–19
    Cinnamon Apples, 120–21, *122*
    Creamed Spinach, 123–24
B.R. Blast, Baskin-Robbins, 526–27
B.R.C. Burrito, El Pollo Loco, 163
Breads
    Cinnamon Rolls, Cinnabon, 139–41, *142*
    See also Bagels; Biscuits; Muffins
Breakfast Burrito, McDonald's, 189–90, *191*
Brownie
    Bars, Fudge, Nabisco Snackwell's, 89–90, *91*
    Sundae, Applebee's, 249–50, *251*
Bubble Gum Shooter, Planet Hollywood, 674
Buddha's Dream, P.F. Chang's, 667
Buffalo

Boneless Wings, Chili's, 373–74, *375*
    Chicken Sandwich, Bennigan's, 344–45, *346*
    Chicken Wings, Hooters, 166–68, *168*
    Shrimp, Hooter's, 169–70, *171*
Burger King
    Big King, 128–29, *130*
    BK Broiler, 125–26, *127*
    Whopper, 131–32, *133*
Burrito
    El Pollo Loco
        B.R.C., 163
        Classic Chicken, 164
        Loco Grande, 164
        Spicy Hot Chicken, 164
    McDonald's, Breakfast, 189–90, *191*
    Taco Bell
        Beef, Supreme, 441–42, *443*
        Grilled Chicken, 222–23, *224*
Buttercrumb Cinnamon, Dolly Madison, 149–50, *151*
Butterfinger McFlurry, McDonald's, 539
Buttermilk Biscuits, KFC, 175–76, *177*
Butternut Squash, Boston Market, 118–19
Butter-Tini Funtini, Red Lobster, 679
Cabbage
    KFC Cole Slaw, 178, *179*
Cacao, Crème de, Liqueur, Hiram Walker, 589
Caesar
    Chicken, Fresh Stuffed Pita, Wendy's, 456–57, *458*
    Salad Dressing, Outback Steakhouse, 416–17
Café Vienna, General Foods International Coffees, 558
Cake(s) and Cupcakes
    Chi-Chi's Sweet Corn Cake, 137–38
    Dolly Madison
        Buttercrumb Cinnamon, 137–38
        Carrot, 152–53, *154*
    Entenmann's
        Cheese-Filled Crumb Coffee Cake, 47–49, *50*
        Golden Loaf, 51–52, *53*
    Hostess Lights
        Cupcakes, Low Fat, 62–65, *65*
        Twinkies, Low-Fat, 66–68, *69*
    Shoney's Hot Fudge, 213–15, *216*
    T.G.I. Friday's Fat-Free Cheesecake, 103–5, *105*

California Pizza Kitchen
  Dakota Smashed Pea & Barley Soup, 254–55
  Grilled Eggplant Cheeseless Pizza, 256–58, 259
  Sedona White Corn Tortilla Soup, 347–48
  Tuscan Hummus, 252–53
  Vegetarian Pizza, 260–62, 263
Calypso Cooler, Chili's, 626, 627
Candy
  Butterfinger McFlurry, McDonald's, 539
  M&M's McFlurry, McDonald's, 540
  Reese's McFlurry, McDonald's, 540–41
  Tootsie Roll Midgees, 335–36, 337
  Whoppers, in Dairy Queen Whopp'N'Wild Blizzard, 536–37
Caramel Frozen Frappuccino, Starbucks, 550
Caribbean
  Cooler, The Cheesecake Factory, 615
  Magic, Bahama Breeze, 607
Carl's Jr.
  Bacon Swiss Crispy Chicken Sandwich, 359–61, 362
  Charbroiled Chicken Club Sandwich, 353–54, 355
  Charbroiled Santa Fe Chicken Sandwich, 356–57, 358
  Ranch Crispy Chicken Sandwich, 349–51, 352
Carrot Cake, Dolly Madison, 152–53, 154
Catalina Dressing, Kraft Free, 74–75
Chambord 1800 Margarita, Chili's, 628
Charbroiled Chicken Club Sandwich, Carl's Jr., 353–54, 355
Charbroiled Santa Fe Chicken Sandwich, Carl's Jr., 356–57, 358
Cheddar Bay Biscuits, Red Lobster, 209–19, 211
Cheddar cheese, See Cheese, cheddar
Cheese
  Nabisco Reduced-Fat Cheese Nips, 83–85, 85
  See also specific types of cheese
Cheese, American
  Burger King Big King, 128–29, 130
  Denny's Moons Over My Hammy, 143–44, 145
  McDonald's
    Arch Deluxe, 394–96, 397
    Egg McMuffin, 398–99, 400
  Wendy's
    Bacon Cheeseburger, Junior, 462–63, 464
    Single with Cheese, 228–29, 230
Cheese, cheddar
  Applebee's
    Baja Potato Boats, 115–17, 117
    Low-Fat Veggie Quesadilla, 22–23, 24
    Tequila Lime Chicken, 341–42, 343
  El Pollo Loco Burritos
    B.R.C., 163
    Classic Chicken, 164
    Loco Grande, 164
    Spicy Hot Chicken, 164
  KFC Macaroni & Cheese, 388–89, 390
  Kraft Light Deluxe Macaroni & Cheese Dinner, 80–81, 82
  Red Lobster Cheddar Bay Biscuits, 209–19, 211
  Taco Bell
    Beef Soft Taco, 219–20, 221
    Grilled Chicken Burrito, 222–23, 224
    Mexican Pizza, 225–26, 227
  T.G.I. Friday's Potato Skins, 453–54, 455
Cheese, cream, See Cream cheese
Cheese, feta
  Gardenburger Classic Greek Veggie Patty, 272–74, 275
  Wendy's Classic Greek Fresh Stuffed Pita, 459–60, 461
Cheese, Monterey Jack
  Applebee's Tequila Lime Chicken, 341–42, 343
  Chili's Southwestern Eggrolls, 384–86, 387
  Outback Steakhouse Alice Springs Chicken, 418–20, 421
  Taco Bell
    Grilled Chicken Burrito, 222–23, 224
    Mexican Pizza, 225–26, 227
Cheese, mozzarella
  Applebee's
    Baja Potato Boats, 115–17, 117
    Low-Fat Veggie Quesadilla, 22–23, 24
  Boston Market Creamed Spinach, 123–24
  California Pizza Kitchen Vegetarian Pizza, 260–62, 263

Gardenburger
    Classic Greek Veggie Patty, 272–74, 275
    Fire-Roasted Vegetable Veggie Patty, 276–78, 279
    Original Veggie Patty, 58–60, 61
    Savory Mushroom Veggie Patty, 280–82, 283
Cheese, provolone
    Boston Market Creamed Spinach, 123–24
    Olive Garden Chicken Parmigiana Sandwich, 401–2, 403
Cheese, Swiss
    Boston Market Creamed Spinach, 123–24
    Denny's
        Moons Over My Hammy, 143–44, 145
        The Super Bird, 146–47, 148
Cheeseburgers
    Wendy's
        Bacon, Junior, 462–63, 464
        Single with Cheese, 228–29, 230
    White Castle, 232–33, 234
    See also Hamburgers
Cheesecake, T.G.I. Friday's, 103–5, 105
Cheesecake Factory, The
    Caribbean Cooler, 615
    J.W. Pink Lemonade, 617
    Key Lime Martini, 616
    Tropical Martini, 619
    Twilight Zone, 618
Cheeseless Pizza, Grilled Eggplant, California Pizza Kitchen, 256–58, 259
Cheese Nips, Nabisco Reduced-Fat, 83–85, 85
Cherry
    Limeade, Sonic Drive-In, 490
    Slurpee, 7-Eleven, 568–69
Chevys
    Fresh Salsa, 264–66
    Garlic Mashed Potatoes, 363–64
    House Rocks Margarita, 621
    Lava Lamp Margarita, 622
    Mesquite-Grilled BBQ Chicken Quesadilla, 369–71, 372
    100% Blue Agave Margarita, 620
    The Sunburn Margarita, 623
    Texas BBQ Wrap, 365–67, 368
    Ultimate Orange Margarita, 624
    Watermelon Fresh Fruit (On the Rocks) Margarita, 625
Chi-Chi's
    Mexican "Fried" Ice Cream, 134–35, 136
    Sweet Corn Cake, 137–38
Chicken
    Alice Springs, Outback Steakhouse, 418–20, 421
    Burrito
        El Pollo Loco, 164
        Taco Bell, 222–23, 224
    Flame-Broiled
        El Pollo Loco, 159–60
        Skinless, Original, Koo Koo Roo, 292–94, 294
    Orange-Flavored, Panda Express, 422–24
    Pasta, Dijon, T.G.I. Friday's, 450–52
    Quesadilla, Mesquite-Grilled BBQ, Chevys, 369–71, 372
    Roast, Tender, KFC, 182–83, 184
    Salad
        Asian, Applebee's, 247–48
        Guiltless, Chili's Guiltless Grill, 30–32
    Sandwich(es)
        Bacon Swiss Crispy, Carl's Jr., 359–61, 362
        BK Broiler, Burger King, 125–26, 127
        Buffalo, Bennigan's, 344–45, 346
        Caesar, Olive Garden, 192–93, 194
        Caesar Fresh Stuffed Pita, Wendy's, 456–57, 458
        Club, Charbroiled, Carl's Jr., 353–54, 355
        Crispy, Ranch, Carl's Jr., 349–51, 352
        Fillet, Spicy, Wendy's, 465–66, 467
        Guiltless, Chili's Guiltless Grill, 33–34, 35
        Parmigiana, Olive Garden, 401–2, 403
        Roast, Deluxe, Arby's, 25–26, 27
        Santa Fe, Charbroiled, Carl's Jr., 356–57, 358
        Tropical Chicken Quartet, Rainforest Cafe, 425–27, 428
    Soft Taco, Taco Bell, 444–45, 446
    Tequila Lime, Applebee's, 341–42, 343
    Texas BBQ Wrap, Chevys, 365–67, 368
    Wings
        BBQ, T.G.I. Friday's, 447–48, 449
        Buffalo, Boneless, Chili's, 373–74, 375
        Buffalo, Hooters, 166–68, 168

Chili's
- Boneless Buffalo Wings, 373–74, *375*
- Calypso Cooler, 626, *627*
- Chambord 1800 Margarita, 628
- Fajita Salad, 376–78
- Guiltless Grill
  - Guiltless Chicken Salad, 30–32
  - Guiltless Chicken Sandwich, 33–34, *35*
  - Guiltless Pasta Primavera, 36–38
- Jamaican Paradise, 629
- Mandrin Blush, 630
- Margarita Grilled Tuna, 379–82, *383*
- Margarita Presidente, 631
- Southwestern Eggrolls, 384–86, *387*
- Tropical Sunburn, 632
- Twisted Lemonade, 633

Chillin' Mango Smoothie, Red Robin, 515

Chocolate
- Almond Amoré, Olive Garden, 657
- Brownie
  - Bars, Fudge, Nabisco Snackwell's, 89–90, *91*
  - Sundae, Applebee's, 249–50, *251*
- Café, Viennese, General Foods International Coffees, 560
- Cream Pie Shake, Sonic Drive-In, 546
- Drink, Yoo-hoo, 575
  - -Banana Mix-Up, 576
  - -Mint Mix-Up, 576
  - -Strawberry Mix-Up, 577
- Éclair, Weight Watchers Smart Ones, 109–11
- Fudge Pudding, Swiss Miss Fat-Free, 99–100
- Grahams, Nabisco Honey Maid, 304–5
- Shake, McDonald's, 542, 543

Chocolate Chip
- Blizzard, Dairy Queen, 535
- Cookie Dough Blizzard, Dairy Queen, 535
- Cookies, Nabisco Snackwell's, 86–87, *88*
- Muffins, Otis Spunkmeyer, 408–9, *410*

Chunky Tomato, Mushroom & Garlic Pasta Sauce, Healthy Choice, 288–89

Cinnabon
- Cinnamon Rolls, 139–41, *142*
- Icescape
  - Mochalatta, 529
  - Orange, 529
  - Strawberry, 528
- Mochalatta Chill, 530

Strawberry Lemonade, 557

Cinnamon
- Apple(s)
  - Boston Market, 120–21, *122*
  - Muffins, Otis Spunkmeyer, 203–4, *205*
- Brown Sugar Pop-Tarts, Frosted, Kellogg's Low-Fat, 70–72, *73*
- Buttercrumb, Dolly Madison, 149–50, *151*
- Gourmet Rolls, Entenmann's, 269–71, *271*
- Grahams, Nabisco Honey Maid, 302–3
- Rolls, Cinnabon, 139–41, *142*
- Sugar Bagels, Einstein Bros., 42–43
- Sweet Rolls, Raisin, Entenmann's, 266–68, *268*

Citrus Squeeze, Jamba Juice, 507, *508*

Claim Jumper
- Absolutely Electric Lemonade, 634
- Bermuda Sunset, 635
- Hawaiian Punch, 636
- Mai Tai, 637
- Otter Pop, 638
- Root Beer Float, 639
- Shark on the Beach, 640
- Tropical Storm, 641

Classic Chicken Burrito, El Pollo Loco, 164

Classic Greek, *See* Greek, Classic

Coca-Cola, 483–85, *486*

Cocktails
- Applebee's
  - Bananaberry Split, 602
  - Blue Skies, 603
  - Perfect Margarita, 604
  - Summer Squeeze, 605
- Bahama Breeze
  - Bahama Mama, 606
  - Caribbean Magic, 607
  - Malimbo Breeze, 608
  - Verry Berry Good, 609
- Bennigan's
  - Emerald Isle Iced Tea, 610
  - Irish Coffee, 611, *612*
  - O'Malley's Orange Cooler, 613
  - Raspberry Road Iced Tea, 614
- The Cheesecake Factory
  - Caribbean Cooler, 615
  - J.W. Pink Lemonade, 617
  - Key Lime Martini, 616
  - Tropical Martini, 619
  - Twilight Zone, 618

Chevys
   House Rocks Margarita, 621
   Lava Lamp Margarita, 622
   100% Blue Agave Margarita, 620
   The Sunburn Margarita, 623
   Ultimate Orange Margarita, 624
   Watermelon Fresh Fruit Margarita (On the Rocks), 625
Chili's
   Calypso Cooler, 626, *627*
   Chambord 1800 Margarita, 628
   Jamaican Paradise, 629
   Mandrin Blush, 630
   Margarita Presidente, 631
   Tropical Sunburn, 632
   Twisted Lemonade, 633
Claim Jumper
   Absolutely Electric Lemonade, 634
   Bermuda Sunset, 635
   Hawaiian Punch, 636
   Mai Tai, 637
   Otter Pop, 638
   Root Beer Float, 639
   Shark on the Beach, 640
   Tropical Storm, 641
Hard Rock Cafe
   The Hard Rock Hurricane, 642
   Lemon Drop Shooter, 644, *645*
   Lynchburg Lo-Rider, 643
   Purple Hooter Shooter, *645*, 646
House of Blues
   Eve's Revenge Martini, 647
   HOB Blue Martini, 648
   HOB Cruiser, 649
   Mo' Betta Blues, 650
Joe's Crab Shack
   Joe Makin' Me Java, 651
   Joe's Ya Ya, 652
   Red Snapper, 653
   Secret Passion Punch, 654
   Shark Tooth, 655
   Swamp Moss, 656
Olive Garden
   Chocolate Almond Amoré, 657
   Italian Margarita, 658
   Strawberry Siciliano, 659
   Venetian Sunset, 660
Outback Steakhouse
   Coral Reef 'Rita, 661
   Don't Koala Me, I'll Koala You Cooler, 662
   Great Barrier Punch, 663
   Melbourne Cooler, 664
   Wallaby Darned, 665, *666*
P.F. Chang's
   Buddha's Dream, 667
   Heat Wave, 668
   Nutty Uncle Chang's Favorite, 669
   The Poolside, 670
Planet Hollywood
   Blue Hawaii Shooter, 674
   Bubble Gum Shooter, 674
   The Comet, 671
   Cool Running, 672
   Grape Crush Shooter, 674
   Meet Jack Black, 673
   Peanut Butter & Jelly Shooter, 675
   Sweet Death Becomes Her, 676
   Terminator, 677
Red Lobster
   Bahama Mama, 678
   Butter-Tini Funtini, 679
   The Hawaiian Funtini, 680
   Red Passion Colada, 681
Red Robin
   Absolut Lemonade, 682
   Jamaican Shake, 683
   Sand in Your Shorts, 684, *685*
   T.N.T., 686
T.G.I. Friday's
   Banana Split Blender Blaster, 687
   Electric Lemonade, 688
   Hawaiian Volcano, 689
   June Bug, 690
   Lights of Havana, 691
   Strawberry Shortcake Blender Blaster, 692
Z'Tejas
   Famous Chambord Raspberry Margarita, 695, *696*
   Z'Big Stick Margarita, 693–94
Coconut Cream Pie Shake, Sonic Drive-In, 546–47
Cod, Nantucket Baked, Red Lobster, 97–98
Coffee Cake, Cheese-Filled Crumb, Entenmann's, 47–49, *50*
Coffee(s)
   Bennigan's Irish, 611, *612*
   General Foods International Coffees
      Café Vienna, 558
      French Vanilla Café, 559
      Hazelnut Belgian Café, 559
      Suisse Mocha, 560
      Viennese Chocolate Café, 560

Coffee(s) (cont.)
    Joe's Crab Shack Joe Makin' Me Java, 651
    Kahlúa Liqueur, 594
    Starbucks Frozen Frappuccino, 548, *549*
        Caramel, 550
        Mocha, 550
Cole Slaw, KFC, 178, *179*
Comet, The, Planet Hollywood, 671
Cookie Dough, Chocolate Chip, Blizzard, Dairy Queen, 535
Cookies
    Entenmann's Oatmeal Raisin, 54–55, *56*
    Girl Scout Cookies Lemon Pastry Cremes, 284–86
    Keebler Pecan Sandies, 290–91, *291*
    Little Debbie Oatmeal Delights, 298–99, *300*
    Nabisco Old Fashion Ginger Snaps, 307–8, *309*
    Nabisco Oreo, 310–12, *313*
        McFlurry, McDonald's, 540
        Shake, Jack in the Box, 538
    Nabisco Snackwell's Chocolate Chip, 86–87, *88*
Cool Running, Planet Hollywood, 672
Coral Reef 'Rita, Outback Steakhouse, 661
Corn
    Cake, Sweet, Chi-Chi's, 137–38
    White, Tortilla Soup, Sedona, California Pizza Kitchen, 347–48
    See also Popcorn
Country Fried Steak, Shoney's, 217–18
Crackers, Nabisco
    Cheese Nips, 83–85, *85*
    Honey Maid Grahams, 301–5, *306*
Cranberry
    Craze, Jamba Juice, 509
    Iced Tea, Snapple, 570, 572
Cream Cheese
    Einstein Bros. Shmear
        Jalapeño Salsa, 157
        Maple Walnut Raisin, 157–58
        Roasted Garlic, 155–56
        Strawberry, 156
    Entenmann's Cheese-Filled Crumb Coffee Cake, 47–49, *50*
    Olive Garden Tiramisu, 199–202, *201*
    T.G.I. Friday's Fat-Free Cheesecake, 103–5, *105*
Creamed Spinach, Boston Market, 123–24
Cream Pie Shakes, Sonic Drive-In
    Banana, 545
    Chocolate, 546
    Coconut, 546–47
    Strawberry, 547
Cream Soda, A&W, 480
Crème
    de Banana Liqueur, Hiram Walker, 588
    de Cacao Liqueur, Hiram Walker, 589
    de Strawberry Liqueur, Hiram Walker, 591
Crispy Chicken Sandwich, Ranch, Carl's Jr., 349–51, *352*
Crumb Coffee Cake, Cheese-Filled, Entenmann's, 47–49, *50*
Cupcakes, *See* Cake(s) and Cupcakes
Dairy Queen Blizzard, 531–37, *533*
    Baby Ruth, 532
    Banana
        Berry, 534
        Pudding, 532
        Split, 534
    Chocolate Chip, 535
        Cookie Dough, 535
    Hawaiian, 536
    Whopp'N'Wild, 536–37
    Yukon Cruncher, 537
Dakota Smashed Pea & Barley Soup, California Pizza Kitchen, 254–55
DeKuyper Thrilla Vanilla French Vanilla Liqueur, 584
Denny's
    Moons Over My Hammy, 143–44, *145*
    The Super Bird, 146–47, *148*
Diet Lemon Iced Tea, Snapple, 570, 572
Dijon Chicken Pasta, T.G.I. Friday's, 450–52
Disaronno Amaretto, 585
Dolly Madison
    Buttercrumb Cinnamon, 149–50, *151*
    Carrot Cake, 152–53, *154*
Don't Koala Me, I'll Koala You Cooler, Outback Steakhouse, 662
Dressing, *See* Salad Dressing
Éclair, Chocolate, Weight Watchers Smart Ones, 109–11
Eggplant, Grilled, Cheeseless Pizza, California Pizza Kitchen, 256–58, *259*
Eggrolls, Southwestern, Chili's, 384–86, *387*
Egg(s)
    McMuffin, McDonald's, 398–99, *400*
    Moons Over My Hammy, Denny's, 143–44, *145*

Einstein Bros.
  Bagels, 39, *40*
    Chopped Garlic, 44
    Chopped Onion, 45
    Cinnamon Sugar, 42–43
    Everything, 45–46
    Jalapeño, 43–44
    Plain, 41–42
  Cream Cheese Shmear
    Jalapeño Salsa, 157
    Maple Walnut Raisin, 157–58
    Roasted Garlic, 155–56
    Strawberry, 156
Electric Lemonade, T.G.I. Friday's, 688
El Pollo Loco
  Burrito
    B.R.C., 163
    Classic Chicken, 164
    Loco Grande, 164
    Spicy Hot Chicken, 164
  Flame-Broiled Chicken, 159–60
  Pinto Beans, 161
  Salsa, 57
  Spanish Rice, 162
Emerald Isle Iced Tea, Bennigan's, 610
Entenmann's
  Cheese-Filled Crumb Coffee Cake, 47–49, *50*
  Cinnamon Raisin Sweet Rolls, 266–68, *268*
  Golden Loaf, 51–52, *53*
  Gourmet Cinnamon Rolls, 269–71, *271*
  Oatmeal Raisin Cookies, 54–55, *56*
Everything Bagels, Einstein Bros., 45–46
Eve's Revenge Martini, House of Blues, 647
Fagioli, Pasta e, Olive Garden, 197–98
Fajita Salad, Chili's, 376–78
Famous Chambord Raspberry Margarita, Z'Tejas, 695, *696*
Fat grams, 237–44
Fat of the Land, The (Fumento), 240
Fettucine Alfredo, Olive Garden, 404–5
Fiddle Faddle, Planters, 320–21, *322*
Fire-Roasted Vegetable Veggie Patty, Gardenburger, 276–78, *279*
Fish, *See names of fish*
Flame-Broiled Chicken
  El Pollo Loco, 159–60
  Skinless, Original, Koo Koo Roo, 292–94, *294*
Frappuccino, Frozen, Starbucks, 548, *549*
  Caramel, 550
  Mocha, 550
Freckled Lemonade, Red Robin, 566
French Vanilla
  Café, General Foods International Coffees, 559
  Liqueur, Thrilla Vanilla, DeKuyper, 584
Fresh Salsa, Chevys, 264–66
Fresh Stuffed Pita, Wendy's
  Chicken, 456–57, *458*
  Classic Greek, 459–60, *461*
Frosted Brown Sugar Cinnamon Pop-Tarts, Kellogg's Low-Fat, 70–72, *73*
Frosty, Wendy's
  frozen dessert version, 231
  shake version, 551
Frozen Frappuccino, Starbucks, 548, *549*
  Caramel, 550
  Mocha, 550
Fruit, *See* Fruit juice drinks; *names of specific fruits*
Fruit juice drinks
  Hawaiian Punch Fruit Juicy Red, 561
  Red Robin Strawberry Ecstacy, 567
  Sunny Delight, 573, *574*
  See also Smoothies
Fudge
  Brownie Bars, Nabisco Snackwell's, 89–90, *91*
  Chocolate, Pudding, Swiss Miss Fat-Free, 99–100
  Hot, Cake, Shoney's, 213–15, *216*
Gardenburger
  Classic Greek Veggie Patty, 272–74, *275*
  Fire-Roasted Vegetable Veggie Patty, 276–78, *279*
  Original Veggie Patty, 58–60, *61*
  Savory Mushroom Veggie Patty, 280–82, *283*
Garlic
  Chopped, Bagels, Einstein Bros., 44
  Chunky Tomato & Mushroom Pasta Sauce, Healthy Choice, 288–89
  Mashed Potatoes, Chevys, 363–64
  Roasted, Cream Cheese Shmear, Einstein Bros., 155–56
General Foods International Coffees
  Café Vienna, 558
  French Vanilla Café, 559
  Hazelnut Belgian Café, 559
  Suisse Mocha, 560
  Viennese Chocolate Café, 560
Ginger Snaps, Old Fashion, Nabisco, 307–8, *309*

721

Girl Scout Cookies Lemon Pastry Cremes, 284–86
Golden
   Loaf, Entenmann's, 51–52, *53*
   Snack Bars, Nabisco Snackwell's, 92–93, *94*
Gourmet Cinnamon Rolls, Entenmann's, 269–71, *271*
Grahams, Nabisco Honey Maid, 301–5, *306*
Grand Marnier Liqueur, 586
Grape Crush Shooter, Planet Hollywood, 674
Gravy, Mashed Potatoes &, KFC, 180–81
Great Barrier Punch, Outback Steakhouse, 663
Greek, Classic
   Fresh Stuffed Pita, Wendy's, 459–60, *461*
   Veggie Patty, Gardenburger, 272–74, *275*
Grilled
   Chicken Burrito, Taco Bell, 222–23, *224*
   Eggplant Cheeseless Pizza, California Pizza Kitchen, 256–58, *259*
   Tuna, Margarita, Chili's, 379–82, *383*
Groovy Smoothie, Red Robin, 516
Ham
   Moons Over My Hammy, Denny's, 143–44, *145*
Hamburgers
   Burger King
     Big King, 128–29, *130*
     Whopper, 131–32, *133*
   McDonald's
     Arch Deluxe, 394–96, *397*
     Big Mac, 185–87, *188*
   Sonic Drive-In
     Hickory, 435–36, *437*
     Jalapeño Burger, 438–39, *440*
     No. 1, 432–33, *434*
   See also Cheeseburgers
Hard Rock Cafe
   The Hard Rock Hurricane, 642
   Lynchburg Lo-Rider, 643
   Shooters
     Lemon Drop, 644, *645*
     Purple Hooter, *645*, 646
Hard Rock Hurricane, The, Hard Rock Cafe, 642
Hawaiian
   Blizzard, Dairy Queen, 536
   Funtini, The, Red Lobster, 680

Punch, Claim Jumper, 636
Volcano, T.G.I. Friday's, 689
Hawaiian Punch Fruit Juicy Red, 561
Hazelnut Belgian Café, General Foods International Coffees, 559
Healthy Choice
   Chunky Tomato, Mushroom & Garlic Pasta Sauce, 288–89
   Traditional Pasta Sauce, 287
Heat Wave, P.F. Chang's, 668
Hickory Burger, Sonic Drive-In, 435–36, *437*
Hiram Walker
   Anisette Liqueur, 587
   Crème de Banana Liqueur, 588
   Crème de Cacao Liqueur, 589
   Crème de Menthe Liqueur, 590
   Crème de Strawberry Liqueur, 591
   Razz Attack Raspberry Schnapps, 592
   Root Beer Schnapps, 593
HOB Blue Martini, House of Blues, 648
HOB Cruiser, House of Blues, 649
Honey Grahams, Nabisco Honey Maid, 301–2
Honey Maid Grahams, Nabisco, 301–5, *306*
Hooters
   Buffalo Chicken Wings, 166–68, *168*
   Buffalo Shrimp, 169–70, *171*
Hostess Lights Low-Fat
   Cupcakes, 62–65, *65*
   Twinkies, 66–68, *69*
Hot Dog on a Stick Muscle Beach Lemonade, 562, *563*
Hot Fudge Cake, Shoney's, 213–15, *216*
House of Blues
   Eve's Revenge Martini, 647
   HOB Blue Martini, 648
   HOB Cruiser, 649
   Mo' Betta Blues, 650
House Rocks Margarita, Chevys, 621
Hummus, Tuscan, California Pizza Kitchen, 252–53
Ice Cream
   Applebee's Brownie Sundae, 249–50, *251*
   Chi-Chi's Mexican "Fried," 134–35, *136*
   Wendy's Frosty, 231
   See also Shakes
Iced Tea, See Tea, Iced
Icescape, Cinnabon
   Mochalatta, 529
   Orange, 529

Strawberry, 528
Irish
    Coffee, Bennigan's, 611, *612*
    Cream, Original, Bailey's, 583
Italian
    Dressing, Viva, Seven Seas, 333–34
    Margarita, Olive Garden, 658
    Salad Dressing, Olive Garden, 195–96
Jack Daniel's Grill Salmon, T.G.I. Friday's, 106–8
Jack in the Box Oreo Cookie Shake, 538
Jalapeño
    Bagels, Einstein Bros., 43–44
    Burger, Sonic Drive-In, 438–39, *440*
    Salsa Cream Cheese Shmear, Einstein Bros., 157
Jamaican
    Paradise, Chili's, 629
    Shake, Red Robin, 683
Jamba Juice
    Banana Berry, 506
    Citrus Squeeze, 507, *508*
    Cranberry Craze, 509
    Orange-A-Peel, 510
    Peach Pleasure, 511
    Strawberries Wild, 512
Jamocha Shake, Arby's, 525
Joe Makin' Me Java, Joe's Crab Shack, 651
Joe's Crab Shack
    Joe Makin' Me Java, 651
    Joe's Ya Ya, 652
    Red Snapper, 653
    Secret Passion Punch, 654
    Shark Tooth, 655
    Swamp Moss, 656
Joe's Ya Ya, Joe's Crab Shack, 652
Julius
    Orange, 513
    Pineapple, 514
    Strawberry, 514
June Bug, T.G.I. Friday's, 690
Junior Bacon Cheeseburger, Wendy's, 462–63, *464*
J.W. Pink Lemonade, The Cheesecake Factory, 617
Kahlúa Coffee Liqueur, 594
Keebler Pecan Sandies, 290–91, *291*
Kellogg's
    Frosted Brown Sugar Cinnamon Pop-Tarts, 70–72, *73*
    Rice Krispies Treats, 172–73, *174*
Key Lime Martini, The Cheesecake Factory, 616

KFC
    Buttermilk Biscuits, 175–76, *177*
    Cole Slaw, 178, *179*
    Macaroni & Cheese, 388–89, *390*
    Mashed Potatoes & Gravy, 180–81
    Potato Salad, 391–92, *393*
    Tender Roast Chicken, 182–83, *184*
Koo Koo Roo
    Original Skinless Flame-Broiled Chicken, 292–94, *294*
    Santa Fe Pasta, 295–96, *297*
Kraft
    Free
        Catalina Dressing, 74–75
        Thousand Island Dressing, 78–79
    Light Deluxe Macaroni & Cheese Dinner, 80–81, *82*
Lava Lamp Margarita, Chevys, 622
Lemon
    Iced Tea, Snapple, 571, *572*
        Diet, 570, *572*
    Natural, Flavored Iced Tea, Nestea, 565
    Pastry Cremes, Girl Scout Cookies, 284–86
    -Pepper Grilled Mahi-Mahi, Red Lobster, 95–96
Lemonade
    Absolut, Red Robin, 682
    Absolutely Electric, Claim Jumper, 634
    All Natural, Minute Maid, 564
    Electric, T.G.I. Friday's, 688
    Freckled, Red Robin, 566
    J.W. Pink, The Cheesecake Factory, 617
    Muscle Beach, Hot Dog on a Stick, 562, *563*
    Strawberry, Cinnabon, 557
    Twisted, Chili's, 633
Lemon Drop Shooters, Hard Rock Cafe, 644, *645*
Lights of Havana, T.G.I. Friday's, 691
Lime
    Key, Martini, The Cheesecake Factory, 616
    Tequila Chicken, Applebee's, 341–42, *343*
Limeade, Sonic Drive-In
    Cherry, 490
    Strawberry, 491
Liqueurs
    Bailey's Original Irish Cream, 583
    DeKuyper Thrilla Vanilla French Vanilla, 584
    Disaronno Amaretto, 585

723

Liqueurs (cont.)
  Grand Marnier, 586
  Hiram Walker
    Anisette, 587
    Crème de Banana, 588
    Crème de Cacao, 589
    Crème de Menthe, 590
    Crème de Strawberry, 591
  Kahlúa Coffee, 594
  Marie Brizard Watermelon, 595
  Midori Melon, 596
Little Debbie Oatmeal Delights, 298–99, *300*
Lynchburg Lo-Rider, Hard Rock Cafe, 643
Macaroni & Cheese
  Dinner, Kraft Light Deluxe, 80–81, *82*
  KFC, 388–89, *390*
Mahi-Mahi, Lemon-Pepper Grilled, Red Lobster, 95–96
Mai Tai, Claim Jumper, 637
Mai tai mix, restaurant-style, 703
Malimbo Breeze, Bahama Breeze, 608
M&M's McFlurry, McDonald's, 540
Mandrin Blush, Chili's, 630
Mango Smoothie, Chillin', Red Robin, 515
Maple Walnut Raisin Cream Cheese Shmear, Einstein Bros., 157–58
Mara Simple Syrup, 700
Margarita Grilled Tuna, Chili's, 379–82, *383*
Margaritas, See Cocktails
Marie Brizard Watermelon Liqueur, 595
Martinis, See Cocktails
Mashed Potatoes
  Garlic, Chevys, 363–64
  & Gravy, KFC, 180–81
McDonald's
  Arch Deluxe, 394–96, *397*
  Big Mac, 185–87, *188*
  Breakfast Burrito, 189–90, *191*
  Egg McMuffin, 398–99, *400*
  McFlurry
    Butterfinger, 539
    M&M's, 540
    Oreo Cookie, 540
    Reese's, 540–41
  Shakes
    Chocolate, 542, 543
    Shamrock, 544
    Strawberry, 542, 543
    Vanilla, 542–43
McFlurry, McDonald's
  Butterfinger, 539

M&M's, 540
Oreo Cookie, 540
Reese's, 540–41
Meet Jack Black, Planet Hollywood, 673
Melbourne Cooler, Outback Steakhouse, 664
Melon
  Liqueur, Midori, 596
  See also Watermelon
Menthe, Crème de, Liqueur, Hiram Walker, 589
Mesquite-Grilled BBQ Chicken Quesadilla, Chevys, 369–71, *372*
Mexican
  "Fried" Ice Cream, Chi-Chi's, 134–35, *136*
  Pizza, Taco Bell, 225–26, *227*
Midgees, Tootsie Roll, 335–36, *337*
Midori Melon Liqueur, 596
Milk shakes, See Shakes
Mint
  -Chocolate Yoo-hoo Mix-Up, 576
  Crème de Menthe Liqueur, Hiram Walker, 590
  in McDonald's Shamrock Shake, 544
Minute Maid All Natural Lemonade, 564
Mixers
  Beau Rivage Bloody Mary Mix, 699
  Mara Simple Syrup, 700
  Mr & Mrs T
    Bloody Mary Mix, 701
    Sweet & Sour Mix, 702
  restaurant-style
    mai tai mix, 703
    piña colada mix, 704
    sweet & sour mix, 705
Mix-Ups, Yoo-hoo
  Chocolate-Banana, 576
  Chocolate-Mint, 576
  Chocolate-Strawberry, 577
Mo' Betta Blues, House of Blues, 650
Mocha
  Frozen Frappuccino, Starbucks, 550
  Suisse, General Foods International Coffees, 560
Mochalatta Chill, Cinnabon, 530
Mochalatta Icescape, Cinnabon, 529
Monterey Jack cheese, See Cheese, Monterey Jack
Moons Over My Hammy, Denny's, 143–44, *145*
Mozzarella cheese, See Cheese, mozzarella

Mr & Mrs T
  Bloody Mary Mix, 701
  Sweet & Sour Mix, 702
Muffins
  McDonald's Egg McMuffin, 398–99, *400*
  Otis Spunkmeyer
    Apple Cinnamon, 203–4, *205*
    Banana Nut, 206–7, *208*
    Chocolate Chip, 408–9, *410*
    Wild Blueberry, 411–12, *413*
Muscle Beach Lemonade, Hot Dog on a Stick, 562, *563*
Mushroom(s)
  Chunky Tomato & Garlic Pasta Sauce, Healthy Choice, 288–89
  The Plant Sandwich, Rainforest Cafe, 325–26, *327*
  Veggie Patty, Savory, Gardenburger, 280–82, *283*
Nabisco
  Honey Maid Grahams, 301–5, *306*
  Old Fashion Ginger Snaps, 307–8, *309*
  Oreo Cookie(s), 310–12, *313*
    McFlurry, McDonald's, 540
    Shake, Jack in the Box, 538
  Reduced-Fat Cheese Nips, 83–85, *85*
  Snackwell's
    Apple Raisin Snack Bars, 314–15, *316*
    Banana Snack Bars, 317–18, *319*
    Chocolate Chip Cookies, 86–87, *88*
    Fudge Brownie Bars, 89–90, *91*
    Golden Snack Bars, 92–93, *94*
Nantucket Baked Cod, Red Lobster, 97–98
Natural Lemon Flavored Iced Tea, Nestea, 565
Nestea Natural Lemon Flavored Iced Tea, 565
No. 1 Burger, Sonic Drive-In, 432–33, *434*
November Sea Breeze, T.G.I. Friday's, 494
Nut, Banana, Muffins, Otis Spunkmeyer, 206–7, *208*
Nutty Uncle Chang's Favorite, P.F. Chang's, 669
Oatmeal
  Delights, Little Debbie, 298–99, *300*
  Raisin Cookies, Entenmann's, 54–55, *56*
Ocean Water, Sonic Drive-In, 491
Old Fashion Ginger Snaps, Nabisco, 307–8, *309*
Olive Garden
  Chicken Caesar Sandwich, 192–93, *194*
  Chicken Parmigiana Sandwich, 401–2, *403*
  Chocolate Almond Amoré, 657
  Fettucine Alfredo, 404–5
  Italian Margarita, 658
  Italian Salad Dressing, 195–96
  Pasta e Fagioli, 197–98
  Strawberry Siciliano, 659
  Tiramisu, 199–202, *201*
  Venetian Sunset, 660
  Zuppa Toscana, 406–7
O'Malley's Orange Cooler, Bennigan's, 613
100% Blue Agave Margarita, Chevys, 620
Onion
  Chopped, Bagels, Einstein Bros., 45
  Walkabout Soup, Outback Steakhouse, 414–15
Orange
  Cooler, O'Malley's, Bennigan's, 613
  -Flavored Chicken, Panda Express, 422–24
  Iced Tea, Snapple, 571, *572*
  Icescape, Cinnabon, 529
  Julius, 513
  Margarita, Ultimate, Chevys, 624
  Slice, 487
Orange-A-Peel, Jamba Juice, 510
Orange juice
  Citrus Squeeze, Jamba Juice, 507, *508*
  O'Malley's Orange Cooler, Bennigan's, 613
  Orange-A-Peel, Jamba Juice, 510
  Orange Icescape, Cinnabon, 529
  Orange Julius, 513
Oreo Cookie(s), Nabisco, 310–12, *313*
  McFlurry, McDonald's, 540
  Shake, Jack in the Box, 538
Original Skinless Flame-Broiled Chicken, Koo Koo Roo, 292–94, *294*
Otis Spunkmeyer
  Banana Nut Muffins, 206–7, *208*
  Chocolate Chip Muffins, 408–9, *410*
  Wild Blueberry Muffins, 411–12, *413*
Otter Pop, Claim Jumper, 638
Outback Steakhouse
  Alice Springs Chicken, 418–20, *421*
  Caesar Salad Dressing, 416–17
  Coral Reef 'Rita, 661
  Don't Koala Me, I'll Koala You Cooler, 662
  Great Barrier Punch, 663
  Melbourne Cooler, 664
  Walkabout Soup, 414–15
  Wallaby Darned, 665, *666*

Panda Express Orange-Flavored Chicken, 422–24
Parmigiana, Chicken, Sandwich, Olive Garden, 401–2, *403*
Pasta
　Chicken, Dijon, T.G.I. Friday's, 450–52
　e Fagioli, Olive Garden, 197–98
　Fettucine Alfredo, Olive Garden, 404–5
　Guiltless Primavera, Chili's Guiltless Grill, 36–38
　Macaroni & Cheese
　　Dinner, Kraft Light Deluxe, 80–81, *82*
　　KFC, 388–89, *390*
　Santa Fe, Koo Koo Roo, 295–96, *297*
Pasta Sauce, Healthy Choice
　Chunky Tomato, Mushroom & Garlic, 288–89
　Traditional, 287
Pastry Cremes, Lemon, Girl Scout Cookies, 284–86
Pea & Barley Soup, Smashed, Dakota, California Pizza Kitchen, 254–55
Peach
　Iced Tea, Snapple, 571, 572
　Pleasure, Jamba Juice, 511
　Smoothie, Baskin-Robbins, 502
Peanut Butter
　Cups, Reese's, in McDonald's McFlurry, 540–41
　& Jelly Shooter, Planet Hollywood, 675
Pecan Sandies, Keebler, 290–91, *291*
Pepper-Lemon Grilled Mahi-Mahi, Red Lobster, 95–96
Perfect Margarita, Applebee's, 604
P.F. Chang's
　Buddha's Dream, 667
　Heat Wave, 668
　Nutty Uncle Chang's Favorite, 669
　The Poolside, 670
Piña colada mix, restaurant-style, 704
Pineapple Julius, 514
Pink Lemonade, J.W., The Cheesecake Factory, 617
Pinto Beans, El Pollo Loco, 161
Pita
　Fresh Stuffed, Wendy's
　　Chicken Caesar, 456–57, *458*
　　Classic Greek, 459–60, *461*
　Turkey, Rumble in the Jungle, Rainforest Cafe, 328–29, *330*
Pizza
　California Pizza Kitchen

Grilled Eggplant Cheeseless, 256–58, *259*
　Vegetarian, 260–62, *263*
　Mexican, Taco Bell, 225–26, *227*
Plain Bagels, Einstein Bros., 41–42
Planet Hollywood
　The Comet, 671
　Cool Running, 672
　Meet Jack Black, 673
　Shooters
　　Blue Hawaii, 674
　　Bubble Gum, 674
　　Grape Crush, 674
　　Peanut Butter & Jelly, 675
　Sweet Death Becomes Her, 676
　Terminator, 677
Plant, The, Sandwich, 325–26, *327*
Planters Fiddle Faddle, 320–21, *322*
Plant Sandwich, The, Rainforest Cafe, 325–26, *327*
Poolside, The, P.F. Chang's, 670
Popcorn
　Planters Fiddle Faddle, 320–21, *322*
　Zonkers, Screaming Yellow, 429–30, *431*
Pop-Tarts, Frosted Brown Sugar Cinnamon, Kellogg's, 70–72, *73*
Potato(es)
　Boats, Baja, Applebee's, 115–17, *117*
　Mashed
　　Garlic, Chevys, 363–64
　　& Gravy, KFC, 180–81
　Salad, KFC, 391–92, *393*
　Skins, T.G.I. Friday's, 453–54, *455*
Pudding, Swiss Miss Fat-Free
　Chocolate Fudge, 99–100
　Tapioca, 101–2
Purple Hooter Shooter, Hard Rock Cafe, *645*, 646
Quesadilla
　Chicken, Mesquite-Grilled BBQ, Chevys, 369–71, *372*
　Veggie, Applebee's, 22–23, *24*
Rainforest Cafe
　The Plant Sandwich, 325–26, *327*
　Reggae Beat Seasoning, 323–24
　Rumble in the Jungle Turkey Pita, 328–29, *330*
　Tropical Chicken Quartet, 425–27, *428*
Raisin
　Apple, Snack Bars, Nabisco Snackwell's, 314–15, *316*

Cinnamon, Sweet Rolls, Entenmann's,
266–68, *268*
Maple Walnut, Cream Cheese Shmear,
Einstein Bros., 157–58
Oatmeal, Cookies, Entenmann's, 54–55,
56
Ranch Crispy Chicken Sandwich, Carl's Jr.,
349–51, *352*
Raspberry
  Iced Tea, Snapple, 571, *572*
  Margarita, Famous Chambord, Z'Tejas,
  695, *696*
  Road Iced Tea, Bennigan's, 614
  Schnapps, Razz Attack, Hiram Walker,
  592
Razz Attack Raspberry Schnapps, Hiram
  Walker, 592
Red Lobster
  Bahama Mama, 678
  Butter-Tini Funtini, 679
  Cheddar Bay Biscuits, 209–19, *211*
  The Hawaiian Funtini, 680
  Lemon-Pepper Grilled Mahi-Mahi,
  95–96
  Nantucket Baked Cod, 97–98
  Red Passion Colada, 681
  Tartar Sauce, 212
Red Passion Colada, Red Lobster, 681
Red Robin
  Absolut Lemonade, 682
  Chillin' Mango Smoothie, 515
  Freckled Lemonade, 566
  Groovy Smoothie, 516
  Jamaican Shake, 683
  Sand in Your Shorts, 684, *685*
  Strawberry Ecstacy, 567
  T.N.T., 686
Red Snapper, Joe's Crab Shack, 653
Red Wine Vinegar Dressing, Seven Seas,
  331–32
Reese's McFlurry, McDonald's, 540–41
Reggae Beat Seasoning, Rainforest Cafe,
  323–24
Restaurant-style
  mai tai mix, 703
  piña colada mix, 704
  sweet & sour mix, 705
Rice
  Margarita Grilled Tuna, Chili's, 379–82,
  383
  Rice Krispies Treats, Kellogg's, 172–73,
  174
  Spanish, El Pollo Loco, 162

Root Beer
  A&W, 481–82
  Float, Claim Jumper, 639
  Schnapps, Hiram Walker, 593
Rumble in the Jungle Turkey Pita,
  Rainforest Cafe, 328–29, *330*
Salad
  Chicken
    Asian, Applebee's, 247–48
    Blackened, Applebee's, 19–21
    Guiltless, Chili's Guiltless Grill, 30–32
  Cole Slaw, KFC, 178, *179*
  Fajita, Chili's, 376–78
  Potato, KFC, 391–92, *393*
Salad Dressing
  Caesar, Outback Steakhouse, 416–17
  Kraft Free
    Catalina, 74–75
    Thousand Island, 78–79
  Olive Garden, Italian, 195–96
  Seven Seas
    Red Wine Vinegar, 331–32
    Viva Italian, 333–34
Salmon, Jack Daniel's Grill, T.G.I. Friday's,
  106–8
Salsa
  El Pollo Loco, 57
  Fresh, Chevys, 264–66
  Jalapeño, Cream Cheese Shmear,
  Einstein Bros., 157
Sand in Your Shorts, Red Robin, 684, *685*
Sandwich(es)
  Chicken
    Bacon Swiss Crispy, Carl's Jr., 359–61,
    362
    BK Broiler, Burger King, 125–26, *127*
    Buffalo, Bennigan's, 344–45, *346*
    Caesar, Olive Garden, 192–93, *194*
    Club, Charbroiled, Carl's Jr., 353–54,
    355
    Crispy, Ranch, Carl's Jr., 349–51, *352*
    Fillet, Spicy, Wendy's, 465–66, *467*
    Guiltless, Chili's Guiltless Grill, 33–34,
    35
    Parmigiana, Olive Garden, 401–2,
    403
    Roast, Deluxe, Arby's, 25–26, *27*
    Santa Fe, Charbroiled, Carl's Jr.,
    356–57, *358*
    Tropical Quartet, Rainforest Cafe,
    425–27, *428*
  Classic Greek Fresh Stuffed Pita,
    Wendy's, 459–60, *461*

Sandwich(es) (cont.)
  Egg
    McMuffin, McDonald's, 398–99, *400*
    Moons Over My Hammy, Denny's, 143–44, *145*
    The Plant, Rainforest Cafe, 325–26, *327*
  Turkey
    Pita, Rumble in the Jungle, Rainforest Cafe, 328–29, *330*
    Roast, Deluxe, Arby's, 28–29, *29*
    The Super Bird, Denny's, 146–47, *148*
  See *also* Hamburgers
Santa Fe
  Chicken Sandwich, Charbroiled, Carl's Jr., 356–57, *358*
  Pasta, Koo Koo Roo, 295–96, *297*
Sauce
  Pasta, Healthy Choice
    Chunky Tomato, Mushroom & Garlic, 288–89
    Traditional, 287
  Tartar, Red Lobster, 212
Savory Mushroom Veggie Patty, Gardenburger, 280–82, *283*
Schnapps, Hiram Walker
  Razz Attack Raspberry, 592
  Root Beer, 593
Screaming Yellow Zonkers, 429–30, *431*
Seasoning, Reggae Beat, Rainforest Cafe, 323–24
Secret Passion Punch, Joe's Crab Shack, 654
Sedona White Corn Tortilla Soup, California Pizza Kitchen, 347–48
7-Eleven Cherry Slurpee, 568–69
Seven Seas
  Red Wine Vinegar Dressing, 331–32
  Viva Italian Dressing, 333–34
7UP, 488–89
Shake(s)
  Arby's Jamocha, 525
  Baskin-Robbins B.R. Blast, 526–27
  Cinnabon Icescape
    Mochalatta, 529
    Orange, 529
    Strawberry, 528
  Cinnabon Mochalatta Chill, 530
  Dairy Queen Blizzard, 531–37, *533*
    Baby Ruth, 532
    Banana Pudding, 532
    Banana Split, 534
    Berry Banana, 534
    Chocolate Chip, 535
    Chocolate Chip Cookie Dough, 535
    Hawaiian, 536
    Whopp'N'Wild, 536–37
    Yukon Cruncher, 537
  Jack in the Box Oreo Cookie, 538
  McDonald's
    Butterfinger McFlurry, 539
    Chocolate, 542, 543
    M&M's McFlurry, 540
    Oreo Cookie McFlurry, 540
    Reese's McFlurry, 540–41
    Shamrock, 544
    Strawberry, 542, 543
    Vanilla, 542–43
  Red Robin Jamaican, 683
  Sonic Drive-In
    Banana Cream Pie, 545
    Chocolate Cream Pie, 546
    Coconut Cream Pie, 546–47
    Strawberry Cream Pie, 547
  Starbucks Frozen Frappuccino
    Caramel, 550
    Coffee, 548, *549*
    Mocha, 550
  Wendy's Frosty, 551
Shamrock Shake, McDonald's, 544
Shark on the Beach, Claim Jumper, 640
Shark Tooth, Joe's Crab Shack, 655
Shoney's
  Country Fried Steak, 217–18
  Hot Fudge Cake, 213–15, *216*
Shrimp, Buffalo, Hooter's, 169–70, *171*
Simple Syrup, Mara, 700
Skinless Flame-Broiled Chicken, Original, Koo Koo Roo, 292–94, *294*
Slurpee, Cherry, 7-Eleven, 568–69
Smart Ones Chocolate Éclair, Weight Watchers, 109–11
Smashed Pea & Barley Soup, Dakota, California Pizza Kitchen, 254–55
Smoothie(s)
  Applebee's Bananaberry Freeze, 500–501
  Baskin-Robbins
    Peach, 502
    Strawberry, 503
    Strawberry Banana, 504
    Wild Berry Banana, 505
  Jamba Juice
    Banana Berry, 506
    Citrus Squeeze, 507, *508*

Cranberry Craze, 509
Orange-A-Peel, 510
Peach Pleasure, 511
Strawberries Wild, 512
Julius
　Orange, 513
　Pineapple, 514
　Strawberry, 514
Red Robin
　Chillin' Mango, 515
　Groovy, 516
Starbucks Tazoberry Tea, 517–18
T.G.I. Friday's Tropical Oasis, 519, *520*
Snack Bars
　Kellogg's Rice Krispies Treats, 172–73, *174*
　Nabisco Snackwell's
　　Apple Raisin, 314–15, *316*
　　Banana, 317–18, *319*
　　Fudge Brownie, 89–90, *91*
　　Golden, 92–93, *94*
Snackwell's, Nabisco
　Apple Raisin Snack Bars, 314–15, *316*
　Banana Snack Bars, 317–18, *319*
　Chocolate Chip Cookies, 86–87, *88*
　Fudge Brownie Bars, 89–90, *91*
　Golden Snack Bars, 92–93, *94*
Snapple Iced Tea
　Cranberry, 570, 572
　Lemon, 571, 572
　　Diet, 570, 572
　Orange, 571, 572
　Peach, 571, 572
　Raspberry, 571, 572
　Strawberry, 571, 572
Sodas
　A&W
　　Cream Soda, 480
　　Root Beer, 481–82
　Coca-Cola, 483–85, *486*
　Orange Slice, 487
　7UP, 488–89
　Sonic Drive-In
　　Cherry Limeade, 490
　　Ocean Water, 491
　　Strawberry Limeade, 491
　Squirt, 493
　T.G.I. Friday's
　　November Sea Breeze, 494
　　Strawberry Surprise, 495
Soft Taco, Taco Bell
　Beef, 219–20, *221*
　Chicken, 444–45, *446*

Sonic Drive-In
　Cherry Limeade, 490
　Cream Pie Shakes
　　Banana, 545
　　Chocolate, 546
　　Coconut, 546–47
　　Strawberry, 547
　Hickory Burger, 435–36, *437*
　Jalapeño Burger, 438–39, *440*
　No. 1 Burger, 432–33, *434*
　Ocean Water, 491
　Strawberry Limeade, 491
Soup
　Dakota Smashed Pea & Barley, California Pizza Kitchen, 254–55
　Pasta e Fagioli, Olive Garden, 197–98
　Tortilla, Sedona White Corn, California Pizza Kitchen, 347–48
　Walkabout, Outback Steakhouse, 414–15
　Zuppa Toscana, Olive Garden, 406–7
Southwestern Eggrolls, Chili's, 384–86, *387*
Spanish Rice, El Pollo Loco, 162
Spicy
　Chicken Fillet Sandwich, Wendy's, 465–66, *467*
　Hot Chicken Burrito, El Pollo Loco, 164
Spinach, Creamed, Boston Market, 123–24
Spirits, *See* Cocktails; Liqueurs; Mixers; Schnapps
Squash, Butternut, Boston Market, 118–19
Squirt, 493
Starbucks
　Frozen Frappuccino, 548, *549*
　　Caramel, 550
　　Mocha, 550
　Tazoberry Tea, 517–18
Steak
　Chili's Fajita Salad, 376–78
　Country Fried, Shoney's, 217–18
Strawberry(ies)
　-Chocolate Yoo-hoo Mix-Up, 577
　Cream Cheese Shmear, Einstein Bros., 156
　Cream Pie Shake, Sonic Drive-In, 547
　Crème de, Liqueur, Hiram Walker, 591
　Ecstacy, Red Robin, 567
　Iced Tea, Snapple, 571, 572
　Lemonade, Cinnabon, 557
　Limeade, Sonic Drive-In, 491

729

Strawberry(ies) (cont.)
  Shake(s)
    Icescape, Cinnabon, 528
    McDonald's, 542, 543
    Shortcake Blender Blaster, T.G.I. Friday's, 692
    Siciliano, Olive Garden, 659
  Smoothie(s)
    Banana, Baskin-Robbins, 504
    Baskin-Robbins, 503
    Julius, 514
    Wild, Jamba Juice, 512
  Surprise, T.G.I. Friday's, 495
Sugar
  Brown, Cinnamon Pop-Tarts, Frosted, Kellogg's Low-Fat, 70–72, *73*
  Cinnamon, Bagels, Einstein Bros., 42–43
Suisse Mocha, General Foods International Coffees, 560
Summer Squeeze, Applebee's, 605
Sunburn Margarita, The, Chevy's, 623
Sundae, Brownie, Applebee's, 249–50, *251*
Sunny Delight, 573, *574*
Super Bird, The, Denny's, 146–47, *148*
Swamp Moss, Joe's Crab Shack, 656
Sweet & Sour Mix
  Mr & Mrs T, 702
  restaurant-style, 705
Sweet Corn Cake, Chi-Chi's, 137–38
Sweet Death Becomes Her, Planet Hollywood, 676
Sweet Rolls, Cinnamon Raisin, Entenmann's, 266–68, *268*
Swiss
  Bacon Crispy Chicken Sandwich, Carl's Jr., 359–61, *362*
  cheese, *See* Cheese, Swiss
  Crispy Chicken Sandwich, Carl's Jr., 359–61, *362*
Swiss Miss Fat-Free
  Chocolate Fudge Pudding, 99–100
  Tapioca Pudding, 101–2
Syrup, Simple, Mara, 700
Taco, Soft, Taco Bell
  Beef, 219–20, *221*
  Chicken, 444–45, *446*
Taco Bell
  Beef Burrito Supreme, 441–42, *443*
  Beef Soft Taco, 219–20, *221*
  Chicken Soft Taco, 444–45, *446*
  Grilled Chicken Burrito, 222–23, *224*
  Mexican Pizza, 225–26, *227*

Tapioca Pudding, Swiss Miss Fat-Free, 101–2
Tartar Sauce, Red Lobster, 212
Tazoberry Tea, Starbucks, 517–18
Tea, Iced
  Arizona
    with Ginseng, 556
    Green, with Ginseng and Honey, 555
  Nestea Natural Lemon Flavored, 565
  Snapple
    Cranberry, 570, 572
    Diet Lemon, 570, 572
    Lemon, 571, 572
    Orange, 571, 572
    Peach, 571, 572
    Raspberry, 571, 572
    Strawberry, 571, 572
  Starbucks Tazoberry, 517–18
Tequila Lime Chicken, Applebee's, 341–42, *343*
Terminator, Planet Hollywood, 677
Texas BBQ Wrap, Chevys, 365–67, *368*
T.G.I. Friday's
  Banana Split Blender Blaster, 687
  BBQ Chicken Wings, 447–48, *449*
  Dijon Chicken Pasta, 450–52
  Electric Lemonade, 688
  Fat-Free Cheesecake, 103–5, *105*
  Hawaiian Volcano, 689
  Jack Daniel's Grill Salmon, 106–8
  June Bug, 690
  Lights of Havana, 691
  November Sea Breeze Fling, 494
  Potato Skins, 453–54, *455*
  Strawberry Shortcake Blender Blaster, 692
  Strawberry Surprise, 495
  Tropical Oasis Smoothie, 519, *520*
Thousand Island Dressing, Kraft Free, 78–79
Thrilla Vanilla French Vanilla Liqueur, DeKuyper, 584
Tiramisu, Olive Garden, 199–202, *201*
T.N.T., Red Robin, 686
Tomato sauce
  Healthy Choice
    Chunky Tomato, Mushroom & Garlic, 288–89
    Traditional Pasta Sauce, 287
  See also Salsa
Tootsie Roll Midgees, 335–36, *337*
Tortilla Soup, Sedona White Corn, California Pizza Kitchen, 347–48

Toscana, Zuppa, Olive Garden, 406–7
Traditional Pasta Sauce, Healthy Choice, 287
Tropical
   Chicken Quartet, Rainforest Cafe, 425–27, *428*
   Martini, The Cheesecake Factory, 619
   Oasis Smoothie, T.G.I. Friday's, 519, *520*
   Storm, Claim Jumper, 641
   Sunburn, Chili's, 632
Tuna, Margarita Grilled, Chili's, 379–82, *383*
Turkey Sandwich
   Pita, Rumble in the Jungle, Rainforest Cafe, 328–29, *330*
   Roast, Deluxe, Arby's, 28–29, *29*
   The Super Bird, Denny's, 146–47, *148*
Twilight Zone, Cheesecake Factory, The, 618
Twinkies, Hostess Lights Low-Fat, 66–68, *69*
Twisted Lemonade, Chili's, 633
Ultimate Orange Margarita, Chevys, 624
Vanilla
   French
     Café, General Foods International Coffees, 559
     Liqueur, Thrilla Vanilla, DeKuyper, 584
   Shake, McDonald's, 542–43
Vegetable(s)
   Applebee's Veggie Quesadilla, 22–23, *24*
   Boston Market
     Butternut Squash, 118–19
     Creamed Spinach, 123–24
   California Pizza Kitchen Vegetarian Pizza, 260–62, *263*
   Gardenburger
     Classic Greek Veggie Patty, 272–74, *275*
     Fire-Roasted Veggie Patty, 276–78, *279*
     Original Veggie Patty, 58–60, *61*
     Savory Mushroom Veggie Patty, 280–82, *283*
   The Plant Sandwich, Rainforest Cafe, 325–26, *327*
   See also names of vegetables

Vegetarian Pizza, California Pizza Kitchen, 260–62, *263*
Venetian Sunset, Olive Garden, 660
Verry Berry Good, Bahama Breeze, 609
Viennese Chocolate Café, General Foods International Coffees, 560
Vinegar, Red Wine, Dressing, Seven Seas, 331–32
Viva Italian Dressing, Seven Seas, 333–34
Vogel, Shawna, 241
Walkabout Soup, Outback Steakhouse, 414–15
Wallaby Darned, Outback Steakhouse, 665, *666*
Walnut, Maple, Raisin Cream Cheese Shmear, Einstein Bros., 157–58
Watermelon
   Fresh Fruit Margarita (On the Rocks), Chevys, 625
   Liqueur, Marie Brizard, 595
Weight Watchers Smart Ones Chocolate Éclair, 109–11
Wendy's
   Chicken Caesar Fresh Stuffed Pita, 456–57, *458*
   Frosty
     frozen dessert version, 231
     shake version, 551
   Junior Bacon Cheeseburger, 462–63, *464*
   Single with Cheese, 228–29, *230*
   Spicy Chicken Fillet Sandwich, 465–66, *467*
White Castle Cheeseburgers, 232–33, *234*
White Corn Tortilla Soup, Sedona, California Pizza Kitchen, 347–48
Whopper, Burger King, 131–32, *133*
Whoppers, in Dairy Queen
   Whopp'N'Wild Blizzard, 536–37
Whopp'N'Wild Blizzard, Dairy Queen, 536–37
Wild Berry Banana Smoothie, Baskin-Robbins, 505
Wild Blueberry Muffins, Otis Spunkmeyer, 411–12, *413*
Wine, Red, Vinegar Dressing, Seven Seas, 331–32
Wrap, Texas BBQ, Chevys, 365–67, *368*
Yoo-hoo Chocolate Drink, 575
   Chocolate-Banana Mix-Up, 576
   Chocolate-Mint Mix-Up, 576
   Chocolate-Strawberry Mix-Up, 577

Yukon Cruncher Blizzard, Dairy Queen, 537
Z'Big Stick Margarita, Z'Tejas, 693–94
Zonkers, Screaming Yellow, 429–30, 431

Z'Tejas
   Famous Chambord Raspberry Margarita, 695, *696*
   Z'Big Stick Margarita, 693–94
Zuppa Toscana, Olive Garden, 406–7